The Playbill® Broadway Yearbook

Eighth Annual Edition
2011-2012

Robert Viagas
Editor

Amy Asch
Assistant Editor

Kesler Thibert
Art Director

Brian Mapp   Joseph Marzullo
Photographers

Theresa Holder   Frank Dain
Production Coordinators

The Playbill Broadway Yearbook: Eighth Annual Edition, June 1, 2011–May 31, 2012
Robert Viagas, Editor

©2012 Playbill® Incorporated

ISBN 978-1-55783-927-5
ISSN 1932-1945

Published by PLAYBILL® BOOKS
525 Seventh Avenue, Suite 1801
New York, NY 10018
Email: yearbook@playbill.com
Internet: www.playbill.com

Exclusively distributed by Applause Theatre & Cinema Books
An Imprint of Hal Leonard Corporation
7777 West Bluemound Road
Milwaukee, WI 53213

Trade Book Division Editorial Offices
33 Plymouth St., Montclair, NJ 07042

Printed in the United States of America

Book design by Kesler Thibert

www.applausebooks.com

Preface to the Eighth Edition

It's five minutes to curtain on the eighth edition of *The Playbill Broadway Yearbook*. We're about to start our annual extravaganza, starring the contents of every PLAYBILL from every show that played on Broadway between June 1, 2011 and May 31, 2012. And there were plenty of them—seventy-two to be exact, the second-highest annual total since we began publishing the *Yearbook* in 2005.

It's the chronicle of a richly diverse season of tuneful new musicals, delirious comedies, hard-hitting dramas and exuberant dances, plus revivals of some of the greatest works in the American theatrical canon: *Death of a Salesman, A Streetcar Named Desire, Porgy and Bess*, in versions that earned their share of controversy, criticism...and several key awards.

Stephen Sondheim, who turned 82 this season, showed he was still in the game, but not by opening a new show (though he is reportedly at work on a musical with David Ives). Sondheim rattled Broadway in summer 2011 by blasting Diane Paulus's new shortened and punched-up version of *Porgy and Bess*, not just for assuming the vanity title *The Gershwins' Porgy and Bess* (elbowing out librettist and co-lyricist DuBose Heyward, Sondheim noted), but for bringing in Pulitzer laureate Suzan-Lori Parks to rewrite the libretto and even to change the show's ending. Sondheim—a Pulitzer-winner himself—excoriated these maulings of the classic. But the result was pleasing enough to win *TGPaB* a Tony Award for Best Revival of a Musical, incidentally beating a noteworthy revival of Sondheim's own *Follies*.

The 2011-2012 season will be remembered for a pyrotechnic display of bravura performances, not least Audra McDonald's Tony-winning turn as Bess. Audiences were thrilled by Danny Burstein's heartbreaking performance as Buddy in *Follies*, Christian Borle as a Groucho-Marxian proto-Captain Hook in *Peter and the Starcatcher*, Nina Arianda as a fake (or maybe not) dominatrix in *Venus in Fur*, Ricky Martin as an audience-pleasing Che in *Evita*, Raúl Esparza as a charismatic con-man in *Leap of Faith*, and Jeremy Jordan in TWO brightly etched lead performances in *Bonnie & Clyde* and *Newsies*; et al.

Even with all these, the showstopper performance of the season was James Corden's breathless clowning turn in *One Man, Two Guvnors*. How good was Corden? In the Tony contest for Best Leading Actor in a Play Corden beat heavyweights Philip Seymour Hoffman, Frank Langella, John Lithgow and James Earl Jones, who were themselves giving stage-shaking performances.

It was a season packed with romance (*Once*), politics (*Gore Vidal's The Best Man*), adventure (*Peter and the Starcatcher*), race relations (*Clybourne Park*), families in crisis (*Other Desert Cities, Stick Fly*) and religion. Lots of religion. Two shows depicted the crucifixion of Jesus, *Godspell* and *Jesus Christ Superstar*. *Leap of Faith* enacted a tent revival. Holdover show *Sister Act* rocked a convent full of nuns singing gospel. Another holdover, *The Book of Mormon* continued to have fun (and earn a million dollars a

YOUR 2011-2012 YEARBOOK COMMITTEE
Top (L-R): Theresa Holder, Editor Robert Viagas, Brian Mapp and David Gewirtzman with dolls from *The Lion King* and "Wonder Woman" representing Kesler Thibert and Amy Asch, respectively.
Bottom (L-R): Joseph Marzullo, Amy Asch, Frank Dain.
Not pictured: Kesler Thibert

week) with the Church of Jesus Christ of Latter-Day Saints.

Once won eight Tony Awards including Best Musical, not just because the bittersweet Irish love story touched so many hearts, but because the show had a unique look and sound. In 1962 Richard Rodgers wrote *No Strings*, a musical that used virtually no strings in the pit. *Once* did the opposite: with a supporting cast of street musicians, it used only strings (plus an accordion/concertina).

And yet, 2011-2012 will be remembered as the season without a blockbuster—unless you count Hugh Jackman's solo show that was so solidly sold out that producers passed on the chance to be nominated for a Tony Award because they needed all the voters' tickets to sell at the box office. They kept the money...and watched as Jackman was given a special Tony Award anyway. But that show was only a limited run, as was the other SRO show, *Death of a Salesman*. *Once, Peter and the Starcatcher* and *Newsies* were some of the biggest hits of the season, but none was solidly sold out until after the Tony Awards. There was no new *Book of Mormon, Jersey Boys* or *The Producers* this year.

Which is not to say that Broadway didn't sell a lot of tickets. Though the number of tickets sold was down slightly, the overall gross for the season was a new record $1.14 billion. It was a roundly booming season with—thank the gods of Comedy and Tragedy—no strike or stock market crashes or similar disasters that challenged some previous seasons.

As all this was going on, *The Playbill Broadway Yearbook* was, as usual, busily poking its nose backstage, to photograph the denizens of Broadway and to let them report on their activities. Among our correspondents were the leading lady of *Lysistrata Jones*, the leading man of *Magic/Bird*, a musician from the ensemble of *Once*, a high-stepping newsboy from *Newsies*, a Tony nominee from *Priscilla Queen of the Desert* and, for the eighth year in a row, the indefatigable Kris Koop Ouellette from *Phantom of the Opera*, who chronicled the night her show played its 10,000th performance, the first Broadway show ever to do so. Along with several of her fellow *Phantom*ites, Kris appeared in a YouTube video about the *Yearbook* in summer 2011. Check it (and them) out at www.youtube.com/watch?v=yyoY_T6OSPc.

As I write this we've already begun work on the ninth edition of the *Yearbook*. See you in 2013!

Robert Viagas
June 2012

Special Thanks

Special thanks to Amy Asch, David Gewirtzman, Theresa Holder, Brian Mapp, Joseph Marzullo, Monica Simoes, Kesler Thibert, Krissie Fullerton, Frank Dain, Pam Karr, Matt Blank, Andrew Gans, Kenneth Jones, Adam Hetrick, Natacha Laniece, Jean Kroeper Murphy, Maria Somma and Debra Candela Novack, whose help made this year's edition possible.

We also thank the Eighth Edition *Yearbook* Correspondents who shared their stories with such wit and insight: Uzo Aduba, Gregg Arst, Pun Bandhu, Rosie Benton, Tanya Birl, Tommy Bracco, Lisa Brescia, Corey Brill, John Carroll, Tug Coker, Jeremy Cohen, Rosalyn Coleman, Luther Creek, Jessica Dickey, James FitzSimmons (for the fourth time), Zach Grenier (for the second time), Brendan Griffin, Bonita J. Hamilton, Roy Harris (for the sixth time), Zach James (for the third time), Tyson Jennette, Chiké Johnson, Celia Keenan-Bolger, Kris Koop (for the eighth time),Bryan Langlitz, Raymond J. Lee, Tony LePage, Christine Lin, Winnie Y. Lok, Emily Mechler, John Moauro, Elizabeth Morton, Patti Murin, Lance Roberts, Jemima Rooper, Jessica Rush, Jay Russell, Tony Sheldon, Lee Siegel, Phumzile Sojola, Zachary Spicer, Brian Spitulnik, Barclay Stiff (for the fourth time), Sarah Stiles, Jesse Swimm, Andy Taylor, Emily Tyra, Jonathan Warren, Jesse Wildman, Gregory Wooddell, Melissa van der Schyff and Katrina Yaukey.

And we thank the folks on each show who shared their photographs and other artwork that lent extra sparkle to the Scrapbook pages: Lisa Brescia, Luther Creek, Kelsey Fowler, Tyson Jennette, John Moauro, Patti Murin, Chelsea Nachman, Eddie Pendergraft, Tony Sheldon, Sarah Stiles, Melissa van der Schyff, Katrina Yaukey and many others.

Also the Broadway press agents who helped set up interviews and photo sessions and helped track down the names of all the people in the crew photos: especially Chris Boneau, Adrian Bryan-Brown, Michael Hartman, Richard Kornberg, Jeffrey Richards, Marc Thibodeau, Philip Rinaldi, Sam Rudy, Tony Origlio, Rick Miramontez, Candi Adams and their respective staffs.

Plus Joan Marcus, Paul Kolnik, Carol Rosegg, Jeremy Daniel, Simon Anand, Dan Jess, Jacob Cohl, Nathan Johnson, Brigitte Lacombe, Michael J. Lutch, Michael McCabe, Ken Howard, Ari Mintz, Johan Persson, Jessica Rush, Anita Shevett, Steve Shevett, Nicole Rivelli, Michael Daniel, Jeremy Daniel, Richard Termine, Deen van Meer, Cylla von Tiedemann and all the fine professional photographers whose work appears on these pages.

And, most of all, thanks to the great show people of Broadway who got into the spirit of the *Yearbook* and took time out of their busy days to pose for our cameras. There's no people like them.

Yearbook User's Manual

Which Shows Are Included? *The Playbill Broadway Yearbook 2011-2012* covers the Broadway season, which ran, as per tradition, from June 1, 2011 to May 31, 2012. Each of the seventy-two shows that played at a Broadway theatre under a Broadway contract during that time are highlighted in this edition. That includes new shows that opened during that time, like *Once*; shows from last season that ran into this season, like *The Book of Mormon*; older shows from seasons past that closed during this season, like *Billy Elliot*; and older shows from seasons past that ran throughout this season and continue into the future (and into the next *Yearbook*), like *Wicked*.

How Is It Decided Which Credits Page Will Be Featured? Each show's credits page (which PLAYBILL calls a "billboard page") changes over the year as cast members come and go. We use the opening-night billboard page for most new shows. For most shows that carry over from the previous season we use the billboard page from the first week in October.

Occasionally, sometimes at the request of the producer, we use a billboard page from another part of the season, especially when a major new star joins the cast.

What Are "Alumni" and "Transfer Students"? Over the course of a season some actors leave a production; others take their place. To follow our *Yearbook* concept, the ones who left a show before the date of the billboard page are listed as "Alumni"; the ones who joined the cast are called "Transfer Students." If you see a photo appearing in both "Alumni" and "Transfer Students" sections, it's not a mistake; it just means that they went in and out of the show during the season and were not present on the billboard date.

What Is a "Correspondent" and How Is One Chosen? We ask each show to appoint a Correspondent to record anecdotes of backstage life at their production. Sometimes the show's press agent picks the Correspondent; sometimes the company manager, the stage manager or the producer does the choosing. Each show

gets to decide for itself. A few shows decline to provide a correspondent, fail to respond to our request, or miss the deadline. Correspondents bring a richness of experience to the job and help tell the story of backstage life on Broadway from many different points of view.

Who Gets Their Picture in the *Yearbook*? Everyone who works on Broadway can get a picture in the *Yearbook*. That includes actors, producers, writers, designers, assistants, stagehands, ushers, box office personnel, stage doormen and anyone else employed at a Broadway show or a support organization. PLAYBILL maintains a database of headshots of all Broadway actors and most creators. We send our staff photographers to all opening nights and all major Broadway-related events. We also offer to schedule in-theatre photo shoots at every production. No one is required to appear in the *Yearbook*, but all are invited. A few shows declined to host a photo shoot this year or were unable to provide material by our deadline. We hope they'll join us in 2013.

TABLE OF CONTENTS

Timeline 2011-2012

Opening Nights, News Headlines and Other Significant Milestones of the Season

June 12, 2011 *The Book of Mormon* is named Best Musical and *War Horse* is named Best Play of the 2010-2011 season in the 65th annual Tony Awards.

June 12, 2011 *Million Dollar Quartet* ends its Broadway run after 489 performances, but six weeks later it transfers to Off-Broadway's New World Stages ten blocks away and continues its run alongside other expatriate Broadway shows, *Avenue Q* and *Rent*.

June 14, 2011 The new season begins with the six-months-delayed opening of the extravaganza musical *Spider-Man: Turn Off the Dark*, following 182 problem-plagued previews—the most in Broadway history. During that period original director/librettist/designer Julie Taymor was joined on the creative team by others. The final book is credited to Taymor, Glen Berger and Roberto Aguirre-Sacasa. The show marks the Broadway debut of songwriters Bono and The Edge from the Irish rock band U2. Reeve Carney stars as the superhero with the powers of a spider in the show which cost a reported $75 million, by far the most expensive in Broadway history.

June 15, 2011 The original cast album of *The Book of Mormon* hits number three on the Billboard album chart, right behind CDs by Adele and Lady Gaga. It marks the first time a cast album has been in the Top 10 since 1969, when the cast recording of *Hair* was number one for 13 weeks.

June 24, 2011 Gay marriage is legalized in New York. Among the first same-sex pairs to say "I do" on the stage of the St. James Theatre when the law goes into effect July 24 are three Broadway couples: actress Terri White and jewelry designer Donna Barnett, actor Ryan Dietz and playwright Josh Levine, and stage doorman John Raymond Barker and usher Jared Pike.

July 7, 2011 Tyne Daly stars as opera diva Maria Callas in a revival of Terrence McNally's Tony-winning play *Master Class*, featuring Sierra Boggess as one of her talented but exasperated pupils.

July 13, 2011 Just a year after closing, the Tony-winning revival of *Hair* caps a national

The Oscar-winning film *Once* becomes the basis for a hit Broadway show of the same title, which won the Tony Award for Best Musical. Steve Kazee and Cristin Milioti (3rd and 4th from left) played the roles originated on film by Glen Hansard and Markéta Irglová (left and 2nd from left), who wrote the score based on their own real-life romance. See March 18, 2012.

tour by returning to Broadway for a two-month engagement.

August 10, 2011 *The New York Times* publishes a letter from composer-lyricist Stephen Sondheim excoriating director Diane Paulus and playwright Suzan-Lori Parks for emendations planned for their upcoming revival of *Porgy and Bess*. Among other things he objects to changing the official title to *The Gershwins' Porgy and Bess*, rewriting DuBose Heyward's libretto to alter the characters, and creating a new ending. Sondheim wrote the alterations were unnecessary because, "These characters are as vivid as any ever created for the musical theatre, as has been proved over and over in productions that may have cut some dialogue and musical passages but didn't rewrite and distort them." Some portions of the original material will be restored prior to the January opening on Broadway.

August 23, 2011 Tremors from an early afternoon 5.8 magnitude earthquake centered in Virginia shake Times Square and much of the Eastern Seaboard of the U.S. It's the biggest to hit New York since 1944. No significant damage to theatres is reported.

August 27-28, 2011 Just days after the earthquake, Hurricane Irene targets New York City. Public transportation is suspended and all Broadway performances are cancelled on Saturday and Sunday.

August 29, 2011 The 1996 revival of *Chicago* becomes the longest-running American musical in Broadway history when it plays its 6138th performance, surpassing the original run of *A Chorus Line*. The Kander & Ebb show is still exceeded by British-originated musicals *Les Misérables*, *Cats*, and the still-running *The Phantom of the Opera*.

September 4, 2011 The stage adaptation of the

musical *Mary Poppins* notches its 2000th performance at the New Amsterdam Theatre.

September 9, 2011 In lieu of the annual "Broadway on Broadway" concert, the casts of Broadway shows gather in Times Square to mark the tenth anniversary of the 9/11 terrorist attacks by singing Kander & Ebb's "New York, New York." The event recreates a similar performance held as a morale booster two weeks after the original attacks.

September 12, 2011 A revival of the Stephen Sondheim/James Goldman musical *Follies* moves to Broadway from a hit engagement at the Kennedy Center in Washington, DC. The production stars Bernadette Peters, Ron Raines, Jan Maxwell and Danny Burstein with supporting roles filled by the likes of Elaine Paige, Jayne Houdyshell and Susan Watson.

October 2, 2011 Disney hosts the first "autism-friendly" performance of *The Lion King*, with sound and light effects dulled, part of a Theatre Development Fund initiative to help those who suffer from the malady.

October 9, 2011 Frank Langella plays a crooked financier whose fall eerily presages that of 21st century ponzi schemer Bernard Madoff, in a revival of Terence Rattigan's 1963 drama *Man and Boy*.

October 13, 2011 Civil rights leader Dr. Martin Luther King, Jr. entertains a supernatural visitor on the night before his assassination in *The Mountaintop*, Katori Hall's drama starring Samuel L. Jackson and Angela Bassett.

October 15, 2011 The "Occupy Wall Street" movement marches uptown to "Occupy Times Square" with a rally to protest income inequity and the wars in Iraq and Afghanistan. Forty-two people are arrested when the crowd, reported by the *Wall Street Journal* as "thousands," refuses to disperse after a three-hour demonstration.

Theatre workers Jared Pike and John Raymond Barker wed on the stage of the St. James Theatre the day gay marriage becomes legal in New York. See June 24, 2011.

Timeline 2011-2012

October 18, 2011 Studio 54, the legendary disco that has operated as a Broadway theatre for more than a decade, reopens for "One Night Only" as a dance hall, reuniting members of the team that worked behind the scenes at the club during its 1977-1981 heyday, along with iconic names chosen from its original guest list.

October 20, 2011 Comedy masters Woody Allen, Ethan Coen and Elaine May each contribute a one-act play to the triple-bill *Relatively Speaking*, which features a cast led by Marlo Thomas, Steve Guttenberg, Danny Hoch, Julie Kavner, Ari Graynor and Mark Linn-Baker.

October 27, 2011 Playwright David Henry Hwang looks at the clash of cultures when an American businessman tries to penetrate the traditional ways behind the booming Chinese economy in *Chinglish*, featuring Gary Wilmes and Jennifer Lim.

nominee for *Born Yesterday*, gets to recreate her star-making 2010 Off-Broadway performance (and win a Tony Award) as an actress who gets a little too much into the role of a dominatrix in David Ives' play, *Venus in Fur*.

November 10, 2011 Tony-winning stage and screen star Hugh Jackman toplines *Hugh Jackman Back on Broadway*, a concert show in which he sings and dances with six chorines. The production sells out most of its two-month run, setting an all-time record $2,056,957 for a single week at any Shubert Organization theatre.

November 14, 2011 The revival of *Chicago* celebrates its 15th anniversary on Broadway.

November 17, 2011 Noël Coward's evergreen comedy *Private Lives* gets its eighth Broadway production, this one starring Kim Cattrall as Amanda and Paul Gross as Elyot, directed by Richard Eyre.

Keys, who is also a co-producer of the show.

December 11, 2011 Director Michael Mayer's radical rethinking of the rarely seen 1965 reincarnation musical *On a Clear Day You Can See Forever* changes the gender of one of the leading characters from female to male. Harry Connick, Jr. stars as a psychiatrist who finds himself falling in love with the female alter-ego of a male patient. The score by Burton Lane (music) and Alan Jay Lerner (lyrics) is enhanced by classics from their film scores for *On a Clear Day You Can See Forever* and *Royal Wedding*. Peter Parnell's new libretto is based on the original book by Lerner.

December 14, 2011 *Lysistrata Jones*, a peppy new musical by Douglas Carter Beane and Lewis Flynn, transposes the action of the Greek classic *Lysistrata* from the Peleponnesian Wars to the world of college basketball. Cheerleaders go on a sex strike to force the laid-back hoopsters to buckle down and play like they mean it. Dan Knechtges directs a cast including Patti Murin, Josh Segarra and Lindsay Nicole Chambers.

December 31, 2011 *The Addams Family* musical closes after 722 performances.

January 3, 2012 *Spider-Man: Turn Off the Dark* rings in the New Year with the highest grossing week in Broadway history—$2,941,790—far outdistancing the previous record of $2,228,235 set by *Wicked* in 2011. The show is helped to that mark by playing an extra performance, and selling out virtually every seat during the week, many at premium prices. The attendance of 17,375 people is also the highest single-week attendance for any single show in Broadway history.

January 8, 2012 The Tony-winning musical *Billy Elliot* closes after a run of 1,312 performances.

January 12, 2012 Diane Paulus' shortened and rewritten *The Gershwins' Porgy and Bess* arrives on Broadway with Norm Lewis and Audra McDonald in the title roles of a crippled beggar and a scarlet woman who find love in the close-knit black enclave of Catfish Row in Charleston, South Carolina. The production, which runs an hour shorter than the full operatic version, also features David Alan Grier, Joshua Henry, Phillip Boykin, Nikki Renée Daniels and NaTasha Yvette Williams.

January 17, 2012 Rosemary Harris, Jim Dale and Carla Gugino star in the Broadway debut of Athol Fugard's *The Road to Mecca*, about an aging female sculptor.

January 24, 2012 The planned spring debut of the musical *Rebecca* suffers the same fate as the *Funny Girl* revival, postponing the production when financing falls through. The adaptation of the classic film was to have starred Sierra Boggess. In March the producers announce the show will be rescheduled to fall 2012.

January 26, 2012 The Broadway premiere of Margaret Edson's Pulitzer Prize-winning play *Wit*, starring Cynthia Nixon.

Comedy titans (L-R) Ethan Coen, Elaine May and Woody Allen contributed original one-acts to the Broadway comedy, *Relatively Speaking*, reflecting the season's overall high-wattage star power. See October 20, 2011.

Photo by Joseph Marzullo/WENN

November 3, 2011 A right-wing Hollywood couple with decidedly left-wing grown children reveals a family secret—but not the one everyone expects—in Jon Robin Baitz's drama *Other Desert Cities*, with a starry cast that includes Stockard Channing, Rachel Griffiths, Judith Light, Stacy Keach and Thomas Sadoski.

November 3, 2011 *Funny Girl*, one of the few golden-age classic musicals never to have had a Broadway reprise, continues its pristine record when an announced revival is cancelled after four investors pull their money. The planned April 2012 production was to have starred Lauren Ambrose as Fanny Brice and Bobby Cannavale as Nick Arnstein.

November 7, 2011 First Broadway revival of *Godspell*, the 1971 Stephen Schwartz/John-Michael Tebelak rock musical that retells *The Gospel According to St. Matthew* with singing, clowning, improvisation and numerous topical references. Daniel Goldstein directs a cast featuring Hunter Parrish, Telly Leung, Uzo Aduba and Nick Blaemire.

November 8, 2011 Nina Arianda, a 2011 Tony

November 20, 2011 Alan Rickman plays a blunt and opinionated teacher hired by a group of young writers to show them the ropes in *Seminar*, Theresa Rebeck's comedy.

November 21, 2011 The Tony-winning co-stars from the original 1979 *Evita* reunite for a concert show titled *An Evening with Patti LuPone and Mandy Patinkin*, singing classic theatre and film tunes.

December 1, 2011 The short, violent career of a pair of Depression-era criminals serves as the plot for the musical *Bonnie & Clyde*, with music by Frank Wildhorn, book by Ivan Menchell and lyrics by Don Black. Laura Osnes and Jeremy Jordan star as the larcenous lovers in Wildhorn's seventh Broadway musical (and, sadly, the fifth in a row to close in the red).

December 8, 2011 A wealthy African-American family gathers at their country house to welcome some new members and to reveal a terrible secret in Lydia R. Diamond's drama *Stick Fly*, starring Dulé Hill, Mekhi Phifer, Tracie Thoms, Ruben Santiago-Hudson and Condola Rashad, with music by pop star Alicia

Timeline 2012-2012

February 6, 2012 Network premiere of "Smash," a TV series that tracks the creation of a new Broadway musical. The show features Broadway stars Christian Borle, Megan Hilty, Brian d'Arcy James and others, and becomes a Monday evening ritual for many theatre fans.

February 11, 2012 *The Phantom of the Opera* becomes the first Broadway show to play 10,000 performances. The historic matinee is presented as a benefit for The Actors Fund.

February 12, 2012 *The Book of Mormon* wins the Grammy Award for Best Musical Theater Album.

February 16, 2012 William Shatner, who made his Broadway debut in the 1956 historical epic *Tamburlaine* and who went on to fame as the two-fisted Captain Kirk in TV's "Star Trek," returns to the stage with *Shatner's World: We Just Live in It*, a tongue-in-cheek solo show about his eventful life.

March 14, 2012 The Tony-winning musical *Memphis* plays its 1000th performance.

March 15, 2012 Philip Seymour Hoffman plays Arthur Miller's iconic antihero, trying to make it in America on a smile and shoeshine in a revival of *Death of a Salesman*, co-starring Linda Emond and Andrew Garfield, directed by Mike Nichols.

March 18, 2012 *Once*, a musical based on the bittersweet film about a romance between an Irish street musician and an enigmatic Czech immigrant woman, comes to Broadway with a full score by Glen Hansard and Markéta Irglová, the original stars/writers of the film.

March 20, 2012 A study commissioned by the Times Square Alliance found that the Broadway theatre district—the area bounded roughly by Sixth and Eighth Avenues from 40th to 53rd Streets—generates $1 of every $9 of economic activity in New York City, about $110 billion overall. That includes not just the theatre industry (just over $1 billion in ticket sales on its own) but the hotels, restaurants, shops, transportation and other economic activities that support the theatre, plus the financial services and media companies that have relocated or expanded there in recent years. The district covers less than 1 percent of the city's land.

March 22, 2012 *Jesus Christ Superstar*, Stratford Shakespeare Festival's production of Andrew Lloyd Webber and Tim Rice's rock musical about Jesus' final days, transfers to Broadway, with direction by Des McAnuff.

March 29, 2012 The new Disney musical *Newsies* officially opens at the Nederlander Theatre following an acclaimed engagement at New Jersey's Paper Mill Playhouse in the fall. Originally a limited engagement, response has been so great that the musical is now playing an open-ended run.

April 1, 2012 Just in time to capitalize on this year's presidential election season comes a revival of Gore Vidal's 1960 play *The Best Man*, about a hard-fought campaign between a ruthless conservative and an idealistic but deter-

The fits, fights, feuds and egos of life backstage at a Broadway musical become the subject of a hit network TV series. See February 6, 2012.

mined liberal, and the effect the process has on their morals and marriages. The all-star cast includes James Earl Jones, Angela Lansbury, Candice Bergen, John Larroquette, Michael McKean, Eric McCormack and Kerry Butler.

April 2, 2012 The final weeks in the life of pop diva Judy Garland are traced in *End of the Rainbow*, Peter Quilter's biographical drama with music, starring Tracie Bennett, which comes to Broadway from the West End.

April 3, 2012 Jeff Goldblum replaces Alan Rickman in *Seminar*.

April 5, 2012 The Broadway revival of Tim Rice and Andrew Lloyd Webber's *Evita* officially opens at the Marquis Theatre. This is the first new Broadway production of the seven-time Tony Award-winning musical since it debuted at the Broadway Theatre over 30 years ago. The Michael Grandage-directed cast is headed by Grammy winner Ricky Martin as Che, Olivier Award winner Elena Roger (repeating her London work) in her Broadway debut as Eva Perón, Tony Award winner Michael Cerveris as Juan Perón, Max von Essen as Magaldi and Rachel Potter as the Mistress.

April 11, 2012 *Lombardi* author Eric Simonson returns to Broadway with another sports-themed drama, *Magic/Bird*, about the friendship and rivalry between Hall of Fame basketball players Larry Bird and Earvin "Magic" Johnson.

April 15, 2012 *Peter and the Starcatcher* is humor columnist Dave Barry's and Ridley Pearson's imagining of how an orphan boy becomes Peter Pan and how a pirate named The Black Stache becomes Captain Hook.

April 16, 2012 *Water by the Spoonful* by Quiara Alegría Hudes wins the Pulitzer Prize for Drama.

April 18, 2012 Broadway transfer of the National Theatre of Great Britain's high-energy farce, *One Man, Two Guvnors*, based on Carlo Goldoni's *The Servant of Two Masters*. James Corden plays the food-loving Francis Henshall, who has the misfortune to be stuck between two murderous criminals as his bosses.

April 19, 2012 Broadway debut of Bruce Norris' 2011 Pulitzer Prize-winner *Clybourne Park*, a sequel of sorts to Lorraine Hansberry's 1959 drama *A Raisin in the Sun*, showing what happens two generations after a black family moves into the all-white Chicago neighborhood of the title.

April 23, 2012 Another London import, *Ghost The Musical* is a high-tech pop adaptation of the Academy Award-winning 1990 film, about a man who tries from beyond the grave to solve his own murder and protect his sweetheart from a similar fate.

April 23, 2012 Also on this date opens the Broadway transfer of Nicky Silver's Off-Broadway comedy *The Lyons*, about a dysfunctional family facing the death of the father. The production stars Linda Lavin and Dick Latessa as a bickering couple.

April 24, 2012 *Nice Work If You Can Get It* is an updated version of the 1926 Gershwin musical comedy *Oh, Kay!*, about romance in Gatsby-era upper-crust Long Island. Stars Matthew Broderick, Kelli O'Hara, Judy Kaye, Jennifer Laura Thompson, Michael McGrath and Estelle Parsons.

April 25, 2012 John Lithgow embodies influential 1960s-era political writer Joseph Alsop in David Auburn's drama, *The Columnist*.

April 26, 2012 The further misadventures of Robert and Bernard from Marc Camoletti's Tony-winning British sex farce *Boeing-Boeing* are chronicled in a revival of the same author's *Don't Dress for Dinner*.

April 26, 2012 Raúl Esparza plays a traveling preacher with a lot more than heaven on his mind in *Leap of Faith*, a musical adaptation of the popular film. It's the second new Alan Menken musical to debut on Broadway in less than a month.

May 22, 2012 Actor Michael McKean is injured when he is struck by a car at the intersection of West 86th Street and Broadway. An understudy steps into his role in *Gore Vidal's The Best Man*; Mark Blum eventually takes over the part, permanently.

May 31, 2012 Broadway ends its most lucrative season on record, selling $1,139,311,457 worth of tickets as of May 27, according to the Broadway League, up 5.4 percent from the previous season. Total attendance is down slightly to 12,334,312, from 12,534,595 in 2010-2011.

June 10, 2012 The 66th Annual Tony Awards are given at the Beacon Theatre. *Clybourne Park* is named Best Play and *Once* is named Best Musical.

—*Robert Viagas*

Head of the Class

Trends, Extraordinary Achievements and Peculiar Coincidences of the Season

Most Tony Awards to a Play: *Peter and the Starcatcher* (5).

Most Tony Awards to a Musical: *Once* (8).

Shortest Regular Run: *Leap of Faith* (19 performances).

Shortest Limited Run: *Shatner's World: We Just Live in It...* (17 performances)

Long Runs Say Farewell: *Billy Elliot* (1312 performances), *The Addams Family* (722 performances).

Stars You Could Have Seen on Broadway This Season: Angela Bassett, Candice Bergen, Christian Borle, Matthew Broderick, Kerry Butler, Norbert Leo Butz, Kim Cattrall, Michael Cerveris, Stockard Channing, Harry Connick Jr., James Corden, Jim Dale, Tyne Daly, Raúl Esparza, Sutton Foster, Joel Grey, Steve Guttenberg, Rosemary Harris, Philip Seymour Hoffman, Hugh Jackman, Samuel L. Jackson, Nick Jonas, James Earl Jones, Stacy Keach, Frank Langella, Angela Lansbury, John Larroquette, Linda Lavin, John Leguizamo, Judith Light, John Lithgow, Patti LuPone, Ricky Martin, Eric McCormack, Audra McDonald, Michael McKean, Donna Murphy, Cynthia Nixon, Kelli O'Hara, Elaine Paige, Mandy Patinkin, Hunter Parrish, Adam Pascal, Bernadette Peters, Daniel Radcliffe, Alan Rickman, Mark Rylance, William Shatner, Brooke Shields, Raven-Symoné, Marlo Thomas, Blair Underwood and Robin Williams, among many more.

Awards They Should Give: #1 Best New Showtune: Our nominees: "If the World Should End" from *Spider-Man*, "Dyin' Ain't So Bad" from *Bonnie & Clyde*, "Falling Slowly" and "Gold" from *Once*, "King of New York" from *Newsies*, "Mermaid Outta Me" from *Peter and the Starcatcher*, "I Can Read You" from *Leap of Faith*.

Jumpin' Jesus: The Christian Son of God was portrayed in three different musicals this season: as the central character in *Godspell* and *Jesus Christ Superstar*, and as a cameo in *The Book of Mormon*.

Angels, Ghosts and Nuns: *The Mountaintop*, *Ghost*, *Follies*, *The Lyons*, *Leap of Faith*, *Sister Act*, *Newsies*, *Billy Elliot*, *Bengal Tiger at the Baghdad Zoo*, *The Addams Family*, *The People in the Picture*.

Operational Basketball Courts Onstage: *Lysistrata Jones*, *Magic/Bird*.

Prequels, Sequels and Follow-ups: *Peter and Starcatcher*, *Clybourne Park*, *Magic/Bird*, *Wicked*.

Awards They Should Give: #2 Best Special Effect: Our nominees: The airborne battle above the Chrysler Building in *Spider-Man*. Jesus makes His entrance walking on a pool of water in *Godspell*. Martin Luther King sees the future in *The Mountaintop*. The giant croc attacks in *Peter and the Starcatcher*. Richard Fleeshman dematerializes from center stage in *Ghost The Musical*.

Kings of New York: Two composers had three musicals playing simultaneously: Alan Menken had *Sister Act*, *Newsies* and *Leap of Faith*.

Andrew Lloyd Webber had *Jesus Christ Superstar*, *Evita* and *Phantom of the Opera*. But no one tops John Gromada who designed sound for six new Broadway shows: *Clybourne Park*, *The Columnist*, *Gore Vidal's The Best Man*, *Man and Boy*, *The Road to Mecca* and *Seminar*.

Two Hats: Jeremy Jordan starred in two musicals: *Bonnie & Clyde* and *Newsies*. Theresa Rebeck, wrote Broadway's *Seminar* and scripts to the TV series "Smash!" Christian Borle co-starred in "Smash!" and *Peter and the Starcatcher*. The Gershwin brothers had their work sung in both *Porgy and Bess* and *Nice Work If You Can Get It*. Sixteen years after *Rent*, New York Theatre Workshop sent two more hits to Broadway: *Once* and *Peter and the Starcatcher*.

Pulitzer-Winning Plays, Old and New: *Death of a Salesman*, *A Streetcar Named Desire*, *How to Succeed in Business Without Really Trying*, *Wit*, *Clybourne Park*. Off-Broadway: *Beyond the Horizon*, *Lost in Yonkers*, *How I Learned to Drive*, *Rent*. *Harvey* was in Broadway previews as the season ended.

Awards They Should Give: #3 Best New Rendition of an Old Song in a Revival or Jukebox Musical: Our nominees: "Day by Day" in *Godspell*. "April in Fairbanks" in *An Evening with Patti LuPone and Mandy Patinkin*. "Soliloquy" in *Hugh Jackman: Back on Broadway*. "Ev'ry Night at Seven" in *On a Clear Day*. "Oh, What a Circus" in *Evita*. "Someone to Watch Over Me" in *Nice Work If You Can Get*

It. "Losing My Mind" in *Follies*. "Buddy's Blues" in *Follies*.

Daddy Has a Secret: *Chinglish*, *Man and Boy*, *Other Desert Cities*, *Stick Fly*, *Death of a Salesman*, *Clybourne Park*.

Erector Set Sets: *Jesus Christ Superstar*, *Newsies*.

Celebrity Composers Doing Incidental Music: Branford Marsalis for *The Mountaintop*. Alicia Keys for *Stick Fly*.

Awards They Should Give: #4 Best Acting Ensemble: Our nominees: *Once*; *Newsies*; *The Gershwins' Porgy and Bess*; *Other Desert Cities*; *Stick Fly*; *Peter and the Starcatcher*.

Creative Use of Luggage: Trunks full of sand/Star Stuff in *Peter and the Starcatcher*. Unliftable trunk in *One Man, Two Guvnors*. Rainbow Tour trunks and girl's suitcase in *Evita*. Stanley rifling the trunk full of Blanche's belongings in *A Streetcar Named Desire*. Samples case in *Death of a Salesman*. Peter Parker's backpack in *Spider-Man*. Bags full of S&M costumes in *Venus in Fur*. Cases of hooch in *Nice Work If You Can Get It*. Offstage bag of drugs in *End of the Rainbow*.

Petite Leading Ladies: Tracie Bennett (5' 2") in *End of the Rainbow*. Elena Roger (just over 5 feet) in *Evita*.

Eva Peron in *Evita* or Magic Johnson in *Magic/Bird*: Kid from a small town rises to the top, takes many lovers then, at the peak of fame, develops a career-ending illness.

Coups de Theatre: Samuel L. Jackson has a cell phone talk with God in *The Mountaintop*. James Corden tries to serve dinner to his two employers (and feed himself) in *One Man, Two Guvnors*. Frank Wood finally loses patience and laces into his racist guest in *Clybourne Park*. Mandy Patinkin and Patti LuPone dance on wheeled office chairs in *An Evening....* The title character of *Spider-Man* flies up to the balcony for the first time. Tyne Daly and Sierra Boggess battle over how to play a scene in *Master Class*. Harry Connick Jr., Jessie Mueller and David Turner do a three-handed waltz to "You're All The World to Me" in *On a Clear Day You Can See Forever*. The cast of *Godspell* takes to the air on tiny trampolines to "We Beseech Thee." Newsboys dance on pages of their own newspapers in *Newsies*. The orchestra dances to "Gold" in *Once*. A few deft pulls transform Spencer Kayden's French maid costume into a slinky evening gown in *Don't Dress for Dinner*. Christian Borle shows how Captain Hook really lost his hand in *Peter and the Starcatcher*. Tom Edden falling down stairs repeatedly in *One Man, Two Guvnors*. An inebriated Judy Kaye literally swings on a chandelier in *Nice Work If You Can Get It*. John Larroquette reveals the surprise title character in the climax of *Gore Vidal's The Best Man*. Elena Roger makers her entrance in a pristine sparkly dress to sing "Don't Cry for Me Argentina" in *Evita*. College girls resolve to go on a sex strike in *Lysistrata Jones*. Kelli O'Hara sings "Someone To Watch Over Me" with a very capable-looking rifle in her hands in *Nice Work If You Can Get It*.

Autographs

The Addams Family

First Preview: March 8, 2010. Opened: April 8, 2010.
Closed December 31, 2011 after 35 Previews and 722 Performances.

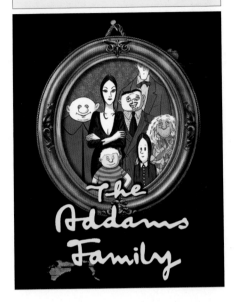

PLAYBILL

The creepy, kooky gothic horror-comedy Addams Family faces a crisis when daughter Wednesday, now grown up, brings home the young man she wants to marry. As Gomez and Morticia prepare to welcome his "normal" family for a get-acquainted dinner in their haunted house, they also face their own aging and the possibility of trouble in their own marriage.

CAST

THE ADDAMS FAMILY

Gomez Addams	ROGER REES
Morticia Addams	BROOKE SHIELDS
Uncle Fester	BRAD OSCAR
Grandma	JACKIE HOFFMAN
Wednesday Addams	RACHEL POTTER
Pugsley Addams	ADAM RIEGLER
Lurch	ZACHARY JAMES

THE BEINEKE FAMILY

Mal Beineke	ADAM GRUPPER
Alice Beineke	HEIDI BLICKENSTAFF
Lucas Beineke	JESSE SWENSON

THE ADDAMS ANCESTORS

BECCA AYERS, TOM BERKLUND,
MO BRADY, ERICK BUCKLEY,
STEPHANIE GIBSON, FRED INKLEY,
LISA KARLIN, REED KELLY,
ALLISON THOMAS LEE, JESSICA LEA PATTY,
LOGAN ROWLAND

All puppetry is performed by members of the
Addams Family Company.

Continued on next page

⇒N⇐ LUNT–FONTANNE THEATRE

UNDER THE DIRECTION OF
JAMES M. NEDERLANDER AND JAMES L. NEDERLANDER

Stuart Oken   Roy Furman   Michael Leavitt   Five Cent Productions
Stephen Schuler   Decca Theatricals   Scott M. Delman   Stuart Ditsky   Terry Allen Kramer   Stephanie P. McClelland
James L. Nederlander   Eva Price   Jam Theatricals/Mary Lu Roffe   Pittsburgh CLO/Gutterman-Swinsky
Vivek Tiwary/Gary Kaplan   The Weinstein Company/Clarence, LLC   Adam Zotovich/Tribe Theatricals

by Special Arrangement with
Elephant Eye Theatrical

present

Roger Rees   Brooke Shields

in

The Addams Family

A NEW MUSICAL COMEDY

Book by
Marshall Brickman & **Rick Elice**

Music and Lyrics by
Andrew Lippa

Based on Characters Created by
Charles Addams

With

Heidi Blickenstaff   Adam Grupper   Zachary James   Brad Oscar
Rachel Potter   Adam Riegler   Jesse Swenson and **Jackie Hoffman**

Merwin Foard   Becca Ayers   Tom Berklund   Jim Borstelmann   Mo Brady
Erick Buckley   Mike Cannon   Valerie Fagan   Stephanie Gibson
Fred Inkley   Lisa Karlin   Reed Kelly   Allison Thomas Lee
Jessica Lea Patty   Logan Rowland   Samantha Sturm

Lighting Design by	Sound Design by	Puppetry by
Natasha Katz	**Acme Sound Partners**	**Basil Twist**

Hair Design by	Make-up Design by	Special Effects by
Tom Watson	**Angelina Avallone**	**Gregory Meeh**

Orchestrations	Music Director	Dance Arrangements	Vocal Arrangements & Incidental Music
Larry Hochman	**Mary-Mitchell Campbell**	**August Eriksmoen**	**Andrew Lippa**

Casting	Press Representative	Marketing	Music Coordinator
Telsey + Company	**The Publicity Office**	**Type A Marketing**	**Michael Keller**

Production Stage Manager	Production Management	General Management
Scott Taylor Rollison	**Aurora Productions**	**101 Productions, Ltd.**

Creative Consultant
Jerry Zaks

Choreography by
Sergio Trujillo

Directed and Designed by
Phelim McDermott & **Julian Crouch**

10/3/11

(L-R): Brooke Shields, Zachary James,
Rachel Potter and Jesse Swenson

Photo by Jeremy Daniel

1

The Addams Family

MUSICAL NUMBERS

ACT ONE

Overture	Orchestra
"When You're an Addams"	The Addams Family, Ancestors
"Where Did We Go Wrong"	Morticia, Gomez
"Pulled"	Wednesday, Pugsley
"One Normal Night"	Company
"Morticia"	Gomez, Male Ancestors
"What If"	Pugsley
"Full Disclosure"	Company
"Waiting"	Alice
"Full Disclosure – Part 2"	Company

ACT TWO

Entr'acte	Orchestra
"Just Around the Corner"	Morticia, Ancestors
"The Moon and Me"	Uncle Fester, Female Ancestors
"Happy/Sad"	Gomez
"Crazier Than You"	Wednesday, Lucas
"Let's Not Talk About Anything Else But Love"	Mal, Gomez, Uncle Fester, Grandma
"In the Arms"	Mal, Alice
"Live Before We Die"	Gomez, Morticia
"Tango de Amor"	Morticia, Gomez, Company
"Move Toward the Darkness"	Company

(L -R): Heidi Blickenstaff, Zachary James, Adam Grupper

Photo by Jeremy Daniel

Cast Continued

STANDBY

Standby for Gomez Addams and Mal Beineke: MERWIN FOARD

UNDERSTUDIES

For Gomez Addams: JIM BORSTELMANN
For Morticia Addams: BECCA AYERS, STEPHANIE GIBSON
For Uncle Fester: JIM BORSTELMANN, ERICK BUCKLEY
For Wednesday Addams: LISA KARLIN, JESSICA LEA PATTY
For Pugsley Addams: LOGAN ROWLAND
For Grandma: BECCA AYERS, VALERIE FAGAN
For Lurch: TOM BERKLUND, FRED INKLEY
For Mal Beineke: FRED INKLEY
For Alice Beineke: BECCA AYERS, VALERIE FAGAN
For Lucas Beineke: MO BRADY, MIKE CANNON

SWINGS

JIM BORSTELMANN, MIKE CANNON, VALERIE FAGAN, TESS SOLTAU, SAMANTHA STURM, CHARLIE SUTTON

Dance Captain: REED KELLY
Puppet Performance Captain: MIKE CANNON
Assistant Dance Captain: MIKE CANNON

ORCHESTRA

Conductor: MARY-MITCHELL CAMPBELL
Associate Conductor: MARCO PAGUIA
Concertmaster: VICTORIA PATERSON
Violin: SEAN CARNEY
Viola: HIROKO TAGUCHI
Cello: ALLISON SEIDNER
Lead Trumpet: JOHN CHUDOBA
Trumpet: BUD BURRIDGE
Trombones/Tuba: ROBERT STUTTMANN
Reed 1: ERICA VON KLEIST
Reed 2: CHARLES PILLOW
Reed 3: FRANK SANTAGATA
French Horn: ZOHAR SCHONDORF
Drums: DAMIEN BASSMAN
Bass: DAVE KUHN
Keyboard 1: MARCO PAGUIA
Keyboard 2: DAVE PEPIN
Guitars: JIM HERSHMAN
Percussion: BILLY MILLER

Music Coordinator: MICHAEL KELLER
Music Copying: KAYE-HOUSTON MUSIC/ ANNE KAYE & DOUG HOUSTON

The Addams Family

Roger Rees
Gomez Addams

Brooke Shields
Morticia Addams

Heidi Blickenstaff
Alice Beineke

Adam Grupper
Mal Beineke

Jackie Hoffman
Grandma

Zachary James
Lurch

Brad Oscar
Uncle Fester

Rachel Potter
Wednesday Addams

Adam Riegler
Pugsley Addams

Jesse Swenson
Lucas Beineke

Merwin Foard
Standby Gomez, Standby Mal Beineke

Becca Ayers
Ancestor

Tom Berklund
Ancestor

Jim Borstelmann
Swing

Mo Brady
Ancestor

Erick Buckley
Ancestor

Mike Cannon
Swing

Valerie Fagan
Swing

Stephanie Gibson
Ancestor

Fred Inkley
Ancestor

Lisa Karlin
Ancestor

Reed Kelly
Ancestor

Allison Thomas Lee
Ancestor

Jessica Lea Patty
Ancestor

Logan Rowland
Ancestor

Tess Soltau
Swing

Samantha Sturm
Swing

Charlie Sutton
Swing

Marshall Brickman
Book

Rick Elice
Book

Andrew Lippa
Music and Lyrics

Phelim McDermott
Director/Designer

Julian Crouch
Director/Designer

Sergio Trujillo
Choreographer

Natasha Katz
Lighting Designer

The Addams Family

Basil Twist
Puppetry

Sten Severson, Tom Clark, Mark Menard and Nevin Steinberg
Acme Sound Partners
Sound Designer

Tom Watson
*Hair and Wig
Designer*

Angelina Avallone
Make-up Designer

Gregory Meeh
*Special Effects
Designer*

Mary-Mitchell
Campbell
Music Director

Larry Hochman
Orchestrations

August Eriksmoen
*Dance
Arrangements*

Bernard Telsey
Telsey + Company
Casting

Michael Keller
Music Coordinator

Beverley Randolph
*Production
Supervisor, 2009-11*

Wendy Orshan
101 Productions, Ltd.
*General
Management*

Stuart Oken
Producer

Roy Furman
Producer

Michael Leavitt
Producer

Stuart Ditsky/Ditsky
Production, LLC
Producer

Terry Allen Kramer
Producer

Stephanie P.
McClelland
Green Curtain
Productions
Producer

James L.
Nederlander
Producer

Eva Price/Maximum
Entertainment
Producer

Arny Granat
Jam Theatricals
Producer

Steve Traxler
Jam Theatricals
Producer

Mary Lu Roffe
Producer

Van Kaplan
Pittsburgh CLO
Producer

Jay and Cindy Gutterman
Producer

Morton Swinsky
Producer

Vivek J. Tiwary
Producer

Bob Weinstein
The Weinstein
Company
Producer

Harvey Weinstein
The Weinstein
Company
Producer

Adam Zotovich
Producer

Carl Moellenberg
Tribe Theatricals
Producer

Wendy Federman
Tribe Theatricals
Producer

The Addams Family

Jamie deRoy
Tribe Theatricals
Producer

Larry Hirschhorn
Tribe Theatricals
Producer

Colin Cunliffe
*Dance Captain,
Puppet Performance
Captain, Swing*

Matthew Gumley
Ancestor

Dontee Kiehn
Swing

Bebe Neuwirth
Morticia Addams

Liz Ramos
Swing

Cortney Wolfson
Ancestor

Michael Buchanan
Swing

Photo by Jeremy Daniel

The cast late in the run (foreground L-R): Jackie Hoffman, Zachary James, Roger Rees, Rachel Potter, Brooke Shields, Brad Oscar and Adam Riegler, with ghosts of Addams ancestors.

STAFF FOR *THE ADDAMS FAMILY*

GENERAL MANAGEMENT
101 PRODUCTIONS, LTD.
Wendy Orshan   Jeffrey M. Wilson
David Auster
Elie Landau

COMPANY MANAGER
Tracy Geltman

PRODUCTION MANAGEMENT
AURORA PRODUCTIONS
Gene O'Donovan, Ben Heller,
Stephanie Sherline, Jarid Sumner, Liza Luxenberg,
Ryan Stanisz, Jason Margolis, Melissa Mazdra

GENERAL PRESS REPRESENTATIVE
THE PUBLICITY OFFICE
Marc Thibodeau
Jeremy Shaffer   Michael S. Borowski

CASTING
TELSEY + COMPANY
Bernie Telsey CSA, Will Cantler CSA, David Vaccari CSA,
Bethany Knox CSA, Craig Burns CSA,
Tiffany Little Canfield CSA, Rachel Hoffman CSA,
Justin Huff CSA, Patrick Goodwin CSA,
Abbie Brady-Dalton, David Morris, Cesar A. Rocha

Production Supervisor, 2009-2011
Beverley Randolph

The Addams Family

Production Stage Manager ....Scott Taylor Rollison
Stage Manager ....Alison A. Lee
Assistant Stage Manager ....Zac Chandler
Associate Company Manager ....Aaron Quintana
Associate Directors ....Heidi Miami Marshall,
Steve Bebout
Drama League Directing Fellow ....David F. Chapman
Associate Choreographer ....Dontee Kiehn
Associate Scenic Designer ....Frank McCullough
Associate Costume Designers ....MaryAnn D. Smith,
David Kaley
Associate Lighting Designer ....Yael Lubetzky
Automated Lighting Programmer ....Aland Henderson
Associate Sound Designer ....Jason Crystal
Associate Special Effects Designer ....Jeremy Chernick
Associate Puppetry Designer ....Ceili Clemens
Assistant Scenic Designers ....Lauren Alvarez,
Jeffrey Hinchee, Christine Peters,
Rob Thirtle
Assistant Costume Designer ....Sarah Laux
Assistant Lighting Designer ....Joel Shier
Assistant Make-up Designer ....Jorge Vargas
Costume Assistant ....Jennifer A. Jacob
Assistant in Puppetry ....Meredith Miller
Production Carpenter ....Paul T. Wimmer
Assistant Carpenter/Automation ....Bill Partello
Flyman ....Bryan S. Davis
Production Electrician ....J. Michael Pitzer
Head Electrician ....Mike Hyman
Assistant Electrician ....Christopher Kurtz
Lead Follow Spot ....Brent Oakley
Production Props ....Denise J. Grillo
Assistant Props ....Kevin Crawford
Production Sound ....David Gotwald
Assistant Sound ....Scott Silvian
Advance Sound ....Darin Stillman
Wardrobe Supervisor ....Linda Lee
Assistant Wardrobe Supervisor ....Andrea Gonzalez
Mr. Rees' Dresser ....Ken Brown
Ms. Shields' Dresser ....Paula Davis
Dressers ....Jennifer Barnes, Ceili Clemens,
Joe Hickey, Betsy Waddell, John Webber
Hair & Make-up Supervisor ....Barry Ernst
Hair Dressers ....Kevin Phillips, Robin Baxter
Music Coordinator ....Michael Keller
Music Preparation ....Kaye-Houston Music, Inc./
Anne Kaye, Doug Houston
Music Preparation Assistants...............Russell Driscoll,
Ernst Ebell, III,
Arthur Koening, Barry Lille
Electronic Music Programmer ....James Abbott
Additional Orchestrations ....August Eriksmoen,
Danny Troob
Additional Drum & Percussion
Arrangements ....Damien Bassman
Music Interns ....Ben Krauss, Tim Rosser,
Adam Wiggins
Children's Guardian ....Katy Lathan
Stage Management
Production Assistants ....CJ LaRoche, Jenn McNeil,
Alison Roberts, Deanna Weiner
Company Management
Assistants ....Johnny Milani, Kathleen Mueller
Lighting Design Production Assistant ....Alec Thorne
Sound Design Production Assistant ....Jessica Bauer
Assistant to Mr. Oken ....Missy Greenberg
Assistant to Mr. Furman ....Eileen Williams

Assistant to Mr. Leavitt ....Erlinda Vo
Assistant to Mr. Lippa ....Will Van Dyke
Legal Counsel ....Levine, Plotkin & Menin LLP/
Loren Plotkin, Esq., Susan Mindell,
Conrad Rippy, Cris Criswell
Accountant ....Rosenberg, Neuwirth,
& Kuchner, CPAs/ Christopher Cacace
Comptroller ....Jana Jevnikar
Advertising ....Serino Coyne/
Sandy Block, Angelo Desimini,
Matt Upshaw
Marketing ....Type A Marketing/
Anne Rippey, Elyce Henkin,
Sarah Ziering
Interactive Marketing ....Situation Interactive/
Damian Bazadona, John Lanasa,
Jeremy Kraus, Brian Hawe
Educational Program ....Camp Broadway
101 Productions, Ltd. Staff ....Beth Blitzer,
Clinton Kennedy, Kathy Kim,
Heidi Neven, Michael Rudd, Mary Six Rupert
101 Productions, Ltd. Interns ....Annora Brennan,
Aislinn Curry, Max Kelsten
Children's Tutoring ....On Location Education/
Alan Simon, Muriel Kester
Banking ....City National Bank/Anne McSweeney
Insurance ....DeWitt Stern, Inc./Peter Shoemaker
Physical Therapy ....PhysioArts/Jennifer R. Green
Orthopedist ....David S. Weiss, MD
Immigration ....Traffic Control Group, Inc./David King
Merchandising ....Encore Merchandising, Inc./
Joey Boyles, Chris Paseka, Maryanna Geller
Production Photographers .....Joan Marcus, Jeremy Daniel
Payroll Services ....Castellana Services, Inc.

www.theaddamsfamilymusical.com

CREDITS

Scenery by Hudson Scenic Studios, Inc., Showman
Fabricators, Chicago Scenic Studios, Inc. Automated
scenery by Hudson Scenic Studios. Lighting equipment and
special lighting effects from PRG Lighting. Sound
equipment from Masque Sound. Costumes executed by Eric
Winterling, Carelli Costumes, Jennifer Love. Costume
painting by Jeffrey Fender. Props by the Paragon Innovation
Group, Jerard Studios, Craig Grigg, Daedalus Design &
Production, Zoe Morsette, ICBA, Inc. Men's shirts by Cego
Custom Shirt. Millinery by Hugh Hanson for Carelli
Costumes and Arnold S. Levine, Inc. Custom footwear by
LaDuca Productions, Ltd.; Pluma Handmade Dance
Footwear; Worldtone Dance; and Sam Vasili Custom Shoes.
"Fester" custom work by Izquierdo Studio. "Grandma's"
shawl by Vanessa Theriault. Additional men's tailoring by
Paul Chang, Chicago. Special effects by Jauchem & Meeh,
Inc. Flying by Foy Aerographic® Services. Make-up
provided by M•A•C. Mr. Grupper's wardrobe provided by
Brooks Brothers. Cell phones courtesy of Nokia. Emergen-
C super energy booster provided by Alacer Corp. Onstage
merchandising by George Fenmore.

"Addams Family Theme" by Vic Mizzy, published by
Unison Music Company (ASCAP). Administered by Next
Decade Entertainment, Inc. All rights reserved, used by
permission.

THE ADDAMS FAMILY rehearsed at
New 42nd Street Rehearsal Studios.

PUPPETRY BUILT BY
TANDEM OTTER PRODUCTIONS
Barbara Busackino, Project Manager
Ceili Clemens, Build Manager
BUILDERS: TV Alexander, Liz Cherry, Duncan Gillis,
Kristin Gdula, Michael Kerns, Matthew Leabo, Vito
Leanza, Nara Lesser, Laura Manns, Eric Novak, Adam
Pagdon, Travis Pickett, Jon Mark Ponder, Jessica Scott, Ted
Southern, Nikki Taylor, Will Pike

MUSIC CREDITS
"For What It's Worth" (Stephen Stills), ©1967 (renewed),
Richie Furay Music (BMI), Springalo Toones (BMI), Ten
East Music (BMI) and Cotillion Music Inc. (BMI). All
rights administered by Warner-Tamerlane Publishing Corp.
All rights reserved. Used by permission. **"Maniac"** (Dennis
Matkosky and Michael Sembello), ©1983 WB Music Corp.
(ASCAP), Sony/ATV Harmony (ASCAP) and Intersong-
USA, Inc. (ASCAP). All rights administered by WB Music
Corp. All rights reserved. Used by permission. **"Puff (The
Magic Dragon)"** (Peter Yarrow, Leonard Lipton), ©1963
(renewed), 1991 Silver Dawn Music (ASCAP) and Honalee
Melodies (ASCAP). All rights on behalf of Silver Dawn
Music administered by WB Music Corp. Worldwide rights
for Honalee Melodies administered by Cherry Lane Music
Publishing Company, Inc. (ASCAP). All rights reserved.
Used by permission. **"So Long, Farewell"** (music by
Richard Rodgers, lyrics by Oscar Hammerstein II). This
selection is used by special arrangement with The Rodgers
and Hammerstein Organization. All rights reserved. Used
by permission.

Souvenir merchandise by
Encore Merchandising, Inc.

Original cast album now available on
Decca Records.

For booking information, contact Meredith Blair:
www.thebookinggroup.com

NEDERLANDER

Chairman ....**James M. Nederlander**
President ....**James L. Nederlander**

Executive Vice President
Nick Scandalios

Vice President   Senior Vice President
Corporate Development   Labor Relations
Charlene S. Nederlander   **Herschel Waxman**

Vice President   Chief Financial Officer
Jim Boese   **Freida Sawyer Belviso**

STAFF FOR THE LUNT-FONTANNE
House Manager ....**Tracey Malinowski**
Treasurer ....Joe Olcese
Assistant Treasurer ....Gregg Collichio
House Carpenter ....Terry Taylor
House Electrician ....Dennis Boyle
House Propertyman ....Andrew Bentz
House Flyman ....Matt Walters
House Engineers ....Robert MacMahon,
Joseph Riccio III

The Addams Family
SCRAPBOOK

Photo by Joseph Marzullo/WENN

①

Correspondent: Zachary James, "Lurch"
Most Vivid Memory of the Final Performance: Singing "Auld Lang Syne" with the audience.
Memorable Notes and Gifts in the Final Weeks: Douglas Sills sent us brownies from the road tour. Also, the touring cast faxed us a congratulatory poster which they all signed with personal messages.
Farewell Parties and/or Gifts: The producers gave us a puzzle of the show poster. Our closing party was at the Paramount Hotel Library Bar on 46th Street.
Special Backstage Rituals: "Word of the Day," Reed Kelly's Project Runway Design Challenge Barbie.
Favorite Moment During the Final Weeks: As we counted down the final performances, remembering the conception of the show years back and how each scene, moment, character was given birth.
Favorite In-Theatre Gathering Places: Heidi Blickenstaff's dressing room, The Hair Room.
Favorite Off-Site Hangouts: Port Authority Bowling Alley, Glass House Tavern.
Favorite Snack Food: Birthday cake.
Mascot: Bernice the Squid, R.I.P.
Favorite Therapy: Physical therapy from PhysioArts.
Memorable Ad-Lib: "Grandma can't get enough Dick...Clark."
Fastest Costume Changes: The ladies from ghosts to bathing beauties to puppeteers. Tom Berklund from Thing to Pilgrim.
Catchphrase Only the Company Would Recognize: "Yes."
Orchestra Member Who Played the Most

②

Photos courtesy Zachary James

③

④

1. The cast celebrates the show's 500th performance on stage by plunging a knife into the heart of a specially designed cake (L-R): Jesse Swenson, Becca Ayers, Rachel Potter, Adam Grupper, Bebe Neuwirth, Roger Rees, Brad Oscar, Adam Riegler, Jackie Hoffman and *Yearbook* correspondent Zachary James.
2. (L-R): *Yearbook* correspondent Zachary James shares a jaw-dropping moment in Times Square with Adam Riegler and Mo Brady.
3. Members of the ghostly ancestors ensemble gather backstage.
4. A somewhat more somber pastry to mark the final performance.

Instruments: Damien Bassman, percussion.
Orchestra Member Who Played the Most Consecutive Performances Without a Sub: Allison Seidner, cello.
Best In-House Parody Lyrics: "Move toward the exit." "When you're an Addams, you have

white makeup on your cell phone."
Memorable Directorial Note: Stand still with your two feet underneath you and tell the truth.
Coolest Thing About Being in This Show: Bringing Charles Addams' iconic characters to life.

Anything Goes

First Preview: March 10, 2011. Opened: April 7, 2011.
Still running as of May 31, 2012.

When Billy Crocker learns that the girl of his dreams, Hope Harcourt, is sailing off to Europe to marry a rich twit, Billy stows away and adopts a series of disguises in hopes of winning her away from her fiancé and her disapproving mother. Along the way Billy gets help from gangster Moonface Martin and nightclub singer Reno Sweeney in a series of farcical plots that eventually win Hope's heart and hand.

CAST

(in order of appearance)

Elisha Whitney .... JOHN McMARTIN
Fred, a bartender .... DEREK HANSON
Billy Crocker .... BILL ENGLISH
Reno Sweeney .... STEPHANIE J. BLOCK
Captain .... WALTER CHARLES
Ship's Purser .... ROBERT CREIGHTON
Crew .... LAWRENCE ALEXANDER,
BRANDON BIEBER, WARD BILLEISEN,
DANIEL J. EDWARDS, DEREK HANSON,
KEVIN MUNHALL, BRANDON RUBENDALL,
WILLIAM RYALL
A Reporter .... LAWRENCE ALEXANDER
A Photographer .... BRANDON BIEBER
Henry T. Dobson, a minister ...... WILLIAM RYALL
Luke .... ANDREW CAO
John .... RAYMOND J. LEE
Angels
Purity .... SHINA ANN MORRIS
Chastity .... BRITTANY MARCIN
Charity .... JENNIFER SAVELLI
Virtue .... HAYLEY PODSCHUN

Continued on next page

Continued on next page

STEPHEN SONDHEIM THEATRE

ROUNDABOUTTHEATRECOMPANY

Todd Haimes, Artistic Director
Harold Wolpert, Managing Director
Julia C. Levy, Executive Director

Presents

Stephanie J. Block *and* Joel Grey

ANYTHING GOES

Music & Lyrics by
Cole Porter

Original Book by
P.G. Wodehouse & Guy Bolton
and Howard Lindsay & Russel Crouse

New Book by
Timothy Crouse & John Weidman

with

Bill English   Erin Mackey   Robert Petkoff   Jessica Stone
Walter Charles   Robert Creighton   Andrew Cao   Raymond J. Lee

Lawrence Alexander   Leslie Becker   Brandon Bieber   Ward Billeison   Daniel J. Edwards
Justin Greer   Derek Hanson   Tari Kelly   Michelle Loucadoux   Brittany Marcin
Shina Ann Morris   Kevin Munhall   Mary Michael Patterson   Hayley Podschun
Brandon Rubendall   William Ryall   Jennifer Savelli   Kiira Schmidt   Vanessa Sonon

with

John McMartin
and
Julie Halston

Set Design Derek McLane	*Costume Design* Martin Pakledinaz	*Lighting Design* Peter Kaczorowski	*Sound Design* Brian Ronan
Additional Orchestrations Bill Elliott	*Original Orchestrations* Michael Gibson	*Dance Arrangements* David Chase	*Music Director/Conductor* James Lowe	*Music Coordinator* Seymour Red Press
Hair & Wig Design Paul Huntley	*Makeup Design* Angelina Avallone	*Production Stage Manager* Peter Hanson	*Casting* Jim Carnahan, C.S.A. & Stephen Kopel
Associate Director Marc Bruni	*Associate Choreographer* Vince Pesce	*Technical Supervisor* Steve Beers	*Executive Producer* Sydney Beers
Press Representative Boneau-Bryan/Brown	*Director of Marketing & Sales Promotion* Thomas Mygatt	*Director of Development* Lynne Gugenheim Gregory	*Founding Director* Gene Feist	*Associate Artistic Director* Scott Ellis

Music Supervisor/Vocal Arranger
Rob Fisher

Directed and Choreographed by
Kathleen Marshall

Proud Sponsor BANK OF AMERICA

*Anything Goes benefits from Roundabout's Musical Theatre Fund with gifts from Marty and Perry Granoff, HRH Foundation, Ted and Mary Jo Shen, Peter and Leni May, Tom and Diane Tuft, The Kaplen Foundation, and one anonymous donor. Roundabout thanks the Henry Nias Foundation, courtesy of Dr. Stanley Edelman, for their support of Anything Goes. *Generously underwritten by Margot Adams, in memory of Mason Adams.*

Anything Goes was produced by Lincoln Center Theater in 1987.

3/12/12

Stephanie J. Block with Sailors (L-R): Clyde Alves, Josh Franklin, Anthony Wayne, Ward Billeisen (kneeling), Adam Perry (standing), Kevin Munhall

Photo by Joan Marcus

Anything Goes

SCENES & MUSICAL NUMBERS

ACT ONE

Overture

Scene 1: **A Smoky Manhattan Bar**
"I Get a Kick Out of You" ....Reno Sweeney

Scene 2: **The Afterdeck of an Ocean Liner**
"There's No Cure Like Travel" ....Captain, Purser and Sailors
"Bon Voyage" ....Sailors and Passengers

Scene 3: **On Deck, that evening**
"You're the Top" ....Reno Sweeney and Billy Crocker
"Easy to Love" ....Billy Crocker
Reprise: "Easy to Love" ....Hope Harcourt

Scene 4: **Whitney's Stateroom/Moon's Adjacent Cabin**
"The Crew Song" ....Elisha Whitney

Scene 5: **On Deck, mid-morning**
"There'll Always Be a Lady Fair" (Sailor's Chantey) ....Quartet
"Friendship" ....Moonface Martin and Reno Sweeney

Scene 6: **Evelyn's Stateroom**

Scene 7: **On Deck, at twilight**
"It's De-lovely" ....Billy Crocker and Hope Harcourt

Scene 8: **On Deck, early the following morning**
"Anything Goes" ....Reno Sweeney, Sailors and Passengers

ACT TWO

Entr'Acte

Scene 1: **The Ship's Nightclub**
"Public Enemy Number One" ....Captain, Purser and Passengers
"Blow, Gabriel, Blow" ....Reno Sweeney, Angels and Passengers
"Goodbye, Little Dream, Goodbye" ....Hope Harcourt

Scene 2: **The Ship's Brig**
"Be Like the Blue Bird" ....Moonface Martin
"All Through the Night" ....Billy Crocker, Hope Harcourt and Quartet

Scene 3: **On Deck, later that night**
"The Gypsy in Me" ....Lord Evelyn Oakleigh and Reno Sweeney

Scene 4: **The Ship's Brig**

Scene 5: **On Deck**
"Buddie, Beware" ....Erma and Sailors
Finale ....Full Company

ORCHESTRA

Conductor:
JAMES LOWE
Associate Conductor:
DAVID GURSKY
Music Coordinator:
SEYMOUR RED PRESS
Reeds:
JIM ERCOLE, RON JANNELLI,
RALPH OLSEN, DAVE YOUNG
Trumpets:
EARL GARDNER, KEN RAMPTON,
STU SATALOF
Trombone:
LARRY FARRELL, ROB FOURNIER,
WAYNE GOODMAN

Piano:
DAVID GURSKY
Bass:
JEFF CARNEY
Drums:
JOHN REDSECKER
Percussion:
BILL HAYES
Guitar:
ERIC DAVIS
Synthesizer Programmer:
BRUCE SAMUELS
Music Copying:
EMILY GRISHMAN MUSIC PREPARATION—
KATHARINE EDMONDS/EMILY GRISHMAN

Cast Continued

Hope Harcourt ....ERIN MACKEY
Mrs. Evangeline Harcourt ....JULIE HALSTON
Lord Evelyn Oakleigh ....ROBERT PETKOFF
FBI Agents ....KEVIN MUNHALL,
                            BRANDON RUBENDALL
Erma ....JESSICA STONE
Moonface Martin ....JOEL GREY
Old Lady in a Wheelchair ....LESLIE BECKER
Quartet ....WARD BILLEISEN,
        DANIEL J. EDWARDS, DEREK HANSON,
                                 WILLIAM RYALL
Ship's Passengers ......LAWRENCE ALEXANDER,
        LESLIE BECKER, BRANDON BIEBER,
        WARD BILLEISEN, DANIEL J. EDWARDS,
        DEREK HANSON, TARI KELLY,
                              KEVIN MUNHALL,
        MARY MICHAEL PATTERSON,
                            BRANDON RUBENDALL,
        WILLIAM RYALL, KIIRA SCHMIDT

SWINGS

JUSTIN GREER, MICHELLE LOUCADOUX,
VANESSA SONON

UNDERSTUDIES

For Reno Sweeney:
TARI KELLY, KIIRA SCHMIDT
For Billy Crocker & Evelyn Oakleigh:
DEREK HANSON
For Moonface Martin:
ROBERT CREIGHTON
For Hope Harcourt:
MICHELLE LOUCADOUX,
MARY MICHAEL PATTERSON
For Mrs. Evangeline Harcourt:
LESLIE BECKER, TARI KELLY
For Elisha Whitney & Captain:
WILLIAM RYALL
For the Purser:
BRANDON BIEBER, JUSTIN GREER
For Erma:
TARI KELLY, HAYLEY PODSCHUN
For Luke:
BRANDON BIEBER, DANIEL J. EDWARDS
For John:
ANDREW CAO, DANIEL J. EDWARDS

Dance Captain: JENNIFER SAVELLI
Assistant Dance Captain: JUSTIN GREER

Production Stage Manager: PETER HANSON
Stage Manager: JON KRAUSE
Assistant Stage Manager: RACHEL BAUDER

Anything Goes

Stephanie J. Block
Reno Sweeney

Joel Grey
Moonface Martin

John McMartin
Elisha Whitney

Julie Halston
Mrs. Evangeline Harcourt

Bill English
Billy Crocker

Erin Mackey
Hope Harcourt

Robert Petkoff
Lord Evelyn Oakleigh

Jessica Stone
Erma

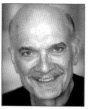

Walter Charles
Captain

Robert Creighton
Ship's Purser

Andrew Cao
Luke

Raymond J. Lee
John

Lawrence Alexander
Crew, Reporter, Passenger

Leslie Becker
Old Lady in a Wheelchair, Passenger

Brandon Bieber
Crew, Photographer, Passenger

Ward Billeisen
Crew, Passenger, Quartet

Daniel J. Edwards
Crew, Quartet

Justin Greer
Swing

Derek Hanson
Fred, Crew, Passenger, Quartet

Tari Kelly
Passenger

Michelle Loucadoux
Swing

Brittany Marcin
Chastity

Shina Ann Morris
Purity

Kevin Munhall
FBI Agent, Passenger

Mary Michael Patterson
Passenger

Hayley Podschun
Virtue

Brandon Rubendall
Crew, Passenger

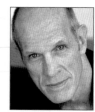

William Ryall
Crew, Henry T. Dobson, Passenger, Quartet

Jennifer Savelli
Charity, Dance Captain

Kiira Schmidt
Passenger

Vanessa Sonon
Swing

Cole Porter
Music & Lyrics

Guy Bolton
Original Book

P.G. Wodehouse
Original Book

Timothy Crouse
Co-Author of the New Book

10

Anything Goes

John Weidman
New Book

Kathleen Marshall
*Director &
Choreographer*

Derek McLane
Scenic Design

Martin Pakledinaz
Costume Design

Peter Kaczorowski
Lighting Design

Brian Ronan
Sound Design

Rob Fisher
*Musical Supervisor,
Vocal Arranger*

Bill Elliott
*Additional
Orchestrations*

Seymour Red Press
Musical Coordinator

David Chase
Dance Arranger

James Lowe
*Musical Director/
Conductor*

Paul Huntley
Hair & Wig Design

Angelina Avallone
Make-Up Design

Kathy Fabian/
Propstar
*Properties
Coordinator*

Marc Bruni
Associate Director

Vince Pesce
*Associate
Choreographer*

Jim Carnahan
Casting

Gene Feist
*Founding Director,
Roundabout Theatre
Company*

Todd Haimes
*Artistic Director,
Roundabout Theatre
Company*

ALUMNI
2011-2012

Clyde Alves
*Photographer, Crew,
Passenger*

Kelly Bishop
*Mrs. Evangeline
Harcourt*

Joyce Chittick
Virtue

Nikki Renée Daniels
Passenger

Colin Donnell
Billy Crocker

Kimberly Fauré
Chastity

Sutton Foster
Reno Sweeney

Josh Franklin
*Fred, Passenger,
Quartet*

Kearran Giovanni
Chastity

Adam Godley
Lord Evelyn Oakleigh

Linda Mugleston
*Old Lady in a
Wheelchair,
Passenger*

Laura Osnes
Hope Harcourt

Adam Perry
*Crew, FBI Agent,
Passenger*

Jessica Walter
*Mrs. Evangeline
Harcourt*

Anthony Wayne
*Crew, Passenger,
Photographer,*

Anything Goes

Kristen Beth
Williams
Passenger

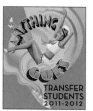

Janine DiVita
Passenger

Ed Dixon
Captain

Colin Donnell
Billy Crocker

John Horton
Elisha Whitney

Kaitlin Mesh
Virtue

Photos by Brian Mapp

CREW
Stairs (Top-Bottom):
Erika Warmbrunn (Followspot Operator),
John Patrick "JP" Nord (Deck Carpenter),
William Craven (Flyman), Paul Ashton
(Automation Operator), Nelson Vaughn
(Properties Running Crew),
Jessica Morton (Followspot Operator)

Left of Stairs (L-R):
Dan Mendeloff (Properties Running Crew),
Josh Weitzman (Production
Electrician/Moving Light Programmer)

Right of Stairs (Clockwise from Top):
Matt Gratz (Followspot Sub),
Donald "Buck" Roberts (Deck Carpenter),
Andrew Forste (House Properties),
Steve Beers (Production Carpenter),
Christopher Ford (Properties Running
Crew Sub), Shannon Slaton (Production
Sound Engineer/Sound Mixer),
Dorion Fuchs (Followspot Operator)

HAIR DEPARTMENT
(L-R): Kelli Reid
(Hair Assistant),
Jessie Mojica
(Hair Assistant),
Heather Wright
(Hair Assistant),
Nathaniel Hathaway
(Hair & Wig Supervisor)

BOX OFFICE STAFF
(Clockwise from Top): Ron Tobia (Box Office), Andrew Clements
(Assistant Box Office Manager), Carlos Morris (Box Office)

Not pictured: Jaime Perlman (Head Treasurer)

Anything Goes

Photos by Brian Mapp

WARDROBE
Stairs (Top-Bottom): Nadine Hettel (Wardrobe Supervisor), Emily Merriweather (Dresser), Tara Delahunt (Dresser), Ruth Goya (Dayworker), Polly Noble (Dayworker/Dresser Sub), Kevin Mark Harris (Dresser), Jessie St. George (Dayworker)

Left of Stairs (L-R): Suzanne Delahunt (Dresser), Julien Havard (Dresser)

Right of Stairs (L-R): Pamela Pierzina (Dresser), James Cavanaugh (Dayworker)

ORCHESTRA
Stairs (Top-Bottom): Bill Hayes (Percussion), James Lowe (Music Director/ Conductor), John Redsecker (Drums), James Ercole (Reeds)

Left of Stairs (L-R): Earl Gardner (Trumpet), Ronald Jannelli (Reeds), Wayne Goodman (Trombone)

Right of Stairs (L-R): David Gursky (Associate Conductor/Keyboard), Stu Satalof (Trumpet), Ken Rampton (Trumpet), David Young (Reeds)

STAGE MANAGEMENT/COMPANY MANAGEMENT
(Clockwise from Top): Peter Hanson (Production Stage Manager), Jon Krause (Stage Manager), Doug Gaeta (Company Manager), Rachel Bauder (Assistant Stage Manager), Jeffrey Rodriguez (Stage Management Sub)

Not Pictured: David Solomon (Assistant Company Manager)

FRONT OF HOUSE STAFF
Standing on Stairs (Top-Bottom): Megan Kosmoski, Jehan O. Young, Caroline Carbo, Michael Portman, Karen Murray

Seated on Stairs (L-R): Jessica Alverson, Billy Peña (Usher Sub)

Left of Stairs (L-R): Christopher Ruth, Johannah-Joy Magyawe (House Manager)

Right of Stairs: Delores Danska (Usher Sub)

Anything Goes

Anything Goes
SCRAPBOOK

Correspondent: Raymond J. Lee, "John"

Memorable Notes, Faxes or Fan Letters: We're coming up on our first anniversary and we still have all of our opening night faxes from the other Broadway shows on our callboard and on the walls backstage. All of us love walking past the hallway of faxes and letters because it reminds us how lucky we are to be working on Broadway and also shows how warm the entire theatre community is. I know Sutton Foster also gets a lot of cool fan art!

Parties, Celebrations and Gifts: We had a fantastic Christmas Party. Roundabout gave us Virgil's barbecue and we had ribs, brisket, barbecued chicken, mac-and-cheese…the works! We were definitely "food coma-ing" during that evening's show. It took a lot of coffee to get through it. We also had our first Secret Santa reveal after the party, where each person got to open their present in front of everyone else and got two guesses before their Secret Santa revealed who they were. We had a barrel of laughs watching people try to decipher who it might be. Our favorite reveal was when Kelly Bishop said, "Well, the wrapping on my present is so amazing, it has to be a lady." One of the male dressers stood up and said, "I'm your lady!"

Most Exciting Celebrity Visitors: President Clinton, Secretary of State Hillary Clinton, and their daughter Chelsea came to see the show and we were all pretty excited about that. It was cool to see them clapping along and having a great time, and we were all in a nervous huddle when they came backstage. Liza Minnelli also came to see the show and during the curtain call, it was so heart-warming to see her and Joel pointing at each other, giving each other a thumbs-up, and blowing kisses to each other. That was really cool!

Actor Who Has Done the Most Shows: Joyce Chittick received the Gypsy Robe on Opening Night, so she probably has been in the most Broadway shows. She designed our portion of the Gypsy Robe beautifully.

Actor Who Performed the Most Roles in This Show: William Ryall seems to play the most roles, including Reverend Dobson, a sailor, a member of the Quartet, and a first class passenger. Several members of the ensemble also play many roles. They may start as one character, then run offstage, change and come back as another character, all in the same scene! This show has people quick-changing like crazy. Thank God we have a stellar wardrobe team

Laura Osnes and Colin Donnell recording the cast album.

Photo by Krissie Fullerton

that makes sure we are taken care of.

Special Backstage Rituals: So many! Sometimes I think we have an even better show backstage than the one on stage. Everybody has their own special rituals and we all seem to have specific moments backstage where we entertain one another. Andrew Cao, Jess Stone and I have a moment where we try and do a little dance for

---

MANAGING DIRECTOR

EMERITUS .... Ellen Richard

Roundabout Theatre Company
231 West 39th Street, New York, NY 10018
(212) 719-9393.

GENERAL PRESS REPRESENTATIVE
BONEAU/BRYAN-BROWN
Adrian Bryan-Brown
Matt Polk   Jessica Johnson   Amy Kass

CREDITS FOR *ANYTHING GOES*

Company Manager .... Karl Baudendistel
Assistant Company Manager .... David Solomon
Production Stage Manager .... Peter Hanson
Assistant Stage Manager ....Rachel Bauder
Stage Manager .... Jon Krause
Dance Captain ....Jennifer Savelli
Assistant Dance Captain .... Justin Greer
Assistant Choreographer .... David Eggers
Assistant Set Designer ....Erica Hemminger
Associate Costume Designer ....Sara Jean Tosetti
Costume Design Assistant ....Carisa Kelly
Assistant to the
    Costume Designer .... Justin Hall
Costume Interns ....Hannah Kittel, Shannon Smith,
    Heather Mathiesen
Associate Lighting Designer ....Paul Toben
Assistant Lighting Designer ....Gina Scherr
Associate Wig and
    Hair Designer ....Giovanna Calabretta
Makeup Design Associate ....Jorge Vargas
Assistant Sound Designer ....John Emmett O'Brien
Production Sound Engineer ....Shannon Slaton
Music Department
    Interns ....Molly Gachignard, Ian Weinberger
Production Carpenter ....Steve Beers

Automation Operator ....Paul Ashton
Flyman .... William Craven
Deck Carpenters ....Donald Roberts, John Patrick Nord
Production Electrician/
    Moving Light Programmer ....Josh Weitzman
Assistant Production Electricians ....John Wooding,
    Jocelyn Smith
Sound Mixer..............................Shannon Slaton
Followspot Operators ....Dorion Fuchs,
    Erika Warmbrunn, Jessica Morton
Deck Electricians ....Jocelyn Smith,
    Francis Elers
House Properties ....Andrew Forste
Properties Running Crew ....Dan Mendeloff,
    Nelson Vaughn
Associate Production Properties ....Carrie Mossman
Prop Artisans ....Mike Billings, Tim Ferro,
    Cathy Small, Mary Wilson
Wardrobe Supervisor ....Nadine Hettel
Dressers.................Steve Chazaro, Suzanne Delahunt,
    Tara Delahunt, Emily Merriweather,
    Jean Naughton, Pamela Pierzina,
    Stacy Sarmiento
Hair and Wig Supervisor ....Nathaniel Hathaway
Hair Assistants ....Kelly Reid, Jessie Mojica,
    Shanah-Ann Kendall
SDC Observer .... Adam Cates
Production Assistant ....Hannah Dorfman
Physical Therapy ....Performing Arts Physical Therapy

CREDITS
Scenery fabrication by Hudson Scenic Studio, Inc. Scenic elements constructed by global scenic services, inc., Bridgeport, CT. Lighting equipment by PRG Lighting. Audio equipment by PRG Audio. Costumes by Arel Studio Inc.; Artur & Tailors Ltd.; Carelli Costumes Inc.; Helen Uffner Vintage Clothing, LLC; Krostyne Studio; Parson-

Meares, Ltd; Paul Chang Custom Tailors; Tricorne, Inc. Millinery by Lynne Mackey Studio, Rodney Gordon, Inc. Men's hats by J.J. Hatts Center. Furs by Sharnelle Furs. Shoes by JC Theatrical, LaDuca, Worldtone Dance. Shoe repair by Rostelle Shoe Repair. Mr. McMartin's glasses provided by Myoptics. Special thanks to Bra*Tenders for hosiery and undergarments. Softgoods by I. Weiss. Specialty prop construction by Cigar Box Studios, Inc.; Costume Amour; Craig Grigg; Anne Guay; Aardvark Interiors. Flame treatment by Turning Star, Inc.

Flying by Foy

STEPHEN SONDHEIM THEATRE
SYDNEY BEERS   GREG BACKSTROM
General Manager   Associate Managing Director
VALERIE SIMMONS
Operations Manager

Make-up provided by M•A•C

STEPHEN SONDHEIM THEATRE STAFF
Operations Manager .... Valerie D. Simmons
House Manager .... Johannah-Joy G. Magyawe
Assistant House Manager ....Molly McQuilkin
Head Treasurer .... Jaime Perlman
Associate Treasurer .... Andrew Clements
Assistant Treasurers .... Kiah Johnson, Carlos Morris,
    Ronnie Tobia
House Carpenter ....Steve Beers
House Electrician ....Josh Weitzman
House Properties ....Andrew Forste
Engineer .... Deosarran
Security .... Gotham Security
Maintenance .... C+W Cleaning Services Inc.
Lobby Refreshments by .... Sweet Concessions

Anything Goes
SCRAPBOOK

the sailors exiting stage right. The actors playing the Harcourt Family, including Kelly Bishop and Erin Mackey, hang out near the greenroom and chat together before the show starts. Before "Blow, Gabriel, Blow," we all gather together on stage and it almost becomes a quick catch-up party. Runway Sundays has also been a tradition before our Sunday matinees. And of course we make sure to sing "Happy Trails" right after the curtain comes down, to a company member who is leaving us.

Favorite Moment: Definitely has to be our curtain call. It is such a rush to see the sea of smiling faces and the standing ovation we've received after every show. The audience really seems to enjoy *Anything Goes* and that's the biggest payoff of all.

Favorite In-Theatre Gathering Place: Dressing Room #4, which I share with Robert Creighton, Walter Charles and Andrew Cao, seems to be a huge hangout room. I don't know if it's the enormous amounts of candy Colin Donnell leaves in our room or the Wii Ping Pong or Dr. Mario tournaments we have, but we LOVE having people in our room!

Favorite Off-Site Hangout: HB Burger and Un Deux Trois are probably our two favorite hangout places for drinks after a show or a bite in between.

Favorite Snack Foods: Sour Patch Kids, jelly beans, chocolate covered ANYTHING, bagels and cream cheese (courtesy of Sutton Foster)…basically anything sweet and edible.

Mascot: Our Four Show Babies (Lua, Juliet, RJC3, & Helena) and, of course, our official show mascot is Cheeky.

Favorite Therapies: Physical Therapy, foam rollers, Emergen-C, massage, coffee and Chipotle.

Memorable Ad-Libs: "If they ever swipe your teeth and you lose your nose…Irish Clothes"— Joel Grey. (Original: "If you ever lose your teeth when you're out to dine, borrow mine.")
"Wire confirmation with the information of the finalization of the amalgamated sale at once."— John McMartin. (Followed by Colin Donnell having to remember and recite the entire thing!)
"Christians don't use….many things."— William Ryall

Memorable Press Encounter: Our six sailor boys and their sexy photo shoot on top of the Intrepid aircraft carrier on a hot sunny day. We have some ridiculously attractive male ensemble members!

Memorable Stage Door Fan Encounter: Darci Caitlin Faye is our biggest fan. She has been to our show several times and it is such a pleasure to see her smiling face at the stage door. We are lucky to have fans like her.

Web Buzz: We have a wonderful web buzz on our show! People on the various message boards seem to really enjoy it and the critics loved our show and gave us some awesome reviews. Checking on the Roundabout Facebook page, there seem to be many happy people who come to see *Anything Goes*.

Members of the cast celebrate the show's 400th performance onstage on March 21, 2012 (L-R): Daniel J. Edwards, Robert Creighton, Joel Grey, Stephanie J. Block, Julie Halston, Jennifer Savelli, Brittany Marcin, Vanessa Sonon and *Yearbook* correspondent Raymond J. Lee.

Photo by Joseph Marzullo/WENN

Fastest Costume Change: Colin Donnell probably has the fastest costume changes in our show. Whether it's right after "I Get a Kick Out of You" or from his various sailor to fake Evelyn Oakleigh costume changes, he is definitely going at full speed to make sure he makes his entrances.

Heaviest/Hottest Costume: William Ryall wears three layers of costumes at the very top of the show. Passenger clothes underneath sailor clothes underneath his Reverend Dobson costume.

Who Wore the Least: Sutton Foster and the Angels during "Blow, Gabriel, Blow" definitely wear the sexiest costumes in the show. And there have been no complaints!

Catchphrases Only the Company Would Recognize: "Boxcars Craps!" "We are the Caution Bros." "Ooh Child." "Count Your Coin." "Ring Them Bells." "Runway Sunday."

Sweethearts Within the Company: Andrew Cao & Raymond J. Lee (but more like an old bickering married couple).

Orchestra Member Who Played the Most Instruments: Our Percussionist Bill Hayes wins this numbers contest! He plays 21 instruments total: vibes, xylophone, glock, chimes, timpani, bongos, field drum, triangle, 2 tambourines, claves, castanets, temple blocks, wood block, suspended cymbal, pair of cymbals, gong, cabasa, crotale, ship's bell and bird whistle.

Orchestra Member Who Played the Most Consecutive Performances Without a Sub: Ron Jannelli went 92 shows before his first sub, unmatched by anyone since.

Company Legends: John McMartin has not missed a performance due to illness yet! That is such a fantastic accomplishment and he was awarded his own Squigs caricature for being the last man standing.

Tale From the Put-in: Justin Greer as Reno Sweeney was kind of amazing. He knew all the steps and jumped right in there for Sutton

during one of our January Put-In Rehearsals.

Understudy Anecdote: Jeffrey Schecter probably holds the record for the least time ever from the start of rehearsal to debut: 48 hours! That has got to be a Broadway record. He started the show on a Thursday morning and went in the following Friday evening performance. The best part was the fact that he still hadn't learned the words to "Public Enemy" and had to mouth his words as best as possible. The cast members on stage right had the hardest time singing because we were laughing so hard.

Nicknames: Crasians (Andrew Cao & Raymond J. Lee). Club Angel (Kimberly Fauré, Shina Ann Morris, Hayley Podschun). Munhrrr/Kansas (Kevin Munhall). Puhsuh-san (Robert Creighton). Table 6 (Ward Billeisen, Jessica Stone & Kevin Munhall). And JG (Joel Grey).

Embarrassing Moments: Mark Ledbetter, one of our amazing swings, had to go on for Reverend Dobson, but they accidentally gave him William Ryall's costume. William is probably one of the tallest men in our cast so poor Mark looked like the kid from *Big* at the end of the movie. The suit was definitely too big for him.

Coolest Thing About Being in This Show: The fact that it's still running in spring 2012! We were supposed to end July 2011!

Also: Oh, I have to tell the story of "Bloody Saturday." It was moments before "Buddy Beware" was supposed to begin and Josh Franklin and Anthony Wayne, two of our sailors, collided in the hallway and immediately started bleeding. In a matter of a couple seconds, Mark Ledbetter and Justin Greer ended up throwing on their costumes (and parts of Josh and Anthony's costumes), raced upstairs, and got on stage as fast as you could snap your fingers. And from the audience's point of view, nothing seemed wrong at all! That is how Broadway works, people!

Baby It's You!

First Preview: March 26, 2011. Opened: April 27, 2011.
Closed September 4, 2011 after 33 Previews and 148 Performances.

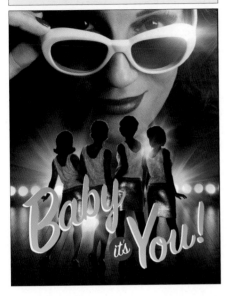

New Jersey housewife Florence Greenberg escapes a stifling marriage and becomes a major record producer when the group she represents, The Shirelles, rockets to the top of the pop charts in the early 1960s.

CAST

Florence Greenberg	BETH LEAVEL
Luther Dixon	ALLAN LOUIS
Jocko, Chuck Jackson, Ronald Isley, Gene Chandler	GENO HENDERSON
Micki, Romantic, Dionne Warwick	ERICA ASH
Mary Jane Greenberg, Lesley Gore	KELLI BARRETT
Beverly, Ruby	KYRA DA COSTA
Millie	ERICA DORFLER
Street Singer	JAHI A. KEARSE
Bernie Greenberg, Milt Gabler	BARRY PEARL
Shirley	CHRISTINA SAJOUS
Doris, Romantic	CRYSTAL STARR
Stanley Greenberg, Murray Schwartz, Kingsman	BRANDON URANOWITZ

Dance Captain: ERICA DORFLER

STANDBYS

For Florence Greenberg:
ALISON CIMMET
For Luther Dixon:
KEN ROBINSON, JAHI A. KEARSE
For Jocko/Chuck Jackson/
Ronald Isley/Gene Chandler:
JAHI A. KEARSE, KEN ROBINSON

Continued on next page

235 West 44th Street
A Shubert Organization Theatre

Philip J. Smith, *Chairman*   Robert E. Wankel, *President*

WARNER BROS. THEATRE VENTURES & AMERICAN POP ANTHOLOGY

in association with
UNIVERSAL MUSIC GROUP & PASADENA PLAYHOUSE

Present

Baby it's You!

Book by **FLOYD MUTRUX & COLIN ESCOTT**

Conceived by **FLOYD MUTRUX**

Starring
BETH LEAVEL
ALLAN LOUIS   GENO HENDERSON

Featuring
ERICA ASH   KELLI BARRETT   KYRA Da COSTA
ERICA DORFLER   JAHI A. KEARSE   BARRY PEARL
CHRISTINA SAJOUS   CRYSTAL STARR   BRANDON URANOWITZ

Scenic Design	Costume Design	Lighting Design	Sound Design
ANNA LOUIZOS	LIZZ WOLF	HOWELL BINKLEY	CARL CASELLA

Projection Design	Hair & Wig Design	Casting	Production Stage Manager
JASON H. THOMPSON	DAVID H. LAWRENCE	TELSEY + COMPANY	JOSHUA HALPERIN

Music Supervisor & Arrangements	Orchestrations	Music Director	Music Coordinator
RAHN COLEMAN	DON SEBESKY	SHELTON BECTON	JOHN MILLER

Marketing Direction	Advertising	Consulting Producer	Producer for American Pop Anthology
TYPE A MARKETING ANNE RIPPEY	SPOTCO	RICHARD PERRY	JONATHAN SANGER

Press Representative	Technical Director	General Management
THE HARTMAN GROUP	BRIAN LYNCH	ALAN WASSER • ALLAN WILLIAMS AARON LUSTBADER

Choreographed by
BIRGITTE MUTRUX

Directed by
FLOYD MUTRUX
&
SHELDON EPPS

BABY IT'S YOU was originally produced at Pasadena Playhouse.
Sheldon Epps, Artistic Director; Stephen Eich, Executive Director

The producers wish to express their appreciation to Theatre Development Fund for its support of this production.

9/4/11

(L-R): Christina Sajous, Erica Ash, Kyra DaCosta, Crystal Starr Knighton, Brandon Uranowitz, Beth Leavel

Baby It's You!

SONG LIST

ACT ONE

"Mr. Lee," "Book of Love," "Rockin' Robin," "Dance With Me"	The Company
"Mama Said"	Florence
"Yakety Yak"	Bernie
"Get a Job"	Stanley
"I Met Him on a Sunday"	Shirley, Beverly, Doris, Micki
"Dedicated to the One I Love"	Florence, Stan, Shirley, Beverly, Doris, Micki
"Dedicated to the One I Love" (Reprise)*	Florence, Stanley
"Sixteen Candles"	Luther
"Tonight's the Night"	Luther, Shirley, Beverly, Doris, Micki
"Dedicated to the One I Love"	Shirley, Beverly, Doris, Micki
"Dedicated to the One I Love" (Reprise)	Mary Jane
"Since I Don't Have You"	Chuck Jackson
"Big John"	Shirley, Beverly, Doris, Micki
"He's So Fine"	Doris, Shirley, Beverly, Micki
"Soldier Boy"	Florence, Luther, Shirley, Beverly, Doris, Micki

ACT TWO

"Shout"	Ron Isley, Shirley, Beverly, Doris, Micki
"Mama Said"	Shirley, Beverly, Doris, Micki, Luther, Florence
"Duke of Earl"	Gene Chandler, Shirley, Micki, Beverly, Doris
"Foolish Little Girl"	Micki, Shirley, Beverly, Doris
"It's My Party"	Lesley Gore
"Our Day Will Come"	Ruby & The Romantics
"The Dark End of the Street"	Luther, Florence, Chuck Jackson, Shirley
"Rhythm of the Rain"	Stanley, Mary Jane, Florence
"You're So Fine"	Chuck Jackson, Doris, Shirley, Beverly, Micki
"Hey Paula"	Chuck Jackson, Shirley, Beverly, Doris, Micki
"Louie, Louie"	Kingsman, Chuck Jackson, Shirley, Beverly, Doris, Micki
"You Really Got a Hold on Me"	Chuck Jackson, Beverly, Mary Jane, Florence, Shirley, Doris, Micki
"Baby It's You"	Shirley, Beverly, Doris, Micki, Florence, Luther
"A Thing of the Past"	Beverly, Micki, Shirley
"Don't Make Me Over"	Dionne Warwick, Florence
"Walk on By"	Dionne Warwick, Florence, Luther
"Baby It's You" (Reprise)	Shirley, Beverly, Doris, Micki
"Tonight's the Night" (Reprise)	Shirley, Beverly, Doris, Micki
"Dedicated to the One I Love" (Reprise)	Shirley, Beverly, Doris, Micki, Florence
"I Say a Little Prayer"	The Company
"Shout" (Reprise), "Twist and Shout"	The Company

Arrangement by Adam Irizarry

Cast Continued

For Bernie Greenberg/Milt Gabler:
ADAM HELLER
For Mary Jane Greenberg/Lesley Gore:
LIZ BYRNE
For Stanley Greenberg/Murray Schwartz/Kingsman:
ZACHARY PRINCE
For Shirley: ERICA DORFLER,
BERLANDO DRAKE
For Beverly/Ruby:
ERICA DORFLER, BERLANDO DRAKE,
ANNETTE MOORE
For Doris/Romantics:
ERICA DORFLER, ANNETTE MOORE
For Micki/Bobbette/Romantics/Dionne Warwick:
BERLANDO DRAKE, ANNETTE MOORE
For Millie:
BERLANDO DRAKE, ANNETTE MOORE

Although this play is inspired by actual events, some material has been fictionalized for dramatic purposes.

SETTING
1958 - 1965
Passaic, New Jersey and New York City

ORCHESTRA
Conductor: SHELTON BECTON
Associate Conductor: JOEL SCOTT
Music Coordinator: JOHN MILLER
Reeds: TOM MURRAY
Trumpet/Flugel: RAVI BEST
Drums: RAYMOND POUNDS
Electric Bass: FRANCISCO CENTENO
Guitar: MICHAEL AARONS
Percussion: CHARLIE DESCARFINO
Synth 1: SHELTON BECTON
Synth 2/Associate Conductor: JOEL SCOTT
Synthesizer Programmer: KARL MANSFIELD
Music Copying: EMILY GRISHMAN

MUSIC PREPARATION
EMILY GRISHMANMUSIC PREPARATION—
EMILY GRISHMAN, KATHARINE EDMONDS

Photo by Colleen Croft

ORCHESTRA
Front Row (L-R): Francisco Centeno, Joel Scott, Shelton Becton, Rahn Coleman, Don Sebesky

Back Row (L-R): John Miller, Raymond Pounds, Charlie Descarfino, Ravi Best, Tom Murray, Emily Grishman, Michael Aarons

Baby It's You!

Beth Leavel
Florence Greenberg

Allan Louis
Luther Dixon

Geno Henderson
Jocko, Chuck Jackson, Ronald Isley, Gene Chandler

Erica Ash
Micki, Romantic, Dionne Warwick

Kelli Barrett
Mary Jane Greenberg, Lesley Gore

Kyra Da Costa
Beverly, Ruby

Erica Dorfler
Dance Captain, Millie

Jahi A. Kearse
Street Singer

Barry Pearl
Bernie Greenberg, Milt Gabler

Christina Sajous
Shirley

Crystal Starr
Doris, Romantic

Brandon Uranowitz
Stanley Greenberg, Murray Schwartz, Kingsman

Liz Byrne
Standby Mary Jane Greenberg, Lesley Gore

Alison Cimmet
Standby for Florence Greenberg

Berlando Drake
Standby Shirley, Micki, Romantics, Dionne Warwick, Millie

Adam Heller
Standby Bernie Greenberg, Milt Gabler

Annette Moore
Standby Beverly, Ruby, Doris, Micki, Dionne Warwick, Millie, School Yard Dancer

Zachary Prince
Standby Stanley Greenberg, Murray Schwartz

Ken Robinson
Standby Luther Dixon, Jocko, Chuck Jackson, Ronald Isley, Gene Chandler

Birgitte Mutrux and Floyd Mutrux
Choreography; Co-Author, Co-Director, Conceiver

Colin Escott
Co-Author

Sheldon Epps
Co-Director; Artistic Director, Pasadena Playhouse

Shelton Becton
Music Director

John Miller
Music Coordinator

Anna Louizos
Scenic Design

Howell Binkley
Lighting Design

Carl Casella
Sound Design

David Lawrence
Hair Design

Jason H. Thompson
Projections Design

Don Sebesky
Orchestrations

Brian Lynch
(Theatretech, Inc.)
Production/Technical Supervisor

Bernard Telsey
Telsey + Company
Casting

Alan Wasser
General Manager

Allan Williams
General Manager

Baby It's You!

COMPANY MANAGEMENT
(L-R): Matthew Sherr, Maia Sutton

STAGE MANAGEMENT
(L-R): Jason Brouillard, Joshua Halperin,
Matthew Aaron Stern

HAIR
(L-R): Linda Rice, Renee Kelly (in front),
David Lawrence, Patricia Marcus, Richard Fabris

WARDROBE

DOORMAN
Joe Trapasso

CREW
Front Row (L-R): Keith Buchanan, Brian Bullard,
Gregg Maday (Producer), Chris Kluth,
Janet Smith

Back Row (L-R): Jeff Turner, Patrick Harrington,
Rob Brenner, Leon Stieb, Chris Doornbos,
Charlie DeVerna, Ronnie Vitelli, Ty Lackey

Baby It's You!

BOX OFFICE
(L-R): Noreen Morgan, Manny Rivera

Photo by Brian Mapp

STAFF FOR *BABY IT'S YOU!*

FOR WARNER BROS.
Chairman & CEO ....Barry Meyer
President & COO ....Alan Horn

WARNER BROS. THEATRE VENTURES
Executive Vice President,
  Lead Producer ....Gregg Maday
Senior Vice President, Development and
  Head of Operations.......................Raymond Wu
Chief Financial Officer ....Laura Valan
Senior Vice President, Finance ....Mark Coker
Director, Finance ....Maria Gonzalez
Senior Financial Analyst ....Arthur Yang
Staff ....Carol Wood, Jennifer Kim,
                Rachel Spenst, Susan Gary

AMERICAN POP ANTHOLOGY
Producer.......................................Jonathan Sanger
Executive Producer ....Gerald Katell
Historical Consultant ....Artie Ripp
Executive Angels.........................Abraham Aguchi,
    Annette Tapert Allen, Knut Bjorum,
    Richard & Lauren Schuler Donner,
    Joel & Jolie Keyser, Tom Pape,
    Yvonne & Brian Perera, Claudia Potamkin,
    Dorothy & Jill Schoelin,
    Mark Singer, Lynne Wasserman

THE PASADENA PLAYHOUSE

| **Sheldon Epps** | **Stephen Eich** |
| Artistic Director | Executive Director |

Director of Development ....Jennifer Berger
Director of Major Gifts ....Patti Eisenberg
Director of Marketing and
  Communications ....Patty Onagan
Controller ....Stephanie Surabian
Operations Manager ....Victoria Watson
Patron Services Manager ....Carrie Gergely

GENERAL MANAGEMENT
ALAN WASSER ASSOCIATES
Alan Wasser   Allan Williams
Aaron Lustbader   Mark Shacket

GENERAL PRESS REPRESENTATIVE
THE HARTMAN GROUP
Michael Hartman   Wayne Wolfe   Nicole Capatasto

MARKETING DIRECTION
TYPE A MARKETING
Anne Rippey   Elyce Henkin
Sarah Ziering

COMPANY MANAGER
Matthew Sherr

PRODUCTION MANAGEMENT
Brian Lynch

CASTING
TELSEY + COMPANY
Bernie Telsey CSA, Will Cantler CSA, David Vaccari CSA,
Bethany Knox CSA, Craig Burns CSA,
Tiffany Little Canfield CSA, Rachel Hoffman CSA,
Justin Huff CSA, Patrick Goodwin CSA,
Abbie Brady-Dalton, David Morris, Cesar A. Rocha

PRODUCTION STAGE MANAGER
Joshua Halperin

Stage Manager ....Matthew Aaron Stern
Assistant Stage Manager ....Jason Brouillard
Assistant Company Manager ....Maia Sutton
Assistant to Mr. Epps ....Courtney Harper
Assistant to Mr. Mutrux ....Ashley Mutrux
Assistant Choreographer ....Tyrone A. Jackson
Dance Captain ....Erica Dorfler
Associate Scenic Designers ....Aimee B. Dombo,
                Jeremy W. Foil
Assistant Scenic Designer ....Melissa Shakun
Associate Costume Designer ....Sarah Sophia Lidz
Assistant Costume Designer ....Amanda Bujak
Costume Design Assistant ....Elizabeth Van Buren
Costume Design Interns ....Stella Mutrux, Laura Rios,
                Taylor Martin
Associate Lighting Designer ....Ryan O'Gara
Assistant to Howell Binkley ....Michael Rummage
Associate Sound Designer ....Wallace Flores
Assistant Sound Designers ....Josh Liebert,
                Robert Hanlon
Assistant Projections Designers ....Jeff Teeter,
                Resa Deverich
Automated Lighting Programmer ....David Arch
Associate Make-up Designer ....Oslyn Holder
Assistant Hair Designer ....Linda Rice
House Carpenter ....Brian McGarty
Production Carpenter/TheatreTech Assoc. .....Chris Kluth
Automation Carpenter ....Robert Hentze
House Flyman ....Brian Bullard
House Electrician ....Charlie DeVerna
Production Electrician ....Keith Buchanan
Spotlight Operator ....Patrick Harrington
Moving Light Programmer ....David Arch
Projection Programmer ....Matthew Mellinger
House Properties ....Ronnie Vitelli
Production Properties ....George Wagner
Production Sound Supervisor ....James Wilkinson
Production Sound Engineer ....Ty Lackey
Synthesizer Programmer ....Karl Mansfield
Wardrobe Supervisor ....James Hall
Dressers ....Jason Blair, Kay Gowenlock,
    Franklin Hollenbeck, Ginny Hounsel,
    Susan Kroeter, Yleana Nuñez, Katherine Sorg
Stitchers ....Angela Lehrer, Liam O'Brien
Hair Supervisor ....Renee Kelly

Hairstylists ....Patricia Marcus, Richard Fabris,
                Linda Rice
Music Coordinator ....John Miller
Assistant to John Miller ....Jennifer Coolbaugh
Production Assistant ....Lisa Susanne Schwartz
Music Intern ....Rachel Lee
Music Clearances ....Jill Meyers Music
Projection Image Clearances ....Jay Floyd

Advertising ....Spotco/
    Drew Hodges, Jim Edwards,
    Tom Greenwald, Tom McCann,
    Josh Fraenkel
Theatre Displays..............BAM Signs Inc./Adam Miller
Website Design & Internet Marketing ....Spotco/
    Sara Fitzpatrick, Matt Wilstein,
    Michael Crowley, Marc Mettler,
    Christina Sees
Legal Counsel ....Loeb & Loeb, LLP/
    Seth Gelblum, Esq.
Audience Development ....Walk Tall Girl Productions/
    Marcia Pendelton, Diane Sanders;
    Walker International Communications Group Inc./
    Donna Walker-Kuhne, Cherine Anderson
Accounting ....Rosenberg, Neuwirth & Kuchner/
    Chris Cacace, Ruthie Skochil
General Management Associates ....Mark Barna,
    Dawn Kusinski
General Management Office ....Hilary Ackerman,
    Jake Hirzel, Nina Lutwick,
    Jennifer O'Connor

Production Photographer ....Ari Mintz
Rehearsal Pianist ....Seth Farber
Insurance ....Reiff & Associates, LLC
Banking ....Signature Bank/
    Barbara von Borstel, Margaret Monigan,
    Mary Ann Fanelli, Janett Urena,
    Alicia Williams
Payroll ....Castellana Services, Inc.
Merchandising ....The Araca Group
Opening Night Coordination .....The Lawrence Company
Group Sales ....Broadway InBound/212-302-0995

CREDITS
Scenery and Automation by Hudson Scenic Studios. Lighting equipment from PRG Lighting. Sound and video by Sound Associates, Inc. Custom men's Tailoring by Arel Studio and Western Costume Company. Millinery by Harry Rotz. Custom knitwear by Maria Ficalora Knitwear Ltd. Custom shoes by Worldtone Dance and LaDuca. Costumes by Euro Co Costumes, Inc.; Donna Langman Costumes; Jennifer Love Costumes Inc.; Katrina Patterns; Timberlake Studios, Inc.; Tricorne, Inc. Special thanks to Bra*Tenders for hosiery and undergarments. Custom fabric printing by First2Print. Fur by Fur and Furgery. Custom fabric painting by Jeff Fender. Custom fabric dyeing by Ellen Steingraber and Eric Winterling, Inc. Eyewear by Fabulous Fanny's and Myoptics. Men's shirts by Anto and L. Allmeier Inc. Souvenir merchandise designed and created by The Araca Group.

MUSIC CREDITS
"Mr. Lee" (Reather E. Dixon, Helen Gathers, Jannie Pought, Laura E. Webb, Emma Ruth Pought), ©1957 (renewed) Unichappell Music Inc. (BMI) and Pre Music Company (BMI). All rights administered by Unichappell

---

Baby It's You!

Music Inc. All rights reserved. Used by permission. "**Book of Love**" (Warren Davis, George Malone, Charles Patrick). Published and administered by EMI Longitude Music (BMI) and Conrad Music, a division of Arc Music Corp. All rights reserved. Used by permission. "**Dance With Me**" written by Jerry Leiber, Mike Stoller, Lewis Lebish, George Treadwell, Irving Nahan. ©1959 Sony/ATV Music Publishing LLC. All rights administered by Sony/ATV Music Publishing LLC, 8 Music Square West Nashville, TN 37203. All rights reserved. Used by permission. "**Mama Said**" (Luther Dixon and Willie Denson). Published and administered by EMI Longitude Music and ABKCO Music, Inc. www.abkco.com. All rights reserved. Used by permission. "**Yakety Yak**" written by Jerry Leiber, Mike Stoller. ©1958 Sony/ATV Music Publishing LLC. All rights administered by Sony/ATV Music Publishing LLC, 8 Music Square West Nashville, TN 37203. All rights reserved. Used by permission. "**Get a Job**" (Earl Beal, Richard Lewis, Raymond Edwards, William Horton). Published and administered by EMI Longitude Music. All rights reserved. Used by permission. "**I Met Him on a Sunday**" (Ronde Ronde, Shirley Owens, Addie Harris, Doris Coley, Beverly Lee). TRO - ©1957 (renewed) and 1958 (renewed) Ludlow Music, Inc. and Mickey & Mac Music Co., New York, NY. All rights reserved. Used by permission. "**Dedicated to the One I Love**" (Ralph Bass, Lowman Pauling). ©1957 (renewed) Fort Knox Music, Inc. (BMI) c/o Carlin America, Inc., Trio Music Company (BMI) a Bug Music Company and Songs of Universal, Inc. (BMI). All rights reserved. Used by permission. "**Sixteen Candles**" (Luther Dixon, Allyson Khent). ©1958 (renewed) Warner-Tamerlane Publishing Corp. (BMI), Mijac Music (BMI) and Unichappell Music Inc. (BMI) All rights administered by Unichappell Music Inc. and Warner-Tamerlane Publishing Corp. All rights reserved. Used by permission. "**Tonight's the Night**" (Luther Dixon and Shirley Owens). Published and administered by EMI Longitude Music and ABKCO Music, Inc. www.abkco.com. All rights reserved. Used by permission. "**Since I Don't Have You**" (Joe Rock, James Beaumont & The Skyliners). ©1959 (renewed) by Bonnyview Music Corporation. Southern Music Publishing Co. administers on behalf of Bonnyview Music Corporation. All rights reserved. Used by permission. "**Big John**" (John Patton and Amiel Sommers). Published and administered by EMI Longitude Music and ABKCO Music, Inc. www.abkco.com. All rights reserved. Used by permission. "**He's So Fine**" (Ronald Mack). Published by Harrisongs Ltd. All rights reserved. Used by permission. "**Soldier Boy**" (Florence Green and Luther Dixon). Published and administered by EMI Longitude Music and ABKCO Music, Inc. www.abkco.com. All rights reserved. Used by permission. "**Shout**" (Ronald Isley, Rudolph Isley and O'Kelly Isley). Published and administered by EMI Longitude Music. All rights reserved. Used by permission. "**Twist and Shout**" written by Bert Burns, Phil Medley. ©1962 Sony/ATV Music Publishing LLC, Unichappell Music Inc., Sloopy II Music. All rights on behalf of Sony/ATV Music Publishing LLC, Unichappell Music Inc. administered by Sony/ATV Music Publishing LLC, 8 Music Square West Nashville, TN 37203. All rights reserved. Used by permission. "**Duke of Earl**" (Eugene Dixon, Bernice Williams, Earl Edwards). Published by Conrad Music, a division of Arc Music Corp. All rights reserved. Used by permission. "**Foolish Little Girl**" (Howard Greenfield, Helen Miller). Published and administered by Screen Gems-EMI Music Inc. ©Universal Music – Careers (ASCAP, BMI). All rights reserved. Used by permission. "**It's My Party**" (Wiener Herb, Gottlieb Seymour, John Gluck Jr., Wally Gold). ©1963 (renewed) Chappell & Co., Inc. (ASCAP). All rights reserved. Used by permission. "**Our Day Will Come**" (words by Bob Hilliard, music by Mort Garson). Published and administered by Better Half Music, a division of Bourne Co. ©Universal Music Corp. All rights reserved. Used by permission. "**The Dark End of the Street**" (Dan Penn, Chips Moman). Published and administered by Screen Gems-EMI Music Inc. (BMI). All rights reserved. Used by permission. "**Rhythm of the Rain**" (John C. Gummoe). ©1963 (renewed) Warner-Tamerlane Publishing Corp. (BMI). All rights reserved. Used by permission. "**You're So Fine**" (Lance Finnie, Willie Schoefield). Published and administered by C and B West Publishing Co. dba Lupine Music, (BMI) affiliates and Harrisongs Ltd. All rights reserved. Used by permission. "**Hey Paula**" (Ray Hildebrand). Speckle Music administered by Spirit One Music (BMI). All rights reserved. Used by permission. "**Louie Louie**" (Richard Berry). Published and administered by Screen Gems-EMI Music Inc. All rights reserved. Used by permission. "**You've Really Got a Hold on Me**" (Smokey Robinson). Published and administered by Jobete Music Co., Inc. All rights reserved. Used by permission. "**Baby It's You**" (Barney Williams, Mack David, Burt F. Bacharach). ©New Hidden Valley Music (ASCAP), Polygram International Publishing Inc. (ASCAP) and EMI U Catalog Inc. (ASCAP). All rights on behalf of New Hidden Valley Music (ASCAP) administered by WB Music Corp. (ASCAP) All rights reserved. Used by permission. "**A Thing of the Past**" (Irwin Levin, Robert Brass). Published by We Three Music, Inc. All rights reserved. Used by permission. "**Don't Make Me Over**" (Burt Bacharach, Bob Hilliard). ©1962 (renewed) New Hidden Valley Music Company (ASCAP) and Casa David Music (ASCAP). All rights on behalf of New Hidden Valley Music Company administered by WB Music Corp. (ASCAP). All rights reserved. Used by permission. "**Walk on By**" (Burt Bacharach, Hal David). ©1964 (renewed) New Hidden Valley Music Company (ASCAP) and Casa David Music (ASCAP). All rights on behalf of New Hidden Valley Music Company administered by WB Music Corp. All rights reserved. Used by permission. "**Stop in the Name of Love**" (Brian Holland, Lamont Herbert Dozier, Edward Holland, Jr.). Published and administered by Jobete Music Company, Stone Agate Music, Inc., Stone Diamond Music (BMI). All rights reserved. Used by permission. "**I Say a Little Prayer**" (Burt Bacharach, Hal David). ©1966 (renewed) New Hidden Valley Music (ASCAP) and Casa David Music (ASCAP). All rights on behalf of New Hidden Valley Music Company administered by WB Music Corp. All rights reserved. Used by permission.

PHOTO CREDITS

Photo of Esquire Theatre Courtesy of Esquire Theatre, Cincinnati, Ohio. *Pillow Talk* images courtesy of Universal Studios Licensing LLP. *LIFE Magazine* Cover ©1958 Time Inc. *LIFE* is a registered trademark of Time Inc. Photos and footage courtesy of Getty Images. Photos and footage courtesy of Corbis Images. Photos courtesy of Classic Stock. Photos courtesy of Associated Press. Some backdrop images of Atlanta and New York City seen during the production were made available by the Charles W. Cushman Collection: Indiana University Archives, Bloomington, IN. *Ben Hur* poster licensed by Warner Bros. Entertainment Inc. and Turner Entertainment Co. Photo courtesy of Jamie Goldsmith.

Billy Elliot

First Preview: October 1, 2008. Opened: November 13, 2008.
Closed January 8, 2012 after 40 Previews and 1,312 Performances.

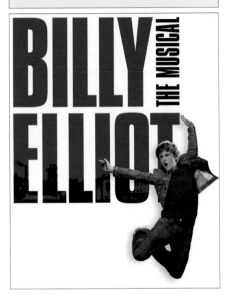

Young Billy has grown up in a union family living in a grim northern English coal-mining town torn by a year-long strike. Like a flower growing in a vacant lot, Billy conceives a desire to be a ballet dancer. He endures the teasing of his friends, the disapproval of his family and the derision of the town at large. But when it becomes apparent that Billy has a chance to get into the Royal Ballet Academy, the townsfolk pool their pennies so Billy can be the one among them who will get to fulfill his dream.

CAST

Billy	TADE BIESINGER, JULIAN ELIA, JOSEPH HARRINGTON, PETER MAZUROWSKI
Mrs. Wilkinson	EMILY SKINNER
Dad	DANIEL JENKINS
Grandma	KATHERINE McGRATH
Tony	PATRICK MULVEY
George	WILLIAM YOUMANS
Michael	JACK BRODERICK, CAMERON CLIFFORD
Debbie	LILLA CRAWFORD
Small Boy	ALEX DREIER, ZACHARY MAITLIN
Big Davey	DANNY RUTIGLIANO
Lesley	STEPHANIE KURTZUBA
Scab/Posh Dad	DREW McVETY
Mum	LAURA MARIE DUNCAN
Mr. Braithwaite	THOMMIE RETTER
Tracey Atkinson	ANNABELLE KEMPF
Older Billy/Scottish Dancer	STEPHEN HANNA
Pit Supervisor	AUSTIN LESCH

Continued on next page

---

⑤ IMPERIAL THEATRE

249 West 45th Street
A Shubert Organization Theatre

Philip J. Smith, *Chairman*   **Robert E. Wankel,** *President*

UNIVERSAL PICTURES STAGE PRODUCTIONS   WORKING TITLE FILMS   OLD VIC PRODUCTIONS
in association with WEINSTEIN LIVE ENTERTAINMENT present

BILLY ELLIOT THE MUSICAL

Based on the Universal Pictures/Studio Canal Film

EMILY SKINNER   DANIEL JENKINS
KATHERINE McGRATH   PATRICK MULVEY

And Introducing

TADE BIESINGER   JULIAN ELIA   JOSEPH HARRINGTON   PETER MAZUROWSKI

With

JACK BRODERICK • CAMERON CLIFFORD • LILLA CRAWFORD • LAURA MARIE DUNCAN • STEPHEN HANNA • THOMMIE RETTER • WILLIAM YOUMANS
OLIVIA ALBOHER • MICHAEL ARNOLD • JASON BABINSKY • BRAD BRADLEY • STEPHEN CARRASCO • AVA DeMARY • ALEX DREIER
C.K. EDWARDS • EBONI EDWARDS • MAKENZI RAE FISCHBACH • BRIANNA FRAGOMENI • ERIC GUNHUS • AARON KABURICK
ANNABELLE KEMPF • CARA KJELLMAN • DAVID KOCH • STEPHANIE KURTZUBA • DAVID LARSEN • AUSTIN LESCH • IAN LIBERTO
MERLE LOUISE • ZACHARY MAITLIN • MARIA MAY • DREW McVETY • MARINA MICALIZZI • LIZ PEARCE • ROBBIE ROBY
DANNY RUTIGLIANO • NICHOLAS SIPES • HEATHER TEPE • KAYLA VANDERBILT • NATALIE WISDOM

Press Representative	General Management	Advertising
THE HARTMAN GROUP	BESPOKE THEATRICALS	aka

Production Stage Manager	Music Contractor	Resident Music Director	Production Supervisors
BONNIE L. BECKER	MICHAEL KELLER	SHAWN GOUGH	ARTHUR SICCARDI PATRICK SULLIVAN

Adult Casting Director	Children's Casting Director	Associate Director (U.S.)	Resident Director
TARA RUBIN CASTING	NORA BRENNAN	JUSTIN MARTIN	GINA RATTAN

Associate Set Designer	Associate Costume Designer	Associate Lighting Designer (Programmer)	Associate Sound Designer
PAUL ATKINSON	CLAIRE MURPHY	VIC SMERDON	JOHN OWENS

Associate Choreographer	Resident Choreographers	Assistant Choreographer	Hair, Wig and Make-Up Designer
KATHRYN DUNN	SARA BRIANS KURT FROMAN	NIKKI BELSHER	CAMPBELL YOUNG

Musical Supervision and Orchestrations by   Music Director
MARTIN KOCH   DAVID CHASE

Costume Design by	Lighting Design by	Sound Design by
NICKY GILLIBRAND	RICK FISHER	PAUL ARDITTI

Executive Producers
DAVID FURNISH   ANGELA MORRISON

Produced by
TIM BEVAN   ERIC FELLNER   JON FINN   SALLY GREENE

Associate Director
JULIAN WEBBER

Set Design by
IAN MacNEIL

Choreography by
PETER DARLING

Directed by
STEPHEN DALDRY

Book and Lyrics by
LEE HALL

Music by
ELTON JOHN

12/12/11

Peter Mazurowski (center, kneeling, in helmet); Emily Skinner (C); and Ballet Girls

Photo by Carol Rosegg

Billy Elliot

MUSICAL NUMBERS

ACT 1
"The Stars Look Down" (The Eve of the Miners' Strike 1984) ....Full Company
"Shine"...Mrs. Wilkinson, Ballet Girls, Billy
"We'd Go Dancing" ....Grandma, Men's Ensemble
"Solidarity" ....Full Company
"Expressing Yourself" ....Billy, Michael, Ensemble
"Dear Billy" (Mum's Letter) ....Billy, Mrs. Wilkinson, Mum
"Born to Boogie" ....Billy, Mrs. Wilkinson, Mr. Braithwaite
"Angry Dance" ....Billy, Men's Ensemble

ACT 2
Six Months Later
"Merry Christmas, Maggie Thatcher" ....Full Company
"Deep Into the Ground"..Dad, Full Company
"He Could Go and He Could Shine" ....Dad, Tony, Ensemble
"Electricity" ....Billy
"Once We Were Kings" ....Full Company
"Dear Billy" (Billy's Reply) ....Billy, Mum
"Company Celebration" ....Full Company

STAGE AND COMPANY MANAGEMENT
Front Row (L-R): Carol M. Oune, Andrew C. Gottlieb, Scott Rowen
Back Row (L-R): Charlene Speyerer, Gregg Arst, Bonnie L. Becker

Photo by Brian Mapp

ORCHESTRA
Resident Music Director/
  Conductor: SHAWN GOUGH
Associate Conductor: ANNBRITT DUCHATEAU
Assistant Conductor: HOWARD JOINES,
  JOSEPH JOUBERT
Reeds: EDDIE SALKIN, RICK HECKMAN,
  MIKE MIGLIORE, JAY BRANDFORD
Trumpets: JAMES DELA GARZA, JOHN DENT,
  ALEX HOLTON
Trombones: DICK CLARK, JACK SCHATZ
French Horns: EVA CONTI, LARRY DIBELLO
Keyboards: ANNBRITT DUCHATEAU,
  JOSEPH JOUBERT
Guitar: JJ McGEEHAN
Bass: RANDY LANDAU

Drums: GARY SELIGSON
Percussion: HOWARD JOINES
Music Coordinator: MICHAEL KELLER

In addition to playing trumpets, French horns and trombones, the brass section of the *Billy Elliot* Orchestra is also playing cornets, flugel horns, tenor horns and euphoniums. These unique brass instruments are the same instruments played in the Easington Colliery Band, which was founded in 1913. Brass players with band experience were encouraged by management to come from the west of Durham to work in the Colliery and play in the band, which continues to perform to this day.

Cast Continued

Tall Boy/Posh Boy ....TADE BIESINGER,
  JULIAN ELIA,
  JOSEPH HARRINGTON,
  PETER MAZUROWSKI
Clipboard Woman ....LIZ PEARCE
"Expressing Yourself" Dancers ....
  MICHAEL ARNOLD, JASON BABINSKY,
  BRAD BRADLEY, C.K. EDWARDS,
  STEPHANIE KURTZUBA,
  DAVID LARSEN, AUSTIN LESCH,
  NICHOLAS SIPES

ENSEMBLE
MICHAEL ARNOLD, JASON BABINSKY,
BRAD BRADLEY, LAURA MARIE DUNCAN,
C.K. EDWARDS, ERIC GUNHUS,
STEPHEN HANNA, AARON KABURICK,
STEPHANIE KURTZUBA, DAVID LARSEN,
AUSTIN LESCH, MERLE LOUISE,
DREW McVETY, LIZ PEARCE,
THOMMIE RETTER, DANNY RUTIGLIANO,
NICHOLAS SIPES

BALLET GIRLS
AVA DeMARY, EBONI EDWARDS,
MAKENZI RAE FISCHBACH,
BRIANNA FRAGOMENI,
ANNABELLE KEMPF, MARIA MAY,
MARINA MICALIZZI, KAYLA VANDERBILT

SWINGS
OLIVIA ALBOHER, STEPHEN CARRASCO,
CARA KJELLMAN, DAVID KOCH,
IAN LIBERTO, ROBBIE ROBY,
HEATHER TEPE, NATALIE WISDOM

UNDERSTUDIES
For Mrs. Wilkinson: LAURA MARIE DUNCAN,
  LIZ PEARCE
For Dad: DREW McVETY,
  WILLIAM YOUMANS
For Grandma: MERLE LOUISE
For Tony: DAVID LARSEN, AUSTIN LESCH
For George: ERIC GUNHUS,
  DANNY RUTIGLIANO
For Debbie: BRIANNA FRAGOMENI,
  MARIA MAY
For Mum: STEPHANIE KURTZUBA,
  LIZ PEARCE
For Mr. Braithwaite: MICHAEL ARNOLD,
  ERIC GUNHUS, AARON KABURICK
For Older Billy/Scottish Dancer: IAN LIBERTO,
  NICHOLAS SIPES

DANCE CAPTAINS
CARA KJELLMAN, ROBBIE ROBY

Billy Elliot

Emily Skinner
Mrs. Wilkinson

Daniel Jenkins
Dad

Katherine McGrath
Grandma

Patrick Mulvey
Tony

Tade Biesinger
Billy

Julian Elia
Billy

Joseph Harrington
Billy

Peter Mazurowski
Billy

Jack Broderick
Michael

Cameron Clifford
Michael

Lilla Crawford
Debbie

Laura Marie Duncan
Mum

Stephen Hanna
*Older Billy,
Scottish Dancer*

Thommie Retter
Mr. Braithwaite

William Youmans
George

Olivia Alboher
Swing

Michael Arnold
Ensemble

Jason Babinsky
*Ensemble/Fight
Captain*

Brad Bradley
Ensemble

Stephen Carrasco
Swing

Ava DeMary
Ballet Girl

Alex Dreier
Small Boy

C.K. Edwards
Ensemble

Eboni Edwards
Ballet Girl

Makenzi Rae
Fischbach
Ballet Girl

Brianna Fragomeni
Ballet Girl

Eric Gunhus
Ensemble

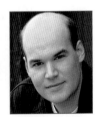
Aaron Kaburick
Ensemble

Annabelle Kempf
Tracey Atkinson

Cara Kjellman
*Swing/Dance
Captain*

David Koch
Swing

Stephanie Kurtzuba
Lesley/Ensemble

David Larsen
Ensemble

Austin Lesch
*Pit Supervisor/
Ensemble*

Ian Liberto
Swing

Billy Elliot

Merle Louise
Ensemble

Zachary Maitlin
Small Boy

Maria May
Ballet Girl

Drew McVety
Posh Dad/Scab

Marina Micalizzi
Ballet Girl

Liz Pearce
*Clipboard Woman/
Ensemble*

Robbie Roby
*Swing/Dance
Captain*

Danny Rutigliano
Big Davey/Ensemble

Nicholas Sipes
Ensemble

Heather Tepe
Swing

Kayla Vanderbilt
Ballet Girl

Natalie Wisdom
Swing

Elton John
Music

Lee Hall
Book & Lyrics

Stephen Daldry
Director

Peter Darling
Choreographer

Ian MacNeil
Set Design

Nicky Gillibrand
Costume Design

Rick Fisher
Lighting Designer

Paul Arditti
Sound Design

Martin Koch
*Musical Supervision
& Orchestrations*

David Chase
Music Director

Michael Keller
Music Coordinator

Sara Brians
*Resident
Choreographer*

Kurt Froman
*Resident
Choreographer*

Tara Rubin Casting
Casting

Nora Brennan
Children's Casting

Gina Rattan
Resident Director

William Conacher
*Supervising Dialect
Coach*

Ben Furey
*Resident Dialect
Coach*

David S. Leong
Fight Director

Arthur Siccardi
Theatrical Services,
Inc.
*Production
Supervisor*

Sally Greene
Old Vic Productions
PLC
Producer

David Furnish
Executive Producer

Maggie Brohn
Bespoke Theatricals
*General
Management*

Billy Elliot

Amy Jacobs
Bespoke Theatricals
General Management

Devin Keudell
Bespoke Theatricals
General Management

Nina Lannan
Bespoke Theatricals
General Management

Michael Arnold
u/s George

Giuseppe Bausilio
Billy, Tall Boy/Posh Boy

Kevin Bernard
Ensemble, Expressing Yourself Dancer, Mr. Wilkinson

Aly Brier
Ballet Girl, u/s Debbie

Jacob Clemente
Billy, u/s Michael

Ben Cook
u/s Michael

Jeremy Davis
Expressing Yourself Dancer, Ensemble

Myles Erlick
Billy, Tall Boy/Posh Boy, u/s Michael

Seth Fromowitz
Small Boy

Joel Hatch
George, u/s Dad

Gregory Jbara
Dad

David Koch
Big Davey

Alison Levenberg
Dance Captain, Swing

Neil McCaffrey
Michael

Brad Nacht
Big Davey, Ensemble

Ruby Rakos
Tracey Atkinson, Ballet Girl

Carole Shelley
Grandma

Ryan Steele
Older Billy/Scottish Dancer, Swing

Kendra Tate
Ballet Girl

Holly Taylor
Ballet Girl

Grant Turner
Expressing Yourself Dancer, Older Billy/Scottish Dancer, Ensemble

Thad Turner Wilson
Ensemble, u/s George

Christopher Brian Williams
Ensemble

Caroline Workman
Swing

Katrina Yaukey
Clipboard Woman, Ensemble, u/s Mrs. Wilkinson, u/s Mum

FRONT OF HOUSE STAFF
Front Row (L-R): Frances Barberetti, Lois Fernandez, Joan Seymour, Dennis Norwood, Cooper Jordan
Back Row (L-R): Julia Pazmino, Marilyn Wassbotten, Lawrence Scharld, Edward Phillins, Janet Kaye

DOORMAN
Alfonso Lee

Photos by Brian Mapp

Billy Elliot

Photo by Brian Mapp

CREW
Front Row Sitting (L-R): Justin Sanok, Joby Horrigan, Renee Mariotti, Duduzile Ndlovu-Mitall, Kirsten Solberg
Second Row Kneeling (L-R): Robert Breheny, Matt Gratz, Billy Rowland, Darryl Mull, Chad Heulitt, Jay Gill, David Bornstein, Jessica Scoblick, Terri Purcell, Nanette Golia, Heidi Brown
Third Row Standing (L-R): Paul Dean, Reginald Vessey, Pete Donovan, John Croissant, Anthony Ferrer, Walter Ballard, Richie Fullam, David Mitchell, Michael Berglund

STAFF FOR *BILLY ELLIOT THE MUSICAL*

GENERAL MANAGEMENT
BESPOKE THEATRICALS
Devin Keudell
Maggie Brohn   Amy Jacobs   Nina Lannan

COMPANY MANAGER
Gregg Arst
Associate Company Manager ....Carol M. Oune

GENERAL PRESS REPRESENTATIVE
THE HARTMAN GROUP
Michael Hartman
Juliana Hannett   Emily McGill

CHILDREN'S CASTING
NORA BRENNAN CSA

ADULT CASTING
TARA RUBIN CASTING
Tara Rubin CSA, Eric Woodall CSA
Laura Schutzel CSA, Merri Sugarman CSA,
Dale Brown CSA
Kaitlin Shaw, Lindsay Levine

Production Stage Manager ....Bonnie L. Becker
Stage Manager ....Scott Rowen
Assistant Stage Managers ....Charlene Speyerer,
Andrew C. Gottlieb

Supervising Dialect Coach (UK) ....William Conacher
Resident Dialect Coach ....Ben Furey

Resident Choreographers ....Sara Brians, Kurt Froman
Dance Captains ....Cara Kjellman, Robbie Roby
Fight Captain ....Jason Babinsky
Original Resident Director ....BT McNicholl
Choreographic Supervision ....Ellen Kane
Staging and Dance Assistant ....Lee Proud

Associate Set Designer ....Paul Atkinson
Assistant Set Designer ....Jaimie Todd
Associate Costume Designer (UK) ....Claire Murphy
Associate Costume Designer (US) ....Brian Russman
Assistant Costume Designer (US) ....Rebecca Lustig
Assistant to Ms. Gillibrand ....Rachel Attridge
Associate Lighting Designer (UK) ....Vic Smerdon
Associate Lighting Designer (US) ....Daniel Walker
Assistant Lighting Designer (US) ....Kristina Kloss
Associate Sound Designer (UK) ....John Owens
Associate Sound Designer (US) ....Tony Smolenski IV
Moving Light Programmer (US) ....David Arch
Costume Shopper (UK) ....Bryony Fayers
Props Shoppers (UK) ....Kathy Anders, Lisa Buckley

Fight Director ....David S. Leong

Production Carpenter ....Gerard Griffin
Production Flyman ....Brian Hutchinson
Production Automation Carpenter ......Charles Heulitt III
Assistant Carpenter ....John Croissant
Production Electrician ....Jimmy Maloney, Jr.
Head Electrician ....Kevin Barry
Assistant Electrician ....Matt Gratz
Production Props Supervisor ....Joseph Harris, Jr.
Head Propmaster ....David Bornstein
Assistant Propmaster ....Reginald Vessey
Production Sound..........................Michael Wojchik
Assistant Production Sound ....Stephanie Vetter
Special Effects Consultant ....Greg Meeh

Wardrobe Supervisor ....Terri Purcell
Associate Wardrobe Supervisor ....Nanette Golia
Dressers.............Michael Berglund, Tina Marie Clifton,
Margiann Flanagan, Jay Gill,
Joby Horrigan, Peggie Kurz,
Kyle LaColla, Renee Mariotti,
Marcia McIntosh, Duduzile Ndlovu-Mitall,
David Mitchell, Lisa Preston,
Jessica Scoblick, Kirsten Solberg

Hair & Makeup Supervisor ....Susan Corrado
Assistant Hair Supervisor ....Jackie Pietro
Hair Dresser ....Jeffrey Brannon Gray
Head Children's Guardian ....Robert Wilson
Assistant Head Guardian ....Amanda Grundy
Guardians ....Sandi DiGeorge, John V. Fahey,
John Funk, Andy Gale,
Alissa Zulvergold
Production Assistants ....Emily Andres,
Andrew Gottlieb, Alison M. Roberts
Rehearsal Pianists ....Joseph Joubert, Aron Accurso
Music Copying/
Library Services (US) ....Emily Grishman
Music Preparation
Children's Tutoring ....On Location Education/
Alan Simon, Jodi Green
Tutors ....Jennifer Cutler, Abigale Dyer,
Diane Hallman, Irene Karasik,
Kim Karim, Lillian Purpi
Box Office Staff ....Bill Carrick, Paul Blaber,
Carlin Blum, Greer Bond, Bryan Cobb,
Kiki Lenoue, John Zameryka
Ballet Instructors ....Miranda Barker, Finis Jhung,
Francois Perron
Acrobatic Instructor ....Hector Salazar
Physical Therapy ....PhysioArts/Jenni Green
Company Physical Therapists ....Sarah Bigham,
Ryanne Glasper, Suzanne Lynch
Orthopedic Consultant ....Dr. Phillip Bauman
Pediatric/ENT Consultant ....Dr. Barry Kohn
Health & Safety Consultants ....Eric D. Wallace,
Greg Petruska

Advertising/Marketing ....aka/
Scott A. Moore, Melissa Marano,
Jennifer Sims, Adam Jay, Sara Rosenzweig
Online/Interactive......................................aka/
Erin Rech, Caleb Custer,
Jen Taylor, Kelly Russin

Billy Elliot

Production Videographer ....Suspension Productions/
Joe Locarro
Production Photographers ....David Scheinmann,
Carol Rosegg
Accountant ....FK Partners/Robert Fried
Comptroller ....Sarah Galbraith and Co./
Sarah Galbraith
Immigration ....Kramer Levin Naftalis & Frankel LLP/
Mark D. Koestler, Esq., Allison Gray, Esq.
Legal Counsel ....Loeb & Loeb/
Seth Gelblum
Franklin, Weinrib, Rudell & Vassallo, PC/
Elliot H. Brown
General Management Associates ....Steve Dow,
David Roth, Danielle Saks
General Management Intern ....Rodney Roth
Production Supervisor Intern ....Lenora Hartley
Lighting Intern ....Trent Suidgeest
Sound Intern ....Rachel O'Connor
Press Associates ....Nicole Capatasto, Tom D'Ambrosio,
Leslie Baden Papa, Matt Ross,
Frances White, Wayne Wolfe
Children's Casting Assistant ....Jennifer Rogers
Payroll Services ....Castellana Services, Inc.
Travel Agent ....Tzell Travel/
The "A" Team, Andi Henig
Housing ....Premier Relocation Solutions/
Angela Rivera
Banking ....Bank of America
Insurance ....AON/
Albert G. Ruben Insurance Services, Inc./
Susan M. Weiss
Structural Engineering
Consultant ....McLaren Engineering Group/
Bill Gorlin
Demolition
Services ....JRM Construction Management, LLC/
Philip R. Arnold, Jr.
Theatre Displays ....BAM Signs
Merchandising ....Encore Merchandising/
Elie Berkowitz, Joey Boyles, Maryanna Geller,
Jessie Bello, Claire Newhouse
Opening Night
Coordination ....The Lawrence Company Events, Inc./
Michael Lawrence

FOR UNIVERSAL PICTURES
STAGE PRODUCTIONS
President and COO,
Universal Studios Inc. ....Ron Meyer
Chairman ....Adam Fogelson
Co-Chairman ....Donna Langley
President, Universal Pictures ....Jimmy Horowitz
President of Marketing......................Eddie Egan
SVP, Production Finance ....Arturo Barquet
Legal Affairs ....Keith Blau

FOR WORKING TITLE FILMS
Marketing Director ....Susan Butterly
President of Production (U.S.) ....Liza Chasin
Head of Production ....Michelle Wright
Head of Legal and Business Affairs ....Sheeraz Shah
Finance Director ....Tim Easthill
Assistant to Eric Fellner ....Katherine Pomfret
Assistant to Tim Bevan ....Chloe Dorigan
Associate Producer ....Marieke Spencer
Head of Finance, *Billy Elliot* ....Shefali Ghosh

FOR OLD VIC PRODUCTIONS
Chief Executive ....Sally Greene
Executive Producer ....Joseph Smith
Assistant Producer ....Becky Barber
Administrator ....Fiona Finlow
Finance Director ....Conor Marren
Management Accountant ....Bina Tankaria
Management Accountant
(Maternity Cover) ....Tessa Baker
Project Advisor to Sally Greene ....Emily Blacksell
Assistant to Sally Greene ....Sara White
Administrative Assistant
to Sally Greene ....Naomi Davenport
Legal Representative ....David Friedlander

CREDITS
Scenery constructed and automation equipment provided by Hudson Scenic Studios, Inc. Back wall by Souvenir Scenic Studios, Ltd. Miners' banner by Alaister Brotchie. Flying by Foy. Lighting equipment from PRG Lighting. Sound equipment by Masque Sound. Puppets designed and contracted by the Wright Stuff Theatre of Puppets. Costumes constructed by Mark Costello, London; Tricorne NYC; Jennifer Love Costumes; Baracath Customwear; Douglas Earl Costumes; David Quinn. Custom knitwear by Maria Ficalora and Karen Eifert. Custom footwear by T.O. Dey and Capezio. Millinery and costume crafts by Rodney Gordon, Inc. Undergarments provided by Bra*Tenders. "Express" dress puppet frames and Maggie Thatcher tank by Sophie Jones. Dancing dresses by Phil Reynolds Costumes, London. Ballet Girls clothing by Airy Fairy Costuming. Fabric painting and costume distressing by Nicola Killeen Textiles and Jeff Fender. Wigs made by Campbell Young Associates. Incidental and small props by the Spoon Group. Soft goods props by Mariah Hale. Musical instruments provided by Manny's Music, Pearl Drums, Mesa Boogie Guitar Amplifiers, Eden Electronics and Ernie Ball. Rehearsed at New 42nd Street Studios. Rehearsal scenery and props by the Technical Office Pty, Australia, and Adelaide Festival Centre Trust Workshops. Coal mining footage used by permission of British Pathé and BFI National Archive.

Billy Elliot on Broadway originally rehearsed at the Little Shubert Theatre, NYC; Ripley-Grier Studios, NYC; 3 Mills Studio, London.

Make-up Provided by
MAKE UP FOR EVER

To learn more about the production, please visit
www.BillyElliotBroadway.com

To become the next Billy Elliot, please visit
www.BeBilly.com

SPECIAL THANKS
The producers wish to thank the following partners for their generous support: CAPEZIO, STEPS ON BROADWAY. Special thanks to Cass Jones (technical director Aus.); Stephen Rebbeck (technical director UK); Dennis Crowley; Maggie Brohn; Mark Vogeley, Michael Stewart and staff of the Little Shubert Theatre; Stanislav Iavroski and the staff of Ripley-Grier Studios; Steve Roath and the staff of Chelsea Studios; Chuck Vassallo and the staff of the Professional Performing Arts School, New York City; American Ballet Theatre; Youth America Grand Prix (YAGP); Ann Willis

Ratray (Acting Consultant); Joan Lader; Ray Hesselink; Tim Federle; Callie Carter; Sara Brians; Stacy Caddell; Fred Lassen; Dorothy Medico and Dorothy's School of Dance – Long Island; Laurie Rae Waugh of Acocella Group; Lisa Schuller of Halstead Property, LLC; Marie Claire Martineau of Maison International; the "Victoria Posse": Jackie Morgan, John Caswell, Tiffany Horton, Donald Ross, Peter Waterman, Gemma Thomas, Sarah Askew, Marian Lynch, Sian Farley; Treagus Stoneman Associates, Ltd.; Louise Withers and Associates; David Blandon; Diane Dawson; Donna Distefano Jewelry. With thanks to the National Coal Mining Museum for England, Wakefield, W. Yorkshire.
Working Title Films would like to thank Ron Meyer, Jimmy Horowitz, Donna Langley, Rick Finkelstein, Arturo Barquet, Allison Ganz, Stephanie Sperber, Stephanie Testa, Hazel Brown and Jonathan Treisman at Universal Pictures; Peter Bennett-Jones and Greg Brenman at Tiger Aspect Pictures; David Thompson at the BBC and Tessa Ross; Luke Lloyd Davies; Janine Shalom; all at Working Title Films for their continuing help and support, and especially to all the people who worked on the film *Billy Elliot*.
Old Vic Productions would like to thank Eric Fellner, Tim Bevan, Elton John, David Furnish, Lee Hall, Stephen Daldry, Peter Darling, Angela Morrison, Jon Finn and all at Working Title Films, Arthur Cohen, David Friedlander, Robert Reed, Marieke Spencer, Jimmy Horowitz, John Barlow, Adam Kenwright, Janine Shalom, and most of all, to David, Kiril and Trent.
Elton John would like to thank Lee Hall, Stephen Daldry, David Furnish, Matt Still, Eric Fellner, Tim Bevan, Jon Finn, Sally Greene, Angela Morrison, Frank Presland, Keith Bradley, Clive Banks, Todd Interland, Davey Johnstone, Bob Birch, Guy Babylon, John Mahon, Nigel Olsen. And a special thanks to Liam, James and George for bringing Billy to life on stage.

Energy-efficient washer/dryer courtesy of
LG Electronics.

THE SHUBERT ORGANIZATION, INC.
Board of Directors

Philip J. Smith	**Robert E. Wankel**
Chairman	President
Wyche Fowler, Jr.	**Diana Phillips**
Lee J. Seidler	**Michael I. Sovern**

Stuart Subotnick

Chief Financial Officer ....Elliot Greene
Sr. Vice President, Ticketing ....David Andrews
Vice President, Finance ....Juan Calvo
Vice President, Human Resources ....Cathy Cozens
Vice President, Facilities ....John Darby
Vice President, Theatre Operations ....Peter Entin
Vice President, Marketing ....Charles Flateman
Vice President, Audit ....Anthony LaMattina
Vice President, Ticket Sales ....Brian Mahoney
Vice President, Creative Projects ........D.S. Moynihan
Vice President, Real Estate ....Julio Peterson

House Manager ....Joseph Pullara

Billy Elliot
SCRAPBOOK

Correspondent: Gregg Arst, Company Manager

Vivid Memories of the Final Performance: It was such a magical performance. We had a great collection of people at the final show. We extended an invitation for each of the alumni to come back as an audience member. Many original principals including Greg Jbara, Carole Shelley and Haydn Gwynne were there, and lots of former principals and Billys in addition to the originals, who we asked to perform in a specially choreographed finale. The spirit of *Billy Elliot* is family and community, and that's how we wanted the final show to be as well. We loved having many alumni return to the Imperial to celebrate one final time. For the alumni kids, it was thrilling to see the transformation because we'd watched those kids grow up before our eyes.

The final performance sold out immediately after we announced it. The audience was divided between alumni and the paying public who came to pay tribute to our three-year run. We did something unusual for the final performance: we utilized all eight kids by weaving all our Billys into the show. Sometimes it was as simple as alternating scenes, but the true enjoyment was in situations where multiple actors were on stage at the same time. It was an amazing show unto itself! Every time a new Billy came on stage there was raucous applause with three or four standing ovations throughout the show. We sat there thinking that while this was a bittersweet performance, it was also one of the most exhilarating performances we ever did and the audiences had ever seen. It perfectly bookended the excitement of opening night. If that's the last memory we have of *Billy Elliot*, that's a great memory to have.

Memorable Quotes from Farewell Stage Speeches: Writer Lee Hall and Director Stephen Daldry were in attendance and gave speeches before the final performance. Lee talked about how thankful he was that Broadway accepted and loved *Billy Elliot*. Both gentlemen gave heartfelt thanks to the Broadway community and New York audiences for embracing the show. Stephen then brought the audience in on the surprise about the rotating Billy performance they were about to see, and the audience climbed on board with the idea with many "oooohs and ahhhs" and applause.

Special Farewell Gift: When the closing was announced the producers thought of how they could time-capsule the show and pay tribute to hardworking cast and crew over 3-plus years. So we created a video yearbook that goes back to the casting of the original three boys all the way through our closing announcement. In order to fully capture the true meaning of the show, the producers wanted to hear directly from the cast and crew. So we spent over a week interviewing

1. The cast welcomes the 1,500,000th person to see the show, Caty Dougherty (center, in navy blue) of Philadelphia, at the June 22, 2011 matinee.
2. Original Broadway cast member Carole Shelley shows off her tutu at the June 22 performance.
3. A reunion of young men who had played the title character at the December 6, 2011 "Gypsy of the Year" competition. *Billy Elliot's* farewell performance earned the Best Stage Presentation prize at the event.

company and alumni about what *Billy Elliot* meant to them. Plus, alumni were encouraged to submit their own videos and/or photos so their memories were shared as well. The video is titled *Billy Is...* and was presented to the cast at Christmas 2011 as a final present. It was also given to any and all alumni at the final performance or via mail so the entire *Billy* family—especially the kids—could have a lasting memento of the time when they were with us.

Special Backstage Ritual: One of the daily routines before each performance was a warmup for the ballet girls and the performing Billy and Michael. Since the final performance featured all the kids and many alumni Billys, the warm-up before the final performance

became a popular attraction for the cast to watch and absorb the special day that was about to come. On that Sunday afternoon, we all got to witness a very rare sight of all the kids warming up together and being all together one final time.

Farewell Party: We had a private party at Lucky Strike bowling for anyone who had been a part of the show. It was a perfect space for our cast, since there was something for both the adults and the kids to do together, so they could mingle. It was a great way to say goodbye.

Favorite Moment During the Final Performance (On Stage or Off): Believe it or not, it was the first time my 6-year-old daughter watched the entire show. She was 3

Billy Eliott
SCRAPBOOK

Photos by Joseph Marzullo/WENN

1. Curtain call at the final performance.
2. The marquee of the Imperial Theatre on closing night.
3. A dozen young men who had played the title role appeared onstage together. The four current Billys are at center.
4. A reunion of the three original Tony-winning Broadway Billys (L-R) Kiril Kulish, Trent Kowalik and David Alvarez on closing night.

when the show opened. She would visit from time to time, but never sat through the entire show. But finally she got to see the whole thing and she was mesmerized. She watched from one of the box seats where I sat with her and from that angle I had an amazing experience watching her experience the entire show. I could see her reaction the whole time, and I will never forget the look of wonder and delight on her face.

Favorite In-Theatre Gathering Place: We had another tradition that whenever someone would leave the show, we'd gather on the stage behind the closed curtain and sing "Happy Trails." I think we intended to do that at the final performance too, but when the curtain came down, everyone hugged and cried and took pictures of each other in costume for the last time.

Favorite Snack: We had a tradition that every Saturday was "Bagel Saturday." Our final performance was on a Sunday, so for that weekend only we had "Bagel Sunday" as well. Also, during the final week the producers delivered a bottle of champagne to everyone in the building (the kids got non-alcoholic drinks).

Company In-Jokes: There was a lot of tongue-in-cheek humor at the final performance. We didn't change a lot of dialogue, but, for example, we had to deal with the multiple actors playing Billy, which meant we had to figure ways to get one off and the next one on. One time two Billys were on stage at the same time, so to remove one, the kids played "Rock, Paper, Scissors" and the loser had to leave while the other stayed and played the scene. Another great moment was at the end of "Solidarity" where Billy usually does a solo ballet spin. At the final performance all four Billys came out and did the spin at the same time. The next line comes from Dad upon entering the ballet studio. He says "What the [bleep] is going on here?!?" That same line had extra meaning when addressed to multiple sons.

Memorable Ad-Lib: The show ends with Billy and his friend Michael saying goodbye. "See ya, Billy." "See ya, Michael." At the final performance, all four Billys "left" and Michael used their real names instead.

Coolest Thing About Being in This Show: I was with *Billy Elliot* for its entire Broadway run, and it was truly the most amazing professional experience. I am so grateful to the producers at Working Title Films and Universal. I wouldn't be here without the support of Nina Lannan and Devin Keudell who guided me from day one. I'm eternally grateful to Carol M. Oune for her hard work helping me. I also want to thank each and every one of the cast and crew, especially the parents who devoted their lives to the dreams of their own kids. I honestly believe there will never be a show or structure like *Billy Elliot*, and I will always remember how fortunate I was to work on such an exciting and rewarding show.

Bonnie & Clyde

First Preview: November 4, 2011. Opened: December 1, 2011.
Closed December 30, 2011 after 33 Previews and 36 Performances.

A musical about the short, violent, passionate careers of two romantically-involved criminals who become media darlings during a colorful crime spree that disrupts (and sometimes ends) the grinding, colorless lives of people in Depression-era West Texas.

CAST
(in order of appearance)

Bonnie Parker	LAURA OSNES
Clyde Barrow	JEREMY JORDAN
Young Bonnie	KELSEY FOWLER
Emma Parker	MIMI BESSETTE
Minister	DANIEL COONEY
Young Clyde	TALON ACKERMAN
Cumie Barrow	LESLIE BECKER
Henry Barrow	VICTOR HERNANDEZ
Buck Barrow	CLAYBOURNE ELDER
First Judge	TAD WILSON
Ted Hinton	LOUIS HOBSON
Blanche Barrow	MELISSA VAN DER SCHYFF
Eleanore	GARRETT LONG
Trish	MARISSA McGOWAN
Stella	ALISON CIMMET
Sheriff Schmid	JOE HART
Bud	MATT LUTZ
Preacher	MICHAEL LANNING
Second Judge	MICHAEL LANNING
First Penitentiary Guard	DANIEL COONEY
Shopkeeper	JON FLETCHER
Deputy Johnson	JON FLETCHER
Bank Teller	TAD WILSON

Continued on next page

GERALD SCHOENFELD THEATRE
236 West 45th Street
A Shubert Organization Theatre

Philip J. Smith, *Chairman*   Robert E. Wankel, *President*

KATHLEEN RAITT   JERRY FRANKEL   JEFFREY RICHARDS
BARRY SATCHWELL SMITH   MICHAEL A. JENKINS

HOWARD CAPLAN   BERNIE ABRAMS/MICHAEL SPEYER   HOWARD KAGAN
BARRY & CAROLE KAYE   TERRY SCHNUCK   NEDERLANDER PRESENTATIONS
COREY BRUNISH/BRISA TRINCHERO   ALDEN BADWAY PODELL/THE BROADWAY CONSORTIUM
PATTY BAKER   BAZINET & COMPANY   UNITEUS ENTERTAINMENT   KEN MAHONEY
JEREMY SCOTT BLAUSTEIN

In Association with

STAGEVENTURES 2011 LIMITED PARTNERSHIP   DARREN BAGERT   ROBERT G. BARTNER/AMBASSADOR THEATRE GROUP
BGM   BROADWAY ACROSS AMERICA   MICHAEL D. COIT   MARY COSSETTE   RONALD FRANKEL   LLOYD FRUGE
BRUCE ROBERT HARRIS/JACK W. BATMAN   CYNTHIA STROUM   DSM/GABRIEL KAMEL   IRVING WELZER

Present

BONNIE & CLYDE

Book by	Lyrics by	Music by
IVAN MENCHELL	DON BLACK	FRANK WILDHORN

Starring

LAURA OSNES   JEREMY JORDAN
MELISSA VAN DER SCHYFF   CLAYBOURNE ELDER
JOE HART   LOUIS HOBSON

With

TALON ACKERMAN   ROZI BAKER   LESLIE BECKER   MIMI BESSETTE   ALISON CIMMET
DANIEL COONEY   JON FLETCHER   KELSEY FOWLER   VICTOR HERNANDEZ   SEAN JENNESS
KATIE KLAUS   MICHAEL LANNING   GARRETT LONG   MATT LUTZ   MARISSA McGOWAN
CASSIE OKENKA   JUSTIN MATTHEW SARGENT   JACK TARTAGLIA   TAD WILSON

Scenic & Costume Design	Lighting Design	Sound Design	Projection Design
TOBIN OST	MICHAEL GILLIAM	JOHN SHIVERS	AARON RHYNE

Casting	Hair & Wig Design	Makeup Design	Fight Director
TELSEY + COMPANY	CHARLES LAPOINTE	ASHLEY RYAN	STEVE RANKIN

Technical Supervisor	Production Stage Manager	Associate Director	Press Agent/Marketing
NEIL A. MAZZELLA/ HUDSON THEATRICAL ASSOCIATES	PAUL J. SMITH	COY MIDDLEBROOK	JEFFREY RICHARDS ASSOCIATES IRENE GANDY/ALANA KARPOFF

Music Director	Music Contractor	General Management	Advertising
JASON HOWLAND	DAVID LAI	BESPOKE THEATRICALS	SERINO/COYNE

Music Supervision/Arrangements/Orchestrations
JOHN McDANIEL

Direction and Choreography
JEFF CALHOUN

World Premiere of Bonnie & Clyde Produced by La Jolla Playhouse
Christopher Ashley, Artistic Director & Michael S. Rosenberg, Managing Director
Subsequently produced at Asolo Repertory Theatre, Sarasota, FL,
Michael Donald Edwards, Producing Artistic Director & Linda DiGabriele, Managing Director

12/1/11

(L-R): Melissa van der Schyff, Claybourne Elder, Jeremy Jordan, Laura Osnes

Photo by Nathan Johnson

Bonnie & Clyde

MUSICAL NUMBERS

ACT ONE

"Picture Show" ....Young Bonnie, Young Clyde, Bonnie, Clyde
"This World Will Remember Me" ....Clyde, Bonnie
"You're Goin' Back to Jail" ....Blanche, Buck, Salon Women
"How 'Bout a Dance" ....Bonnie
"When I Drive" ....Clyde, Buck
"God's Arms Are Always Open" ....Preacher, Congregation
"You Can Do Better Than Him" ....Ted, Clyde
"You Love Who You Love" ....Bonnie, Blanche
"Raise a Little Hell" ....Clyde
"This World Will Remember Us" ....Clyde, Bonnie

ACT TWO

"Made in America" ....Preacher, Ensemble
"Too Late to Turn Back Now" ....Clyde, Bonnie
"That's What You Call a Dream" ....Blanche
"What Was Good Enough for You" ....Clyde, Bonnie
"Bonnie" ....Clyde
"Raise a Little Hell" (Reprise) ....Clyde, Buck, Ted
"Dyin' Ain't So Bad" ....Bonnie
"God's Arms Are Always Open" (Reprise) ....Blanche, Preacher
"Picture Show" (Reprise) ....Young Bonnie, Young Clyde
"Dyin' Ain't So Bad" (Reprise) ....Bonnie, Clyde

(L-R): Laura Osnes, Jeremy Jordan

Photo by Nathan Johnson

Cast Continued

Governor Ferguson ....LESLIE BECKER
Captain Frank Hamer.................TAD WILSON
Detective Alcorn ....DANIEL COONEY

Ensemble ....ALISON CIMMET,
    DANIEL COONEY, JON FLETCHER,
    MICHAEL LANNING, GARRETT LONG,
    MATT LUTZ, MARISSA McGOWAN,
    TAD WILSON

SWINGS

KATIE KLAUS, SEAN JENNESS,
CASSIE OKENKA,
JUSTIN MATTHEW SARGENT

UNDERSTUDIES

For Young Bonnie: ROZI BAKER
For Young Clyde: JACK TARTAGLIA
For Bonnie Parker: MARISSA McGOWAN,
    CASSIE OKENKA
For Clyde Barrow: JON FLETCHER,
    JUSTIN MATTHEW SARGENT
For Buck Barrow: MATT LUTZ,
    JUSTIN MATTHEW SARGENT
For Blanche Barrow: ALISON CIMMET,
    KATIE KLAUS, GARRETT LONG
For Sheriff Schmid: DANIEL COONEY,
    TAD WILSON
For Ted Hinton: MATT LUTZ,
    JUSTIN MATTHEW SARGENT
For Emma Parker, Cumie Barrow & Governor
    Ferguson: ALISON CIMMET,
    GARRETT LONG
For Henry Barrow: SEAN JENNESS,
    JUSTIN MATTHEW SARGENT

ORCHESTRA

Musical Director/
    Conductor/Piano: JASON HOWLAND
Associate Conductor/Synthesizer: JEFF TANSKI
Violin: CENOVIA CUMMINS
Drums: CLINT deGANON
Bass: CHRIS LIGHTCAP
Guitar 1: BRIAN KOONIN
Guitar 2/Banjo/
    Pedal Steel: GORDON TITCOMB
Woodwinds: ROB JACOBY, DAN WILLIS
Synthesizer Programmer: RANDY COHEN

Bonnie & Clyde

Laura Osnes
Bonnie Parker

Jeremy Jordan
Clyde Barrow

Melissa Van Der Schyff
Blanche Barrow

Claybourne Elder
Buck Barrow

Joe Hart
Sheriff Schmid

Louis Hobson
Ted Hinton

Talon Ackerman
Young Clyde

Leslie Becker
Cumie Barrow, Governor Ferguson

Mimi Bessette
Emma Parker

Alison Cimmet
Stella, Ensemble

Daniel Cooney
Minister, First Penitentiary Guard, Detective Alcorn, Fight Captain, Ensemble

Jon Fletcher
Shopkeeper, Deputy Johnson, Ensemble

Kelsey Fowler
Young Bonnie

Victor Hernandez
Henry Barrow

Michael Lanning
Preacher, Second Judge, Ensemble

Garrett Long
Eleanore, Ensemble

Matt Lutz
Bud, Ensemble

Marissa McGowan
Trish, Ensemble

Tad Wilson
First Judge, Bank Teller, Captain Frank Hamer, Ensemble

Rozi Baker
Young Bonnie Standby

Sean Jenness
Swing

Katie Klaus
Swing

Cassie Okenka
Swing

Justin Matthew Sargent
Swing

Jack Tartaglia
Young Clyde Standby

Ivan Menchell
Book

Don Black
Lyrics

Frank Wildhorn
Music

Jeff Calhoun
Director/ Choreographer

John McDaniel
Music Supervision/ Arrangements/ Orchestrations

Tobin Ost
Scenic & Costume Design

Michael Gilliam
Lighting Design

John Shivers
Lighting Design

Aaron Rhyne
Projection Design

Bernard Telsey, Telsey + Company
Casting

Bonnie & Clyde

Charles G. LaPointe
Hair & Wig Design

Ashley Ryan
Makeup Design

Steve Rankin
Fight Direction

Neil A. Mazzella/
Hudson Theatrical
Associates
*Technical
Supervision*

Coy Middlebrook
Associate Director

Jason Howland
Musical Director

David Lai
Music Contractor

Maggie Brohn,
Bespoke Theatricals
*General
Management*

Amy Jacobs,
Bespoke Theatricals
*General
Management*

Devin Keudel,l
Bespoke Theatricals
*General
Management*

Nina Lannan,
Bespoke Theatricals
*General
Management*

Corey Brunish
*Assistant Director,
Producer*

J. Scott Lapp
Assistant Director

Shane Ann Younts
Dialect Consultant

Kathleen Raitt
Producer

Jerry Frankel
Producer

Jeffrey Richards
Producer

Michael A. Jenkins
Producer

Bernard Abrams
Producer

Michael Speyer
Producer

Terry Schnuck
Producer

James M.
Nederlander,
Nederlander
Presentations
Producer

James L.
Nederlander,
Nederlander
Presentations
Producer

Brisa Trinchero
Producer

Michael A. Alden
Producer

Dale Badway
Producer

Van Dean, Kenny Howard,
The Broadway Consortium
Producers

Patty Baker
Producer

Tena Clark,
Uniteus
Entertainment
Producer

Ken Mahoney
Producer

Jeremy Scott
Blaustein
Producer

Christopher Ashley,
Artistic Director,
La Jolla Playhouse

Michael S.
Rosenberg,
Managing Director,
La Jolla Playhouse

Bonnie & Clyde

Photo by Nathan Johnson

(Foreground L-R):
Jeremy Jordan,
Joe Hart and
Louis Hobson in a
scene from the show..

COMPANY AND STAGE MANAGEMENT AND CHILD WRANGLER
(L-R): Jason Brouillard, Doug Gaeta, Megan Schneid, Paul J. Smith, Roseanna Sharrow, Vanessa Brown

Photos by Brian Mapp

DOORMAN
Dave McGaughran

THE CAST
Front Row (L-R): Michael Lanning, Mimi Bessette, Tad Wilson, Marissa McGowan, Jon Fletcher, Matt Lutz, Cassie Okenka

Middle Row (L-R): Alison Cimmet, Katie Klaus, Rozi Baker, Talon Ackerman, Kelsey Fowler, Jack Tartaglia, Leslie Becker

Back Row (L-R): Daniel Cooney, Victor Hernandez, Justin Matthew Sargent, Louis Hobson, Laura Osnes, Jeremy Jordan, Joe Hart, Claybourne Elder, Melissa van der Schyff

Not Shown: Sean Jenness, Garrett Long

Bonnie & Clyde

FRONT OF HOUSE STAFF

Photos by Brian Mapp

HAIR & WARDROBE
Front Row (L-R): Keith Shaw, Franklin Hollenbeck, Susan Checklick, Carrie Kamerer, Tamara Kopko

Back Row (L-R): Meredith Benson, Jennifer Hohn, Jake Fry, Carrie Rohm, Pat Marcus

CREW
Front Row (L-R): Dan Tramontozzi, Glenn Ingram, Tim McWilliams, Brian Schweppe

Back Row (L-R): Peter Guernsey, Marc Schmittroth, Leslie Ann Kilian, Nick Borisjuk, Brien Brannigan, Brad Robertson, Steve McDonald, Neil Rosenberg

ORCHESTRA AND MUSIC
(L-R): Jeff Tanski, Gordon Titcomb, Cenovia Cummins, John McDaniel, Rob Jacoby

Bonnie & Clyde

(L-R): Claybourne Elder, Jeremy Jordan

Photo by Nathan Johnson

Bonnie & Clyde
SCRAPBOOK

Correspondent: Melissa Van Der Schyff, "Blanche Barrow"

Memory of the Final Performance: The audience response at the end of each number. The applause was so hearty and prolonged that we had to keep holding and holding. I also think everyone was really savoring the melodies and taking a moment to look into each others' eyes. Some of us have been with this show for three or four years. It was our way of saying goodbye to old friends, yet staying in character.

Memorable Farewell Speech: Jeff didn't do a curtain speech to the audience, but he did speak with the cast and crew just before the curtain rose on the final performance. We stood in a circle and everybody held hands. He told us how proud he was of the show and that he hoped we all were as proud. There were a lot of emotions, but people tried to hold back tears so we could go and do the show without blotchy eyes.

Memorable Fan Appreciation: The last week we had overwhelming fan support. We got flowers, letters and candy all week. The Superfans, as we call them, were there in droves all that week, so we saw a lot of familiar faces at the stage door. We all got beautiful letters from the creative team including composer Frank Wildhorn and associate director Coy Middlebrook. And instead of writing a letter, book-writer Ivan Menchell flew in and surprised us all on the last day. He didn't speak at the circle, but he came and talked to us all individually and gave us all a big hug.

Farewell Party and Gifts: We had our closing party at the Irish Rogue on 44th Street. Besides the other nice gifts, when we first found out we were closing, one fan named Abby made us a cake with a car on top and figures of the four members of the Barrow Gang all made out of cake! At first nobody wanted to eat it because it was so beautiful, but during the show backstage I would walk by and see a head or a leg had gone. It was a metaphor for what was happening with the show I guess. We were eating ourselves in cake form.

Most Exciting Celebrity Visitors: One was our neighbor, Hugh Jackman. He dropped by the theatre on our first day to welcome us. He hid behind Jeff who told the gathered cast that he wanted to introduce Clyde's new understudy, then Hugh jumped out. Another exciting guest was Dolly Parton. She saw the show, then came on stage afterward and said hello to everyone and let us take photos with her. She spoke to me personally and said, "Oh, darlin' you must be from the South." And I said, "Oh gosh, thanks, but I'm from Canada!" We both laughed.

Special Backstage Rituals: We had a few. One was "Push-ups with Dan Cooney." He started doing push-ups backstage before the show and gradually more and more people joined him. Another one was something called "Buck's Bits." Each night Clay, who played my husband Buck, would come off stage covered in blood and bits of brain. For some reason he decided to save these and he would put them in a jar he labeled "Buck's Bits." By the end of the run it was filled with blood and we all signed the jar. Clay and I had

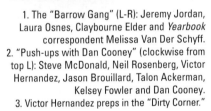

1. The "Barrow Gang" (L-R): Jeremy Jordan, Laura Osnes, Claybourne Elder and *Yearbook* correspondent Melissa Van Der Schyff.
2. "Push-ups with Dan Cooney" (clockwise from top L): Steve McDonald, Neil Rosenberg, Victor Hernandez, Jason Brouillard, Talon Ackerman, Kelsey Fowler and Dan Cooney.
3. Victor Hernandez preps in the "Dirty Corner."

one more ritual. We would meet before the show for a few minutes of talking and getting back in touch. We called it our "Couples Counseling." We did it so that Buck and Blanche were ready to be husband and wife for that performance.

Favorite Moments (On Stage or Off): During the song "That's What You Call a Dream" I had a nice moment just sitting in Clay's lap. I loved having that quiet moment in a show that had a lot of activity. I also loved singing "God's Arms" because it was the first time the majority of the cast was on stage at the same time. We finally had a moment we could celebrate singing together.

Favorite In-Theatre Gathering Place: Our theatre had dressing rooms on six different floors connected only by staircases. So if you were on the upper floors, once you left your dressing room you tried hard not to go back. Leslie Becker, who played Cumie, and Victor Hernandez who played Henry spent a lot of the

show covered in dirt. So Leslie set up "Leslie's Dirty Corner" in the basement where they could put on their dirt. There was a funny parallel in the show where Clyde remembers the family living under a viaduct in the Depression. That's what it felt like.

Favorite Off-Site Hangout: For a while the cast had a "Bring Back Sardi's" campaign and would go there between matinee and evening performances. We also went to Elsewhere on 43rd Street and the Glass House Tavern on 47th.

Favorite Snack Foods: We had cookies and brownies—a lot of brownies. It also seemed like we had birthday cake a couple of times a week. Luckily, with all those stairs, we got to work off the cake, so it all balanced out.

Mascot: Tad Wilson gave us Teddy the Tunesmith, a bear figurine who would play a Christmas song on a toy piano when you pushed a button.

Bonnie & Clyde
SCRAPBOOK

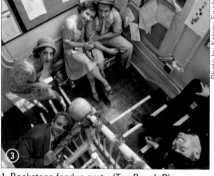

1. Backstage fondue party: (Top Row L-R): Carrie Kamerer, Joe Hart, Jack Tartaglia, Melissa Van Der Schyff, Alison Cimmet; (Bottom Row L-R): Talon Ackerman, Kelsey Fowler, Laura Osnes, Rozi Baker.
2. An eerie foreshadowing (L-R): Jeremy Jordan, Matt Lutz, Laura Osnes, Garrett Long.
3. In a backstage stairwell (ascending): Joe Hart, Alison Cimmet, Marissa McGowan, Jon Fletcher.

Favorite Therapies: Laura Osnes got walkie-talkies for the four members of the Barrow Gang (Laura, Jeremy, Clay and myself) because we all had dressing rooms on different floors. We used them for Joke Therapy. We would make up jokes before the show—usually involving a horrible pun—so we could have a little laughter before going on stage. Here's one of mine: What do you call a puppet made out of pasta? Pin-gnocchi-o! I was also a big fan of ginger lemon honey tea with cayenne pepper. It helped to ward off colds and invigorate a tired voice.

Memorable Ad-Lib: Sometimes Michael Lanning would ad-lib when he was singing "God's Arms." The first line was "God's arms are always open," but every now and then he would start speaking in tongues. It was hilarious and still kind of appropriate.

Technological Interruptions: We didn't have a lot of cell phones ringing, but we did see a lot of

camera lights. People thought they were getting away with it, but of course we could see them. Much more intrusive was all the coughers. I guess it's because we were performing in cold and flu season. I wish we could have passed out Ricolas.

Memorable Press Encounter: Being interviewed and photographed on the red carpet opening night was amazing. We finally made it to Broadway! That was a sweet memory.

Memorable Stage Door Fan Encounter: We had our Superfans Jennifer and Susan who we could always see looking up at us from the front row. They became a regular part of *Bonnie & Clyde* life. I had one fan who asked me to sign his arm with a Sharpie. I have a really long name, so I only put my initials so he didn't get toxic poisoning! That was the first limb that I ever signed.

Fastest Costume Changes: There were two, and both involved water. At the end of the bathtub

scene Jeremy is wet and almost naked, but he has only about thirty seconds to get dry and into a three-piece suit including socks and shoes, for the next scene. Clay had about the same amount of time to go from being fully immersed in the baptism scene to wearing a dry three-piece suit for the next scene.

Catchphrases Only the Company Would Recognize: "I have tape…on my face." "What happens on the field stays on the field." "Boobie and Clyde." "Zombie and Died."

Sweethearts Within the Company: Our established couple was Jeff and Katie, and the love-in-bloom was Jon and Marissa.

Orchestra Members Who Played the Most Instruments: Two were tied with seven each: Gordon Titcomb played seven strings including banjo. Rob Jacoby played seven woodwinds.

Orchestra Member Who Played the Most Consecutive Performances Without a Sub: Gordon Titcomb subbed out only once, to watch the show.

Best In-House Parody Lyrics: Instead of "He stole—wouldn't you" we said, "He stole—wooden shoes." When Clyde sang about "Ed Crowder," we would sing "Clam Chowder."

Memorable Directorial Note: We all loved this one: "This is a collaboration—the best idea wins." Jeff once asked Matt to "die faster." At the beginning of rehearsals, Jeff asked us to introduce ourselves to the stage crew so we could get to know each other. It was a small thing, but it really served to bring us all together in a very unique way.

Understudy Anecdote: Sean Jenness understudied the preacher. During early previews we hadn't yet had full understudy rehearsals, but Sean was called upon to go on one day with just a quick rehearsal. Things were going fine until we got to the scene where Clay gets baptized. Clay got on his knees in the pool and Sean pushed him backward into the water—but then had no idea how to get him back up! Clay was stuck down there for a few seconds until somehow they got him back up. Sean was very grateful that he didn't drown one of our stars!

Nicknames: The Barrow Gang had walkie-talkie nicknames. Laura was "Lolo Bird." Jeremy was "You're an Animal" (from a line in the show). Clay was "Buck O'Brown." Mine was "Big Blanche."

Embarrassing Moments: In the scene where Leslie and Victor are burying Buck, they had to roll him into the burial hole and place planks over it. One night a plank fell through and the "dead" Buck had to lift it up and hand it back to them. Also, the fake blood was very slippery so almost everyone at some point fell or slipped on the raked stage.

Superstitions That Turned Out To Be True: I guess in hindsight there was some foreshadowing that the show may have a short run. We had the lyric "A short and loving life—that ain't so bad." At the beginning of Act II Matt Lutz held a sign that said "Who will help me get a job?"

Coolest Thing About Being in This Show: It was the nicest group of people you could ever want to work with.

The Book of Mormon

First Preview: February 24, 2011. Opened: March 24, 2011.
Still running as of May 31, 2012.

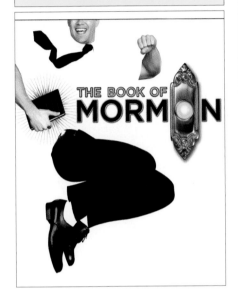

PLAYBILL

THE BOOK OF MORMON

Elder Price, the smartest, most devout and most handsome young Mormon in missionary school, is stunned to find himself assigned, not to Orlando, Florida, as he had prayed, but to a small, miserable village in Africa. He's also shocked to find himself partnered with the dorkiest missionary student, Elder Cunningham. Things go from bad to worse—until Cunningham starts making up his own additions to the Mormon Bible.

CAST

(in order of appearance)

Mormon	JASON MICHAEL SNOW
Moroni	RORY O'MALLEY
Elder Price	ANDREW RANNELLS
Elder Cunningham	JOSH GAD
Missionary Training Center Voice	LEWIS CLEALE
Price's Dad	LEWIS CLEALE
Cunningham's Dad	KEVIN DUDA
Mrs. Brown	REMA WEBB
Guards	JOHN ERIC PARKER, TOMMAR WILSON
Mafala Hatimbi	MICHAEL POTTS
Nabulungi	NIKKI M. JAMES
Elder McKinley	RORY O'MALLEY
Joseph Smith	LEWIS CLEALE
General	BRIAN TYREE HENRY
Doctor	MICHAEL JAMES SCOTT
Mission President	LEWIS CLEALE
Ensemble	SCOTT BARNHARDT, JUSTIN BOHON, DARLESIA CEARCY, KEVIN DUDA, ASMERET GHEBREMICHAEL, CLARK JOHNSEN, JOHN ERIC PARKER, BENJAMIN SCHRADER,

Continued on next page

EUGENE O'NEILL THEATRE
A JUJAMCYN THEATRE

JORDAN ROTH
President

PAUL LIBIN
Executive Vice President

JACK VIERTEL
Senior Vice President

ANNE GAREFINO   SCOTT RUDIN

ROGER BERLIND   SCOTT M. DELMAN   JEAN DOUMANIAN
ROY FURMAN   IMPORTANT MUSICALS   STEPHANIE P. McCLELLAND
KEVIN MORRIS   JON B. PLATT   SONIA FRIEDMAN PRODUCTIONS

EXECUTIVE PRODUCER STUART THOMPSON

PRESENT

THE BOOK OF MORMON

BOOK, MUSIC AND LYRICS BY

TREY PARKER, ROBERT LOPEZ AND MATT STONE

WITH

JOSH GAD   ANDREW RANNELLS

NIKKI M. JAMES   RORY O'MALLEY   MICHAEL POTTS

LEWIS CLEALE   BRIAN TYREE HENRY   SCOTT BARNHARDT   JUSTIN BOHON
GRAHAM BOWEN   DARLESIA CEARCY   KEVIN DUDA   JARED GERTNER
ASMERET GHEBREMICHAEL   TYSON JENNETTE   CLARK JOHNSEN   VALISIA LeKAE
DOUGLAS LYONS   MATTHEW MARKS   JOHN ERIC PARKER   NIC ROULEAU
BENJAMIN SCHRADER   MICHAEL JAMES SCOTT   BRIAN SEARS   JASON MICHAEL SNOW
NICK SPANGLER   LAWRENCE STALLINGS   REMA WEBB   MAIA NKENGE WILSON   TOMMAR WILSON

SCENIC DESIGN	COSTUME DESIGN	LIGHTING DESIGN	SOUND DESIGN
SCOTT PASK	**ANN ROTH**	**BRIAN MacDEVITT**	**BRIAN RONAN**

HAIR DESIGN	CASTING	PRODUCTION STAGE MANAGER
JOSH MARQUETTE	**CARRIE GARDNER**	**KAREN MOORE**

ORCHESTRATIONS	DANCE MUSIC ARRANGEMENTS	MUSIC COORDINATOR
LARRY HOCHMAN & STEPHEN OREMUS	**GLEN KELLY**	**MICHAEL KELLER**

ASSOCIATE PRODUCER	PRESS REPRESENTATIVE	PRODUCTION MANAGEMENT	GENERAL MANAGEMENT
ELI BUSH	**BONEAU/ BRYAN-BROWN**	**AURORA PRODUCTIONS**	**STP/DAVID TURNER**

MUSIC DIRECTION AND VOCAL ARRANGEMENTS
STEPHEN OREMUS

CHOREOGRAPHED BY
CASEY NICHOLAW

DIRECTED BY
CASEY NICHOLAW AND TREY PARKER

2/27/12

(L-R): Nikki M. James, Josh Gad

Photo by Joan Marcus

The Book of Mormon

Cast Continued

MICHAEL JAMES SCOTT, BRIAN SEARS,
JASON MICHAEL SNOW,
LAWRENCE STALLINGS,
REMA WEBB, MAIA NKENGE WILSON,
TOMMAR WILSON

UNDERSTUDIES

For Elder Price:
KEVIN DUDA, NICK SPANGLER
For Elder Cunningham:
BENJAMIN SCHRADER
For Missionary Training Center Voice/Price's
Dad/Joseph Smith/Mission President:
GRAHAM BOWEN, KEVIN DUDA,
BENJAMIN SCHRADER
For Mafala Hatimbi:
TYSON JENNETTE, JOHN ERIC PARKER
For Nabulungi:
ASMERET GHEBREMICHAEL,
VALISIA LeKAE
For Elder McKinley:
SCOTT BARNHARDT, GRAHAM BOWEN,
BRIAN SEARS
For the General:
TYSON JENNETTE, DOUGLAS LYONS,
JOHN ERIC PARKER

Standby for Elder Cunningham:
JARED GERTNER
Standby for Elder Price:
NIC ROULEAU

SWINGS

GRAHAM BOWEN, TYSON JENNETTE,
VALISIA LeKAE, DOUGLAS LYONS,
MATTHEW MARKS, NICK SPANGLER

Dance Captain:
GRAHAM BOWEN
Assistant Dance Captain:
ASMERET GHEBREMICHAEL

ORCHESTRA

Conductor:
STEPHEN OREMUS
Associate Conductor:
ADAM BEN-DAVID

Keyboards:
STEPHEN OREMUS, ADAM BEN-DAVID
Guitars:
JAKE SCHWARTZ

Bass:
DAVE PHILLIPS
Drums/Percussion:
SEAN McDANIEL
Reeds:
BRYAN CROOK
Trumpet:
RAUL AGRAZ
Trombone:
RANDY ANDOS
Violin/Viola:
ENTCHO TODOROV

Music Coordinator:
MICHAEL KELLER
Keyboard Programmer:
RANDY COHEN
Copyist:
EMILY GRISHMAN MUSIC PREPARATION

Josh Gad
Elder Cunningham

Andrew Rannells
Elder Price

Nikki M. James
Nabulungi

Rory O'Malley
Elder McKinley

Michael Potts
Mafala Hatimbi

Lewis Cleale
*Missionary Training,
Center Voice, Price's
Dad, Joseph Smith*

Brian Tyree Henry
General

Scott Barnhardt
Ensemble

Justin Bohon
Ensemble

Graham Bowen
*Swing, Dance
Captain*

Darlesia Cearcy
Ensemble

Kevin Duda
Ensemble

Jared Gertner
*Standby Elder
Cunningham*

Asmeret
Ghebremichael
*Ensemble, Assistant
Dance Captain*

The Book of Mormon

Tyson Jennette
Swing

Clark Johnsen
Ensemble

Valisia LeKae
Swing

Douglas Lyons
Swing

Matthew Marks
Swing

John Eric Parker
Ensemble

Nic Rouleau
Standby Elder Price

Benjamin Schrader
Ensemble

Michael James Scott
Ensemble

Brian Sears
Ensemble

Jason Michael Snow
Ensemble

Nick Spangler
Swing

Lawrence Stallings
Ensemble

Rema Webb
Ensemble

Maia Nkenge Wilson
Ensemble

Tommar Wilson
Ensemble

Matt Stone and Trey Parker
Book, Music, and Lyrics;
Co-Director, Book, Music, Lyrics

Robert Lopez
Book, Music, Lyrics

Casey Nicholaw
Co-Director and
Choreographer

Scott Pask
Scenic Design

Ann Roth
Costume Design

Brian MacDevitt
Lighting

Brian Ronan
Sound Design

Stephen Oremus
Music Director/
Vocal Arranger/
Co-Orchestrator

Larry Hochman
Co-Orchestrator

Josh Marquette
Hair Design

Randy Houston
Mercer
Makeup Design

Michael Keller
Music Coordinator

Jennifer Werner
Associate Director

John MacInnis
Associate
Choreographer

Gene O'Donovan,
Aurora Productions
Production
Management

Ben Heller,
Aurora Productions
Production
Management

Anne Garefino
Producer

Scott Rudin
Producer

The Book of Mormon

Roger Berlind
Producer

Jean Doumanian
Producer

Sonia Friedman
Productions Ltd.
Producer

Roy Furman
Producer

Stephanie P.
McClelland
Producer

Jon B. Platt
Producer

Stuart Thompson
Producer

ALUMNI 2011-2012

Melanie Brezill
Swing

Ta'Rea Campbell
Swing

TRANSFER STUDENTS 2011-2012

Will Blum
*Standby for
Elder Cunningham*

Tamika Sonja
Lawrence
*Mrs. Brown,
Ensemble*

Allison Semmes
Swing

Photos by Brian Mapp

WARDROBE
(L-R): Jeff McGovney, unidentified, unidentified, Dolly Williams, James Martin Williams Gunn, unidentified, unidentified, Frank Scaccia, unidentified, Veneda Truesdale, Michael Harrell

HAIR DEPARTMENT
(L-R): Joel Hawkins (Hair Dresser), Matthew Wilson (Hair Dresser), Josh Marquette (Hair Designer), Tod McKim (Hair Supervisor)

The Book of Mormon

Photos by Brian Mapp

BOX OFFICE
(L-R): Stan Shaffer (Treasurer),
Gloria Diabo, Robert Ricchiuti,
Rusty Owen (Assistant Treasurer)

ORCHESTRA
Front Row (L-R): Raul Agraz (Trumpet), Stephen Oremus (Conductor/Keyboard 1),
Sean McDaniel (Drums)
Back Row (L-R): Randy Andos (Trombone), Adam Ben-David (Associate Conductor/Keyboard 2),
Entcho Todorov (Violin/Viola), Jake Schwartz (Guitars), Bryan Crook (Reeds)
Not pictured: Dave Phillips (Bass)

STAGE MANAGEMENT
(L-R): Karen Moore, Michael P. Zaleski, Rachel S. McCutchen

STAGE CREW

The Book of Mormon

Photo by Brian Mapp

FRONT OF HOUSE
Standing (L-R): Tim Murphy, Bruce Lucoff, Bill Mayo, Sean Chambers
Second Row (L-R): Charlotte Brauer, Verna Hobson, Lorraine Wheeler
Fourth Row (L-R): John Nascenti, Heather Jewels, Heather Gilles, Byron Vargas
Sixth Row (L-R): Leslie Morgenstern, Travis Navarra, Megan Rozak, Mili Vela
Top Row (L-R): Jeremy Plyburn, Jeremy Benson

First Row (L-R): Jesse Schanzenbach, Brian Busby, Mair Heller, Dwane Upp, Emily Hare
Third Row (L-R): Giovanni Monserrate, Sandra Palmer, Saime Hodzic
Fifth Row (L-R): Dorothy Lennon, Scott Rippe, Raymond Millan
Seventh Row (L-R): Jared St. Gelais, Kami Martin, Alana Linchner

---

STAFF FOR THE BOOK OF MORMON

GENERAL MANAGEMENT
STUART THOMPSON PRODUCTIONS
Stuart Thompson   David Turner   Patrick Gracey
Kevin Emrick   Andrew Lowy
Christopher Taggart   Brittany Weber   James Yandoli

COMPANY MANAGER
Adam J. Miller

PRODUCTION MANAGEMENT
AURORA PRODUCTIONS INC.
Gene O'Donovan   Ben Heller
Stephanie Sherline   Jarid Sumner   Liza Luxenberg
Anita Shah   Rebecca Zuber   Steven Dalton
Eugenio Saenz Flores   Isaac Katzanek
Melissa Mazdra

PRESS REPRESENTATIVE
BONEAU/BRYAN-BROWN
Chris Boneau   Jim Byk   Christine Olver

MAKEUP DESIGNER
Randy Houston Mercer

ASSOCIATE DIRECTOR
Jennifer Werner

ASSOCIATE CHOREOGRAPHER
John MacInnis

SCOTT RUDIN PRODUCTIONS
Max Grossman   Jessica Held   Adam Klaff
Julie Oh   Nick Reimond   Jason Sack   Dan Sarrow

Production Stage Manager .... **Karen Moore**

Stage Manager ....Rachel S. McCutchen
Assistant Stage Manager ....Michael P. Zaleski
Assistant Company Manager ....Megan Curren
Dance Captain ....Graham Bowen
Assistant Dance Captain ....Asmeret Ghebremichael
Associate Scenic Designer ....Frank McCullough
Assistant Scenic Designers ....Lauren Alvarez,
                                              Christine Peters
Associate Costume Designers ....Matthew Pachtman,
                                              Michelle Matland
Costume Design Assistant ....Irma Escobar
Associate Lighting Designer ....Benjamin C. Travis
Assistant Lighting Designer ....Carl Faber
Associate Sound Designer ....Ashley Hanson
Production Carpenter ....Mike Martinez
Production Electrician...........................Dan Coey
Head Electrician ....Drayton Allison
Production Sound Engineer ....Chris Sloan

The Book of Mormon

Moving Light Programmer ....David John Arch
Lead Front Electrics ....Damian Caza-Cleypool
Sound Engineer ....Jason McKenna
Deck Automation ....Andrew Lanzarotta
Fly Automation ....Scott Dixon
Production Props ....Ken Keneally
Properties Coordinator ....Pete Sarafin
Wardrobe Supervisor ....Dolly Williams
Assistant Wardrobe Supervisor ....Fred Castner
Hair Supervisor ....Tod L. McKim

Dressers ....D'Ambrose Boyd, Michael Harrell,
Eugene Nicks, Melanie McClintock,
Jeff McGovney, Virginia Neinenger,
Veneda Truesdale
Hair Dressers ....Joel Hawkins, Matthew Wilson
Associate Musical Director ....Adam Ben-David
Electronic Music Programmer ....Randy Cohen
Drum Programmer ....Sean McDaniel
Rehearsal Pianist ....Brian Usifer
Assistant to the Producers ....Kurt Nickels
Production Assistants ....Sara Cox Bradley,
Derek DiGregorio
Music Department Assistant ....Matthew Aument
Costume Shoppers ....Brenda Abbandandolo,
Kate Friedberg
Assistant to Ms. Roth ....Jonathan Schwartz
Research Assistant to Ms. Roth ....Debbe DuPerrieu
Assistants to Mr. MacDevitt ....Ariel Benjamin,
Jonathan Dillard
Prop Shopper ....Buist Bickley
Casting Associate ....Kate S. Boka
Company Management Assistant ....Stuart Shefter
General Management Intern ....Michael Holt
Marketing Director ....Steven Cardwell
Banking..................................City National Bank/
Erik Piecuch, Michele Gibbons
Payroll ....Castellana Services, Inc.
Accountant ....Fried & Kowgios CPA's LLP/
Robert Fried, CPA
Controller ....J.S. Kubala
Insurance ....DeWitt Stern Group
Legal Counsel ....Lazarus & Harris LLP/
Scott Lazarus, Esq.,
Robert C. Harris, Esq.
Advertising ....Serino/Coyne/
Scott Johnson, Nancy Coyne,
Sandy Block, Greg Corradetti,
Robert Jones, Vanessa Javier
Digital Outreach ....Serino/Coyne/
Kevin Keating, Laurie Connor,
Chip Meyrelles, Crystal Chase,
Jacqui Kaiser
Marketing ....Serino/Coyne/
Leslie Barrett, Mike Rafael,
Diana Salameh
Website Design..............South Park Digital Studios/aka
Production Photographer ....Joan Marcus
Company Physical Therapists ....PhysioArts
Company Orthopaedist ....David S. Weiss, M.D.
Theatre Displays ....BAM Signs, Inc.
Transportation ....IBA Limousines

CREDITS

Scenery fabrication by PRG-Scenic Technologies, a division
of Production Resource Groups, LLC, New Windsor, NY.
Lighting equipment provided by PRG Lighting, Secaucus,

NJ. Sound equipment provided by Masque Sound.
Costumes by Eric Winterling, Inc.; Gilberto Designs, Inc.;
Katrina Patterns; Izquierdo Studios, Ltd.; Studio Rouge,
Inc. Millinery by Rodney Gordon, Inc. Military clothing
provided by Kaufman's Army & Navy. Custom military
ammunition by Weapons Specialists, Ltd. Custom fabric
printing by First 2 Print LLC. Custom fabric dyeing and
painting by Jeff Fender. Eyewear provided by Dr. Wayne
Goldberg. Custom footwear by LaDuca Shoes, Inc.;
Worldtone Dance. Props executed by Cigar Box Studios,
Tom Carroll Scenery, Jerard Studios, Daedalus Design and
Production, Joe Cairo, J&M Special Effects, Jeremy Lydic,
Josh Yocom. Wigs made by Hudson Wigs. Makeup
provided by M•A•C Cosmetics. Keyboards from Yamaha
Corporation of America.

SPECIAL THANKS

John Barlow, Lisa Gajda, Angela Howard, Bruce Howell,
Beth Johnson-Nicely, Sarah Kooperkamp, Kristen
Anderson-Lopez, Katie Lopez, Annie Lopez, Kathy Lopez,
Frank Lopez, Billy Lopez, Brian Shepherd, Eric Stough,
Boogie Tillmon, The Vineyard Theatre, Darlene Wilson

Souvenir merchandise designed and created by
The Araca Group.

Rehearsed at the New 42nd Street Studios

JUJAMCYN THEATERS

JORDAN ROTH
President

PAUL LIBIN
Executive Vice President

JACK VIERTEL
Senior Vice President

MEREDITH VILLATORE
Chief Financial Officer

JENNIFER HERSHEY
Vice President,
Building Operations

MICAH HOLLINGWORTH
Vice President,
Company Operations

HAL GOLDBERG
Vice President,
Theatre Operations

Director of Business Affairs ....Albert T. Kim
Director of Human Resources ....Michele Louhisdon
Director of Ticketing Services ....Justin Karr
Theatre Operations Managers ....Willa Burke,
Susan Elrod, Emily Hare,
Jeff Hubbard, Albert T. Kim
Theatre Operations Associates ....Carrie Jo Brinker,
Brian Busby, Michael Composto,
Anah Jyoti Klate
Accounting ....Cathy Cerge, Erin Dooley, Amy Frank
Executive Producer, Red Awning ....Nicole Kastrinos
Director of Marketing, Givenik.com ....Joe Tropia
Marketing Associate, Givenik.com ....Ben Cohen
Building Operations Associate ....Erich Bussing
Executive Coordinator ....Ed Lefferson
Executive Assistants ....Clark Mims Tedesco,
Julia Kraus, Beth Given
Receptionist ....Lisa Perchinske
Maintenance ....Ralph Santos, Ramon Zapata
Security ....Rasim Hodzic, John Acero
Interns ....Maggie Baker, Alaina Bono,
Erin Carr, Hunter Chancellor, Cindy Vargas,
Kelvin Veras, Luke Weidner, Margaret White

Andrew Rannells

Photo by Joan Marcus

The Book of Mormon

SCRAPBOOK

Correspondent: Tyson Jennette, Swing

Memorable Fan Letter: "So very impressed with your incredible show! Cheers!!" —Julia Roberts.

Milestone Gifts: Gigantic live wild orchid from Jim Carrey.

Cases of Champagne from Jack Nicholson.

A mountain of cookies, cakes and sweet treats from Whoopi Goldberg.

Milestone Celebration: The *BOM* Tony party was fantastic!

Most Exciting Celebrity Visitor: Oprah Winfrey: She loved it. She stayed afterward for 20 minutes taking pictures with the company backstage. So gracious.

Actor Who Performed the Most Roles in This Show: Tyson Jennette: 8 (4 ensemble African men, 2 women, 2 principals).

Who Has Done the Most Performances: Lawrence Stallings: 408 as of 3/3/12, including 28 previews.

Special Backstage Rituals: Myra Angelou (see Josh Gad for details).

Favorite Moment During Each Performance (On Stage or Off): Onstage: When Nikki James sings "Sal Tla Kasiti."

Offstage: Gussie Mae's Vestibule Cabaret during intermission (See Maia Nkenge Wilson for set list and menu).

Favorite In-Theatre Gathering Place: Stage Management Office: It's not just for birthdays anymore.

Favorite Off-Site Hangouts: Lillie's, for the smothered pulled-pork French fries.

Inc. Lounge @ The Time Hotel.

Molloy's.

Favorite Snack Foods: M&M's, Donkey Balls.

Mascot: FROGS...definitely frogs.

Favorite Therapy: Coconut water.

Memorable Ad-Libs: "Black Friday," "New York Giants," "Irene," "Non-Equity," "Newt Gingrich" (all names substituted for "Nabulungi" over the last year by Josh Gad)

Record Number of Cell Phone Rings, Cell Phone Photos or Texting Incidents During a Performance: 4.

Memorable Press Encounter: People Magazine photo shoot: Matt and Trey and cast in full costume on a double-decker tour bus in front of the Eugene O'Neill Theater.

Memorable Stage Door Fan Encounter: After her seventh time seeing the show, a fan who wanted to "feel Rory O'Malley's energy" waited at the stage door and grabbed his forearms and stated that she was "recharging."

Latest Audience Arrival: During "Spooky Mormon Hell Dream" (second song in Act II)!

Fastest Costume Change: Rema Webb: 3 seconds (From baptisee to Kafe bartender).

Who Wore the Heaviest/Hottest Costume: Tommar Wilson as Darth Vader.

Who Wore the Least: Lawrence Stallings: Bare-chested vest and Mambo pants. Honorable mention goes to Andrew Rannells and his antics in hospital gown.

1. Talk show host Oprah Winfrey (C) visits the cast on stage.
2. Brian Sears and Jason Michael Snow put their hearts into recording the cast album.
3. (L-R): Anne Garefino, Robert Lopez, Stephen Oremus and Trey Parker accept the 2012 Grammy Award for Best Musical Theater Album.

Catchphrases Only the Company Would Recognize: "Pokey people to places please."

Sweethearts Within the Company: Were eaten on Valentine's day.

Orchestra Who Member Played the Most Instruments: Bryan Crook: Oboe, Clarinet, Flute, Piccolo, Alto Sax, Tenor Sax and four Recorders.

Orchestra Member Who Played the Most Consecutive Performances Without a Sub: Sean McDaniel: Percussion/Drums.

Memorable Directorial Note: "KEEP IT HONEST."

Company In-Joke: *DAS BOOT* is Das *BOM*.

Understudy Anecdote: There was a fire that spilled over from the hotel next door during understudy rehearsal one afternoon. We were well into running Act II amid a strange acrid smell of smoke but didn't halt until seven random firefighters, clad in full gear and axes, crossed the stage during scene work. Then it was necessary for our dedication to be paused to assess the situation.

Nicknames: "Raoul": Nic Rouleau.

"Brah": Brian Sears.

"Chocolate Hipster:" Douglas Lyons.

Ghostly Encounters Backstage: Whoopi Goldberg pic that she posted on "The View" the next morning.

Coolest Things About Being in This Show: Playing to packed houses eight times a week. Knowing that our tickets are in demand.

Most-Worked Swing: Nick Spangler: 150 out of 411 shows, as of 3/4/12.

Most Consecutive Shows: 282 by Michael James Scott, including 28 previews.

Disasters: In one week early on we endured two fires and several floods that enveloped dressing rooms and our basement. We questioned if the gods were a bit miffed.

Also: Keith Olbermann has seen us nine times...and counting

Kevin Duda's backstage concerts as an illuminated Jesus are epic.

Our first full cast brush-up rehearsal was '80s themed.

Born Yesterday

First Preview: March 31, 2011. Opened: April 24, 2011.
Closed June 26, 2011 after 28 Previews and 73 Performances.

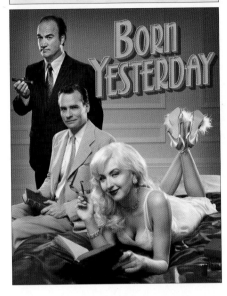

Billie Dawn, an ex-chorus girl derided as a dumb blonde by her crooked boyfriend, gets tutored by a handsome writer in the ways of Washington, DC —and the world—and turns out to be smarter than anyone expected.

CAST OF CHARACTERS
(in order of appearance)

Helen, a Maid ....JENNIFER REGAN
Paul Verrall ....ROBERT SEAN LEONARD
Eddie Brock ....MICHAEL McGRATH
Bellhop ....FRED ARSENAULT
Another Bellhop ....DANNY RUTIGLIANO
A Third Bellhop ....BILL CHRIST
Harry Brock ....JIM BELUSHI
Assistant Manager ....ANDREW WEEMS
Billie Dawn ....NINA ARIANDA
Ed Devery ....FRANK WOOD
Barber ....BILL CHRIST
Manicurist ....LIV ROOTH
Bootblack ....DANNY RUTIGLIANO
Senator Norval Hedges ....TERRY BEAVER
Mrs. Hedges....................PATRICIA HODGES

UNDERSTUDIES

For Billie Dawn: LIV ROOTH
Harry Brock: BILL CHRIST
Paul Verrall: FRED ARSENAULT
Ed Devery: CHRIS BARNES
Eddie Brock: DANNY RUTIGLIANO
Senator Norval Hedges: ANDREW WEEMS
Mrs. Hedges: JENNIFER REGAN
Assistant Manager, Bellhops, Barber, Bootblack:
CHRIS BARNES

ⓈCORT THEATRE
138 West 48th Street
A Shubert Organization Theatre

Philip J. Smith, *Chairman*   Robert E. Wankel, *President*

Philip Morgaman   Anne Caruso   Vincent Caruso   Frankie J. Grande
James P. MacGilvray   Brian Kapetanis   Robert S. Basso
in association with Peter J. Puleo

present

JIM BELUSHI   ROBERT SEAN LEONARD   NINA ARIANDA

in

Born Yesterday

a comedy by

GARSON KANIN

with

Frank Wood

Terry Beaver   Patricia Hodges   Michael McGrath
Fred Arsenault   Bill Christ   Jennifer Regan
Liv Rooth   Danny Rutigliano   Andrew Weems

Scenic Design	Costume Design	Lighting Design	Original Music/Sound Design
John Lee Beatty	Catherine Zuber	Peter Kaczorowski	David Van Tieghem

Hair/Wig Design	Casting	Fight Director	Production Stage Manager
Tom Watson	Jay Binder/ Jack Bowdan	J. David Brimmer	Tripp Phillips

Press Representative	Technical Supervisor	Company Manager	General Management
Richard Kornberg & Associates	Larry Morley	Brig Berney	Richards/Climan, Inc.

Directed by

Doug Hughes

The Producers wish to express their appreciation to Theatre Development Fund for its support of this production.

6/26/11

(L-R): Robert Sean Leonard, Nina Arianda, Jim Belushi

Photo by Carol Rosegg

Born Yesterday

The play is set in Washington, D.C.
The year is 1946.

ACT ONE
September

ACT TWO
About two months later

ACT THREE
Later that night

James Belushi
Harry Brock

Robert Sean Leonard
Paul Verrall

Nina Arianda
Billie Dawn

Frank Wood
Ed Devery

Terry Beaver
Senator Norval Hedges

Patricia Hodges
Mrs. Hedges

Michael McGrath
Eddie Brock

Fred Arsenault
A Bellhop

Bill Christ
A Third Bellhop, Barber

Jennifer Regan
Helen

Liv Rooth
Manicurist

Danny Rutigliano
Another Bellhop, Bootblack

Andrew Weems
Assistant Hotel Manager

Chris Barnes
u/s Ed Devery, Assistant Manager, Bellhops, Barber, Bootblack

Garson Kanin
Playwright

Doug Hughes
Director

John Lee Beatty
Scenic Designer

Catherine Zuber
Costume Designer

Peter Kaczorowski
Lighting Designer

David Van Tieghem
Original Music/ Sound Designer

Tom Watson
Hair/Wig Designer

Jay Binder C.S.A.
Casting

Jack Bowdan C.S.A.
Casting

J. David Brimmer
Fight Director

Richard Kornberg & Associates
Press Representative

Philip Morgaman
Producer

David R. Richards and Tamar Haimes
Richards/Climan, Inc.
General Management

Anne Caruso
Producer

Vincent Caruso
Producer

Frankie J. Grande
Producer

Robert Emmet Lunney
u/s Bootblack, Ed Devery

50

Born Yesterday

FRONT OF HOUSE STAFF

STAGE AND COMPANY MANAGEMENT
(L-R): Jason Hindelang, Tripp Phillips,
Brig Berney

BOX OFFICE STAFF
(L-R): Larry Staroff, Pete Damen

STAGE DOORMAN
Hills Smith

Born Yesterday

CREW
(L-R): David Levenberg, Scott DeVerna, Shannon January, Lonnie Gaddy

HAIR AND WARDROBE
(L-R): Carmel A. Vargyas, Lo Marriott, Claire Verlaet, Steve Chazaro

STAFF FOR *BORN YESTERDAY*

GENERAL MANAGEMENT
RICHARDS/CLIMAN INC.
David R. Richards   Tamar Haimes
Michael Sag   Kyle Bonder   Cesar Hawas

COMPANY MANAGER
Brig Berney

GENERAL PRESS REPRESENTATIVES
RICHARD KORNBERG & ASSOCIATES
Richard Kornberg   Don Summa   Billy Zavelson
Danielle McGarry

CASTING
BINDER CASTING
Jay Binder CSA,
Jack Bowdan CSA, Mark Brandon CSA,
Nikole Vallins CSA
Assistant: Patrick Bell

PRODUCTION STAGE MANAGER .TRIPP PHILLIPS
Stage Manager ....Jason Hindelang
Assistant Director ....Alexander Greenfield
Fight Captain ....Fred Arsenault
Associate Scenic Designer ....Kacie Hultgren
Assistant Costume Designers ....Patrick Bevilacqua,
Nicole Moody, Ryan Park
Assistant Lighting Designer ....Jake DeGroot
Associate Sound Designer ....David Sanderson
Lighting Programmer ....Jay Penfield
Assistant Fight Director ....Turner Smith
Production Carpenter ....Edward Diaz
Production Electrician ....Shannon M.M. January
Production Sound ....Jens McVoy
Head Electrician ....Scott DeVerna
Head Props ....Lonnie Gaddy
Props Coordinators ....Scott Laule, Buist Bickley
Props Supervisor ....David Levenberg
Wardrobe Supervisor ....Patrick Bevilacqua
Hair Supervisor ....Carmel A. Vargyas
Make-Up Design ....Ashley Ryan

Dressers ....Erin Byrne, Steve Chazaro,
Lo Marriott, Claire Verlaet
Production Assistants ....Robbie Peters, John Bantay
Legal Counsel ....Frankfurt, Kurnit, Klein & Selz PC
S. Jean Ward
Advertising ....Serino-Coyne/
Greg Corradetti, Joe Alesi, Sandy Block,
Tom Callahan, Joaquin Esteva,
Sarah Marcus, Peter Gunther
Marketing Services ....Type A Marketing/
Anne Rippey, Michael Porto,
John McCoy
Digital Outreach, Online Media,
Video Production, Website Design ....Serino-Coyne/
Jim Glaub, Chip Meyrelles,
Laurie Connor, Kevin Keating,
Ryan Greer, Crystal Chase, Brad Coffman
Accountant ....Fried & Kowgios, CPAs, LLP/
Robert Fried, CPA
Controller.................................Elliott Aronstam
Insurance ....DeWitt Stern Group/
Pete Shoemaker, Anthony Pittari
Banking.................................City National Bank/
Michele Gibbons, Erik Piecuch
Payroll ....Castellana Services
Merchandise ....Broadway Merchandising LLC
Production Photographer ....Carol Rosegg
Additional Photography ....Joan Marcus
Event & Party Planner ....Jennifer Pate Gilbert

CREDITS
Scenery constructed by Showman Fabricators. Lighting equipment from LUCS Lighting. Sound Equipment from Masque Sound. Costumes built by Parsons Meares Costumes, Timberlake Studios, John Cowles, Brian Hemesath and DL Cerney. Shoes by JC Theatrical Custom Shoes. Millinery by Rodney Gordon and Arnold Levine. Some costumes provided by Angels of London. Undergarments by Bra*Tenders. Special thanks to M•A•C Cosmetics.

MUSIC RIGHTS
"Anything Goes" music and lyrics by Cole Porter, copyright

1934 (renewed) by Warner Bros., Inc., used by permission of the Cole Porter Musical and Literary Property Trusts. "Well Git It!" written by Cy Oliver. Embassy Music (BMI). Courtesy of Music Sales Corporation/G. Schirmer, Inc.

Born Yesterday rehearsed at the
Roundabout Rehearsal Studios.

Energy-efficient washer/dryer courtesy of
LG Electronics.

CORT THEATRE
House Manager ....Joseph Traina

Catch Me If You Can

First Preview: March 11, 2011. Opened: April 10, 2011.
Closed September 4, 2011 after 32 Previews and 166 Performances.

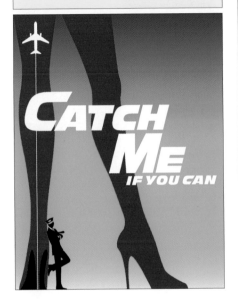

Based on a true story, this musical traces the life of Frank Abagnale, Jr., a young man who turns his father's twisted philosophy into a life of crime, becoming a master con man and forger and successfully posing as everything from an airline pilot to a doctor and a lawyer. He is pursued by dogged FBI agent Carl Hanratty, with whom he establishes a kind of respect and even affection, until Frank makes the fatal mistake of falling in love.

CAST
(in order of appearance)

Frank Abagnale, Jr.	AARON TVEIT
Agent Branton	JOE CASSIDY
Agent Dollar	BRANDON WARDELL
Agent Carl Hanratty	NORBERT LEO BUTZ
Agent Cod	TIMOTHY McCUEN PIGGEE
Frank Abagnale, Sr.	TOM WOPAT
Paula	RACHEL de BENEDET
Cheryl Ann	RACHELLE RAK
Brenda	KERRY BUTLER
Roger Strong	NICK WYMAN
Carol Strong	LINDA HART
Jack Barnes	BOB GAYNOR
Nerd	CHARLIE SUTTON
Jock	ALEKS PEVEC
Principal Owings	JENNIFER FRANKEL
Betty	ALEX ELLIS
Judge	MICHAEL X. MARTIN
Railroad Agent	TIMOTHY McCUEN PIGGEE
Swiss Army Knife Assistant	ANGIE SCHWORER
India Ink Assistant	KEARRAN GIOVANNI
Elmer's Glue Assistant	SARRAH STRIMEL

Continued on next page

NEIL SIMON THEATRE
UNDER THE DIRECTION OF JAMES M. NEDERLANDER AND JAMES L. NEDERLANDER

Margo Lion   Hal Luftig

Stacey Mindich   Yasuhiro Kawana   Scott & Brian Zellinger   The Rialto Group   The Araca Group
Michael Watt   Barbara & Buddy Freitag   Jay & Cindy Gutterman/Pittsburgh CLO   Elizabeth Williams
Johnny Roscoe Productions/Van Dean   Fakston Productions/Solshay Productions   Patty Baker/Richard Winkler
Nederlander Presentations Inc. and Warren Trepp

IN ASSOCIATION WITH

Remmel T. Dickinson   Paula Herold/Kate Lear   Stephanie P. McClelland   Jamie deRoy   Barry Feirstein   Rainerio J. Reyes
Rodney Rigby   Loraine Boyle   Amuse Inc.   Joseph & Matthew Deitch/Cathy Chernoff   Joan Stein/Jon Murray

The 5th Avenue Theatre

PRESENT

Norbert Leo Butz   **Aaron Tveit**

CATCH ME IF YOU CAN
THE MUSICAL
Based on the DreamWorks Motion Picture

BOOK BY	MUSIC BY	LYRICS BY
Terrence McNally	**Marc Shaiman**	**Scott Wittman & Marc Shaiman**

STARRING

Tom Wopat

Rachel de Benedet	Linda Hart	Nick Wyman	Jay Armstrong Johnson
Joe Cassidy	Timothy McCuen Piggee		Brandon Wardell

Sara Andreas	Alex Ellis	Will Erat	Jennifer Frankel	Lisa Gajda
Bob Gaynor	Kearran Giovanni	Nick Kenkel	Grasan Kingsberry	Michael X. Martin
Aleks Pevec	Kristin Piro	Rachelle Rak	Joe Aaron Reid	Angie Schworer
Sabrina Sloan	Sarrah Strimel	Charlie Sutton	Katie Webber	Candice Marie Woods

AND

Kerry Butler

SCENIC DESIGN	COSTUME DESIGN	LIGHTING DESIGN	SOUND DESIGN
David Rockwell	**William Ivey Long**	**Kenneth Posner**	**Steve Canyon Kennedy**

CASTING	WIG & HAIR DESIGN	ASSOCIATE DIRECTOR	ASSOCIATE CHOREOGRAPHERS
Telsey + Company	**Paul Huntley**	**Matt Lenz**	**Joey Pizzi Nick Kenkel**

PRODUCTION STAGE MANAGER	MUSIC COORDINATOR	TECHNICAL SUPERVISOR
Rolt Smith	**John Miller**	**Chris Smith/Smitty**

ASSOCIATE PRODUCERS	ADVERTISING	PRESS REPRESENTATIVE	GENERAL MANAGER
Brian Smith T. Rick Hayashi	**SpotCo**	**The Hartman Group**	**The Charlotte Wilcox Company**

ARRANGEMENTS BY	ORCHESTRATIONS BY
Marc Shaiman	**Marc Shaiman & Larry Blank**

MUSIC DIRECTION BY
John McDaniel

CHOREOGRAPHED BY
Jerry Mitchell

DIRECTED BY
Jack O'Brien

The World Premiere of *Catch Me If You Can* was produced by The 5th Avenue Theatre,
David Armstrong, Executive Producer and Artistic Director; Bernadine Griffin, Managing Director; Bill Berry, Producing Director
The producers wish to express their appreciation to the Theatre Development Fund for its support of this production.

8/22/11

Aaron Tveit and Ladies

Photo by Joan Marcus

Catch Me If You Can

MUSICAL NUMBERS

ACT I

OVERTURE
"Live in Living Color" .... Frank, Jr. and Company
"The Pinstripes Are All That They See" .... Frank, Sr., Frank, Jr., Ladies
"Someone Else's Skin" .... Frank, Jr. and Company
"Jet Set" .... Frank, Jr. and Company
"Live in Living Color" (Reprise) .... Frank, Jr.
"Don't Break the Rules" .... Hanratty and Company
"The Pinstripes Are All That They See" (Reprise) .... The Ladies
"Butter Outta Cream" .... Frank, Sr., Frank, Jr.
"The Man Inside the Clues" .... Hanratty
"Christmas Is My Favorite Time of Year" .... Partygoers
"My Favorite Time of Year" .... Hanratty, Frank, Jr., Frank, Sr., Paula

ACT II

ENTR'ACTE
"Doctor's Orders" .... Nurses
"Live in Living Color" (Reprise) .... Frank, Jr.
"Don't Be a Stranger" .... Paula, Frank, Sr.
"Little Boy, Be a Man" .... Frank, Sr., Hanratty
"Seven Wonders" .... Frank, Jr., Brenda
"(Our) Family Tree" .... Carol, Roger, Brenda, Frank, Jr. and Strong Family Singers
"Fly, Fly Away" .... Brenda, Women
"Good-Bye" .... Frank, Jr.
"Strange But True" .... Frank, Jr., Hanratty

SWINGS
SARA ANDREAS, WILL ERAT,
NICK KENKEL, KRISTIN PIRO

DANCE CAPTAIN
NICK KENKEL

ORCHESTRA
Conductor:
JOHN McDANIEL
Associate Conductor:
LON HOYT
Woodwinds:
TODD GROVES, RICK HECKMAN,
ALDEN BANTA
Trumpets:
DAVE TRIGG, TREVOR NEUMANN
Trombone:
ALAN FERBER
Guitar:
LARRY SALTZMAN
Bass:
VINCENT FAY
Drums:
CLINT DE GANON
Percussion:
JOSEPH PASSARO
Keyboards:
LON HOYT, JASON SHERBUNDY

Kerry Butler
Photo by Joan Marcus

Keyboard/Guitar:
BRIAN KOONIN
Concert Master:
RICK DOLAN
Violin:
BELINDA WHITNEY
Cello:
CLAY RUEDE

Music Coordinator:
JOHN MILLER
Keyboard Programmer:
SYNTHLINK LLC, JIM HARP

Cast Continued

Briefcase Assistant .... JENNIFER FRANKEL
Diane, Bank Teller .. CANDICE MARIE WOODS
Cindy .... ANGIE SCHWORER
Pan Am Executive .... BOB GAYNOR
Tailor .... MICHAEL X. MARTIN
Skyway Man Stewardess .... SABRINA SLOAN
Motel Manager .... MICHAEL X. MARTIN
Party Doctor #1
    at Riverbend Apartments .... JOE AARON REID
Ben Casey .... BOB GAYNOR
Ben Casey Intern .... JOE CASSIDY
Dr. Wanamaker .... MICHAEL X. MARTIN
First Bartender in
    New Rochelle Bar .... ALEKS PEVEC
Mitch Miller .... MICHAEL X. MARTIN
The Frank Abagnale, Jr. Players ...... JOE CASSIDY,
    ALEX ELLIS, JENNIFER FRANKEL,
    LISA GAJDA, BOB GAYNOR,
    KEARRAN GIOVANNI,
    GRASAN KINGSBERRY,
    MICHAEL X. MARTIN, ALEKS PEVEC,
    TIMOTHY McCUEN PIGGEE,
    RACHELLE RAK, JOE AARON REID,
    ANGIE SCHWORER, SABRINA SLOAN,
    SARRAH STRIMEL, CHARLIE SUTTON,
    BRANDON WARDELL, KATIE WEBBER,
    CANDICE MARIE WOODS

Standby for Frank Abagnale, Jr.:
JAY ARMSTRONG JOHNSON

UNDERSTUDIES
For Frank Abagnale, Jr.: BRANDON WARDELL
For Agent Carl Hanratty: JOE CASSIDY,
    WILL ERAT
For Frank Abagnale, Sr.: BOB GAYNOR,
    MICHAEL X. MARTIN
For Paula: RACHELLE RAK,
    ANGIE SCHWORER
For Brenda: ALEX ELLIS, KATIE WEBBER
For Carol Strong: JENNIFER FRANKEL,
    LISA GAJDA
For Roger Strong: WILL ERAT,
    MICHAEL X. MARTIN
For Cheryl Ann: LISA GAJDA, KATIE WEBBER
For Jack Barnes, Judge, Pan Am Executive, Tailor,
    Motel Manager, Ben Casey, Ben Casey Intern,
    Dr. Wanamaker, Mitch Miller: WILL ERAT,
    NICK KENKEL
For Agent Cod & Railroad Agent: WILL ERAT,
    GRASAN KINGSBERRY
For Principal Owings, Betty, Swiss Army Knife Asst.,
    India Ink Asst., Elmer's Glue Asst., Briefcase Asst.,
    Cindy, Diane, Skyway Man Stewardess:
    SARA ANDREAS, KRISTIN PIRO
For Jock, Nerd, Party Doctor, First Bartender in
    New Rochelle Bar: NICK KENKEL

Catch Me If You Can

Norbert Leo Butz
Agent Carl Hanratty

Aaron Tveit
Frank Abagnale, Jr.

Tom Wopat
Frank Abagnale, Sr.

Kerry Butler
Brenda Strong

Rachel de Benedet
Paula Abagnale

Linda Hart
Carol Strong

Nick Wyman
Roger Strong

Jay Armstrong Johnson
Standby for Frank Abagnale, Jr.

Joe Cassidy
Agent Branton

Timothy McCuen Piggee
Agent Cod

Brandon Wardell
Agent Dollar

Sara Andreas
Swing

Alex Ellis
Ensemble

Will Erat
Swing

Jennifer Frankel
Ensemble

Lisa Gajda
Ensemble

Bob Gaynor
Ensemble

Kearran Giovanni
Ensemble

Nick Kenkel
Associate Choreographer, Swing

Grasan Kingsberry
Ensemble

Michael X. Martin
Ensemble

Aleks Pevec
Ensemble

Kristin Piro
Swing

Rachelle Rak
Cheryl Ann, Ensemble

Joe Aaron Reid
Ensemble

Angie Schworer
Ensemble

Sabrina Sloan
Ensemble

Sarrah Strimel
Ensemble

Charlie Sutton
Ensemble

Katie Webber
Ensemble

Candice Marie Woods
Ensemble

Terrence McNally
Book

Marc Shaiman
Music/Lyrics/ Arrangements/ Orchestrations

Scott Wittman
Lyrics

Jack O'Brien
Director

Catch Me If You Can

Jerry Mitchell
Choreographer

David Rockwell
Scenic Design

William Ivey Long
Costume Design

Kenneth Posner
Lighting Design

Steve Canyon
Kennedy
Sound Design

Paul Huntley
Wig & Hair Design

John McDaniel
Music Director

Larry Blank
Co-Orchestrator

Matt Lenz
Associate Director

John Miller
Music Coordinator

Chris Smith/Smitty
Technical Supervisor

Bernard Telsey,
Telsey + Company
Casting

The Charlotte Wilcox
Company
General Manager

Margo Lion
Producer

Hal Luftig
Producer

Yasuhiro Kawana
Producer

Scott Zeilinger
Producer

Brian Zeilinger
Producer

Lauren Stevens,
The Rialto Group
Producer

Wendy Federman,
The Rialto Group
Producer

Carl Moellenberg,
The Rialto Group
Producer

Michael Rego, Hank Unger, Matthew Rego,
The Araca Group
Producers

Barbara Freitag
Producer

Buddy Freitag
Producer

Jay Gutterman & Cindy Gutterman
Producers

Van Kaplan
Pittsburgh CLO
Producer

Elizabeth Williams
Producer

Van Dean
Producer

Lorenzo Thione,
Sing Out, Louise!
Productions
Producer

Jay Kuo,
Sing Out, Louise!
Productions
Producer

Adam Blanshay,
Solshay Productions
Producer

Patty Baker
Producer

Richard Winkler
Producer

Catch Me If You Can
Scrapbook

1. Celebrating the 100th performance July 6, 2011 (L-R): Kerry Butler, Norbert Leo Butz, Aaron Tveit, lyricist Scott Wittman, composer Marc Shaiman.
2. Autographing the original cast album at Barnes & Noble (L-R): Rachel de Benedet and Kerry Butler.
3. Norbert Leo Butz performs at the CD signing at Barnes & Noble.

Photo by Joseph Marzullo/WENN

Photo by Krissie Fullerton

Photo by Krissie Fullerton

James M. Nederlander, Nederlander Presentations
Producer

James L. Nederlander, Nederlander Presentations
Producer

Remmel T. Dickinson
Producer

Paula Herold
Producer

Kate Lear
Producer

Stephanie P. McClelland
Producer

Jamie deRoy
Producer

Rainerio J. Reyes
Producer

Loraine Alterman Boyle
Producer

Joseph Deitch
Producer

Matthew Deitch
Producer

Brian Smith
Associate Producer

T. Rick Hayashi
Associate Producer

David Armstrong, Executive Producer and Artistic Director, 5th Avenue Theatre
Originating Theatre

Bernadine Griffin, Managing Director 5th Avenue Theatre
Originating Theatre

Bill Berry, Producing Director, 5th Avenue Theatre
Originating Theatre

Catch Me If You Can

Photos by Brian Mapp

FRONT OF HOUSE STAFF
Front Row (L-R): Sierra Waxman, Marilyn Christie, Jean Manso, Grace Darbasie, Sally Dillon, Evie Gonzalez

Middle Row (L-R): Lauren Arellano, Joanne DeCicco, Robyn Corrigan, Evelyn Olivero, Kim Raccioppi, Rebecca Henning, Dorothy Marquette, Michelle Smith

Back Row (L-R): Tara Delasnueces, Ryan Conn (Bar), Steven Ouellette (House Manager), Angel Diaz (Chief Usher), Eddie Cuevas, Omar Aguilar (Porter), Peter Hodgson and Jared St. Gelais (Merchandise), Amy Carcaterra

Photo courtesy Christopher Langdon

(L-R): Jose Lopez (Porter), Chris Langdon (Ticket Taker)

SOUND ENGINEER/BOARD OP
Daniel Tramontozzi

BOX OFFICE
Marc Needleman, unidentified

HAIR, PROPS, WARDROBE
Front Row (L-R): Mark Trezza (Wardrobe), Douglas Petitjean (Wardrobe), Samantha Lawrence (Wardrobe), Edward J. Wilson (Hair), Steven Kirkham (Hair)

Back Row (L-R): John Rinaldi (Wardrobe), Julie Tobia (Wardrobe), Dede LaBarre (Wardrobe), Scotty Cain (Wardrobe), Anna Hoffman (Hair), Lolly Totero (Wardrobe), Pete Drummond (Props)

STAGE MANAGEMENT
Lisa Ann Chernoff, Carly J. Price, Andrea O. Saraffian, Rolt Smith

Not Pictured: Holly Coombs

Catch Me If You Can

Chicago

First Preview: October 23, 1996. Opened: November 14, 1996.
Still running as of May 31, 2012.

Aspiring vaudeville performer Roxie Hart kills her lover and finds herself plunged into the corrupt legal system of late 1920s Chicago. As fast-talking lawyer Billy Flynn and fellow murderess Velma Kelly teach her that razzle-dazzle outdoes justice, Roxie's whole world starts to look more and more like show business.

THE CAST

(in order of appearance)

Velma Kelly	AMRA-FAYE WRIGHT
Roxie Hart	BIANCA MARROQUIN
Fred Casely	BRIAN O'BRIEN
Sergeant Fogarty	ADAM ZOTOVICH
Amos Hart	RAYMOND BOKHOUR
Liz	NICOLE BRIDGEWATER
Annie	CRISTY CANDLER
June	DONNA MARIE ASBURY
Hunyak	NILI BASSMAN
Mona	DYLIS CROMAN
Matron "Mama" Morton	CAROL WOODS
Billy Flynn	MARCO ZUNINO
Mary Sunshine	R. LOWE
Go-To-Hell Kitty	MELISSA RAE MAHON
Harry	PETER NELSON
Doctor	JASON PATRICK SANDS
Aaron	RYAN WORSING
The Judge	JASON PATRICK SANDS
Bailiff	AMOS WOLFF
Martin Harrison	PETER NELSON
Court Clerk	AMOS WOLFF
The Jury	MICHAEL CUSUMANO

Continued on next page

---

⑧ AMBASSADOR THEATRE

A Shubert Organization Theatre

Philip J. Smith, *Chairman*   Robert E. Wankel, *President*

Barry & Fran Weissler
in association with
Kardana/Hart Sharp Entertainment
present

**Bianca Marroquin   Amra-Faye Wright
Marco Zunino
Raymond Bokhour**

in

CHICAGO

Lyrics by   Music By   Book by
Fred Ebb   John Kander   Fred Ebb & Bob Fosse

Original Production Directed and Choreographed by **Bob Fosse**

Based on the play by Maurine Dallas Watkins

with

Carol Woods   R. Lowe

and

Donna Marie Asbury   Nili Bassman   Nicole Bridgewater
Cristy Candler   Dylis Croman   Michael Cusumano   Jennifer Dunne
David Kent   J. Loeffelholz   Melissa Rae Mahon   Sharon Moore
Peter Nelson   Brian O'Brien   Jason Patrick Sands
Brian Spitulnik   Amos Wolff   Ryan Worsing   Adam Zotovich

Supervising Music Director	Music Director
Rob Fisher	**Leslie Stifelman**

Scenic Design	Costume Design	Lighting Design
John Lee Beatty	**William Ivey Long**	**Ken Billington**

Sound Design	Orchestrations	Dance Music Arrangements
Scott Lehrer	**Ralph Burns**	**Peter Howard**

Script Adaptation	Musical Coordinator	Hair Design
David Thompson	**Seymour Red Press**	**David Brian Brown**

Casting	Original Casting
Duncan Stewart and Company	**Jay Binder**

Technical Supervisor	Dance Supervisor	Production Stage Manager
Arthur Siccardi	**Gary Chryst**	**Rolt Smith**

Executive Producer	Presented in association with
Alecia Parker	**Broadway Across America**

General Manager	Press Representative
B.J. Holt	**Jeremy Shaffer**
	The Publicity Office

Based on the presentation by City Center's Encores!℠

Choreography by
Ann Reinking
in the style of Bob Fosse

Directed by
Walter Bobbie

Cast Recording on RCA Victor

3/5/12

Amra-Faye Wright (center) and the cast

Photo by Catherine Ashmore

Chicago

MUSICAL NUMBERS

ACT I

"All That Jazz"	Velma and Company
"Funny Honey"	Roxie
"Cell Block Tango"	Velma and the Girls
"When You're Good to Mama"	Matron
"Tap Dance"	Roxie, Amos and Boys
"All I Care About"	Billy and Girls
"A Little Bit of Good"	Mary Sunshine
"We Both Reached for the Gun"	Billy, Roxie, Mary Sunshine and Company
"Roxie"	Roxie and Boys
"I Can't Do It Alone"	Velma
"My Own Best Friend"	Roxie and Velma

ACT II

Entr'acte	The Band
"I Know a Girl"	Velma
"Me and My Baby"	Roxie and Boys
"Mister Cellophane"	Amos
"When Velma Takes the Stand"	Velma and Boys
"Razzle Dazzle"	Billy and Company
"Class"	Velma and Matron
"Nowadays"	Roxie and Velma
"Hot Honey Rag"	Roxie and Velma
Finale	Company

(L-R): Ryan Worsing, Bianca Marroquin, Michael Cusumano

Photo by Jeremy Daniel

Cast Continued

THE SCENE:

Chicago, Illinois. The late 1920s.

UNDERSTUDIES

For Roxie Hart:
DYLIS CROMAN, MELISSA RAE MAHON
For Velma Kelly:
DONNA MARIE ASBURY,
    NICOLE BRIDGEWATER
For Billy Flynn:
BRIAN O'BRIEN, JASON PATRICK SANDS
For Amos Hart:
JASON PATRICK SANDS, ADAM ZOTOVICH
For Matron "Mama" Morton:
DONNA MARIE ASBURY,
    NICOLE BRIDGEWATER
For Mary Sunshine:
J. LOEFFELHOLZ
For Fred Casely:
DAVID KENT, JASON PATRICK SANDS,
    BRIAN SPITULNIK
For "Me and My Baby":
DAVID KENT, BRIAN SPITULNIK

For all other roles:
JENNIFER DUNNE, DAVID KENT,
    SHARON MOORE, BRIAN SPITULNIK

Dance Captain:
DAVID KENT

"Tap Dance" specialty performed by
JASON PATRICK SANDS, AMOS WOLFF
and RYAN WORSING.

"Me and My Baby" specialty performed by
MICHAEL CUSUMANO and RYAN WORSING.

"Nowadays" whistle performed by
JASON PATRICK SANDS

Original Choreography for "Hot Honey Rag" by
BOB FOSSE

ORCHESTRA

Orchestra Conducted by
LESLIE STIFELMAN
Associate Conductor:
SCOTT CADY
Assistant Conductor:
JOHN JOHNSON
Woodwinds:
SEYMOUR RED PRESS, JACK STUCKEY,
RICHARD CENTALONZA

Trumpets:
GLENN DREWES, DARRYL SHAW
Trombones:
DAVE BARGERON, BRUCE BONVISSUTO
Piano:
SCOTT CADY
Piano, Accordion:
JOHN JOHNSON

Banjo:
JAY BERLINER
Bass, Tuba:
DAN PECK
Violin:
MARSHALL COID
Drums, Percussion:
RONALD ZITO

Chicago

Bianca Marroquin
Roxie Hart

Amra-Faye Wright
Velma Kelly

Marco Zunino
Billy Flynn

Raymond Bokhour
Amos Hart

Carol Woods
Matron "Mama" Morton

R. Lowe
Mary Sunshine

Donna Marie Asbury
June

Nili Bassman
Hunyak

Nicole Bridgewater
Liz

Cristy Candler
Annie

Dylis Croman
Mona

Michael Cusumano
The Jury

Jennifer Dunne
Swing

David Kent
Swing, Dance Captain

J. Loeffelholz
Standby Mary Sunshine

Melissa Rae Mahon
Go-To-Hell Kitty

Sharon Moore
Swing

Peter Nelson
Harry/Martin Harrison

Brian O'Brien
Fred Casely

Jason Patrick Sands
Doctor/The Judge

Brian Spitulnik
Swing

Amos Wolff
Bailiff/Court Clerk

Ryan Worsing
Aaron

Adam Zotovich
Sergeant Fogarty

John Kander and Fred Ebb
Music; Book/Lyrics

Bob Fosse
Book

Walter Bobbie
Director

Ann Reinking
Choreographer

John Lee Beatty
Set Design

William Ivey Long
Costume Designer

Ken Billington
Lighting Designer

Scott Lehrer
Sound Design

David Thompson
Script Adaptation

Rob Fisher
Supervising Music Director

Chicago

Leslie Stifelman
Musical Director

Seymour Red Press
Music Coordinator

Duncan Stewart,
Duncan Stewart
and Company
Casting

Benton Whitley,
Duncan Stewart and
Company
Casting

Arthur Siccardi,
Theatrical Services
Inc.
Technical Supervisor

Gary Chryst
Dance Supervisor

Alecia Parker
Executive Producer

Barry and Fran Weissler
Producers

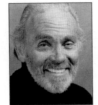
John N. Hart,
Evamere
Entertainment
Producer

Morton Swinsky,
Kardana Productions
Producer

John Gore,
CEO,
Broadway Across
America
Producer

Thomas B. McGrath,
Chairman,
Broadway Across
America
Producer

Brent Barrett
Billy Flynn

Eddie Bennett
*Bailiff, Court Clerk,
Swing*

Christie Brinkley
Roxie Hart

Charlotte d'Amboise
Roxie Hart

Kara DioGuardi
Roxie Hart

Kate Dunn
Hunyak

Babriela Garcia
Annie

James Harkness
Fred Casely

Bahiyah Hibah
(a.k.a. Bahiyah
Sayyed Gaines)
Velma Kelly

James T. Lane
Sergeant Fogarty

Nikka Graff
Lanzarone
Velma Kelly

Jill Nicklaus
Annie

John O'Hurley
Billy Flynn

Roz Ryan
*Matron "Mama"
Morton*

Christopher Sieber
Billy Flynn

T.W. Smith
Mary Sunshine

Chris Sullivan
Amos Hart

Tonya Wathen
*Annie, Hunyak,
Swing*

Tony Yazbeck
Billy Flynn

Chicago

Terra C. MacLeod
Velma Kelly

D. Micciche
Mary Sunshine

Roz Ryan
Matron "Mama" Morton

Tracy Shayne
Roxie Hart

Tony Yazbeck
Billy Flynn

FRONT OF HOUSE STAFF
Front Row (L-R): Ellen Cogan, Timothy Newsome, Arlene Peters, Manuel Levine (House Manager), Allison Martin, Matthew Rodriguez
Second Row (L-R): Lori McElroy, Olga Campos
Third Row (L-R): Subhadra Robert, Dorothea Bentley, Tasha Allen
Back Row (L-R): Kasha Williams, Michael Heitzler, Jack Donaghy, Belen Bekker, Beatrice Carney

Photos by Jeremy Shaffer

WARDROBE AND HAIR
Front Row (L-R): Sue Stepnik (Dresser), Cleopatra Matheos (Dresser)
Back Row (L-R): Patrick Rinn (Dresser), Kevin Woodworth (Wardrobe Supervisor), Jeff Silverman (Hair), Rick Meadows (Dresser)

CREW
Front Row (L-R): John Montgomery (Sound Engineer), Tim McIntyre (Stage Crew), Fred Phelan (Props), Mike Guggino (Front Light Op.), Mike Phillips (Stage Crew)
Back Row (L-R): Lee Iwanski (House Electrician), Jim Werner (Front Light Op.), Luciana Fusco (Head Electrician), Bob Hale (Front Light Op.)

Chicago

STAGE MANAGEMENT AND COMPANY MANAGEMENT
(L-R): Terrence Witter (Stage Manager), Mindy Farbrother (Stage Manager), Rina Saltzman (Company Manager), Rolt Smith (Production Stage Manager)

STAFF FOR *CHICAGO*

GENERAL MANAGEMENT
B.J. Holt, General Manager
Nina Skriloff, International Manager

PRESS REPRESENTATIVE
THE PUBLICITY OFFICE
Jeremy Shaffer   Marc Thibodeau   Michael Borowski

CASTING
DUNCAN STEWART AND COMPANY
Duncan Stewart, CSA; Benton Whitley;
Andrea Zee

COMPANY MANAGER
Rina L. Saltzman

Production Stage Manager	**Rolt Smith**
Stage Managers	Terrence J. Witter,
	Mindy Farbrother, Scott Faris
Associate General Manager	Matthew Rimmer
General Management	
Associate	Stephen Spadaro
Assistant Director	Jonathan Bernstein
Associate Lighting Designer	John McKernon
Assistant Choreographer	Debra McWaters
Assistant Set Designers	Eric Renschler,
	Shelley Barclay
Wardrobe Supervisor	Kevin Woodworth
Hair Supervisor	Jenna Brauer
Costume Assistant	Donald Sanders
Personal Asst to Mr. Billington	Jon Kusner
Assistant to Mr. Lehrer	Thom Mohrman
Production Carpenter	Joseph Mooneyham
Production Electrician	James Fedigan
Head Electrician	Luciana Fusco
Front Lite Operator	Michael Guggino
Production Sound Engineer	John Montgomery
Production Props	Fred Phelan

Dressers	Sue Stepnik,
	Kathy Dacey, Cleopatra Matheos,
	Rick Meadows, Patrick Rinn
Banking	City National Bank,
	Stephanie Dalton, Michele Gibbons
Music Prep	Chelsea Music Services, Inc.
	Donald Oliver & Evan Morris
Payroll	Castellana Services, Inc.
Accountants	Rosenberg, Neuwirth & Kuchner
	Mark D'Ambrosi, Marina Flom
Insurance	Industrial Risk Specialists
Counsel	Seth Gelblum/Loeb & Loeb
Art Design	Spot Design
Advertising	SpotCo: Drew Hodges,
	Jim Edwards, Sara Fitzpatrick,
	Beth Watson, Tim Falotico
Press Assistant	Lauren Wolman
Education	Students Live/Amy Weinstein
Merchandising	Dewynters Advertising Inc.
Displays	King Display

NATIONAL ARTISTS MANAGEMENT CO.

Chief Financial Officer	Bob Williams
Head of Marketing Strategy	Clint Bond Jr.
Manager of Accounting/Admin	Marian Albarracin
Associate to the Weisslers	Brett England
Assistant to Mrs. Weissler	Nikki Pelazza
Executive Assistant to Mr. Weissler	Irene Cabrera
Assistant to B.J. Holt	Katharine Hayes
Executive Assistant	Laura Sisk
Director of Marketing	Ken Sperr

SPECIAL THANKS
Additional legal services provided by Jay Goldberg, Esq. and Michael Berger, Esq. Dry cleaning by Ernest Winzer Cleaners. Hosiery and undergarments provided by Bra*Tenders. Tuxedos by Brioni.

CREDITS
Lighting equipment by PRG Lighting. Scenery built and painted by Hudson Scenic Studios. Specialty Rigging by United Staging & Rigging. Sound equipment by PRG Audio. Shoulder holster courtesy of DeSantis Holster and Leather Goods Co. Period cameras and flash units by George Fenmore, Inc. Colibri lighters used. Bible courtesy of Chiarelli's Religious Goods, Inc. Black pencils by Dixon-Ticonderoga. Gavel courtesy of The Gavel Co. Zippo lighters used. Garcia y Vega cigars used. Hosiery by Donna Karan. Shoes by T.O. Dey. Orthopaedic Consultant, David S. Weiss, M.D.

Energy-efficient washer/dryer courtesy of
LG Electronics.

 THE SHUBERT ORGANIZATION, INC.
Board of Directors

Philip J. Smith	**Robert E. Wankel**
Chairman	President
Wyche Fowler, Jr.	**Diana Phillips**
Lee J. Seidler	**Michael I. Sovern**
Stuart Subotnick	

Chief Financial Officer	Elliot Greene
Sr. Vice President, Ticketing	David Andrews
Vice President, Finance	Juan Calvo
Vice President, Human Resources	Cathy Cozens
Vice President, Facilities	John Darby
Vice President, Theatre Operations	Peter Entin
Vice President, Marketing	Charles Flateman
Vice President, Audit	Anthony LaMattina
Vice President, Ticket Sales	Brian Mahoney
Vice President, Creative Projects	D.S. Moynihan
Vice President, Real Estate	Julio Peterson
House Manager	Manuel Levine

Chicago
SCRAPBOOK

Correspondent: Brian Spitulnik, Swing

Memorable Directorial Note: "We know the outcome. It's only in the telling that it's interesting." –Walter Bobbie to Chris Sullivan

Anniversary Parties: On August 27, 2011 we surpassed *A Chorus Line* as the Longest Running American Musical on Broadway, and on November 14, 2011 *Chicago* celebrated 15 years on Broadway. To celebrate, we got shuttled around Times Square on "The Ride" and were treated to a swanky evening at The Lambs Club after the show. We also received a very classy engraved champagne glass from our choreographer, Ann Reinking.

Exciting Celebrity Guest: Billy Joel visited backstage at intermission when seeing his former wife, Christie Brinkley, perform the role of Roxie Hart. Before asking if he could use the bathroom in her dressing room, the piano man was heard to say, "See, I told you you could sing."

Actor Who Played the Most Roles: Aside from the Swings, who cover the ensemble, Jason Patrick Sands has played Amos, Billy, Fred Casely, and his usual track of the Judge this year, sometimes all in one week.

Actor Who Has Done the Most Shows: We've got some winners for annual attendance, but the award for the cast member who has been with the show the longest goes to Donna Marie Asbury (though asking the exact number of performances is a bit like asking a lady her age).

Backstage Rituals: There is a wall near the stage that we decorate in accordance with the season or the holiday at hand. Company members express their individual creativity with pumpkins, hand-traced turkeys, snowflakes, etc.

Favorite Moment During the Show: On Stage: The opening number is always thrilling to perform, no matter how many times you've done it that week (or that decade). Off-stage: Olga Vahginavah (Michael Cusumano's alter ego) gives a sex education class before "Razzle Dazzle" at every show. It's not to be missed.

Favorite In-Theatre Gathering Place: The Ambassador is a pretty tiny theater, so we all tend to gather around the Wardrobe Table in the basement, where our wardrobe supervisor Kevin holds court. When Nikka Lanzarone was playing Velma Kelly, the boys in the ensemble made a ritual of sitting on the couch in her dressing room before the show and making her entertain them.

Off-Site Hang Out: Toloache (best Margaritas in midtown), Natsumi (the spicy crunchy tuna roll is flawless), and E&E Grill House (they named a cocktail after us).

Favorite Snack Foods: Kevin, our wardrobe supervisor, keeps a jar full of very evil miniature chocolate bars on hand at all times.

Mascot: There was once an assortment of cast member's dogs that regularly visited the theatre. Pets were banned from the theatre, however, after one had a little accident in a dressing room and the Shuberts mandated that, for the sake of their carpets, we keep them out. But still, we'll say all the dogs who have come and gone

1. In fine Merry Murderess tradition, Bebe Neuwirth (R) plunges a knife into the heart of a cake marking the night the show surpassed *A Chorus Line* to become the longest-running American musical on Broadway, witnessed by (L-R): Christopher Sieber, Nikka Graff Lanzarone and Charlotte d'Amboise.
2. Taking bows at the 15th anniversary show (L-R front): producers Barry and Fran Weissler, script adaptor David Thompson, leading lady Bebe Neuwirth, director Walter Bobbie and composer John Kander.

through our stage door are our honorary mascots.

Favorite Therapy: Daily body-dysmorphia counseling in the men's dressing rooms.

Memorable Ad-lib: "Miss Velma Kelly, in an act of…disarray." —Carol Woods

Cell Phone Disturbance: It is not so much the ringing anymore as it is the glow of the faces reading texts during the show.

Memorable Press Encounter: Pictures with Amra-Faye Wright and Christie Brinkley posing with a very happy Pamela Anderson.

Memorable Stage Door Fan Encounter: With the addition of Peruvian Television Star Marco Zunino, we have expanded our reach into another Latin American market with his fans waving Peru's flag as we exit the theater.

Internet Buzz on the Show: We were pleased to see that when the press came to review Kara DioGuardi they were effusive about what great shape the show was in after 15 years.

Latest Arrival: Being that we have 2:30 p.m. matinees on Sunday we get the occasional, "Oops, we thought the show was at 3" arrivals.

Fastest Costume Change: Ryan Worsing changing from his street clothes into his costume at the places call.

Busiest Day at the Box Office: *Chicago* broke a box office record with a weekly gross of $1,065,501 during Christmas.

Heaviest Costume: Mary Sunshine (extra points for all that makeup).

Who Wore the Least: Dylis Croman

Catchphrase Only a Company Member Would Recognize: "There's a snitch."

Sweethearts in the Company: It depends on the week. Leslie Stifelman and Melissa Rae Mahon just celebrated their second wedding anniversary.

Best In-House Parody Lyrics: "OOOH YOU'RE GONNA SEE BAHIYAH HIBAH SHAKE…."

Company In-Jokes: Ratchet! Boom!

Company Legends: Anytime Annie Reinking, Bebe Neuwirth, Joel Grey, or any other member of the original cast walks in the building, it's pretty cool.

Tales from Put-In: Roz Ryan performing her song wearing sunglasses.

Understudy Anecdote: After playing Amos Hart for a week, Jason Patrick Sands was back to playing his regular track (Doctor/The Judge), and the leading lady—who had been playing his wife the day before—welcomed him back and asked with 100 percent sincerity if he had had a nice holiday.

Nicknames: Olga, B.O.B, D.M.A.

Coolest Thing About Being in This Show: Wearing see-through clothing (and being part of theatre history).

Other Stories and Memories: Our own Mikey Cusumano won the Broadway Beauty Pageant representing *Chicago*; we had the world's most beautiful woman (Christie Brinkley) and the sassiest "American Idol" judge (Kara DioGuardi) playing Roxie Hart, and, as it is every year, the best day of the year was spent in Westchester at the Weisslers' Summer Pool Party.

Chinglish

First Preview: October 11, 2011. Opened: October 27, 2011.
Closed January 29, 2012 after 19 Previews and 109 Performances.

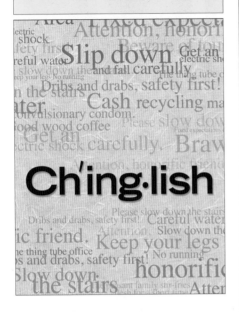

An American businessman with a dark spot on his past tries to start over again in China, only to find himself quickly embroiled in a clash of commercial, political and romantic cultures.

CAST

(in order of appearance)

Daniel Cavanaugh	GARY WILMES
Peter Timms	STEPHEN PUCCI
Minister Cai Guoliang	LARRY LEI ZHANG
Xi Yan	JENNIFER LIM
Miss Qian/Prosecutor Li	ANGELA LIN
Miss Zhao	CHRISTINE LIN
Bing/Judge Xu Geming	JOHNNY WU

SETTING

The present. An American assembly room and the city of Guiyang, China.

UNDERSTUDIES/STANDBYS

For Daniel Cavanaugh:
TONY CARLIN
For Xi Yan:
ANGELA LIN
For Miss Zhao; Miss Qian/Prosecutor Li:
VIVIAN CHIU
For Peter Timms, Bing/Judge Xu Geming, Minister Cai Guoliang:
BRIAN NISHII

⊗ LONGACRE THEATRE
220 West 48th Street
A Shubert Organization Theatre

Philip J. Smith, *Chairman*   **Robert E. Wankel,** *President*

Jeffrey Richards   Jerry Frankel
Jay & Cindy Gutterman/Cathy Chernoff   Heni Koenigsberg/Lily Fan   Joseph & Matthew Deitch
Dasha Epstein   Ronald & Marc Frankel   Barry & Carole Kaye   Mary Lu Roffe
The Broadway Consortium   Ken Davenport   Filerman Bensinger   Herbert Goldsmith   Jam Theatricals
Olympus Theatricals   Playful Productions   David & Barbara Stoller   Roy Gottlieb   Mary Casey   Hunter Arnold

In association with
the Goodman Theatre

presents

Ch'ing·lish

by

David Henry Hwang

with

Jennifer Lim   Gary Wilmes

Angela Lin   Christine Lin   Stephen Pucci   Johnny Wu   Larry Lei Zhang

Scenic Design	Costume Design	Lighting Design	Sound Design
David Korins	Anita Yavich	Brian MacDevitt	Darron L West

Projection Design	Technical Supervision	Casting
Jeff Sugg	Hudson Theatrical Associates	Telsey + Company
Shawn Duan		Jordan Thaler & Heidi Griffiths
		Adam Belcuore

Cultural Advisors	Mandarin Chinese Translations	Production Stage Manager
Joanna C. Lee	Candace Chong	Stephen M. Kaus
Ken Smith		

Press/Marketing	Associate Producer	General Management
Jeffrey Richards Associates	Jeremy Scott Blaustein	Richards/Climan, Inc.
Irene Gandy/Alana Karpoff		

Directed by

Leigh Silverman

CHINGLISH was first developed at the Lark Play Development Center, New York City.
Developed in association with The Public Theater (Oskar Eustis, Artistic Director).
CHINGLISH was first presented by the Goodman Theatre
(Robert Falls, Artistic Director; Roche Schulfer, Executive Director) in Chicago on June 18, 2011.
The Producers wish to express their appreciation to the Theatre Development Fund for its support of this production.

10/27/11

(L-R): Jennifer Lim, Gary Wilmes

Photo by Michael McCabe

Chinglish

Jennifer Lim
Xi Yan

Gary Wilmes
Daniel Cavanaugh

Angela Lin
*Miss Qian/
Prosecutor Li*

Christine Lin
Miss Zhao

Stephen Pucci
Peter Timms

Johnny Wu
*Bing/Judge Xu
Geming*

Larry Lei Zhang
*Minister Cai
Guoliang*

Tony Carlin
*u/s Daniel
Cavanaugh*

Vivian Chiu
*u/s Miss Zhao, Miss
Qian/Prosecutor Li*

Brian Nishii
*u/s Peter Timms,
Bing/Judge Xu
Geming, Cai
Guoliang*

David Henry Hwang
Playwright

Leigh Silverman
Director

David Korins
Scenic Design

Anita Yavich
Costume Design

Brian MacDevitt
Lighting Design

Darron L. West
Sound Design

Neil A. Mazzella,
Hudson Theatrical
Associates
*Technical
Supervision*

Bernard Telsey,
Telsey + Company
New York Casting

Jeffrey Richards
Producer

Jerry Frankel
Producer

Joseph Deitch
Producer

Jay & Cindy Gutterman
Producers

Matthew Deitch
Producer

Dasha Epstein
Producer

Mary Lu Roffe
Producer

Van Dean, Kenny Howard,
The Broadway Consortium
Producers

Ken Davenport
Producer

Michael Filerman
Producer

Chris Bensinger
Producer

Arny Granat,
Jam Theatricals
Producer

Steve Traxler,
Jam Theatricals
Producer

Lily Fan
Producer

Jeremy Scott
Blaustein
Associate Producer

Chinglish

FRONT OF HOUSE
Standing (L-R): Bob Reilly,
Pamela Loetterle,
Kathleen Reiter,
John Barbaretti,
Rosetta Jlelaty

Seated (L-R): Janice Jenkins,
Keith Gartner, Patricia Roehrich,
John Mallon, Elsie Grosvenor,
Rowland Andrews

Front Row: Monica Caraballo

STAGE MANAGEMENT AND CREW
Back Row (L-R): Barry Doss, McBrien Dunbar, Kevin Fedorko, Wilbur Graham,
John Lofgren, Ric Rogers

Front Row (L-R): Carly J. Price, Jillian M. Oliver, Bryen Shannon, Jamie Englehart,
Stephen M. Kaus

SECURITY/DOORMAN
Rick Bozzacco

**2011-2012
AWARD**

THEATRE WORLD
AWARD
For Outstanding
Broadway
or Off-Broadway
Debut
(Jennifer Lim)

SCRAPBOOK

Correspondents: Christine Lin ("Miss Zhao") and Johnny Wu ("Bing"/"Judge Xu Geming")
Memorable Opening Night Note: "Joyous Cavity!!!" (Chinglish for "Happy Opening!")
Opening Night Gifts: Trapeze lesson certificate, 2 dice and playing cards "from one high-roller to another" (from Gary Wilmes).
Most Exciting Celebrity Visitor and What They Did/Said: Ang Lee liked the show (at opening)!
Actors Who Performed the Most Roles in This Show: Angela, Johnny and Christine are tied with four roles each.

Special Backstage Ritual: *Chinglish* cheer by Brian MacDevitt: "Let's go Chinglish!" Clap, Clap, ClapClapClap!
Favorite Moment During Each Performance: "Frog loves pee" –Daniel (Gary Wilmes) trying to say "I love you" in Chinese.
Favorite In-Theatre Gathering Place: Angela and Christine's dressing room is rather festive! :)
Favorite Off-Site Hangout: Hurley's Saloon next door.
Memorable Ad-Lib: "Maybe you left it in the bathroom." —Jennifer during previews,

covering for the cell phone that was not preset in Gary's pants.
Fastest Costume Change: Gary stripping down to his underwear for one scene and then getting dressed into a full suit for the next one.
Who Wore the Least: Jennifer in her bra and underwear. (Gary wears boxers, too.)
Catchphrase Only the Company Would Recognize: "Gao wu!" coined by Stephen Pucci, the literal Chinese translation for "High five!"
Sweethearts Within the Company: What happens in Guiyang STAYS in Guiyang!

Chinglish

(L-R): Stephen Pucci, Gary Wilmes, Angela Lin, Larry Lei Zhang

Photo by Michael McCabe

Clybourne Park

First Preview: March 26, 2012. Opened: April 19, 2012.
Still running as of May 31, 2012.

The Pulitzer Prize-winning "sequel" to Lorraine Hansberry's 1959 classic A Raisin in the Sun, which was about the black Younger family, and the mother's resolve to move into a house in an all-white Chicago suburb despite racist pressure to stay out. Act I of Clybourne Park shows what was happening in the lives of the white family living in the house that made them decide to sell their home to the Youngers over the objections of their neighbors. Act II of Clybourne Park jumps ahead to 2009 to show what happens when a white family tries to buy the same house and move into what has now become an all-black neighborhood.

CAST

(in alphabetical order)

Francine/Lena ....CRYSTAL A. DICKINSON
Jim/Tom/Kenneth ....BRENDAN GRIFFIN
Albert/Kevin.....................DAMON GUPTON
Bev/Kathy ....CHRISTINA KIRK
Betsy/Lindsey ....ANNIE PARISSE
Karl/Steve ....JEREMY SHAMOS
Russ/Dan ....FRANK WOOD

TIME:

ACT ONE: 1959
ACT TWO: 2009

Continued on next page

Continued on next page

♀ WALTER KERR THEATRE
A JUJAMCYN THEATRE

JORDAN ROTH
President

PAUL LIBIN
Executive Vice President

JACK VIERTEL
Senior Vice President

JUJAMCYN THEATERS

JANE BERGÈRE   ROGER BERLIND/QUINTET PRODUCTIONS   ERIC FALKENSTEIN/DAN FRISHWASSER

RUTH HENDEL/HARRIS KARMA PRODUCTIONS   JTG THEATRICALS

DARYL ROTH   JON B. PLATT   CENTER THEATRE GROUP

in association with

LINCOLN CENTER THEATER

Present

THE PLAYWRIGHTS HORIZONS PRODUCTION OF

By

BRUCE NORRIS

With

CRYSTAL A. DICKINSON   BRENDAN GRIFFIN   DAMON GUPTON
CHRISTINA KIRK   ANNIE PARISSE   JEREMY SHAMOS   FRANK WOOD

Scenic Design	Costume Design	Lighting Design	Sound Design
DANIEL OSTLING	ILONA SOMOGYI	ALLEN LEE HUGHES	JOHN GROMADA

Hair & Wig Design	Casting	Production Management	Production Stage Manager
CHARLES LaPOINTE	ALAINE ALLDAFFER	AURORA PRODUCTIONS	C.A. CLARK

General Manager	Press Representative	Advertising	Executive Producer
BESPOKE THEATRICALS	O&M CO.	SERINO/COYNE	RED AWNING

Directed by

PAM MacKINNON

The Producers wish to express their appreciation to Theatre Development Fund for its support of this production.

4/19/12

L-R: Frank Wood, Annie Parisse, Christina Kirk, Jeremy Shamos, Damon Gupton, Crystal A. Dickinson

Photo by Nathan Johnson

Clybourne Park

Cast Continued

UNDERSTUDIES AND STANDBYS

For Francine/Lena:
APRIL YVETTE THOMPSON
For Jim/Tom/Kenneth:
RICHARD THIERIOT
For Albert/Kevin:
BRANDON J. DIRDEN
For Bev/Kathy:
CARLY STREET
For Betsy/Lindsey:
CARLY STREET
For Karl/Steve:
RICHARD THIERIOT
For Russ/Dan:
GREG STUHR

2011-2012 AWARDS

TONY AWARD
Best Play

THEATRE WORLD AWARD
For Outstanding Broadway
or Off-Broadway Debut
(Crystal A. Dickinson)

Christina Kirk
and Frank Wood

Photo by Nathan Johnson

Crystal A. Dickinson
Francine/Lena

Brendan Griffin
Jim/Tom/Kenneth

Damon Gupton
Albert/Kevin

Christina Kirk
Bev/Kathy

Annie Parisse
Betsy/Lindsey

Jeremy Shamos
Karl/Steve

Frank Wood
Russ/Dan

Brandon J. Dirden
Albert/Kevin u/s

Richard Thieriot
*Karl/Steve and
Jim/Tom u/s*

Carly Street
*Bev/Kathy and
Betsy Lindsey u/s*

April Yvette
Thompson
Francine/Lena u/s

Greg Stuhr
Russ/Dan u/s

Bruce Norris
Playwright

Pam MacKinnon
Director

Daniel Ostling
Scenic Designer

Ilona Somogyi
Costume Designer

Allen Lee Hughes
Lighting Designer

John Gromada
Sound Designer

Charles LaPointe
*Hair and Wig
Designer*

Alaine Alldaffer
Casting

Clybourne Park

Maggie Brohn
Bespoke Theatricals
General Manager

Amy Jacobs
Bespoke Theatricals
General Manager

Devin Keudell
Bespoke Theatricals
General Manager

Nina Lannan
Bespoke Theatricals
General Manager

Jordan Roth
President
Jujamcyn Theaters
Producer

Jane Bergère
Producer

Roger Berlind
Producer

Sue Vaccaro
Quintet Productions
Producer

Ricky Stevens
Quintet Productions
Producer

Catherine Schreiber
Quintet Productions
Producer

Bruce Robert Harris
Quintet Productions
Producer

Jack W. Batman
Quintet Productions
Producer

Wendell Pierce
Quintet Productions
Producer

Eric Falkenstein
Producer

Dan Frishwasser
Producer

Ruth Hendel
Producer

Dede Harris
Harris Karma
Productions
Producer

Sharon Karmazin
Harris Karma
Productions
Producer

John Pinckard
JTG Theatricals
Producer

Terry Schnuck
JTG Theatricals
Producer

Gregory Rae
JTG Theatricals
Producer

Daryl Roth
Producer

Jon B. Platt
Producer

Michael Ritchie,
Artistic Director
Center Theatre
Group
Producer

Edward L. Rada,
Managing Director
Center Theatre
Group
Producer

Douglas C. Baker,
Producing Director
Center Theatre
Group
Producer

André Bishop and Bernard Gersten,
Artistic Director and Executive Producer,
Lincoln Center Theater
Producer

Tim Sanford,
Artistic Director
Playwrights Horizons
Originating Theatre

Leslie Marcus,
Managing Director
Playwrights Horizons
Producer

Nicole Kastrinos
Red Awning
Executive Producer

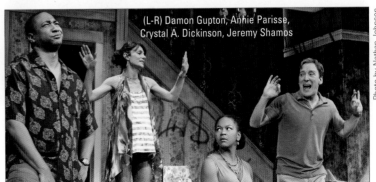
(L-R) Damon Gupton, Annie Parisse,
Crystal A. Dickinson, Jeremy Shamos

Photo by Nathan Johnson

Clybourne Park

FRONT OF HOUSE
Front Row (L-R): Robert Zwaschka, Michelle Fleury, T.J. D'Angelo

Second Row (L-R): Juliett Cipriati, Katie Siegmund, Alison Traynor

Third Row (L-R): Ilir Velovic, Mallory Sims, Aaron Kendall

Top Row (L-R): Martine Sigue, Manuel Sandridge

BOX OFFICE TREASURERS
(L-R): Michael Loiacono, Joe Smith

CREW
Front Row (Seated L-R): Ed Chapman, Christina Ainge

Middle Row (L-R): Ron Fleming, Vincent J. Valvo, George E. Fullum, Timothy Bennet, Peter J. Iacoviello

Back Row (L-R): Carol Clark, Francine Schwartz-Buryiak, Chad Heulitt, Mike "Moose" Johnson, Heidi Neven, Pat Marcus, James Latus, Jill Johnson

Clybourne Park

STAFF FOR *CLYBOURNE PARK*

GENERAL MANAGEMENT
BESPOKE THEATRICALS
Amy Jacobs, Nina Lannan
Maggie Brohn, Devin Keudell

COMPANY MANAGER
Heidi Neven

PRESS REPRESENTATIVE
O&M CO.
Rick Miramontez

Joyce Friedmann	Ryan Ratelle
Andy Snyder	Michael Jorgensen

PRODUCTION MANAGEMENT
AURORA PRODUCTIONS
Gene O'Donovan, Ben Heller,
Stephanie Sherline, Anita Shah, Jarid Sumner,
Liza Luxenberg, Anthony Jusino, Steven Dalton,
Eugenio Saenz Flores, Isaac Katzanek,
Melissa Mazdra

CASTING
Alaine Alldaffer, CSA
Associate Casting Director .... Lisa Donadio

Production Stage Manager .... C.A. Clark
Stage Manager .... James Latus
Assistant Director .... Kimberly Faith Hickman
Associate Costume Designer .... Jessica Wegener Shay
Associate Lighting Designer .... Xavier Pierce
Assistant Lighting Designer .... Miriam Crowe
Associate Sound Designer .... Chris Cronin
Associate Hair Designer .... Leah Loukas

Production Carpenter .... Chad Heulitt
Production Electrician .... Michael Pitzer
Production Props Supervisor .... Faye Armon
Production Props .... Jill Johnson
Production Sound Engineer .... Ed Chapman
Wardrobe Supervisor .... Christina Ainge
Dressers .... Ron Fleming, Francine Schwartz-Buryiak
Hair Supervisor .... Pat Marcus
Moving Light Programmer .... Jeremy Wahlers
Scenic Consultant .... Brenda Sabakta-Davis
Advertising .... Serino/Coyne/
Greg Corradetti, Tom Callahan,
Danielle Boyle, Drew Nebrig, Doug Ensign
Digital Outreach & Website .... Serino/Coyne/
Jim Glaub, Chip Meyrelles,
Laurie Connor, Kevin Keating, Mark Seeley
Marketing .... Serino/Coyne/
Leslie Barrett, Diana Salameh
Legal Counsel .... Sendroff & Baruch/
Jason Baruch, Esq.
Accountant .... FK Partners/Robert Fried
Comptroller .... Sarah Galbraith and Co./
Sarah Galbraith, Kenny Noth
General Management Associates .... Steve Dow,
Ryan Conway, Libby Fox,
David Roth, Danielle Saks
General Management Interns .... Michelle Heller,
Jimmy Wilson, Sean Coughlin
Production Assistant .... Matthew Lutz
Costume Shopper .... Kristina Makowski

Press Associates .... Sarah Babin, Molly Barnett,
Jaron Caldwell, Philip Carrubba,
Jon Dimond, Richard Hillman,
Yufen Kung, Chelsea Nachman,
Ryan Ratelle, Elizabeth Wagner
Payroll Services .... Checks and Balances Payroll Inc.
Travel Agent .... Tzell Travel/
The "A" Team, Andi Henig
Banking .... City National Bank/Michele Gibbons
Insurance .... Dewitt Stern Group, Inc./Peter Shoemaker
Theatre Displays .... King Displays, Inc.
Merchandise .... Max Merchandising

CREDITS
Scenery constructed by F&D Scene Changes. Lighting equipment supplied by PRG. Sound equipment supplied by Sound Associates. Costumes by the Center Theatre Group Costume Shop; Paul Chang Custom Tailors & Shirtmakers; Tiia Torchia; Eric Winterling, Inc.; Sarah Reever; Bobby Tilley; Harry Johnson. Props from Lincoln Center Theater. Special thanks to Bra*Tenders for hosiery and undergarments.

MUSIC CREDITS
"Confidential" by the Fleetwoods.
"It's Too Soon to Know" by Pat Boone.
"Catch a Falling Star" by Perry Como.

To learn more about the production, please visit
www.ClybournePark.com

CENTER THEATRE GROUP
Michael Ritchie, Artistic Director
Edward L. Rada, Managing Director
Douglas C. Baker, Producing Director
Kelley Kirkpatrick and Neel Keller,
Associate Artistic Directors
Nausica Stergiou, General Manager,
Mark Taper Forum

LINCOLN CENTER THEATER
André Bishop, Artistic Director
Bernard Gersten, Executive Director
Adam Siegel, Managing Director
Hattie Jutagir, Executive Director of
Development & Planning
Linda Mason Ross, Director of Marketing

PLAYWRIGHTS HORIZONS
Tim Sanford, Artistic Director
Leslie Marcus, Managing Director
Carol Fishman, General Manager

JUJAMCYN THEATERS

JORDAN ROTH
President

PAUL LIBIN	**JACK VIERTEL**
Executive Vice President	Senior Vice President
MEREDITH VILLATORE	**JENNIFER HERSHEY**
Chief Financial Officer	Vice President,
	Building Operations
MICAH HOLLINGWORTH	**HAL GOLDBERG**
Vice President,	Vice President,
Company Operations	Theatre Operations

Director of Business Affairs .... Albert T. Kim
Director of Human Resources .... Michele Louhisdon
Director of Ticketing Services .... Justin Karr
Theatre Operations Managers .... Willa Burke,
Susan Elrod, Emily Hare,
Jeff Hubbard, Albert T. Kim
Theatre Operations Associates .... Carrie Jo Brinker,
Brian Busby, Michael Composto,
Anah Jyoti Klate
Accounting .... Cathy Cerge, Erin Dooley,
Amy Frank
Executive Producer, Red Awning .... Nicole Kastrinos
Director of Marketing, Givenik.com .... Joe Tropia
Marketing Associate, Givenik.com .... Ben Cohen
Building Operations Associate .... Erich Bussing
Executive Coordinator .... Ed Lefferson
Executive Assistants .... Clark Mims Tedesco,
Beth Given, Julia Kraus
Receptionist .... Lisa Perchinske
Maintenance .... Ralph Santos, Ramon Zapata
Security .... Rasim Hodzic, John Acero
Interns .... Maggie Baker, Alaina Bono,
Erin Carr, Hunter Chancellor,
Cindy Vargas, Kelvin Veras,
Luke Weidner, Margaret White

STAFF FOR THE WALTER KERR THEATRE FOR *CLYBOURNE PARK*
Theatre Manager .... Susan Elrod
Treasurer .... Harry Jaffie
Head Carpenter .... George E. Fullum
Head Propertyman .... Timothy Bennet
Head Electrician .... Vincent J. Valvo
Flyman .... Peter J. Iacoviello
Propertyman .... Moose Johnson
Engineer .... Brian DiNapoli
Assistant Treasurers .... Michael Loiacono,
Joseph Smith, Gail Yerkovich
Head Usher .... T.J. D'Angelo
Director .... Michelle Fleury
Tickets Takers .... Alison Traynor, Robert Zwaschka
Ushers .... Jason Aguirre, Florence Arcaro,
Juliett Cipriati, Aaron Kendall,
Victoria Lauzun, Ilir Velovic
Doormen .... Brandon Houghton, Kevin Wallace
Head Porter .... Marcio Martinez
Porter .... Rudy Martinez
Head Cleaner .... Sevdija Pasukanovic
Cleaner .... Lourdes Perez

Lobby refreshments by Sweet Concessions

Security provided by GBA Consulting Inc.

Jujamcyn Theatres is a proud member of the
Broadway Green Alliance

Clybourne Park
Scrapbook

①

③

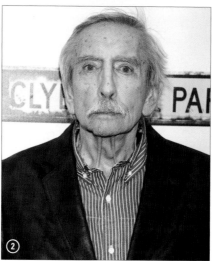

②

Correspondent: Brendan Griffin, "Jim/Tom/Kenneth"

Memorable Opening Night Faxes: The faxes from the other shows were really incredible. I still look them over when I have a few minutes to spare. I'll admit a few of us definitely studied them to see if the super celebrities in some of the other shows signed. Some did not, I'll have you know.

Opening Night Gifts: A lot of really beautiful key chains. Huh. In fact I think one was from Tiffany's. I went into that store once but nobody would speak to me.

Most Exciting Celebrity Visitors: Geez, take your pick: Jon Hamm, Whoopi, Blythe Danner. They were there all at once. I thought I might go blind. Henry Winkler was rendered a little speechless. That was cool.

Actor Who Performed the Most Roles in This Show: That would be me, as I play three. But I can't tell you about the third one.

Fastest Costume Change: Me again!!

Who Has Done the Most Shows in Their Career: Frank's like a million years old so it's probably him. But, Jeremy's very industrious, so you never know.

Special Backstage Ritual: We take turns giving Frank dutch rubs on his wrists and ankles before the top of each show. While they are excruciating, we have to consistently remind him that the damage is purely emotional and not physical. None of this is true, by the way.

Favorite Moment During Each Performance: I love the section in Act II we have lovingly come to refer to as "The Joke Section." I don't have much to say, so I get to sit back and watch some of the best actors I've ever met say some of the most offensive shit I've ever heard.

Favorite In-Theatre Gathering Places: There are a couple of spots. Christina's dressing room is a fun place because it's like a Whole Foods, except I don't lose entire paychecks there as she is very generous with her plethora of healthy snacks. Her essential oils create a very calming atmosphere as well. But she gets all uppity at half hour and literally shoves us out the door. She once did that when I was in the middle of a sentence.

Favorite Off-Site Hangout: I'm a true believer in Deacon Brodie's. Although, I could throw a rock through the front door of Hurley's from my dressing room. So that's a never-fail.

Favorite Snack Food: Toenail clippings.

Mascot: Frank Wood.

Favorite Therapy: Olympic weightlifting. I'm serious.

Memorable Ad-Lib: I dropped a line once and Damon literally cued me to speak. I realized we were sitting in silence and he tapped me on the shoulder and said "Hey, man, jump in," or something like that.

Record Number of Cell Phone Rings, Cell Phone Photos or Texting Incidents During a Performance: This is an awesome one. During the L.A. run the audience sounded like the floor of the stock exchange with all the phones going

off. Crystal has a line in the second act that addresses such a disturbance that is something to the effect of, "Maybe we should all turn off our phones." I'm pretty sure she played it directly to the audience.

Memorable Press Encounter: This question is entrapment and I refuse to answer it.

Memorable Stage Door Fan Encounter: Crystal gave her autograph to someone who then complained they couldn't read it and requested she write it more clearly. She declined.

What the Cast Thought of the Internet Buzz on the Show: What's the "internet"?

Latest Audience Arrival: This is twofold since it happened twice in the same show. A guy came in about halfway through the first act and he was wearing a jacket that was made from some sort of reflective material. Think of those reflective strips on the vests highway workers wear, but an entire jacket. It looked like C3PO was being seated in the tenth row. He was all I could see for the rest of the act. Then, at the top of the second act, a latecomer obviously thought that her seat was in the first row when it was really in the second. She passed through the entire front

row, everyone standing to let her by, mind you, and then again in the second. It looked like the audience was doing the wave really slowly.

Who Wore the Heaviest/Hottest Costume: I'll fall on that one. I've got a heavy Donegal tweed suit complete with a wool clerical vest and collar.

Who Wore the Least: I could answer this but I'd be talking about another play.

Memorable Directorial Note: "Annie, your objective is to behead your husband."

Company Legend: Bruce Norris is the kind of legend who drinks bourbon and rides the subway.

Understudy Anecdote: Man, Richard Thieriot single-handedly keeps the tobacco industry in the black.

Nicknames: I like to call Christina "Kirkles." I think it makes her feel a combination of love and discomfort.

Sweethearts Within the Company: Everyone's married so unless we're talking about platonic love then I think it's safe to say the temperature backstage is pretty monastic.

Ghostly Encounters Backstage: Uhhhhh...what?

1. Cast members (L-R): Annie Parisse, Frank Wood, Damon Gupton, Christina Kirk, Jeremy Shamos, Crystal A. Dickinson and *Yearbook* correspondent Brendan Griffin at Gotham Hall for the opening night party.
2. Three-time Pulitzer-winning playwright Edward Albee was a guest at the premiere.
3. Producer Jordan Roth, director Pam MacKinnon and author Bruce Norris at Gotham Hall.

Photos by Joseph Marzullo/WENN

The Columnist

First Preview: April 4, 2012. Opened: April 25, 2012.
Still running as of May 31, 2012.

PLAYBILL®

The Columnist

A portrait of real-life syndicated political columnist Joseph Alsop, who was the scourge of politicians on both sides of the aisle from the 1930s to the 1970s while carefully trying to conceal his homosexuality from the world. David Auburn's drama focuses on Alsop's personal and professional crises of the 1960s.

CAST

(in order of appearance)

Joseph Alsop	JOHN LITHGOW
Andrei	BRIAN J. SMITH
Susan Mary Alsop	MARGARET COLIN
Stewart Alsop	BOYD GAINES
Abigail	GRACE GUMMER
Halberstam	STEPHEN KUNKEN
Philip	MARC BONAN

Stage Manager	DENISE YANEY

UNDERSTUDIES

For Andrei:
MARC BONAN
For Susan Mary Alsop:
CHARLOTTE MAIER
For Joseph Alsop:
ANTHONY NEWFIELD
For Philip:
BRIAN J. SMITH
For Abigail:
ADRIA VITLAR
For Stewart Alsop/Halberstam:
TONY WARD

Manhattan Theatre Club
Samuel J. Friedman Theatre

Artistic Director
Lynne Meadow

Executive Producer
Barry Grove

Presents

THE Columnist

by

David Auburn

with

John Lithgow
Margaret Colin   Boyd Gaines   Stephen Kunken
Marc Bonan   Grace Gummer   Brian J. Smith

Scenic Design	Costume Design	Lighting Design
John Lee Beatty	**Jess Goldstein**	**Kenneth Posner**

Original Music & Sound Design	Projection Design	Hair & Wig Design
John Gromada	**Rocco DiSanti**	**Charles G. LaPointe**

Casting	Production Stage Manager
David Caparelliotis	**Jane Grey**

Directed by

Daniel Sullivan

Artistic Producer
Mandy Greenfield

General Manager
Florie Seery

Director of Artistic Development	Director of Marketing	Press Representative	Production Manager
Jerry Patch	**Debra Waxman-Pilla**	**Boneau/Bryan-Brown**	**Joshua Helman**

Director of Casting	Artistic Line Producer	Director of Development
Nancy Piccione	**Lisa McNulty**	**Lynne Randall**

Lead support for *The Columnist* is provided by MTC's Producing Fund Partner, ANDREW MARTIN-WEBER.

Additional support is provided by THE BLANCHE AND IRVING LAURIE FOUNDATION
and the NATIONAL ENDOWMENT FOR THE ARTS.
The Columnist is a recipient of an EDGERTON FOUNDATION New American Plays Award.
Special thanks to THE HAROLD AND MIMI STEINBERG CHARITABLE TRUST for supporting Manhattan Theatre Club.
The Columnist was developed with the support of TENNESSEE REPERTORY THEATRE
through its Ingram New Works Fellowship and Residency.
Manhattan Theatre Club wishes to express its appreciation to Theatre Development Fund for its support of this production.

4/25/12

(L-R): John Lithgow, Boyd Gaines

Photo by Joan Marcus

The Columnist

John Lithgow
Joseph Alsop

Brian J. Smith
Andrei

Margaret Colin
Susan Mary Alsop

Boyd Gaines
Stewart Alsop

Grace Gummer
Abigail

Stephen Kunken
Halberstam

Marc Bonan
Philip

Charlotte Maier
u/s Susan Mary Alsop

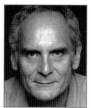

Anthony Newfield
u/s Joseph Alsop

Adria Vitlar
u/s Abigail

Tony Ward
u/s Stewart Alsop/ Halberstam

David Auburn
Playwright

Daniel Sullivan
Director

John Lee Beatty
Scenic Design

Jess Goldstein
Costume Design

Kenneth Posner
Lighting Design

John Gromada
Original Music & Sound Design

John Lithgow as Joseph Alsop

Photo by Joan Marcus

Charles G. LaPointe
Hair and Wig Design

Thomas Schall
Fight Director

David Caparelliotis/ Melcap Casting
Casting

Lynne Meadow
Artistic Director, Manhattan Theatre Club

Barry Grove
Executive Producer, Manhattan Theatre Club

Andrew Martin-Weber
Producing Fund Partner

Photo by Brian Mapp

BOX OFFICE
(L-R): David Dillon (Head Treasurer), P. Dustin Eastwood (Assistant Treasurer)

The Columnist
SCRAPBOOK

Correspondent: Marc Bonan, "Philip"
Opening Night Gifts: Posters, cast drawings, chocolates, Veuve Clicquot, orchids, books.
Who Has Done the Most Shows in Their Career: John Lithgow, Boyd Gaines
Favorite Moment During Each Performance: When the character of Philip enters.
Phrases Said Prior to Top of Show:
"Hey good looking, don't you ever die."
"Thumbs up."
"Knock their dicks in the dirt."
Company Legends: John Lithgow, four-time Tony Winner Boyd Gaines.

Favorite In-Theatre Gathering Place: The Clubhouse (dressing room of Bonan, Kunken & Smith).
Favorite Snack Food: Deviled eggs.
Favorite Therapy: Yoga, jelly beans, kombucha, nap time and spooning.
Memorable Ad-Libs: "Understudy of Defense" instead of Under-Secretary (said by John Lithgow to Adria Vitlar, when Adria went on as an understudy for Grace Gummer).
"I looked for you over at the Carousel" instead of Caravelle, a Saigon Hotel (said by Stephen Kunken to Boyd Gaines).

Who Wore the Least: John Lithgow, who is naked in the Moscow Hotel Room scene.
Catchphrases from *The Columnist* Only the Company Would Recognize:
"Here's to being fucked."
"The Johnson pick."
"He uses a cigarette holder for Christ's sake."
"You've been pretty tough on Johnson lately."
"I'll tell you where I get off."
"Johnson continues to escalate."
"To uncover or lay bare?"
"The missile gap."
"You put him in a terrible position."

FRONT OF HOUSE
Seated (L-R): Lyanna Alvarado, Joshua Diaz, Wendy Wright, Jan Rosenberg, Richard Ponce
Standing (L-R): Jackson Ero, John Wyffels, Patricia Polhill, Dinah Glorioso, Ed Brashear, Christine Snyder, Jim Joseph

CREW
In Front of Desk (L-R): John Fullum, Jane Grey, Timothy Walters
Sitting at Desk (L-R): Erin Moeller, Denise Yaney
Standing (L-R): Samuel Patt, Jeff Dodson, Louis Shapiro, Vaughn Preston, Chris Wiggins, Richard Klinger, Jeremy Von Deck

The Columnist

Photo by Joan Marcus

John Lithgow,
Margaret Colin

Death of a Salesman

First Preview: February 14, 2012. Opened: March 15, 2012.
Still running as of May 31, 2012.

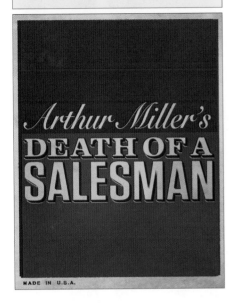

PLAYBILL®

Arthur Miller's DEATH OF A SALESMAN

MADE IN U.S.A.

In Arthur Miller's iconic portrait of an American Everyman, traveling salesman Willy Loman has lived his life on a smile and a shoeshine, adhering faithfully to the belief that it's not so important that you be good at something as long as you are "well-liked." Willy relies on his ever-suffering wife Linda to help him raise his pride and joy—his two boys Biff and Happy. But as he approaches late middle age Willy finds himself losing his touch, losing his grip and likely losing everything that meant anything to him.

CAST
(in order of appearance)

Willy Loman	PHILIP SEYMOUR HOFFMAN
Linda Loman	LINDA EMOND
Biff Loman	ANDREW GARFIELD
Happy Loman	FINN WITTROCK
Bernard	FRAN KRANZ
The Woman	MOLLY PRICE
Charley	BILL CAMP
Ben	JOHN GLOVER
Howard Wagner	REMY AUBERJONOIS
Jenny	KATHLEEN McNENNY
Stanley	GLENN FLESHLER
Miss Forsythe	STEPHANIE JANSSEN
Letta	ELIZABETH MORTON
Second Waiter	BRAD KOED

Continued on next page

ⓈETHEL BARRYMORE THEATRE
243 West 47th Street
A Shubert Organization Theatre

Philip J. Smith, *Chairman*   Robert E. Wankel, *President*

SCOTT RUDIN   STUART THOMPSON
JON B. PLATT   COLUMBIA PICTURES   JEAN DOUMANIAN
MERRITT FORREST BAER   ROGER BERLIND   SCOTT M. DELMAN   SONIA FRIEDMAN PRODUCTIONS
RUTH HENDEL   CARL MOELLENBERG   SCOTT & BRIAN ZEILINGER   ELI BUSH

Present

PHILIP SEYMOUR
HOFFMAN

LINDA   ANDREW
EMOND   GARFIELD

Arthur Miller's

DEATH OF A SALESMAN

FINN WITTROCK   FRAN KRANZ

REMY AUBERJONOIS   GLENN FLESHLER   STEPHANIE JANSSEN
BRAD KOED   KATHLEEN McNENNY   ELIZABETH MORTON   MOLLY PRICE
BILL CAMP   JOHN GLOVER

SCENIC DESIGN JO MIELZINER	COSTUME DESIGN ANN ROTH	LIGHTING DESIGN BRIAN MacDEVITT	SOUND DESIGN SCOTT LEHRER
HAIR & WIG DESIGN DAVID BRIAN BROWN	MAKEUP DESIGN IVANA PRIMORAC	ORIGINAL MUSIC BY ALEX NORTH	MUSIC SUPERVISOR GLEN KELLY
SCENIC DESIGN PREPARED BY BRIAN WEBB	CASTING BY MELCAP CASTING	FIGHT DIRECTOR THOMAS SCHALL	PRODUCTION STAGE MANAGER JILL CORDLE
PRODUCTION MANAGEMENT AURORA PRODUCTIONS	PRESS REPRESENTATIVE BONEAU/BRYAN-BROWN		GENERAL MANAGEMENT STP/PATRICK GRACEY

DIRECTED BY

Mike Nichols

3/15/12

(L-R): Andrew Garfield, Finn Wittrock, Philip Seymour Hoffman, Linda Emond

Death of a Salesman

Cast Continued

Time
The late 1940s

Setting
Willy Loman's house and yard, and various places in
New York City and Boston

UNDERSTUDIES

For Linda Loman:
KATHLEEN McNENNY
For Biff Loman, Happy Loman, Bernard:
BRAD KOED
For Willy Loman:
GLENN FLESHLER
For Ben, Charley:
JULIAN GAMBLE
For Howard Wagner, Stanley, Second Waiter:
THOMAS MICHAEL HAMMOND
For The Woman, Jenny, Miss Forsythe, Letta:
MEREDITH HOLZMAN

MUSICIANS

Conductor:
DAVID LOUD
Flute, Alto Flute:
KATHERINE FINK
Cello:
SARAH SEIVER
Trumpet, Flugelhorn:
DON DOWNS
Clarinet, Bass Clarinet:
MARK THRASHER

Philip Seymour Hoffman

Photo by Brigitte Lacombe for New York Magazine

Philip Seymour
Hoffman
Willy Loman

Linda Emond
Linda Loman

Andrew Garfield
Biff Loman

John Glover
Ben

Bill Camp
Charley

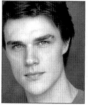

Finn Wittrock
Happy Loman

Fran Kranz
Bernard

Remy Auberjonois
Howard Wagner

Glenn Fleshler
Stanley

Stephanie Janssen
Miss Forsythe

Brad Koed
Second Waiter

Kathleen McNenny
Jenny

Elizabeth Morton
Letta

Molly Price
The Woman

Julian Gamble
u/s Ben, Charley

Thomas Michael
Hammond
*u/s Howard Wagner,
Stanley, Second
Waiter*

Meredith Holzman
*u/s The Woman,
Jenny, Miss
Forsythe, Letta*

Arthur Miller
Author

Mike Nichols
Director

Jo Mielziner
Scenic Design

Death of a Salesman

Ann Roth
Costume Design

Brian MacDevitt
Lighting Design

Scott Lehrer
Sound Design

David Brian Brown
Hair & Wig Design

Alex North
Original Music

Thomas Schall
Fight Director

Gene O'Donovan,
Aurora Productions
*Production
Management*

Ben Heller,
Aurora Productions
*Production
Management*

Scott Rudin
Producer

Stuart Thompson
Producer

Jon B. Platt
Producer

Jean Doumanian
Producer

Roger Berlind
Producer

Sonia Friedman
Productions
Producer

Ruth Hendel
Producer

Carl Moellenberg
Producer

Scott Zeilinger
Producer

Brian Zeilinger
Producer

(L-R) Linda Emond and
Andrew Garfield

Photo by Brigitte Lacombe for New York Magazine

2011-2012 AWARDS

TONY AWARDS
Best Revival of a Play
Best Direction of a Play
(Mike Nichols)

THEATRE WORLD AWARD
For Outstanding Broadway
or Off-Broadway Debut
(Finn Wittrock)

DRAMA DESK AWARDS
Outstanding Revival of a Play
Outstanding Director of a Play
(Mike Nichols)
Outstanding Lighting Design
(Brian MacDevitt)

OUTER CRITICS CIRCLE AWARD
Outstanding Revival of a Play

THE DRAMA LEAGUE AWARD
Distinguished Revival of a Play

CLARENCE DERWENT AWARD
Most Promising Male Performer
(Finn Wittrock)

Death of a Salesman

CREW
Seated (L-R): Mitchell Beck (Hair & Wig
Supervisor),
David Stollings (Head Sound)

Standing (L-R): Mike Hyman (Head Electrician),
John Glover (Cast "Uncle Ben"),
Jason Clark (Head Carpenter),
Andrew Meeker (Head Properties),
Phillip Feller (House Properties)
Gerry Pavon (Spot Operator)

**STAGE
MANAGEMENT**
(L-R): Jill Cordle,
Matt Stern

DRESSERS
(L-R): Cathy Cline, Kelly Saxon, Claire Verlaet

BOX OFFICE
(L-R): Steven DeLuca (Treasurer), Diane Heatherington (Head Treasurer),
Danny D'Elia (Treasurer)

FRONT OF HOUSE
Front Row: (L-R): Troy Scarborough,
Devin Elting (Concessions),
Dan Landon (Barrymore Theatre Manager)

Second Row: (L-R): Mike Reilly, Marizol Lugo,
Justin Roman, John Cashman (Ushers)

Back Row: (L-R): Wambui Bahati (Infa-red Hearing),
John Barbaretti (Asst. Mgr.- Ticket Taker),
Sherry McIntyre (Head Usher),
Brandon Fleming (Concessions)

Photos by Brian Mapp

Death of a Salesman

Photo by Brigitte Lacombe for New York Magazine

(L-R) Bill Camp, Linda Emond, Finn Wittrock, Andrew Garfield

STAFF FOR *DEATH OF A SALESMAN*

GENERAL MANAGEMENT
STUART THOMPSON PRODUCTIONS
Stuart Thompson   Patrick Gracey   David Turner
Kevin Emrick   Christopher Taggart
Andrew Lowy   Brittany Weber   James Yandoli

SCOTT RUDIN PRODUCTIONS
Steven Cardwell   Donald Devcich   Jessica Held
Adam Klaff   Kim Lessing   Julie Oh
Nick Reimond   Jason Sack   Dan Sarrow

COMPANY MANAGER
Jennifer Hindman Kemp

PRODUCTION MANAGEMENT
AURORA PRODUCTIONS INC.
Gene O'Donovan   Ben Heller
Stephanie Sherline   Jarid Sumner   Liza Luxenberg
Anita Shah   Anthony Jusino   Steven Dalton
Eugenio Saenz Flores   Isaac Katzanek
Aneta Feld   Melissa Mazdra

PRESS REPRESENTATIVE
BONEAU/BRYAN-BROWN
Chris Boneau   Jim Byk   Kelly Guiod

MELCAP CASTING
Mele Nagler   David Caparelliotis
Lauren Port   Candice Alustiza   Felicia Rudolph

Production Stage Manager	Jill Cordle
Stage Manager	Matthew Aaron Stern
Assistant Director	Kathy Hendrickson
Vocal Coach	Grace Zandarski
Associate Costume Designer	Matthew Pachtman
Associate Lighting Designer	Jennifer Schriever
Associate Sound Designer	Will Pickens
Production Electrician	Dan Coey
Production Props	Jen Dunlap
Assistant to the Lighting Designer	Coby Chasman-Beck
Moving Light Programmer	Michael Hill
Head Carpenter	Jason Clark
Head Properties	Andrew Meeker

Head Electrician	Mike Hyman
Sound Engineer	David Stollings
Wardrobe Supervisor	Kay Grunder
Hair Supervisor	Mitchell Beck
Dressers	Kimberly Prentice, Kelly Saxon, Claire Verlaet
Production Assistants	Ariel C. Osborne, Amy Steinman
General Management Intern	Michael Holt

Advertising	Serino/Coyne Nancy Coyne, Sandy Block, Scott Johnson, Joaquin Esteva, Nicole Francois
Digital Outreach & Website	Serino/Coyne Kevin Keating, Chip Meyrelles, Laurie Connor, Jim Glaub, Ian Weiss
Marketing	Serino/Coyne Leslie Barrett, Abby Wolbe
Logo and Artwork Design	BLT Communications, Inc.
Press Associates	Adrian Bryan-Brown, Jackie Green, Linnae Hodzic, Jessica Johnson, Kevin Jones, Amy Kass, Holly Kinney, Emily Meagher, Aaron Meier, Christine Olver, Joe Perrotta, Matt Polk, Amanda Sales, Heath Schwartz, Michael Strassheim, Susanne Tighe
Accountant	Fried & Kowgios CPA's LLP/ Robert Fried, CPA
Controller	J.S. Kubala
Insurance	DeWitt Stern Group
Legal Counsel	Loeb & Loeb, LLP Seth Gelblum, Esq.
Banking	City National Bank/Michele Gibbons
Payroll	Castellana Services, Inc.
Theatre Displays	King Displays, Inc.
Transportation	IBA Limousine

PRODUCTION CREDITS
Scenery and scenic effects built, painted, electrified and automated by Show Motion, Inc., Milford, CT. Lighting equipment from PRG Lighting, a division of Production Resource Group, LLC, New Windsor, NY. Sound equipment by Masque Sound. Specialty props by Joe Cairo, Craig Grigg and Metal Dimensions LLC. Costumes by Eric Winterling, Inc. and Giliberto Designs, Inc. Custom knitwear by Danielle Matland. Fabric painting and dyeing by Jeff Fender Studios. Millinery by Rodney Gordon, Inc. Custom footwear by LaDuca Shoes. Susanna Sandke – Western Costume Company, Gary Franke – Steppin' Out Vintage Clothing, Daybreak Vintage and Bra*Tenders for undergarments & hosiery.

RECORDED VOICES PROVIDED BY
Justis Bolding, Stephanie Janssen, Matthew Mindler and Sue-Anne Morrow.

Rehearsed at the New 42nd Street Studios and the Clark Studio Theatre at Lincoln Center for the Performing Arts.

www.deathofasalesmanbroadway.com

 THE SHUBERT ORGANIZATION, INC.
Board of Directors

Philip J. Smith Chairman	**Robert E. Wankel** President
Wyche Fowler, Jr.	**Diana Phillips**
Lee J. Seidler	**Michael I. Sovern**

Stuart Subotnick

Chief Financial Officer	Elliot Greene
Sr. Vice President, Ticketing	David Andrews
Vice President, Finance	Juan Calvo
Vice President, Human Resources	Cathy Cozens
Vice President, Facilities	John Darby
Vice President, Theatre Operations	Peter Entin
Vice President, Marketing	Charles Flateman
Vice President, Audit	Anthony LaMattina
Vice President, Ticket Sales	Brian Mahoney
Vice President, Creative Projects	D.S. Moynihan
Vice President, Real Estate	Julio Peterson

Staff for The Ethel Barrymore

House Manager	Dan Landon

Death of a Salesman
SCRAPBOOK

Photos by Joseph Marzullo/WENN

Correspondent: Elizabeth Morton, "Letta"

Opening Night Gifts: Engraved glass footballs from Tiffany, Tiffany lockets and gold pens.

Most Exciting Celebrity Visitors: Meryl Streep came opening night and returned the following week with her pal, Hillary Clinton.

Actor Who Performed the Most Roles in This Show: "Second Waiter" Brad Koed understudies Biff, Happy and Bernard.

Who Has Done the Most Shows in Their Career: John Glover is our true actor veteran.

Special Backstage Ritual: Philip Seymour Hoffman spends the half hour pre show in the Loman House. Linda Emond joins him for part of that time.

Favorite Moment During Each Performance: Bill Camp's many quick changes in and out of a toupee and knickers.

Favorite In-Theatre Gathering Place: Linda Emond's anteroom.

Favorite Off-Site Hangout: Glass House Tavern.

Favorite Snack Food: Lots of pies brought by our fabulous house electrician!

Cell Phone Rings, Cell Phone Photos or Texting Incidents During a Performance: Notorious amount of cell phones ringing during the pin-drop quiet Requiem scene.

Latest Audience Arrival: No late seating!

Fastest Costume Change: Fran Kranz from nerdy teen Bernard to successful lawyer Bernard.

Who Wore the Heaviest/Hottest Costume: Philip Seymour Hoffman: a wool suit for the entire show.

Who Wore the Least: Finn Wittrock: Boxers and a t-shirt.

Catchphrases Only the Company Would Recognize: "Delicious coffee, mean in itself!"

Company In-Jokes: Bill Camp, who plays Charley and says, "Knock a homer, Biff, knock a homer" is the star softball player in the Broadway League and "knocks" more homers than anyone!

Company Legends: Costume designer Ann Roth, director Mike Nichols. 'Nuff said.

Coolest Thing About Being in This Show: Mike Nichols is the coolest. He referred to this production as the happiest time of his life.

1. (L-R): Finn Wittrock, Linda Emond, Philip Seymour Hoffman, John Glover and Andrew Garfield take bows on opening night.
2. Also at curtain call (L-R): Remy Auberjonois, Molly Price, Glenn Fleshler.
3. Director Mike Nichols gives a thumbs-up to photographers at the premiere.
4. Exterior of the Ethel Barrymore Theatre during the run of *Death of a Salesman*.

Don't Dress for Dinner

First Preview: March 30, 2012. Opened: April 26, 2012.
Still running as of May 31, 2012.

PLAYBILL

Marc Camoletti's sequel to his hit farce Boeing-Boeing *shows the philandering Bernard, again with his old pal Robert by his side, trying to conceal his mistress from his wife during a dinner party at his home near Paris. What he doesn't know is that his wife is having an affair too—and so is Robert. With the help of a tipsy French cook, they weave ever more tangled webs of doomed comic deceit.*

CAST
(in order of appearance)

Bernard	ADAM JAMES
Jacqueline	PATRICIA KALEMBER
Robert	BEN DANIELS
Suzette	SPENCER KAYDEN
Suzanne	JENNIFER TILLY
George	DAVID ARON DAMANE

PLACE & TIME

1960: A country home northwest of Paris

Ben Daniels is appearing with the permission of
Actors' Equity Association.

UNDERSTUDIES

For Robert:
TOM GALANTICH
For Jacqueline, Suzette, Suzanne:
FRANCES MERCANTI-ANTHONY
For Bernard, George:
JAMES ANDREW O'CONNOR

Production Stage Manager: BARCLAY STIFF
Stage Manager: KELLY BEAULIEU

AMERICAN AIRLINES THEATRE

ROUNDABOUTTHEATRECOMPANY

Todd Haimes, Artistic Director
Harold Wolpert, Managing Director
Julia C. Levy, Executive Director

In association with

Damian Arnold

Presents

Ben Daniels   Adam James   Patricia Kalember *and* Jennifer Tilly
in

DON'T DRESS FOR DINNER

By

Marc Camoletti

Adapted by

Robin Hawdon

with

Spencer Kayden   David Aron Damane

Set Design John Lee Beatty	*Costume Design* William Ivey Long	*Lighting Design* Ken Billington	*Sound Design* David Van Tieghem
Hair & Wig Design Paul Huntley	*Fight Director* Thomas Schall	*Production Stage Manager* Barclay Stiff	*Production Management* Aurora Productions

Casting
Jim Carnahan, CSA/Carrie Gardner, CSA
Stephen Kopel/Laura Stanczyk, CSA

General Manager
Denise Cooper

Press Representative
Boneau/Bryan-Brown

Associate Managing Director Greg Backstrom	*Director of Marketing & Sales Promotion* Thomas Mygatt	*Director of Development* Lynne Gugenheim Gregory	*Founding Director* Gene Feist	*Adams Associate Artistic Director** Scott Ellis

Directed by

John Tillinger

Roundabout gratefully acknowledges partial underwriting from Douglas and Karen McKeel Calby.
*Generously underwritten by Margot Adams, in memory of Mason Adams.
Roundabout Theatre Company is a member of the League of Resident Theatres.
www.roundabouttheatre.org

4/26/12

(L-R): Spencer Kayden,
Ben Daniels,
Patricia Kalember

Photo by Joan Marcus

Don't Dress for Dinner

Ben Daniels
Robert

Adam James
Bernard

Patricia Kalember
Jacqueline

Jennifer Tilly
Suzanne

Spencer Kayden
Suzette

David Aron Damane
George

Tom Galantich
u/s Robert

Frances Mercanti-
Anthony
*u/s Jacqueline,
Suzette, Suzanne*

James Andrew
O'Connor
u/s Bernard, George

Marc Camoletti
Playwright

Robin Hawdon
Adaptation

John Tillinger
Director

John Lee Beatty
Scenic Design

William Ivey Long
Costume Design

Ken Billington
Lighting Design

David Van Tieghem
Sound Design

Thomas Schall
Fight Director

Paul Huntley
*Hair and Wig
Designer*

Gene O'Donovan,
Aurora Productions
*Production
Management*

Ben Heller,
Aurora Productions
*Production
Management*

Jim Carnahan
Casting

Damian Arnold,
Executive Producer
of the British Stage
Company
Producer

Gene Feist
*Founding Director
Roundabout
Theatre Company*

Todd Haimes,
Artistic Director
*Roundabout Theatre
Company*

(L-R): Adam James,
Ben Daniels

Photo by Joan Marcus

Photo by Brian Mapp

BOX OFFICE
(L-R) Ted Osborne,
Mead Margulies

Don't Dress for Dinner

CREW

Seated (L-R): Manuela LaPorte, Susan Fallon, Dale Carman, Kat Martin, Carly DiFulvio, Robert W. Dowling II

Standing (L-R): Dann Wojnar, Glenn Merwede, Jillian Tully, Brian Maiuri, Hannah Overton, Barclay Stiff, Davin DeSantis

ROUNDABOUT THEATRE COMPANY STAFF
ARTISTIC DIRECTOR ....TODD HAIMES
MANAGING DIRECTOR ....HAROLD WOLPERT
EXECUTIVE DIRECTOR ....JULIA C. LEVY
ADAMS ASSOCIATE
    ARTISTIC DIRECTOR ....SCOTT ELLIS

ARTISTIC STAFF
DIRECTOR OF ARTISTIC DEVELOPMENT/
    DIRECTOR OF CASTING ....Jim Carnahan
Artistic Consultant ....Robyn Goodman
Resident Director ....Doug Hughes
Associate Artists ....Mark Brokaw, Scott Elliott,
    Sam Gold, Bill Irwin, Joe Mantello,
    Kathleen Marshall, Theresa Rebeck
Literary Manager ....Jill Rafson
Senior Casting Director.....................Carrie Gardner
Casting Director ....Stephen Kopel
Casting Associate ....Jillian Cimini
Casting Assistant ....Michael Morlani
Artistic Associate ....Amy Ashton
Literary Associate ....Josh Fiedler
The Blanche and Irving Laurie Foundation
    Theatre Visions Fund
      Commissions........................David West Read,
      Nathan Louis Jackson
Educational Foundation of
    America Commissions...............Bekah Brunstetter,
    Lydia Diamond, Diana Fithian,
    Julie Marie Myatt

New York State Council
    on the Arts Commission ....Nathan Louis Jackson
Roundabout Commissions..............Helen Edmundson,
    Andrew Hinderaker, Stephen Karam,
    Steven Levenson, Matthew Lopez,
    Kim Rosenstock
Casting Interns ....Stanzi Davis, Kyle Eberlein,
    Rebecca Henning, Rachel Reichblum,
    Krystal Rowley
Script Readers ....Jay Cohen, Shannon Deep,
    Ben Izzo, Alexis Roblan
Artistic Apprentice ....Joshua M. Feder

EDUCATION STAFF
EDUCATION DIRECTOR ....Greg McCaslin
Associate Education Director ....Jennifer DiBella
Education Program Manager ....Aliza Greenberg
Education Program Associate ....Sarah Malone
Education Assistant ....Holly Sansom
Education Dramaturg ....Ted Sod
Teaching Artists ....Josh Allen, Cynthia Babak,
    Victor Barbella, LaTonya Borsay,
    Mark Bruckner, Eric C. Dente, Joe Doran,
    Elizabeth Dunn-Ruiz, Carrie Ellman-Larsen,
    Deanna Frieman, Sheri Graubert, Melissa Gregus,
    Adam Gwon, Devin Haqq, Carrie Heitman,
    Karla Hendrick, Jason Jacobs, Alana Jacoby,
    Lisa Renee Jordan, Jamie Kalama Wood, Alvin Keith,
    Erin McCready, James Miles, Nick Moore,
    Meghan O'Neil, Nicole Press, Leah Reddy,

Amanda Rehbein, Nick Simone, Joe Skowronski,
    Heidi Stallings, Daniel Sullivan, Carl Tallent,
    Vickie Tanner, Laurine Towler, Jennifer Varbalow,
    Leese Walker, Gail Winar, Chad Yarborough
Teaching Artist Emeritus ....Reneé Flemings
Education Apprentice ....Kimberley Oria

EXECUTIVE ADMINISTRATIVE STAFF
ASSOCIATE MANAGING
    DIRECTOR...............................Greg Backstrom
Assistant Managing Director ....Katharine Croke
Assistant to the Managing Director ....Zachary Baer
Assistant to the Executive Director ....Nicole Tingir

MANAGEMENT/ADMINISTRATIVE STAFF
GENERAL MANAGER ....Sydney Beers
General Manager,
    American Airlines Theatre ....Denise Cooper
General Manager,
    Steinberg Center ....Nicholas J. Caccavo
Human Resources Director ....Stephen Deutsch
Operations Manager ....Valerie D. Simmons
Associate General Manager ....Maggie Cantrick
Office Manager ....Scott Kelly
Archivist ....Tiffany Nixon
Receptionists ....Dee Beider, Emily Frohnhoefer,
    Elisa Papa, Allison Patrick
Messenger ....Darnell Franklin
Management Apprentice ....Christina Pezzello

Don't Dress for Dinner

FINANCE STAFF
DIRECTOR OF FINANCE ....Susan Neiman
Payroll Director ....John LaBarbera
Accounts Payable Manager ....Frank Surdi
Payroll Benefits Administrator ....Yonit Kafka
Manager Financial Reporting ....Joshua Cohen
Business Office Assistant ....Jackie Verbitski
Business Apprentice ....Kimberly Lucia

DEVELOPMENT STAFF
DIRECTOR OF
   DEVELOPMENT ....Lynne Gugenheim Gregory
Assistant to the
   Director of Development ....Liz Malta
Director, Institutional Giving ....Liz S. Alsina
Director, Individual Giving ....Christopher Nave
Director, Special Events ....Lane Hosmer
Associate Director, Individual Giving ....Tyler Ennis
Manager, Telefundraising ....Gavin Brown
Manager, Corporate Relations ....Sohyun Kim
Manager, Friends of Roundabout ....Marisa Perry
Manager, Donor Information Systems ....Lise Speidel
Special Events Associate ....Natalie Corr
Individual Giving Officer ....Joseph Foster
Individual Giving Officer ....Sophia Hinshelwood
Institutional Giving Assistant ....Brett Barbour
Development Assistant ....Martin Giannini
Development Apprentice ....Julie Erhart
Special Events Apprentice ....Genevieve Carroll

INFORMATION TECHNOLOGY STAFF
DIRECTOR OF INFORMATION
   TECHNOLOGY ....Daniel V. Gomez
System Administrator ....Jim Roma
IT Associate ....Cary Kim

MARKETING STAFF
DIRECTOR OF MARKETING AND
   SALES PROMOTION ....Thomas Mygatt
Associate Director of Marketing ....Tom O'Connor
Senior Marketing Manager ....Shannon Marcotte
Marketing Associate ....Eric Emch
Marketing Assistant ....Bradley Sanchez
Web Producer ....Mark Cajigao
Web Developer ....Daniel V. Gomez
Website Consultant ....Keith Powell Beyland
Director of Telesales
   Special Promotions ....Marco Frezza
Telesales Manager ....Patrick Pastor
Telesales Office Coordinator ....Nicholas Ronan
Marketing Apprentices........................Julie Boor,
     Bethany Nothstein

AUDIENCE SERVICES STAFF
DIRECTOR OF
   AUDIENCE SERVICES ....Wendy Hutton
Subscription Manager ....Bill Klemm
Box Office Managers ....Edward P. Osborne,
     Jaime Perlman, Krystin MacRitchie,
     Nicole Nicholson
Group Sales Manager ....Jeff Monteith
Assistant Box Office Managers ....Robert Morgan,
     Joseph Clark, Andrew Clements,
     Catherine Fitzpatrick
Assistant Audience Services Managers ....Robert Kane,
     Lindsay Ericson,
     Jessica Pruett-Barnett

Customer Services Coordinator ....Thomas Walsh
Audience Services ....Solangel Bido, Michael Bultman,
     Lauren Cartelli, Adam Elsberry,
     Joe Gallina, Kara Harrington,
     Lindsay Hoffman, Nicki Ishmael,
     Kiah Johnson, Kate Longosky,
     Michelle Maccarone, Mead Margulies,
     Laura Marshall, Chuck Migliaccio,
     Carlos Morris, Kaia Rafoss, Josh Rozett,
     Ben Schneider, Heather Siebert,
     Nalane Singh, Ron Tobia,
     Michael Valentine, Hannah Weitzman
Audience Services Apprentice ....Jennifer Almgreen

SERVICES
Counsel ....Paul, Weiss,
     Rifkind, Wharton and Garrison LLP,
     Charles H. Googe Jr., Carol M. Kaplan
Counsel ....Rosenberg & Estis
Counsel ....Andrew Lance,
     Gibson, Dunn, & Crutcher, LLP
Counsel ....Harry H. Weintraub,
     Glick and Weintraub, P.C.
Counsel ....Stroock & Stroock & Lavan LLP
Counsel ....Daniel S. Dokos,
     Weil, Gotshal & Manges LLP
Counsel ....Claudia Wagner/
     Manatt, Phelps & Phillips, LLP
Immigration Counsel ....Mark D. Koestler and
     Theodore Ruthizer
House Physicians ....Dr. Theodore Tyberg,
     Dr. Lawrence Katz
House Dentist ....Neil Kanner, D.M.D.
Insurance ....DeWitt Stern Group, Inc.
Accountant ....Lutz & Carr CPAs, LLP
Advertising ....Spotco/
     Drew Hodges, Jim Edwards,
     Tom Greenwald, Kyle Hall, Josh Fraenkel
Interactive Marketing ....Situation Interactive/
     Damian Bazadona, John Lanasa,
     Eric Bornemann, Mollie Shapiro
Events Photography ....Anita and Steve Shevett
Production Photographer ....Joan Marcus
Theatre Displays.............King Displays, Wayne Sapper
Lobby Refreshments ....Sweet Concessions
Merchandising ....Spotco Merch/
     James Decker

MANAGING DIRECTOR
   EMERITUS ....Ellen Richard

Roundabout Theatre Company
231 West 39th Street, New York, NY 10018
(212) 719-9393.

GENERAL PRESS REPRESENTATIVE
BONEAU/BRYAN-BROWN
Adrian Bryan-Brown
Matt Polk   Jessica Johnson   Amy Kass

CREDITS FOR *DON'T DRESS FOR DINNER*
Company Manager ....Carly DiFulvio
Production Stage Manager ....Barclay Stiff
Stage Manager ....Kelly Beaulieu
Production Management by ......Aurora Productions Inc./
     Gene O'Donovan, Ben Heller,
     Stephanie Sherline, Jarid Sumner,

     Anthony Jusino, Anita Shah,
     Liza Luxenberg, Steven Dalton,
     Eugenio Saenz Flores, Isaac Katzanek,
     Melissa Mazdra
Assistant Director ....Jessica Creane
Associate Scenic Designer ....Kacie Hultgren
Associate Costume Designer ....Cathy Parrott
Director of
   William Ivey Long Studios ....Donald Sanders
Costume Intern ....Emily Winokur
Associate Lighting Designer ....John Demous
Associate Sound Designer ....Dave Sanderson
Fight Director ....Thomas Schall
Make-up Designer ....Angelina Avallone
Make-up Assistant ....Valentina Celada
Tango Instructor ....Dardo Galletto,
     Dardo Galletto Studios
Production Properties Supervisor ....Peter Sarafin
Assistant Production Properties ....Buist Bickley
Production Carpenter ....Glenn Merwede
Production Electrician ....Brian Maiuri
Running Properties ....Robert W. Dowling II
Sound Operator ....Dann Wojnar
Wardrobe Supervisor ....Susan J. Fallon
Dressers ....Dale Carman, Kat Martin
Wardrobe Dayworker ....Jillian Tully
Hair and Wig Supervisor ....Manuela Laporte
Production Assistant ....Davin De Santis
Physical Therapy ....PhysioArts

CREDITS
Scenery constructed by Showman Fabricators, Inc., Long Island City, NY. Additional scenery and properties by R Ramos Upholstery and Sightlines Scenery. Lighting equipment by PRG Lighting. Sound equipment by Sound Associates. Costumes constructed by Euroco, Giliberto Designs, Katrina Patterns and Tricorne, Inc. Millinery by Rodney Gordon. Dance shoes by WorldTone Dance Shoes. Special thanks to Bra*Tenders for hosiery and undergarments. Makeup by M•A•C Cosmetics and Make Up For Ever. "Hit the Road Jack" (Percy Mayfield) is licensed courtesy of Tangerine Music.

AMERICAN AIRLINES THEATRE STAFF
Company Manager ....Carly DiFulvio
House Carpenter ....Glenn Merwede
House Electrician ....Brian Maiuri
House Properties ....Robert W. Dowling II
House Sound ....Dann Wojnar
IA Apprentice ....Hannah Overton
Wardrobe Supervisor ....Susan J. Fallon
Box Office Manager ....Ted Osborne
Assistant Box Office Manager ....Robert Morgan
House Manager ....Stephen Ryan
Associate House Manager .... Zipporah Aguasvivas
Head Usher ....Crystal Suarez
House Staff............ Lance Andrade, Christopher Busch,
     Jeanne Coutant, Anne Ezell,
     Denise Furbert, Maria Graves,
     Lee Henry, Rebecca Knell,
     Taylor Martin, Enrika Nicholas,
     Jazmine Perez, Samantha Rivera,
     Celia Torres, Alvin Vega, Felisha Whatts
Security ....Julious Russell

Don't Dress for Dinner
SCRAPBOOK

Photos by Monica Simoes

Correspondent: Barclay Stiff, Production Stage Manager

Memorable Opening Night Faxes: The best part of an opening night on Broadway is when the fax machine in the SM office starts lighting up the night before. One by one, faxes come in from practically every Broadway show. A single sheet of paper with the warmest of wishes from fellow cast and crew. To me this is the highlight of all the opening night festivities. A chance to read some lovely notes from everyone in the Broadway community and beyond.

Opening Night Gifts: The Roundabout Theatre gave the entire company the traditional silver frame with a photo of the "Family Portrait" we took just before our first preview. The photo included everyone onstage and backstage. The show name and date was also engraved on the front of the frame. A wonderful way to remember working at RTC. Spencer Kayden also gave the company small containers of "monkey fart" flavored lip balm. Everyone raved how great the lip balm worked and tasted like strawberries. Awesome!

Special Backstage Rituals: The fight call seemed to be the nightly ritual for the entire cast. We came together an hour before the show and worked through all the many physical moments throughout the play (more than 18 of them, created by Tom Schall). Over time the fight call evolved into a chance for everyone to check in with others and tell dirty jokes. Great fun had by all!

Favorite Moment During Each Performance: Spencer Kayden and Ben Daniels open the second act of the play with a tango dance that is truly a wonder to behold. It includes spins, jumps, and kicks all within a 90 second dance. The final bit of the dance includes Ben catching Spencer in a lift that sends the two of them over the back of the onstage couch. Spencer falls in such a way that her crotch lands square on Ben's face. Spencer then says her line: "The dance

makes me moist!" The audience roars with laughter. The rest of the cast loved watching it offstage on the monitors. Great fun!

Favorite Snack Food: Sour Patch Kids and Gummy Bears. We all ate them by the truckload!

Fastest Costume Change: It actually happens onstage in full view of the audience. Spencer Kayden enters wearing a full waitress costume. Adam James and Ben Daniels ultimately transform her costume into a tiny little cocktail dress. They achieve this by simultaneously removing her apron and wrist cuffs. They turn her body upstage and pull off her shirt that splits up the middle. They then pull her skirt up and over her bust line. Adam finally pulls out a hair pin and lets her hair fall down to her shoulders. Spencer turns around facing the audience looking dazed and bewildered about what just happened. This quick change always earns huge applause and laughter from the audience. William Ivey Long designed an incredible set of costumes to pull this transformation off. He deservedly received a Tony nomination for his work.

Company In-Jokes: "Thank you for the gorgeous, gorgeous, gorgeous coat, you gorgeous, gorgeous man. Suzy!"

1. Curtain call on opening night (L-R): Patricia Kalember, Adam James, Jennifer Tilly, Ben Daniels, Spencer Kayden and David Aron Damane.
2. The same cast (plus director John Tillinger, second from left) in "civvies" on the way to the cast party.

"We will can always add that in for the world tour."

Memorable Directorial Notes: From John Tillinger (director) to Ben Daniels: "I think you could get arrested for doing that to Spencer onstage. I love it! Do it more!"
To Adam James: "Quit looking at Jennifer's breasts so much!"

2011-2012 AWARD

OUTER CRITICS CIRCLE AWARD
Outstanding Featured Actress in a Play
(Spencer Kayden)

End of the Rainbow

First Preview: March 19, 2012. Opened: April 2, 2012.
Still running as of May 31, 2012.

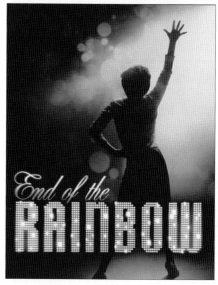

Tracie Bennett recreates her award-winning London performance as tragic film and concert diva assoluta Judy Garland in Peter Quilter's biographical drama. The play with music traces the last sad weeks of Garland's life, and gives her a chance to perform many of her standards, including "Over the Rainbow," which at last takes its rightful place as a Broadway showtune.

CAST

Judy Garland ....TRACIE BENNETT
Anthony ....MICHAEL CUMPSTY
Mickey Deans ....TOM PELPHREY
BBC Interviewer/Porter/ASM ....JAY RUSSELL

STANDBYS

Standby for Judy Garland:
SARAH URIARTE BERRY
Standby for Mickey Deans:
ERIK HEGER
Standby for Anthony,
BBC Interviewer/Porter/ASM:
DON NOBLE

TIME:
December 1968.
PLACE:
The Ritz Hotel, London.

MUSICIANS

Bass ....Louis Bruno
Trombone.............................Wayne Goodman
Drums ....Richard Rosenzweig
Woodwind ....Edward Salkin
Trumpet ....David Stahl

❀ BELASCO THEATRE
111 West 44th Street
A Shubert Organization Theatre

Philip J. Smith, *Chairman*   Robert E. Wankel, *President*

LEE DEAN   LAURENCE MYERS   JOEY PARNES
ELLIS GOODMAN   SHADOWCATCHER ENTERTAINMENT/ALHADEFF PRODUCTIONS   NATIONAL ANGELS U.S. INC.
CHARLES DIAMOND/JENNY TOPPER   MYLA LERNER/ANDREW BRYAN   SPRING SIRKIN/CANDY GOLD   HILARY WILLIAMS
and S.D. WAGNER   JOHN JOHNSON
in association with
GUTHRIE THEATRE
present

TRACIE BENNETT
in

BY
PETER QUILTER

with

TOM PELPHREY   JAY RUSSELL
and
MICHAEL CUMPSTY

SCENIC & COSTUME DESIGN	LIGHTING DESIGN	SOUND DESIGN
WILLIAM DUDLEY	CHRISTOPHER AKERLIND	GARETH OWEN

ORCHESTRATIONS	MUSICAL ARRANGEMENTS	MUSICAL DIRECTION	MUSIC COORDINATOR
CHRIS EGAN	GARETH VALENTINE	JEFFREY SAVER	SEYMOUR RED PRESS

CASTING	PRODUCTION STAGE MANAGER
PAT McCORKLE	MARK DOBROW

PRESS REPRESENTATIVE	ADVERTISING & MARKETING
O&M CO.	aka

DIRECTED BY
TERRY JOHNSON

Originally presented in the UK at Royal & Derngate, Northampton, Laurie Sansom, Artistic Director, Martin Sutherland, Executive Director and subsequently in the
West End at Trafalgar Studios produced by Lee Dean, Jenny Topper, Laurence Myers, Charles Diamond, Hilary Williams and David Bailey for Pinstripe Productions.

American premiere presented by the Guthrie Theater Joe Dowling, Artistic Director.

The producers wish to express their appreciation to Theatre Development Fund for its support of this production.

4/2/12

(L-R): Michael Cumpsty, Tracie Bennett, Tom Pelphrey

Photo by Carol Rosegg

End of the Rainbow

Tracie Bennett
Judy Garland

Michael Cumpsty
Anthony

Tom Pelphrey
Mickey Deans

Jay Russell
*BBC Interviewer/
Porter/ASM*

Sarah Uriarte Berry
*Standby Judy
Garland*

Erik Heger
*Standby Mickey
Deans*

Don Noble
*Standby Anthony,
BBC Interviewer/
Porter/ASM*

Peter Quilter
Playwright

Terry Johnson
Director

William Dudley
*Set and Costume
Design*

Christopher Akerlind
Lighting Design

Gareth Owen
Sound Design

Seymour Red Press
Music Coordinator

Kate Wilson
Dialect Coach

Pat McCorkle
McCorkle Casting,
Ltd. C.S.A.
Casting

Joey Parnes
Producer

Chase Mishkin
Producer

Marleen Alhadeff
Alhadeff Productions
Producer

Kenny Alhadeff
Alhadeff Productions
Producer

Myla Lerner
Producer

Barbara Freitag
Producer

Buddy Freitag
Producer

Spring Sirkin
Producer

Tracie Bennett
as Judy
Garland

Photo by Carol Rosegg

2011-2012 AWARDS

DRAMA DESK AWARD
Outstanding Actress in a Play
(Tracie Bennett)

OUTER CRITICS CIRCLE AWARD
Outstanding Actress in a Play
(Tracie Bennett)

THEATRE WORLD AWARD
For Outstanding Broadway
or Off-Broadway Debut
(Tracie Bennett)

Hilary Williams
Producer

Joe Dowling
The Guthrie Theater
Producer

End of the Rainbow

Photo by Brian Mapp

CREW

Front Row (L-R): Joseph Pittman, Pamela Loetterle, Julian Andres Arango, Eugenia Raines, Maria Lugo

Middle Row (L-R): Joe Luongo, Matt Maloney, Mark Dobrow, Rachel Zack

Back Row (L-R): Stephanie Wallis, Jon Jordan, Stephen Hills, Joanna Lynne Staub, Elizabeth Coleman, Mike Smanko, Del Miskie, Mike Martinez, Carlos Jaramillo, Michele Moyna, Carole Hollenbeck, Dexter Luke

---

STAFF FOR *END OF THE RAINBOW*

GENERAL MANAGEMENT
JOEY PARNES PRODUCTIONS
Joey Parnes

S.D. Wagner   John Johnson
Kim Sellon   Kit Ingui
Nathan V. Koch

PRESS REPRESENTATIVE
O&M Co.
Rick Miramontez   Andy Snyder

UK GENERAL MANAGER FOR LEE DEAN
Mardi Metters

FOR THE GUTHRIE THEATER
Joe Dowling, Director
Jacques Brunswick, Chief Administrative Officer
Dianne Brennan, Development Director
Frank Butler, Production Director
Trish Santini, External Relations Director
John Miller-Stephany, Associate Artistic Director

CASTING
Pat McCorkle, Casting Director
Joe Lopick, Casting Associate
Carter Niles, Casting Associate

Production Stage Manager ....Mark Dobrow
Stage Manager ....Rachel Zack
Company Manager ....Kim Sellon
Assistant Company Manager ....Kit Ingui

Management Associate ....Nathan V. Koch
Associate Lighting Designer ....Caroline Chao
Associate Sound Designer ....Joanna Lynne Staub
Assistant Director ....Benjamin Shaw
Dialect Coach ....Kate Wilson
Production Carpenter ....Larry Morley
Production Properties ....Mike Smanko
Production Electrician ....Dan Coey
Moving Light Programmer ....Michael Hill
Production Sound/A1 ....Joanna Lynne Staub
Deck Sound/A2 ....Liz Coleman
Wardrobe Supervisor ....Roberto Bevenger Gonzalez
Dressers ....Julian Andres Arango, Del Miskie
Hair Supervisor ....Jon Jordan
UK Technical Supervisor ....Leigh Porter
Music Copyist ....Emily Grishman
Production Assistants ....Sarah Howell,
Bethany Wood
Management Assistant ....Chie Morita
Management Intern ....Emily DaSilva
Advertising, Marketing & Sales ....aka/
Elizabeth Furze, Scott A. Moore,
Andrew Damer, Pippa Bexon,
Bashan Aquart, Mary Littell, Adam Jay,
Janette Roush, Shane Marshall Brown
Interactive ....aka/Erin Rech, Jen Taylor
Press Associates ....Molly Barnett,
Jaron Caldwell, Philip Carrubba,
Jon Dimond, Joyce Friedmann,
Richard Hillman, Yufen Kung,
Chelsea Nachman, Elizabeth Wagner,
Sarah Babin, Michael Jorgensen

Legal Counsel ....Loeb & Loeb LLP/
Seth Gelblum, Esq.,
David Schmerler, Esq.,
Jack S. Yeh, Esq.
Music Rights Acquisition ....Abigail Kende/
Tele-Cinema
Accountants ....Rosenberg, Neuwirth &
Kuchner/Mark A. D'Ambrosi,
Patricia M. Pedersen
Banking ....City National Bank/
Stephanie Dalton, Michele Gibbons
Insurance ....AON/Albert G. Ruben,
George Walden, Claudia B. Kaufman
Payroll ....Castellana Services Inc./
Lance Castellana, James Castellana,
Norman Sewell
Housing Coordination ....Road Concierge/
Lisa Morris
Visa Coordination ....Elise-Ann Konstantin/
E-AK Visa Services, LLC
Physical Therapy ....Performing Arts Physical Therapy
Production Photographer ....Carol Rosegg
Opening Night
Coordination ....The Lawrence Company/
Michael Lawrence
Car Service.....................................IBA Limousine

---

CREDITS
Scenery built and painted by Guthrie Theater Scene Shop. Automation and show control by Show Motion, Inc., Milford, CT, using the AC2 computerized motion control system. Lighting equipment from Hudson Sound and Light

End of the Rainbow

Correspondent: Jay Russell, "BBC Interviewer/Porter/ASM"

Opening Night Gifts: The day we left for the Guthrie Theater, the producers got us all fab fleece sweatshirts with the show's logo. First day at the Belasco they got us all pillows embroidered with red shoes and a wand saying "There's no Place Like Home." For the opening night on Broadway, Tracie got us all Crystal Beer Steins from Tiffany's (you can never have enough!). EOTR Water Bottles from stage management, gorgeous handmade glittery Judy ornaments from Jon Jordan (Hair), glitter snow globe with ruby slippers from Terry Johnson.

Most Exciting Celebrity Visitor: Favorite so far would have to be Elaine Stritch. On opening night four of us were raising a glass of bubbly in our "Rainbow Room" when she walked in and surprised us all. I've been a fan for so long and loved her in her one-woman show, *At Liberty*. Since that show I often quote her, especially when Noël Coward used to call her "Stritchy." So, when she walked in, I didn't think and just blurted out "STRITCHY!!" like she was an old friend. Having never met me before, she looked at me like I had three heads. Happily she loved the show and loved Tracie's performance so my faux pas passed without too much ado. Elaine's comment to Tracie that night was, "Don't let the producers know I said this but...Don't do matinees".

Actor Who Performed the Most Roles in This Show: That would be me, with three roles.

Broadway Debuts: Tracie, Tom, Don Noble and Erik Heger!!!

Special Backstage Rituals: Tom, Michael and I have a ritual where we gather offstage left to watch Tracie do the encore every time she does it. We love watching it and continually are in awe of her energy and stamina and even after all these months constantly say to each other, "How does she do it?!" We greet her as she exits

Tracie Bennett throws herself into the Encore on opening night.

and then we all tend to follow her backstage to our dressing rooms like three little ducklings following Mama Duck.

Favorite Moments During Each Performance: I'd have to say watching Tracie do "Over the Rainbow" each night from off stage right. Just love it and feel so lucky to have such a great view of it each night. We also all love hearing Tom Pelphrey's laugh on and off the stage. It is huge and infectious and so genuine. Tracie is constantly stunned at how he can laugh so genuinely and so truthfully every night in the play. Not such an easy thing to do. Tom also talks about the moment in Act II when he forces Judy to swallow the pills, and the often very vocal response from the audience each night—everything from "No! NO, don't do it!" to boos and hisses. One night he got a distinct feeling from some audience members that they might rush the stage to stop him. We LOVE live theatre!!

Favorite Opening Night Memory: At the curtain call Tracie was given HUGE bouquets of roses and then single roses were thrown up onto the stage covering it and her. It was unlike anything we've ever seen. Truly a gorgeous sight and she was so genuinely moved. However, she still had the Encore to do and couldn't do it on a stage floor covered in flowers. Eventually when all of us had our hands full of roses and they were still throwing them she said, "Please, you've got to stop! I've got another number to do!" It was incredible.

Favorite In-Theatre Gathering Place: The smokers in the company would probably say the back alley outside the stage door, but I'd have to say The Rainbow Room. This incredible room next to Tracie's dressing room was designed as a post show 'receiving room'. Pictures of Judy, tix stubs, posters, an old trunk that was transformed into a bar, and a wall of red roses (just like in *A Star Is Born*) for photo ops with celebs.

Favorite Off-Site Hangout: Coffee from Gregory's Coffee. Post-show our favorite place is probably The Long Room across the street though we have been known to frequent the Lamb's Club, Café Un Deux Trois and the Bistro as well. We tend to stay right near the theatre and have yet to really venture out of the 'hood. I think we all got used to staying close while we were at the Guthrie where there was a great bar/restaurant IN the theatre complex, so that was our nightly ritual.

Favorite Birthday Rituals: Whoever's birthday it is is greeted offstage right immediately after the show with the cake/pie/cupcakes of their choice and some good quality Champers courtesy of our producers.

Most-Asked Questions: Is Tracie really singing? Answer: Yes.
Is Michael really playing the piano? Answer: No.
How does Tracie do what she does eight times a

LLC. Sound equipment from PRG Audio. Costumes constructed by Guthrie Theater Costume Shop.

Rehearsed at Foxwoods Theatre Rehearsal Studios.

Tracie Bennett Sings Judy: Songs From End of the Rainbow *and Other Garland Classics* available from Masterworks Broadway.

Souvenir merchandise provided by Encore Merchandising, Inc.

SPECIAL THANKS

Silkstone (Jamie DuMont, Phil Winser, Ben Towill), Julian Christenberry, Amy Carothers, Louise Foisy, Barry Rosenberg, Stuart Levy, Jeff Harris, Ken Lundie, Jane Pfeffer

MUSIC RIGHTS

"I Can't Give You Anything But Love," Dorothy Fields and Jimmy McHugh. Shapiro, Bernstein & Co., Inc. on behalf of Aldi Music Company, EMI April Music Inc. "Just in Time," Betty Comden, Adolph Green, Jule Styne. Chappell & Co., Inc. on behalf of Stratford Music Corporation. "The Trolley Song," Hugh Martin and Ralph Blane. EMI Feist Catalog Inc. "The Man That Got Away," Ira Gershwin and Harold Arlen. WB Music Corp. on behalf of New World Music Company Ltd., Harwin Music Co. "When You're Smiling (The Whole World Smiles With You)," Mark Fisher, Joe Goodwin, Larry Shay. EMI Mills Music, Inc., Music by Shay. "Blue Skies," Irving Berlin. Irving Berlin Music Corp. "Dancing in the Dark," Arthur Schwartz and Howard Dietz. Arthur Schwartz Music Publishing Ltd., WB Music Corp. "Come Rain or Come Shine," Johnny Mercer and Harold Arlen. WB Music Corp. on behalf of the Johnny Mercer Foundation, S.A. Music LLC. "Over the Rainbow," E.Y. "Yip" Harburg and Harold Arlen. EMI Feist Catalog Inc. "By Myself," Arthur Schwartz and Howard Dietz. Arthur Schwartz Music Publishing Ltd., Chappell & Co., Inc.

End of the Rainbow
SCRAPBOOK

(L-R): Tom Pelphrey, Tracie Bennett and Michael Cumpsty cope with a cascade of roses on opening night,

Photo by Joseph Marzullo/WENN

week? Answer: God knows.

Favorite Therapies: Tracie has quick-change stations on each side of the stage stocked with Ricolas, Vitamin Water Zero, as well as Manuka Honey that keep her going.

We all love the Keurig Coffee Maker in the basement as well.

Favorite Post-show Therapy: This is all about the Tracie Bennett Cosmopolitan (at the Long Room they now just call it a 'Bennett'). Substitute Triple Sec with a drop of Cointreau and you've got a Bennett!

Memorable Ad-Lib: When Judy is asking what the BBC Interviewer is like in Act I her line is supposed to be, "What's he gonna do? Piss on me, or Kiss my Ass?!" In performance one night, she famously said, "What's he gonna do? Kiss me, or Piss on my Ass?!" All I can say is I'm glad I wasn't on stage then as Tom and Tracie were unable to look at each other for the rest of the scene.

Cell Phone Rings, Cell Phone Photos or Texting Incidents During a Performance: Tracie is amazed at how vocal and aggressive folks get in the audiences here in New York when a cell phone goes off (which is quite often). She says in the UK people sigh and groan but that is usually the extent of it. Here there are full on arguments starting with "Turn off the damn phone!" and often escalating from there. All while the show is going on. Also, Tracie says at the top of Act II every night when she goes out in the dark to her place the entire audience is lit up as everyone finishes their texts and tweets and calls and turns off their phones. She looks out and sees all their faces lit up.

Memorable Press Encounter: At the Plaza Hotel on opening night when Tracie arrived (covered in Verdura jewels) we all gathered to take company pictures. Our lovely press guys, Rick and Andy, said the three of us should pick

her up. We all looked at them like they were nuts and Rick said, "It'll be the shot that is shown around the world" and so we did, laughing like crazy. And it was everywhere for days after.

Memorable Curtain Call: An older gentleman in the front row was up on his feet before we even got onstage and was screaming at the top of his lungs towards Tracie, "THANK YOU! THANK YOU!!! WELCOME TO AMERICA! JUST ONE MORE!!!" It was quite something.

Memorable Stage Door Fan Encounters: The Judy Fans surpass almost any fans I've ever seen. They all want to meet Tracie and tell her their personal stories about having seen Judy onstage, or loving her since childhood, et cetera. It is so great to see their reactions to how different Tracie looks offstage (blonde, Manchester accent, et cetera). But she signs every single program and poster every night, takes photos and hears all their stories. Tracie says the support and respect she receives nightly just blows her away. People talk about what Judy went through and just recently she said one man asked her if she "can feel the warmth from the audience towards her?" Humbling for sure.

My own personal stage door fave is when folks actually do recognize me as the guy who played the three small roles in the show. Just recently there was a bunch of folks as I went down the line signing. They were so complimentary about the characters I had played, with very specific comments about them. I was flying high and feeling pretty special...until the last lady in line said, "You were SO wonderful! That goodbye scene just broke my heart!" and then I realized she thought I was Michael Cumpsty!

Fastest Costume Change: Tracie getting into the red dress. Del, her dresser, says it's about seven seconds. Though the most complicated is from her copper beaded pantsuit (the one Judy famously stole from *Valley of the Dolls* when she

was fired) into the nightie.

Busiest Day at the Box Office: The day after opening when the *New York Times* review came out.

Catchphrases Only the Company Would Recognize: "C'mon, just come for one!!!" "Not gonna do it!

Mascot: Tracie's dear (and incredibly generous) friend John Addy whom we have all nicknamed "Miss Addy." He is a huge fan of the show and a great supporter of all of us with his incredible gifts of orchids, champagne, perfume and cologne...the list goes on and on.

Nicknames: For Tracie: Herself, Dame Bennett.
For Tom: Mrs. Pelphrey
For Michael: Mrs. Cumpsty
For me: Monty
For Erik Heger: Mrs. Viking

Ghostly Encounter Backstage: Tracie had a pretty extraordinary one. The Belasco is famously known for being haunted by the ghost of David Belasco. Though when she came to New York about a year or so before we opened to look at possible Broadway Theatres she had no idea of the legend. The Belasco was the first of five theatres she saw. She arrived before the producers and others. Patrick, the security guy, let her in and let her onto the stage by herself. In the UK they don't have ghost lights like we do so the only way they know them is from *Gypsy*. Tracie went out onto the darkened stage, grabbed the ghost light and sang a bit of "I had a dream." She was just overwhelmed by the whole thing and was in tears and felt that even though she had four more theatres to see she just had a feeling that this was going to be the one. After she had a bit of a tour with the producers she asked Patrick if she could see the dressing room she would have if they chose this theatre. Patrick jingled all his keys and let her into the star dressing room. Then Tracie said she felt a presence. She didn't see anything but felt the very strong presence of a man. Not too tall, with dark hair. Patrick asked if she was all right and when she described what she felt he said, "That'll be Mr. Belasco, ma'am." Tracie felt this man studying her, checking her out, wary of her. She went into the dressing room and had a bit of a 'chat' with him. She said she felt his energy changing from judgement and wariness to one that was more twinkly and a bit flirty, and then a very powerful feeling of warmth as if he seemed to say, "I approve".

Coolest Thing About Being in This Show: Besides all of us having our own dressing rooms? Mmmmm.... Would have to say that we are all bowled over by the audience response each night—especially at the curtain call. Standing ovations seem *de rigueur* on Broadway in recent years. But watching the audiences leap to their feet and scream the way they do each night is unlike anything I've ever seen (as an actor or an audience member). It truly feels like they have seen Judy Garland and are so grateful and overwhelmed by it and seeing and hearing that each night is just beyond compare.

An Evening with Patti LuPone and Mandy Patinkin

First Preview: November 16, 2011. Opened: November 21, 2011.
Closed January 13, 2011 after 6 Previews and 57 Performances.

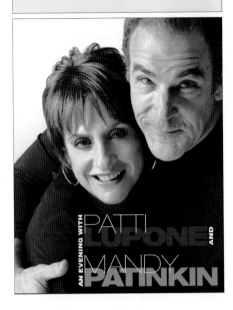

Two-person concert show of Broadway and pop hits featuring the onetime co-stars of Evita.

CAST
(in alphabetical order)

PATTI LuPONE
MANDY PATINKIN

ORCHESTRA
PAUL FORD: Music Director, Piano
JOHN BEAL: Bass

⊛ ETHEL BARRYMORE THEATRE
243 West 47th Street
A Shubert Organization Theatre

Philip J. Smith, *Chairman*   Robert E. Wankel, *President*

STACI LEVINE   THE DODGERS   JON B. PLATT   JESSICA R. JENEN

Present

Conceived by MANDY PATINKIN and PAUL FORD

Production Design DAVID KORINS	Lighting Design ERIC CORNWELL	Sound Design DANIEL J. GERHARD
Costume Design JON CAN COSKUNSES	Production Stage Manager MATTHEW AARON STERN	Production Manager AURORA PRODUCTIONS
Press Representative BONEAU/BRYAN-BROWN	Advertising and Marketing SERINO/COYNE	Company Manager JENNIFER HINDMAN KEMP

General Manager
RICHARDS/CLIMAN, INC.

Executive Producer
GROUNDSWELL THEATRICALS, INC.

Music Director
PAUL FORD

Dance Consultant
ANN REINKING

Director
MANDY PATINKIN

1/2/12

(L-R): Mandy Patinkin,
Patti LuPone

An Evening with Patti LuPone and Mandy Patinkin

MUSICAL NUMBERS

ACT I

"Another Hundred People" ....Stephen Sondheim (*Company*)
"When"...Stephen Sondheim (*Evening Primrose*)
"A Cockeyed Optimist"* ....Richard Rodgers & Oscar Hammerstein II (*South Pacific*)
"Twin Soliloquies" ....Richard Rodgers & Oscar Hammerstein II (*South Pacific*)
"Some Enchanted Evening"..................Richard Rodgers & Oscar Hammerstein II (*South Pacific*)
"Some Enchanted Evening" Reprise ....Richard Rodgers & Oscar Hammerstein II (*South Pacific*)
"Getting Married Today" ....Stephen Sondheim (*Company*)
"Loving You" ....Stephen Sondheim (*Passion*)
"A Cockeyed Optimist" Reprise ....Richard Rodgers & Oscar Hammerstein II (*South Pacific*)
"I'm Old Fashioned" ....Jerome Kern & Johnny Mercer (*You Were Never Lovelier*)
"I Have the Room Above Her" ....Jerome Kern & Oscar Hammerstein II (*Show Boat*)
"Baby It's Cold Outside" ....Frank Loesser (*Neptune's Daughter*)
"Everybody Says Don't" ....Stephen Sondheim (*Anyone Can Whistle*)
"A Quiet Thing" ....John Kander & Fred Ebb (*Flora, the Red Menace*)
"It Takes Two" ....Stephen Sondheim (*Into the Woods*)
"I Won't Dance" ....Jerome Kern (*Roberta*)
"I Want a Man" ....Vincent Youmans & Oscar Hammerstein II (*Rainbow*)
"April in Fairbanks" ....Murray Grand (*New Faces of 1956*)

ACT II

"Old Folks" ....John Kander & Fred Ebb (*70, Girls, 70*)
"Everything's Coming Up Roses"....................Jule Styne & Stephen Sondheim (*Gypsy*)
"The God-Why-Don't-You-Love-Me Blues" ....Stephen Sondheim (*Follies*)
"The Hills of Tomorrow" ....Stephen Sondheim (*Merrily We Roll Along*)
"Merrily We Roll Along" ....Stephen Sondheim (*Merrily We Roll Along*)
"Old Friends" ....Stephen Sondheim (*Merrily We Roll Along*)
"Like It Was" ....Stephen Sondheim (*Merrily We Roll Along*)
"Oh What a Circus" ....Sir Andrew Lloyd Webber & Tim Rice (*Evita*)
"Don't Cry for Me Argentina" ....Sir Andrew Lloyd Webber & Tim Rice (*Evita*)
"Somewhere That's Green" ....Howard Ashman & Alan Menken (*Little Shop of Horrors*)
"In Buddy's Eyes" ....Stephen Sondheim (*Follies*)
"You're a Queer One,
  Julie Jordan"** ....Richard Rodgers & Oscar Hammerstein II (*Carousel*)
"If I Loved You" ....Richard Rodgers & Oscar Hammerstein II (*Carousel*)
"If I Loved You" Reprise ....Richard Rodgers & Oscar Hammerstein II (*Carousel*)
"What's the Use of Wond'rin'" ....Richard Rodgers & Oscar Hammerstein II (*Carousel*)
"If I Loved You" Reprise ....Richard Rodgers & Oscar Hammerstein II (*Carousel*)
"You'll Never Walk Alone" ....Richard Rodgers & Oscar Hammerstein II (*Carousel*)

SOUTH PACIFIC. Music by Richard Rodgers. Lyrics by Oscar Hammerstein II. Book by Oscar Hammerstein II and Joshua Logan. Adapted from the Pulitzer Prize-winning novel *Tales of the South Pacific* by James A. Michener.

**CAROUSEL.* Music by Richard Rodgers. Book and Lyrics by Oscar Hammerstein II. Based on Ferenc Molnar's play *Liliom* as adapted by Benjamin F. Glazer. Original Dances by Agnes de Mille. These selections are used by special arrangement with Rodgers and Hammerstein: an Imagem Company, www.rnh.com. All rights reserved.

All selections by Stephen Sondheim are used by special arrangement with Stephen Sondheim.

Patti LuPone
Performer

Mandy Patinkin
*Performer,
Director*

Ann Reinking
Dance Consultant

David Korins
Production Design

Paul Ford
*Music Director,
Piano*

Staci Levine
Producer

Patti LuPone and Mandy Patinkin

Photo by Joan Marcus

An Evening with Patti LuPone and Mandy Patinkin

David R. Richards, Tamar Haimes
Richards/Climan, Inc.
General Manager

Michael David,
The Dodgers
Producer

Edward Strong,
The Dodgers
Producer

Rocco Landesman,
The Dodgers
Producer

Des McAnuff,
The Dodgers
Producer

Jon B. Platt
Producer

STAFF FOR
*AN EVENING WITH PATTI LuPONE
AND MANDY PATINKIN*

EXECUTIVE PRODUCER
GROUNDSWELL THEATRICALS, INC.
Staci Levine
Tim Hurley   Richard Cerato

GENERAL MANAGER
RICHARDS/CLIMAN, INC.
David R. Richards   Tamar Haimes
Michael Sag   Kyle Bonder
Jessica Fried   Jaqueline Kolek

COMPANY MANAGER
Jennifer Hindman Kemp

PRODUCTION MANAGER
AURORA PRODUCTIONS
Gene O'Donovan, Ben Heller,
Stephanie Sherline, Jarid Sumner, Liza Luxenberg,
Anita Shah, Anthony Jusino, Steven Dalton,
Eugenio Saenz Flores, Isaac Katzanek, Melissa Mazdra

PRESS REPRESENTATIVE
BONEAU/BRYAN-BROWN
Adrian Bryan-Brown   Susanne Tighe   Christine Olver

PRODUCTION STAGE
MANAGER ....Matthew Aaron Stern
Stage Manager ....Laura Skolnik
Producer Associate ....Tim Hurley
Assistant Dance Consultant ....Jim Borstelmann
Associate Scenic Designer ....Rod Lemmond
Assistant Lighting Designer ....Cory Pattak
Assistant to the
    Lighting Designer ....Amy Francis Schott
Assistant to the Sound Designer ....Alexis Parsons
Production Electrician ....Craig Caccamise
Production Sound Engineers ....Phil Lojo,
                                          Paul Delcioppo
Assistant Sound Engineer ....Dan Hochstine
Head Sound/Mixer ....Mark Fiore
Lead Followspot ....Brian Renoni
Wardrobe Supervisor ....Lyle Jones
Hair/Wig Supervisor ....Ruth Carsch
Draper ....Georgia Theodosis
Moving Light Programmer ....Sean Beach
Publicist for Miss LuPone ....Philip Rinaldi
Assistant to Miss LuPone ....Pamela Lyster
Advertising ....Serino/Coyne/
                              Greg Corradetti, Sandy Block
                          Andrei Oleinik, Kim Hewski,
                            Jon Erwin, Brian Wright

Digital Outreach & Website ....Serino/Coyne/
                            Jim Glaub, Chip Meyrelles,
                        Laurie Connor, Kevin Keating,
                        Whitney Creighton, Crystal Chase
Press Associates ....Chris Boneau, Jim Byk,
                        Jackie Green, Joe Perrotta,
                    Matt Polk, Aaron Meier, Jessica Johnson,
                    Heath Schwartz, Amy Kass, Kelly Guiod,
                    Emily Meagher, Michael Strassheim,
                        Linnae Hodzic, Kevin Jones,
                        Holly Kinney, Amanda Sales
Press Interns ....Derek Downs, Dayna Johnson,
                                          Caryn Savitz
Banking ....JPMorganChase/
                                          Grace Correa
Insurance ....DeWitt Stern Group/
                        Anthony Pittari, Peter Shoemaker
Accountants ....Schall & Ashenfarb CPAs LLP/
                              Ira Schall, Lauren White
Comptroller ....Elliott Aronstam
Legal Counsel ....Davis, Wright, Tremaine LLP/
                        M. Graham Coleman, Andrew Owens
Payroll ....Castellana Services, Inc.
Merchandising ....The Araca Group
Opening Night Coordination ....John Haber
Production Photographer ....Joan Marcus
Production Photos ....Brigitte Lacombe
Tour Marketing & Press Rep .....CMajor Marketing, Inc./
                                          Catherine Major

The touring production of
***AN EVENING WITH
PATTI LUPONE AND MANDY PATINKIN***
is represented by
AVID TOURING GROUP, LTD
L. GLENN POPPLETON
Jessica Francis

CREDITS
Lighting and sound equipment from Production Resource Group. Scenery fabrication by PRG-Scenic Technologies, a division of Production Resource Group, LLC, New Windsor, NY. Miss LuPone's car service provided by Novelride, Inc. Mr. Patinkin's clothes provided by Giorgio Armani. Makeup provided by M•A•C. Special thanks to Bra*Tenders for undergarments and hosiery. Piano generously provided by Steinway & Sons.

SPECIAL THANKS
Victoria Traube, Carol Kaplan, Lois Smith, Nicole Borrelli Hearn and Opus 3 Artists, Amy Rogers, Cathryn Salamone, Matthew Curiano, Bruce MacPherson, Angelina Avallone, Roman Kusayev

Many thanks to past and present members of the Patti-Mandy Tour:

Theoni Aldredge (in loving memory), John Beal, Jim Borstelmann, Jeff Carney, Richard Cerato, Eric Cornwell, Barbara Crompton, Judith Daitsman, Paul Ford, Mark Fiore, Jessica Francis, Dick Gallagher (in loving memory), Dan Gerhard, Ron Gubin, Ann Hould-Ward, Tim Hurley, Gayle Jeffery, Lyle Jones, Ingrid Kloss, David Korins, Woody Lane, Rod Lemmond, Staci Levine, Pam Lyster, Catherine Major, Otts Munderloh, Alexis Parsons, L. Glenn Poppleton, Ann Reinking, Bob Rendon, Laura Skolnik, Matt Stern, Danielle Vignevich, Peter Wolf and Michael David, Sally Morse and everyone at the Dodgers who helped birth the concert in 2002.

For more information on
An Evening with Patti LuPone and Mandy Patinkin,
visit their websites:
www.pattiandmandyonbroadway.com
www.pattiandmandy.com
www.pattilupone.net
and
www.mandypatinkin.org

An Evening with Patti LuPone and Mandy Patinkin
SCRAPBOOK

Photos by Joseph Marzullo/WENN

1. Patti LuPone and Mandy Patinkin share a curtain call on opening night.
2. LuPone and Patinkin accept flowers and an ovation.
3. LuPone (C) with her son Joshua Johnston (L) and husband Matthew Johnston at the cast party at Glass House Tavern. Joshua's 21st birthday was celebrated from the stage at the premiere.
4. LuPone at Glass House Tavern.
5. LuPone and Patinkin flank lead producer Staci Levine.

Evita

First Preview: March 12, 2012. Opened: April 5, 2012.
Still running as of May 31, 2012.

PLAYBILL®

Beautiful, passionate and ambitious Eva Duarte grows up in poverty in backwater Argentina. She tries to improve her lot in life by bedding a series of powerful men, eventually allying herself with army colonel Juan Perón. Using the mass media to touch the common people, the descamisados ("shirtless ones"), who call her "Evita," she builds a powerful political base to get Perón elected president. However, the real power behind his throne is Evita, whose dreams for enriching herself, Perón and Argentina know no bounds. Is this woman a gangster, a saint—or a combination of both?

CAST
(in order of appearance)

Che	RICKY MARTIN
Eva	ELENA ROGER
Eva (at Wed. eve. and Sat. mat. performances)	CHRISTINA DeCICCO
Magaldi	MAX VON ESSEN
Perón	MICHAEL CERVERIS
Mistress	RACHEL POTTER
Child	MAYA JADE FRANK or ISABELA MONER

ENSEMBLE

ASHLEY AMBER, GEORGE LEE ANDREWS,
ERIC L. CHRISTIAN, KRISTINE COVILLO,
COLIN CUNLIFFE, MARGOT DE LA BARRE,
BRADLEY DEAN, REBECCA EICHENBERGER,
MELANIE FIELD,
CONSTANTINE GERMANACOS,

Continued on next page

⇒N⇐ MARQUIS THEATRE
UNDER THE DIRECTION OF JAMES M. NEDERLANDER AND JAMES L. NEDERLANDER

HAL LUFTIG   SCOTT SANDERS PRODUCTIONS

ROY FURMAN   YASUHIRO KAWANA   ALLAN S. GORDON/ADAM S. GORDON   JAMES L. NEDERLANDER
TERRY ALLEN KRAMER   GUTTERMAN FULD CHERNOFF/PITTSBURGH CLO   THOUSAND STARS PRODUCTIONS
ADAM BLANSHAY   ADAM ZOTOVICH   ROBERT AHRENS   STEPHANIE P. McCLELLAND   CAROLE L. HABER
RICARDO HORNOS   CAROL FINEMAN   BRIAN SMITH   WARREN & JÂLÉ TREPP

RICKY MARTIN   ELENA ROGER   MICHAEL CERVERIS

EVITA

Lyrics by		Music by
TIM RICE		**ANDREW LLOYD WEBBER**

MAX VON ESSEN   *with*   RACHEL POTTER

and at certain performances
CHRISTINA DeCICCO
plays the role of "Eva"

ASHLEY AMBER   GEORGE LEE ANDREWS   WENDI BERGAMINI   ERIC L. CHRISTIAN   KRISTINE COVILLO   COLIN CUNLIFFE
MARGOT DE LA BARRE   BRADLEY DEAN   REBECCA EICHENBERGER   MELANIE FIELD   JENNIE FORD   MAYA JADE FRANK
CONSTANTINE GERMANACOS   LAUREL HARRIS   BAHIYAH HIBAH   NICK KENKEL   BRAD LITTLE   ERICA MANSFIELD
EMILY MECHLER   ISABELA MONER   SYDNEY MORTON   JESSICA LEA PATTY   ALEKS PEVEC   KRISTIE DALE SANDERS
TIMOTHY SHEW   MICHAELJON SLINGER   JOHNNY STELLARD   ALEX MICHAEL STOLL   DANIEL TORRES   MATT WALL

Scenic & Costume Design	Lighting Design	Sound Design
CHRISTOPHER ORAM	**NEIL AUSTIN**	**MICK POTTER**
Wig & Hair Design	Projection Design	Casting
RICHARD MAWBEY	**ZACHARY BOROVAY**	**TELSEY + COMPANY**
Technical Supervisor	Production Stage Manager	Associate Director	Associate Choreographer
CHRISTOPHER C. SMITH	**MICHAEL J. PASSARO**	**SETH SKLAR-HEYN**	**CHRIS BAILEY**
Advertising	Press	Marketing Services	General Management
SPOTCO	**THE HARTMAN GROUP**	**TYPE A MARKETING / ANNE RIPPEY**	**BESPOKE THEATRICALS**
Music Supervisor/Conductor	Orchestrations	Dance Arrangements	Music Coordinator
KRISTEN BLODGETTE	**ANDREW LLOYD WEBBER & DAVID CULLEN**	**DAVID CHASE**	**DAVID LAI**

Choreographed by
ROB ASHFORD

Directed by
MICHAEL GRANDAGE

ORIGINALLY PRODUCED BY ANDRÉ PTASZYNSKI FOR THE REALLY USEFUL THEATRE COMPANY.
WORLD PREMIERE OF *EVITA* DIRECTED BY HAROLD PRINCE IN 1978.

4/5/12

Elena Roger

Photo by Richard Termine

Evita

MUSICAL NUMBERS

ACT I

"Requiem"	The Company
"Oh, What a Circus"	Che and Company
"On This Night of a Thousand Stars"	Magaldi
"Eva, Beware of the City"	Magaldi, Eva, Che and Family
"Buenos Aires"	Eva, Che and Company
"Goodnight and Thank You"	Che, Eva and Lovers
"The Art of the Possible"	Perón, Eva and Officers
"Charity Concert"	Magaldi, Che, Perón and Company
"I'd Be Surprisingly Good for You"	Eva and Perón
"Another Suitcase in Another Hall"	Mistress
"Perón's Latest Flame"	Che and Company
"A New Argentina"	Perón, Eva, Che and Company

ACT II

"On the Balcony of the Casa Rosada"	Perón and Company
"Don't Cry for Me Argentina"	Eva
"High Flying, Adored"	Che and Eva
"Rainbow High"	Eva and Valets
"Rainbow Tour"	Perón, Che, Eva and Company
"The Chorus Girl Hasn't Learned"	Eva and Company
"And the Money Kept Rolling In"	Che and Company
"Santa Evita"	Child and Company
"Waltz for Eva and Che"	Eva and Che
"You Must Love Me"	Eva
"She Is a Diamond"	Perón and Officers
"Dice Are Rolling"	Perón and Eva
"Eva's Final Broadcast"	Eva
"Montage"	The Company
"Lament"	Eva

ORCHESTRA

Conductor: KRISTEN BLODGETTE
Associate Conductor: WILLIAM WALDROP
Woodwinds: JAMES ERCOLE,
    KATHLEEN NESTER
Trumpets: JAMES DE LA GARZA,
    ALEX HOLTON
Trombone: TIM ALBRIGHT
French Horn: SHELAGH ABATE
Guitar: MICHAEL AARONS
Bass: JEFF COOPER
Drums: BILL LANHAM
Percussion: DAVE ROTH
Keyboards: ANDY EINHORN,
    WILLIAM WALDROP
Keyboards/Accordion: EDDIE MONTEIRO
Violins: VICTOR COSTANZI,
    KATHERINE LIVOLSI-LANDAU,
    SUZY PERELMAN
Viola: DAVID BLINN
Cello: MAIRI DORMAN-PHANEUF

Music Coordinator: DAVID LAI
Synthesizer Programmer: STUART ANDREWS
Music Copyist: ROB MEFFE

Cast Continued

LAUREL HARRIS, BAHIYAH HIBAH,
NICK KENKEL, BRAD LITTLE,
ERICA MANSFIELD, EMILY MECHLER,
SYDNEY MORTON, JESSICA LEA PATTY,
ALEKS PEVEC, RACHEL POTTER, KRISTIE
DALE SANDERS, TIMOTHY SHEW,
JOHNNY STELLARD, ALEX MICHAEL
STOLL, DANIEL TORRES

UNDERSTUDIES
For Eva:
CHRISTINA DeCICCO, LAUREL HARRIS,
JESSICA LEA PATTY
For Che:
MAX VON ESSEN, DANIEL TORRES
For Perón:
BRADLEY DEAN, BRAD LITTLE
For Magaldi:
CONSTANTINE GERMANACOS,
MATT WALL
For Mistress:
EMILY MECHLER, SYDNEY MORTON

SWINGS
WENDI BERGAMINI, JENNIE FORD,
MICHAELJON SLINGER, MATT WALL

ASSISTANT DANCE CAPTAIN
MATT WALL

DANCE CAPTAIN
JENNIE FORD

*Elena Roger appears courtesy of Actors' Equity
Association.*

SETTING:
Junin and Buenos Aires, Argentina
TIME:
1934-1952

Ricky Martin (front) and
the Company

Photo by Richard Termine

Evita

Ricky Martin
Che

Elena Roger
Eva

Michael Cerveris
Perón

Christina DeCicco
Eva Alternate

Max Von Essen
Magaldi

Rachel Potter
Mistress/Ensemble

Ashley Amber
Ensemble

George Lee Andrews
Ensemble

Wendi Bergamini
Swing

Eric L. Christian
Ensemble

Kristine Covillo
Ensemble

Colin Cunliffe
Ensemble

Margot De La Barre
Ensemble

Bradley Dean
Ensemble

Rebecca
Eichenberger
Ensemble

Melanie Field
Ensemble

Jennie Ford
*Swing/Dance
Captain*

Maya Jade Frank
Child

Constantine
Germanacos
Ensemble

Laurel Harris
Ensemble

Bahiyah Hibah
Ensemble

Nick Kenkel
Ensemble

Brad Little
Ensemble

Erica Mansfield
Ensemble

Emily Mechler
Ensemble

Isabela Moner
Child

Sydney Morton
Ensemble

Jessica Lea Patty
Ensemble

Aleks Pevec
Ensemble

Kristie Dale Sanders
Ensemble

Timothy Shew
Ensemble

Michaeljon Slinger
Swing

Johnny Stellard
Ensemble

Alex Michael Stoll
Ensemble

Daniel Torres
Ensemble

Evita

Matt Wall
Swing/Assistant Dance Captain

Andrew Lloyd Webber
The Really Useful Group
Licensor, Music and Orchestrations

Tim Rice
Book and Lyrics

Michael Grandage
Director

Rob Ashford
Choreographer

Christopher Oram
Scenic and Costume Design

Neil Austin
Lighting Design

Mick Potter
Sound Design

Richard Mawbey
Wig and Hair Design

Zachary Borovay
Projection Design

Bernard Telsey
Telsey + Company
Casting

Jason Goldsberry
Makeup Design

David Cullen
Co-Orchestrator

Kristen Blodgette
Music Supervisor/ Conductor

David Chase
Dance Arrangements

Seth Sklar-Heyn
Associate Director

David Lai
Music Coordinator

Christopher C. Smith
Technical Supervisor

Maggie Brohn
Bespoke Theatricals
General Management

Amy Jacobs
Bespoke Theatricals
General Management

Devin Keudell
Bespoke Theatricals
General Management

Nina Lannan
Bespoke Theatricals
General Management

Hal Luftig
Producer

Scott Sanders
Scott Sanders Productions
Producer

Roy Furman
Producer

Yasuhiro Kawana
Producer

Allan S. Gordon
Producer

Adam S. Gordon
Producer

James L. Nederlander
Producer

Terry Allen Kramer
Producer

Jay & Cindy Gutterman
Gutterman Fuld Chernoff/Pittsburgh CLO
Producers

James Fuld, Jr.
Gutterman Fuld Chernoff/Pittsburgh CLO
Producer

Van Kaplan,
Exec. Producer
Pittsburgh CLO
Producer

Wendy Federman
Thousand Stars Productions
Producer

Evita

Van Dean, Kenny Howard
The Broadway Consortium,
Thousand Stars Productions
Producers

Carl Moellenberg
Thousand Stars
Productions
Producer

Antonio Marion
Thousand Stars
Productions
Producer

Barbara
Manocherian
Thousand Stars
Productions
Producer

Michael A. Alden
Thousand Stars
Productions
Producer

Adam Blanshay
Producer

Adam Zotovich
Producer

Robert Ahrens
Producer

Stephanie P.
McClelland
Producer

Carole L. Haber
Producer

Ricardo Hornos
Producer

BOX OFFICE
Gary Flynn, Nick Kapovic

STAGE MANAGEMENT TEAM
Pat Sosnow (Stage Manager)
Michael J. Passaro (Production Stage Manager)
Jim Athens (Assistant Stage Manager)
Seth Sklar-Heyn (Associate Director)

STAGE DOOR
Juan Garcia

Evita

USHERS

Front Row (L-R): Rosaire Caso, Phyllis Weinsaft, Barbara Newsome, Jesse White

Middle Row (L-R): George Fitze, Michael Mejias, David Calhoun, Stanley Seidman, Iskritsa Ognianova, Mariea Crainiciuc

Back Row (L-R): Mamie Spruell, Sonia Torres, Heidi Giovine, Odalis Concepcion

CREW, WARDROBE, HAIR

Front Row (L-R): Scotty Cain, Jeannie Naughton, Vera Pizzarelli, Jay Woods, Katie Chick, Sean McMahon

Middle Row (L-R): Douglas Petitjean, Samantha Lawrence, Adam Girardet, Kathleen Mack, Rick Caroto, Jake Fry, Joe Valentino

Back Row (L-R): Kenny Sheehan, Brian Aman, Joe Sardo, Scott Mecionis, Derek Healy, Emilia Martin, Nathan Gehan, Jenny Pendergraft, Tanya Guercy-Blue, Deirdre LaBarre, Erick Mendinilla, Freddy Mecionis

Evita

STAFF FOR *EVITA*

GENERAL MANAGEMENT
BESPOKE THEATRICALS
Amy Jacobs
Maggie Brohn   Devin Keudell   Nina Lannan
Associate General Manager ....David Roth

COMPANY MANAGER
Nathan Gehan
Assistant Company Manager ....Kate Egan

GENERAL PRESS REPRESENTATIVE
THE HARTMAN GROUP
Michael Hartman
Leslie Baden Papa   Whitney Holden Gore

CASTING
TELSEY + COMPANY
Bernie Telsey CSA, Will Cantler CSA,
David Vaccari CSA, Bethany Knox CSA,
Craig Burns CSA, Tiffany Little Canfield CSA,
Rachel Hoffman CSA, Justin Huff CSA,
Patrick Goodwin CSA, Abbie Brady-Dalton CSA,
David Morris, Cesar A. Rocha, Andrew Femenella,
Karyn Casl, Kristina Bramhall, Jessie Malone

MARKETING SERVICES
TYPE A MARKETING
Anne Rippey   Elyce Henkin   Melissa Cohen

PRODUCTION STAGE
   MANAGER ....Michael J. Passaro
Stage Manager ....Pat Sosnow
Assistant Stage Manager ....Jim Athens
Associate Director ....Seth Sklar-Heyn
Associate Choreographer ....Chris Bailey
Dance Captain ....Jennie Ford
Assistant Dance Captain ....Matt Wall
Associate Scenic Designer ....Bryan Johnson
UK Scenic Associate ....Richard Kent
UK Scenic Assistants ....David Woodhead,
     Andrew Riley, Simon Anthony Wells
Associate Costume Designer ....Barry Doss
Assistant Costume Designers ....Christina Cocchiara,
     Robert J. Martin
Associate Lighting Designer ....Dan Walker
Assistant Lighting Designer ....Kristina Kloss
Lighting Programmer ....Rob Halliday
Associate Sound Designer ....Anthony Smolenski
Associate Projection Designer ....Driscoll A. Otto
Assistant Projection Designer ....Daniel Vatsky
Assistant to the Hair Designer ....Susan Pedersen
Makeup Designer ....Jason Goldsberry
Production Carpenter ....Donald J. Oberpriller
Fly Automation ....David Elmer
Production Electrician ....Jimmy Maloney
Associate Production Electrician ....Kevin Barry
Head Followspot ....Brian Aman
Production Sound ....Paul Delcioppo, Phil Lojo
Head Sound ....George Huckins
Assistant Sound ....John Dory
Production Properties/
   Head Properties ....Vera Pizzarelli
Wardrobe Supervisor ....Douglas Petitjean
Assistant Wardrobe Supervisor ....Deirdre LaBarre
Dresser for Mr. Martin ....Scotty Cain

Dresser for Ms. Roger ....Jeannie Naughton
Dresser for Mr. Cerveris ....Erick Medinilla
Dressers ....Tracey Diebold, Jake Fry,
     Adam Girardet, Tanya Guercy-Blue,
     Samantha Lawrence, Kathleen Mack,
     Jay Woods
Hair Supervisor ....Wanda Gregory
Hair Assistants ....Rick Caroto,
     Jenny Pendergraft, Emilia Martin
Assistant Synthesizer Programmer ....Dave Weiser
Children's Guardian ....Bridget Mills
Projection Research ....Sheila Maniar
Costume Production Assistant ....Carly J. Price
Costume Shoppers ....Adam Adelman,
     Edgar Contreras
UK Costume Design Liaison ....Stephanie Arditti
Costume Stitchers/
   Construction ....Katie Chick, Adam Girardet,
     Jamie Englehart, Libby Villanova,
     Erin Brooke Roth, Sandy Vojta
Costume Interns ....Kayla Quiter, Jana Violante,
     Aaron Simms, Cim Roesener,
     Elizabeth Gleason, Anne Liberman,
     Ryan Dodson, Todd Phillips, Maggie Ronck
Production Assistants ....Lee Micklin,
     Derric Nolte, Michael Ulreich
SDC Observer ....Stephen Kaliski
Associate to Mr. Luftig ....Brian Smith
Assistant to Mr. Sanders ....Jamie Quiroz
Children's Tutoring ....On Location Education/
     Alan Simon, Jodi Green
Physical Therapy ....Marc Hunter Hall
Production Photographer ....Richard Termine
Advertising ....SpotCo/Drew Hodges,
     Jim Edwards, Tom Greenwald,
     Tom McCann, Laura Ellis
Website & Online Marketing ....SpotCo/
     Sara Fitzpatrick, Marc Mettler,
     Michael Crowley, Meghan Ownbey
Accountant ....Robert Fried CPA/Fried &
     Kowgios CPAS LLP
Comptroller ....Galbraith & Company/
     Sarah Galbraith
General Management Associates ....Danielle Saks,
     Libby Fox
General Management Interns...............Michelle Heller,
     Jimmy Wilson
Press Representative Staff ....Katie Britton,
     Nicole Capatasto, Tom D'Ambrosio,
     Juliana Hannett, Bethany Larsen, Emily McGill,
     Matt Ross, Frances White, Wayne Wolfe
Insurance ....AON/Albert G. Ruben Insurance
     Services, Inc./Claudia Kaufman
Banking ....City National Bank/Michele Gibbons
Payroll ....Checks and Balances Payroll Inc.
Travel Agent ....Tzell Travel/The "A" Team,
     Andi Henig
Legal Counsel ....Franklin, Weinrib, Rudell &
     Vassallo, P.C.
Immigration Counsel ....Kramer Levin Naftalis &
     Frankel, LLP
Visa Consultant ....Lisa Carr
Merchandising ....Broadway Merchandising, LLC/
     Adam S. Gordon, David Eck
Opening Night
   Coordination ....The Lawrence Company

Opening Night Creative Consultant ....Susan Holland

Official Airline of *Evita* ....Delta

www.EvitaOnBroadway.com

CREDITS
Scenery and automation constructed by Show Motion. Set built by Terry Murphy Scenery. Costumes by Siobhan Nestor; Artur & Tailors; Cygnet Studio, Inc.; John Kristiansen; Sarah Timberlake; Jennifer Love; House of Savoia; Scafati; Jodek International Ltd. - David Douek, Daniel Webster; Costume Armour; Kaufman's Army & Navy; Beckenstein's Men's Fabric Czar. Handmade shoes by Fred Longtin, J.C. Theatrical, T.O.Dey custom made shoes, Worldtone Dance Shoes, Capezio Theatricals, LaDuca Shoes. Eva Perón's jewelry by Marcelo Toledo. Millinery by Anne Guay & Stetson Hats, Arnold S. Levine. Lighting equipment by PRG Lighting, Inc. Sound equipment by Sound Associates. Projection equipment by Scharff Weisberg, Inc. Props by Props Is Tops, Propstar, Tom Carroll Scenery, John Creech Design & Production. Soft goods by iWeiss Theatrical Solutions. Wigs made by Wig Specialities, London. Additional costume support provided by Tony Craney, Melissa Crawford, Shahnaz Khan, Alyce Gilbert, Kevin Hucke. Housing by ABA-Elizabeth Helke. Historical footage provided by Associated Press, ArenaPAL, Fondo Documental Museo Evita/Archivo General de la Nacion and Producers Library. Yamaha pianos provided courtesy of Yamaha Artist Services, New York. Drum heads provided by Remo, Inc. Drum sticks and mallets provided by Vic Firth Inc. Cymbals provided by Paiste America. Makeup provided by M•A•C Cosmetics. Event photography provided by Bruce Glikas.

SPECIAL THANKS
Diagio Americas, Inc., Swarovski Elements and
Steven Rivellino/8th Sea Inc.

Evita rehearsed at the
New 42nd Street Studios

Performance rights to *Evita*
are licensed by R&H Theatricals:
www.rnh.com

NEDERLANDER
Chairman ....**James M. Nederlander**
President ....**James L. Nederlander**

Executive Vice President
Nick Scandalios

Vice President Corporate Development **Charlene S. Nederlander**	Senior Vice President Labor Relations **Herschel Waxman**
Vice President **Jim Boese**	Chief Financial Officer **Freida Sawyer Belviso**

STAFF FOR THE MARQUIS THEATRE
Manager ....David Calhoun
Associate Manager ....Jesse White
Treasurer ....Rick Waxman
Assistant Treasurer ....John Rooney
Carpenter ....Joseph P. Valentino
Electrician ....James Mayo
Property Man ....Scott Mecionis

Evita
SCRAPBOOK

Correspondent: Emily Mechler, Ensemble

Opening Night Gifts/Party: Our Opening Night Party was at the Marriott Marquis Hotel —how convenient for us! This cast went all out for opening night gifts, it was like Christmas morning. Ricky Martin gave everyone the newest iTouch with Evita 2012 engraved on the back, Elena Roger had everyones' names hand-painted beautifully for our dressing stations, Michael Cerveris gave everyone a maté tea gourd (which is a famous Argentine tea that was a big part of this company's routine), our producers gave us customized sweatshirts, and Max von Essen got specialized "Magaldi" Malbec made for us. There were beautiful cards, shirts, posters and even "LIVIN' *EVITA* LOCA" shot glasses given.

Most Exciting Celebrity Visitor: Ricky Martin is our star. We get to hang out with him every night—does it get better than that?

Actors Who Perform the Most Roles: Colin Cunliffe and Brad Little transform into about nine different characters throughout the show.

Who Has Done the Most Shows in Their Career: Matt Wall earned the Gypsy Robe for *Evita,* his eleventh Broadway show. *Evita* marks Tim Shew's tenth Broadway show—often as a principal.

Special Backstage Ritual: Ricky leads an energy circle before curtain every night to all come together to tell our story. "Love and Light!" There are bodies all over the stage stretching, smaller prayer circles, and other people taking moments to prepare themselves in the back of the catacombs.

Favorite Moment During Each Performance: Personally, I love doing "A New Argentina." The whole company gets to come together and so many personalized moments have been created. It is also unreal to gaze up at Elena Roger every night on that balcony singing "Don't Cry for Me, Argentina" so beautifully.

Favorite In-Theatre Gathering Place: For opening night, Melanie, Johnny, Sydney, Rachel and my "gift" to the company was to redecorate the greenroom. We re-covered the sofas, built a bar, got wall art and a chalkboard and hung twinkle lights. The entire cast is constantly rolling out and stretching in there and on Saturday night we have a rockin' dance party for S.N.O.B. (Saturday Night on Broadway!)

Favorite Off-Site Hangout: Lillie's

Favorite Snack Food: Candy basket in wig room.

Mascot: Melting Tiger Hidden Dragon.

Favorite Therapies: "Rollin' on Out" and PT with Marc.

Cell Phone Photos During a Performance: Every night during curtain call people shamelessly whip out their cell phones and walk down the aisles to snap as many pictures as they can of our three leads. It's like the paparazzi!

Fastest Costume Change: Rebecca, Colin and Bradley's "Requiem" into "Junin" change.

Who Wore the Heaviest/Hottest Costume:

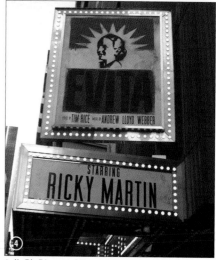

1. (L-R): Director Michael Grandage with leads Michael Cerveris, Elena Roger and Ricky Martin at a press conference after the first Broadway preview.
2. Ladies of the ensemble including, second from right, *Yearbook* correspondent Emily Mechler.
3. Lyricist/librettist Tim Rice with composer Andrew Lloyd Webber.
4. Marquee of the Marquis Theatre in April 2012.

Tim (Gaucho under opening mourning).

Catchphrases Only the Company Would Recognize: "Broadway's Hard!" —Rob Ashford "Don't Count on Me Argentina." —Elena Roger

"Head-Ba!"—Kristen Blodgette

Best In-House Parody Lyrics: "Rice-a-Roni" / "Dice are rolling."

Memorable Directorial Note: "Just remember, you could be changing a person's life, and the person next to them might be losing the will to live: so remember to stay secure in our story."

Company In-Jokes: "PERON!"

Company Legend: George Lee Andrews— need I say more?

Sweethearts Within the Company: Erica Mansfield (cast member) and Dave Roth (Percussionist).

Embarrassing Moment: Sydney Morton had an incident with a hairpin in her panty hose. It was a comical version of Buenos Aires!

Coolest Thing About Being in This Show: I feel so blessed by being in the company of these incredible human beings and getting to tell our story every night!

Photos by Joseph Marzullo/WENN

Follies

First Preview: August 7, 2011. Opened: September 12, 2011.
Closed January 22, 2012 after 38 Previews and 152 Performances.

PLAYBILL®

Decades after the heyday of the glittering Weismann Follies, *the old theatre is being demolished. Weismann hosts one last reunion of the many dancers, singers and showgirls who paraded across its stage. Now middle-aged or elderly, the Weismann Girls (and Boys) gather for the party, but soon find that some old emotional wounds have never healed. Housewife Sally who was in love with Ben (now a diplomat) settled for Buddy. But Buddy knows where his wife's heart has always been, and it eats him up inside. Ben, meanwhile, married Phyllis, but their marriage has decayed into a loveless, bitter husk. The reunion gives them a chance to reexamine the mistakes they made and the roads they didn't take. Raw emotions rise to the surface as the proceedings are watched over by the unseen ghosts of their younger selves.*

⇒N⇐ MARQUIS THEATRE
UNDER THE DIRECTION OF JAMES M. NEDERLANDER AND JAMES L. NEDERLANDER

THE JOHN F. KENNEDY CENTER FOR THE PERFORMING ARTS
DAVID M. RUBENSTEIN, CHAIRMAN   MICHAEL M. KAISER, PRESIDENT   MAX A. WOODWARD, VICE PRESIDENT
NEDERLANDER PRESENTATIONS, INC.   ADRIENNE ARSHT   HRH FOUNDATION
ALLAN WILLIAMS, EXECUTIVE PRODUCER

BERNADETTE PETERS   JAN MAXWELL
DANNY BURSTEIN   RON RAINES

FOLLIES

BOOK BY   MUSIC AND LYRICS BY
JAMES GOLDMAN   **STEPHEN SONDHEIM**

STARRING

ELAINE PAIGE as Carlotta

ALSO STARRING

DON CORREIA   CHRISTIAN DELCROIX   ROSALIND ELIAS
COLLEEN FITZPATRICK   LORA LEE GAYER
MICHAEL HAYES   LEAH HOROWITZ   JAYNE HOUDYSHELL
FLORENCE LACEY   MARY BETH PEIL   DAVID SABIN
KIRSTEN SCOTT   FREDERICK STROTHER
NICK VERINA   SUSAN WATSON   TERRI WHITE

WITH

LAWRENCE ALEXANDER	BRANDON BIEBER	JOHN CARROLL	MATHEW deGUZMAN	SARA EDWARDS
LESLIE DONNA FLESNER	JENIFER FOOTE	SUZANNE HYLENSKI	DANIELLE JORDAN	AMANDA KLOOTS-LARSEN
JOSEPH KOLINSKI	BRITTANY MARCIN	ERIN N. MOORE	PAMELA OTTERSON	CLIFTON SAMUELS
KIIRA SCHMIDT	BRIAN SHEPARD	JESSICA SHERIDAN	AMOS WOLFF	ASHLEY YEATER

SCENIC DESIGN	COSTUME DESIGN	LIGHTING DESIGN	SOUND DESIGN
DEREK McLANE	**GREGG BARNES**	**NATASHA KATZ**	**KAI HARADA**
HAIR & WIG DESIGN	MAKE-UP DESIGN	PRODUCTION STAGE MANAGER	ASSOCIATE DIRECTOR
DAVID BRIAN BROWN	**JOSEPH DULUDE II**	**ARTHUR GAFFIN**	**DAVID RUTTURA**
ORCHESTRATIONS	DANCE MUSIC ARRANGER	MUSIC COORDINATOR	CASTING
JONATHAN TUNICK	**JOHN BERKMAN**	**JOHN MILLER**	**LAURA STANCZYK CASTING, CSA**
PRODUCTION MANAGER	PRESS REPRESENTATIVE	MARKETING SERVICES	GENERAL MANAGEMENT
JUNIPER STREET PRODUCTIONS	**BONEAU/BRYAN-BROWN**	**TYPE A MARKETING**	**ALAN WASSER – ALLAN WILLIAMS** **MARK SHACKET**

MUSIC DIRECTION BY
JAMES MOORE

CHOREOGRAPHY BY
WARREN CARLYLE

DIRECTED BY
ERIC SCHAEFFER

9/12/11

The *Weismann Follies* girls reunite.

Photo by Joan Marcus

Follies

MUSICAL NUMBERS

1971 — The stage of the Weismann Theater

ACT ONE

Prologue .... Orchestra
"Beautiful Girls" .... Roscoe and Company
"Don't Look at Me" .... Sally and Ben
"Waiting for the Girls Upstairs" .... Buddy, Ben, Phyllis, Sally,
Young Buddy, Young Ben, Young Phyllis, Young Sally
"Rain on the Roof" .... Emily and Theodore
"Ah, Paris!" .... Solange
"Broadway Baby" .... Hattie
"The Road You Didn't Take" .... Ben
"In Buddy's Eyes" .... Sally
"Who's That Woman" .... Stella and The Ladies
"I'm Still Here" .... Carlotta
"Too Many Mornings" .... Ben and Sally

ACT TWO

"The Right Girl" .... Buddy
"One More Kiss" .... Heidi and Young Heidi
"Could I Leave You?" .... Phyllis

LOVELAND

The Folly of Love
  "Loveland" .... The Ensemble
The Folly of Youth
  "You're Gonna Love Tomorrow" .... Young Ben, Young Phyllis, Young Buddy, Young Sally
Buddy's Folly
  "The God-Why-Don't-You-Love-Me Blues" .... Buddy, "Margie," "Sally"
Sally's Folly
  "Losing My Mind" .... Sally
Phyllis's Folly
  "The Story of Lucy and Jessie" .... Phyllis and Gentlemen of the Ensemble
Ben's Folly
  "Live, Laugh, Love" .... Ben and Company

CAST
(in order of appearance)

Sally Durant Plummer ....BERNADETTE PETERS
Young Sally.........................LORA LEE GAYER
Sandra Crane ....FLORENCE LACEY
Young Sandra ....KIIRA SCHMIDT
DeeDee West............COLLEEN FITZPATRICK
Young DeeDee ....LESLIE DONNA FLESNER
Solange LaFitte ....MARY BETH PEIL
Young Solange.....................ASHLEY YEATER
Hattie Walker ....JAYNE HOUDYSHELL
Young Hattie ....JENIFER FOOTE
Roscoe ....MICHAEL HAYES
Stella Deems ....TERRI WHITE
Young Stella ....ERIN N. MOORE
Max Deems ....FREDERICK STROTHER
Heidi Schiller ....ROSALIND ELIAS
Young Heidi ....LEAH HOROWITZ
Emily Whitman ....SUSAN WATSON
Young Emily ....DANIELLE JORDAN
Theodore Whitman ....DON CORREIA
Carlotta Campion ....ELAINE PAIGE
Young Carlotta ....PAMELA OTTERSON

Phyllis Rogers Stone ....JAN MAXWELL
Young Phyllis ....KIRSTEN SCOTT
Benjamin Stone ....RON RAINES
Buddy Plummer ....DANNY BURSTEIN
Dimitri Weismann ....DAVID SABIN
Young Buddy ....CHRISTIAN DELCROIX
Young Ben ....NICK VERINA
Kevin ....CLIFTON SAMUELS
Buddy's Blues "Margie" ....KIIRA SCHMIDT
Buddy's Blues "Sally" ....JENIFER FOOTE

ENSEMBLE

LAWRENCE ALEXANDER,
BRANDON BIEBER, JOHN CARROLL,
LESLIE DONNA FLESNER, JENIFER FOOTE,
LEAH HOROWITZ, SUZANNE HYLENSKI,
DANIELLE JORDAN,
AMANDA KLOOTS-LARSEN,
BRITTANY MARCIN, ERIN N. MOORE,
PAMELA OTTERSON, CLIFTON SAMUELS,
KIIRA SCHMIDT, BRIAN SHEPARD,
AMOS WOLFF, ASHLEY YEATER

SWINGS
MATHEW deGUZMAN, SARA EDWARDS

DANCE CAPTAIN
SARA EDWARDS

ASSISTANT DANCE CAPTAIN
AMOS WOLFF

Elaine Paige is appearing with the permission of
Actors' Equity Association.

UNDERSTUDIES
For Roscoe, Young Buddy: BRANDON BIEBER
For Buddy Plummer: DON CORREIA
For DeeDee West, Buddy's Blues "Sally"
  and "Margie": SARA EDWARDS
For Phyllis Rogers Stone, Solange LaFitte:
  COLLEEN FITZPATRICK
For Young Heidi: LESLIE DONNA FLESNER
For Sandra Crane, DeeDee West, Solange LaFitte:
  JENIFER FOOTE
For Emily Whitman, Young Sally:
  DANIELLE JORDAN
For Buddy Plummer, Benjamin Stone, Max
  Deems, Dimitri Weismann, Theodore Whitman:
  JOSEPH KOLINSKI
For Sally Durant Plummer, Carlotta Campion:
  FLORENCE LACEY
For Young Phyllis: KIIRA SCHMIDT
For Young Ben: BRIAN SHEPARD
For Hattie Walker, Heidi Schiller, Sandra Crane,
  Carlotta Campion, Stella Deems:
  JESSICA SHERIDAN
For Kevin: AMOS WOLFF

ORCHESTRA
Conductor: JAMES MOORE
Associate Conductor: MARVIN LAIRD
Assistant Conductor: VINCENT J. FANUELE
Music Coordinator: JOHN MILLER
Concertmaster: RICK DOLAN
Violins: ASHLEY HORNE, ROB SHAW,
  UNA TONE, KARL KAWAHARA,
  KIKU ENOMOTO
Violas: KENNETH BURWARD-HOY,
  DAVID CRESWELL
Celli: LAURA BONTRAGER,
  SARAH HEWITT-ROTH
Bass: RAY KILDAY
Harp: BARBARA BIGGERS
Woodwinds: TODD GROVES, DAVE NOLAND,
  LES SCOTT, RICK HECKMAN,
  CHAD SMITH
Trumpets: TREVOR D. NEUMANN,
  MATT PETERSON,
  JEREMY MILOSZEWICZ
French Horn: WILL DEVOS
Trombones: KEITH O'QUINN, DAN LEVINE,
  VINCENT FANUELE
Percussion: CHARLES DESCARFINO
Drums: RICH ROSENZWEIG
Guitar: GREG UTZIG
Keyboard: MARVIN LAIRD

Follies

Bernadette Peters
Sally Durant Plummer

Jan Maxwell
Phyllis Rogers Stone

Danny Burstein
Buddy Plummer

Ron Raines
Benjamin Stone

Elaine Paige
Carlotta Campion

Don Correia
Theodore Whitman

Christian Delcroix
Young Buddy

Rosalind Elias
Heidi Schiller

Colleen Fitzpatrick
DeeDee West

Lora Lee Gayer
Young Sally

Michael Hayes
Roscoe

Leah Horowitz
Young Heidi

Jayne Houdyshell
Hattie Walker

Florence Lacey
Sandra Crane

Mary Beth Peil
Solange LaFitte

David Sabin
Dimitri Weismann

Kirsten Scott
Young Phyllis

Frederick Strother
Max Deems

Nick Verina
Young Ben

Susan Watson
Emily Whitman

Terri White
Stella Deems

Lawrence Alexander
Ensemble

Brandon Bieber
Ensemble

John Carroll
Ensemble

Mathew deGuzman
Swing

Sara Edwards
Swing, Dance Captain

Leslie Donna Flesner
Ensemble

Jenifer Foote
Ensemble

Suzanne Hylenski
Ensemble

Danielle Jordan
Ensemble

Amanda Kloots-Larsen
Ensemble

Joseph Kolinski
Understudy

Brittany Marcin
Ensemble

Erin N. Moore
Ensemble

Pamela Otterson
Ensemble

Follies

Clifton Samuels
Kevin, Ensemble

Kiira Schmidt
Ensemble

Brian Shepard
Ensemble

Jessica Sheridan
Understudy

Amos Wolff
*Ensemble, Asst.
Dance Captain*

Ashley Yeater
Ensemble

James Goldman
Book

Stephen Sondheim
Music & Lyrics

Eric Schaeffer
Director

Warren Carlyle
Choreographer

James Moore
*Music Director,
Conductor*

Derek McLane
Set Design

Gregg Barnes
Costume Design

Natasha Katz
Lighting Design

Kai Harada
Sound Design

David Brian Brown
Hair & Wig Design

Joseph Dulude II
Make-up Design

David Ruttura
Associate Director

John Miller
Music Coordinator

Laura Stanczyk, CSA
Casting

Alan Wasser
General Manager

Ana Rose Greene, Guy Kwan, Joe DeLuise,
Hillary Blanken
Juniper Street Productions
Production Manager

Allan Williams
*General Manager
and Executive
Producer*

David M. Rubenstein
*Chairman, John F.
Kennedy Center for
the Performing Arts,
Producer*

Michael M. Kaiser
*President, John F.
Kennedy Center for
the Performing Arts,
Producer*

Max A. Woodward
*Vice President,
John F. Kennedy
Center for the
Performing Arts,
Producer*

James M.
Nederlander
Producer

James L.
Nederlander
Producer

Adrienne Arsht
Producer

2011-2012 AWARDS

Tony Award
Best Costume Design of a Musical
(Gregg Barnes)

Drama Desk Awards
Outstanding Revival of a Musical
Outstanding Actor in a Musical
(Danny Burstein)
Outstanding Costume Design
(Gregg Barnes)

Outer Critics Circle Awards
Outstanding Revival of a Musical
Outstanding Actor in a Musical
(Danny Burstein)

Drama League Award
Distinguished Revival of a Musical

Follies

FRONT OF HOUSE STAFF
Front Row (L-R): George Fitze, unidentified, Jesse White
Second Row (L-R): unidentified, David Calhoun, unidentified, Rosaire Lulu Caso
Third Row (L-R): unidentified, unidentified, Stanley Seidman, unidentified, unidentified
Back Row (L-R): Odalis Concepcion, Phyllis Weinsaft, Nancy Diaz, unidentified

Photos by Brian Mapp

CREW
Front Row (L-R): Ken Sheehan, Steve Reid,
Eric Norris, Steve Long
Second Row (L-R): Derek Healy, Elizabeth Coleman,
Patrick Pummill
Next Row (L-R): Dave Elmer, Joel DeRuyter
Top Row (L-R): Scott Mecionis, Jacob White

HAIR
(L-R): Danny Koye, Richard Orton, Mitchell Beck

WARDROBE
Front Row (L-R): Mary Miles, Julienne Schubert-Blechman,
Kelly Saxon, Paul Ludick, Danny Paul, Cece Cruz, Lolly Totero
Second Row (L-R): Rick Kelly, Jenny Barnes, Ron Fleming,
Franc Weinperl
Back Row (L-R): Patti Luther, Cathy Cline, Phillip Rolfe,
Christina Ainge

COMPANY MANAGERS
(L-R): Kim Kelley, Michael Altbaum

DOORMAN
Rey Concepcion

STAGE MANAGERS
Front Row (L-R): Lee Micklin, Laurie Goldfeder,
Jamie Greathouse
Back Row: (L-R) Artie Gaffin (Stage Manager),
Patty Saccente (Bernadette Peters' Assistant)

Follies

STAFF FOR *FOLLIES*

GENERAL MANAGEMENT
ALAN WASSER ASSOCIATES
Alan Wasser   Allan Williams
Mark Shacket   Aaron Lustbader

GENERAL PRESS REPRESENTATIVE
BONEAU/BRYAN-BROWN
Adrian Bryan-Brown   Heath Schwartz
Michael Strassheim

COMPANY MANAGER
Kimberly Kelley

MARKETING
TYPE A MARKETING
Anne Rippey   John McCoy   DJ Martin
Robin Steinthal

CASTING
LAURA STANCZYK CASTING, CSA
Meryl Ballew, Tony Tilli, Alicia Newkirk,
Anika Chapin, Kate Freeman, Sarah Johnston

PRODUCTION MANAGEMENT
JUNIPER STREET PRODUCTIONS
Hillary Blanken   Guy Kwan
Ana Rose Greene   Joseph DeLuise

Production Stage Manager ....Arthur Gaffin
Stage Manager ....Laurie Goldfeder
Assistant Stage Manager ....Jamie Greathouse
Assistant Company Manager ....Michael Altbaum
Assistant Choreographer/
  Dance Captain ....Sara Edwards
Assistant Dance Captain ....Amos Wolff
Associate Scenic Designers ....Erica Hemminger,
                                        Shoko Kambara
Assistant Scenic Designer ....Brett Banakis
Associate Costume Designer ....Matthew Pachtman
Assistant Costume Designers ....Irma Escobar,
                                        Sky Switser
Costume Interns ....Elise Tollefsen, Molly Deale
Associate Lighting Designer ....Yael Lubetzky
Assistant Lighting Designer ....Joel Shier
Associate Sound Designer ....Jana Hoglund
Moving Lighting Programmer ....Marc Polimeni
Production Carpenter ....Fred Gallo
Head Carpenter ....Scott "Gus" Poitras
Flyman ....David J. Elmer
Production Electricians ....Randall Zaibek,
                                        James Fedigan
Head Electrician ....Eric Norris
Assistant Electrician ....Stephen Long
Production Properties
  Supervisor ....Matthew Elias Hodges
Properties Coordinator ....Jeremy Lydic
Head Properties Supervisor ....Andrew Meeker
Production Sound Engineer ....Patrick Pummill
Deck Audio ....Elizabeth Coleman
Wardrobe Supervisor ....Rick Kelly
Assistant Wardrobe Supervisor ....Paul Ludick
Ms. Peters' Dresser ....Lolly Totero
Dressers ....Christina Ainge, Jenny Barnes,
                    Gary Biangone, Cathy Cline,

Cece Cruz, Ron Fleming, Patti Luther,
Danny Paul, Phillip Rolfe, Kelly Saxon,
Julienne Schubert-Blechman, Franc Weinperl
Associate Hair/Wig Designer/
  Hair Supervisor ....Richard Orton
Assistant Hair Supervisor ....Mitchell Beck
Hair Dressers ....Chelsea Roth, Danny Koye
Production Assistants ....Melissa Hansen,
          Johnny Kruger, Lee Micklin, Lindsey Turteltaub
Music Coordinator ....John Miller
Assistant to John Miller ....Nichole Jennino
Rehearsal Pianist.............................Mat Eisenstein
Rehearsal Drummer ....Rich Rosenzweig
Music Department Intern ....Anthony DeAngelis
NIDA Production Secondment (Sound) ......Remy Woods
Advertising ....Serino/Coyne
                    Sandy Block, Greg Corradetti,
                    Robert Jones, Danielle Boyle,
                    David Barrineau
Digital Outreach & Website ....Serino/Coyne
                    Jim Glaub, Chip Meyrelles,
                    Laurie Connor, Kevin Keating,
                    Whitney Manalio Creighton, Mark Seeley
Theatre Displays ....King Displays
Legal Counsel ....Elliot H. Brown, Jonathan A. Lonner/
          Franklin, Weinrib, Rudell & Vassallo, P.C.
Accounting ....Rosenberg, Neuwirth & Kuchner/
                    Marina Flom
General Management Associates ....Lane Marsh,
                    Thom Mitchell
General Management Office ....Hilary Ackerman,
                    Mark Barna, Jake Hirzel,
                    Nina Lutwick, Jennifer O'Connor
Production Artwork ....Frank Verlizzo
Production Photographer ....Joan Marcus
Assistant to Mr. Sondheim ....Steve Clar
Assistant to Ms. Peters ....Patty Saccente
Athletic Trainer ....Alan Kroll, MS, ACT
Orthopedist ....David S. Weiss, M.D.
Insurance ....Ventura Insurance Brokerage
Banking ....Signature Bank/
          Barbara von Borstel, Margaret Monigan
Payroll ....Castellana Services, Inc.
Opening Night ....The Lawrence Company/
                    Michael P. Lawrence
Group Sales ....Broadway Inbound
Transportation ....Get Services LLC

CREDITS AND ACKNOWLEDGEMENTS
Scenery fabricated and painted by Global Scenic Services, Inc. Bridgeport, CT. Show control and scenic motion control featuring Stage Command® Systems by PRG Scenic Technologies, a division of Production Resource Group, LLC, New Windsor, NY. Lighting equipment by PRG Lighting. Audio equipment by PRG Audio. Costumes by Arel Studio, Inc.; Armando Farfan, Jr.; Carelli Costumes, Inc.; Donna Langman Costumes; Euroco Costumes, Inc.; Lynne Baccus; Michael Stanton; Primadonna; Stephen Stratton; Thomas Slack; Tricorne Costumes, Inc. Millinery by Lynne Mackey Studios and Rodney Gordon, Inc. Costume fabric dyeing and painting by Jeff Fender Studios. Costume beading by Polly Isham Kinney, Bessie Nelsen, Josie Spano, Mystic Beading, Silvia's Costumes and Douglas Esselmann. Custom costume, wigs by Independent Wig Co. Metalwork by Den Design Studio. Custom footwear by LaDuca Shoes and Worldtone Dance. Women's hosiery

provided by Bra*Tenders. Makeup provided by Make Up for Ever.

THE JOHN F. KENNEDY CENTER FOR THE PERFORMING ARTS STAFF FOR *FOLLIES*
General Manager ....John J. Hance
Associate General Manager ....Joe Christopher
Executive Vice President ....Claudette Donlon
Vice President for Marketing and
  Sales Services ....David Kitto
Vice President for Development ....Marie Mattson
Vice President of Finance ....Lynne Pratt
General Counsel ....Maria Kersten
Director of Press Office ....John Dow*
Press Representative ....Stephanie O'Neill
                    *Member of ATPAM

Piano by Steinway & Sons

Rehearsed at MTC

Souvenir merchandise by
The Kennedy Center

Merchandise operations by
The Araca Group.

---

www.FolliesBroadway.com

Chairman ....James M. Nederlander
President ....James L. Nederlander

Executive Vice President
Nick Scandalios

Vice President	Senior Vice President
Corporate Development	Labor Relations
Charlene S. Nederlander	**Herschel Waxman**

| Vice President | Chief Financial Officer |
| **Jim Boese** | **Freida Sawyer Belviso** |

STAFF FOR THE MARQUIS THEATRE
Manager ....David Calhoun
Associate Manager ....Jesse White
Treasurer ....Rick Waxman
Assistant Treasurer ....John Rooney
Carpenter..............................Joseph P. Valentino
Electrician..............................James Mayo
Property Man ....Scott Mecionis

Follies
SCRAPBOOK

Correspondent: John Carroll, Male Ensemble

Opening Night Gifts: A puzzle from Stephen Sondheim with the logo of the show and each puzzle cut out with everyone's initials, which was crazy and really cool. Bernadette Peters gave necklaces, and the Kennedy Center producers gave engraved silver *Follies* jewelry boxes.

Most Exciting Celebrity Visitors: Barbra Streisand and Elaine Stritch. Elaine came down to the orchestra screaming "Bravo!" throughout the curtain call.

Who Got the Gypsy Robe: Jenifer Foote

"Gypsy of the Year" Skit: "A Farewell to *Follies*" by Brandon Bieber, Jenifer Foote, Jan Maxwell and Amos Wolff.

Special Backstage Rituals: Elaine Paige tells a joke, usually dirty, before every show. Mary Beth Peil gives a spit-blessing to everyone she sees.

Favorite Moment During Each Performance: When the amazing 28-piece orchestra starts the show.

Favorite In-Theatre Gathering Place: The greenroom.

Favorite Off-Site Hangout: The Glass House Tavern.

Favorite Snacks: Leah Horowitz's mother's cookies. She does everything from brownies to chocolate chip to oatmeal raisin and all that good stuff.

Favorite Therapy: Physical therapy whenever we can get it.

Most Memorable Ad-Lib: Ron Raines called Danny Burstein by his real name onstage instead of "Buddy."

Latest Audience Arrival: During "The Right Girl," which is in Act II.

Fastest Costume Change: The Ensemble boys out of "The Story of Lucy and Jessie" into "Live, Laugh, Love." We get maybe a minute. It's so quick, it's ridiculous.

Heaviest Costume: Ashley Yeater plays one of the ghosts and she appears at the very top of the show in her showgirl skirt that has a humongous train attached to one of her arms.

Actors Who Wore the Least: The ponies, Kiira Schmidt and Leslie Donna Flesner wear little bra tops and short shorts.

Catchphrase: "I'm loving the show."

Nicknames: "BP" is Bernadette Peters, "EP" is Elaine Paige, and "MBP" is Mary Beth Peil.

Embarrassing Moments: Clifton Samuels falling down in "Live, Laugh, Love."

Superstitions That Turned Out To Be True: "We are going to Broadway!"

Coolest Thing About Being in This Show: Working with theatre legends like Bernadette Peters.

1. The leads take bows on opening night.
2. Elaine Paige takes a curtain call.
3. Ensemble members Sara Edwards, Pamela Otterson and Kiira Schmidt at the opening night party at the Marriott Marquis Hotel.
4. (L-R): Christian Delcroix, Lora Lee Gayer, Nick Verina and Kirsten Scott at the Marriott Marquis.
5. Stephen Sondheim and Bernadette Peters at the Dec. 1, 2011 cast album signing at Barnes & Noble.
6. Men of the chorus at the debut.

The Gershwins' Porgy and Bess

First Preview: December 17, 2011. Opened: January 12, 2012.
Still running as of May 31, 2012.

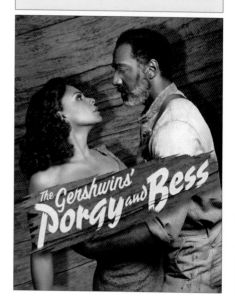

PLAYBILL

In the Charleston, South Carolina ghetto of Catfish Row poor beggar Porgy falls in love with Bess, a scarlet woman who is the consort of the powerful and murderous bully Crown. Bess finds herself falling in love with the kind goodness of Porgy, and she tries to turn her back on her old life, especially after it appears that Crown has died in a hurricane. But when Crown returns to claim her, Porgy knows he has to find a way to fight for the woman he loves, or lose her forever.

CAST

(in order of appearance)

Clara	NIKKI RENÉE DANIELS
Jake	JOSHUA HENRY
Mariah	NaTASHA YVETTE WILLIAMS
Sporting Life	DAVID ALAN GRIER
Mingo, the Undertaker	J.D. WEBSTER
Serena	BRYONHA MARIE PARHAM
Robbins	NATHANIEL STAMPLEY
Porgy	NORM LEWIS
Crown	PHILLIP BOYKIN
Bess	AUDRA McDONALD
Detective	CHRISTOPHER INNVAR
Policeman	JOSEPH DELLGER
The Strawberry Woman	ANDREA JONES-SOJOLA
Peter, the Honey Man	PHUMZILE SOJOLA
The Crab Man	CEDRIC NEAL
Fishermen	ROOSEVELT ANDRÉ CREDIT, TREVON DAVIS, WILKIE FERGUSON III
Women of Catfish Row	ALLISON BLACKWELL, HEATHER HILL, ALICIA HALL MORAN, LISA NICOLE WILKERSON

Continued on next page

RICHARD RODGERS THEATRE

UNDER THE DIRECTION OF JAMES M. NEDERLANDER AND JAMES L. NEDERLANDER

Jeffrey Richards   Jerry Frankel   Rebecca Gold   Howard Kagan

Cheryl Wiesenfeld/Brunish Trinchero/Meredith Lucio TBC   Joseph & Matthew Deitch
Mark S. Golub & David S. Golub   Terry Schnuck   Freitag Productions/Koenigsberg Filerman
The Leonore S. Gershwin 1987 Trust   Universal Pictures Stage Productions   Ken Mahoney
Judith Resnick   Tulchin/Bartner/ATG   Paper Boy Productions   Alden Badway
Broadway Across America   Christopher Hart   Irene Gandy   Will Trice

PRESENT

AUDRA
McDONALD

NORM
LEWIS

DAVID ALAN
GRIER

in the AMERICAN REPERTORY THEATER production of

THE GERSHWINS'®
PORGY AND BESS®

by
George Gershwin, DuBose and Dorothy Heyward and Ira Gershwin

Adapted by
Suzan-Lori Parks   Diedre L. Murray

with

Phillip Boykin   Nikki Renée Daniels   Joshua Henry
Christopher Innvar   Bryonha Marie Parham   NaTasha Yvette Williams

Allison Blackwell   Roosevelt André Credit   Trevon Davis   Joseph Dellger   Wilkie Ferguson III   Carmen Ruby Floyd
Heather Hill   David Hughey   Andrea Jones-Sojola   Alicia Hall Moran   Cedric Neal   Phumzile Sojola   Nathaniel Stampley
Julius Thomas III   J.D. Webster   Lisa Nicole Wilkerson

Scenic Design	Costume Design	Lighting Design	Sound Design
Riccardo Hernandez	ESosa	Christopher Akerlind	Acme Sound Partners

Wig/Hair/Makeup Design	Music Supervisor	Music Director and Conductor	Music Coordinator
J. Jared Janas and Rob Greene	David Loud	Constantine Kitsopoulos	John Miller

Casting	Associate Director/Production Stage Manager	Technical Supervision
Telsey + Company	Nancy Harrington	Hudson Theatrical Associates

Press Representative	Company Manager	General Management
Jeffrey Richards Associates Irene Gandy/Alana Karpoff	Bruce Klinger	Richards/Climan, Inc.

Associate Producers
Ronald Frankel   James Fuld Jr.   Allan S. Gordon   INFINITY Stages
Shorenstein Hays-Nederlander Theatres LLC   David & Barbara Stoller   Michael & Jean Strunsky   Theresa Wozunk

Orchestrations by
William David Brohn and Christopher Jahnke

Choreographed by
Ronald K. Brown

Directed by
Diane Paulus

First performed at the American Repertory Theater August 17, 2011
Diane Paulus, Artistic Director and Diane Borger, Producer
The worldwide copyrights in the works of George Gershwin and Ira Gershwin for this presentation are licensed by the Gershwin Family.

1/12/12

(L-R): Audra McDonald as Bess and Norm Lewis as Porgy

Photo by Michael J. Lutch

The Gershwins' Porgy and Bess

MUSICAL NUMBERS

ACT I

"Overture"
"Summertime" .... Clara and Jake
"A Woman Is a Sometime Thing" .... Jake and Ensemble
"Crap Game" .... Ensemble
"Gone, Gone, Gone" .... Ensemble
"My Man's Gone Now" .... Serena
"Leaving for the Promised Land" .... Bess and Ensemble
"It Takes a Long Pull" .... Jake and the Fishermen
"I Got Plenty of Nothing" .... Porgy
"I Hates Your Strutting Style" .... Mariah
"Bess, You Is My Woman Now" .... Porgy and Bess
"Oh, I Can't Sit Down" .... Ensemble

ACT II

"Entr'acte"
"It Ain't Necessarily So" .... Sporting Life and Ensemble
"What You Want With Bess?" .... Bess and Crown
"It Takes a Long Pull" (Reprise) .... Jake and the Fishermen
"Oh, Doctor Jesus" .... Serena and Ensemble
"Street Cries" .... Strawberry Woman, Honey Man, Crab Man
"I Loves You, Porgy" .... Bess and Porgy
"Oh, The Lord Shake the Heaven" .... Ensemble
"A Red Headed Woman" .... Crown and Ensemble
"Clara, Don't You Be Downhearted" .... Ensemble
"There's a Boat That's Leaving Soon" .... Sporting Life
"Where's My Bess?" .... Porgy, Mariah, Serena
"I'm on My Way" .... Porgy and Ensemble

ORCHESTRA

Conductor:
CONSTANTINE KITSOPOULOS
Associate Conductor:
PAUL MASSE
Woodwinds:
KATHY FINK, LYNNE COHEN,
STEVE KENYON, JONATHAN LEVINE,
JILL M. COLLURA
Trumpets:
NICK MARCHIONE, DAN URNESS
Trombone:
KEITH O'QUINN
Bass Trombone/Tuba:
JENNIFER WHARTON
French Horns:
R.J. KELLEY, ERIC DAVIS

Concert Master:
BELINDA WHITNEY
Violins:
ORLANDO WELLS, KARL KAWAHARA,
PHILIP PAYTON
Violas:
CRYSTAL GARNER, LIUH-WEN TING
Cellos:
SARAH SEIVER, SUMMER BOGGESS
Bass:
BILL ELLISON
Drums/Percussion:
CHARLES DESCARFINO
Piano/Celeste/Accordion:
PAUL MASSE
Music Coordinator:
JOHN MILLER

Cast Continued

SWINGS
CARMEN RUBY FLOYD, DAVID HUGHEY,
JULIUS THOMAS III

UNDERSTUDIES
For Porgy: NATHANIEL STAMPLEY
For Bess: ALICIA HALL MORAN
For Sporting Life: DAVID HUGHEY
For Crown: NATHANIEL STAMPLEY
For Clara: ANDREA JONES-SOJOLA
For Jake: TREVON DAVIS, DAVID HUGHEY
For Detective: JOSEPH DELLGER
For Serena: ANDREA JONES-SOJOLA
For Mariah: ALLISON BLACKWELL,
    CARMEN RUBY FLOYD
For The Crab Man: JULIUS THOMAS III,
    WILKIE FERGUSON III
For Mingo: JULIUS THOMAS III
For Robbins: WILKIE FERGUSON III,
    DAVID HUGHEY, PHUMZILE SOJOLA
For Peter: JULIUS THOMAS III
For The Strawberry Woman: HEATHER HILL

DANCE CAPTAIN
LISA NICOLE WILKERSON

SETTING
Time: Late 1930s
Place: Catfish Row and Kittawah Island
Charleston, South Carolina

Audra McDonald

Photo by Michael J. Lutch

The Gershwins' Porgy & Bess

Audra McDonald
Bess

Norm Lewis
Porgy

David Alan Grier
Sporting Life

Phillip Boykin
Crown

Nikki Renée Daniels
Clara

Joshua Henry
Jake

Christopher Innvar
Detective

Bryonha Marie Parham
Serena

NaTasha Yvette Williams
Mariah

Allison Blackwell
Woman of Catfish Row

Roosevelt André Credit
Fisherman

Trevon Davis
Fisherman

Joseph Dellger
Policeman

Wilkie Ferguson III
Fisherman

Carmen Ruby Floyd
Swing

Heather Hill
Woman of Catfish Row

David Hughey
Swing

Andrea Jones-Sojola
The Strawberry Woman

Alicia Hall Moran
Woman of Catfish Row

Cedric Neal
The Crab Man

Phumzile Sojola
Peter, the Honey Man

Nathaniel Stampley
Robbins

Julius Thomas III
Swing

J.D. Webster
Mingo, the Undertaker

Lisa Nicole Wilkerson
Woman of Catfish Row, Dance Captain, Fight Captain

George Gershwin
Music

DuBose & Dorothy Heyward
Libretto/Lyrics

Ira Gershwin
Lyrics

Diane Paulus
Director

Suzan-Lori Parks
Adapter/Additional Scenes

Diedre L. Murray
Musical Adapter

Ronald K. Brown
Choreographer

ESosa
Costume Design

Christopher Akerlind
Lighting Design

The Gershwins' Porgy and Bess

Sten Severson, Tom Clark, Mark Menard and Nevin Steinberg
Acme Sound Partners
Sound Design

David Loud
Music Supervisor

Constantine Kitsopolous
Music Director and Conductor

John Miller
Music Coordinator

William David Brohn
Orchestrations

Christopher Jahnke
Orchestrations

Bernard Telsey
Telsey + Company
Casting

Denise Woods
Dialect Coach

Mia Walker
Assistant Director

Neil A. Mazzella
Hudson Theatrical Associates
Technical Supervision

David R. Richards, Tamar Haimes
Richards/Climan, Inc
General Management

Jeffrey Richards
Producer

Jerry Frankel
Producer

Rebecca Gold
Producer

Cheryl Wiesenfeld
Producer

Brisa Trinchero
Producer

Meredith Lucio
Producer

Joseph Deitch
Producer

Van Dean, Kenny Howard
The Broadway Consortium
Producers

Matthew Deitch
Producer

Mark S. Golub
Producer

Barbara and Buddy Freitag
Freitag Productions
Producers

Michael Filerman
Producer

Ken Mahoney
Producer

Judith Resnick
Producer

Will Dombrowski
Paper Boy Productions
Producer

Bruston Kade Manuel
Paper Boy Productions Producer

Michael A. Alden
Producer

Dale Badway
Producer

John Gore
Broadway Across America
Producer

Irene Gandy
Producer

The Gershwins' Porgy and Bess

Sumayya Ali
Swing

Gavin Gregory
Swing

Photo by Lisa Pacino

COMPANY MANAGEMENT
(L-R): Bruce Klinger, Caitlin Fahey

2011-2012 AWARDS

TONY AWARDS
Best Revival of a Musical
Best Performance by an Actress
in a Leading Role in a Musical
(Audra McDonald)

DRAMA DESK AWARDS
Outstanding Actress in a Musical
(Audra McDonald)
Outstanding Sound Design of a Musical
(Acme Sound Partners)

OUTER CRITICS CIRCLE AWARD
Outstanding Actress in a Musical
(Audra McDonald)

DRAMA LEAGUE AWARDS
Distinguished Performance
(Audra McDonald)
Founders Award for Excellence in Directing
(Diane Paulus)

THEATRE WORLD AWARD
For Outstanding Broadway
or Off-Broadway Debut
(Phillip Boykin)

FRED AND ADELE ASTAIRE AWARDS
Excellence in Choreography on Broadway
(Ronald K. Brown)
Best Female Dancer on Broadway
(Lisa Nicole Wilkerson)

Photo by Brian Mapp

CREW

Front Row (L-R): Julie Baldauff, Brendan O'Neal, Justin Rathbun, Steve Carver, Sharika Niles, Vangeli Kaseluris

Middle Row (L-R): Worth Strecker, Nancy Harrington

Back Row (L-R): Kate Sorg, Steve DeVerna, Yleana Nuñez, Thomas Augustine, Jim Wilkinson, Kevin Camus, Justin Freeman, Tim Rossi

The Gershwins' Porgy and Bess

ORCHESTRA
(L-R): Constantine Kitsopolous, Lynne Cohen, Rob Shaw, Summer Boggess, Liuh-Wen Ting, Laura Bontrager, Katherine Fink, Orlando Wells, Fred Lassen, Charles Descarfino, Crystal Garner, Eric C. Davis, Bill Ellison, Janet Lantz, Keith O'Quinn, Karl Kawahara, Philip Payton, Don McGeen, Steve Kenyon, Jonathan Levine, Dan Urness, Max Seigel

FRONT OF HOUSE STAFF
Front Row (L-R): Carla Cherry (Concessions), Barbara Rodell, Lori Miata, Derrick Darby, Carmen Frank (Ushers), Dorothy Darby (Directress), Destiny Bivona (Usher), Rosanne Kelly (Matron)

Middle Row (L-R): Larry Purvis (Concessions), Brenda Schwarz, Roxanne Gayol (Ushers), Timothy Pettolina (House Manager)

Back Row (L-R): Colum Meehan (Usher), Richard Lester (Concessions), Maureen Gonzalez, Frank Holmes, Beverly Thornton, Giovanny Lopez (Ushers)

The Gershwins' Porgy and Bess

David Alan Grier as Sporting Life

Photo by Michael J. Lutch

STAFF FOR THE GERSHWINS' PORGY AND BESS

GENERAL MANAGEMENT
RICHARDS/CLIMAN, INC.
David R. Richards   Tamar Haimes
Michael Sag   Kyle Bonder
Jessica Fried   Jaqueline Kolek

COMPANY MANAGER
Bruce Klinger

GENERAL PRESS REPRESENTATIVE
JEFFREY RICHARDS ASSOCIATES
Irene Gandy/Alana Karpoff
Ryan Hallett   Elon Rutberg

PRODUCTION MANAGEMENT
HUDSON THEATRICAL ASSOCIATES
Neil Mazzella   Sam Ellis   Irene Wang
Walter Murphy   Corky Boyd

CASTING
TELSEY + COMPANY
Bernie Telsey CSA, Will Cantler CSA,
David Vaccari CSA, Bethany Knox CSA,
Craig Burns CSA, Tiffany Little Canfield CSA,
Rachel Hoffman CSA, Justin Huff CSA,
Patrick Goodwin CSA, Abbie Brady-Dalton CSA,
David Morris, Cesar A. Rocha, Andrew Femenella,
Karyn Casi, Kristina Bramhall

PRODUCTION STAGE
  MANAGER ....NANCY HARRINGTON
Stage Manager ....Julie Baldauff
Assistant Stage Manager ....Sharika Niles
Assistant Company Manager ....Caitlin Fahey
Assistant Director ....Mia Walker
Assistant Choreographer ....Arcell Cabuag
Dance Captain/Fight Captain ....Lisa Nicole Wilkerson
Assistant Producer ....Michael Crea
Dialect Coach ....Denise Woods
Fight Director ....J. Steven White
Associate Scenic Designer ....Maruti Evans
Associate Costume Designer ....Cathy Parrott
Associate Lighting Designer ....Caroline Chao
Assistant to Mr. Akerlind ....Seth Reiser
Lighting Programmer ....Warren Flynn
Video Programmers......................C. Andrew Bauer,
                                        Daniel Brodie
Associate Sound Designer ....Jason Crystal

Production Assistant ....Christopher Windom
Production Carpenter ....Francis Rapp
Head Carpenter ....Tim Rossi
Flyman ....Ronald Knox
Production Electrician ....Jimmy Maloney
Head Electrician ....Justin Freeman
Followspot Operators ....William Walters, John Carton,
                                        Brian Frankel
Production Properties Supervisor ....Worth Strecker
Sound Engineer ....Justin Rathbun
Deck Audio ....James Wilkinson
Advance Sound ....Darin Stillman
Wardrobe Supervisor ....Jesse Galvan
Dressers ....Vangeli Kaseluris, Kurt Keilmann,
                        Angela Lehrer, Yleana Nuñez, Kate Sorg
Hair Supervisor ....Thomas Augustine
Hair Dresser ....Brendan O'Neal
Assistant to Diedre L. Murray ....Randall Eng
Music Preparation Services ....Larry H. Abel,
                        Music Preparation International, Inc.
Assistant to the Orchestrators/
  Music Assistant ....Neil Douglas Reilly
Assistant to John Miller ....Nichole Jennino
Music Assistant ....Nehemiah Luckett
Advertising ....Serino Coyne, Inc./
                        Greg Corradetti, Tom Callahan,
                        Danielle Boyle, Peter Gunther, Drew Nebrig
Website Design/Online Marketing ....SpotCo/
                        Michael Crowley, Meghan Ownbey
Interactive Marketing
  Service ....Broadway's Best Shows/
                        Andy Drachenberg, Christopher Pineda
Banking...............................City National Bank/
                        Michele Gibbons, Erik Piecuch
Insurance ....DeWitt Stern Group Inc./
                        Peter Shoemaker, Anthony Pittari
Accountants.................Fried & Kowgios, CPA's LLP,
                        Robert Fried, CPA
Comptroller ....Elliott Aronstam
Legal Counsel ....Lazarus & Harris LLP./
                        Scott R. Lazarus, Esq.,
                        Robert C. Harris, Esq.
Payroll ....CSI/Lance Castellana
Production Photographer....................Michael Lutch
Merchandise.........................Max Merchandising/
                        Randi Grossman
Company Mascots ....Skye, Franco, Butler

CREDITS
Scenery constructed and automated by Hudson Scenic Studio, Inc. Lighting equipment from Hudson Sound & Light LLC. Sound equipment from Sound Associates. Projection equipment from Scharff Weisberg. Costumes constructed by Giliberto Designs, Jennifer Love Costumes, Katrina Patterns, Tricorne, ART Costume Shop. Fabric dying and distressing by Hochi Asiatico. Millinery by Arnold Levine and Denise Wallace. Dance shoes by Worldtone. Undergarments by Bra*Tenders. Makeup provided by M·A·C.

Rehearsed at the New 42nd Street Studios

SPECIAL THANKS
To all at A.R.T., particularly Diane Borger, Chris DeCamillis, Anna Fitzloff, Jared Fine, Kati Mitchell, Brendan Shea, Lauren Antler, Mark Lunsford, Patricia Quinlan, Ryan McKittrick, Jenna Clark Embrey and the production staff. Karmaloop for A.R.T. production sponsorship. The A.R.T. Board of Trustees and Advisors and the Porgy and Bess Leadership Circle. Ashley Farra, Elizabeth Van Buren, Isabelle Simone.

www.PorgyAndBessOnBroadway.com

✹N✹
NEDERLANDER

Chairman	**James M. Nederlander**
President	**James L. Nederlander**

Executive Vice President
Nick Scandalios

Vice President	Senior Vice President
Corporate Development	Labor Relations
Charlene S. Nederlander	**Herschel Waxman**

Vice President	Chief Financial Officer
Jim Boese	**Freida Sawyer Belviso**

HOUSE STAFF FOR
THE RICHARD RODGERS THEATRE
House Manager ....Timothy Pettolina
Box Office Treasurer ....Fred Santore Jr.
Assistant Treasurer ....Corinne Dorso
Electrician ....Steve Carver
Carpenter ....Kevin Camus
Propertymaster ....Stephen F. DeVerna
Engineer ....Sean Quinn

The Gershwins' Porgy and Bess
Scrapbook

Correspondents: Phumzile Sojola, "Peter, The Honey Man," and Andrea Jones-Sojola, "The Strawberry Woman"

Opening Night Gifts: Pendant from Audra and Norm with *Porgy and Bess* engraved on it. CD with soulful arrangements of *Porgy and Bess* by Josh Henry.

Opening Night Party: They served a Strawberry Woman cocktail and Honey Man hush puppies named after our characters.

Most Exciting Celebrity Visitor and What He Said: Sam Jackson Tweet: "Saw *Porgy and Bess* tonight! Some sangin' muhfuggahhhhs up in there! Great show!"

Actor Who Has Done the Most Shows in Their Career: David Alan Grier has done a TON of shows!

Special Backstage Rituals: Prayer at 5 minutes. Roll Dem Bones chant in guys' dressing room. Nikki's Red Leather, Yellow Leather.

Favorite Moment During Each Performance (On Stage or Off): Dance hype before Kittiwah.

Favorite In-Theatre Gathering Place: Guys' dressing room, Warm-up room.

Favorite Off-Site Hangouts: Liberty Hotel, Dean and Deluca, Patzeria.

Mascot: Hurri-Cane

Favorite Therapies: Foam rollers, PT.

Most Memorable Ad-Libs: Mariah: "Struttin' free-style." Bess: "Leave Me Be, Leave Me Be." Allison: "Porgy, Porgy, Porgy, Porgy."

What We Thought of the Web Buzz on Our Show: Thank you, Mr. Sondheim.

Memorable Press Encounters: Proclamation of both *Porgy and Bess* Days—and all the funny things that happened, like that police-escorted school bus ride. Woof!

Memorable Stage Door Fan Encounters: Although they are not fans, the Anti-Scientology protesters have serenaded us with a few obscene Christmas carols.

Fastest Costume Change: Audra—going to the picnic and "Fisherman" after funeral.

Catchphrases Only the Company Would Recognize: "Flying in Diane, on the wings of egrets" and "Not Ash Wednesday but Ashy Wednesday where African-Americans are allowed to leave the house without emollients," —David Alan Grier. "Look at God" —Nate. Allison's lexicon.

Best In-House Parody Lyrics: "I seen him in the morning with his work clothes GONE" — Heather

Memorable Directorial Notes: "Clock that." "Organic." "Nate, who's standing behind you? Trevon? Oh, all right. Good." "Puma, WHAT are you doing?"

Company In-Jokes: Ghost Whisperer.

Sweethearts Within the Company: Phumzile Sojola and Andrea Jones-Sojola, Nancy Harrington and Worth Strecker, Bryonha Parham and Sharika Niles

Embarrassing Moment: NaTasha's babies throwing up on Nikki!

1. Curtain call on opening night (L-R): NaTasha Yvette Williams, Phillip Boykin, Audra McDonald, Norm Lewis, David Alan Grier, Bryonha Marie Parham and cast.
2. (L-R): Trevon Davis, Gavin Gregory, NaTasha Yvette Williams, B. Smith, Cedric Neal and Nathaniel Stampley at a post-show reception February 21, 2012 to benefit Givenik.com and Broadway Cares/Equity Fights AIDS, held at B. Smith's Restaurant.
3. Lewis and McDonald at the McKittrick Hotel for the cast party.
4. Members of the creative team join the cast on opening night (L-R) Boykin, director Diane Paulus, McDonald, adapter Suzan-Lori Parks and Lewis.

Nickname: "Butterscotch."

Coolest Thing About Being in This Show: We're family.

Fan Club Info: porgyandbessonbroadway.com Facebook: The Gershwins' *Porgy and Bess* on Broadway. http://twitter.com/#!/porgybessonbway

Also: One night Porgy's cane flew into the orchestra pit. It levitated up from the orchestra and a man from the audience grabbed it and put it back onstage! The cane was autographed and presented to that man during the curtain call. He was in tears. That's the effect *Porgy and Bess* has on the audience. GO TEAM PORGY!

Ghost: The Musical

First Preview: March 15, 2012. Opened: April 23, 2012.
Still running as of May 31, 2012.

A pop-musical adaptation of the Oscar-winning 1990 film of the same title. This supernatural romance tells the story of a murder victim who returns as a ghost (with the help of an unwilling medium) to discover the plot behind his murder and to stop his killers from visiting a similar fate on his girlfriend. This transfer from London is memorable for its eerie special effects—including a leading man who vanishes from center stage—created by a team of holograph technicians.

CAST

Sam Wheat	RICHARD FLEESHMAN
Molly Jensen	CAISSIE LEVY
Oda Mae Brown	DA'VINE JOY RANDOLPH
Carl Bruner	BRYCE PINKHAM
Willie Lopez	MICHAEL BALDERRAMA
Subway Ghost	TYLER McGEE
Hospital Ghost	LANCE ROBERTS
Clara	MOYA ANGELA
Louise	CARLY HUGHES
Bank Assistant	JENNIFER NOBLE
Minister	JASON BABINSKY
Mrs. Santiago	JENNIFER SANCHEZ
Officer Wallace	MOYA ANGELA
Detective Beiderman	JASON BABINSKY
Orlando	DANIEL J. WATTS
Ortisha	VASTHY MOMPOINT
Bank Officer	ALISON LUFF
Lionel Furgeson	JEREMY DAVIS
Nuns	CARLY HUGHES, ALISON LUFF

Continued on next page

LUNT–FONTANNE THEATRE
UNDER THE DIRECTION OF
JAMES M. NEDERLANDER AND JAMES L. NEDERLANDER

COLIN INGRAM   HELLO ENTERTAINMENT/DAVID GARFINKLE
DONOVAN MANNATO   MJE PRODUCTIONS   PATRICIA LAMBRECHT
ADAM SILBERMAN

in association with

COPPEL/WATT/WITHERS/BEWICK   FIN GRAY/MICHAEL MELNICK   MAYERSON/GOULD HAUSER/TYSOE
RICHARD CHAIFETZ & JILL CHAIFETZ   JEFFREY B. HECKTMAN   LAND LINE PRODUCTIONS
GILBERT PRODUCTIONS/MARION/SHAHAR   FRESH GLORY PRODUCTIONS/BRUCE CARNEGIE-BROWN

by special arrangement with PARAMOUNT PICTURES

present

GHOST
THE MUSICAL

Book & Lyrics
BRUCE JOEL RUBIN

Music & Lyrics
DAVE STEWART & GLEN BALLARD

Based on the Paramount Pictures film written by Bruce Joel Rubin

"Unchained Melody" written by Hy Zaret and Alex North
Courtesy of Frank Music Corp. (ASCAP)

General Management	Production Management	Advertising & Marketing
BESPOKE THEATRICALS	**AURORA PRODUCTIONS**	**SPOTCO**
Press Agent	Casting Director (US)	Casting Director (UK)
THE HARTMAN GROUP	**TARA RUBIN CASTING**	**DAVID GRINDROD**
Musical Director	Associate Director	Production Stage Manager
DAVID HOLCENBERG	**THOMAS CARUSO**	**IRA MONT**

Additional Movement Sequences **LIAM STEEL**

Musical Supervisor, Arranger & Orchestrator	Video & Projection Designer
CHRISTOPHER NIGHTINGALE	**JON DRISCOLL**

Lighting	Illusions	Sound
HUGH VANSTONE	**PAUL KIEVE**	**BOBBY AITKEN**

Designer	Choreographer
ROB HOWELL	**ASHLEY WALLEN**

Director
MATTHEW WARCHUS

4/23/12

Richard Fleeshman

Photo by Joan Marcus

Ghost: The Musical

MUSICAL NUMBERS

ACT I

"Here Right Now"	Sam, Molly
"Unchained Melody"	Sam
"More"	Sam, Carl, Ensemble
"Three Little Words"	Sam, Molly
"You Gotta Let Go"	Hospital Ghost, Ensemble
"Are You a Believer?"	Clara, Louise, Oda Mae
"With You"	Molly
"Suspend My Disbelief/I Had a Life"	Molly, Carl, Sam, Ensemble

ACT II

"Rain/Hold On"	Molly, Sam, Ensemble
"Life Turns on a Dime"	Carl, Molly, Sam
"Focus"	Subway Ghost
"Talkin' 'Bout a Miracle"	Hospital Ghost, Oda Mae, Ensemble
"Nothing Stops Another Day"	Molly
"I'm Outta Here"	Oda Mae, Ensemble
"Unchained Melody" (Reprise)	Sam, Molly

Da'Vine Joy Randolph

Photo by Joan Marcus

ORCHESTRA

Conductor:
DAVID HOLCENBERG
Associate Conductor:
ANDY GROBENGIESER

Keyboard 1:
DEBORAH ABRAMSON
Keyboard 2:
ANDY GROBENGIESER
Guitars:
ERIC DAVIS, J.J. McGEEHAN
Bass:
RANDY LANDAU
Drums:
HOWARD JOINES
Trumpet:
JOHN REID

Trombone:
BRUCE EIDEM
Woodwinds:
HIDEAKI AOMORI
Horn:
ZOHAR SCHONDORF
Concertmaster:
ELIZABETH LIM-DUTTON
Violins:
CENOVIA CUMMINS, JIM TSAO,
ROBIN ZEH
Violin/Viola:
JONATHAN DINKLAGE, HIROKO TAGUCHI
Cello:
JEANNE LeBLANC

Music Copying: Emily Grishman Music
Preparation/Emily Grishman, Katharine Edmonds
Music Coordinator: Howard Joines

Cast Continued

ENSEMBLE
MOYA ANGELA, JASON BABINSKY,
JEREMY DAVIS, SHARONA D'ORNELLAS,
JOSH FRANKLIN, ALBERT GUERZON,
AFRA HINES, CARLY HUGHES, ALISON
LUFF, TYLER McGEE, VASTHY MOMPOINT,
JENNIFER NOBLE, JOE AARON REID,
LANCE ROBERTS, CONSTANTINE
ROUSOULI, JENNIFER SANCHEZ,
DANIEL J. WATTS

SWINGS
MIKE CANNON, STEPHEN CARRASCO,
KAREN HYLAND, JESSE WILDMAN

DANCE CAPTAIN
JAMES BROWN III

ASSISTANT DANCE CAPTAIN
AFRA HINES

UNDERSTUDIES
For Sam Wheat:
JOSH FRANKLIN,
CONSTANTINE ROUSOULI
For Molly Jensen:
ALISON LUFF, JENNIFER NOBLE
For Oda Mae Brown:
MOYA ANGELA, CARLY HUGHES
For Carl Bruner:
JASON BABINSKY,
CONSTANTINE ROUSOULI
For Subway Ghost:
JOE AARON REID, DANIEL J. WATTS
For Hospital Ghost:
STEPHEN CARRASCO, DANIEL J. WATTS
For Willie Lopez:
MIKE CANNON, JOE AARON REID
For Clara and Louise:
AFRA HINES, VASTHY MOMPOINT

SETTING
New York City, modern day

Richard Fleeshman is appearing with the support of
Actors' Equity Association.
The producers gratefully acknowledge Actors' Equity
Association for its assistance with this production.

Ghost: The Musical

Richard Fleeshman
Sam Wheat

Caissie Levy
Molly Jensen

Da'Vine Joy
Randolph
Oda Mae Brown

Bryce Pinkham
Carl Bruner

Michael Balderrama
Willie Lopez

Tyler McGee
*Subway Ghost/
Ensemble*

Lance Roberts
*Hospital Ghost/
Ensemble*

Moya Angela
*Clara/Officer
Wallace/Ensemble,*

Carly Hughes
*Louise/Nun/
Ensemble*

Jason Babinsky
*Detective
Beiderman/
Minister/Ensemble*

James Brown III
*Dance Captain/
Fight Captain*

Mike Cannon
Swing

Stephen Carrasco
Swing

Jeremy Davis
*Lionel Furgeson/
Ensemble*

Sharona D'Ornellas
Ensemble

Josh Franklin
Ensemble

Albert Guerzon
Ensemble

Afra Hines
*Ensemble/Assistant
Dance Captain*

Karen Hyland
Swing

Alison Luff
*Bank Officer/
Nun/Ensemble*

Vasthy Mompoint
Ortisha/Ensemble

Jennifer Noble
*Bank Assistant/
Ensemble*

Joe Aaron Reid
Ensemble

Constantine Rousouli
Ensemble

Jennifer Sanchez
*Mrs. Santiago/
Ensemble*

Daniel J. Watts
Orlando/Ensemble

Jesse Wildman
Swing

Bruce Joel Rubin
Book & Lyrics

Dave Stewart
Music & Lyrics

Glen Ballard
Music & Lyrics

Ashley Wallen
Choreographer

Christopher
Nightingale
*Musical Supervisor,
Arranger &
Orchestrator*

Hugh Vanstone
Lighting

Jon Driscoll
*Video & Projection
Designer*

Bobby Aitken
Sound Designer

Ghost: The Musical

Paul Kieve
Illusionist

Rob Howell
Designer

Matthew Warchus
Director

Liam Steel
Additional Movement Sequences

Campbell Young and Luc Verschueren
Campbell Young Associates
Hair, Wig & Makeup Designer

Thomas Caruso
Associate Director

David Holcenberg
Music Director/ Conductor

Howard Joines
Music Coordinator

Sunny Walters
Associate Choreographer

Daryl A. Stone
Associate Costume Designer

Tim Lutkin
Associate Lighting Designer

Joel Shier
Associate Lighting Designer

Simon King
Associate Sound Designer

Joanie Spina
Associate Illusionist

Tara Rubin Casting
Casting

David Grindrod
UK Casting

Gene O'Donovan
Aurora Productions
Production Management

Ben Heller
Aurora Productions
Production Management

Maggie Brohn
Bespoke Theatricals
General Management

Amy Jacobs
Bespoke Theatricals
General Management

Devin Keudell
Bespoke Theatricals
General Management

Nina Lannan
Bespoke Theatricals
General Management

Colin Ingram
Lead Producer

Hello Entertainment/ David Garfinkle
Lead Producer

Michael Edwards
MJE Productions
Producer

Carole Winter
MJE Productions
Producer

Matthew Gordon
MJE Productions
Producer

Adam Silberman
Executive Producer

Michael Coppel
Producer

Michael Watt
Producer

Louise Withers
Producer

Linda Bewick
Producer

Fin Gray
Producer

Frederic H. Mayerson
Producer

Ghost: The Musical

James M. Gould
Producer

Ron Tysoe
Producer

Richard A. Chaifetz
Producer

Jill Chaifetz
Producer

Jeffrey B. Hecktman
Producer

Jordan Scott Gilbert
Gilbert Productions,
LLC
Co-Producer

Liz Torres
Gilbert Productions,
LLC
Co-Producer

Martin Peacock
Gilbert Productions,
LLC
Co-Producer

John Yonover
Gilbert Productions,
LLC
Co-Producer

Antonio R. Marion
Co-Producer

Guy Shahar
Shahar Productions
Co-Producer

Jonathan Shahar
Shahar Productions
Co-Producer

Marc Goldman
Shahar Productions
Co-Producer

David Goldman
Shahar Productions
Co-Producer

Dave Broitman
Shahar Productions
Co-Producer

Rosalind Cressy
Fresh Glory
Productions
Co-Producer

Bruce
Carnegie-Brown
Co-Producer

2011-2012 AWARDS

DRAMA DESK AWARD
Outstanding Set Design
(Jon Driscoll, Rob Howell and Paul Kieve)

OUTER CRITICS CIRCLE AWARD
Outstanding Lighting Design
(Hugh Vanstone)

(L-R): Richard Fleeshman
and Caissie Levy

Photo by Joan Marcus

128

Ghost: The Musical

Photos by Brian Mapp

WARDROBE
Front Row (L-R): Duduzile Mitall, Michael Berglund

Middle Row (L-R): Peggie Kurz, Marcia McIntosh, Joby Horrigan, Jessica Scoblick, Lisa Preston, Margiann Flanagan, Nanette Golia

Back Row (L-R): Tina Clifton, Terri Purcell, Jaymes Gill, Ken Brown, David Mitchell

STAGE MANAGEMENT
(L-R): Ira Mont, Julia P. Jones, Kate Croasdale, Matthew Lacey

BOX OFFICE
(L-R): Thomas Waxman and Joe Olcese

Photo by www.jeremydavis photography.com

ORCHESTRA, COMPOSERS, ORCHESTRATOR, MUSICAL COORDINATOR
Front Row (L-R): Dave Stewart, Cenovia Cummins, Elizabeth Lim-Dutton, Chris Nightingale, Glen Ballard

Middle Row (L-R): Emily Grishman, Jonathan Dinklage, Hiroko Taguchi, Robin Zeh, David Holcenberg, Howard Joines, Deborah Abramson, Zohar Schondorf, Jim Tsao, JJ McGeehan

Back Row (L-R): Hideaki Aomori, Jeanne LeBlanc, Bruce Eidem, John Reid, Andy Grobengieser, Randy Landau, Eric Davis, Phij Adams

Ghost: The Musical

HAIR DEPARTMENT
(L-R): Susan Corrado, Elisa Acevedo

CREW
Kneeling (L-R): Steve Long, John Sheppard, Mike Cornell, David Brickman, David Bornstein, Danny Terrill, Andy Bentz

Back Row (L-R): Joseph Pfifferling, Colle Bustin, Brendan Lynch, Joel DeRuyter, Chris Kurtz, Mike Wojchik, Danny Kearon, Fran Rapp

FRONT OF HOUSE
Front Row (L-R): Kirstin DeCicco, Rosalee Cortez, Marienell Clavano, Stephanie Colon, Stephanie Martinez, Vincent Diaz
Middle Row (L-R): Jessica Gonzalez (Chief Usher), Rosalinda Liclican, Honey Owen, Angalic Cortes, Carmella Cambio, Tracey Malinowski (House Manager), Barry Jenkins (Head Porter)
Back Row (L-R): Sharon Grant, Sheron James-Richardson, Kayla Christie, Seth Augsberger, Anthony Marcello, Melissa Ocasio, Charles Thompson, Paul Perez, Philip Zhang, Joey Cintron, Richard Darbasie, Roberto Calderon, Samana Gharzeddine, Ray West, Lauren Banyai, Diane Mashburn

---

STAFF FOR *GHOST*

GENERAL MANAGEMENT
BESPOKE THEATRICALS
Nina Lannan   Devin Keudell
Maggie Brohn   Amy Jacobs
Associate General Manager ....Steve Dow

COMPANY MANAGEMENT
Company Manager ....Shaun Moorman
Associate Company Manager ....Roseanna Sharrow

PRODUCTION MANAGEMENT
AURORA PRODUCTIONS
Gene O'Donovan, Ben Heller
Stephanie Sherline, Jarid Sumner, Liza Luxenberg,

Anita Shah, Anthony Jusino, Steven Dalton,
Eugenio Saenz Flores, Isaac Katzanek, Aneta Feld,
Melissa Mazdra

GENERAL PRESS REPRESENTATIVE
THE HARTMAN GROUP
Michael Hartman
Juliana Hannett   Emily McGill

Ghost: The Musical

CASTING (U.S.)
TARA RUBIN CASTING
Tara Rubin CSA, Eric Woodall CSA
Merri Sugarman CSA, Dale Brown CSA,
Stephanie Yankwitt CSA
Kaitlin Shaw, Lindsay Levine

CASTING (UK)
DAVID GRINDROD
Casting Associates..........Will Burton, Stephen Crockett

COLIN INGRAM PRODUCTIONS
Producer...Colin Ingram
Associate General Manager.....................Simon Ash
Financial Controller.......................Louise Waldron
Production Assistant........................Daisy Campey

HELLO ENTERTAINMENT
Producer...David Garfinkle
Executive Producer.......................Adam Silberman
Chief Financial Officer....................Michael Lowen
Executive Assistant...........................Clay Martin
Special Projects Director.........................PJ Miller

Production Stage Manager........................Ira Mont
Stage Manager..............................Julia P. Jones
Assistant Stage Manager....................Matthew Lacey
Consulting Stage Manager (UK)..............Natalie Wood
Associate Director.........................Thomas Caruso
Associate Choreographer.....................Sunny Walters
Dance Captain.............................James Brown III
Assistant Dance Captain........................Afra Hines
Fight Director..................................Terry King
Fight Captain.............................James Brown III
Associate Scenic Designer.............Rosalind Coombes
Associate Scenic Designer.....................Paul Weimer
Associate Costume Designer................Daryl A. Stone
Assistant Costume Designer...............Rachel Attridge
Costume Design Assistant.................Audrey Nauman
Associate Lighting Designer.....................Tim Lutkin
Associate Lighting Designer.......................Joel Shier
Associate Sound Designer.....................Simon King
Associate Sound Designer......................Garth Helm
Associate Video &
  Projection Designer.................Gemma Carrington
Associate Video &
  Projection Designer.......................Michael Clark
Associate Illusionist............................Joanie Spina
Hair, Wig & Makeup
  Designer...................Campbell Young Associates
Hair, Wig & Makeup Associate............Luc Verschueren
Head Carpenter.................................Francis Rapp
Fly Automation Carpenter..................John Croissant
Deck Automation Carpenter................Joel DeRuyter
Head Electrician.............................Mike Cornell
Production Electricians....................Randall Zaibek,
                                              Jimmy Fedigan
Moving Light Technician........................Steve Long
Moving Light Programmer.....................David Arch
Production Property Master.................David Bornstein
U.K. Props Supervisors.........Lisa Buckley, Lizzie Frankl
Props Shopper.............................Christina Gould
Production Sound Engineer..................Mike Wojchik
Assistant Sound Engineer.......................Colle Bustin
Production Sound Mixer UK.....................Ben Evans
Advance Sound...................................Drew Levy
Associate Music Director (UK)...............Laurie Perkins

Music Technology................................Phij Adams
Music Technology Associate............Andy Grobengieser
Digital Arrangements & Programming........Ned Douglas
Video System Consultant.........................Alan Cox
Production Video Technician...............Jason Lindahl
Video/Projections Programmers..............Laura Frank,
                                              Emily Harding
Video Technician...............................Chris Kurtz
Special Effects Coordinators...............Randall Zaibek,
                                              Jimmy Fedigan
Wardrobe Supervisor..........................Terri Purcell
Associate Wardrobe Supervisor.............Nanette Golia
Dressers....................Michael Berglund, Ken Brown,
                  Tina Clifton, Margiann Flanagan,
                  Jaymes Gill, Joby Horrigan,
                  Peggie Kurz, Marcia McIntosh,
                  Duduzile Mitall, Lisa Preston,
                  Jessica Scoblick
Hair Supervisor.............................Susan Corrado
Assistant Hair Supervisor...................Monica Costea
Hairdresser..................................Lisa Acevedo
Music Copying.............................Emily Grishman
Music Copying (UK).............................Tom Kelly
Vocal Coach................................Deborah Hecht
Physical Therapy................................PhysioArts
Production Assistants.......................Kate Croasdale,
                  Cody Renard Richard,
                  Kristen Torgrimson
SDC Directing Intern...................Stephen Brotebeck
SDC Observer..................................Ryan Emmons
Lottery Administrator.....................Benny Enfinger
General Management Associates................Libby Fox,
                                              Danielle Saks
General Management Interns..............Sean Coughlin,
                  Michelle Heller, Jimmy Wilson
Advertising......................................SPOTCO/
                  Drew Hodges, Jim Edwards,
                  Tom Greenwald, Stephen Sosnowski,
                  Nora Tillmanns
Marketing..SPOTCO/
                  Nick Pramik, Kristen Rathbun,
                  Julie Wechsler, Caroline Newhouse
Online/Digital Interactive......................SPOTCO/
                  Kristen Bardwil, Cory Spinney,
                  Rebecca Cohen, Marisa Delmore,
                  Sara Fitzpatrick, Marc Mettler,
                  Jennifer Sacks, Christina Sees,
                  Matt Wilstein
Ticket Services.................SPOTCO/Stephen Santore
Production Photographer U.S...............Joan Marcus
Production Photographer UK.......Sean Ebsworth Barnes
Accountant.........................FK Partners/Robert Fried
Controller................Galbraith & Co./Sarah Galbraith
Legal Counsel UK
  and Worldwide.....Harbottle & Lewis LLP/Neil Adleman
Legal Counsel U.S...........Davis Wright Tremaine LLP/
                  M. Graham Coleman, Robert J. Driscoll
                  Kramer Levin Naftalis & Frankel LLP/
                  Mark D. Koestler
                  Biegelman, Feiner and Feldman PC/
                  Ron Feiner
Payroll Services.........................Checks & Balances
Banking......................................Signature Bank/
                  Barbara von Borstel, Margaret Monigan
Insurance...............Aon/Albert G. Ruben Company/
                  Claudia Kaufman

Opening Night
  Coordination................Stamp Event Management
                  Jason Burlingame, Margaret Crisostomo
Merchandise..............................The Araca Group
Travel Agent.......Tzell Travel/The "A" Team/Andi Henig
Housing.................................ABA/Elizabeth Helke
Hotel Accommodations............The Time/Kanvar Singh

CREDITS
Scenery fabrication and show control and scenic motion control, featuring Stage Command Systems® by PRG - Scenic Technologies, a division of Production Resource Group, LLC. Scenery painted by Scenic Arts Studio. Lighting equipment from PRG Lighting. Sound and video equipment from Sound Associates, Inc. Flying by Foy. Costumes by Tricorne Inc.; Artur & Tailors; Gene Mignola, Inc.; Maria Ficalora Knitwear; Jeff Fender Studios; Arnold Levine Millinery; Barak Stribling; Beckenstein Shirts; Hochi Asiatico. Shoes by LaDuca Shoes, T.O. Dey, Center Shoes. Custom dance shoes by LaDuca. Makeup provided by M•A•C. Guitar supplies provided by D'Addario Strings and Ernie Ball. Portions of the video used were filmed at New 42nd Street Studios.

SPECIAL THANKS
American Airlines, Totes Isotoner, Mud Sweat and Tears Pottery, The Time Hotel, Frozen Ghost, Harlem Brewery, Hilco, Ivanka Trump Fine Jewelry, Magnolia Bakery, Russell Nardozza and Geoffrey Beene, Joseph P. Harris, Jr., Ruth Carney, and James McKeon

In memory of Tony Adams
In memory of Tom Lambrecht

Rehearsed at the New 42nd Street Studios

N
NEDERLANDER

Chairman........................**James M. Nederlander**
President.........................**James L. Nederlander**

Executive Vice President
Nick Scandalios

Vice President	Senior Vice President
Corporate Development	Labor Relations
Charlene S. Nederlander	**Herschel Waxman**

Vice President	Chief Financial Officer
Jim Boese	**Freida Sawyer Belviso**

STAFF FOR THE LUNT-FONTANNE
House Manager........................**Tracey Malinowski**
Treasurer...Joe Olcese
Assistant Treasurer............................Kevin Lynch
House Carpenter..................................Terry Taylor
House Electrician..............................Dennis Boyle
House Propertyman.........................Andrew Bentz
House Flyman.................................Matt Walters
House Engineers...................Robert MacMahon,
                                              Joseph Riccio III

Ghost: The Musical
SCRAPBOOK

Correspondent: Jesse Wildman, Swing

Opening Night Gifts/Party: It felt like Christmas! Our stations were all covered in gifts, cards, and flowers from each other and friends and family. Notably, we were all given a really lovely journal from the producers, which seemed fitting since this really has been a journey. From auditioning, to seeing the show in London as a cast, to rehearsals, to our long set of previews, to opening—through both injuries and awesomeness, it's been a remarkable journey. The party was at The Tunnel. Lots of food, lots of booze, lots of love.

Most Exciting Celebrity Visitors: Beyoncé! She was really interested in the technology employed in the show. And David Copperfield came at one point during previews. Considering we do quite a bit of magic in the show, that was pretty huge. Lisa Niemi Swayze came to Opening. Reading the kind words she had to say about our production was incredibly touching and an amazing affirmation that we're doing the story justice. We would all love for Whoopi to come! We're waiting for you, Whoops.

Who Wrote the "Easter Bonnet" Sketch: We didn't do the Easter Bonnet. We were coming up on Opening night and there was just no time. Next year! The business of opening was messing with our Broadway social life.

Actor Who Performed the Most Roles in This Show: Oh gosh, this question gets so sticky, as there's a lot of internal covering of the smaller feature parts. If we're going strictly by the PLAYBILL, it'd be Jason Babinsky—he's in the ensemble, has two featured parts, and covers the role of Carl. He's a pretty incredible performer. Like all of our understudies (who are also extraordinary humans), I can't wait to see him go on. This cast is far from talent-lite.

Who Has Done the Most Shows in Their Career: I don't know if this is meant to include *Rock Around the World* at Busch Gardens or what but, for the sake of this questionnaire, I'm going to go with our Gypsy Robe winner—James Brown. He's had an awesome and varied career that spans seven Broadway shows. He's a pretty big deal, if I do say so myself.

Special Backstage Rituals: The majority of the time backstage is spent in the quick-change areas—there's a whole lot of dressing going on. Pre-show, the men in the fourth floor changing room can be found drinking espresso—the elixir of life. There's almost always music coming from the fifth floor men's dressing room. In the girls' room, Moya and Vasthy are undoubtedly causing trouble. Before "Transition 1," there's some Wing 1 dancing going on. As a Swing, I'm sure there are a bunch I'm leaving out here.

Favorite Moments During Each Performance: This is going to seem small but there's a transitional musical moment that Sam (Richard) has that I think is just awesome. It comes during "Suspend My Disbelief," the finale of Act I. It's right after he's really come to

Leads and creators meet the press (L-R): librettist Bruce Joel Rubin, Caissie Levy, Richard Fleeshman, Da'Vine Joy Randolph, Bryce Pinkham, and songwriters Dave Stewart and Glen Ballard.

Photo by Joseph Marzullo/WENN

realize that his best friend, Carl (Bryce Pinkham), betrayed him. He's singing his face off, the orchestra (led by the awesome David Holcenberg) is rocking out, and I literally, involuntarily can't help but move every time I hear it. The ending is truly beautiful, too. It stills makes me cry. I, also, love "With You." Caissie Levy's voice is truly a phenomenon, one of the best I have ever heard on stage. Off stage, I think my favorites might be the musical stylings of Josh Franklin and Albert Guerzon. Josh has an amazing "bad singing" voice and uses it...a lot—which is made more hilarious given that his actual voice is stunning! Albert likes to sing the music from the show in a Filipino accent...need I say more?

Favorite In-Theatre Gathering Place: This is definitely dictated by where your dressing room is located. My and Karen's dressing room is on the fifth floor, so I'm partial to the men's room on the fourth floor. It feels like they have a little living room in there. Plus, by the time you've walked up four flights of stairs, you need a rest stop!

Favorite Snack Food: Daniel Watts likes UTZ natural, lightly salted, kettle cooked, gourmet potato chips, to be vague. Alison Luff & I are food twins—we like most anything that's usually considered to be on the "crunchy granola" side of things. Jason likes chewy Spree. Jeremy wouldn't be mad at you if you made him cookies. Vasthy likes meat. Karen likes Australian red licorice. Michael likes liquor (okay, that's not a snack food but the bar in Lance's and his dressing room is tricked out!). Stephen likes everything. Carly likes candy of the neon colored variety. Deb never met a gummi bear she didn't like.

Mascot: I don't think we have one. We should work on that.

Favorite Therapies: There are lots of yoga lovers in the cast and a bunch of people who like Entertainer's Secret throat spray.

What the Cast Thought of the Web Buzz on the Show: More so than web buzz, I think we've all been really happy with the reactions of our friends and family. Of course, not everyone is

going to love what we're doing but it's really special to hear how much the show touches people, how effectively all the technical elements come off, and how surprised people are by how much they really, really enjoyed themselves. With something like this, an iconic movie turned musical, there's certainly an element of "I really don't know what to expect" when people walk into it. It's really great to hear that we're surpassing expectation and really touching the average theatergoer and our peers.

Fastest Costume Change: Afra changes into her Outta Here costume in 12 seconds. She completely changes her suit, puts sunglasses on, and enters the stage in a backbend, on a box, on a moving travelator...in 12 seconds.

Catchphrases Only the Company Would Recognize: I wish I could include a video to answer this question because a description doesn't do it justice. It's not so much a catchphrase as it is a gesture. You take one hand and cover your mouth (or "shade your grill," as I like to say), the other hand is up above your head, you say, "aaaaaaahhhhhhh!" and you jump around a bit. I am fully aware of how ridiculous that sounds in writing—you just have to see it. You'd probably still think it's ridiculous...but you'd absolutely want to do it, too.

Company Legends: Vasthy Mompoint is pretty legendary.

Nicknames: Connie Rousouli seems to have a nickname for everyone—all of which are awesome and many of which change on a daily basis. Boo Mama, SOS, Dickie, Va-Va....

Sweethearts Within the Company: Both Connie and Caissie have an uncanny ability to brighten any room they're in.

Ghostly Encounters Backstage: Ironically, there actually hasn't been any paranormal activity...yet.

Coolest Thing About Being in This Show: That we're in the show! It's also pretty cool to know the secrets behind the magic.

Fan Club Info: While there's no Jesse Wildman fan club, I support any and all who would like to takes the reins on that one. And follow *Ghost* on Facebook and Twitter!

Godspell

First Preview: October 13, 2011. Opened: November 7, 2011.
Still running as of May 31, 2012.

Revival of the 1970s musical, adapted from the Gospel of St. Matthew. A tribe of sweet-tempered clownlike performers retell the New Testament story of Jesus' life, parables and crucifixion through a series of songs and partially-improvised skits.

CAST

HUNTER PARRISH
as Jesus
WALLACE SMITH
as John and Judas
UZO ADUBA
NICK BLAEMIRE
CELISSE HENDERSON
MORGAN JAMES
TELLY LEUNG
LINDSAY MENDEZ
GEORGE SALAZAR
ANNA MARIA PEREZ DE TAGLE

UNDERSTUDIES

JOAQUINA KALUKANGO, ERIC MICHAEL
KROP, COREY MACH, JULIA MATTISON

Dance Captain: JULIA MATTISON

CIRCLE IN THE SQUARE

UNDER THE DIRECTION OF
THEODORE MANN and PAUL LIBIN
SUSAN FRANKEL, General Manager

KEN DAVENPORT
and
HUNTER ARNOLD   BROADWAY ACROSS AMERICA   LUIGI CAIOLA   ROSE CAIOLA   EDGAR LANSBURY
MIKE McCLERNON   THE TOLCHIN FAMILY   GUILLERMO WIECHERS & JUAN TORRES
and
THE PEOPLE OF GODSPELL
present

GODSPELL

CONCEIVED AND ORIGINALLY DIRECTED BY
JOHN-MICHAEL TEBELAK

MUSIC AND NEW LYRICS BY
STEPHEN SCHWARTZ

STARRING
HUNTER PARRISH   WALLACE SMITH

UZO ADUBA   NICK BLAEMIRE   CELISSE HENDERSON   MORGAN JAMES
TELLY LEUNG   LINDSAY MENDEZ   GEORGE SALAZAR   ANNA MARIA PEREZ DE TAGLE
JOAQUINA KALUKANGO   ERIC MICHAEL KROP   COREY MACH   JULIA MATTISON

SCENIC DESIGN	COSTUME DESIGN	LIGHTING DESIGN	SOUND DESIGN
DAVID KORINS	**MIRANDA HOFFMAN**	**DAVID WEINER**	**ANDREW KEISTER**

CASTING BY   SPECIAL EFFECTS DESIGN
TELSEY + COMPANY   **CHIC SILBER**

ORCHESTRATIONS AND VOCAL ARRANGEMENTS   MUSIC COORDINATOR
MICHAEL HOLLAND   **JOHN MILLER**

PRESS REPRESENTATIVE   MARKETING
THE PUBLICITY OFFICE   **DAVENPORT THEATRICAL**
JEREMY SHAFFER   **ENTERPRISES**

PRODUCTION STAGE MANAGER   PRODUCTION MANAGEMENT   GENERAL MANAGEMENT
DAVID O'BRIEN   **JUNIPER STREET**   **THE CHARLOTTE WILCOX**
                          PRODUCTIONS, INC.   **COMPANY**

ASSOCIATE PRODUCERS
DENNIS GRIMALDI PRODUCTIONS   TODD MILLER   PIVOT ENTERTAINMENT GROUP   CHRIS WELCH   CEDRIC YAU

MUSIC DIRECTOR
CHARLIE ALTERMAN

CHOREOGRAPHED BY
CHRISTOPHER GATTELLI

DIRECTED BY
DANIEL GOLDSTEIN

The producers wish to express their appreciation to Theatre Development Fund for its generous support of this production.

11/7/11

Uzo Aduba (center) with Hunter Parrish and Company

Photo by Jeremy Daniel

Godspell

ORCHESTRA

Conductor: CHARLIE ALTERMAN
Associate Conductor: MATT HINKLEY
Guitars: MICHAEL AARONS,
    THAD DeBROCK
Guitar/Keyboard: MATT HINKLEY
Bass: STEVE MILLHOUSE
Drums: SHANNON FORD
Piano/Keyboard: CHARLIE ALTERMAN
Music Coordinator: JOHN MILLER

MUSICAL NUMBERS

ACT I

Prologue	Company
"Prepare Ye"	John and Company
"Save the People"	Jesus and Company
"Day by Day"	Anna Maria and Company
"Learn Your Lessons Well"	Celisse and Company
"Bless the Lord"	Lindsay and Company
"All for the Best"	Jesus, Judas and Company
"All Good Gifts"	Telly and Company
"Light of the World"	George and Company

ACT II

"Turn Back, O Man"	Morgan and Company
"Alas for You"	Jesus
"By My Side"*	Uzo and Company
"We Beseech Thee"	Nick and Company
"Beautiful City"	Jesus and Company
"On the Willows"	Judas and the Band
Finale	Jesus and Company

* Music by Peggy Gordon, lyrics by Jay Hamburger

Hunter Parrish
Jesus

Wallace Smith
John/Judas

Uzo Aduba

Nick Blaemire

Celisse Henderson

Morgan James

Telly Leung

Lindsay Mendez

George Salazar

Anna Maria Perez
De Tagle

Joaquina Kalukango
Understudy

Eric Michael Krop
Understudy

Corey Mach
Understudy

Julia Mattison
Understudy

Nick Blaemire (with guitar) leads the cast in bounching on mini trampolines for "We Beseech Thee"

Photo by Jeremy Daniel

Godspell

John-Michael Tebelak
Conceiver and Original Director

Stephen Schwartz
Music and New Lyrics

Daniel Goldstein
Director

Christopher Gattelli
Choreographer

David Korins
Scenic Designer

Miranda Hoffman
Costume Designer

David Weiner
Lighting Designer

Andrew Keister
Sound Designer

Chic Silber
Special Effects Designer

Michael Holland
Orchestrator

Charlie Alterman
Music Director/ Conductor

John Miller
Music Coordinator

Ana Rose Greene, Guy Kwan, Joe DeLuise, Hillary Blanken
Juniper Street Productions
Production Manager

Bernard Telsey
Telsey + Company
Casting

Charlotte Wilcox
The Charlotte Wilcox Company
General Manager

Ken Davenport
Producer

John Gore
Broadway Across America
Producer

Thomas B. McGrath
Broadway Across America
Producer

Edgar Lansbury
Producer

Mike McClernon
Producer

The Tolchin Family
Producer

Guillermo Wiechers
Producer

Juan Torres
Producer

Dennis Grimaldi
Dennis Grimaldi Productions
Associate Producer

Cedric Yau
Associate Producer

Theodore Mann
Artistic Director Circle in the Square

Paul Libin
President of Circle in the Square Theatre and Theatre School

Corbin Bleu
Jesus

Hannah Elless
Cast

Amina S. Robinson
Understudy

STAGE MANAGEMENT AND COMPANY MANAGEMENT
(L-R): Ryan Lympus (Company Manager),
David O'Brien, (Production Stage Manager),
Colleen Danaher (Stage Manager),
Stephen R. Gruse (Stage Manager)

Godspell

Photos by Brian Mapp

FRONT OF HOUSE STAFF
Front Row (L-R): Susan Frankel, Wendy Porter, Lindsey Freeman, Nirvana Diaz

Second Row (L-R): Panagiota Thomatos, Laurel Brevoort, Sophie Koufakis, Michele Monya, Laura Middleton

Back Row (L-R): Georgia Keghlian, Samuel Keghlian, Heidi Giovine, Julia Ward, Joseph Pittman

STAGE CREW
Front Row (L-R):
Tony Menditto (House Carpenter),
Cat Dee (Wardrobe),
Jason Blair (Wardrobe),
Owen Parmele (House Props),
John Albin (Props)

Back Row (L-R):
Liam O'Brien (Wardrobe),
Rob Dagna (Props),
James Hall (Wardrobe Supervisor),
Jake Hall (Sound),
Jim Bay (Sound),
Stewart Wagner (House Electrics)

BAND
Top Row (L-R): Matt Hinkley,
Steve Millhouse,
Thad DeBrock,
Shannon Ford
Bottom Row: Charlie Alterman

Godspell

Celisse Henderson sings "Learn Your Lessons Well"

Photo by Jeremy Daniel

Godspell
SCRAPBOOK

Correspondent: Uzo Aduba, Ensemble

Opening Night Gift: Nick Blaemire gave us some great chocolate. It worked out to be a great snack over the next days after opening. The gift that just kept on giving.

Actor Who Has Done the Most Shows in His Career: Wallace Smith. He's always workin'!

Favorite Snack Food: Anything Anna Maria Perez de Tagle's mother makes for us to eat for dinner during our two-show days, and then we FEAST and hang in Anna's room!

Mascot: We have a small plastic doll we use in one of our parables during the show. George Salazar named it "Mildred." She never blinks. That's mainly because she's a doll. We all find Mildred absolutely terrifying. Julia Mattison never looks her in the eye or challenges her to a staring contest because Mildred is off-putting and will always win. Because she can't blink.

Sweethearts Within the Company: George Salazar and Mildred (see above).

Embarrassing Moment: When Julia lost a staring contest to Mildred.

Most Memorable Ad-Lib: This award goes to Eric Krop for his "Prodigal Son" interpretive dance.

Memorable Stage Door Fan Encounter: We have two teams of fans who come see our show multiple times a week. We love and appreciate their support for our show.

Fastest Costume Change: Lindsay Mendez from Lindsay to the fatted calf. She has a mere four minutes to go off stage, put on a headband with cow ears attached to it, and get back on stage for her entrance. Yeah, I don't know how she does it either. #sarcasm

Who Wore the Heaviest/Hottest Costume: That's a tie between Hunter Parrish's pre-dressed wife-beater/boxer getup and Telly Leung's wife-beater/suspenders concoction he wore during previews. For the record, I understand that's probably not what PLAYBILL meant when they wrote "hottest." ;-)

Who Wore the Least: See above. Then, add Morgan James.

Understudy Anecdote: Our killer swing Joaquina Kalukango stepped up and went on for a second act performance and did a beautiful show! Also, Corey Mach playing The Father in "Prodigal Son." He did a wonderful job making it his own!

Nickname: Celisse Henderson: "Carte Blanche." 'Nuff said.

Coolest Thing About Being in This Show: The cast. Then the trampolines, then the water, and then the confetti. In that order.

1. Hunter Parrish (C) in the opening night finale.
2. "Family Photo" of the cast and creators in the rehearsal hall.
3. (L-R): Julia Mattison, Celisse Henderson, Lindsay Mendez, *Yearbook* correspondent Uzo Aduba, Anna Maria Perez de Tagle, Morgan James and Hunter Parrish at the opening night cast party at Planet Hollywood.

Gore Vidal's The Best Man

First Preview: March 6, 2012. Opened: April 1, 2012.
Still running as of May 31, 2012.

A starry revival of Vidal's drama, which opens the door on back-room politics during a fictional presidential party convention set in 1960. The ruthless Senator Cantwell will do anything including throw mud to secure his party's nomination. His more thoughtful and restrained opponent, Secretary Russell, wants to win on his merits, but is told that he'll never get the chance to win unless he gets in the gutter with Cantwell. The candidates tell each other "May the best man win," but Vidal's script keeps the audience guessing until the last minute about exactly who will be title character.

CAST

The Party

Former President
  Arthur "Artie" Hockstader .JAMES EARL JONES
Mrs. Sue-Ellen Gamadge,
  Chairman of the
  Women's Division .... ANGELA LANSBURY
Senator Clyde Carlin .... DAKIN MATTHEWS

The Candidates

Secretary William Russell .JOHN LARROQUETTE
Alice Russell, *his wife* .... CANDICE BERGEN
Dick Jensen,
  his campaign manager .... MICHAEL McKEAN
Catherine, *a campaign aide* ...... ANGELICA PAGE
Senator Joseph Cantwell ...... ERIC McCORMACK
Mabel Cantwell, *his wife* .... KERRY BUTLER
Mrs. Cantwell, *his mother* ..... DONNA HANOVER
Don Blades, *his campaign manager* ... COREY BRILL

Continued on next page

GERALD SCHOENFELD THEATRE
236 West 45th Street
A Shubert Organization Theatre

Philip J. Smith, *Chairman*   Robert E. Wankel, *President*

Jeffrey Richards   Jerry Frankel   INFINITY Stages

Universal Pictures Stage Productions   Barbara Manocherian/Michael Palitz
The Broadway Consortium/Ken Mahoney   Kathleen K. Johnson   Andy Sandberg
Fifty Church Street Productions   Larry Hirschhorn/Bennu Productions
Patty Baker   Paul Boskind and Martian Entertainment   Wendy Federman
Mark S. Golub & David S. Golub   Cricket Hooper Jiranek   Stewart F. Lane & Bonnie Comley
Carl Moellenberg   Harold Thau   Will Trice

Present

JAMES EARL JONES   JOHN LARROQUETTE
CANDICE BERGEN   ERIC McCORMACK
KERRY BUTLER   JEFFERSON MAYS   MICHAEL McKEAN
and ANGELA LANSBURY

in

with

CURTIS BILLINGS   COREY BRILL   TONY CARLIN   DONNA HANOVER
SHERMAN HOWARD   OLJA HRUSTIC   BILL KUX   JAMES LECESNE
DAKIN MATTHEWS   ANGELICA PAGE   FRED PARKER   AMY TRIBBEY

Scenic Design	Costume Design	Lighting Design	Original Music/Sound Design	Projection Design
Derek McLane	Ann Roth	Kenneth Posner	John Gromada	Peter Nigrini

Hair Design	Casting	Technical Supervision	Production Stage Manager
Josh Marquette	Telsey + Company Will Cantler, CSA	Hudson Theatrical Productions	Matthew Farrell

Press Representative	Company Manager	General Manager	Associate Producer
Jeffrey Richards Associates Irene Gandy/Alana Karpoff	Brig Berney	Richards/Climan, Inc.	Stephanie Rosenberg

Directed by
MICHAEL WILSON

4/1/12

(L-R): John Larroquette, James Earl Jones, Jefferson Mays, Michael McKean

Photo by Joan Marcus

Gore Vidal's The Best Man

Cast Continued

The Visitors
Dr. Artinian, *a psychiatrist* ....BILL KUX
Sheldon Marcus ....JEFFERSON MAYS

The Press
John Malcolm,
    the *News commentator* ...SHERMAN HOWARD
Howie Annenberg, *a reporter from*
    the Philadelphia Inquirer ....FRED PARKER
Frank Pearson, *a reporter from*
    the New York Daily Mirror ....TONY CARLIN
Barbara Brinkley, *a reporter from*
    United Press International ...DONNA HANOVER
Mitch Graham, *a reporter from*
    the Washington Post ....JAMES LECESNE

The Hotel Staff
Bellboy ....CURTIS BILLINGS
Cleaning Woman.....................AMY TRIBBEY
Security ....TONY CARLIN

Additional Press, Hotel Staff, Campaign Workers, and
    Delegates ....CURTIS BILLINGS,
        TONY CARLIN, OLJA HRUSTIC,
        BILL KUX, JAMES LECESNE,
        FRED PARKER, AMY TRIBBEY

UNDERSTUDIES

For Frank Pearson, a reporter from the *New York Daily Mirror*; Security; Howie Annenberg, a reporter from the *Philadelphia Inquirer*; Mitch Graham, a reporter from the *Washington Post*:
CURTIS BILLINGS

For Senator Joseph Cantwell, News Commentator:
TONY CARLIN

For Alice Russell, Mrs. Sue-Ellen Gamadge:
DONNA HANOVER

For Secretary William Russell, Dick Jensen:
SHERMAN HOWARD

For Assistant to Barbara Brinkley, Cleaning Woman:
OLJA HRUSTIC

For Senator Clyde Carlin, Bellboy, Photographer, Campaign Worker, Bell Person, Cameraperson:
BILL KUX

For Dick Jensen, Sheldon Marcus, Dr. Artinian, Additional Hotel Staff, Reporter:
JAMES LECESNE

For Ex-President Arthur "Artie" Hockstader:
DAKIN MATTHEWS

For Mabel Cantwell, Alice Russell:
ANGELICA PAGE

For Don Blades, News Commentator:
FRED PARKER

For Barbara Brinkley, a reporter from *United Press International*; Mrs. Cantwell; Catherine; Additional Hotel Staff; Reporter; Mabel Cantwell:
AMY TRIBBEY

SETTING

TIME: July, 1960

PLACE: The Presidential Convention, Philadelphia, Pennsylvania

(L-R): Angela Lansbury, Candice Bergen

(L-R): Eric McCormack, Kerry Butler

Photos by Joan Marcus

Gore Vidal's The Best Man

James Earl Jones
*Former President
Arthur Hockstader*

Angela Lansbury
*Mrs. Sue-Ellen
Gamadge*

John Larroquette
*Secretary William
Russell*

Candice Bergen
Alice Russell

Eric McCormack
*Senator Joseph
Cantwell*

Kerry Butler
Mabel Cantwell

Jefferson Mays
Sheldon Marcus

Michael McKean
Dick Jensen

Curtis Billings
*Bellboy,
Photographer,
Delegate, Campaign
Worker*

Corey Brill
Don Blades

Tony Carlin
*Frank Pearson,
Delegate, Hotel
Security*

Donna Hanover
*Barbara Brinkley,
Mrs. Cantwell*

Sherman Howard
*John Malcolm, The
News Commentator*

Olja Hrustic
*Bell Person,
Cameraperson*

Bill Kux
*Dr. Artinian,
Delegate*

James Lecesne
*Mitch Graham
Delegate*

Dakin Matthews
Senator Clyde Carlin

Angelica Page
Catherine

Fred Parker
*Howie Annenberg,
Delegate*

Amy Tribbey
*Assistant to Barbara
Brinkley, Cleaning
Woman*

Gore Vidal
Playwright

Michael Wilson
Director

Derek McLane
Set Design

Ann Roth
Costume Design

Kenneth Posner
Lighting Design

John Gromada
*Composer/Sound
Design*

Peter Nigrini
Projection Design

Josh Marquette
Hair Design

Neil A. Mazzella/
Hudson Theatrical
Associates
*Technical
Supervision*

Bernard Telsey
Telsey + Company
Casting

David R. Richards, Tamar Haimes
Richards/Climan, Inc.
General Management

Jeffrey Richards
Producer

Jerry Frankel
Producer

Darren Bagert
Infinity Stages
Producer

Gore Vidal's The Best Man

Barbara Manocherian
Producer

Van Dean, Kenny Howard
The Broadway Consortium
Producers

Ken Mahoney
Producer

Kathleen K. Johnson
Producer

Larry Hirschhorn
Producer

Matthew Masten
Bennu Productions
Producer

Steven Baker
Bennu Productions
Producer

Patty Baker
Producer

Paul Boskind and Martian Entertainment
Producer

Wendy Federman
Producer

Mark S. Golub
Producer

Stewart F. Lane, Bonnie Comley
Producers

Carl Moellenberg
Producer

Harold Thau
Producer

2011-2012 AWARDS

DRAMA DESK AWARD
Outstanding Sound Design
in a Play
(John Gromada)

OUTER CRITICS CIRCLE AWARD
Outstanding Featured Actor
in a Play
(James Earl Jones)

PAUL ROBESON AWARD
(James Earl Jones)

Photo by Brian Mapp

CREW
Lying Down: Ken McGee
Seated (L-R): Kim Butler-Gilkeson, Lolly Totero, Flynn Earl Jones, Danny Paul, Andrea Gonzalez, Matthew Farrell
Standing (L-R): Tim McWilliams, Steve McDonald, Wayne Smith, Leslie Ann Kilian, Maeve Butler, Laura Beattie, Linda Lee, Marc Jones, Jeanette Harrington, Jay Penfield

Gore Vidal's The Best Man

Photos by Brian Mapp

FRONT OF HOUSE
Front Row (L-R):
Roz Nyman, Lisa Boyd,
Amber Hill

Second Row (L-R):
David Conte, Raya Konyk,
Rosetta Jlelaty,
Alexandria Williams

Third Row (L-R): Shatail
Williams, Denise Demirjian

Fourth Row (L-R): Michael
Rhodus, Michael Santoro,
Jennifer Ewing, James Teal

Top Row (L-R): Pep Speed,
Anthony Martinez,
Paul Brown

MANAGEMENT
(L-R): Matthew Farrell,
Ken McGee,
Brig Berney

STAFF FOR *GORE VIDAL'S THE BEST MAN*

GENERAL MANAGEMENT
RICHARDS/CLIMAN, INC.

David R. Richards	Tamar Haimes
Michael Sag	Kyle Bonder
Jessica Fried	Ashley Rodbro

COMPANY MANAGER
Brig Berney

GENERAL PRESS REPRESENTATIVE
JEFFREY RICHARDS ASSOCIATES
Irene Gandy   Alana Karpoff   Ryan Hallett

PRODUCTION MANAGEMENT
HUDSON THEATRICAL ASSOCIATES
Neil A. Mazzella   Sam Ellis   Irene Wang
Walter Murphy   Corky Boyd   Jillian Oliver

CASTING
TELSEY + COMPANY
Bernie Telsey CSA, Will Cantler CSA,
David Vaccari CSA, Bethany Knox CSA,
Craig Burns CSA, Tiffany Little Canfield CSA,
Rachel Hoffman CSA, Justin Huff CSA,
Patrick Goodwin CSA, Abbie Brady-Dalton CSA,
David Morris, Cesar A. Rocha, Andrew Femenella,
Karyn Casl, Kristina Bramhall, Jessie Malone

PRODUCTION STAGE MANAGER ....Matthew Farrell
Stage Manager ....Kenneth J. McGee
Assistant Director ....David Alpert
Assistant Producer ....Michael Crea
SDC Observer ....Jessica Rose McVay
Makeup Designer ....Angelina Avallone
Dialect Coach ....Kate Wilson
Associate Scenic Designer ....Aimee B. Dombo
Assistant Scenic Designer ....Erica Hemminger
Associate Costume Designer ....Matthew Pachtman
Assistant to Ms. Roth ....Irma Escobar
Associate Lighting Designer ....John Viesta
Associate Projection Designer ....C. Andrew Bauer
Assistant Projection Designer ....Dan Scully
Projection Programmer ....Benjamin Keightley

Associate Sound Designer ....Alex Neumann
Sound Intern ....Chet Miller
Production Carpenter ....Robert Griffin
Carpenter/Deck Automation ....McBrien Dunbar
Production Electrician ....James Maloney
Associate Production Electrician ....Brian Maiuri
Electrician ....Jay Penfield
Production Sound Engineer ....Wayne Smith
Production Properties Coordinator ....Peter Sarafin
Assistant Properties Coordinator ....Buist Bickley
Wardrobe Supervisor ....Linda Lee
Dressers ....Laura Beattie, Kimberly Butler,
Maeve Fiona Butler, Andrea Gonzalez,
Daniel Paul, Lolly Totero
Hair/Wig Supervisor ....Carole Morales
Assistant Hair Supervisor ....Linda Rice
Production Assistants......................Lori Lundquist,
Shelley Miles, Sean Lyons
Assistant to Mr. Bagert ....Matthew Masten
Press Intern ....Thomas Raynor
Advertising ....Serino/Coyne/
Greg Coradetti, Tom Callahan,
Danielle Boyle, Drew Nebrig
Website Design/
Online Marketing Strategy ....Situation Interactive/
Damien Bazadona, John Lanasa,
Brian Hawe, Victoria Gettler,
Tom Lorenzo, Bizzy Coy, Lisa Cecchini
Interactive Marketing
Service ....Broadway's Best Shows/
Andy Drachenberg, Christopher Pineda
Banking...............................City National Bank/
Michele Gibbons, Erik Piecuch
Insurance ....DeWitt Stern Group, Peter Shoemaker,
Anthony Pittari
Accountants ....Fried & Kowgios CPAs LLP/
Robert Fried, Anthony Moore
Comptroller ....Elliott Aronstam
Legal Counsel ....Lazarus and Harris LLP/
Scott Lazarus, Esq., Robert C. Harris, Esq.
Legal Clearance and Permissions
provided by ....License It
Payroll ....Castellana Services
Production Photographer ....Joan Marcus
Merchandise ....Max Merchandising

Company Mascots ....Skye, Franco, Jerry, Phyllis

CREDITS
Scenery constructed and automated by Hudson Scenic Studio. Lighting equipment from Hudson Sound and Light LLC. Sound Equipment from Sound Associates. Video projection system provided by Worldstage/Scharff Weisberg, Inc. Costumes by Eric Winterling, Inc. and Giliberto Designs, Inc. Miss Lansbury and Miss Bergen's wigs by Paul Huntley. Other wigs by Hudson Wigs LLC. Millinery by Rodney Gordon, Inc. Prop fabricators: C and R Designs, Joseph Cairo, Jeremy Lydic, Craig Grigg, Enhance a Colour, Anna Light, Joshua Yocom. Furniture painted and finished by Stephanie Dedes.

This production is dedicated to Howard Austen.

Rehearsed at the New 42nd Street Studios

 THE SHUBERT ORGANIZATION, INC.
Board of Directors

Philip J. Smith	**Robert E. Wankel**
Chairman	President
Wyche Fowler, Jr.	**Diana Phillips**
Lee J. Seidler	**Michael I. Sovern**

Stuart Subotnick

Chief Financial Officer ....Elliot Greene
Sr. Vice President, Ticketing ....David Andrews
Vice President, Finance ....Juan Calvo
Vice President, Human Resources ....Cathy Cozens
Vice President, Facilities ....John Darby
Vice President, Theatre Operations ....Peter Entin
Vice President, Marketing ....Charles Flateman
Vice President, Audit ....Anthony LaMattina
Vice President, Ticket Sales ....Brian Mahoney
Vice President, Creative Projects ............D.S. Moynihan
Vice President, Real Estate ....Julio Peterson

---

Theatre Manager ....David M. Conte

Gore Vidal's The Best Man
SCRAPBOOK

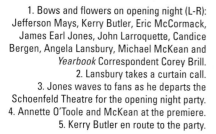

1. Bows and flowers on opening night (L-R): Jefferson Mays, Kerry Butler, Eric McCormack, James Earl Jones, John Larroquette, Candice Bergen, Angela Lansbury, Michael McKean and *Yearbook* Correspondent Corey Brill.
2. Lansbury takes a curtain call.
3. Jones waves to fans as he departs the Schoenfeld Theatre for the opening night party.
4. Annette O'Toole and McKean at the premiere.
5. Kerry Butler en route to the party.

Correspondent: Corey Brill, "Don Blades"

Actor Who Has Done the Most Shows in Their Career: That's a tough call—I would guess it's a tight race between James Earl Jones, Angela Lansbury and Dakin Matthews.

Special Backstage Rituals: My own ritual for a while was to read the copy of *To Kill a Mockingbird* that was on one of the sets, backstage. Once I was finished reading that I suddenly didn't know what to do with myself. And after each evening's show, Eric McCormack and I would split a beer in the dressing room. We'd take turns buying the six-packs.

Favorite Moment During Each Performance: Onstage (But Viewed From the Wings): Candice has the most hilarious reaction to seeing a photo of Eric McCormack and Kerry Butler's (apparently quite ugly) children. Just priceless.

Favorite Off-Site Hangout: Plenty of us go to the Glass House Tavern (hey Chris!) often enough to warrant having our paychecks sent directly to them.

Favorite Snack Food: There are almonds and olives used as props in the show and I'm thinking of writing a *Best Man* diet book.

Favorite Therapy: We have an optional warm-up before each show. Well, optional for everyone but me, since I was asked to lead it. First time I've ever done that for a cast on a regular basis, and I don't know that I'll ever get over the fact that James Earl Jones looks to me to help him warm up his voice! He never misses the warm-up.

Most Memorable Ad-Lib: During rehearsal instead of calling for "line," I remember JEJ saying, "Now. . . what do I say to that shit?"

Catchphrase Only the Company Would Recognize: "F#$% this orange!" (John Larroquette).

Nicknames: Fred Parker plays a photographer, and, as Fred is the youngest member of the cast, Michael Wilson dubbed him "Cub." I think it's stuck.

Superstition That Turned Out To Be True: Jefferson Mays a few nights ago quoted The Scottish Play. . . he went through all of the required atonements, but sure enough, halfway through a scene in Act III, all of the power went off onstage and off. Coincidence?

Coolest Thing About Being in This Show: I've been lucky to work with some amazing talents over the years, but this takes the cake—watching these luminaries tackle Vidal's text, each with their own way of working but toward a common goal. . . I can not believe my luck!

Also: On our first preview, Larroquette accidently bumped his head into one of the wall sconces early in act one. He stood there for a moment staring at it, then said his next line. And it just so happened that his next line was "Sorry we're in such close quarters"! Just one of those perfect moments that can only happen onstage.

Hair

First Preview: July 5, 2011. Opened: July 13, 2011.
Closed September 10, 2011 after 11 Previews and 67 Performances.

HAIR
HAIR
HAIR
HAIR

Return engagement of the rock musical about a tribe of hippies living on the streets of New York, and how they react when one of their members is drafted and goes off to fight in Vietnam.

CAST

(in order of appearance)

Dionne	PHYRE HAWKINS
Berger	STEEL BURKHARDT
Woof	MATT DeANGELIS
Hud	DARIUS NICHOLS
Claude	PARIS REMILLARD
Sheila	CAREN LYN TACKETT
Jeanie	KACIE SHEIK
Crissy	KAITLIN KIYAN
Mother	ALLISON GUINN
Dad	JOSH LAMON
Principal	LEE ZARRETT
Margaret Mead	JOSH LAMON
Hubert	LEE ZARRETT
Abraham Lincoln	LULU FALL
John Wilkes Booth	LEE ZARRETT
Buddhadalirama	ALLISON GUINN
Tribe Members	SHALEAH ADKISSON, NICHOLAS BELTON, MARSHAL KENNEDY CAROLAN, MIKE EVARISTE, LULU FALL, NKRUMAH GATLING, ALLISON GUINN, SARA KING, JOSH LAMON, JOHN MOAURO, CHRISTINE NOLAN, EMMY RAVER-LAMPMAN, ARBENDER ROBINSON, CAILAN ROSE, JEN SESE, LEE ZARRETT

Continued on next page

🎭 ST. JAMES THEATRE

A JUJAMCYN THEATRE

JORDAN ROTH
President

PAUL LIBIN
Executive Vice President

JACK VIERTEL
Senior Vice President

THE PUBLIC THEATER
Oskar Eustis, Artistic Director
NEDERLANDER PRODUCTIONS INC.   CARL MOELLENBERG/WENLARBAR PRODUCTIONS
REBECCA GOLD/MYLA LERNER   RICK COSTELLO   JOY NEWMAN & DAVID SCHUMEISTER
PAUL G. RICE/PAUL BARTZ   DEBBIE BISNO   CHRISTOPHER HART PRODUCTIONS   JOHN PINCKARD   TERRY SCHNUCK
JOEY PARNES
by special arrangement with
ELIZABETH IRELAND McCANN

present

HAIR

The American Tribal Love-Rock Musical

Book & Lyrics by
GEROME RAGNI & JAMES RADO

Music by
GALT MacDERMOT

with

STEEL BURKHARDT   MATT DeANGELIS   PHYRE HAWKINS   KAITLIN KIYAN
DARIUS NICHOLS   PARIS REMILLARD   KACIE SHEIK   CAREN LYN TACKETT

and

SHALEAH ADKISSON   EMILY AFTON   NICHOLAS BELTON   LARKIN BOGAN   COREY BRADLEY
MARSHAL KENNEDY CAROLAN   LAURA DREYFUSS   MIKE EVARISTE   LULU FALL
TRIPP FOUNTAIN   NKRUMAH GATLING   ALLISON GUINN   SARA KING
JOSH LAMON   JOHN MOAURO   CHRISTINE NOLAN   EMMY RAVER-LAMPMAN
ARBENDER ROBINSON   CAILAN ROSE   TANESHA ROSS   JEN SESE   LEE ZARRETT

Scenic Design **SCOTT PASK**	Costume Design **MICHAEL McDONALD**	Lighting Design **KEVIN ADAMS**	Sound Design **ACME SOUND PARTNERS**
Orchestrations **GALT MacDERMOT**	Music Supervisor **NADIA DiGIALLONARDO**	Music Director **DAVID TRUSKINOFF**	Music Coordinator **SEYMOUR RED PRESS**
Wig Design **GERARD KELLY**	Production Supervisor **NANCY HARRINGTON**	Production Stage Manager **WILLIAM JOSEPH BARNES**	Casting **JORDAN THALER HEIDI GRIFFITHS**
Press Representative **O&M CO.**	Marketing **ALLIED LIVE, LLC**	Advertising **SPOTCO**	Tour Booking **BROADWAY BOOKING OFFICE NYC**

Associate Producers
JENNY GERSTEN   S.D. WAGNER   JOHN JOHNSON

Choreography by
KAROLE ARMITAGE

Directed by
DIANE PAULUS

ORIGINALLY PRODUCED IN 1967 AND SUBSEQUENTLY REVIVED IN 2008 BY THE PUBLIC THEATER
OSKAR EUSTIS, ARTISTIC DIRECTOR

7/13/11

(L-R): Paris Remillard and Steel Burkhardt (center) with the cast

Photo by Joan Marcus

Hair

MUSICAL NUMBERS

ACT I

"Aquarius" .... Dionne and Tribe
"Donna" .... Berger and Tribe
"Hashish" .... Tribe
"Sodomy" .... Woof and Tribe
"Colored Spade" .... Hud and Tribe
"Manchester, England" .... Claude and Tribe
"I'm Black" .... Hud, Woof, Berger, Claude and Tribe
"Ain't Got No" .... Woof, Hud, Dionne and Tribe
"Sheila Franklin" .... Tribe
"I Believe in Love" .... Sheila, Cailan, Sara, Shaleah
"Ain't Got No" .... Tribe
"Air" .... Jeanie, Crissy and Dionne
"The Stone Age" .... Berger
"I Got Life" .... Claude and Tribe
"Initials" .... Tribe
"Going Down" .... Berger and Tribe
"Hair" .... Claude, Berger and Tribe
"My Conviction" .... Margaret Mead
"Easy to Be Hard" .... Sheila
"Don't Put It Down" .... Berger, Woof, Arbender
"Frank Mills" .... Crissy
"Hare Krishna" .... Tribe
"Where Do I Go" .... Claude and Tribe

ACT II

"Electric Blues" .... Allison, Josh, Nick, Shaleah
"Oh Great God of Power" .... Tribe
"Black Boys" .... Christine, Jen, Sara
"White Boys" .... Dionne, Emmy, Lulu
"Walking in Space" .... Tribe
"Minuet" .... Orchestra
"Yes, I's Finished on Y'alls Farmlands" .... Hud, Arbender, Mike, Nkrumah
"Four Score and Seven Years Ago"/
  "Abie Baby" .... Abraham Lincoln, Hud, Arbender, Mike, Nkrumah
"Give Up All Desires" .... Buddhadalirama, Crissy, Sheila, Woof
"Three-Five-Zero-Zero" .... Tribe
"What a Piece of Work Is Man" .... Tribe
"Good Morning Starshine" .... Sheila and Tribe
"Ain't Got No" (Reprise) .... Claude and Tribe
"The Flesh Failures" .... Claude
"Manchester"/"Eyes Look Your Last" .... Claude, Crissy, Dionne, Jeanie, Woof
"Flesh Failures"/"Let the Sun Shine In" .... Sheila, Dionne, Jeanie, Sara and Tribe

Cast Continued

UNDERSTUDIES

For Claude: LARKIN BOGAN, MARSHAL
    KENNEDY CAROLAN, MATT DeANGELIS
For Berger: NICHOLAS BELTON,
    MATT DeANGELIS
For Woof: LARKIN BOGAN, JOHN MOAURO
For Hud: COREY BRADLEY, MIKE EVARISTE
For Sheila: LAURA DREYFUSS, SARA KING,
    JEN SESE
For Dionne: EMMY RAVER-LAMPMAN,
    TANESHA ROSS
For Jeanie: ALLISON GUINN, JEN SESE
For Crissy: LAURA DREYFUSS, CAILAN ROSE
For Mother: EMILY AFTON,
    CHRISTINE NOLAN
For Dad, Margaret Mead: TRIPP FOUNTAIN,
    LEE ZARRETT
For Principal, Hubert, John Wilkes Booth:
    LARKIN BOGAN, TRIPP FOUNTAIN
For Buddhadalirama: EMILY AFTON,
    CHRISTINE NOLAN
For Abraham Lincoln: SHALEAH ADKISSON,
    EMMY RAVER-LAMPMAN

Dance Captain: JOHN MOAURO
Assistant Dance Captain: EMILY AFTON

TRIBE SWINGS

EMILY AFTON, LARKIN BOGAN,
COREY BRADLEY, LAURA DREYFUSS,
TRIPP FOUNTAIN, TANESHA ROSS

MUSICIANS

Conductor/Keyboard: DAVID TRUSKINOFF
Associate Conductor/Keyboards: JARED STEIN
Guitar: JOSH WEINSTEIN
Bass: FRANK CANINO
Woodwinds: DANIEL BLOCK
Trumpet: ROBERT MILLIKAN,
    RONALD BUTTACAVOLI, ELAINE BURT
Trombone: CHARLES GORDON
Percussion: SEAN RITENAUER
Drums: WAYNE DUNTON

The Tribe

Photo by Joan Marcus

Hair

Steel Burkhardt
Berger

Matt DeAngelis
Woof

Phyre Hawkins
Dionne

Kaitlin Kiyan
Crissy

Darius Nichols
Hud

Paris Remillard
Claude

Kacie Sheik
Jeanie

Caren Lyn Tackett
Sheila

Shaleah Adkisson
Tribe

Emily Afton
Swing

Nicholas Belton
Tribe

Larkin Bogan
Swing

Corey Bradley
Swing

Marshal Kennedy Carolan
Tribe

Laura Dreyfuss
Swing

Mike Evariste
Tribe

Lulu Fall
*Tribe/
Abraham Lincoln*

Tripp Fountain
Swing

Nkrumah Gatling
Tribe

Allison Guinn
*Tribe/Mother/
Buddhadalirama*

Sara King
Tribe

Josh Lamon
*Tribe/Dad/
Margaret Mead*

John Moauro
Tribe

Christine Nolan
Tribe

Emmy Raver-
Lampman
Tribe

Arbender Robinson
Tribe

Cailan Rose
Tribe

Tanesha Ross
Swing

Jen Sese
Tribe

Lee Zarrett
*Tribe/Principal/
Hubert/
John Wilkes Booth*

Gerome Ragni
Co-Creator

James Rado
Co-Creator

Galt MacDermot
Composer

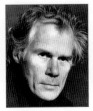
Diane Paulus
Director

Karole Armitage
Choreographer

Hair

Scott Pask
Scenic Design

Michael McDonald
Costume Design

Kevin Adams
Lighting Design

Sten Severson, Tom Clark, Mark Menard and Nevin Steinberg,
Acme Sound Partners
Sound Designer

David Truskinoff
*Music Director/
Conductor*

Seymour Red Press
Music Coordinator

Jordan Thaler/
Heidi Griffiths
Casting

Christine O'Grady
*Associate
Choreographer*

Oskar Eustis,
Artistic Director,
Public Theater
Productions
Producer

Joey Parnes,
Interim Executive
Director,
Public Theater
Productions
Producer

James L.
Nederlander
Producer

Carl Moellenberg
Producer

Wendy Federman
Producer

Larry Hirschhorn
Producer

Barbara
Manocherian
Producer

(L-R): Matt DeAngelis,
Caren Lyn Tackett
and Paris Remillard

Photo by Joan Marcus

Rebecca Gold
Producer

Myla Lerner
Producer

Debbie Bisno
Producer

John Pinckard
Producer

Terry Schnuck
Producer

Elizabeth Ireland
McCann
Producer

Hair

CREW

Standing (L-R): Dave Brown, Ryan McDonough, Mike Eickmeyer, Tim McDonough, Jr., Tim McDonough Sr., Greg Pott, Stuart Metcalf, Bonnie Runk, Tree Sarvay, Lane Elms

Kneeling (L-R): Dawn Marcoccia, Edgar Vanegas, Joe Lenihan, Ginny Headrick, Sue Pelkofer, Kimberly Mark, David Grevengoed, Bob Miller

MANAGEMENT

(Top to Bottom): Chris Zaccardi, Kathryn L. McKee, Kit Ingui, Billy Barnes, Jennifer Graves, Lola Graves (Black Dog)

HAIR DEPARTMENT

(L-R): Monica Costea, Lisa Ann Fraley, Brittnye Batchelor

BAND

(L-R): Ronnie Nelson, David Truskinoff, Frank Canino, Sean Ritenauer, Elaine Burt, Wayne Dunton

USHERS

Front Row (L-R): Heather Jewels, Katie Siegmund, Margaret McElroy, Rebecca Segarra, Quinton Menendez, Catherine Junior, Andrew Mackay

Middle Row (L-R): Donna Vanderlinden, Cindy Lopiano, Rita Richardson, Joann Mariani, Kendra McDuffie, Lenny Baron, Jim Barry

Back Row (L-R): Thomas Murdoch, Jeff Hubbard, Julia Furay, Katie Schmidt, Barbara Kagan, Aaron Kendall

Hair

STAFF FOR *HAIR*

GENERAL MANAGEMENT
Joey Parnes
John Johnson   S.D. Wagner
Kim Sellon

COMPANY MANAGER
Jennifer R. Graves

FOR THE PUBLIC THEATER
Artistic Director ....Oskar Eustis
Interim Executive Director ....Joey Parnes
Associate Artistic Director ....Mandy Hackett

GENERAL PRESS REPRESENTATIVE
O&M CO.
Rick Miramontez
Molly Barnett   Elizabeth Wagner

**TOUR BOOKING &
ENGAGEMENT MANAGEMENT**
BROADWAY BOOKING OFFICE NYC
Steven Schnepp   Temah Higgins   David Freeland
Alexander Parra   Julia D'Angelo

ASSOCIATE CHOREOGRAPHER
Christine O'Grady

Production Stage Manager ....William Joseph Barnes
Stage Manager ....Chris Zaccardi
Assistant Stage Manager ....Kathryn McKee
Assistant Company Manager ....Kit Ingui
Management Associates ....Kristen Luciani, Nate Koch
Associate Set Designer ....Paul Weimer
Associate Lighting Designer ....Joel Silver
Assistant Lighting Designer ....Andy Fritsch
Associate Costume Designer ....Lisa Zinni
Associate Sound Designer ....David Thomas
Casting Associate ....Amber Wakefield
Production Carpenter ....Larry Morley
Head Carpenter ....Greg Pott
Assistant Carpenter ....Michael Eickmeyer
Production Properties ....Mike Smanko
Head Properties ....Stuart Metcalf
Assistant Properties ....Genevieve Headrick
Production Electrician ....Richie Mortell
Head Electrician ....Thomas "Whitey" Ford
Assistant Electrician ....Jeff Brewer
Moving Light Programmers ....Paul J. Sonnleitner,
Thomas Hague
Production Sound ....Jim Wilkinson
Head Sound Engineer ....Mark Clark
Monitor Mixer ....Alex Ritter
Deck Sound ....Lane Elms
Wardrobe Supervisor ....Rob Bevenger
Assistant Wardrobe Supervisor ....Julian Andres Arango
Hair Supervisor ....Lisa Ann Fraley
Production Assistant ....Rebecca Spinac
Assistant to Production Carpenter ......Amanda Raymond
Assistant to Oskar Eustis ....Jesse Alick
Assistant to the
Interim Executive Director ....Rosalind Barbour
Advertising ....SpotCo/
Drew Hodges, Jim Edwards,
Y. Darius Suyama, Erin Moeller

Marketing ....Allied Live/
Laura Matalon, Tanya Grubich,
Ronni Seif, Kelly Estrella, Julian Ramirez
Interactive Marketing
and Website Design ....Situation Interactive/
Damian Bazadona, John Lanasa,
Jeremy Kraus, Miriam Naggar
Merchandise ....Creative Goods/
Pete Milano, Kyle McGinley
Touring Merch Rep ....Erica Porch
Press Associates ....Jaron Caldwell, Philip Carrubba,
Sam Corbett, Jon Dimond,
Richard Hillman, Yufen Kung,
Andy Snyder
Press Interns ....Michael Jorgensen, Chelsea Nachman
Legal Counsel ....Lazarus & Harris LLP/
Scott Lazarus, Esq., Robert Harris, Esq.
Public Theater Counsel ....Paul, Weiss, Rifkind,
Wharton & Garrison LLP/
Charles H. Googe Jr., Carolyn J. Casselman,
Michael Bogner
Accountants ....Rosenberg, Neuwirth & Kuchner/
Mark A. D'Ambrosi, Patricia M. Pedersen,
Ruthie Skochil
Banking ....City National Bank/
Stephanie Dalton, Michele Gibbons
Insurance ....AON/Albert G. Ruben/
George Walden, Claudia B. Kaufman
Payroll ....Castellana Services Inc./
Lance Castellana, James Castellana,
Norman Sewell
Housing Coordination ....Road Concierge/Lisa Morris
Physical Therapy
Consultants ....Performing Arts Physical Therapy
Production Photographer ....Joan Marcus

CREDITS
Scenery and scenic effects built, painted and electrified by Showmotion, Inc. Lighting equipment by PRG Lighting. Sound equipment by Sound Associates. Costumes executed by the Public Theater Costume Shop; John Kristiansen, New York Inc.; Timberlake Studios; Marc Happel; Giliberto Custom Tailors. Specialty costumes by Fritz Masten and Barbara Brust. Millinery by Lynne Mackey Studio and T. Michael Hall. Custom embroidery by Jason Hadley. Knitware by Clarion Overmoyer. Custom leatherware by David Samuel Menkes. Select vintage clothing courtesy of Scaramouche. Military uniforms and accessories supplied by Kaufman's Army & Navy, NYC.

Rehearsed at the New 42nd Street Studios.

Synthesizers provided by
Yamaha Corporation of America.

Original cast recording available on
Ghostlight Records.

SPECIAL THANKS
Bumble and bumble, Leslie Glassburn,
Trini Huschle, Maddie Felix, Lola,
Steve Sosnowski, Meghan Ownbey

Energy-efficient washer/dryer courtesy of
LG Electronics

JUJAMCYN THEATERS

JORDAN ROTH
President

PAUL LIBIN   **JACK VIERTEL**
Executive Vice President   Senior Vice President
MEREDITH VILLATORE   **JENNIFER HERSHEY**
Chief Financial Officer   Vice President,
Building Operations

MICAH HOLLINGWORTH   **HAL GOLDBERG**
Vice President,   Vice President,
Company Operations   Theatre Operations

Director of Business Affairs ....Albert T. Kim
Theatre Operations Managers ....Willa Burke,
Susan Elrod, Hal Goldberg,
Jeff Hubbard, Albert T. Kim
Theatre Operations Associates ....Carrie Jo Brinker,
Emily Hare, Anah Jyoti Klate
Accounting ....Cathy Cerge, Erin Dooley,
Christian Sislian
Executive Producer, Red Awning ....Nicole Kastrinos
Director of Marketing, Givenik.com ....Joe Tropia
Marketing Associate, Givenik.com ....Ben Cohen
Building Operations Associate ....Erich Bussing
Assistant to Jordan Roth ....Ed Lefferson
Assistant to Paul Libin ....Clark Mims Tedesco
Assistant to Jack Viertel ....Marisol Rosa-Shapiro
Receptionist ....Kate Garst
Maintenance ....Ralph Santos, Ramon Zapata
Security ....Rasim Hodzic, John Acero
Interns ....Anna Barth, Mike Composto,
Stephanie Ditman, Garrett Ellison,
Audrey Frischman, Joanna Kamien,
Jonathan Meyers, Justin Noga,
Tori Piersanti, Olivia Rubino-Finn

Staff for the St. James Theatre for *Hair*
Manager ....Jeff Hubbard
Treasurer ....Vincent Sclafani
Head Carpenter ....Timothy B. McDonough
Head Propertyman ....Timothy McDonough
Head Electrician ....Albert Sayers
Flyman ....David Brown
Engineer ....Michael Tooze
Assistant Treasurers ....Carmine Loiacono,
Thomas Motylenski,
Vincent Siniscalchi
Propertyman ....Ryan McDonough
Electricians ....Joe Lenihan, Tom Maloney,
Bob Miller, Sue Pelkofer
Head Usher ....Cynthia Lopiano
Ticket-takers/Directors/
Ushers ....Len Baron, James Barry,
Murray Bradley, Barbara Carroll,
Julia Furay, Heather Jewels,
Catherine Junior, Barbara Kagan,
Andrew Mackay, Kendra McDuffie,
Margaret McElroy, Katie Schmidt, Katie Siegmund,
Jessica Theisen, Donna Vanderlinden, Brian Veith
Doormen ....Russell Buenteo, Adam Hodzic
Head Porter ....Jacobo Medrano
Porters ....Rafael Liriano, Francisco Medina,
Donnette Niles
Head Cleaner ....Carmela Tenebruso
Cleaners ....Juana Medrano, Antonia Moreno

Hair
SCRAPBOOK

Correspondent: John Moauro, "Tribe Member" and Dance Captain

Memorable Fan Letter: When I was doing *Hair* on the West End (and the Broadway company had just closed) a fan sent me my face, from a picture on the doors outside the Hirschfeld Theatre. He said he was walking by and didn't want it to just end up in the trash, so he cut it off. He wrote that he thought it was something I would like to have as a memory. It was very sweet.

Memorable Party: Our opening night on Broadway was definitely the best party. The night was filled with excitement and joy. We had 12 cast members making their Broadway debut that night.

Most Exciting Celebrity Visitor: Diane Keaton. She stayed long after the dance party was over to say hi, and tell us how much she enjoyed the show, and briefly talked about being in the original production, and understudying Sheila. She was very nice, and pretty!!

Special Backstage Rituals: As dance captain I am usually running around giving notes or fixing little staging or traffic issues. I love hanging in the men's ensemble dressing room. We have a good time together. I always need my coffee before the show!

Favorite Moment: It's hard to pick just one, but if I had to, it would be at the top of "Good Morning Starshine." I always whisper something in Kacie Sheik's ear and we either laugh or cry together.

Favorite In-Theatre Gathering Place: On the road our company managers Jennifer and Kit ALWAYS have candy in their office...the cast is usually lingering around there. :) At the St. James I love to chill in Kacie Sheik's dressing room OR in my dressing room with Marshal, Arbender, and Nkrumah.

Favorite Off-Site Hangout: Kodama (on 45th Street) is a big hangout between shows for the cast. We LOVE Kodama!!! Those of us that were in the original revival company across the street at the Hirschfeld were there every day...it's a *Hair* staple.

Favorite Snack Foods: I love gummi bears and thanks to our company managers I now have a passion for M&M's Pretzel. Yum!

Mascots: The dogs that travel with us on the road. Nick Belton's dog Charlie (who sadly passed away, when we were on tour this past spring) and Lola, our company manager Jennifer's dog, whom you can always hear barking throughout the theatre.

Favorite Therapy: Ricola AND Orbit Mist Raspberry Lemon Dew gum. Our stage is always filled with a thin layer of fog and the dust that accumulates on the carpet on our stage makes it very dry during the show. The gum helps keep my throat lubricated.

Memorable Ad-Lib: Josh Lamon as Margaret Mead is the king of ad-libbing. The moment that Crissy rushes to Margaret and says "She's gonna sing" and Josh replies "If we're talking,

Curtain call on opening night (L-R): Kacie Sheik, Phyre Hawkins, Paris Remillard, Steel Burkhardt, Caren Lyn Tackett, Matt DeAngelis, Kaitlin Kiyan and Marshal Kennedy Carolan

Photo by Joseph Marzullo/WENN

One of the couples wed on the stage of the St. James Theatre July 25, 2011 after gay marriage was legalized in New York.

Photo by Monica Simoes

we aren't listening"—it started as an ad-lib and now it's in the script.

Latest Audience Arrival: We had a couple come in during the yellow shirt scene. That's about 45 minutes into the show.

Fastest Costume Change: Allison Guinn's change from Buddhadalirama into Fantasy Mom. It takes 23 seconds!!

Busiest Day at the Box Office: On Monday, July 25, 2011 we were lucky enough to host the union of three same-sex couples. The St. James Theatre was packed with love and support from the community. Those three couples were among the first in New York State to be married after the state legislature passed the bill. Colman Domingo officiated the ceremonies. And afterwards we all proudly sang "Let the Sun Shine In."

Heaviest/Hottest Costume: Kacie Sheik as Jeanie!! She has on a tank top and shorts under the pregnancy belly and a tank top, a dress and a long sleeved shirt on top of that heavy padded

Belly. She wins!

Who Wore the Least: There are 19 cast members naked onstage every performance. They ALL wear the least!!!!

Catchphrase Only the Company Would Recognize: "CLAM!!"

Sweethearts Within the Company: It is one big love fest in our cast.

Orchestra Member Who Played the Most Instruments: Percussionist Sean Ritenauer plays the congas, the bongo, the timbales, many cymbals and gongs, the tambourine, the water phone, the washboard, the bell tree, a marimba and many more toys. He also has some great moves! Watch him dance during "Abie Baby."

Orchestra Member Who Played the Most Consecutive Performances Without a Sub: Wayne Dunton, our drummer, has never missed a show! We love Wayne.

Memorable Directorial Note: It's always funny during rehearsals when we are doing

Hair
SCRAPBOOK

1. Josh Lamon playing around in Matt DeAngelis' 'Woof' costume in a dressing room.
2. Some of the Tribe on stage at the St. James Theatre.
3. Kacie Sheik and *Playbill Broadway Yearbook* correspondent John Moauro.
4. Matt DeAngelis and Kacie Sheik.
5. Swings Laura Dreyfuss and Emily Afton show off their hair backstage.
6. Producer Jordan Roth, director Diane Paulus and Public Theater Artistic Director Oskar Eustis at the opening night party at Sky Bar.

sexual acts with each other. Diane [Paulus] once told us that we were humping each other too hard during "S-E-X Y-O-U." She yelled on the God mic, "You all need to hump softer there. Save it for 'Sodomy'." Rehearsing those moments always makes me blush a little.

Company Legend: One of the worst things that could happen to an actor came true one night during "White Boys." In the original cast on Broadway I had created this moment, with Megan Lawrence. It was during my BIG paddle turn section of the song (haha). Caissie Levy (who played Sheila) ran a little too close to me and I accidentally punched her in the face...twice. Her nose immediately started bleeding and she ran off stage right. I was mortified. I finished the song and ran backstage

to check on her and was told that she was going to the hospital. I felt horrible. We improvised a few new lines and Nicole Lewis (who was one of our Sheila covers) jumped in to save the day and belt out a beautiful "Good Morning Starshine." Caissie ended up with a bruise. Nothing was broken, thank goodness. It made for a very interesting second act. We now look back and laugh about it.

Nicknames: Our "hippie" names are a regular go-to: Smokie, Sensei, Butterbean, Willow, Earthquake...

Embarrassing Moments: On more than one occasion as we ran off stage naked, cast members have tripped over clothes on the ground and fallen. It's embarrassing enough to fall on stage with clothes on...

Ghostly Encounter Backstage: While we were in Chicago at the Oriental Theatre, Josh Lamon, Caren Tackett and Lisa Ann Fraley (head of our hair department) were taken on an actual Ghost Hunt in the famously haunted theatre. They were led by James Card, who has a paranormal investigative team there. Caren said "He had a bunch of gear that did readings and all kinds of things I can't explain, and the results were pretty jarring." They were definitely believers after that experience.

Coolest Things About Being in This Show: Not having a fourth wall. I LOVE going into the house and seeing the audience's faces up close, messing with their hair and giving high fives. The dance party at the end of the show is a favorite as well.

How to Succeed in Business Without Really Trying

First Preview: February 26, 2011. Opened: March 27, 2011.
Closed May 20, 2012 after 30 Previews and 473 Performances.

PLAYBILL®

J. Pierrepont Finch is a lowly window washer at the World Wide Wicket Company, but he's got a dream. He bought himself the book "How to Succeed in Business Without Really Trying," and decides to follow its precepts and see how far they take him. Starting in the mailroom, he uses a combination of flattery, insincere friendship-building and bare-faced chutzpah to leap upward through the ranks in just a few days, dazzling stenographer Rosemary, who sets her cap for him, and horrifying the older climbers in the company hierarchy as he breezes past them on the way to the president's chair. Just before J. Pierrepont takes over the company completely, he makes one fatally flawed move that threatens to send him plunging to the mailroom. But not to worry: his magical book has the right answer for everything.

CAST

(in order of appearance)

The Voice of the Narrator . ANDERSON COOPER
J. Pierrepont Finch .... NICK JONAS
Mr. Gatch .... NICK MAYO
Mr. Jenkins .... CHARLIE WILLIAMS
Mr. Johnson/TV Announcer ...... KEVIN COVERT
Mr. Matthews .... RYAN WATKINSON
Mr. Peterson .... MARTY LAWSON
Mr. Tackaberry .... TIMOTHY J. ALEX
Mr. Toynbee .... TAYLOR FREY
Mr. Andrews .... ANDREW MADSEN
J.B. Biggley .... BEAU BRIDGES
Rosemary Pilkington .... ROSE HEMINGWAY
Mr. Bratt .... MICHAEL PARK
Smitty .... MARY FABER
Miss Jones .... ELLEN HARVEY

Continued on next page

9 AL HIRSCHFELD THEATRE
A JUJAMCYN THEATRE

JORDAN ROTH
President

PAUL LIBIN
Executive Vice President

JACK VIERTEL
Senior Vice President

BROADWAY ACROSS AMERICA   CRAIG ZADAN   NEIL MERON
JOSEPH SMITH   MICHAEL McCABE
CANDY SPELLING   TAKONKIET VIRAVAN / SCENARIO THAILAND   HILARY A. WILLIAMS
JEN NAMOFF / FAKSTON PRODUCTIONS   TWO LEFT FEET PRODUCTIONS / POWER ARTS
HOP THEATRICALS, LLC / PAUL CHAU / DANIEL FRISHWASSER / MICHAEL JACKOWITZ
MICHAEL SPEYER - BERNIE ABRAMS / JACKI BARLIA FLORIN - ADAM BLANSHAY / ARLENE SCANLAN / TBS SERVICE

NICK JONAS   BEAU BRIDGES

HOW TO SUCCEED IN BUSINESS WITHOUT REALLY TRYING

Music & Lyrics by
FRANK LOESSER

Book by
**ABE BURROWS, JACK WEINSTOCK
& WILLIE GILBERT**

Based on the book by SHEPHERD MEAD

TAMMY BLANCHARD

ROB BARTLETT   MARY FABER   ELLEN HARVEY   MICHAEL PARK

TIMOTHY J. ALEX   CLEVE ASBURY   TANYA BIRL   HOLLY ANN BUTLER   ABBY CHURCH
KEVIN COVERT   J. AUSTIN EYER   PAIGE FAURE   TAYLOR FREY   ROBERT HAGER   MARTY LAWSON
SHANNON LEWIS   IAN LIBERTO   ANDREW MADSEN   NICK MAYO   SARAH O'GLEBY
STEPHANIE ROTHENBERG   RYAN WATKINSON   CHARLIE WILLIAMS   SAMANTHA ZACK

with
MICHAEL URIE

and introducing
ROSE HEMINGWAY

featuring
ANDERSON COOPER
as the Voice of the Narrator

Scenic Design by **DEREK McLANE**	Costume Design by **CATHERINE ZUBER**	Lighting Design by **HOWELL BINKLEY**	Sound Design by **JON WESTON**
	Hair & Wig Design by **TOM WATSON**	Orchestrations by **DOUG BESTERMAN**	Music Coordinator **HOWARD JOINES**
Production Stage Manager **KRISTEN HARRIS**	Associate Director **STEPHEN SPOSITO**	Associate Choreographer **CHRISTOPHER BAILEY**	Assistant Choreographers **SARAH O'GLEBY** **CHARLIE WILLIAMS**
Casting by **TARA RUBIN CASTING**	Production Manager **JUNIPER STREET PRODUCTIONS**	Press Representative **THE HARTMAN GROUP**	Marketing **TYPE A MARKETING** **ANNE RIPPEY**
General Management **ALAN WASSER - ALLAN WILLIAMS** **MARK SHACKET**	Associate Producers **STAGE VENTURES** **2010 LIMITED PARTNERSHIP**		Executive Producer **BETH WILLIAMS**

Music Direction & Arrangements by
DAVID CHASE

Directed & Choreographed by
ROB ASHFORD

2/20/12

(L-R:) Nick Jonas and Beau Bridges

Photo by Joan Marcus

How to Succeed in Business Without Really Trying

MUSICAL NUMBERS

ACT I

"Overture" ....Orchestra
"How to Succeed" ....Finch and Company
"Happy to Keep His Dinner Warm" ....Rosemary
"Coffee Break" ....Bud, Smitty and Company
"Company Way" ....Finch and Twimble
"Company Way" (Reprise) ....Bud and Company
"Rosemary's Philosophy" ....Rosemary
"A Secretary Is Not a Toy" ....Bratt, Smitty, Bud and Company
"Been a Long Day" ....Smitty, Finch, Rosemary and Company
"Been a Long Day" (Reprise) ....Biggley, Bud and Hedy
"Grand Old Ivy" ....Finch and Biggley
"Paris Original" ....Rosemary, Smitty, Miss Krumholtz, Miss Jones and the Secretaries
"Rosemary" ....Finch and Rosemary
"Act I Finale" ....Finch, Rosemary and Bud

ACT II

"Cinderella Darling" ....Smitty and the Secretaries
"Happy to Keep His Dinner Warm" (Reprise) ....Rosemary
"Love From a Heart of Gold" ....Biggley and Hedy
"I Believe in You" ....Finch and the Men
"Pirate Dance" ....Company
"I Believe in You" (Reprise) ....Rosemary
"Brotherhood of Man" ....Finch, Miss Jones, Wally Womper and Men
"Finale" ....Company

ORCHESTRA

Conductor:
MATT PERRI
Associate Conductor:
LAWRENCE GOLDBERG
Music Coordinator:
HOWARD JOINES
Reeds:
STEVE KENYON, LAWRENCE FELDMAN,
MARK THRASHER
Trumpets:
NICHOLAS MARCHIONE,
SCOTT WENDHOLT
Trombones:
JOHN ALLRED, GEORGE FLYNN
Horn:
DAVID PEEL
Drums:
LARRY LELLI
Bass:
MICHAEL BLANCO
Guitars:
SCOTT KUNEY
Percussion:
ERIK CHARLSTON
Harp:
GRACE PARADISE

Piano/Synth/Associate Conductor:
LAWRENCE GOLDBERG
Keyboard Programmer:
RANDY COHEN
Music Preparation:
ANIXTER RICE MUSIC SERVICE

Cast Continued

Miss Krumholtz ....SHANNON LEWIS
Bud Frump ....MICHAEL URIE
Mr. Twimble/Wally Womper .....ROB BARTLETT
Hedy La Rue ....TAMMY BLANCHARD
Mr. Davis ....ROBERT HAGER
Meredith ....STEPHANIE ROTHENBERG
Kathy/Scrub Woman ....ABBY CHURCH
Miss Grabowski/Scrub Woman ......PAIGE FAURE
Nancy ....TANYA BIRL
Lily ....SAMANTHA ZACK
Mr. Ovington ....CLEVE ASBURY

Dance Captain: SARAH O'GLEBY
Assistant Dance Captain: CHARLIE WILLIAMS

SWINGS

HOLLY ANN BUTLER, J. AUSTIN EYER,
IAN LIBERTO, SARAH O'GLEBY

UNDERSTUDIES

For J. Pierrepont Finch:
TAYLOR FREY, ROBERT HAGER
For J.B. Biggley:
CLEVE ASBURY, ROB BARTLETT,
MICHAEL PARK
For Rosemary Pilkington:
ABBY CHURCH, STEPHANIE ROTHENBERG
For Bud Frump: CHARLIE WILLIAMS
For Hedy La Rue:
HOLLY ANN BUTLER, PAIGE FAURE
For Smitty:
TANYA BIRL, HOLLY ANN BUTLER
For Miss Jones:
HOLLY ANN BUTLER, PAIGE FAURE
For Twimble/Womper:
CLEVE ASBURY, KEVIN COVERT
For Bert Bratt:
TIMOTHY J. ALEX, NICK MAYO

Daniel Radcliffe PLAYBILL Cover

Darren Criss PLAYBILL Cover

How to Succeed in Business Without Really Trying

Nick Jonas
J. Pierrepont Finch

Beau Bridges
J.B. Biggley

Rose Hemingway
Rosemary Pilkington

Tammy Blanchard
Hedy La Rue

Michael Urie
Bud Frump

Rob Bartlett
Mr. Twimble/Wally Womper

Mary Faber
Smitty

Ellen Harvey
Miss Jones

Michael Park
Bert Bratt

Anderson Cooper
The Voice of the Narrator

Timothy J. Alex
Mr. Tackaberry

Cleve Asbury
Mr. Ovington

Tanya Birl
Nancy

Holly Ann Butler
Swing

Abby Church
Kathy/Scrub Woman

Kevin Covert
Mr. Johnson/TV Announcer

J. Austin Eyer
Swing

Paige Faure
Miss Grabowski/ Scrub Woman

Taylor Frey
Mr. Toynbee

Robert Hager
Mr. Davis

Marty Lawson
Mr. Peterson

Shannon Lewis
Miss Krumholtz

Ian Liberto
Swing

Andrew Madsen
Mr. Andrews

Nick Mayo
Mr. Gatch

Sarah O'Gleby
Swing/Dance Captain

Stephanie Rothenberg
Meredith

Ryan Watkinson
Mr. Matthews

Charlie Williams
Mr. Jenkins/Asst. Dance Captain

Samantha Zack
Lily

Frank Loesser
Music and Lyrics

Abe Burrows
Book

Shepherd Mead
Original Author

Rob Ashford
Director/ Choreographer

Derek McLane
Scenic Design

How to Succeed in Business Without Really Trying

Catherine Zuber
Costume Designer

Howell Binkley
Lighting Design

Tom Watson
Hair and Wig Design

Stephen Sposito
Associate Director

Doug Besterman
Orchestrations

David Chase
Music Director and Arranger

Howard Joines
Music Contractor

Ana Rose Greene, Guy Kwan, Joe DeLuise, Hillary Blanken
Juniper Street Productions
Production Manager

Tara Rubin Casting
Casting

Alan Wasser
General Manager

Allan Williams
General Manager

John Gore,
CEO,
Broadway Across America
Producer

Thomas B. McGrath,
Chairman
Broadway Across America
Producer

Craig Zadan
Producer

Neil Meron
Producer

Joseph Smith
Producer

Candy Spelling
Producer

Hilary A. Williams
Producer

Joel Dodge
Two Left Feet
Productions
Producer

Jonathan Feder
Two Left Feet
Productions
Producer

Larry Kaye
Hop Theatricals, LLC
Producer

Paul Chau
Producer

Dan Frishwasser
Producer

Michael Jackowitz
Producer

Michael Speyer
Producer

Nick Jonas
sings "I Believe
in You."

Photo by Joan Marcus

Bernie Abrams
Producer

Jacki Barlia Florin
Producer

Adam Blanshay
Producer

Arlene Scanlan
Producer

Beth Williams
Executive Producer

How to Succeed in Business Without Really Trying

Cameron Adams
Kathy/Scrub Woman

Darren Criss
J. Pierrepont Finch

David Hull
Mr. Toynbee

Justin Keyes
Mr. Davis

John Larroquette
J.B. Biggley

Lorin Latarro
Swing

Colt Prattes
Mr. Matthews

Daniel Radcliffe
J. Pierrepont Finch

Megan Sikora
Miss Krumholtz

Michaeljon Slinger
Swings

Joey Sorge
Mr. Tackaberry

Matt Wall
Swing

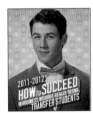

Synthia Link
Meredith

Charlie Sutton
Mr. Jenkins

Karl Warden
Swing

HAIR SUPERVISORS
(L-R): Katie Beatty and Carla Muniz

DOORMAN
Henry E. Menendez

Michael Urie sings "Company Way."

How to Succeed in Business Without Really Trying

STAGE MANAGEMENT
(L-R): Jeff Siebert (Assistant Stage Manager),
Glynn David Turner (Stage Manager),
Kristen Harris (Production Stage Manager),
Shannon Hammons (Assistant Stage Manager)

Photos by Brian Mapp

WARDROBE
Front Row (L-R): Joshua Burns,
Shana Albery, Dora Suarez,
Jeff Johnson, Rick Ortiz

Second Row (L-R): Barry Hoff

Back Row (L-R):
Tony Hoffman, Marybeth Irons, Mark Romer

CREW
Front Row (L-R): Erik Hansen, Scott "Gus" Poitras, John Blixt, Gretchen Metzloff, Emile LaFargue, Charlie Grieco, Michele Gutierrez

Back Row (L-R): Brian Dawson, Tom Burke, Rocco Williams, Joseph Mooneyham, Chris Conrad, Jason Strangfeld, Will Sweeney, Gabe Harris, Chris Pantuso, Sal Sclafani, Richard Anderson

Camera Shy: Joseph Maher

How to Succeed in Business Without Really Trying

FRONT OF HOUSE STAFF
Front Row (L-R): Mike Wirsch, Ross Larkin, Alexander Gutierrez, Hollis Miller, Tristan Blacer

Middle Row (L-R): Donald Royal, Jennifer DiDonato, Mary Marzan, Janice Rodriguez, Lorraine Feeks, Jose Nunez, Albert T. Kim (Theatre Manager)

Back Row (L-R): Lise Greaves, Alison Traynor, unidentified, Lawrence Levens, William Meyers, Terry Monahan, Carrie Jo Brinker

---

STAFF FOR
HOW TO SUCCEED IN BUSINESS
WITHOUT REALLY TRYING

GENERAL MANAGEMENT
ALAN WASSER ASSOCIATES
Alan Wasser   Allan Williams
Mark Shacket   Aaron Lustbader

GENERAL PRESS REPRESENTATIVE
THE HARTMAN GROUP
Michael Hartman
Wayne Wolfe   Matt Ross   Nicole Capatasto

COMPANY MANAGER
Penelope Daulton

MARKETING
TYPE A MARKETING
Anne Rippey
Elyce Henkin   Sarah Ziering

CASTING
TARA RUBIN CASTING
Tara Rubin CSA, Merri Sugarman CSA
Eric Woodall CSA, Laura Schutzel CSA, Dale Brown CSA
Lindsay Levine, Kaitlin Shaw

PRODUCTION MANAGEMENT
JUNIPER STREET PRODUCTIONS
Hillary Blanken   Guy Kwan
Joseph DeLuise   Kevin Broomell   Ana Rose Greene

Production Stage Manager ....Kristen Harris
Stage Manager ....Glynn David Turner
Assistant Stage Manager ....Shannon Hammons
Assistant Stage Manager ....Jeff Siebert
Associate Company Manager ....Cathy Kwon
Dance Captain ....Sarah O'Gleby
Assistant Dance Captain ....Charlie Williams
SDC Traube Fellow ....Sara-Ashley Bischoff
Associate Scenic Designer ....Shoko Kambara

Assistant Scenic Designer ....Brett Banakis
Scenic Design Assistant ....Paul Depoo
Assistant Costume Designers ....Nicole Moody,
     David Newell, Liam O'Brian, Ryan Park
Costume Design Intern ....Peter Dolhas
Associate Lighting Designer ....Ryan O'Gara
Assistant Lighting Designers ....Sean Beach,
     Amanda Zieve
Associate Sound Designer/
     Sound Engineer ....Jason Strangfeld
Assistant Sound Designer ....Michael Eisenberg
Moving Lights Programmer ....Eric Norris
Make-up Design ....Ashley Ryan
Aerial Design ....Sonja Rzepski
Stunt Coordinator ....Mike Russo
Production Carpenter ....Erik Hansen
Automation Carpenter ....Scott "Gus" Poitras
Production Electricians ....James J. Fedigan,
     Randall Zaibek
Head Electrician ....Brian Dawson
Production Properties
     Supervisor ....Christopher Pantuso
Assistant Properties Supervisor ....Jim Kane
Production Sound Engineers ....Paul Delcioppo,
     Phil Lojo
Deck Audio ....Charles Grieco
Wardrobe Supervisor ....Debbie Cheretun
Assistant Wardrobe Supervisor ....Brendan Cooper
Mr. Jonas' Dresser ....Sandy Binion
Mr. Bridges' Dresser ....Barry Hoff
Dressers ....Shana Albery, Joshua Burns,
     Tracey Diebold, Lisa Gosnell,
     Anthony Hoffman, Marybeth Irons,
     Jeffrey Johnson, Nesreen Mahmoud,
     Trevor McGinness
Hair Supervisor ....Katie Beatty
Hair Dressers ....Carla Muniz, Gabrielle Vincent
Music Coordinator ....Howard Joines
Music Copying ....Anixter Rice Music Service/
     Russ Anixter
Advertising ....Serino/Coyne/

Nancy Coyne, Sandy Block,
Greg Corradetti, Robert Jones,
Vanessa Javier, Ryan Cunningham,
David Barrineau
International Marketing ....Joe Public
Theatre Displays ....King Displays

Digital Outreach, Online Media,
     Video Production, Website Design ....Serino/Coyne/
     Jim Glaub, Chip Meyrelles,
     Laurie Connor, Kevin Keating,
     Whitney Manalio Creighton,
     Mark Seeley, John Lagomarsino
Legal Counsel ....Levine Plotkin & Menin LLP/
     Loren Plotkin, Esq.;
     Susan Mindell; Cris Criswell
Accounting ....Rosenberg, Neuwirth & Kuchner/
     Chris Cacace, Ruthie Skochil
General Management Associates ....Lane Marsh,
     Steve Greer
General Management Office ....Hilary Ackerman,
     Mark Barna, Chris D'Angelo,
     Jake Hirzel, Nina Lutwick,
     Jennifer O'Connor
Production Photographer ....Ari Mintz
Production Assistants ....Steve Chazaro,
     Melissa Hansen, Morgan Holbrook,
     Jason Pelusio, Jeff Siebert
Physical Therapist ....Encore Physical Therapy PC/
     Marc Hunter-Hall
Orthopaedist ....David S. Weiss, MD
Insurance ....Ventura Insurance Brokerage/
     Christine Sadofsky
Banking ....Signature Bank/
     Barbara von Borstel, Margaret Monigan
Payroll.............................Castellana Services, Inc.
Opening Night
     Coordination ....Serino Coyne, LLC/
     Suzanne Tobak, Gail Perlman
Group Sales ....Broadway Inbound/212-302-0995
Transportation ....IBA Limousine

How to Succeed in Business Without Really Trying
SCRAPBOOK

Correspondent: Tanya Birl, "Ensemble"

Memorable Fan Letter: Our very own Rose Hemingway plays Rosemary and has the amazing and interesting job of playing opposite some of the world's biggest stars! She received a fan letter that was filled with some rather interesting compliments. It read: "I stood in the middle of a crowded sidewalk for about an hour to get a pic with you and an autograph. Dan [Radcliffe] had long gone and people started to leave. I finally pushed my way to the front of the crowd. I waited and then asked someone if you had come out, and they told me, 'Who? Was she in the show?' I had to explain that, yes you were in the show and you played Rosemary!" She obviously meant well, but it was still hilarious to say the least!

Memorable Party: We've been invited to some pretty cool events, but a highlight for me was having a private viewing of the final Harry Potter film. Daniel Radcliffe invited us to a screening studio a few weeks before it came out in theatres. We were all so excited and happy for Dan and I know he was nervous and excited to share the final movie with all of us.

Most Exciting Celebrity Visitor: I think having Robert Morse (the original Finch) at the

(L-R): Producer Craig Zadan, Michael Urie, Director Rob Ashford, Nick Jonas and Producer Neil Meron at Glass House Tavern for the party celebrating Jonas' and Urie's opening.

show was pretty exciting. A lot of us are also huge fans of his on "Mad Men." It's interesting how the worlds of both shows are so closely related.

Who Had Done the Most Performances: Daniel Radcliffe! He didn't miss ONE day for the entire year that he was with the show. He set such a high bar for the rest of the cast.

Special Backstage Rituals: Before the curtain goes up every night we all gather on stage in a huddle and yell "SAY WICKETS"! It's an inside joke from previews when our music director David Chase asked the cast to count the amount of times the word "SAY" was used in the play. He stressed that it was an important beginning to many lines in the show. Wickets

---

CREDITS AND ACKNOWLEDGEMENTS

Scenery constructed and show control and scenic motion control featuring Stage Command® Systems by PRG Scenic Technologies, a division of Production Resources Group, LLC, New Windsor, NY. Scenery constructed by Global Scenic Services, Bridgeport, CT. Lighting equipment provided by PRG Lighting. Audio equipment provided by PRG Audio. Props built by the Spoon Group, the Ken Larson Co. TV camera provided by the Museum of Broadcast Technology, Paul Beck, Pres. Costumes by Parsons-Meares, Ltd.; EuroCo Costumes, Inc., John Cowles; Center Stage Costume Shop. Millinery by Rodney Gordon, Inc.; Arnold Levine Millinery. Men's tailoring by Brooks Brothers, Brian Hemesath, Edward Dawson. Men's shirts by Cego Custom Shirts, Jared Bleese. Custom footwear by JC Theatrical and Custom, T.O. Dey, World Tone Dance. Fabric painting and dyeing by Jeffrey Fender. Custom knitwear by Maria Ficalora. Custom jewelry by Larry V'rba. Vintage eyewear by Fabulous Franny's. Special thanks to Bra*Tenders for hosiery and undergarments. Dry cleaning by Ernest Winzer Cleaners.

Makeup provided by M·A·C Cosmetics

Piano by Steinway & Sons

Rehearsed at the New 42nd Street Studios

Souvenir Merchandise designed and created by Creative Goods Merchandise

---

Energy efficient washer/dryer courtesy of LG Electronics.

Special thanks to Michael J. Passaro.

---

www.HowToSucceedBroadway.com

JUJAMCYN THEATERS

JORDAN ROTH
President

PAUL LIBIN	JACK VIERTEL
Executive Vice President	Senior Vice President
MEREDITH VILLATORE	**JENNIFER HERSHEY**
Chief Financial Officer	Vice President, Building Operations
MICAH HOLLINGWORTH	**HAL GOLDBERG**
Vice President, Company Operations	Vice President, Theatre Operations

Director of Business Affairs . . . . Albert T. Kim
Director of Human Resources . . . . Michele Louhisdon
Director of Ticketing Services . . . . Justin Karr
Theatre Operations Managers . . . . Willa Burke, Susan Elrod, Emily Hare, Jeff Hubbard, Albert T. Kim
Theatre Operations Associates . . . . Carrie Jo Brinker, Brian Busby, Michael Composto, Anah Jyoti Klate
Accounting . . . . Cathy Cerge, Erin Dooley, Amy Frank
Executive Producer, Red Awning . . . . Nicole Kastrinos
Director of Marketing, Givenik.com . . . . Joe Tropia
Marketing Associate, Givenik.com . . . . Ben Cohen
Building Operations Associate . . . . Erich Bussing
Executive Coordinator . . . . Ed Lefferson
Executive Assistants . . . . Clark Mims Tedesco, Julia Kraus, Beth Given
Receptionist . . . . Lisa Perchinske
Maintenance . . . . Ralph Santos, Ramon Zapata
Security . . . . Rasim Hodzic, John Acero
Interns . . . . Maggie Baker, Alaina Bono, Erin Carr, Hunter Chancellor, Cindy Vargas, Kelvin Veras, Luke Weidner, Margaret White

---

Staff for the Al Hirschfeld Theatre for
How to Succeed in Business Without Really Trying

Theatre Manager . . . . Albert T. Kim
Associate Theatre Manager . . . . Carrie Jo Brinker
Treasurer . . . . Carmine LaMendola
Head Carpenter . . . . Joseph J. Maher, Jr.
Head Propertyman . . . . Sal Sclafani
Head Electrician . . . . Michele Gutierrez
Flyman . . . . Gabe Harris
Engineer . . . . Kevin Farrelly
Assistant Treasurers . . . . Vicci Stanton, Gloria Diabo, Jeffrey Nevin, Janette Wernegreen
Carpenters . . . . Joe Mooneyham, Chris Conrad
Propertymen . . . . Will Sweeney, Richard Anderson
Electricians . . . . John Blixt, Tom Burke, Emile LaFargue, Gretchen Metzloff, Rocco Williams
Head Usher . . . . Janice Rodriguez
Ticket-Takers . . . . Tristan Blacer, Lorraine Feeks
Doormen . . . . Henry E. Menendez, Neil Perez
Front of House Directors . . . . Julie Burnham, Lawrence Levens, William Meyers
Head Porter . . . . Jose Nunez
Head Cleaner . . . . Bethania Alvarez
Ushers . . . . Peter Davino, Jennifer DiDonato, Alexander Gutierrez, Theresa Lopez, Mark Maciejewski, Mary Marzan, Hollis Miller, Sonia Moreno, Donald Royal, Bart Ryan
Porters . . . . Tereso Avila, Roberto Ellington
Cleaners . . . . Michelina Annarumma, Mirjan Aquino

---

Lobby refreshments by Sweet Concessions.

Security provided by P and P Security.

Jujamcyn Theaters is a proud member of the Broadway Green Alliance.

How to Succeed in Business Without Really Trying

SCRAPBOOK

are simply what we sell at the World Wide Wicket Company. We all have our own ideas of what "wickets" are. You can decide for yourself!

Favorite Moment During Each Performance: Onstage, it would have to be the opening number. It's really exciting to have the curtain go up and the entire cast is dancing like crazy! Offstage, it would have to be anytime that there is a break for snacks! Our cast is not ashamed of our love of food! Rob Bartlett (who plays Twimble/Womper) brings bagels every Saturday morning and has even gone as far as bringing a fully loaded hot dog bar!

Favorite In-Theatre Gathering Place: We have a weekly ritual called TH.N.O.B. It stands for Thursday Night On Broadway. We gather in either the girls' or boys' dressing room and a different cast member makes a specialty drink for that night. It has become so popular that our friends in other shows often ask if they can come and hang out.

Favorite Off-Site Hangout: If I had to choose one I'd say the downstairs lounge at Southern Hospitality. We've had many gatherings there and it's private enough so that our Finches can come without being mauled.

Favorite Snack Foods: I can only speak for the women's ensemble when I say that we are strictly pescetarian. We are addicted to flavor-blasted Goldfish and Swedish Fish.

Mascots: Our cast mascot is the beaver. He hangs on the callboard and dons many different outfits throughout the year. Right now he is wearing a Mardi Gras outfit.

Our women's dressing room mascot is Darryl the vegan shark. He lives in our quick change room in the basement. Our dresser Shana made him from a blue towel. He even has his own theme song!

Favorite Therapy: I would say that the foam roller is our best friend!

Memorable Ad-Lib: John Larroquette liked to ad-lib quite a bit in the show. One of them being "10 out of 9 people are dyslexic."

Memorable Press Encounter: Being that Daniel Radcliffe was in the show during the release of the last Harry Potter film, some people experienced paparazzi following them to ask for info on how to get to Dan.

Memorable Stage Door Fan Encounter: When Darren [Criss] was in the show, we would have "Glee" fans singing at the top of their lungs waiting for him to come outside. This would often happen between shows, and I'm not ashamed to say that a few choice words were yelled from the upstairs dressing rooms when we were all trying to take a nap.

Web Buzz: I thought that we had some pretty impressive web buzz. We have some very dedicated fans and they aren't afraid to voice their opinions. Good or bad! A lot of our fans like to get a behind-the-scenes look at what we do when we're not onstage. We took pictures of us "planking" and our press department would post them to our Facebook page. We had a few fans that took offense to it and it started a

(L-R Front): Michael Urie, Rose Hemingway, Nick Jonas, Beau Bridges and Tammy Blanchard with the cast take curtain call on Jonas' opening night, January 24, 2012.

HUGE Facebook feud! They were quickly removed.

Fastest Costume Change: That would be Rose Hemingway who changes her entire costume onstage while singing "Paris Original"

Heaviest/Hottest Costume: The guys have to wear full on three-piece wool suits while performing (in my opinion) the hardest choreography on Broadway! I'm sure their dressers have a fun time with that!

Who Wore the Least: Since the majority of the show takes place at the office, there isn't anything too risqué, but Tammy Blanchard (who plays Hedy La Rue) wears a pretty skimpy towel in Mr. Biggley's office!

Catchphrases Only the Company Would Recognize: "Broadway Shapes!" "Find the leg." "K-hole."

Sweethearts Within the Company: Megan Sikora and Barrett Martin. They were both in the original cast and have since moved on to other projects. Megan just gave birth to their first child, Elliot!

Orchestra Member Who Played the Most Instruments: Mark Thrasher is the orchestra's in-house contractor and plays in the reed section. He plays the clarinet, bass clarinet, contrabass clarinet, flute, alto flute and bassoon.

Orchestra Member Who Played the Most Consecutive Performances Without a Sub: Grace Paradise who plays the harp. She's also the only woman in the orchestra!

Best In-House Parody Lyrics: "We were raised on you, Jesus, and we've loved you all the same!" – Associate choreographer Chris Bailey

Memorable Directorial Note: Rob Ashford has some pretty brilliant analogies for this show. Some of them being:
"World Wide Wickets is an ivory tower."
"Always stay front-footed through the performance."
"This show is a snack."
"We're always playing black and white. NO grey!"

Company In-Jokes: During previews we had an epic five-minute pirate number that eventually got cut down to 90 seconds. At the end of the number the girls had to "row a boat" across the stage. The first night of previews, the automation didn't work and we had to "Flintstone" the boat off stage ourselves! It took us forever and we all had egg on our face, but Cameron Adams cut the tension by yelling "I Love Boats!" The audience loved it and it has been a joke in the company ever since!

Nicknames: This isn't so much a nickname as it is a special character in the show. Nick Mayo plays Mr. Gatch but has also created his alter ego Si. He works in the mailroom at the World Wide Wicket Company. He immigrated from Mexico and is a very important part of the company! He's even saved the day and came to Bud Frump's rescue when he almost fell to his death off a pile of boxes in "Company Way!"

Embarrassing Moments: I'll have to speak for Charlie Williams on this one. During the pirate number, the women lift the men while they are upside down in a handstand. One night Charlie went a bit too far and flipped into the orchestra pit! The entire audience was on their feet looking to see if he was alright and the rest of us onstage had to keep dancing while watching this all happen right in front of us. Luckily no one was hurt and he landed safely below, but he did say that the embarrassment was way worse than the fall!

Ghostly Encounters Backstage: Our doorman Neil has some crazy ghost stories from the past 10 years of being at the Al Hirschfeld Theatre. The freakiest one being a large man that paces the spotlight booth at the back of the house. Neil describes him as wearing a white t-shirt with overalls and a very thick beard. He has seen him whenever the theatre is empty and he's locking up at night!

Coolest Thing About Being in This Show: I know it's a cliché, but it really is the people. We really have a super tight group and I have heard from multiple people that it reads onstage.

Hugh Jackman Back on Broadway

First Preview: October 25, 2011. Opened: November 10, 2011.
Closed January 1, 2012 after 18 Previews and 61 Performances.

PLAYBILL

A concert show of pop and Broadway standards performed by the star of The Boy From Oz, A Steady Rain *and filmdom's* The X-Men *series.*

CAST

HUGH JACKMAN

Ensemble .... ROBIN CAMPBELL,
KEARRAN GIOVANNI,
ANNE OTTO, LARA SEIBERT,
HILARY MICHAEL THOMPSON,
EMILY TYRA

Vocalists .... CLIFTON BIEUNDURRY,
OLIVE KNIGHT

Didgeridoo Players .... PAUL BOON,
NATHAN MUNDRABY

ORCHESTRA

Conductor: PATRICK VACCARIELLO
Associate Conductor: JIM LAEV
Piano/Synth: JIM LAEV
Concert Master: MARTIN AGEE
Violins: FRITZ KRAKOWSKI,
DANA IANCULOVICI
Celli: PETER PROSSER, VIVIAN ISRAEL
Reeds: BEN KONO, ADAM KOLKER,
DAVID YOUNG, RON JANNELLI
Trumpets: TREVOR NEUMANN,
SCOTT WENDHOLT
Trombones: TIM ALBRIGHT, JACK SCHATZ
Drums: BRIAN BRAKE
Bass: PAUL NOWINSKI
Guitars: JJ McGEEHAN
Piano vocal score preparation by Tim Brown
Music copying by Kaye-Houston Music Inc.

---

⑥ BROADHURST THEATRE
235 West 44th Street
A Shubert Organization Theatre

Philip J. Smith, *Chairman*   Robert E. Wankel, *President*

ROBERT FOX and THE SHUBERT ORGANIZATION

Present

HUGH JACKMAN
Back on Broadway

Scenic Consultant	Costume Design	Lighting Design
JOHN LEE BEATTY	WILLIAM IVEY LONG	KEN BILLINGTON

Sound Design	Video Design
JOHN SHIVERS	ALEXANDER V. NICHOLS

Music Direction
PATRICK VACCARIELLO

Direction & Choreography
WARREN CARLYLE

11/10/11

(L-R): Emily Tyra, Hugh Jackman, Lara Seibert, Kearran Giovanni

Photo by Joan Marcus

Hugh Jackman Back on Broadway

The songs you will hear at this performance have been written by some of the greatest artists of the Broadway and pop music world, including Marcel Eugene Ageron, Peter W. Allen, Richard Alleyne, Adrienne Anderson, Harold Arlen, Georges Abel, Louis Auric, Burt Bacharach, G. Becand, Boudleaux Bryant, Felice Bryant, Shawn C. Carter, Eddie J. Cooley, Christopher C. Cross, John Davenport, Mac Davis, John Albert Denicola, William Engvick, Sammy Fain, Dorothy Fields, Milt Gabler, George Gershwin, Ira Gershwin, Barry Gibb, Maurice Gibb, Robin Gibb, Oscar Hammerstein, Otto A. Harbach, Yip Harburg, Thaddis Laphonia Harrell, Jerry Herman, Herman Hupfeld, Elton John, The Jonas Brothers, Bert Kaempfert, Irving Kahal, Jerome Kern, Manny Kurtz, Albert Abraham Lasry, Jack Lawrence, Leiber & Stoller, John Lennon, Frank Loesser, Donald Jay Markowitz, Richard Marx, Paul McCartney, Jimmy McHugh, Albert Phillip McKay, Johnny Mercer, Freddy Mercury, Terius Youngdell Nash, Randy Newman, Dean Pitchford, Cole Porter, Franke Jon Previte, Tim Rice, Richard Rodgers, Carole Sager, Christopher A. Stewart, Billy Strange, Linda Thompson, Louis Trenet, Maurice White and Allee Willis.

They have been lovingly arranged and orchestrated by the talents of August Eriksmoen, Michael Gibson, Larry Hochman, Mark Hummel, Michael John La Chiusa, Jim Laev, Richard Mann, Richard Marx, JJ McGeehan, Danny Troob, Patrick Vaccariello, Don Walker and Harold Wheeler.

Hugh Jackman

Robin Campbell
Ensemble

Kearran Giovanni
Ensemble

Anne Otto
Ensemble

Lara Seibert
Ensemble

Hilary Michael Thompson
Ensemble

Emily Tyra
Ensemble

Clifton Bieundurry
Vocalist

Paul Boon
Didgeridoo Player

Olive Knight
Vocalist

Nathan Mundraby
Didgeridoo Player

John Lee Beatty
Scenic Consultant

Ken Billington
Lighting Design

William Ivey Long
Costume Design

John Shivers
Sound Design

Alexander V. Nichols
Projection and Video Design

Patrick Vaccariello
Music Direction

Warren Carlyle
Direction & Choreography

Angie Canuel
Associate Director

Jim Laev
Associate Conductor

Neil A. Mazzella/ Hudson Theatrical Associates
Technical Supervision

Tara Rubin
Tara Rubin Casting
Casting

Robert Fox
Producer

Philip J. Smith
The Shubert Organization
Producer

Robert E. Wankel
The Shubert Organization
Producer

2011-2012 AWARD

TONY AWARD
Special Award
(Hugh Jackman)

Hugh Jackman Back on Broadway

CAST, ORCHESTRA, CREW

Front Row (L-R): John Hobson, Danielle Banyai, Nancy Reyes, Karen Diaz, Emily Tyra, Robin Campbell, Lara Seibert, Hilary Michael Thompson, Kearran Giovanni, Anne Otto, JJ McGeehan

Second Row (L-R): Charlie Underhill, Carlos Parra, Paul Boon, Rose Keough, James Laev, Nathan Mundraby

Third Row (L-R): Debbie Eng, Tony Lopez, Vivian Israel, Heidi Neven, Brian "Boomer" Bullard, Charlie DeVerna, Leon Stieb, Kathleen Gallagher, Hugh Barnett, Patrick Vaccariello, David Young, Clifton Bieundurry, Kimberly Vernace

Back Row (L-R): Geoffrey Polischuck, unknown, Ron Schwier, Jonathan Cohen, Brian McGarty, Irving Milgrom, Hugh Jackman, David Patridge, Michael "Jersey" VanNest, Ron Vitelli, Brian Brake

DOORMAN
Joe Trapasso, Jr.

BOX OFFICE
Al Crivelli, Cliff Cobb, Noreen Morgan

Hugh Jackman Back on Broadway

Hugh Jackman

Photo by Joan Marcus

STAFF FOR
HUGH JACKMAN BACK ON BROADWAY

GENERAL MANAGEMENT
BESPOKE THEATRICALS
Maggie Brohn
Amy Jacobs   Devin Keudell   Nina Lannan

COMPANY MANAGER
Heidi Neven

GENERAL PRESS REPRESENTATIVE
BONEAU/BRYAN-BROWN
Adrian Bryan-Brown   Jackie Green   Kelly Guiod

HAIR DESIGN
Edward J. Wilson

CASTING
TARA RUBIN CASTING
Tara Rubin CSA
Eric Woodall CSA, Merri Sugarman CSA,
Dale Brown CSA, Kaitlin Shaw, Lindsay Levine

Production Stage Manager .... Kim Vernace
Stage Manager .... Charles Underhill
Associate Director .... Angie Canuel
Associate Lighting Designers .... John Demous,
                                         Anthony Pearson
Assistant to the Lighting Designer .... Brandon Baker
Associate Scenic Designer .... Kacie Hultgren
Associate Costume Designer .... Martha Bromelmeier
Associate Sound Designer .... David Patridge
Moving Light Programmer .... David Arch
Synthesizer Programmer .... Jim Abbott
Production Assistant .... Lauren Klein
Production Electrician .... Jimmy Maloney, Jr.
Head Electrician .... Ronald Schwier
Production Carpenter .... Fran Rapp
Followspot .... Michael Van Nest
Head Sound .... David Patridge

Wardrobe Supervisor .... Kathleen Gallagher
Mr. Jackman's Dresser .... Geoffrey Polischuck
Dresser .... Rose Keough

Booking Agency for
  Mr. Jackman .... WME Entertainment

Press Representation for
  Mr. Jackman .... Rogers & Cowan, Inc.
Writing Consultant for
  Mr. Jackman .... John Macks
Assistant to Mr. Jackman .... Irving Milgrom
Assistant to Mr. Fox .... Sarah Richardson
Advertising .... SpotCo/
                                         Drew Hodges, Jim Edwards,
                                   Tom Greenwald, Y. Darius Suyama,
                                              Caraline Sogliuzzo
Online .... SpotCo/
                                   Sarah Fitzpatrick, Kristen Bardwil,
                                      Meghan Ownbey, Marc Mettler,
                                                   Matt Wilstein
Legal Counsel .... Franklin, Weinrib, Rudell & Vassalo PC/
                              Elliot H. Brown, Jonathan A. Lonner
Accountant .... FK Partners/Robert Fried
Comptroller .... Sarah Galbraith and Co./
                                              Tabitha Falcone
Ticketing and Sales Consultant .... Gregg Arst
General Management Associates .... Steve Dow,
                                      Libby Fox, David Roth,
                                              Danielle Saks
General Management Intern .... Rodney Roth
Press Office Staff .... Chris Boneau, Jim Byk,
                                   Linnae Hodzic, Jessica Johnson,
                                   Kevin Jones, Amy Kass, Holly Kinney,
                                      Emily Meagher, Aaron Meier,
                                      Christine Olver, Joe Perrotta,
                                      Matt Polk, Heath Schwartz,
                                   Michael Strassheim, Susanne Tighe
Payroll Services .... Checks and Balances Payroll Inc.
Travel Agent .... Tzell Travel/
                                      The "A" Team, Andi Henig
Banking .... City National Bank/Michele Gibbons
Immigration Attorney .... Lawrence Yudess, Esq.
Theatre Displays .... King Displays, Inc.
Merchandise .... Araca Merchandise Company
Production Photographer .... Joan Marcus
Physical Therapy .... PhysioArts/Jennifer Green
Orthopaedic Consultant .... Dr. Weiss

CREDITS
Scenery constructed and automation equipment provided
by Hudson Scenic Studios, Inc. Lighting and video
equipment from PRG Lighting. Sound equipment by
Masque Sound. Costumes by Euroco Costumes; Jennifer
Love Costumes, Inc.; Katrina Patterns, Inc.; Worldtone

Dance. Thanks to Bra*Tenders for hosiery and
undergarments.

To learn more about the production, please visit
www.HughJackmanBackonBroadway.com

Hugh Jackman Back on Broadway originally rehearsed
at the Pearl Studios.

SPECIAL THANKS
My wife Deb, Dan Harmon, Rob Schrab, Brent Smith,
Clint Mitchell, Baz Luhrmann, Martin Chalk, James Gray,
Jason Sloan, Howard Altman, Harris Hartman, Patrick
Whitesell, Barry Diller, Rich Ross, Irving Milgrom

Energy-efficient washer/dryer courtesy of
LG Electronics.

THE SHUBERT ORGANIZATION, INC.
Board of Directors

Philip J. Smith	Robert E. Wankel
Chairman	President
Wyche Fowler, Jr.	Diana Phillips
Lee J. Seidler	Michael I. Sovern

Stuart Subotnick

Chief Financial Officer .... Elliot Greene
Sr. Vice President, Ticketing .... David Andrews
Vice President, Finance .... Juan Calvo
Vice President, Human Resources .... Cathy Cozens
Vice President, Facilities .... John Darby
Vice President, Theatre Operations .... Peter Entin
Vice President, Marketing .... Charles Flateman
Vice President, Audit .... Anthony LaMattina
Vice President, Ticket Sales .... Brian Mahoney
Vice President, Creative Projects .... D.S. Moynihan
Vice President, Real Estate .... Julio Peterson

House Manager .... Hugh Barnett

Hugh Jackman Back on Broadway
SCRAPBOOK

Correspondent: Emily Tyra, "Ensemble"

Most Exciting Celebrity Visitors: Oprah!!, Tony Blair, Joan Rivers, Kathie Lee and Hoda, Neil Patrick Harris, Oscar de la Renta and Calvin Klein, to name a few.

Actor Who Has Done the Most Broadway Shows in Their Career: Kearran Giovanni: seven shows!

Special Backstage Rituals: High-fives from Hugh. Overture dance party. Hugh's warm-up throwing a football around on stage before the show.

Favorite Moment During Each Performance (On Stage or Off):
The rotating female jukebox where every night Hugh chose someone to sing a random song while he shook his hips in gold lamé pants as "Peter Allen."
The aboriginal Australians singing and playing the didgeridoo every night.

Favorite In-Theatre Gathering Place: Hugh's dressing room. (I wish!)

Favorite Off-Site Hangout: Anywhere involving Margaritas!

Favorite Snack Food: Sour Patch Kids (Hugh's favorite and available at ALL times).

Mascot: Lauren Klein

Favorite Therapies: Red wine. More Sour Patch Kids.

Most Memorable Ad-Lib: "Gobble gobble." –Kearran Giovanni

Memorable Stage Door Fan Encounter: Every night is a memorable stage door Hugh fan encounter.

Latest Audience Arrival: Never. Hugh filled empty front row seats with people from standing room. "Come on down...it's like 'The Price is Right'!!" And if someone walks in late, Hugh has no problem turning on the house lights, asking them how dinner was, and helping them get to their seats.

Busiest Day at the Box Office: Every day.

Catchphrases Only the Company Would Recognize:
"You're dancing with Hugh Jackman. You better panic-attack it out."
"Chicken pot pie."
"Affirm or interrogate."
"Two Sides."

Understudy Anecdote: "During the last week of the run Kearran let me swing on for the first time during one of the numbers. After the number Hugh stopped the show, announced my Broadway debut to the audience, handed me the mic, and made me sing a solo while the entire orchestra backed me up and I belted 'Hit Me with Your Best Shot.' The most embarrassing and most incredible thing that's ever happened to me!!" –Hilary Michael Thompson

Sweethearts Within the Company: Emily and Hugh, Kearran and Hugh, Lara and Hugh, Anne and Hugh, Robin and Hugh, Hilary and Hugh, and Charlie Red and Hugh.

Embarrassing Moments: Hugh asking Kearran to show off and flex her rear delts to the whole audience.
Hugh playing Emily singing "Chestnuts Roasting..." at age 13 during the show.

Coolest Thing About Being in This Show: Hanging out with Wolverine.

Also: During the run, there were four girls who celebrated their birthday. Not only did he point us out on stage, but he led the entire Broadway audience in singing us "Happy Birthday." Coolest guy ever.

Also: During a particularly wild Peter Allen moment, Hugh took the weave of a woman in the front row and proceeded to dance around with it on his head backwards. When he was through, he turned around and flung it backwards out into the 12th row.

1. The cast backstage (L-R): Robin Campbell, Hilary Michael Thompson, Hugh Jackman, Lara Seibert, *Yearbook* correspondent Emily Tyra, Anne Otto and Kearran Giovanni.
2. The Ladies take cover in a dressing room.
3. Dressed up for opening night.
4. Giovanni (second from left) gets the Gypsy Robe on opening night.
5. The Ladies with Director Warren Carlyle (C).

Jersey Boys

First Preview: October 4, 2005. Opened: November 6, 2005.
Still running as of May 31, 2012.

A musical based on the lives and careers of the close-harmony pop group The Four Seasons. We meet founder Tommy DeVito, a bad boy who is constantly in trouble with the law, supportive Nick Massi, songwriter Bob Gaudio, and finally lead singer Frankie Valli, whose soulful falsetto helps loft the foursome to international success. That success, along with DeVito's troubles with the mob and changes in the public's musical taste, helps splinter the original group. But the indefatigable Valli and the prolific Gaudio help make sure that the music lives on.

CAST

(in alphabetical order)

Nick DeVito, Stosh, Billy Dixon, Norman Waxman,
Charlie Calello (and others) .....MILES AUBREY
Officer Petrillo, Hank Majewski, Crewe's PA,
Joe Long (and others) ....ERIK BATES
Nick Massi..........................MATT BOGART
Mary Delgado,
Angel (and others) ....CARA COOPER
French Rap Star, Detective One, Hal Miller,
Barry Belson, Police Officer,
Davis (and others) ....JOHN EDWARDS
Joey, Recording Studio Engineer
(and others) ....RUSSELL FISCHER
Tommy DeVito ....ANDY KARL
Gyp DeCarlo (and others) ....MARK LOTITO
Church Lady, Miss Frankie Nolan, Bob's Party Girl,
Angel, Lorraine (and others) .....JESSICA RUSH
Frankie Valli (Wed. &
Sat. matinees) ......DOMINIC SCAGLIONE JR.

Continued on next page

9 AUGUST WILSON THEATRE
A JUJAMCYN THEATRE

JORDAN ROTH
President

PAUL LIBIN
Executive Vice President

JACK VIERTEL
Senior Vice President

Dodger Theatricals   Joseph J. Grano   Tamara and Kevin Kinsella   Pelican Group
in association with Latitude Link   Rick Steiner/Osher/Staton/Bell/Mayerson Group

present

JERSEY BOYS

The Story of Frankie Valli & The Four Seasons

Book by	Music by	Lyrics by
Marshall Brickman & Rick Elice	Bob Gaudio	Bob Crewe

with

Matt Bogart   Andy Karl   Jarrod Spector   Quinn VanAntwerp

Miles Aubrey   Brad Bass   Erik Bates   Cara Cooper   Ken Dow   John Edwards
Russell Fischer   Katie O'Toole   Joe Payne   Jessica Rush   Dominic Scaglione Jr.
Nathan Scherich   Sara Schmidt   Taylor Sternberg
with Mark Lotito and Courter Simmons

Scenic Design	Costume Design	Lighting Design	Sound Design
Klara Zieglerova	Jess Goldstein	Howell Binkley	Steve Canyon Kennedy

Projection Design	Wig and Hair Design	Fight Director	Production Supervisor
Michael Clark	Charles LaPointe	Steve Rankin	Richard Hester

Orchestrations	Music Coordinator	Conductor	Production Stage Manager
Steve Orich	John Miller	Andrew Wilder	Michelle Bosch

Technical Supervisor	East Coast Casting	West Coast Casting	Company Manager
Peter Fulbright	Tara Rubin Casting	Sharon Bialy C.S.A. Sherry Thomas C.S.A.	Sandra Carlson

Associate Producers	Executive Producer	Promotions	Press Representative
Lauren Mitchell Rhoda Mayerson Stage Entertainment	Sally Campbell Morse	HHC Marketing	Boneau/Bryan-Brown

Music Direction, Vocal Arrangements & Incidental Music
Ron Melrose

Choreography
Sergio Trujillo

Directed by
Des McAnuff

World Premiere Produced by La Jolla Playhouse, La Jolla, CA
Christopher Ashley, Artistic Director & Michael S. Rosenberg, Managing Director

The producers wish to thank Theatre Development Fund for its support of this production.

1/9/12

(L-R): Matt Bogart, Jarrod Spector, Quinn VanAntwerp, Andy Karl

Photo by Joan Marcus

Jersey Boys

MUSICAL NUMBERS

ACT ONE

"Ces Soirées-La (Oh What a Night)" – Paris, 2000 ....French Rap Star, Backup Group
"Silhouettes" ....Tommy DeVito, Nick Massi, Nick DeVito, Frankie Castelluccio
"You're the Apple of My Eye" ....Tommy DeVito, Nick Massi, Nick DeVito
"I Can't Give You Anything But Love" ....Frankie Castelluccio
"Earth Angel" ....Tommy DeVito, Full Company
"Sunday Kind of Love" ....Frankie Valli, Tommy DeVito, Nick Massi, Nick's Date
"My Mother's Eyes" ....Frankie Valli
"I Go Ape" ....The Four Lovers
"(Who Wears) Short Shorts" ....The Royal Teens
"I'm in the Mood for Love/Moody's Mood for Love" ....Frankie Valli
"Cry for Me" ....Bob Gaudio, Frankie Valli, Tommy DeVito, Nick Massi
"An Angel Cried" ....Hal Miller and The Rays
"I Still Care" ....Miss Frankie Nolan and The Romans
"Trance" ....Billy Dixon and The Topix
"Sherry" ....The Four Seasons
"Big Girls Don't Cry" ....The Four Seasons
"Walk Like a Man" ....The Four Seasons
"December, 1963 (Oh What a Night)" ....Bob Gaudio, Full Company
"My Boyfriend's Back" ....The Angels
"My Eyes Adored You" ....Frankie Valli, Mary Delgado, The Four Seasons
"Dawn (Go Away)" ....The Four Seasons
"Walk Like a Man" (reprise) ....Full Company

ACT TWO

"Big Man in Town" ....The Four Seasons
"Beggin'" ....The Four Seasons
"Stay" ....Bob Gaudio, Frankie Valli, Nick Massi
"Let's Hang On (To What We've Got)" ....Bob Gaudio, Frankie Valli
"Opus 17 (Don't You Worry 'Bout Me)" ....Bob Gaudio, Frankie Valli and The New Seasons
"Bye Bye Baby" ....Frankie Valli and The Four Seasons
"C'mon Marianne" ....Frankie Valli and The Four Seasons
"Can't Take My Eyes Off You" ....Frankie Valli
"Working My Way Back to You" ....Frankie Valli and The Four Seasons
"Fallen Angel" ....Frankie Valli
"Rag Doll" ....The Four Seasons
"Who Loves You" ....The Four Seasons, Full Company

(L-R): Katie O'Toole, Sara Schmidt, Jessica Rush

Photo by Joan Marcus

Cast Continued

Frankie's Mother, Nick's Date, Angel,
    Francine (and others) ....SARA SCHMIDT
Bob Crewe (and others) .....COURTER SIMMONS
Frankie Valli ....JARROD SPECTOR
Bob Gaudio ....QUINN VANANTWERP
Thugs ....KEN DOW, JOE PAYNE

SWINGS
BRAD BASS, KATIE O'TOOLE,
NATHAN SCHERICH, TAYLOR STERNBERG

Dance Captain:
KATIE O'TOOLE
Assistant Dance Captain:
CARA COOPER

UNDERSTUDIES
For Tommy DeVito:
BRAD BASS, ERIK BATES
For Nick Massi:
MILES AUBREY, NATHAN SCHERICH
For Frankie Valli:
RUSSELL FISCHER,
DOMINIC SCAGLIONE JR.,
TAYLOR STERNBERG
For Bob Gaudio:
BRAD BASS, NATHAN SCHERICH
For Gyp DeCarlo:
MILES AUBREY, NATHAN SCHERICH
For Bob Crewe:
BRAD BASS, ERIK BATES,
NATHAN SCHERICH

ORCHESTRA
Conductor:
ANDREW WILDER
Associate Conductor:
DEBRA BARSHA
Keyboards:
DEBRA BARSHA,
STEPHEN "HOOPS" SNYDER
Guitars:
JOE PAYNE
Bass:
KEN DOW
Drums:
KEVIN DOW
Reeds:
MATT HONG, BEN KONO
Trumpet:
DAVID SPIER
Music Coordinator:
JOHN MILLER

Jersey Boys

Matt Bogart
Nick Massi

Andy Karl
Tommy DeVito

Jarrod Spector
Frankie Valli

Quinn VanAntwerp
Bob Gaudio

Mark Lotito
Gyp DeCarlo and others

Courter Simmons
Bob Crewe and others

Miles Aubrey
Norm Waxman and others

Brad Bass
Swing

Erik Bates
Hank Majewski and others

Cara Cooper
Mary Delgado and others

Ken Dow
Thug, Bass

John Edwards
Hal Miller and others

Russell Fischer
Joey, Recording Studio Engineer and others

Katie O'Toole
Swing

Joe Payne
Thug, Guitars

Jessica Rush
Lorraine and others

Dominic Scaglione Jr.
Frankie Valli on Wed. & Sat. Mats.

Nathan Scherich
Swing

Sara Schmidt
Francine and others

Taylor Sternberg
Swing

Marshall Brickman
Book

Rick Elice
Book

Bob Gaudio
Composer

Bob Crewe
Lyricist

Des McAnuff
Director

Sergio Trujillo
Choreographer

Ron Melrose
Music Direction, Vocal Arrangements and Incidental Music

Klara Zieglerova
Scenic Design

Jess Goldstein
Costume Design

Howell Binkley
Lighting Design

Steve Canyon Kennedy
Sound Design

Charles LaPointe
Wig/Hair Design

Steve Rankin
Fight Director

Richard Hester
Production Supervisor

Steve Orich
Orchestrations

John Miller
Music Coordinator

Andrew Wilder
Conductor

Peter Fulbright/Tech
Production Services
Technical Supervisor

Tara Rubin Casting
Casting

Sharon Bialy and Sherry Thomas
West Coast Casting

Stephen Gabis
Dialect Coach

Michael David
Dodger Theatricals
Producer

Edward Strong
Dodger Theatricals
Producer

Rocco Landesman
Dodger Theatricals
Producer

Joseph J. Grano
Producer

Kevin and Tamara Kinsella
Producers

Ivor Royston,
The Pelican Group
Producer

Rick Steiner
Producer

John and Bonnie
Osher
Producer

Dan Staton
Producer

Marc Bell
Producer

Frederic H.
Mayerson
Producer

Lauren Mitchell
Associate Producer

Rhoda Mayerson
Associate Producer

Joop van den Ende,
Stage Entertainment
Associate Producer

Christopher Ashley,
Artistic Director
La Jolla Playhouse
Original Producer

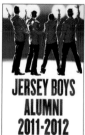

JERSEY BOYS
ALUMNI
2011-2012

Jared Bradshaw
*Swing
u/s Tommy DeVito*

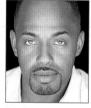

Kris Coleman
Davis (and others)

Matt Bogart
as Nick Massi.

Photo by Joan Marcus

Peter Gregus
*Bob Crewe (and
others)*

Ryan Jesse
Bob Gaudio

Dominic Nolfi
Tommy DeVito

Jake Speck
*Officer Petrillo,
Hank Majewski,
Crewe's PA, Joe
Long and others*

Jersey Boys

Photos by Brian Mapp

STAGE DOOR
Christine Snyder

(L-R): Jonny Massena, Julie Randolph

HAIR
(L-R): Isaac Grnya, Hazel Higgins

STAGE MANAGEMENT
(L-R): Michelle Bosch (Production Stage Manager),
Brendan Fay (Stage Manager), Pam Remler (Asst.
Stage Manager), Leonardo the SM fish (center)

ORCHESTRA
(L-R): Ben Kono, Andrew Wilder, Joe Payne

PROPS
(L-R): John Thompson (top of stairs), Emiliano Pares,
Scott Mulrain, Ken Harris (bottom of stairs)

SOUND AND ELECTRIC
(L-R): Dave Shepherd (holding box), Brian Aman (top of stairs), Bobby Fehribach (standing in
black sweater), Gary Marlin (bottom of stairs), Mike Lyons (holding railing), Kevin Fedigan,
Jan Nebozenko (green shirt)

Jersey Boys

AUTOMATION
(L-R): Peter Wright
Greg Burton,
Ron Fucarino

WARDROBE
Front (L-R):
Lee Austin, Kelly Kinsella
Standing in back (L-R):
Michelle Sesco,
Polly Noble,
Nick Staub

FRONT OF HOUSE STAFF
Front (L-R): Ralph Santos, Rose Balsamo,
Raymond Polanco, Eli Phillips,
Fatima Eljaouhari, Gail Worthman,
Carmella Galante

Back (L-R): Natividad Nery, Sally Lettieri,
Amy Marquez, Russell Saylor,
Ariel Martinez, Willa Burke

STAFF FOR *JERSEY BOYS*

GENERAL PRESS REPRESENTATION
BONEAU/BRYAN-BROWN
Adrian Bryan-Brown   Susanne Tighe
Heath Schwartz

COMPANY MANAGER
Sandra Carlson

PRODUCTION STAGE
   MANAGER ....MICHELLE BOSCH
Stage Manager ....Brendan M. Fay
Assistant Stage Manager ....Pamela Remler
Senior Associate
   General Manager ....Jennifer F. Vaughan
Associate General Manager ....Flora Johnstone
General Management Assistant ....Lauren Freed

Production Manager ....Jeff Parvin
Associate Company Manager ....Tim Sulka
Technical Supervision ....Tech Production Services/
                               Peter Fulbright, Mary Duffe,
                         Colleen Houlehen, Lauren A. Duffy
Music Technical Design ....Deborah N. Hurwitz
Musician Swing ....Steve Gibb
Associate Director ....West Hyler

Jersey Boys

Assistant Director ....Holly-Anne Ruggiero
Second Assistant Director ....Alex Timbers
Associate Choreographers ....Danny Austin,
Kelly Devine
Associate Music Supervisor ....Michael Rafter
Dialect Coach ....Stephen Gabis
Fight Captain ....Erik Bates
Associate Scenic Designers ....Nancy Thun, Todd Ivins
Assistant Scenic Designers ....Sonoka Gozelski,
Matthew Myhrum
Associate Costume Designer ....Alejo Vietti
Assistant Costume Designers ....China Lee,
Elizabeth Flauto
Associate Lighting Designer ....Patricia Nichols
Assistant Lighting Designer ....Sarah E. C. Maines
Associate Sound Designer ....Andrew Keister
Associate Projection Designer ....Jason Thompson
Assistant Projection Designer ....Chris Kateff
Story Board Artist ....Don Hudson
Casting Directors ....Tara Rubin, CSA;
Merri Sugarman, CSA
Casting Associates ....Eric Woodall, CSA;
Laura Schutzel, CSA;
Dale Brown, CSA
Casting Assistants ....Paige Blansfield;
Kaitlin Shaw, Lindsay Levine
Automated Lighting Programmer ....Hillary Knox
Projection Programming ....Paul Vershbow
Set Model Builder ....Anne Goelz
Costume Intern ....Jessica Reed
Production Carpenter ....Michael W. Kelly
Deck Automation ....Greg Burton
Production Electrician ....James Fedigan
Head Electrician ....Brian Aman
Assistant Electrician ....Gary L. Marlin
Production Sound Engineer ....Andrew Keister
Head Sound Engineer ....Julie M. Randolph
Production Props ....Emiliano Pares
Assistant Props ....Kenneth Harris Jr.
Production Wardrobe Supervisor ....Lee J. Austin
Assistant Wardobe Supervisor ....Michelle Sesco
Wardrobe Department ....Davis Duffield,
Kristen Gardner, Kelly Kinsella,
Shaun Ozminski, Nicholas Staub, Ricky Yates
Hair Supervisor ....Frederick C. Waggoner
Hair Department ....Hazel Higgins, Isaac Grnya
Assistant to John Miller ....Charles Butler
Synthesizer Programming ....Deborah N. Hurwitz,
Steve Orich
Music Copying ....Anixter Rice Music Service
Music Production Assistant ....Alexandra Melrose
Dramaturg ....Allison Horsley
Associate to Messrs. Michael David
and Ed Strong ....Pamela Lloyd
Advertising ....Serino Coyne, Inc./
Scott Johnson, Sandy Block, Lauren D'Elia
Marketing ....Dodger Marketing/
Jessica Ludwig, Jessica Morris
Promotions ....HHC Marketing/
Hugh Hysell, Michael Redman
Banking ....Signature Bank/Barbara von Borstel
Payroll ....Castellana Services Inc./
Lance Castellana, Norman Sewell,
James Castellana
Accountants ....Schall and Ashenfarb, C.P.A.
Finance Director ....Paula Maldonado
Insurance ....AON/Albert G. Rubin Insurance Services/

George Walden, Claudia Kaufman
Counsel ....Nan Bases, Esq.
Special Events ....John L. Haber
Travel Arrangements ....The "A" Team at Tzell Travel/
Andi Henig
Information Technology Management ....ITelagen, Inc.
Web Design ....Curious Minds Media, Inc.
Production Photographer ....Joan Marcus
Theatre Displays ....King Displays

DODGERS
DODGER THEATRICALS
Mark Andrews, Richard Biederman, Sandra Carlson, Michael David, Anne Ezell, Lauren Freed, Mariann Fresiello, John L. Haber, Richard Hester, Flora Johnstone, Abigail Kornet, Tony Lance, Pamela Lloyd, James Elliot Love, Jessica Ludwig, Paula Maldonado, Anthony McDonald, Lauren Mitchell, Jessica Morris, Sally Campbell Morse, Taylor Noble, Jeff Parvin, Samuel Rivera, R. Doug Rodgers, Maureen Rooney, Andrew Serna, Bridget Stegall, Edward Strong, Tim Sulka, Ashley Tracey, Ann E. Van Nostrand, Jennifer F. Vaughan, Laurinda Wilson, Josh Zeigler

Dodger Group Sales 1-877-5DODGER
Exclusive Tour Direction ....Steven Schnepp/
Broadway Booking Office NYC

CREDITS
Scenery, show control and automation by ShowMotion, Inc., Norwalk, CT. Lighting equipment from PRG Lighting. Sound equipment by Masque Sound. Projection equipment by Sound Associates. Selected men's clothing custom made by Saint Laurie Merchant Tailors, New York City. Costumes executed by Carelli Costumes, Studio Rouge, Carmen Gee, John Kristiansen New York, Inc. Selected menswear by Carlos Campos. Props provided by The Spoon Group, Downtime Productions, Tessa Dunning. Select guitars provided by Gibson Guitars. Laundry services provided by Ernest Winzer Theatrical Cleaners. Additional set and hand props courtesy of George Fenmore, Inc. Rosebud matches by Diamond Brands, Inc., Zippo lighters used. Rehearsed at the New 42nd Street Studios. Emergen-C by Alacer Corporation. PLAYBILL® cover photo by Chris Callis.

Grammy Award-winning cast album now available on Rhino Records.

www.jerseyboysinfo.com

Scenic drops adapted from *George Tice: Urban Landscapes*/W.W. Norton. Other photographs featured are from *George Tice: Selected Photographs 1953–1999*/David R. Godine. (Photographs courtesy of the Peter Fetterman Gallery/Santa Monica.)

SONG CREDITS
"Ces Soirees-La ("Oh What a Night")" (Bob Gaudio, Judy Parker, Yannick Zolo, Edmond David Bacri). Jobete Music Company Inc., Seasons Music Company (ASCAP). "Silhouettes" (Bob Crewe, Frank Slay, Jr.), Regent Music Corporation (BMI). "You're the Apple of My Eye" (Otis Blackwell), EMI Unart Catalog Inc. (BMI). "I Can't Give You Anything But Love" (Dorothy Fields, Jimmy McHugh), EMI April Music Inc., Aldi Music Company, Cotton Club Publishing (ASCAP). "Earth Angel" (Jesse Belvin, Curtis Williams, Gaynel Hodge), Embassy Music Corporation (BMI). "Sunday Kind of Love" (Barbara Belle, Anita Leanord Nye, Stan Rhodes, Louis Prima), LGL Music Inc./Larry Spier, Inc. (ASCAP). "My Mother's Eyes" (Abel Baer, L. Wolfe Gilbert), Abel Baer Music Company, EMI Feist Catalog Inc. (ASCAP). "I Go Ape" (Bob Crewe, Frank Slay, Jr.), MPL Music Publishing Inc. (ASCAP). "(Who Wears) Short Shorts" (Bob Gaudio, Bill Crandall, Tom Austin, Bill Dalton), EMI Longitude Music, Admiration Music Inc., Third Story Music Inc., and New Seasons Music (BMI). "I'm in the Mood for Love" (Dorothy Fields, Jimmy McHugh), Famous Music Corporation (ASCAP). "Moody's Mood for Love" (James Moody, Dorothy Fields, Jimmy McHugh), Famous Music Corporation (ASCAP). "Cry for Me" (Bob Gaudio), EMI Longitude Music, Seasons Four Music (BMI). "An Angel Cried" (Bob Gaudio), EMI Longitude Music (BMI). "I Still Care" (Bob Gaudio), Hearts Delight Music, Seasons Four Music (BMI). "Trance" (Bob Gaudio), Hearts Delight Music, Seasons Four Music (BMI). "Sherry" (Bob Gaudio), MPL Music Publishing Inc. (ASCAP). "Big Girls Don't Cry" (Bob Gaudio, Bob Crewe), MPL Music Publishing Inc. (ASCAP). "Walk Like a Man" (Bob Crewe, Bob Gaudio), Gavadima Music, MPL Communications Inc. (ASCAP). "December, 1963 (Oh What a Night)" (Bob Gaudio, Judy Parker), Jobete Music Company Inc, Seasons Music Company (ASCAP). "My Boyfriend's Back" (Robert Feldman, Gerald Goldstein, Richard Gottehrer), EMI Blackwood Music Inc. (BMI). "My Eyes Adored You" (Bob Crewe, Kenny Nolan), Jobete Music Company Inc, Kenny Nolan Publishing (ASCAP), Stone Diamond Music Corporation, Tannyboy Music (BMI). "Dawn, Go Away" (Bob Gaudio, Sandy Linzer), EMI Full Keel Music, Gavadima Music, Stebojen Music Company (ASCAP). "Big Man in Town" (Bob Gaudio), EMI Longitude Music (BMI), Gavadima Music (ASCAP). "Beggin'" (Bob Gaudio, Peggy Farina), EMI Longitude Music, Seasons Four Music (BMI). "Stay" (Maurice Williams), Cherio Corporation (BMI). "Let's Hang On (To What We've Got)" (Bob Crewe, Denny Randell, Sandy Linzer), EMI Longitude Music, Screen Gems-EMI Music Inc., Seasons Four Music (BMI). "Opus 17 (Don't You Worry 'Bout Me)" (Denny Randell, Sandy Linzer) Screen Gems-EMI Music Inc, Seasons Four Music (BMI). "Everybody Knows My Name" (Bob Gaudio, Bob Crewe), EMI Longitude Music, Seasons Four Music (BMI). "Bye Bye Baby" (Bob Crewe, Bob Gaudio), EMI Longitude Music, Seasons Four Music (BMI). "C'mon Marianne" (L. Russell Brown, Ray Bloodworth), EMI Longitude Music and Seasons Four Music (BMI). "Can't Take My Eyes Off You" (Bob Gaudio, Bob Crewe), EMI Longitude Music, Seasons Four Music (BMI). "Working My Way Back to You" (Denny Randell, Sandy Linzer), Screen Gems–EMI Music Inc, Seasons Four Music (BMI). "Fallen Angel" (Guy Fletcher, Doug Flett), Chrysalis Music (ASCAP). "Rag Doll" (Bob Crewe, Bob Gaudio), EMI Longitude Music (BMI), Gavadima Music (ASCAP). "Who Loves You?" (Bob Gaudio, Judy Parker), Jobete Music Company Inc, Seasons Music Company (ASCAP).

SPECIAL THANKS
Peter Bennett, Elliot Groffman, Karen Pals, Janine Smalls, Chad Woerner, New 42nd Street Studios, Roundabout Theatre Company, Dan Whitten. The authors, director, cast and company of *Jersey Boys* would like to express their love and thanks to Jordan Ressler.

Jersey Boys
SCRAPBOOK

Correspondent: Jessica Rush, "Lorraine" and other roles

Anniversary Party: Sixth anniversary party at Bowlmor Lanes!

Most Exciting Celebrity Visitors: Brian Dennehy was extremely gracious and Elaine Stritch was a hoot in her sunglasses! We also had a couple of Marines on leave from Afghanistan stop in. So glad we were able to give back to them in our small way.

Actor Who Performed the Most Roles: Sara Schmidt performs the most, at 15.

Actor Who Has Done the Most Shows: Mark Lotito, here from the beginning, who puts his count at around 2500....that's crazy.

Special Backstage Rituals: When the boys are at places for the top of the show, they tap fingers thru the fence. Let's get this going!

Favorite Moment: The one that seems to win out is the finale, the one time we are all onstage together...great energy.

Favorite In-Theatre Gathering Place: Stage Management...all the way.

Favorite Off-Site Hangouts: Sosa Borella, Medi...when we do hang out. Let's be honest, most folks in our show go right home to their kiddos and families. But if we all hang together it's good times for sure.

Favorite Snack Food: Anything anyone brings us. We aren't picky.

Mascot: Leonardo, our Siamese fighting fish.

Favorite Therapy: The Frankies have a warm-up ritual from Katie Agresta that involves lots of tongue pulling and humming...and I think they also enjoy a quick massage from Cara Cooper in one of their scenes.

Memorable Ad-Lib: "Two cars, three Karls,

AIDSWALK 2011 (L-R): Russell Fischer, Katie O'Toole, Dominic Scaglione Jr., Michelle Bosch, Peter Gregus, Brendan Fay and Rachel Spadaro.

Photo courtesy Jessica Rush

(confused look)...four guys?...infinite possibilities."—Nathan Scherich as Bob Gaudio.

Memorable Electronic Device Incident During a Performance: There was that one time a woman was watching something on her iPad down front for a good portion of Act I.

Memorable Press Encounter: Joining other Broadway companies to acknowledge the 10th anniversary of 9/11.

Fastest Costume Change: Nine seconds: Cara Cooper changing from an Angel to Mary Delgado.

Heaviest/Hottest Costumes: Several of the guys underdress two shirts and then add a suit coat and sometimes an overcoat.

Actor Who Wore the Least: Sara Schmidt, bra and panties in the penthouse scene...well, she DOES have a boa, too!

Catchphrase Only the Company Would Recognize: "Ride"—Dominic Scaglione Jr.

Sweethearts Within the Company: Can we count the Bromance between Quinn Van Antwerp and Dominic Scaglione Jr....add Matt Bogart in there for good measure. :)

Orchestra Member Who Played the Most Instruments: Ben Kono, 4: alto sax, clarinet, flute and oboe.

Memorable Directorial Note: "Mark, you need to bend over more in your bow."—Des McAnuff. (That is the ONLY note I've ever heard Mark get, incidentally.)

Nicknames: Thanks to Scags the boys are known as Chance Sutcliff, Richie Bainbridge, Jim Hudson, Sanford McCarthy and Biff Sterling. But...which is which?

Coolest Thing About Being in This Show: How excited the audiences are and their response at the end of the show. It's an awesome way to end the night! They're on their feet and dancing EVERY TIME.

IN MEMORY

It is difficult to imagine producing anything without the presence of beloved Dodger producing associate James Elliot Love. Friend to everyone he met, James stood at the heart of all that is good about the theatrical community. He will be missed, but his spirit abides.

The producers would like to use this space to remember Mark Fearon, and in the spirit of this production, to contemplate the abiding joy of youth.

In memory of Jairo "Jay" Santos

JUJAMCYN THEATERS

JORDAN ROTH
President

PAUL LIBIN
Executive Vice President

JACK VIERTEL
Senior Vice President

MEREDITH VILLATORE
Chief Financial Officer

JENNIFER HERSHEY
Vice President,
Building Operations

MICAH HOLLINGWORTH
Vice President,
Company Operations

HAL GOLDBERG
Vice President,
Theatre Operations

Director of Business Affairs . . . . .Albert T. Kim

Director of Ticketing Services . . . . .Justin Karr
Theatre Operations Managers . . . . .Willa Burke,
Susan Elrod, Emily Hare,
Jeff Hubbard, Albert T. Kim
Theatre Operations Associates . . . . . . .Carrie Jo Brinker,
Michael Composto, Anah Jyoti Klate
Accounting . . . . .Cathy Cerge, Erin Dooley,
Christian Sislian
Executive Producer, Red Awning . . . . . . .Nicole Kastrinos
Director of Marketing, Givenik.com . . . . .Joe Tropia
Marketing Associate, Givenik.com . . . . .Ben Cohen
Building Operations Associate . . . . .Erich Bussing
Executive Coordinator . . . . .Ed Lefferson
Executive Assistants . . . . .Clark Mims Tedesco,
Julia Kraus, Beth Given
Receptionist . . . . .Kate Garst
Maintenance . . . . .Ralph Santos, Ramon Zapata
Security . . . . .Rasim Hodzic, John Acero
Interns . . . . .Jason Blackwell, Stephanie Ditman,
Burton Frey, Sam Chapin,
Emily Petrain, Lisa Perchinske,
Kate Siegel, Mark Smith, Kelsey Wehde

STAFF FOR THE AUGUST WILSON THEATRE

Theatre Manager . . . . .Willa Burke
Associate Theatre Manager . . . . .Anah Jyoti Klate
Treasurer . . . . .Nick Russo
Head Carpenter . . . . .Dan Dour

Head Propertyman . . . . .Scott Mulrain
Head Electrician . . . . .Robert Fehribach
Flyman . . . . .Peter Wright
Engineer . . . . .Ralph Santos
Assistant Treasurers . . . . . . .Kevin Dublynn, Kathryn Fearon,
Matthew Fearon, Tara Giebler,
Jeanne Halal, James Roeder, John Tobin
Fly Automation . . . . .Ron Fucarino
Carpenter . . . . .Alex Gutierrez
Propertyman . . . . .John Thomson
Follow Spot Operators . . . . . . .Andrew Dean, Sean Fedigan,
Michael Lyons
House Sound Engineers . . . . .Jan Nebozenko,
David Shepherd
Head Usher . . . . .Rose Balsamo
Ticket-Takers/Directors/Ushers . . . . .Fatima Eljaouhari,
Helen Flaherty, Robert Fowler,
Carmella Galante, Joan Gilmore,
Barbara Hill, Sally Lettieri, Amy Marquez,
J. Ariel Martinez, Eli Phillips, Raymond Polanco,
Russell Saylor, Gail Worthman
Doorpersons . . . . .Gustavo Catuy, Christine Snyder
Head Porter . . . . .Natividad Nery
Porters . . . . .Pedro Martinez, Lourdes Moreno
Head Cleaner . . . . .Maria Giria
Cleaners . . . . .Antonia Duran, Lorraine Feeks

Jerusalem

First Preview: April 2, 2011. Opened: April 21, 2011
Closed August 21, 2011 after 21 Previews and 141 Performances.

PLAYBILL

Local wild man Johnny "Rooster" Byron drinks, smokes and whores his way through life with joyous abandon surrounded by a tribe of his closest friends and hangers-on until at last the forces of civil order threaten to bulldoze his mobile home and drag him off to justice. Is this any way for a grown man to behave, especially one with an impressionable young son? Byron has to figure out a way to stay true to the legends he has concocted about himself while living up to his responsibilities as a grownup...or not.

CAST

Phaedra	AIMEÉ-FFION EDWARDS
Ms. Fawcett	SARAH MOYLE
Mr. Parsons	HARVEY ROBINSON
Johnny "Rooster" Byron	MARK RYLANCE
Ginger	MACKENZIE CROOK
The Professor	ALAN DAVID
Lee	JAY SULLIVAN
Davey	DANNY KIRRANE
Pea	MOLLY RANSON
Tanya	CHARLOTTE MILLS
Wesley	MAX BAKER
Marky	MARK PAGE

(Tues., Fri., Sat. mat. and eve.)
AIDEN EYRICK
(Wed. mat. and eve., Thurs., Sun.)

Dawn	GERALDINE HUGHES
Troy Whitworth	BARRY SLOANE
Frank Whitworth	JAMES RIORDAN
Danny Whitworth	RICHARD SHORT

⑤ THE MUSIC BOX
239 W. 45th Street
A Shubert Organization Theatre

Philip J. Smith, *Chairman*   Robert E. Wankel, *President*

Sonia Friedman Productions   Stuart Thompson   Scott Rudin   Roger Berlind
Royal Court Theatre Productions   Beverly Bartner/Alice Tulchin   Dede Harris/Rupert Gavin
Broadway Across America   Jon B. Platt   1001 Nights/Stephanie P. McClelland
Carole L. Haber/Richard Willis   Jacki Barlia Florin/Adam Blanshay

present the ROYAL COURT THEATRE production of

Mark Rylance
in

JERUSALEM

by

Jez Butterworth

with

Mackenzie Crook

Max Baker   Alan David   Aimeé-Ffion Edwards   Aiden Eyrick   Geraldine Hughes
Danny Kirrane   Charlotte Mills   Sarah Moyle   Mark Page   Molly Ranson
Harvey Robinson   Barry Sloane   Jay Sullivan
Frances Mercanti-Anthony   Michael Milligan   James Riordan   Richard Short   Libby Woodbridge

Scenic & Costume Design	Lighting Design	Sound Design	Original Music
Ultz	**Mimi Jordan Sherin**	**Ian Dickinson for Autograph**	**Stephen Warbeck**

UK Casting	Casting	Production Stage Manager
Amy Ball	**Jim Carnahan, C.S.A.**	**Jill Cordle**

Press Representative	Production Management	General Management	UK General Management
Boneau/Bryan-Brown	**Aurora Productions**	**STP / David Turner**	**Sonia Friedman Productions**

Directed by

Ian Rickson

The Producers wish to express their appreciation to Theatre Development Fund for its support for this production.

8/21/11

UNDERSTUDIES

For Davey/Troy: RICHARD SHORT
For Dawn/Ms. Fawcett:
FRANCES MERCANTI-ANTHONY
For Ginger/Lee: HARVEY ROBINSON
For Pea/Tanya/Phaedra: LIBBY WOODBRIDGE
For Wesley/The Professor: JAMES RIORDAN
For Mr. Parsons/Frank Whitworth/
Danny Whitworth: MICHAEL MILLIGAN

SETTING

Flintock, Wiltshire, England 2011

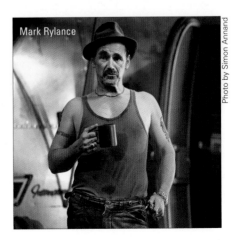

Mark Rylance

Photo by Simon Annand

Jerusalem

Mark Rylance
Johnny "Rooster" Byron

Mackenzie Crook
Ginger

Max Baker
Wesley

Alan David
The Professor

Aimeé-Ffion Edwards
Phaedra

Aiden Eyrick
Marky

Geraldine Hughes
Dawn

Danny Kirrane
Davey

Charlotte Mills
Tanya

Sarah Moyle
Ms. Fawcett

Mark Page
Marky

Molly Ranson
Pea

Harvey Robinson
Mr. Parsons

Barry Sloane
Troy Whitworth

Jay Sullivan
Lee

Frances Mercanti-Anthony
*u/s Dawn,
Ms. Fawcett*

Michael Milligan
*u/s Mr. Parsons,
Frank Whitworth,
Danny Whitworth*

James Riordan
Frank Whitworth

Richard Short
Danny Whitworth

Libby Woodbridge
*u/s Pea, Tanya,
Phaedra*

Jez Butterworth
Playwright

Ian Rickson
Director

Ultz
*Set and Costume
Design*

Mimi Jordan Sherin
Lighting Design

Ian Dickinson
for Autograph
Sound Design

Stephen Warbeck
Composer

Charmian Hoare
*Voice and Dialect
Coach*

David Turner
General Manager

Sonia Friedman
Productions Ltd.
Producer

Stuart Thompson
Producer

Scott Rudin
Producer

Roger Berlind
Producer

Dede Harris
Producer

John Gore,
Broadway Across
America
Producer

Thomas B. McGrath,
Broadway Across
America
Producer

Jerusalem

Jon B. Platt
Producer

Stephanie P.
McClelland
Producer

Richard Willis
Producer

Jacki Barlia Florin
Producer

Adam Blanshay
Producer

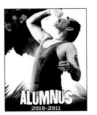

John Gallagher, Jr.
Lee

Photos by Brian Mapp

BOX OFFICE
(L-R): Bob Kelly, John Stange

DOORMAN
Tim Barrett

FRONT OF HOUSE STAFF
Front Row (L-R): John Seid, Laura Scanlon,
Nick Fusco, Jonathan Shulman (House Manager)

Middle Row (L-R): Joe Amato, Tim Shelton,
Lottie Dennis, Tom Murdoch, Mike Composto

Back Row (L-R): Kenny Kelly, Dennis Scanlon

CREW
(L-R): Ken McGee (Stage Manager), Beth Berkeley (Production Sound), Kim Garnett (House Props), Billy Rowland (House Electrician), Dennis Maher (House Carpenter), Mark Diaz (Flyman), Jill Cordle (Production Stage Manager), Chris D'Angelo (Company Manager), Scott Monroe (Production Props)

Jerusalem

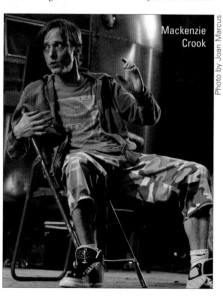

Mackenzie Crook

Photo by Joan Marcus

Jesus Christ Superstar

First Preview: March 1, 2012. Opened: March 22, 2012.
Still running as of May 31, 2012.

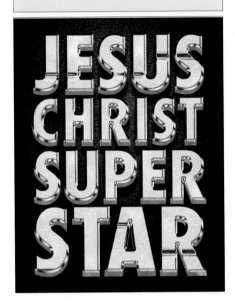

PLAYBILL®

The last days in the life of Jesus Christ portrayed in rock opera style, with an emphasis on showing how much Roman Imperial politics had to do with Jesus' betrayal, arrest, imprisonment, trial, torture and crucifixion. The Resurrection is not shown.

CAST

Jesus Christ	PAUL NOLAN
Judas Iscariot	JOSH YOUNG
Mary Magdalene	CHILINA KENNEDY
Pontius Pilate	TOM HEWITT
King Herod	BRUCE DOW
Caiaphas	MARCUS NANCE
Annas	AARON WALPOLE
Simon Zealotes	LEE SIEGEL
Peter	MIKE NADAJEWSKI
Thaddeus	MATT ALFANO
Matthew, Priest	MARK CASSIUS
Bartholomew	RYAN GIFFORD
James the Lesser, Priest	JEREMY KUSHNIER
Thomas	JAZ SEALEY
John	JASON SERMONIA
James	JULIUS SERMONIA
Phillip	JONATHAN WINSBY
Andrew, Priest	SANDY WINSBY
Jonah/Swing	NICK CARTELL
Elizabeth	MARY ANTONINI
Ruth	KAREN BURTHWRIGHT
Mary (Martha's Sister)	JACQUELINE BURTNEY
Sarah	KAYLEE HARWOOD
Martha, Maid by the Fire	MELISSA O'NEIL
Rachel	LAURIN PADOLINA

Continued on next page

NEIL SIMON THEATRE
UNDER THE DIRECTION OF JAMES M. NEDERLANDER AND JAMES L. NEDERLANDER

The Dodgers and The Really Useful Group
Latitude Link   Tamara and Kevin Kinsella   Pelican Group   Waxman-Dokton

Joe Corcoran   Detsky/Sokolowski/Kassie   Florin-Blanshay-Fan/Broadway Across America
Rich/Caudwell   Shin/Coleman   TheatreDreams North America, LLC

Present

the Stratford Shakespeare Festival's Production of

JESUS CHRIST SUPERSTAR

Lyrics by	Music by
Tim Rice	**Andrew Lloyd Webber**

with

Paul Nolan   Josh Young   Chilina Kennedy
Tom Hewitt   Bruce Dow

Matt Alfano	Mary Antonini	Karen Burthwright	Jacqueline Burtney
Nick Cartell	Mark Cassius	Ryan Gifford	Kaylee Harwood
Jeremy Kushnier	Krista Leis	Mike Nadajewski	Melissa O'Neil
Laurin Padolina	Katrina Reynolds	Matthew Rossoff	Jaz Sealey
Jason Sermonia	Julius Sermonia	Lee Siegel	Matt Stokes
	Jonathan Winsby	Sandy Winsby	

with Marcus Nance and Aaron Walpole

Scenic Design	Costume Design	Lighting Design	Sound Design
Robert Brill	Paul Tazewell	Howell Binkley	Steve Canyon Kennedy

Video Design	Fight Director	Stunt Coordinator
Sean Nieuwenhuis	Daniel Levinson	Simon Fon

Music Coordinator	Production Stage Manager	Company Manager
John Miller	Frank Hartenstein	Kimberly Kelley

Technical Supervisor	New York Casting	Stratford Casting
Hudson Theatricals	Tara Rubin Casting	Beth Russell

Associate Producers	Press Representative	Promotions	Executive Producer
Lauren Mitchell Nederlander Presentations, Inc.	Boneau/Bryan-Brown	Red Rising Marketing	Sally Campbell Morse

Music Direction and Supervision
Rick Fox

Choreography
Lisa Shriver

Directed by
Des McAnuff

3/22/12

(L-R): Chilina Kennedy as Mary Magdalene, Josh Young as Judas, and Paul Nolan as Jesus Christ

Photo by Joan Marcus

Jesus Christ Superstar

MUSICAL NUMBERS

ACT ONE

Overture ....Orchestra
"Heaven on Their Minds"...Judas
"What's the Buzz"...Jesus, Mary, Ensemble
"Strange Thing, Mystifying"...Judas, Jesus, Ensemble
"Everything's Alright"..Mary, Judas, Jesus, Ensemble
"This Jesus Must Die"...Caiaphas, Annas, Priests, Ensemble
"Hosanna"..Caiaphas, Jesus, Ensemble
"Simon Zealotes"..Simon, Ensemble
"Poor Jerusalem"...Jesus
"Pilate's Dream"..Pilate
"The Temple/Make Us Well"..Ensemble, Jesus
"Everything's Alright" (Reprise)...Mary, Jesus
"I Don't Know How to Love Him"...Mary
"Damned for All Time/Blood Money"....................Judas, Caiaphas, Annas, Ensemble

ACT TWO

"The Last Supper"..Jesus, Judas, Apostles
"Gethsemane"..Jesus
"The Arrest"..Jesus, Peter, Caiaphas, Annas, Apostles, Ensemble
"Peter's Denial"...Peter, Maid by the Fire, Mary, Priests
"Pilate and Christ"..Pilate, Jesus, Annas, Ensemble
"Herod's Song"...King Herod
"Could We Start Again Please"...Mary, Peter, Judas
"Judas' Death"..Judas, Caiaphas, Annas, Ensemble
"Trial by Pilate/39 Lashes".....................................Pilate, Caiaphas, Jesus, Ensemble
"Superstar"...Judas, Women
"Crucifixion"..Jesus
"John 19:41"..Orchestra

ORCHESTRA

Conductor:
RICK FOX
Associate Conductor:
MATT GALLAGHER
Assistant Conductor:
SONNY PALADINO
Reeds:
DAVID MANN
Trumpets:
DAVE TRIGG, JEFF WILFORE
Trombone/Tuba:
NATHAN MAYLAND
French Horns:
KATE DENNIS, WILL DeVOS
Guitar 1:
KEVIN RAMESSAR

Guitar 2:
LARRY SALTZMAN
Bass:
FRANCISCO CENTENO
Drums:
CLINT DEGANON
Percussion:
JOSEPH PASSARO
Keyboards:
MATT GALLAGHER, SONNY PALADINO
Piano/Organ:
RICK FOX
Synth Programmer:
GREG DIAKUN

Music Coordinator:
JOHN MILLER

Cast Continued

Esther ....KATRINA REYNOLDS

SWINGS:
KRISTA LEIS, MATTHEW ROSSOFF,
MATT STOKES

DANCE CAPTAIN:
MATTHEW ROSSOFF

ASSISTANT DANCE CAPTAIN:
KRISTA LEIS

FIGHT CAPTAIN:
JULIUS SERMONIA

UNDERSTUDIES
For Jesus:
NICK CARTELL, JEREMY KUSHNIER,
JONATHAN WINSBY
For Judas:
NICK CARTELL, JEREMY KUSHNIER
For Mary:
KAYLEE HARWOOD, MELISSA O'NEIL
For Pontius Pilate:
JEREMY KUSHNIER, MATT STOKES,
SANDY WINSBY
For King Herod:
MIKE NADAJEWSKI, MATT STOKES
For Caiaphas:
MATT STOKES, SANDY WINSBY
For Annas:
NICK CARTELL, MARK CASSIUS

Paul Nolan

Photo by Joan Marcus

Jesus Christ Superstar

Paul Nolan
Jesus

Josh Young
Judas Iscariot

Chilina Kennedy
Mary Magdalene

Tom Hewitt
Pontius Pilate

Bruce Dow
King Herod

Marcus Nance
Caiaphas

Aaron Walpole
Annas

Matt Alfano
Thaddeus

Mary Antonini
Elizabeth

Karen Burthwright
Ruth

Jacqueline Burtney
Mary (Martha's Sister)

Nick Cartell
Jonah, Swing

Mark Cassius
Matthew/High Priest

Ryan Gifford
Bartholomew

Kaylee Harwood
Sarah

Jeremy Kushnier
James the Lesser/Priest

Krista Leis
Swing/Assistant Dance Captain

Mike Nadajewski
Peter

Melissa O'Neil
Martha/Maid by the Fire

Laurin Padolina
Rachel

Katrina Reynolds
Esther

Matthew Rossoff
Swing/Dance Captain

Jaz Sealey
Thomas

Jason Sermonia
John

Julius Sermonia
James/Fight Captain

Lee Siegel
Simon Zealotes

Matt Stokes
Swing

Jonathan Winsby
Phillip

Sandy Winsby
Andrew

Andrew Lloyd Webber
Composer

Tim Rice
Lyricist

Des McAnuff
Director/ Artistic Director Stratford Shakespeare Festival

Lisa Shriver
Choreographer

Rick Fox
Music Director

Robert Brill
Set Design

Jesus Christ Superstar

Paul Tazewell
Costume Design

Howell Binkley
Lighting Design

Steve Canyon
Kennedy
Sound Design

Sean Nieuwenhuis
Video Design

Daniel Levinson
Fight Director

Simon Fon
Stunt Coordinator

John Miller
Music Coordinator

Tara Rubin
Tara Rubin Casting
Casting

Beth Russell
Stratford Casting

Neil A. Mazzella
Hudson Theatrical
Associates
Technical Supervisor

Michael David
The Dodgers
Producer

Edward Strong
The Dodgers
Producer

Rocco Landesman
The Dodgers
Producer

Ralph Bryan
Latitude Link
Producer

Tamara and Kevin Kinsella
Producers

Ivor Royston
The Pelican Group
Producer

Anita Waxman
Producer

Joe Corcoran
Producer

Dan Corcoran
Producer

Jacki Barlia Florin
Florin-Blanshay-Fan
Producer

Adam Blanshay
Florin-Blanshay-Fan
Producer

Lily Fan
Florin-Blanshay-Fan
Producer

John Gore
CEO
Broadway Across
America
Producer

Thomas B. McGrath
Chairman
Broadway Across
America
Producer

John Caudwell
Rich/Caudwell
Producer

Chunsoo Shin
Shin/Coleman
Producer

Joan A. Alper
Theatredreams
North America LLC
Producer

Jill Wilker and Lawrence J. Wilker
Theatredreams North America LLC
Producer

William W. Becker
Theatredreams
North America LLC
Producer

(L-R) Paul Nolan
and Josh Young

Photo by Joan Marcus

Jesus Christ Superstar

Lauren Mitchell
Associate Producer

Antoni Cimolino
*General Director
Stratford
Shakespeare Festival
Original Producer*

TRANSFER STUDENT 2011-2012

Leo Ash Evens
*Phillip
Soldier with Bullwhip*

Photos by Brian Mapp

CREW
Front Row (L-R): Roy Seiler, Polly Noble, CeCe Cruz, Michael Altbaum, Heather Wright, Brian Scott, Matt Walsh, Courtney James, Kelly Martindale, Angela Simpson, Sean McGrath

Back Row (L-R): Hilda Garcia-Suli, Norman Ballard, Scott Westervelt, Kim Kelley, Mia Bienovich, Julie Randolph, Julienne Schubert-Blechman, Keith Buchanan, Artie Lutz, Peter Drummond, John Kelly, Meredith Benson, Angela Lehrer, Ryan Oslak, Mike Bennet, Hector Lugo, Mark Diaz, John Gordon

BOX OFFICE
(L-R): Erich Stollberger, Louis Waldron
Not pictured: Edward Waxman, Treasurer

USHERS, TCKET TAKERS, MERCHANDISE, BARTENDERS
Front Row (L-R): Nan Baldwin, Janice Luca

Second Row (L-R): Evelyn Gutierrez, Marilyn Christie, Dorothy Thimote, Linda DiGloria

Third Row (L-R): Eshautine King, Joanne DeCicco, Chris Langdon, Jane Publik

Fourth Row (L-R): Marisol Olavarria, Tom Tassiello, Michelle Smith, Sharon Hauser

Fifth Row (L-R): Eddie Cuevas, Sarah Schechtman, Grace Darbasie, Lauren Arellano, Tara Delasnueces

Sixth Row (L-R): Vincent Gautieri, Vinnie Diaz, Robyn Corrigan, Steven Ouellette (House Manager)

Jesus Christ Superstar

STAFF FOR *JESUS CHRIST SUPERSTAR*

GENERAL MANAGEMENT
DODGER MANAGEMENT GROUP

COMPANY MANAGER
Kimberly Kelley

NATIONAL PRESS REPRESENTATIVES
BONEAU/BRYAN-BROWN
Adrian Bryan-Brown   Susanne Tighe
Emily Meagher

Production Stage Manager	FRANK HARTENSTEIN
Stage Manager	Brian Scott
Assistant Stage Manager	Kelly A. Martindale
Assistant Company Manager	Michael Altbaum
Technical Supervision	Hudson Theatrical Associates/ Neil Mazzella, Sam Ellis, Irene Wang
Associate Technical Supervisor	John Tiggeloven
Technical Production Assistant	Caitlin McInerney
Assistant Director	Lezlie Wade
Associate Choreographer	Bradley "Shooz" Rapier
Assistant Choreographer	Marc Kimelman
Associate Scenic Designer	Steven Kemp
Assistant Set Designers	Brandon Kleiman, Angrette McCloskey, Dustin O'Neill
Associate Costume Designer	Katie Irish
Assistant Costume Designer	Angela Kahler
Costume Shopper	Dana Burkart
Associate Lighting Designer	Ryan O'Gara
Assistant Lighting Designer	Amanda Zieve
Automated Lighting Programmer	Timothy F. Rogers
Associate Sound Designers	Walter Trarbach, Andrew Keister
Assistant Sound Designer	Jana Hoglund
Assistant Video Designer	Davida Tkach
Casting Directors	Tara Rubin, CSA; Dale Brown, CSA; Merri Sugarman, CSA
Tara Rubin Casting	Eric Woodall, CSA; Stephanie Yankwitt, CSA; Kaitlin Shaw, Lindsay Levine
Production Carpenter	Edward Diaz
Automation Flyman	Ben Horrigan
Advance Electrician	Jae Day
Production Electrician	Keith Buchanan
Production Sound Engineer	Walter Trarbach
Production Sound Mixer	Julie Randolph
Deck Soundman	Matt Walsh
Production Props	Emiliano Pares
Head Props	Pete Drummond
Production Wardrobe Supervisor	Scott Westervelt
Asst. Wardrobe Supervisor	Angela Simpson
Dressers	Meredith Benson, Maria Cecilia Cruz, Hilda Garcia-Suli, Hector Lugo, Polly Noble, Ryan Oslak, Julienne Schubert-Blechman, Roy Seiler
Production Wig Supervisors	Gerry Altenburg, Erica Croft-Fraser
Hair Supervisor	Heather Wright
Assistant Hair Supervisor	Carrie Rohm
Hair Dresser	Tim Miller
Assistant to John Miller	Nichole Jennino
Production Assistants	Courtney James, Ryan Mekenian

Advertising	Serino/Coyne Scott Johnson, Sandy Block, Marci Kaufman, Ryan Cunningham, Sarah Marcus
Promotions	Red Rising Marketing/ Michael Redman, Nicole Pando
Accountants	Schall and Ashenfarb, C.P.A., PC
Banking	Signature Bank/Barbara von Borstel
Payroll	Castellana Services Inc.
Insurance	AON Albert G. Ruben Insurance Services Inc./ George Walden, Claudia Kaufman
Counsel to *JCS*	Seth Gelblum, Esq., Loeb & Loeb LLP
Information Technology Management	ITelagen, Inc.
Web Design/Maintenance	Situation Interactive
Production Photographer	Joan Marcus
Theatre Displays	King Displays

Official Website
www.SuperstarOnBroadway.com

Performance rights to *Jesus Christ Superstar* are
licensed by R&H Theatricals:
www.rnh.com

THE DODGERS
Dodger Properties

President	Michael David
Executive Producer	Sally Campbell Morse
Director of Creative Development	Lauren Mitchell
Director of Business Administration	Pamela Lloyd
Director of Marketing	Jessica Ludwig
Director of Finance	Paula Maldonado
Senior Assoc. General Manager	Jennifer F. Vaughan
Production Manager	Jeff Parvin
Associate General Manager	Flora Johnstone
General Management Assistant	Lauren Freed
Marketing Associates	Jessica Morris, Ann E. Van Nostrand, Tony Lance
Finance Associates	Laurinda Wilson, Mariann Fresiello
Executive Assistants to Mr. David	Andrew Serna, Ashley Tracey
Seat Manager	Andrew Serna
Office & Atelier Manager	Abigail Kornet
Assistant Office Manager	Anne Ezell
Office Assistant	Scott Dennis
Special Events	John Haber
Counsel to Dodger Properties	Nan Bases
CPA to Dodger Properties	Ira Schall

Dodgers-at-Large
Mark Andrews, Michael Camp, Sandra Carlson, Dhyana Colony, Tyler Gabbard, John Gendron, Richard Hester, West Hyler, Deana Marie Kirsch, James Elliot Love, Jennie Mamary, Ron Melrose, Samuel Rivera, R. Doug Rodgers, Maureen Rooney, Bridget Stegall, Edward Strong, Tim Sulka, Ellen Szorady

THE REALLY USEFUL GROUP

Directors	Andrew Lloyd Webber, Madeleine Lloyd Webber
Chairman	Mark Wordsworth
Managing Director	Barney Wragg
Director of Legal and Business Affairs	Jonathan Hull

Chief Financial Officer	Bishu Chakraborty
Head of Production	Patrick Murphy
Executive Assistant to Andrew Lloyd Webber	Jan Eade
Marketing Co-ordinator	Mark Fox
Music Content Manager	Benjamin Frost
Senior Legal Affairs Manager	Richard Gates
Consumer Products Manager	Eve Gee
General Manager	Dan Hinde
Production Assistant	Richard Jones
Managing Editor – Digital	Susan Williamson

CREDITS
Scenery and automation by Hudson Scenic Studio. Lighting by PRG. Sound and projection by Sound Associates. Rehearsed at the New 42nd Street Studios. Costumes by Tricorne Inc., Jennifer Love, Donna Langman, By Barak, and Artur & Tailors. Custom dyeing by Jeff Fender. Costume crafts by Killer and The Leather Man, Inc. Some undergarments by Bra*Tenders.

SPECIAL THANKS
William Apfelbaum, Ralph Bryan, Jim Neil, Richard Pechter, Judith Richardson, Barry Weissler, the Wig and Makeup Department of the Stratford Shakespeare Festival. The La Jolla Playhouse.

IN MEMORY
It is difficult to imagine producing anything without the presence of beloved Dodger producing associate James Elliot Love. Friend to everyone he met, James stood at the heart of all that is good about the theatrical community. He will be missed, but his spirit abides.

NEDERLANDER

Chairman	**James M. Nederlander**
President	**James L. Nederlander**

Executive Vice President
Nick Scandalios

Vice President Corporate Development **Charlene S. Nederlander**	Senior Vice President Labor Relations **Herschel Waxman**
Vice President **Jim Boese**	Chief Financial Officer **Freida Sawyer Belviso**

STAFF FOR THE NEIL SIMON THEATRE

Theatre Manager	Steve Ouellette
Treasurer	Eddie Waxman
Associate Treasurer	Marc Needleman
House Carpenter	John Gordon
Flyman	Douglas McNeill
House Electrician	James Travers, Sr.
House Propman	Danny Viscardo
House Engineer	John Astras

184

The Playbill Broadway Yearbook 2011-2012

Jesus Christ Superstar
SCRAPBOOK

Paul Nolan (C) hands up a bouquet to lyricist Tim Rice and composer Andrew Lloyd Webber during curtain call on opening night. With them are other members of the cast including (fifth from R) *Yearbook* correspondent Lee Siegel.

Photo by Joseph Marzullo/WENN

Correspondent: Lee Siegel, "Simon Zealotes"

Opening Night Gifts/Party: For Opening Night we received bottles of Champagne, one specifically from Tim Rice, which was very nice. Plus a little blue box wrapped in a white ribbon from Mr. McAnuff, and a host of great gifts from the production team and fellow cast members.

Most Exciting Celebrity Visitors: I think for all of us, THE MOST EXCITING celebrities would have to have been Andrew Lloyd Webber and Tim Rice. Although Ben Vereen, Glenn Close, Eric McCormack, Trey Anastasio, Billy Crystal, Mackenzie Phillips, Anthony Rapp were all great to meet, or see. It was an incredible feeling.

Actor Who Performed the Most Roles in This Show: Ryan Gifford definitely had the most costume changes in the show, and some of the quickest. That track became crazy after rehearsals were finished. That said, however, I think Matthew Rossoff, our swing, ended up playing the MOST roles in the show—sometimes two or three mixed roles in a single performance.

Special Backstage Rituals: Everyone has their own "before the show" routine. For the men's dressing room, it's usually music, laughter, and stretches. Sometimes they pass around the Shake Weight. (Yep, that's right.)

Favorite Moment During Each Performance: Seeing the cast gather in the wings to watch Paul Nolan sing "Gethsemane" and watching the female ensemble kick the choreography out of the park during "Jesus Christ Superstar."

Favorite Therapy: Does psychiatric count? I'm pretty sure every member of the company has used every therapy there is...from Ricola to Halls to Throat-Coat Tea to physio therapy to just laying on a couch, talking about Jesus.

Memorable Stage Door Fan Encounter: Like most shows, we've had an entourage of fans who have seen *JCS* an impressive number of times. Upon filling out this questionnaire, I think the highest number (that we know about) is 14

times. (For a show that, at questionnaire time, has only been open a month and a half...that's an impressive number.) We've had MANY who have seen the show four to eight times as well.

Cell Phone Rings, Cell Phone Photos, Tweeting or Texting Incidents During a Performance: LOTS of PHOTOS being taken through a variety of shows, and moments in the show. TURN YOUR CELL PHONES OFF, PEOPLE.

Who Wore the Heaviest/Hottest Costume: The priests in their black leather head-to-floor-length coats were pretty warm. And several people wore THICK wool costumes and coats.

Who Wore the Least: I think that claim to fame goes to Paul Nolan, on the cross in a loincloth. The next step would be pretty much naked.

Fastest Costume Change: Ryan Gifford, a change that comes in under 30 seconds.

Catchphrases Only the Company Would Recognize: "PORK!!!" I don't know why or where it came from but it grew into a backstage epidemic. Just yell, "PORK!"

Best In-House Parody Lyrics: The real lyric is: "We have no king but Caesar." Our in-house parody: "I'll have a Chicken Caesar." Or "Jesus Christ Superstar, do you think you're...." And we'd say: "Cheese and Rice. Cheese and Rice. Two Jalapenos with cheese and rice." Then there may have been a few too dirty for print. Let's just say: "I Don't Know How To Love Him" took on several different renditions.

Memorable Directorial Note: "Don't touch Jesus" and "Don't shoot up on the toilet." With Des McAnuff as our director, there is pretty much a book of Memorable Directorial quotes. A really big book.

Sweethearts Within the Company: Matt Alfano and Melissa O'Neil, Jaz Sealey and Mary Antonini.

Coolest Thing About Being in This Show: Having the show start in Canada at the Stratford Shakespeare Festival, traveling with this incredible group of people to La Jolla,

California, then watching 23 of the 29 cast members make their Broadway debuts, and knowing the show was born and raised in Canada; all of that made being a part of this show something that NO ONE ELSE will ever be able to recreate. Every step was a surprise, and a new experience, and the company continued to grow as a tight family. Some people stepped aside from the ride, and some new faces joined, but the entire experience was one for the books.

Fan Club Info: Many of us can be found on Facebook with (Actor/Director) or (Musician) pages. LIKE those pages, and keep in touch with us. There are also TWO *Jesus Christ Superstar* (Broadway) Facebook pages. One is the official Broadway page; another is the *Superstar* Fan Club page.

Other Stories and Memories: Thank you to all of the family, fans and loved ones who have supported each and every performer and musician on that stage from whatever our humble beginnings were, to finally reaching a dream of performing on Broadway.

For every mom, dad, family member, husband or wife who waited hours in a car for dance rehearsals, or music rehearsals or auditions.

To Rick, Lisa, Bradley, Beth, and Des for seeing something in all of these faces and putting us in a show that forever changed our lives (in one way or another).

To be on Broadway is the dream of a million little kids dancing in their mirrors or idolizing their favorite cast recording, and here we are. Truly blessed. And to those incredible people who give of their hard-earned cash to sit in a Broadway theater and long to be entertained by the living art—Thank you!! We strive to do our jobs above and beyond your expectation, and are hugely appreciative of your time and support. Thank you, PLAYBILL, for gathering all of this information for future Broadway hopefuls to see. Like a time capsule. It's GREAT to be a part of THIS time!

Leap of Faith

First Preview: April 3, 2012. Opened: April 26, 2012.
Closed May 13, 2012 after 25 Previews and 19 Performances.

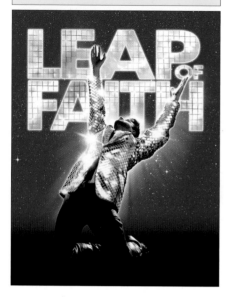

PLAYBILL

In a plot reminiscent of The Music Man, *a con man descends on a small town hoping to gull the rubes with his fast-talking pitch (faith-healing religion, in this case, rather than a boys' band), but finds himself falling for a woman who happens to be the local sheriff, and her disabled son. He's all set to sneak away with his ill-gotten gains—until he pulls off what appears to be a real miracle. Based on the Steve Martin film of the same title.*

CAST

(in order of appearance)

Ida Mae Sturdevant	KECIA LEWIS-EVANS
Isaiah Sturdevant	LESLIE ODOM, JR.
Ornella Sturdevant	KRYSTAL JOY BROWN
Jonas Nightingale	RAÚL ESPARZA
Brother Zak	BRYCE RYNESS
Sam Nightingale	KENDRA KASSEBAUM
Brother Amon	C.E. SMITH
Brother Carl	DENNIS STOWE
Marla McGowan	JESSICA PHILLIPS
Emma Schlarp	ROBERTA WALL
Jake McGowan	TALON ACKERMAN
Susie Raylove	MICHELLE DUFFY
Amanda Wayne	DIERDRE FRIEL

ANGELS OF MERCY

HETTIE BARNHILL, TA'REA CAMPBELL,
LYNORRIS EVANS, BOB GAYNOR,
LUCIA GIANNETTA, ANGELA GROVEY,
TIFFANY JANENE HOWARD,
GRASAN KINGSBERRY,

Continued on next page

---

9 ST. JAMES THEATRE
A JUJAMCYN THEATRE

JORDAN ROTH
President

PAUL LIBIN
Executive Vice President

JACK VIERTEL
Senior Vice President

Michael Manheim James D. Stern Douglas L. Meyer
Marc Routh Richard Frankel Tom Viertel Steven Baruch
Annette Niemtzow Daryl Roth Robert G. Bartner Steven and Shanna Silva
Endgame Entertainment Patricia Monaco Debi Coleman
Dancap Productions, Inc. Steve Kaplan Relativity Media, LLC Rich/Caudwell
and
Center Theatre Group
in association with Michael Palitz Richard J. Stern Melissa Pinsly/Celine Rosenthal Independent Presenters Network Diana Buckhantz
Pamela Cooper Vera Guerin Leading Investment Co., Ltd Christina Papagjika Victor Syrmis Semlitz/Glaser Productions
and
Jujamcyn Theaters

Present

Raúl Esparza
in

LEAP OF FAITH

Based on the motion picture, "Leap of Faith", produced by
Paramount Pictures Corporation and written by Janus Cercone

Music by	Book by		Lyrics by
Alan Menken	**Janus Cercone** and	**Warren Leight**	**Glenn Slater**

with

Jessica Phillips

and

Kendra Kassebaum Kecia Lewis-Evans
Leslie Odom, Jr. Krystal Joy Brown Talon Ackerman

Hettie Barnhill Kyle Brenn Ta'Rea Campbell Michelle Duffy Lynorris Evans
Manoly Farrell Dierdre Friel Bob Gaynor Lucia Giannetta Angela Grovey
Louis Hobson Tiffany Janene Howard Grasan Kingsberry Fletcher McTaggart Maurice Murphy Ian Paget
Terita Redd Eliseo Román Bryce Ryness Ann Sanders C.E. Smith Danny Stiles
Dennis Stowe Betsy Struxness Roberta Wall Virginia Ann Woodruff

Scenery Designed by	Costumes Designed by	Lighting Designed by
Robin Wagner	William Ivey Long	Don Holder

Sound Designed by	Video Coordinator	Wigs & Hair Designed by	Make-Up Designed by	Casting by
John Shivers	Shawn Sagady	Paul Huntley	Angelina Avallone	Telsey + Company

Orchestrations by	Vocal & Incidental Music Arrangements by	Dance Music Arrangements by	Music Direction by
Michael Starobin Joseph Joubert	Michael Kosarin	Zane Mark	Brent-Alan Huffman

Music Coordinator	Associate Director	Associate Choreographer	Production Supervisor
John Miller	Beatrice Terry	Edgar Godineaux	Steven Zweigbaum

General Management	Technical Supervision	Press Representative	Associate Producers
Frankel Green Theatrical Management	Hudson Theatrical Associates	Boneau/Bryan-Brown	Broadway Across America Rebecca Falcon

Music Supervision by
Michael Kosarin

Choreography by
Sergio Trujillo

Directed by
Christopher Ashley

The producers wish to express their appreciation to Theatre Development Fund for its support of this production.

4/26/12

Raúl Esparza and the
Angels of Mercy

Photo by Joan Marcus

Leap of Faith

MUSICAL NUMBERS

ACT ONE

"Rise Up!"	Ida Mae, Ornella, Isaiah, Jonas Nightingale, Sam, Angels of Mercy
"Fox in the Henhouse"	Marla McGowan, Jonas
"Fields of the Lord"	Sam, Jonas, Angels of Mercy
"Step Into the Light"	Ornella, Jonas, Ida Mae, Angels of Mercy, Townspeople
"Walking Like Daddy"	Isaiah
"Lost"	Ida Mae, Angels of Mercy
"I Can Read You"	Marla, Jonas
"Like Magic"	Jake, Jonas
"I Can Read You" (Reprise)	Sam, Jonas
"Dancin' in the Devil's Shoes"	Isaiah, Ornella, Ida Mae, Angels of Mercy
"King of Sin"	Jonas
"Dancin' in the Devil's Shoes" (Reprise)	Isaiah, Ornella, Ida Mae, Angels of Mercy, Townspeople

ACT TWO

"Rise Up!" (Reprise)	Angels of Mercy, Townspeople
"Long Past Dreamin'"	Marla, Jonas
"Are You on the Bus?"	Ornella, Sam, Ida Mae, Isaiah, Jonas
"Like Magic" (Reprise)	Jake, Jonas
"People Like Us"	Sam, Marla
"Last Chance Salvation"	Jonas, Angels of Mercy, Townspeople
"If Your Faith Is Strong Enough"	Jonas, Angels of Mercy, Townspeople
"Jonas' Soliloquy"	Jonas
"Leap of Faith"	The Company

ORCHESTRA

Conductor:
BRENT-ALAN HUFFMAN
Associate Conductor:
JASON MICHAEL WEBB
Assistant Conductor:
JEFF MARDER

(L-R): Raúl Esparza and Jessica Phillips

Photo by Joan Marcus

Woodwinds:
GREGORY THYMIUS, CHARLES PILLOW,
DAVE NOLAND, ROGER ROSENBERG
Trumpets/Flügels:
MATT PETERSON, GREGORY L. GISBERT,
JEREMY MILOSZEWICZ
Trombone/Bass Trombone:
TIMOTHY SESSIONS
Violins:
RICK DOLAN (Concertmaster),
UNA TONE, SHINWON KIM
Viola:
RICHARD BRICE
Cello:
SARAH HEWITT-ROTH
Electric Bass:
LYNN KELLER
Guitar:
DAVID SPINOZZA
Drums/Percussion:
PERRY CAVARI
Piano/Synthesizer:
JASON MICHAEL WEBB
Hammond B3/Synthesizer:
JEFF MARDER

Music Coordinator:
JOHN MILLER

Cast Continued

FLETCHER McTAGGART, ELISEO ROMÁN,
BRYCE RYNESS, C. E. SMITH,
DENNIS STOWE, BETSY STRUXNESS,
VIRGINIA ANN WOODRUFF

TOWNSPEOPLE
MICHELLE DUFFY, DIERDRE FRIEL,
BOB GAYNOR, LOUIS HOBSON,
ANN SANDERS, DANNY STILES,
BETSY STRUXNESS, ROBERTA WALL

OFFSTAGE VOCALISTS
MAURICE MURPHY, TERITA REDD

SWINGS
MANOLY FARRELL, MAURICE MURPHY,
IAN PAGET, TERITA REDD

DANCE CAPTAIN
IAN PAGET

ASSISTANT DANCE CAPTAIN
MANOLY FARRELL

UNDERSTUDIES
For Jonas Nightingale:
LOUIS HOBSON, BRYCE RYNESS
For Ida Mae:
ANGELA GROVEY,
VIRGINIA ANN WOODRUFF
For Ornella:
TA'REA CAMPBELL, TERITA REDD
For Sam:
MICHELLE DUFFY, BETSY STRUXNESS
For Isaiah:
GRASAN KINGSBERRY, MAURICE MURPHY
For Marla McGowan:
MICHELLE DUFFY, ANN SANDERS
For Jake:
KYLE BRENN

All proceeds from the revivals' collection baskets
will be donated to
Broadway Cares/Equity Fights Aids.

PLACE:
The action takes place at the Saint James Theatre,
New York, and Sweetwater, Kansas.

TIME:
The Present

Leap of Faith

Raúl Esparza
Jonas Nightingale

Jessica Phillips
Marla McGowan

Kendra Kassebaum
Sam

Kecia Lewis-Evans
Ida Mae Sturdevant

Leslie Odom, Jr.
Isaiah Sturdevant

Krystal Joy Brown
Ornella Sturdevant

Talon Ackerman
Jake

Hettie Barnhill
Angel of Mercy

Kyle Brenn
u/s Jake

Ta'rea Campbell
Angel of Mercy

Michelle Duffy
Susie Raylove, Townsperson

Lynorris Evans
Angel of Mercy

Manoly Farrell
Swing, Assistant Dance Captain

Dierdre Friel
Amanda Wayne, Townsperson

Bob Gaynor
Angel of Mercy

Lucia Giannetta
Angel of Mercy

Angela Grovey
Angel of Mercy

Louis Hobson
Townsperson

Tiffany Janene Howard
Angel of Mercy

Grasan Kingsberry
Angel of Mercy

Fletcher McTaggart
Fletch, the Camera Guy; Angel of Mercy

Maurice Murphy
Swing, Offstage Vocalist

Ian Paget
Dance Captain, Swing

Terita Redd
Swing, Offstage Vocalist

Eliseo Román
Angel of Mercy

Bryce Ryness
Zak, Angel of Mercy

Ann Sanders
Townsperson

C.E. Smith
Brother Amon, Angel of Mercy

Danny Stiles
Townsperson

Dennis Stowe
Brother Carl, Angel of Mercy

Betsy Struxness
Angel of Mercy, Townsperson

Roberta Wall
Emma Schlarp, Townsperson

Virgina Ann Woodruff
Angel of Mercy

Alan Menken
Composer

Janus Cercone
Book

Leap of Faith

Warren Leight
Book

Glenn Slater
Lyrics

Christopher Ashley
Director

Sergio Trujillo
Choreographer

Michael Kosarin
*Music Supervisor/
Vocal and Incidental
Music Arrangements*

Robin Wagner
Scenic Design

William Ivey Long
Costume Designer

Donald Holder
Lighting Design

John Shivers
Sound Design

Paul Huntley
*Wigs and Hair
Design*

Angelina Avallone
Make-up Designer

Bernard Telsey
Telsey + Company
Casting

Michael Starobin
Orchestrations

Joseph Joubert
Orchestrator

Zane Mark
*Dance Music
Arranger*

John Miller
Music Coordinator

Beatrice Terry
Associate Director

Edgar Godineaux
*Associate
Choreographer*

Richard Frankel
Frankel Green
Theatrical
Management
*General Management/
Producer*

Laura Green
Frankel Green
Theatrical
Management
General Management

Neil A. Mazzella
Hudson Theatrical
Associates
Technical Supervisor

Douglas L. Meyer
Producer

Marc Routh
Producer

Tom Viertel
Producer

Steven Baruch
Producer

Annette Niemtzow
Producer

Daryl Roth
Producer

Aubrey Dan
Dancap Productions
Inc.
Producer

John Caudwell
Rich/Caudwell
Producer

Michael Ritchie,
Artistic Director
Center Theatre
Group
Producer

Jordan Roth
Jujamcyn Theaters
Producer

Christina Papagjika
Producer

John Gore,
CEO
Broadway Across
America
Associate Producer

Thomas B. McGrath,
Chairman
Broadway Across
America
Associate Producer

Diana Buckhantz
Producer

Leap of Faith

FRONT OF HOUSE
Standing (L-R): Jeff Hubbard, Jacobo Medrano, Lenny Baron

First Row (L-R): Rebecca Segarra, Caroline Choi, Heather Jewels

Second Row (L-R): Elizabeth Harvey, Cindy Lopiano, Obias Obiago

Third Row (L-R): Sean Zimmerman, Rochelle Rogers, Jim Barry

Fourth Row (L-R): Quinton Menendez, Barbara Carroll, Andrea Vazquez

Fifth Row (L-R): Tim Perkins, Andrew Mackay, Ebony Ruffin, Tamika Kidd

Sixth Row (L-R): Terry Swiney, Tegan McDuffie, Rita Richardson

Top Row Sitting (L-R): Blake, Adam Young, Rubin

Top Row Standing (L-R): Michael Composto, Donna Vanderlinden

Leap of Faith

Photo by Brian Mapp

WARDROBE
Front Row (L-R): Bonnie Prather, Shonté Walker, Sara Darneille, Kimberly Mark, Rachel Maier (children's guardian)

Back Row (L-R): Kimberly Baird, Susan Cook, Bobbi Morse, Renee Borys, Julie Alderter, Vicki Grecki, Joe Hickey, Robert Guy (Supervisor)

CREW
Front Row (L-R): Jason Muldrow, Paul Coltoff, Robert Valli, Peter Karrer, Tommy Vercetti, Sam Ellis

Back Row (L-R): Eric Castaldo, Ron Schwier, Chris Pravata, Al Sayers, Kevin Kennedy, David Patridge, Tom Maloney, Justin Borowinski, Timmy B. McDonough Joe Lenihan, Ryan McDonough, Todd Frank, Timmy M. McDonough

Leap of Faith

2011-2012 AWARD

FRED AND ADELE ASTAIRE AWARD
Best Male Dancer on Broadway
(Leslie Odom, Jr.)

Leslie Odom, Jr.

Photo by Joan Marcus

Photo by Brian Mapp

WIG DEPARTMENT
(L-R): Jeanette Harrington, Danny Koye, Eddie Wilson (Supervisor), Cheryl Thomas, Alison Wadsworth

STAGE MANAGEMENT
(L-R): Joseph Sheridan, Marisha Ploski, Steven Zweigbaum

BOX OFFICE
(L-R): Vincent Sclafani, Vincent Siniscalchi

STAFF FOR *LEAP OF FAITH*

GENERAL MANAGEMENT
FRANKEL GREEN THEATRICAL MANAGEMENT
Richard Frankel   Laura Green
Joe Watson

COMPANY MANAGER
Kathy Lowe

ASSOCIATE COMPANY MANAGER
Sammy Ledbetter

GENERAL PRESS REPRESENTATIVE
BONEAU/BRYAN-BROWN
Chris Boneau   Jackie Green   Kelly Guiod

CASTING
TELSEY + COMPANY
Bernie Telsey CSA, Will Cantler CSA,
David Vaccari CSA, Bethany Knox CSA,
Craig Burns CSA, Tiffany Little Canfield CSA,
Rachel Hoffman CSA, Justin Huff CSA,
Patrick Goodwin CSA, Abbie Brady-Dalton CSA
David Morris, Cesar A. Rocha, Andrew Femenella,
Karyn Casl, Kristina Bramhall, Jessie Malone

Technical Supervisor ....Sam Ellis
Production Supervisor ....Steven Zweigbaum
Stage Manager ....Joseph Sheridan
Assistant Stage Manager ....Marisha Ploski
Associate Director ....Beatrice Terry
Associate Choreographer ....Edgar Godineaux

Assistant Choreographer ....Dionne Figgins
Dance Captain ....Ian Paget
Assistant Dance Captain ....Manoly Farrell
Illusions Designed
    by Afterglow Group LLC ....Peter Samelson
Associate Scenic Designer ....David Peterson
Assistant Scenic Designer ....Atkin Pace
Associate Costume Designer ....Martha Bromelmeier
Assistant Costume
    Designer ....Brenda Abbandandolo
Assistants to William Ivey Long................Brian Mear,
                    Donald Sanders, Jennifer Raskopf
Associate Lighting Designer ....Jeanne Koenig
Assistant Lighting Designers ....Heather Graff,
                                        Karen Spahn

Leap of Faith

Associate Sound Designer ....David Patridge
Associate Wig Designers ....Giovanna Calabretta,
 Edward J. Wilson
Associate General Manager ....Joshua A. Saletnik
Company Management Assistant ....Katie Pope
Company Management Intern ....Mike McLinden
SDC Observer ....Lindsey Hope Pearlman

Head Carpenter ....Todd Frank
Assistant Carpenters ....Chris Pravata, Robert Valli
Production Electrician ....James Maloney
Associate Production Electrician ....Ron Schwier
Advance Electrician ....Ross Feilhauer
Head Electrician ....Ron Schwier
Moving Light Programmer ....Aland Henderson
Advance Production
 Sound Engineer ....Kevin Kennedy
Head Sound Engineer ....David Patridge
Assistant Sound Engineer ....Peter Karrer
Head Props ....Eric Castaldo
Video Programmer ....Dan Mueller
Wardrobe Supervisor ....Robert Guy
Assistant Wardrobe Supervisor ....Kimberly Baird
Mr. Esparza's Dresser ....Kevin O'Brien
Dressers ....Renée Borys, Susan E. Cook,
 Sara Darneille, Victoria Grecki,
 David Grevengoed, Joseph Hickey,
 Dawn Marcoccia, Kimberly Mark,
 Barbara Morse, Melanie Olbrych,
 Shonté Walker
Hair & Wig Supervisor ....Edward J. Wilson
Assistant Hair & Wig
 Supervisor ....Jeanette Harrington
Hairdressers ....Daniel Koye, Cheryl Thomas,
 Alison Wadsworth
Production Assistants ....Lawrence Copeland,
 T.J. Kearney, Deanna Weiner
Children's Tutoring ....On Location Education/
 Liza Chasin, Irene Karasik
Children's Guardian ....Rachel Maier

Associate Music Director/
 Conductor ....Jason Michael Webb
Synthesizer Programmer ....Jeff Marder
Music Coordinator ....John Miller
Assistant to John Miller ....Nichole Jennino
Music Copying ....Anixter Rice Music Services/
 Russ Anixter, Don Rice
Music Production Assistant ....Scott Wasserman
Rehearsal Musicians ....Perry Cavari, Jesse Kissel

Assistant to James D. Stern ....Karen Bove
Assistant to Marc Routh ....Melissa Pinsly
Assistant to Tom Viertel ....Tania Senewiratne
Assistant to Steve Baruch ....Sonja Soper
Advertising ....Serino/Coyne/
 Sandy Block, Ryan Cunningham,
 Joaquin Esteva, Nicole Francois
Digital Outreach & Website ....Serino/Coyne/
 Jim Glaub, Chip Meyrelles, Laurie Connor,
 Kevin Keating, Ryan Greer, Mark Seeley
Promotions ....blue vista 725/Matt Sicoli
Press Associates ....Adrian Bryan-Brown, Jim Byk,
 Linnae Hodzic, Jessica Johnson,
 Kevin Jones, Amy Kass, Holly Kinney,
 Emily Meagher, Aaron Meier, Dana Moody,
 Christine Olver, Joe Perrotta, Matt Polk,

 Amanda Sales, Heath Schwartz,
 Michael Strassheim, Susanne Tighe
Production Photography ....Joan Marcus
Theatre Displays ....King Displays
Insurance ....DeWitt Stern Group, Inc./
 Anthony Pittari
Legal Counsel ....Patricia Crown, Esq./
 Coblence & Associates
Banking ....JP Morgan Chase Bank/Grace Correa
Payroll Service ....Castellana Services, Inc.
Accounting ....Fried & Kowgios Partners, CPAs, LLP
Opening Night Coordinator ....Anthony Taccetta
Group Sales ....Shubert Group Sales/
 212-239-6262/800-432-7780
 www.telecharge.com/groups

FRANKEL GREEN THEATRICAL MANAGEMENT STAFF

Finance Director ....**Jeffrey Bledsoe**
Assistant to Richard Frankel ....Heidi Libby
Assistant to Laura Green ....Joshua A. Saletnik
Assistant Finance Director ....Sue Bartelt
Finance Associate ....Amanda Hayek
Information Technology Manager ....Ben Bigby
Marketing Director ....**Deirdre Alby**
Director of Business Affairs ....**Michael Sinder**
Business Affairs Assistant ....Dario Dallalasta
Booking ....On the Road Booking, LLC/
 Simma Levine, President
Booking Coordinator ....Allison Engallena
Office Manager ....**Emily Wright**
Receptionists ....Rebekah Hughston, Christina Lowe
Interns ....Shari Council, J.J. Flores, Britt Goodman,
 Sarah Hartman, Liz Krane, Xander Jarowey,
 Kelcie Mohr, Andrew Morton, Lucy Obus,
 Ricky Romano

CREDITS AND ACKNOWLEDGEMENTS

Scenery and automation by Hudson Scenic Studio, Inc.
Rain effect provided by Showman Fabricators, Inc. Lighting
equipment provided by PRG Lighting. Video equipment
provided by PRG Video. Sound equipment provided by
Masque Sound and Recording Corporation. Costumes by
Tricorne, Inc., Jennifer Love and the Murphy Robe
Company. Shoes by LaDuca Productions, Inc., T.O. Dey
and Worldtone Dance. Shirts by Cego. Special thanks to
Bra*Tenders for undergarments and hosiery. Rehearsed at
the New 42nd Street Studios.

Makeup provided by M•A•C Cosmetics.

World premiere produced at the Ahmanson Theatre by
Center Theatre Group, Los Angeles.

Lobby refreshments by Sweet Concessions.

Security provided by GBA Consulting, Inc.

Jujamcyn Theatres is a proud member of
the Broadway Green Alliance.

JUJAMCYN THEATERS
JORDAN ROTH
President

PAUL LIBIN	JACK VIERTEL
Executive Vice President	Senior Vice President
MEREDITH VILLATORE	**JENNIFER HERSHEY**
Chief Financial Officer	Vice President,
	Building Operations
MICAH HOLLINGWORTH	**HAL GOLDBERG**
Vice President,	Vice President,
Company Operations	Theatre Operations

Director of Business Affairs ....Albert T. Kim
Director of Human Resources ....Michele Louhisdon
Director of Ticketing Services ....Justin Karr
Theatre Operations Managers ....Willa Burke,
 Susan Elrod, Emily Hare, Jeff Hubbard, Albert T. Kim
Theatre Operations Associates ....Carrie Jo Brinker,
 Brian Busby, Michael Composto, Anah Jyoti Klate
Accounting ....Cathy Cerge, Erin Dooley, Amy Frank
Executive Producer, Red Awning ....Nicole Kastrinos
Director of Marketing, Givenik.com ....Joe Tropia
Marketing Associate, Givenik.com ....Ben Cohen
Building Operations Associate ....Erich Bussing
Executive Coordinator ....Ed Lefferson
Executive Assistants ....Clark Mims Tedesco,
 Beth Given, Julia Kraus
Receptionist ....Lisa Perchinske
Maintenance ....Ralph Santos, Ramon Zapata
Security ....Rasim Hodzic, John Acero
Interns ....Maggie Baker, Alaina Bono,
 Erin Carr, Hunter Chancellor, Cindy Vargas,
 Kelvin Veras, Luke Weidner, Margaret White

Staff for the St. James Theatre for
Leap of Faith

Manager ....Jeff Hubbard
Associate Manager ....Michael Composto
Treasurer ....Vincent Sclafani
Head Carpenter ....Timothy B. McDonough
Head Propertyman ....Timothy M. McDonough
Head Electrician ....Albert Sayers
Flyman ....David Brown
Carpenters ....Ryan McDonough, Jason Muldrow,
 Tommy Vercetti
Propertymen ....Justin Borowinski, Kevin Kennely
Electrics ....Paul Coltoff, Dave Holliman,
 Joe Lenihan, Tom Maloney,
 Bob Miller, Sue Pelkofer
Engineer ....Zaim Hodzic
Assistant Treasurers ....Carmine Loiacono,
 Thomas Motylenski, Vincent Siniscalchi
Head Usher ....Cynthia Lopiano
Ticket-takers/Directors/Ushers ....Leonard Baron,
 Jim Barry, Murrary Bradley, Barbara Carroll,
 Caroline Choi, Heather Jewels, Barbara Kagan,
 Andrew Mackay, Kendra McDuffie,
 Margaret McElroy, Rebecca Segarra,
 Jessica Theisen, Donna Vanderlinden
Doormen ....Russell Buenteo, Adam Hodzic
Head Porter ....Jacobo Medrano
Porters ....Rafael Liriano, Francisco Medina,
 Donnette Niles
Head Cleaner ....Carmela Tenebruso
Cleaners ....Benita Aliberti, Juana Medrano,
 Antonia Moreno

The Lion King

First Preview: October 15, 1997. Opened: November 13, 1997.
Still running as of May 31, 2012.

PLAYBILL

Disney
PRESENTS
THE LION KING
CELEBRATING 10 YEARS ON BROADWAY

When the evil lion Scar kills his brother Mufasa, and seizes the kingship of the African Pridelands, young prince Simba flees into the wilderness. There he is transformed by some new friends and finally returns to reclaim his crown. Performed by actors in puppetlike costumes designed by director Julie Taymor.

CAST

(in order of appearance)

RAFIKI ....Tshidi Manye
MUFASA ....Alton Fitzgerald White
SARABI ....Jean Michelle Grier
ZAZU ....Jeff Binder
SCAR ....Patrick R. Brown
YOUNG SIMBA ....(Wed. Eve., Thurs., Sat.
Mat., Sun.) Judah Bellamy
(Tue., Wed. Mat., Fri., Sat. Eve.) Niles Fitch
YOUNG NALA ....(Tue., Wed. Mat.,
Sat. Mat., Sun.) Nia Ashleigh
(Wed. Eve., Thurs., Fri., Sat. Eve.) Imani Dia Smith
SHENZI ....Bonita J. Hamilton
BANZAI ....James Brown-Orleans
ED ....Enrique Segura
TIMON ....Fred Berman
PUMBAA ....Ben Jeffrey
SIMBA ....Adam Jacobs
NALA ....Chaunteé Schuler
ENSEMBLE SINGERS.............Alvin Crawford,
Derrick Davis, Lindiwe Dlamini,
Trista Dollison, Bongi Duma, Jean Michelle Grier,
Joel Karie, Ron Kunene, Sheryl McCallum,
S'bu Ngema, Nteliseng Nkhela,
Selloane A. Nkhela, Vusi Sondiyazi

Continued on next page

MINSKOFF THEATRE

UNDER THE DIRECTION OF
JAMES M. NEDERLANDER, JAMES L. NEDERLANDER,
SARA MINSKOFF ALLAN AND THE MINSKOFF FAMILY

Disney
PRESENTS
THE LION KING

Music & Lyrics by
ELTON JOHN & TIM RICE

Additional Music & Lyrics by
LEBO M, MARK MANCINA, JAY RIFKIN, JULIE TAYMOR, HANS ZIMMER

Book by
ROGER ALLERS & IRENE MECCHI

Starring
PATRICK R. BROWN   ALTON FITZGERALD WHITE   TSHIDI MANYE
JEFF BINDER   BEN JEFFREY   FRED BERMAN
ADAM JACOBS   CHAUNTEÉ SCHULER
JAMES BROWN-ORLEANS   BONITA J. HAMILTON   ENRIQUE SEGURA
NIA ASHLEIGH   JUDAH BELLAMY   NILES FITCH   IMANI DIA SMITH

SANT'GRIA BELLO   CAMILLE M. BROWN   ALVIN CRAWFORD   GABRIEL CROOM   DERRICK DAVIS   GARLAND DAYS
CHARITY de LOERA   LINDIWE DLAMINI   TRISTA DOLLISON   BONGI DUMA   ANGELICA EDWARDS   JIM FERRIS
CHRISTOPHER FREEMAN   JEAN MICHELLE GRIER   KENNY INGRAM   NICOLE ADELL JOHNSON   DENNIS JOHNSTON
JOEL KARIE   RON KUNENE   LISA LEWIS   SHERYL McCALLUM   JAYSIN McCOLLUM   RAY MERCER
WILLIA-NOEL MONTAGUE   MATTHEW S. MORGAN   JENNIFER HARRISON NEWMAN   S'BU NGEMA
NTELISENG NKHELA   SELLOANE A. NKHELA   JAMES A. PIERCE III   CHONDRA LA-TEASE PROFIT   VUSI SONDIYAZI
NATALIE TURNER   PHILLIP W. TURNER   DONNA MICHELLE VAUGHN   THOM CHRISTOPHER WARREN

Adapted from the screenplay by
IRENE MECCHI & JONATHAN ROBERTS & LINDA WOOLVERTON

Produced by
PETER SCHNEIDER & THOMAS SCHUMACHER

Scenic Design RICHARD HUDSON	*Costume Design* JULIE TAYMOR	*Lighting Design* DONALD HOLDER	*Mask & Puppet Design* JULIE TAYMOR & MICHAEL CURRY
Sound Design STEVE CANYON KENNEDY	*Hair & Makeup Design* MICHAEL WARD	*Associate Director* JOHN STEFANIUK	*Associate Choreographer* MAREY GRIFFITH
Associate Producer ANNE QUART	*Technical Director* DAVID BENKEN	*Production Stage Manager* RON VODICKA	*Production Supervisor* DOC ZORTHIAN

Music Supervisor CLEMENT ISHMAEL	*Music Director* KARL JURMAN	*Associate Music Producer* ROBERT ELHAI	*Music Coordinator* MICHAEL KELLER	*Orchestrators* ROBERT ELHAI DAVID METZGER BRUCE FOWLER

Music Produced for the *Stage & Additional Score by* MARK MANCINA	*Additional Vocal Score,* *Vocal Arrangements* *& Choral Director* LEBO M	*Casting* BINDER CASTING/ MARK BRANDON, C.S.A.	*Fight Director* RICK SORDELET

Choreography by
GARTH FAGAN

Directed by
JULIE TAYMOR

©Disney

2//27/12

A scene from *The Lion King*.

Photo by Joan Marcus

The Lion King

SCENES AND MUSICAL NUMBERS

ACT ONE

Scene 1	Pride Rock	
	"Circle of Life" with "Nants' Ingonyama"	......................................Rafiki, Ensemble
Scene 2	Scar's Cave	
Scene 3	Rafiki's Tree	
Scene 4	The Pridelands	
Scene 5	Scar's Cave	
Scene 6	The Pridelands	
	"I Just Can't Wait to Be King"	.....................Young Simba, Young Nala, Zazu, Ensemble
Scene 7	Elephant Graveyard	
	"Chow Down"	....Shenzi, Banzai, Ed
Scene 8	Under the Stars	
	"They Live in You"	....Mufasa, Ensemble
Scene 9	Elephant Graveyard	
	"Be Prepared"	...........................Scar, Shenzi, Banzai, Ed, Ensemble
Scene 10	The Gorge	
Scene 11	Pride Rock	
	"Be Prepared" (Reprise)	....Scar, Ensemble
Scene 12	Rafiki's Tree	
Scene 13	The Desert/The Jungle	
	"Hakuna Matata"	..............................Timon, Pumbaa, Young Simba, Simba, Ensemble

ACT TWO

Entr'acte	"One by One"	....Ensemble
Scene 1	Scar's Cave	
	"The Madness of King Scar"	........................Scar, Zazu, Banzai, Shenzi, Ed, Nala
Scene 2	The Pridelands	
	"Shadowland"	....Nala, Rafiki, Ensemble
Scene 3	The Jungle	
Scene 4	Under the Stars	
	"Endless Night"	....Simba, Ensemble
Scene 5	Rafiki's Tree	
Scene 6	The Jungle	
	"Can You Feel the Love Tonight"	.....................Timon, Pumbaa, Simba, Nala, Ensemble
	"He Lives in You" (Reprise)	....Rafiki, Simba, Ensemble
Scene 7	Pride Rock	
	"King of Pride Rock"/"Circle of Life" (Reprise)	...................................Ensemble

SONG CREDITS

All songs by Elton John (music) and Tim Rice (lyrics) except as follows:

"Circle of Life" by Elton John (music) and Tim Rice (lyrics)
with "Nants' Ingonyama" by Hans Zimmer and Lebo M

"He Lives in You" ("They Live in You"): Music and lyrics by Mark Mancina, Jay Rifkin, and Lebo M

"One by One": Music and lyrics by Lebo M

"Shadowland": Music by Lebo M and Hans Zimmer, lyrics by Mark Mancina and Lebo M

"Endless Night": Music by Lebo M, Hans Zimmer, and Jay Rifkin, lyrics by Julie Taymor

"King of Pride Rock": Music by Hans Zimmer, lyrics by Lebo M

ADDITIONAL SCORE

Grasslands chant and Lioness chant by Lebo M
Rafiki's chants by Tsidii Le Loka.

ENSEMBLE DANCERS ....Sant'gria Bello, Camille M. Brown, Gabriel Croom, Charity de Loera, Christopher Freeman, Nicole Adell Johnson, Lisa Lewis, Jaysin McCollum, Ray Mercer, Jennifer Harrison Newman, Phillip W. Turner, Donna Michelle Vaughn

SWINGS AND UNDERSTUDIES

RAFIKI: Angelica Edwards, Sheryl McCallum, Nteliseng Nkhela, Selloane A. Nkhela
MUFASA: Alvin Crawford, Derrick Davis, Vusi Sondiyazi
SARABI: Camille M. Brown, Sheryl McCallum, Chondra La-Tease Profit
ZAZU: Jim Ferris, Enrique Segura, Thom Christopher Warren
SCAR: Jeff Binder, Thom Christopher Warren
SHENZI: Angelica Edwards, Trista Dollison, Nicole Adell Johnson
BANZAI: Garland Days, Kenny Ingram, Joel Karie
ED: Gabriel Croom, Kenny Ingram, Dennis Johnston, Jaysin McCollum
TIMON: Jim Ferris, Enrique Segura
PUMBAA: Jim Ferris, Thom Christopher Warren
SIMBA: Dennis Johnston, Joel Karie, Matthew S. Morgan
NALA: Nicole Adell Johnson, Selloane A. Nkhela, Chondra La-Tease Profit

SWINGS: Garland Days, Angelica Edwards, Kenny Ingram, Dennis Johnston, Willia-Noel Montague, Matthew S. Morgan, James A. Pierce III, Chondra La-Tease Profit, Natalie Turner

DANCE CAPTAINS

Garland Days, Willia-Noel Montague

SPECIALTIES

CIRCLE OF LIFE VOCALS: S'bu Ngema, Vusi Sondiyazi
MOUSE SHADOW PUPPET: Joel Karie
ANT HILL LADY: Donna Michelle Vaughn
GUINEA FOWL: Sant'gria Bello
BUZZARD POLE: Christopher Freeman
GAZELLE WHEEL: Charity de Loera
GAZELLE: Jaysin McCollum
LIONESS CHANT VOCAL: S'bu Ngema
ACROBATIC TRICKSTER: Ray Mercer
STILT GIRAFFE CROSS: Gabriel Croom
GIRAFFE SHADOW PUPPETS: Jaysin McCollum, Vusi Sondiyazi
CHEETAH: Lisa Lewis

Continued on next page

The Lion King

Cast Continued

SCAR SHADOW PUPPETS: Sant'gria Bello,
    Jaysin McCollum, Vusi Sondiyazi
SIMBA SHADOW PUPPETS:
    Christopher Freeman, Ray Mercer,
    Phillip W. Turner
ONE BY ONE VOCAL: Bongi Duma,
    Selloane A. Nkhela
ONE BY ONE DANCE: Bongi Duma,
    Ron Kunene, S'bu Ngema
FIREFLIES: Camille M. Brown
PUMBAA POLE PUPPET: Vusi Sondiyazi
NALA POLE PUPPET: Lisa Lewis
LIONESS/HYENA SHADOW PUPPETS:
    Lindiwe Dlamini, Trista Dollison, Ron Kunene,
    Sheryl McCallum, Nteliseng Nkhela,
    Selloane A. Nkhela

Tshidi Manye, Nteliseng Nkhela, Selloane A. Nkhela
and Vusi Sondiyazi are appearing with the permission
of Actors' Equity Association.

ORCHESTRA

CONDUCTOR–Karl Jurman
KEYBOARD SYNTHESIZER/ASSOCIATE
    CONDUCTOR: Cherie Rosen
SYNTHESIZERS: Ted Baker, Paul Ascenzo
WOOD FLUTE SOLOIST/FLUTE/PICCOLO:
    David Weiss
CONCERTMASTER: Francisca Mendoza
VIOLINS: Krystof Witek, Avril Brown
VIOLIN/VIOLA: Ralph Farris
CELLOS: Eliana Mendoza, Bruce Wang
FLUTE/CLARINET/BASS CLARINET:
    Robert DeBellis
FRENCH HORNS: Patrick Milando,
    Alexandra Cook, Greg Smith
TROMBONE: Rock Ciccarone
BASS TROMBONE/TUBA: Morris Kainuma
UPRIGHT AND ELECTRIC BASSES:
    Tom Barney
DRUMS/ASSISTANT CONDUCTOR:
    Tommy Igoe
GUITAR: Kevin Kuhn
PERCUSSION/ASSISTANT CONDUCTOR:
    Rolando Morales-Matos
MALLETS/PERCUSSION: Valerie Dee Naranjo,
    Tom Brett
PERCUSSION: Junior "Gabu" Wedderburn
MUSIC COORDINATOR–Michael Keller

Based on the Disney film *The Lion King*
Directed by Roger Allers and Rob Minkoff
Produced by Don Hahn
**Special thanks to all the artists and staff
of Walt Disney Feature Animation**

Patrick R. Brown
Scar

Alton Fitzgerald
White
Mufasa

Tshidi Manye
Rafiki

Jeff Binder
Zazu

Ben Jeffrey
Pumbaa

Fred Berman
Timon

Adam Jacobs
Simba

Chaunteé Schuler
Nala

James Brown-
Orleans
Banzai

Bonita J. Hamilton
Shenzi

Enrique Segura
Ed

Nia Ashleigh
*Young Nala
at certain
performances*

Judah Bellamy
*Young Simba
at certain
performances*

Niles Fitch
*Young Simba
at certain
performances*

Imani Dia Smith
*Young Nala
at certain
performances*

Sant'gria Bello
Ensemble

Camille M. Brown
Ensemble

Alvin Crawford
Ensemble

Gabriel Croom
Ensemble

Derrick Davis
Ensemble

The Lion King

Garland Days
Swing, Dance Captain

Charity de Loera
Ensemble

Lindiwe Dlamini
Ensemble

Trista Dollison
Ensemble

Bongi Duma
Ensemble

Angelica Edwards
Swing

Jim Ferris
Standby Zazu, Timon, Pumbaa

Christopher Freeman
Ensemble

Jean Michelle Grier
Sarabi/Ensemble

Kenny Ingram
Swing

Nicole Adell Johnson
Ensemble

Dennis Johnston
Swing

Joel Karie
Ensemble

Ron Kunene
Ensemble

Lisa Lewis
Ensemble

Sheryl McCallum
Ensemble

Jaysin McCollum
Ensemble

Ray Mercer
Ensemble

Willia-Noel Montague
Swing, Dance Captain

Matthew S. Morgan
Swing

Jennifer Harrison Newman
Ensemble

S'bu Ngema
Ensemble

Nteliseng Nkhela
Ensemble

Selloane A. Nkhela
Ensemble

James A. Pierce III
Swing

Chondra La-Tease Profit
Swing

Vusi Sondiyazi
Ensemble

Natalie Turner
Swing

Phillip W. Turner
Ensemble

Donna Michelle Vaughn
Ensemble

Thom Christopher Warren
Standby Scar, Pumbaa, Zazu

Elton John
Music

Tim Rice
Lyrics

Roger Allers
Book

Irene Mecchi
Book

The Lion King

Julie Taymor
Director, Costume Design, Mask/Puppet Co-Design, Additional Lyrics

Garth Fagan
Choreographer

Lebo M
Additional Music & Lyrics, Additional Vocal Score, Vocal Arrangements, Choral Director

Mark Mancina
Additional Music & Lyrics, Music Produced for the Stage, Additional Score

Hans Zimmer
Additional Music & Lyrics

Jay Rifkin
Additional Music & Lyrics

Richard Hudson
Scenic Design

Donald Holder
Lighting Design

Michael Curry
Mask & Puppet Design

Steve Canyon Kennedy
Sound Design

Mark Brandon CSA/Binder Casting
Casting

David Benken
Technical Director

John Stefaniuk
Associate Director

Karl Jurman
Music Director/Conductor

Darren Katz
Resident Director

Ruthlyn Salomons
Resident Dance Supervisor

Robert Elhai
Associate Music Producer, Orchestrator

Michael Keller
Music Coordinator

Thomas Schumacher, Disney Theatrical Productions

ALUMNI 2011-2012

Shaylin Becton
Young Nala

John E. Brady
Pumbaa

Khail Toi Bryant
Young Nala

Ian Yuri Gardner
Ensemble Singer, Giraffe/Scar Shadow Puppet, Pumbaa Pole Puppet

Andrea Jones
Ensemble Singer/Shadow Puppets

Aubrey Omari Joseph
Young Simba

Brian M. Love
Swing

Clifton Oliver
Simba

Cameron Pow
Zazu

Jacqueline René
Swing

Gareth Saxe
Scar

Jeremiah Tatum
Ensemble Dancer, Simba Shadow Puppet

L. Steven Taylor
Ensemble Singer

Jason Veasey
Ensemble Singer

Torya
Ensemble Dancer, Swing, Nala Pole Puppet

The Lion King

Keisha Laren
Clarke Gray
*Dance Captain,
Swing*

Zach Law Ingram
Ensemble Dancer

Charlaine Katsuyoshi
Ensemble Dancer

Jacqueline René
Swing

Arbender J.
Robinson
Swing

Rhea Roderick
Ensemble Dancer

Rema Webb
Ensemble

Syndee Winters
Nala

Camille Workman
Ensemble Dancer

Dashaun Young
Simba

Staff for *THE LION KING* Worldwide

Associate Producer ....Anne Quart
Production Supervisor ....Doc Zorthian
Senior Production Manager ....Myriah Perkins
Production Manager ....Thomas Schlenk
Assistant Production Manager ....Michael Height
Associate Director ....John Stefaniuk
Associate Choreographer ....Marey Griffith
Music Supervisor ....Clement Ishmael
Dance Supervisor ....Celise Hicks
Associate Music Supervisor ....Jay Alger
Associate Scenic Designer ....Peter Eastman
Associate Costume Designer ....Mary Nemecek Peterson
Associate Mask & Puppet Designer ....Louis Troisi
Associate Sound Designer ....John Shivers
Associate Hair & Makeup Designer.......Carole Hancock
Associate Lighting Designer ....Jeanne Koenig
Assistant Lighting Designer ....Marty Vreeland
Assistant Sound Designer ....Shane Cook
Automated Lighting Designer ....Aland Henderson
Production Coordinator ....Tara Engler
Management Assistant ....Kelly Archer

DISNEY ON BROADWAY PUBLICITY
Senior Publicist ....Dennis Crowley
Associate Publicist ....Michelle Bergmann

Staff for *THE LION KING* New York

Company Manager ....THOMAS SCHLENK
Associate Company Manager ....Christopher A. Recker
Production Stage Manager ....Ron Vodicka
Resident Director ....Darren Katz
Resident Dance Supervisor ....Ruthlyn Salomons
Musical Director/Conductor ....Karl Jurman

Stage Managers ....Carmen I. Abrazado,
Antonia Gianino, Arabella Powell,
Tom Reynolds
Dance Captains ......Garland Days, Willia-Noel Montague
Fight Captain ....Ray Mercer
Assistant Choreographers ....Norwood J. Pennewell,
Natalie Rogers
South African Dialect Coach ....Ron Kunene
Casting Associates ....Jack Bowdan, C.S.A.;
Mark Brandon, C.S.A.
Casting Assistant ....Jason Styres
Corporate Counsel ....Michael Rosenfeld
Physical Therapy ....Neuro Tour Physical Therapy/
Tarra Taylor
Consulting Orthopedist ....Neil Roth, M.D.
Child Wrangler ....Rick Plaugher
Executive Travel ....Robert Arnao, Patt McRory
Production Travel ....Jill Citron
Web Design Consultant ....Joshua Noah
Advertising ....Serino/Coyne Inc.
Interactive Marketing..................Situation Marketing

Production Carpenter ....Drew Siccardi
Head Carpenter ....Michael Trotto
House Carpenter ....Patrick Sullivan
Assistant Carpenters ....Kirk Bender, Michael Phillips
Automation Carpenters ....Aldo "Butch" Servilio,
George Zegarsky
Carpenters ....Sean Farrugia, Daniel Macormack,
Duane Mirro
Flying Supervision ....Dave Hearn
Production Flymen ....Kraig Bender, Dylan Trotto
House Flyman ....Richard McQuail
Production Electrician ....James Maloney
House Electrician ....Michael Lynch

Board Operator ....Edward Greenberg
House Assistant Electrician ....Stephen Speer
Automated Lighting Technician ....Sean Strohmeyer
Key Spot Operator ....Doug Graf
Assistant Electricians ....William Brennan,
David Holliman, David Lynch,
Joseph P. Lynch
Production Propman ....Victor Amerling
House Propman ....Frank Illo
Props ....Matthew Lavaia, Michael Lavaia,
Robert McCauley
Head Sound ....Alain Van Achte
Sound Assistants ....Donald McKennan, Scott Scheidt
Production Wardrobe Supervisor ....Kjeld Andersen
Assistant Wardrobe Supervisor ....Cynthia Boardman
Puppet Supervisor ....Anne Salt
Puppet Dayworkers ....Islah Abdul-Rahiim,
Ilya Vett
Mask/Puppet Studio ....Jeff Curry
Dressers ....Meredith Chase-Boyd,
Andy Cook, Tom Daniel,
Theresa DiStasi, Donna Doiron,
Pixie Esmonde, Michelle Gore-Butterfield,
Douglas Hamilton, Mark Houston,
Sara Jablon, Mark Lauer, Dawn Reynolds,
Kathryn Rohe, Rita Santi, Sheila Terrell,
Dave Tisue, Walter Weiner
Stitcher ....Janeth Iverson
Production Hair Supervisor ....Jon Jordan
Assistant Hair Supervisor ....Adenike Wright
Production Makeup Supervisor ....Elizabeth Cohen
Assistant Makeup Supervisor ....Christina Grant
Makeup Artist ....Brenda O'Brien

Music Development ....Nick Glennie-Smith

The Lion King

Music Preparation ....Donald Oliver and Evan Morris/ Chelsea Music Service, Inc.
Synthesizer Programmer ....Ted Baker
Orchestral Synthesizer Programmer ......Christopher Ward
Electronic Drum Programmer ....Tommy Igoe
Addt'l Percussion Arrangements ....Valerie Dee Naranjo
Music Assistant ....Elizabeth J. Falcone
Personal Assistant to Elton John ....Bob Halley
Assistant to Tim Rice ....Eileen Heinink
Assistant to Mark Mancina ....Chuck Choi

Associate Scenic Designer ....Jonathan Fensom
Assistant Scenic Designer ....Michael Fagin
Lighting Design Assistant ....Karen Spahn
Automated Lighting Tracker ....Lara Bohon
Projection Designer ....Geoff Puckett
Projection Art ....Caterina Bertolotto
Assistant Sound Designer ....Kai Harada
Assistant Costume Designer ....Tracy Dorman
Stunt Consultant ....Peter Moore
Children's Tutoring ....On Location Education
Production Photography ....Joan Marcus,
Marc Bryan-Brown
Associate Producer 1996–1998 ....Donald Frantz
Project Manager 1996–1998 ....Nina Essman
Associate Producer 1998–2002 ....Ken Denison
Associate Producer 2000-2003 ....Pam Young
Associate Producer 2002-2007 ....Todd Lacy
Associate Producer 2003-2008 ....Aubrey Lynch
Original Music Director ....Joseph Church

The Lion King is a proud member of the Broadway Green Alliance.

Disney's *The Lion King* is a registered trademark owned by The Walt Disney Company and used under special license by Disney Theatrical Productions.

HOUSE STAFF FOR THE MINSKOFF THEATRE
House Manager ....Victor Irving
Treasurer ....Nicholas Loiacono
Assistant Treasurer ....Cheryl Loiacono

CREDITS
Scenery built and mechanized by Hudson Scenic Studio, Inc. Additional scenery by Chicago Scenic Studios, Inc.; Edge & Co., Inc.; Michael Hagen, Inc.; Piper Productions, Inc.; Scenic Technologies, Inc.; I. Weiss & Sons, Inc. Lighting by Westsun, vari*lite® automated lighting provided by Vari-Lite, Inc. Props by John Creech Design & Production. Sound equipment by Pro-Mix, Inc. Additional sound equipment by Walt Disney Imagineering. Rehearsal Scenery by Brooklyn Scenic & Theatrical. Costumes executed by Parsons-Meares Ltd., Donna Langman, Eric Winterling, Danielle Gisiger, Suzie Elder. Millinery by Rodney Gordon, Janet Linville, Arnold Levine. Ricola provided by Ricola, Inc. Shibori dyeing by Joan Morris. Custom dyeing and painting by Joni Johns, Mary Macy, Parsons-Meares Ltd., Gene Mignola. Additional Painting by J. Michelle Hill. Knitwear by Maria Ficalora. Footwear by Sharlot Battin, Robert W. Jones, Capezio, Vasilli Shoes. Costume development by Constance Hoffman. Special Projects by Angela M. Kahler. Custom fabrics developed by Gary Graham and Helen Quinn. Puppet Construction by Michael Curry Design, Inc. and Vee Corporation. Shadow puppetry by Steven Kaplan. Pumbaa Puppet Construction by Andrew Benepe. Flying by Foy. Trucking by Clark Transfer. Wigs made at The Wigworkshop by Sam Fletcher. Specialist brushes made by Joseph Begley. Cheetah skins and make-up stamps made by Mike Defeo in the USA. Dry cleaning by Ernest Winzer Cleaners. Marimbas by De Morrow Instruments, Ltd. Latin Percussion by LP Music Group. Drumset by DrumWorkshop. Cymbals by Zildjian. Bass equipment by Eden Electronics. Paper products supplied by Green Forest.

Song excerpts (used by permission): "Supercalifragilisticexpialidocious" written by Richard M. Sherman and Robert B. Sherman; "Five Foot Two, Eyes of Blue" written by Sam Lewis, Joe Young, and Ray Henderson; "The Lion Sleeps Tonight" written by Hugo Peretti, George David Weiss, Luigi Creatore and Solomon Linda.

NEDERLANDER

Chairman ....**James M. Nederlander**
President ....**James L. Nederlander**

Executive Vice President
Nick Scandalios

Vice President Corporate Development **Charlene S. Nederlander**	Senior Vice President Labor Relations **Herschel Waxman**
Vice President **Jim Boese**	Chief Financial Officer **Freida Sawyer Belviso**

DISNEY THEATRICAL PRODUCTIONS
President ....Thomas Schumacher
EVP & Managing Director ....David Schrader
Senior Vice President, International ....Ron Kollen
Vice President, International, Europe ....Fiona Thomas
Vice President, International, Australia ....James Thane
Vice President, Operations ....Dana Amendola
Vice President, Publicity ....Joe Quenqua
Vice President, Domestic ....Jack Eldon
Vice President, Human Resources ....June Heindel
Director, Domestic Touring..............Michael Buchanan
Director, Worldwide Publicity ....Michael Cohen
Director, Regional Engagements ....Scott A. Hemerling
Director, Regional Engagements ....Kelli Palan
Director, Regional Engagements ....Deborah Warren
Manager, Domestic Touring & Planning ....Liz Botros
Manager, Human Resources ....Jewel Neal
Manager, Publicity ....Lindsay Braverman
Project Manager ....Ryan Pears
Senior Computer Support Analyst ....Kevin A. McGuire
IT/Business Analyst ....William Boudiette

Creative & Production
Executive Music Producer ....Chris Montan
VP, Creative Development ....Steve Fickinger
VP, Production ....Anne Quart
Director, International Production ....Felipe Gamba
Director, Labor Relations ....Edward Lieber
Associate Director ....Jeff Lee
Production Supervisor ....Clifford Schwartz
Production Manager ....Eduardo Castro
Manager, Labor Relations ....Stephanie Cheek
Manager, Physical Production ....Karl Chmielewski
Manager, Creative Development ....Jane Abramson
Manager, Theatrical Licensing ....David R. Scott

Dramaturg & Literary Manager ....Ken Cerniglia
Manager, Education Outreach ....Lisa Mitchell

Marketing
Senior Vice President ....Andrew Flatt
Director, Creative Resources ....Victor Adams
Director, Synergy & Partnership ....Kevin Banks
Director, Digital Marketing ....Kyle Young
Design Manager ....James Anderer
Manager, Media & Strategy ....Jared Comess
Manager, Creative Services ....Lauren Daghini
Manager, Synergy & Partnership ....Sarah Schlesinger
Manager, Consumer Insights ....Craig Trachtenberg
Manager, Digital Marketing ....Peter Tulba

Sales
Vice President, National Sales ....Bryan Dockett
National Sales Manager ....Victoria Cairl
Sr. Manager, Sales & Ticketing ....Nick Falzon
Manager, Group Sales ....Hunter Robertson

Business and Legal Affairs
Senior Vice President ....Jonathan Olson
Director ....Daniel M. Posener
Director ....Seth Stuhl
Sr. Paralegal ....Jessica White

Finance
VP, Finance/Business Development ....Mario Iannetta
Director, Finance ....Joe McClafferty
Director, Business Development ....Michael Barra
Director, Accounting ....Leena Mathew
Manager, Finance ....Liz Jurist Schwarzwalder
Manager, Production Accounting ....Nick Judge
Manager, Accounting ....Adrineh Ghoukassian
Senior Business Analyst ....Sven Rittershaus
Senior Financial Analyst ....Mikhail Medvedev
Senior Financial Analyst ....Jason Ve
Senior Business Planner ....Jennifer August
Production Accountant ....Joy Sims Brown
Production Accountant ....Angela DiSanti
Assistant Production Accountant ....Isander Rojas

Administrative Staff
Brian Bahr, Sarah Bills, Elizabeth Boulger, Whitney Britt, Jonelle Brown, Amy Caldamone, Michael Dei Cas, Preston Copley, Alanna Degner, Brittany Dobbs, Cara Epstein, Nicholas Faranda, Cristi Finn, Phil Grippe, Greg Josken, Cyntia Leo, Colleen McCormack, Brendan Padgett, Matt Quinones, Jillian Robbins, Kattia Soriano, Lee Taglin, Anji Taylor

DISNEY THEATRICAL MERCHANDISE
Vice President ....Steven Downing
Merchandise Manager ....Neil Markman
District Manager ....Alyssa Somers
Associate Buyer ....Violet Burlaza
Assistant Manager, Inventory ....Suzanne Jakel
On-Site Retail Manager ....Jeff Knizer
On-Site Assistant Retail Manager ....Jana Cristiano

Disney Theatrical Productions
guestmail@disneytheatrical.com

The Lion King
SCRAPBOOK

Cast members perform as part of the "Gypsy of the Year" celebration December 6, 2011 at the New Amsterdam Theatre.

Correspondent: Bonita J. Hamilton, "Shenzi"

Anniversary Parties and Gifts: Our anniversary party was awesome even though we are 15 years old now...and our best gift was a plush terrycloth *Lion King* bathrobe.

Most Exciting Celebrity Visitors: Even though he is no longer with us by far the most exciting celebrity to visit us was Michael Jackson, but Kobe Bryant was pretty cool too.

"Easter Bonnet" Sketch: The Easter Bonnet sketch was written by Kenny Ingram and Peter Candela. The name of the sketch was "Hallelujah Harlem!" It was about Harlem's heyday and it won Best Presentation. The performers were: Nia Ashleigh, Judah Bellamy, Khail Bryant, Alvin Crawford, Trista Dollison, Angelica Edwards, Niles Fitch, Jean Michelle Grier, Aubrey Omari Joseph, Sheryl McCallum, Jaysin McCollum, Matthew Sean Morgan, James A Pierce III, Chondra La-Tease Profit, Imani Dia Smith, Phillip Turner, Donna Michelle Vaughn, Jason Veasey, Rema Webb, Camille Workman.

Actors Who Perform the Most Roles in This Show: Angelica Edwards covers nine tracks; Dennis Johnston covers ten tracks.

Actor Who Has Done the Most Performances in This Show: Camille Brown: 5600, give or take a few.

Special Backstage Ritual: Right before the Mufasa apparition, stage right performers come together, hold hands and say "Kum bi yah" and stomp their right foot.

Favorite Moment During Each Performance: "The Circle of Life."

Favorite In-Theatre Gathering Place: The female ensemble dressing room.

Off-Site Hangout: Intercontinental Hotel

Favorite Snack Foods: Cake and popcorn.

Mascot: The Lion Head.

Favorite Therapy: Natalie Kinghorn and Neurosport Physical Therapy.

Memorable Ad-Lib: During the confrontation scene when Simba is facing off with Scar, Simba's line is supposed to be: "Give me one good reason why I shouldn't rip you apart?" The snafu was: "Give me one good reason why I shouldn't rip your clothes off?"

Fastest Costume Change: Simba has the quickest costume change...he has less than two minutes to get into his corset.

Heaviest/Hottest Costume: Patrick Brown who plays Scar has the heaviest and hottest costume. The costume weighs 45 lbs.

Who Wore the Least: The Antelopes.

Catchphrases Only the Company Would Recognize: "Ain't nobody got time for that."

Best In-House Parody Lyrics: The lyric is: "Ingoyama Nengwe Namabala." The parody is: "Pink pajamas penguins on the bottom."

Sweethearts Within the Company: Bongi Duma and Lindiwe Dlamini.

Memorable Directorial Note: "Your acting is great...but you look like a laundry lady carrying heavy bags....Get more Physical!!!!!"

Company Legends: Camille Brown, Ron Kunene, Lindiwe Dlamini all have been in the show fifteen years.

Nicknames: Bertha for the Elephant, Stiffy for Baby Simba.

Frightening Moment: When Ray Mercer fell in the Giraffe during "The Circle of Life" from 14 feet in the air and a stagehand and The Birdman had to drag him offstage by both feet because he could not get up.

Ghostly Encounters Backstage: We haven't had any at The Minskoff but we used to have visits from Olive Thomas all the time when we were at The New Amsterdam theatre.

Superstition That Turned Out To Be True: The Zulus put a fertility curse on the building. Everyone's pregnant!!!!

Coolest Thing About Being in This Show: The faces of the audience members as they watch "The Circle of Life" and how the show itself speaks to people of different cultures, races, and ages...We are all connected in the great circle of life.

The Lyons

First Preview: April 5, 2012. Opened: April 23, 2012.
Still running as of May 31, 2012.

The neurotic Lyons family gathers beside the deathbed of the father, an old curmudgeon who spends his last hours berating his wife and two grown children about how miserable they made his life. But it turns out to be no worse than what they all thought about him—and about each other.

CAST

(in order of speaking)

Rita Lyons .... LINDA LAVIN
Ben Lyons .... DICK LATESSA
Lisa Lyons .... KATE JENNINGS GRANT
Curtis Lyons .... MICHAEL ESPER
Nurse .... BRENDA PRESSLEY
Brian .... GREGORY WOODDELL

ACT 1

A hospital room

ACT 2

Scene 1: An empty apartment
Scene 2: A hospital room

UNDERSTUDIES

For Curtis/Brian: RICHARD GALLAGHER
For Ben: TIM JEROME
For Lisa/Nurse: EVA KAMINSKY
For Curtis/Brian: JOHN WERNKE

---

⑤ CORT THEATRE
138 West 48th Street
A Shubert Organization Theatre
Philip J. Smith, *Chairman*   Robert E. Wankel, *President*

KATHLEEN K. JOHNSON
PRESENTS
THE VINEYARD THEATRE PRODUCTION
OF

LINDA LAVIN
IN

THE LYONS

WRITTEN BY
NICKY SILVER

WITH

MICHAEL ESPER   KATE JENNINGS GRANT
BRENDA PRESSLEY   GREGORY WOODDELL

ALSO STARRING
DICK LATESSA

SCENIC DESIGN **ALLEN MOYER**	COSTUME DESIGN **MICHAEL KRASS**	LIGHTING DESIGN **DAVID LANDER**
ORIGINAL MUSIC & SOUND DESIGN **DAVID VAN TIEGHEM**	PRODUCTION MANAGEMENT **AURORA PRODUCTIONS**	FIGHT DIRECTOR **THOMAS SCHALL**
PRODUCTION STAGE MANAGER **ROBERT BENNETT**	CASTING **HENRY RUSSELL BERGSTEIN, CSA**	ADVERTISING & MARKETING **aka**

GENERAL MANAGER
NIKO COMPANIES, LTD.

PRESS REPRESENTATIVE
SAM RUDY

DIRECTED BY
MARK BROKAW

THE PRODUCER WISHES TO EXPRESS HER APPRECIATION TO THEATRE DEVELOPMENT FUND FOR ITS SUPPORT OF THIS PRODUCTION.

4/23/12

(L-R): Linda Lavin and Dick Latessa

Photo by Carol Rosegg

The Lyons

Linda Lavin
Rita Lyons

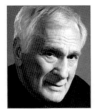
Dick Latessa
Ben Lyons

Michael Esper
Curtis Lyons

Kate Jennings Grant
Lisa Lyons

Brenda Pressley
Nurse

Gregory Wooddell
Brian

Richard Gallagher
u/s Curtis, Brian

Tim Jerome
u/s Ben

Eva Kaminsky
u/s Lisa, Nurse

John Wernke
u/s Curtis, Brian

Nicky Silver
Playwright

Mark Brokaw
Director

Allen Moyer
Set Design

David Lander
Lighting Design

David Van Tieghem
Original Music and Sound Design

Thomas Schall
Fight Director

Gene O'Donovan
Aurora Productions
Production Management

Manny Kladitis
Niko Companies, Ltd
General Manager

Kathleen K. Johnson
Producer

Jonathan Tessero
Associate Producer

Douglas Aibel
Artistic Director,
Vineyard Theatre
Producer

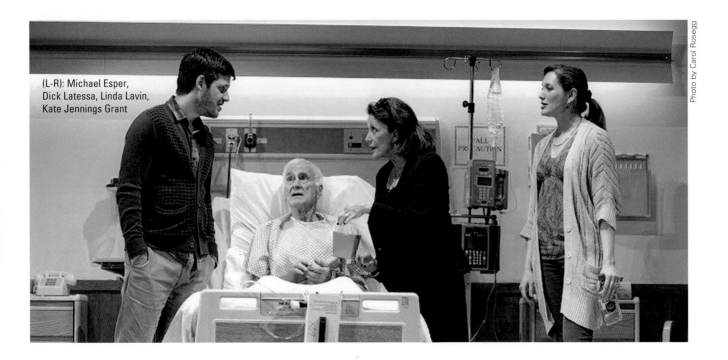

(L-R): Michael Esper, Dick Latessa, Linda Lavin, Kate Jennings Grant

Photo by Carol Rosegg

The Lyons

BOX OFFICE
(L-R): Larry Staroff, Pete Damen

HOUSE STAFF
Front Row (L-R): William Denson, Mario Carillo

Middle Row (L-R): Danielle Smith, Nicole McIntyre, Scott Witebsky

Top Row (L-R): Cody Butler, Marilyn Molina, Steve Simmons, Beth Sacks

CREW
Kneeling (L-R): Lois L. Griffing, Jessica Moy, Jason T. Vanderwoude, Scott DeVerna

Standing (:L-R): Brian Hutchinson, Kathleen K. Johnson, Robert Bennett, Ed Diaz, Tessa Dunning, Lonnie Gaddy, Eileen Miller

The Lyons
SCRAPBOOK

Correspondent: Gregory Wooddell, "Brian"
Opening Night Gifts: *The Lyons* bathrobes!
Celebrity Visitors: Robert De Niro, Martin Short, Joan Rivers, Alan Rickman.
Actors Who Have Done the Most Shows in Their Careers: Linda Lavin (16 Broadway), Dick Latessa (18 Broadway).
Special Backstage Ritual: "It's time to light the music!"
Favorite Moment During Each Performance (On Stage or Off): The audience's reaction to Rita's (Linda Lavin's) line: "You can wish me bon voyage or frankly you can both go fuck yourselves."
Most Memorable Ad-Lib: "Did you notice the recessed lighting?" became "Did you notice the receding hairline?"
Cast Reaction to the Internet Buzz on the Show: Overwhelmed by the positive response.
Fastest Costume Change: Michael Esper: Act II, scene 1 into Act II, scene 2.
Who Wore the Least: Dick Latessa: Hospital gown.
Catchphrase Only the Company Would Recognize: "What else?"
Coolest Thing About Being in This Show: Sharing in Nicky Silver's Broadway debut!!!

Curtain call on opening night (L-R): Brenda Pressley, Kate Jennings Grant, Dick Latessa, Linda Lavin, Michael Esper and Gregory Wooddell.

Photo by Monica Simoes

STAFF FOR *THE LYONS*

GENERAL MANAGEMENT
NIKO COMPANIES, LTD.
Manny Kladitis
Jeffrey Chrzczon   Jason T. Vanderwoude

GENERAL PRESS REPRESENTATIVE
SAM RUDY MEDIA RELATIONS

ADVERTISING AND MARKETING
aka
Scott A. Moore   Liz Furze
Joshua Lee Poole   Jennifer Sims   Adam Jay
Janette Roush   Sara Rosenzweig

DIGITAL AND INTERACTIVE
aka
Erin Rech   Jen Taylor   Flora Pei

CASTING
Henry Russell Bergstein, CSA

PRODUCTION MANAGEMENT
AURORA PRODUCTIONS, INC.
Gene O'Donovan, Ben Heller
Stephanie Sherline, Anita Shah, Jarid Sumner,
Anthony Jusino, Liza Luxenberg, Steven Dalton,
Eugenio Saenz Flores, Isaac Katzanek
Anita Feld, Melissa Mazdra

PRODUCTION STAGE MANAGER	Robert Bennett
Stage Manager	Lois Griffing
Production Assistant	Jessica Johnstone
Assistant to the Producer	Judy Crozier
Assistant Director	Sam Pinkleton
Assistant Set Designer	Warren Karp

Assistant Costume Designer	Brenda Abbandandolo
Assistant Lighting Designer	Travis McHale
Associate Sound Designer	David Sanderson
Assistant Sound Designer	Emma Wilk
Production Carpenter	Ed Diaz
Production Electrician	Scott Deverna
Production Properties	Lonnie Gaddy
Advance Properties Supervisor	Rob Brenner
Sound Board Engineer	Jim Van Bergen
Wardrobe Supervisor	Eileen Miller
Costume Shopper	Annie Sunai
Property Coordinator	Tessa Dunning
Legal Counsel	Levine, Plotkin & Menen/ Loren Plotkin
Accounting	Rosenberg, Neuwirth & Kuchner/ Mark D'Ambrosi, Sarah Krug
Insurance	Insurance Office of America/ Carol Bressi-Cilona
Banking	City National Bank
Production Photographer	Carol Rosegg
Medical Consultants	Fidel Lim, Bev Mitchell

VINEYARD THEATRE

Artistic Director	Douglas Aibel
Executive Producer	Jennifer Garvey-Blackwell
Co-artistic Director	Sarah Stern
Managing Director	Rebecca Habel

CREDITS
Sound equipment provided by Sound Associates. Lighting equipment provided by P.R.G. Scenery by P.R.G. Scenic Technologies. Originally rehearsed at the Davenport Studios.

Linda Lavin's Make-up Design by
J. Roy Helland.

Linda Lavin's Hair Design by
Antonio Soddu.

House Beautiful provided by
Hearst Publications.

SPECIAL THANKS
Ann Palmer, Jeffrey Richards, Jerry Frankel

 THE SHUBERT ORGANIZATION, INC.
Board of Directors

Philip J. Smith Chairman	**Robert E. Wankel** President
Wyche Fowler, Jr.	**Diana Phillips**
Lee J. Seidler	**Michael I. Sovern**
Stuart Subotnick	

Chief Financial Officer	Elliot Greene
Sr. Vice President, Ticketing	David Andrews
Vice President, Finance	Juan Calvo
Vice President, Human Resources	Cathy Cozens
Vice President, Facilities	John Darby
Vice President, Theatre Operations	Peter Entin
Vice President, Marketing	Charles Flateman
Vice President, Audit	Anthony LaMattina
Vice President, Ticket Sales	Brian Mahoney
Vice President, Creative Projects	D.S. Moynihan
Vice President, Real Estate	Julio Peterson

CORT THEATRE

House Manager	Joseph Traina

Lysistrata Jones

First Preview: November 12, 2011. Opened: December 14, 2011.
Closed January 8, 2012 after 34 Previews and 30 Performances.

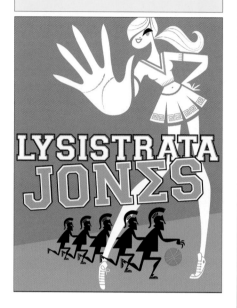

This new musical transposes the action of the Greek classic Lysistrata *from the Peleponnesian Wars to the world of college basketball. Cheerleaders from Athens University go on a sex strike to force their laid-back hoopsters to buckle down and start winning some games. Along the way they learn something about commitment of all kinds with the help of the local brothel's madame, who boasts goddess-like wisdom (and proportions).*

CAST

(in alphabetical order)

'Uardo	ALEXANDER AGUILAR
Tyllis	ATO BLANKSON-WOOD
Lampito	KATIE BOREN
Robin	LINDSAY NICOLE CHAMBERS
Hetaira	LIZ MIKEL
Lysistrata Jones	PATTI MURIN
Cleonice	KAT NEJAT
Mick	JOSH SEGARRA
Myrrhine	LaQUET SHARNELL
Xander	JASON TAM
Harold	TEDDY TOYE
Cinesias	ALEX WYSE

DANCE CAPTAIN
CHARLIE SUTTON

Continued on next page

JORDAN ROTH
President

PAUL LIBIN
Executive Vice President

JACK VIERTEL
Senior Vice President

PAULA HEROLD   ALAN WASSER
JOSEPH SMITH   MICHAEL McCABE   JOHN BREGLIO
TAKONKIET VIRAVAN/SCENARIO THAILAND   HILARY A. WILLIAMS
BROADWAY ACROSS AMERICA   JAMES G. ROBINSON
in association with
TONY MEOLA   MARTIN McCALLUM   MARIANNE MILLS

present

A MUSICAL COMEDY

Book by
DOUGLAS CARTER BEANE

Music and Lyrics by
LEWIS FLINN

PATTI MURIN
JOSH SEGARRA   JASON TAM   LINDSAY NICOLE CHAMBERS
ALEXANDER AGUILAR   ATO BLANKSON-WOOD   KATIE BOREN   KAT NEJAT
LaQUET SHARNELL   TEDDY TOYE   ALEX WYSE
LaVON FISHER-WILSON   LIBBY SERVAIS   CHARLIE SUTTON   BARRETT WILBERT WEED   JARED ZIRILLI
And
LIZ MIKEL

Scenic Design by	Costume Design by	Lighting Design by	Sound Design by
ALLEN MOYER	DAVID C. WOOLARD & THOMAS CHARLES LeGALLEY	MICHAEL GOTTLIEB	TONY MEOLA

Hair & Wig Design by	Associate Choreographer	Casting by	Production Stage Manager
MARK ADAM RAMPMEYER	JESSICA HARTMAN	CINDY TOLAN	LOIS L. GRIFFING

Orchestrations & Arrangements by	Music Director	Music Coordinator
LEWIS FLINN	BRAD SIMMONS	DEAN SHARENOW

Marketing Direction	Press Representative	Production Management	General Management
TYPE A MARKETING ANNE RIPPEY	THE HARTMAN GROUP	JUNIPER STREET PRODUCTIONS	AWA MANAGEMENT ALLAN WILLIAMS • AARON LUSTBADER

Directed and Choreographed by
DAN KNECHTGES

Originally Produced by Dallas Theater Center	New York Premiere produced by Transport Group Theatre Company
Kevin Moriarty, Artistic Director Heather M. Kitchen, Executive Director	Jack Cummings III, Artistic Director Lori Fineman, Executive Director

LYSISTRATA JONES was developed and first presented in New York at THE GYM AT JUDSON.

The Producers wish to express their appreciation to Theatre Development Fund for its support of this production.

1/8/12

The Cast

Photo by Joan Marcus

Lysistrata Jones

MUSICAL NUMBERS

ACT I

Opening – "Right Now"	The Company
"Change the World"	Lysistrata & Girls
"No More Giving It Up!"	Girls
"Lay Low"	Mick & Boys
"I Don't Think So"	Hetaira & Girls
"You Go Your Way"	The Company
"Where Am I Now"	Lysistrata & Company

ACT II

"Writing on the Wall"	Hetaira & Company
"Hold On"	Xander, Lysistrata & Hetaira
"Don't Judge a Book"	Myrrhine & Cinesias
"Right Now Operetta"	The Company
"When She Smiles"	Mick
"Give It Up!"	The Company

Patti Murin (C) and Ladies

Photo by Joan Marcus

CREW
(L-R): Matthew Maloney, Chris Devany, George Fullum, David Holliman, Joel DeRuyter, Paul Valvo, Josh Maszle, Jennifer Bullock, Andy Meeker, Jess Dermody, Scott Westervelt, Scott Cain, Angie Simpson, Meredith Benson

Photo by Brian Mapp

Cast Continued

UNDERSTUDIES

For Lysistrata:
LIBBY SERVAIS
For Hetaira:
LaVON FISHER-WILSON
For Robin:
LIBBY SERVAIS, BARRETT WILBERT WEED
For Myrrhine:
LIBBY SERVAIS, BARRETT WILBERT WEED
For Lampito:
LIBBY SERVAIS, BARRETT WILBERT WEED
For Cleonice:
BARRETT WILBERT WEED
For Mick:
ALEXANDER AGUILAR, JARED ZIRILLI
For Xander:
CHARLIE SUTTON
For Cinesias:
CHARLIE SUTTON, JARED ZIRILLI
For 'Uardo:
CHARLIE SUTTON, JARED ZIRILLI
For Tyllis:
JARED ZIRILLI
For Harold:
CHARLIE SUTTON

Special thanks to Chris & Liz Mullin and
Penny Marshall

BAND

Conductor:
BRAD SIMMONS
Associate Conductor:
CHRIS HABERL
Keyboard 1:
BRAD SIMMONS
Keyboard 2:
CHRIS HABERL
Guitar:
FREDDY HALL
Bass:
ALAN STEVENS HEWITT
Drums:
MARQUES WALLS
Percussion:
WILSON TORRES
Vocalist/Percussion:
BITI STRAUCHN
Music Coordinator:
DEAN SHARENOW
Keyboard and Electronic Drum Programmer:
RANDY COHEN
Music Copyist:
ALEX VORSE

Lysistrata Jones

Patti Murin
Lysistrata Jones

Liz Mikel
Hetaira

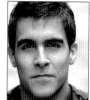
Josh Segarra
Mick

Jason Tam
Xander

Lindsay Nicole Chambers
Robin

Alexander Aguilar
'Uardo

Ato Blankson-Wood
Tyllis

Katie Boren
Lampito

Kat Nejat
Cleonice

LaQuet Sharnell
Myrrhine

Teddy Toye
Harold

Alex Wyse
Cinesias

LaVon Fisher-Wilson
Hetaira u/s

Libby Servais
Lysistrata, Robin, Myrrhine, Lampito u/s

Charlie Sutton
Xander, Cinesias, 'Uardo, Harold u/s

Barrett Wilbert Weed
Robin, Myrrhine, Cleonice, Lampito u/s

Jared Zirilli
Mick, Cinesias, 'Uardo, Tyllis u/s

Lewis Flinn
Music, Lyrics, Arrangements, Orchestrations

Douglas Carter Beane
Book

Dan Knechtges
Director/ Choreographer

Allen Moyer
Set Designer

David C. Woolard
Co-Costume Designer

Thomas Charles LeGalley
Co-Costume Designer

Michael Gottlieb
Lighting Designer

Tony Meola
Sound Designer, Producer

Jessica Hartman
Associate Choreographer/ Resident Choreographer

Brad Simmons
Musical Director

Alan Wasser
AWA Management Services
General Manager and Producer

Ana Rose Greene, Guy Kwan, Joe DeLuise, Hillary Blanken
Juniper Street Productions
Production Manager

Allan Williams
AWA Management Services
General Manager

Paula Herold
Producer

Joseph Smith
Producer

Michael McCabe
Producer

John Breglio
Producer

208

Lysistrata Jones

Hilary A. Williams
Producer

John Gore
Broadway Across
America
Producer

Thomas B. McGrath
Broadway Across
America
Producer

Photos by Brian Mapp

BOX OFFICE
(L-R): Gail Yerkovich, Harry Jaffie

FRONT OF HOUSE
Front Row (L-R): Alison Traynor, Victoria Lauzun
Second Row (L-R): Juliett Cipriati, Jared Pike, Tatiana Gomberg, Mallory Sims
Third Row (L-R): Michelle Fleury, TJ D'Angelo, Ryan Kerr, Chris Gizzi, Brian C. Veith
Back Row (L-R): Ilir Velovic, Rick Cabrera

BAND
(Clockwise from top): Biti Strauchn, Brad Simmons, Alan Stevens Hewitt,
Marques Walls, Freddy Hall, Wilson Torres, Chris Haberl

MANAGEMENT
(L-R): Lois L. Griffing, Meredith Morgan, John E. Gendron,
Thomas Recktenwald, Neveen Mahmoud

Lysistrata Jones

(L-R): Josh Segarra, Patti Murin
Photo by Joan Marcus

STAFF FOR *LYSISTRATA JONES*

GENERAL MANAGEMENT
ALAN WASSER ASSOCIATES
Alan Wasser   Allan Williams
Aaron Lustbader   Mark Shacket

GENERAL PRESS REPRESENTATIVE
THE HARTMAN GROUP
Michael Hartman   Tom D'Ambrosio   Frances White

COMPANY MANAGER
John E. Gendron

MARKETING
TYPE A MARKETING
Anne Rippey   Elyce Henkin
Allison Morrow   David Loughner

CASTING
CINDY TOLAN, CSA
Adam Caldwell, CSA

PRODUCTION MANAGEMENT
JUNIPER STREET PRODUCTIONS
Hillary Blanken   Joseph DeLuise
Guy Kwan   Ana Rose Greene

Production Stage Manager ....Lois L. Griffing
Stage Manager........................Thomas Recktenwald
Assistant Stage Manager ....Neveen Mahmoud
Assistant Company Manager ....Meredith Morgan
Media Design ....Howard Werner/Lightswitch
Assistant Director ....Nick Eilerman
Associate Scenic Designer ....Jonathan Collins
Associate Costume Designer ....Matthew Pachtman
Assistant to the Costume Designers...........Joseph Blaha
Associate Lighting Designer ....Craig Stelzenmuller
Assistant Lighting Designer ....Jeremy Cunningham
Associate Sound Designer ....Zach Williamson
Moving Light Programmer ....David Arch
Video Programmer ....Phil Gilbert
Production Carpenter ....Fred Gallo
Head Carpenter ....David M. Cohen
Advance Carpenter ....David J. Elmer
Production Props ....Susan Barras
Head Props ....Andrew Meeker
Production Electrician ....Rick Baxter
Head Electrician ....Sandra Paradise
Production Sound Engineer ....Joshua Maszle
Deck Audio ....Christina Devany
Wardrobe Supervisor ....Scott Westervelt
Dressers ....Scotty R. Cain, Jessica Dermody,
                                            Angela Simpson

Makeup Consultant ....Brandalyn Fulton
Hair Supervisor ....Jennifer Bullock
Music Coordinator ....Dean Sharenow
Music Copying ....Alex Vorse
Keyboard and Electronic Drum
    Programmer ....Randy Cohen
Assistant to Mr. Flinn ....Alex Vorse
Production Assistant ....Cody Renard Richard
Technical Production Assistant ....Colyn Fiendel
General Management Associates ....Mark Barna,
    Christopher D'Angelo, Jake Hirzel, Lane Marsh
General Management Office ....Hilary Ackerman,
    Nina Lutwick, Jennifer O'Connor
General Management Intern ....Kaitlin Boland
Advertising ....Serino/Coyne/
    Sandy Block, Greg Coradetti,
    Roger Micone, Ryan Cunningham,
    Nick Nolte
Digital Outreach & Website ....Serino/Coyne/
    Jim Glaub, Chip Meyrelles,
    Laurie Connor, Whitney Creighton,
    Mark Seeley, Kevin Keating, Ryan Greer
Opening Night Coordinator ....Serino/Coyne Events/
    Suzanne Tobak, Chrissann Gasparro
Theatre Displays ....King Displays
Accounting ....Rosenberg, Neuwirth & Kuchner/
    Chris Cacace, Ruthie Skochil
Banking ....Signature Bank/
    Barbara von Borstel,
    Margaret Monigan
Insurance ....Ventura Insurance Brokerage
Legal ....Sendroff & Baruch, LLP/
    Mark D. Sendroff, Esq.;
    Jason Baruch, Esq.
Payroll Service ....Castellana Services Inc.
Physical Therapy
    Provider ....Performing Arts Physical Therapy
Orthopedist ....Phillip Bauman, M.D.
Illustrator ....Kristen Ulve
Group Sales ....Broadway.com/Groups
Production Photography ....Joan Marcus

CREDITS
Scenery fabrication, show control and scenic motion control featuring Stage Command Systems by PRG Scenic Technologies, a division of Production Resources Group, LLC, New Windsor, NY. Lighting equipment from PRG Lighting. Audio equipment from PRG Audio. Peacock chariot by Nino Novellino and Costume Armour, Inc. Properties fabricated by Joe Cairo. Costumes executed by John Kristiansen New York Inc.; Cygnet Studio, Inc.; and Tricorne Inc. Selected crafts executed by Arnold S. Levine, Inc.; Matthew Smart; Jeff Fender Studio; Pete's Print Shop; and Vogue Too, Pleating, Stitching & Embroidery. Wigs by Hudson Wigs. Percussion instruments by LP. Cymbals by Sabian. Keyboards by Yamaha. Headphones and microphones by Sennheiser.

Souvenir merchandise designed and created by Max Merchandising/Platypus Productions.

Product consideration furnished by Apple.

SPECIAL THANKS
Cathy Kwon, Suzanne Lindbergh, George Poulios, Carole Morales, Tom Stultz

www.lysistratajones.com

JUJAMCYN THEATERS
JORDAN ROTH
President

PAUL LIBIN   **JACK VIERTEL**
Executive Vice President   Senior Vice President
MEREDITH VILLATORE   **JENNIFER HERSHEY**
Chief Financial Officer   Vice President,
                                            Building Operations
MICAH HOLLINGWORTH **HAL GOLDBERG**
Vice President,   Vice President,
Company Operations   Theatre Operations

Director of Business Affairs ....Albert T. Kim
Director of Ticketing Services ....Justin Karr
Theatre Operations Managers ....Willa Burke,
    Susan Elrod, Emily Hare,
    Jeff Hubbard, Albert T. Kim
Theatre Operations Associates ....Carrie Jo Brinker,
    Michael Composto, Anah Jyoti Klate
Accounting ....Cathy Cerge, Erin Dooley,
    Christian Sislian
Executive Producer, Red Awning ....Nicole Kastrinos
Director of Marketing, Givenik.com ....Joe Tropia
Marketing Associate, Givenik.com ....Ben Cohen
Building Operations Associate ....Erich Bussing
Executive Coordinator ....Ed Lefferson
Executive Assistants ....Clark Mims Tedesco,
    Julia Kraus, Beth Given
Receptionist ....Kate Garst
Maintenance ....Ralph Santos, Ramon Zapata
Security ....Rasim Hodzic, John Acero
Interns ....Jason Blackwell, Stephanie Ditman,
    Burton Frey, Sam Chapin,
    Emily Petrain, Lisa Perchinske,
    Kate Siegel, Mark Smith, Kelsey Wehd

STAFF FOR THE WALTER KERR THEATRE FOR *LYSISTRATA JONES*

Theatre Manager ....Susan Elrod
Treasurer ....Harry Jaffie
Head Carpenter ....George E. Fullum
Head Propertyman ....Timothy Bennet
Head Electrician ....Vincent V. Valvo
Engineer ....Brian DiNapoli
Assistant Treasurers ....Michael Loiacono,
    Joseph Smith, Gail Yerkovich
Flyman ....Michael Bennet
Ticket-Takers/Directors/Ushers ....Jason Aguirre,
    Florence Arcaro, Juliett Cipriati,
    TJ D'Angelo, Michelle Fleury,
    Victoria Lauzun, Alison Traynor,
    Robert Zwaschka
Doorpersons ....Brandon Houghton, Kevin Wallace
Head Porter ....Marcio Martinez
Porter ....Rudy Martinez
Head Cleaner ....Sevdija Pasukanovic
Cleaner ....Lourdes Perez

Lobby refreshments by Sweet Concessions.

Security provided by P and P Security.

Lysistrata Jones
SCRAPBOOK

Photo by Joseph Marzullo/WENN

Photo by Joseph Marzullo/WENN

Photo courtesy Patti Murin

1. Curtain call on opening night.
2. (L-R): Lindsay Nicole Chambers and LaQuet Sharnell at Famous Dave's restaurant for the cast party.
3. Rehearsing downtown: (L-R): Teddy Toye, coach Chris Mullin, Jared Zirilli, Charlie Sutton, Patti Murin, Jason Tam, Josh Segarra, Alex Wyse, Alexander Aguilar.

Correspondent: Patti Murin, "Lysistrata Jones"

Opening Night Party and Gifts: Our party was at the beautiful New Liberty Theatre on 42nd Street. Lots of great college themed gifts were given out, including pint glasses, shot glasses and a great backpack from our Stage Management team. TONS of flowers and baked goods of course!

Most Exciting Celebrity Visitors: We had Rosie O'Donnell and Abby Lee Miller of "Dance Moms" come on the same night, and it was just chaos on the stage afterwards! Rosie LOVES Abby, so she was as excited to meet her as we were. And of course, Rosie was so funny and supportive and she tweeted about us three

times in the next 12 hours, about how much she loved the show.

Who Has Done the Most Shows in Their Career: We were all on principal contracts so we were one of the rare musicals that did NOT get a Gypsy Robe ceremony. But Charlie Sutton, our Dance Captain and one of our male understudies, has done seven Broadway shows, so he would win that prize!

Special Backstage Rituals: Some members of the band and some of the understudies liked to "plank" before every show. Also, as we were waiting to go on for the Opening, Alex Aguilar would give us a "change" for the show that night. They were never real, and he always thought of them on the spot in the 60 seconds

before the music started. The more far fetched, the better! And then we would put our hands in and do a different "1-2-3" every night, like a real basketball team.

Favorite Moment During Each Performance (On Stage or Off): Generally everyone's favorite moment was performing the final number, "Give It Up!" It was just an explosion of energy and joy and happiness, and every single night we got to revel together in what we had just accomplished.

Favorite Off-Site Hangout: Hurley's! The bar/restaurant right across the street from the Walter Kerr. They were so gracious and hosted many of our parties and gatherings.

Favorite Snack Foods: There was always chocolate and candy everywhere, so I don't know that we had a real preference. If there was sugar in it, someone was eating it.

Mascot: Our show actually had a mascot built into it! The Athens Spartan, who was brilliantly brought to life by Jason Tam in the character of Xander.

Favorite Therapies: We had PT once a week. It was always full of our hard-working dancing boys; Ricolas and Patti Murin; steam inhalers for LaQuet Sharnell; Emergen-C for Alex Wyse; naps for Katie Boren; Throat Coat for Josh Segarra; foam rollers for Ato Blankson-Wood and Jason Tam…the list goes on and on! Everyone had their own rituals that worked for them.

Memorable Ad-Libs: "L'Chaim!" —Alex Wyse in the middle of "Don't Judge a Book By Its Cover."

"Oh, I get it now." —Patti Murin on closing night in response to the line "The best theatre always comes from movies. That way, the audience doesn't have to worry about being surprised." Get it? Cause we were closing?

Cell Phone Rings, Cell Phone Photos, Tweeting or Texting Incidents During a Performance: None that were memorable from the audience, but we had ALL of those things happening onstage, within the world of the show of course! We incorporated iPhones and laptops in a realistic way, so everyone had an electronic device that they worked with.

Understudy Anecdote: We only had one understudy go on in the entire run of previews and shows. Libby Servais was thrown on as the character of Myrrhine with just a few hours to prepare, and she was flawless! It was exciting to have her onstage with us after she had worked so hard!

Memorable Stage Door Fan Encounters: We had some amazing drawings made for us by our fans!

Who Wore the Least: The boys in the locker room scene all stripped down to their undies, and the girls stripped down to just tube tops and short shorts. Also, Liz Mikel wore a rather famous catsuit, and Josh Segarra performed a striptease down to his BVDs. So the question really is, who DIDN'T wear the least?

Lysistrata Jones
SCRAPBOOK

1. *Yearbook* correspondent Patti Murin accepts her ovation at the premiere.
2. The cast at basketball camp with Dan Knechtges, Lewis Flinn, Douglas Carter Beane and coach and former NBA player Chris Mullin (tall man, back row, center).
3. Jessica Hartman and Dan Knechtges on the first day of rehearsal.
4. Downtown: (Standing L-R): Lindsay Nicole Chambers, Patti Murin, Chris Mullin, Kat Nejat, Libby Servais and Barrett Wilbert Weed, with LaQuet Sharnell at the bottom.

Catchphrase Only the Company Would Recognize: "Guys, there's a change."
Memorable Directorial Note: "I'm gonna need you to sing...better?" —Brad Simmons, our MD.
Company In-Joke: ASBESTOS.
Fastest Costume Change: All of the girls had approximately 10 seconds to completely change our outfits at the same time at the end of "I Don't Think So," right before we came out strutting our stuff in our protest gear. I'm talking shoe changes, headpiece changes, the whole nine yards. Luckily most of it involved taking clothes off to do our sexy walk downstage!
Who Wore the Heaviest/Hottest Costume: Jason Tam had to wear our Spartan mascot costume, which included a helmet that completely obscured his whole head and face. He had to do an entire dance with it on, while holding and looking at an iPhone. And we're talking Jason Tam dancing, which means it was real dancing!
Nicknames: We had a rather colorful array of nicknames for each other, most of which are not fit for print.
Sweethearts Within the Company: Most of us came into this with significant others, so there was no showmancing happening at this theatre!
Embarrassing Moments: The ONLY TIME basketballs ever went into the audience, it happened twice in the same show. Whoops :)
Coolest Thing About Being in This Show: Getting to transfer from the gym downtown to the Broadway stage all together. We were so blessed to keep our family and continue the adventure.
Memorable Quote from Farewell Stage Speech: "We won....you gotta just believe." —Patti Murin
Most Vivid Memory of the Final Performance: Per college basketball tradition, we cut down the basketball net from our set and we each got to take a piece of it home.
Farewell Party: We went across the street to Hurley's, our favorite spot, and got pretty drunk.

Magic/Bird

First Preview: March 21, 2012. Opened: April 11, 2012.
Closed May 12, 2012 after 24 Previews and 37 Performances.

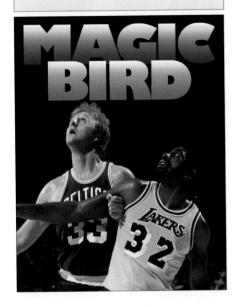

A chronicle of the off-court friendship that blossomed between the two top pro basketball players of the 1980s, Earvin "Magic" Johnson of the Los Angeles Lakers and his main rival, Larry Bird of the Boston Celtics. The two overcome team loyalty, racism and widely divergent backgrounds to allow their initial dislike to moderate into respect and finally into something more.

CAST

Earvin "Magic" Johnson ....KEVIN DANIELS
Larry Bird ....TUG COKER
Pat Riley/Red Auerbach/
   Jerry Buss/Tom/Bob Woolf ....PETER SCOLARI
Dinah Bird/Patricia Moore/Shelly/
   Georgia Bird ....DEIRDRE O'CONNELL
Willy/Bryant Gumbel/Jon Lennox/
   Ron Baxter ....FRANCOIS BATTISTE
Henry Alvarado/Cedric Maxwell/
   Norm Nixon/Frank/Michael Cooper/
   Jeff ....ROBERT MANNING, JR.

THE TIME:
1979-1992

UNDERSTUDIES

For Earvin "Magic" Johnson, Willy, Bryant Gumbel,
Jon Lennox, Ron Baxter, Henry Alvarado,
Cedric Maxwell, Norm Nixon, Frank,
Michael Cooper, Jeff:
ANTHONY HOLIDAY

Continued on next page

ⓢ LONGACRE THEATRE
220 West 48th Street
A Shubert Organization Theatre

Philip J. Smith, *Chairman*   **Robert E. Wankel,** *President*

FRAN KIRMSER   TONY PONTURO

W. SCOTT MCGRAW JOHN MARA, JR. TAMARA TUNIE/JEFFREY DONOVAN
FRIENDS OF MAGIC BIRD

IN ASSOCIATION WITH
NATIONAL BASKETBALL ASSOCIATION

PRESENTS

MAGIC / BIRD

BY
ERIC SIMONSON

STARRING

KEVIN DANIELS   **TUG COKER**
DEIRDRE O'CONNELL   **PETER SCOLARI**
FRANCOIS BATTISTE   **ROBERT MANNING, JR.**

ANNE-MARIE CUSSON   GREGORY JONES   ANTHONY HOLIDAY

SET DESIGN	COSTUME DESIGN	LIGHTING DESIGN	MEDIA DESIGNER
DAVID KORINS	PAUL TAZEWELL	HOWELL BINKLEY	JEFF SUGG

SOUND DESIGN	CASTING	HAIR/WIG DESIGN	DIALECT COACH	TECHNICAL SUPERVISOR
NEVIN STEINBERG	TELSEY + COMPANY	CHARLES G. LAPOINTE	STEPHEN GABIS	DAVID BENKEN

PRESS AND MARKETING	GENERAL MANAGEMENT	PRODUCTION STAGE MANAGER	ADVERTISING	MARKETING OUTREACH
KIRMSER PONTURO GROUP	BESPOKE THEATRICALS	J. PHILIP BASSETT	SPOTCO	WALK TALL GIRL PRODUCTIONS

ASSOCIATE PRODUCERS
RACHEL WEINSTEIN   RICHARD REDMOND & WILLIAM BLOOM

DIRECTED BY
THOMAS KAIL

4/11/12

(L-R): Francois Battiste, Kevin Daniels, Deirdre O'Connell, Peter Scolari, Tug Coker

Photo by Joan Marcus

Magic/Bird

Cast Continued

For Larry Bird, Pat Riley, Red Auerbach,
Jerry Buss, Tom, Bob Woolf:
GREGORY JONES

For Dinah Bird, Patricia Moore,
Shelly, Georgia Bird:
ANNE-MARIE CUSSON

Kevin Daniels
Earvin "Magic" Johnson

Tug Coker
Larry Bird

Deirdre O'Connell
Dinah Bird/Patricia Moore/Shelly/Georgia Bird

Peter Scolari
Pat Riley/Red Auerbach/ Jerry Buss/Tom/Bob Woolf

Francois Battiste
Willy/Bryant Gumbel/ Jon Lennox/ Ron Baxter

Robert Manning, Jr.
Henry Alvarado/ Cedric Maxwell/ Norm Nixon/Frank/ Michael Cooper/Jeff

Anne-Marie Cusson
u/s Dinah Bird/ Patricia Moore/ Shelly/ Georgia Bird

Anthony Holiday
u/s Earvin "Magic" Johnson/Willy/Bryant Gumbel, Jon Lennox, Ron Baxter, et al

Gregory Jones
u/s Larry Bird/ Pat Riley/ Red Auerbach/ Jerry Buss/Tom/ Bob Woolf

Thomas Kail
Director

Eric Simonson
Playwright

David Korins
Scenic Designer

Paul Tazewell
Costume Designer

Howell Binkley
Lighting Designer

Jeff Sugg
Media Design

Charles G. Lapointe
Hair and Wig Design

Stephen Gabis
Dialect Coach

Bernard Telsey
Telsey + Company Casting

David Benken
Technical Supervisor

Maggie Brohn
Bespoke Theatricals General Management

Amy Jacobs
Bespoke Theatricals General Management

Devin Keudell
Bespoke Theatricals General Management

Nina Lannan
Bespoke Theatricals General Management

Fran Kirmser
Producer

Tony Ponturo
Producer

John Mara, Jr.
Producer

Tamara Tunie
Producer

Jeffrey Donovan
Producer

David J. Stern
Commissioner National Basketball Association

FRIENDS OF *MAGIC/BIRD* PRODUCERS

Marty Cargas, Jeff Goodby, Dulé Hill, Earvin "Magic" Johnson, Pamela and Tim Kashani, Tracy Howe and Peter Kraft, Nick Lewin, John Mogur, Bob and Janine Musumeci, David Peacock, James Roday, Lisa Rosenthal, Teri Schindler, Jonathan Tisch, Frank Vuono and Ray Warren.

Magic/Bird
Scrapbook

Correspondent: Tug Coker, "Larry Bird"
Memorable Opening Night Notes: It's wonderful to receive congratulatory notes from the other shows running on Broadway. *Peter and the Starcatcher* sent us a great card saying that "You've been Stached!" but I want to remind them that Larry Bird had a decent "cookie duster" of his own. Getting individual notes from playwright Eric Simonson and director Tommy Kail were notes to cherish.

Opening Night Gifts: Kevin Daniels gave each person in the cast and crew caricature drawings of roles we played in the show. Mine was of me as Larry Bird. I've pretended I was Larry Bird since I was six years old so that's something I'll cherish forever.

Most Exciting Celebrity Visitors: Magic Johnson and Larry Bird both came to opening night. After curtain call, they came on stage and talked about their relationship both on and off court. Then they took a bow with the cast. Seeing Magic and Larry together in the same room is a once-in-a-lifetime moment. No one in the theatre will ever forget that night.

Actor Who Performed the Most Roles in This Show: Didi O'Connell, Francois Battiste, Robert Manning, Jr. and Peter Scolari all played Jackie MacMullan, Michigan State University, Indiana State University, Scientific Mapp, Actors' Equity Association.

STAFF FOR *MAGIC/BIRD*

GENERAL MANAGEMENT
BESPOKE THEATRICALS
Maggie Brohn
Amy Jacobs   Devin Keudell   Nina Lannan
Associate General Manager .... Danielle Saks

COMPANY MANAGER
Doug Gaeta

GENERAL PRESS REPRESENTATIVE
KIRMSER/PONTURO GROUP
Fran Kirmser

PRODUCTION MANAGEMENT
David Benken   Rose Palombo   Martin Pavloff

CASTING
TELSEY + COMPANY
Bernie Telsey CSA, Will Cantler CSA,
David Vaccari CSA, Bethany Knox CSA,
Craig Burns CSA, Tiffany Little Canfield CSA,
Rachel Hoffman CSA, Justin Huff CSA,
Patrick Goodwin CSA, Abbie Brady-Dalton CSA,
David Morris, Cesar A. Rocha, Andrew Femenella,
Karyn Casl, Kristina Bramhall

PRODUCTION STAGE
   MANAGER .... J. PHILIP BASSETT
Stage Manager .... Gregory T. Livoti
Assistant Director .... Patrick Vassel
Dialect Coach .... Stephen Gabis
Original Music .... Nevin Steinberg
Associate Scenic Designer .... Rod Lemmond
Assistant Scenic Designer .... Amanda Stephens
Assistants to the Scenic Designer .... Sarah Muxlow,
                               Emily Inglis
Associate Costume Designer .... Kara Harmon
Associate Lighting Designer .... Ryan O'Gara
Assistant Lighting Designer .... Joe Doran
Associate Sound Designer .... Jason Crystal
Assistant Sound Designers .... Janie Bullard,
                              David Thomas
Associate Media Designer .... Daniel Brodie
Video Programmer .... Patrick Southern
Moving Lights Programmer .... Sean Beach

Production Carpenter/
   Head Carpenter .... David M. Cohen
House Carpenter .... Wilbur Graham
Flyman .... Andre Grey
Advance Rigger .... Jeff Zink
Production Electrician .... Michael LoBue
Head Electrician .... Brent Oakley
House Electrician .... Ric Rogers

Moving Light/Video Technician .... Brian Collins
Production Sound .... Jason Crystal
Sound Engineer .... Nick Borisjuk
Production Properties/
   Head Properties .... Jacob White
House Properties .... John Lofgren
Wardrobe Supervisor .... Susan Checklick
Dressers .... Carrie Kamerer, Paul Ludick
Hair Supervisor .... Amy Neswald
Production Assistants .... Rebecca Spinac,
                              Matthew Lutz

KIRMSER PONTURO GROUP
Production Associates .... Courtney Bottomley,
                              Amanda Zoch
Sports Outreach .... Joe Favorito
Website Design .... Jason Howard
With Special Thanks to .... Jason Marsh

Advertising .... SpotCo/Jim Edwards,
           Drew Hodges, Tom Greenwald,
           Beth Watson, Nora Tillmanns
Comptroller .... Galbraith & Company/
                          Kenny Noth
Accountants .... Robert Fried CPA/
           Fried & Kowgios CPAS, LLP
                   General Management
Associates .... Steve Dow, David Roth,
                              Libby Fox
General Management Interns .... Michelle Heller,
           Jimmy Wilson, Sean Coughlin
Insurance .... Aon/Albert G Ruben,
                      Claudia Kaufman
Banking .... City National Bank/Michele Gibbons
Payroll .... Checks and Balances Payroll Inc.
Travel Agent .... Tzell Travel/
           The "A" Team/Andi Henig
Legal Counsel .... Loeb & Loeb
Merchandising .... Encore Merchandising, Inc./
           Joey Boyles, Elie Berkowitz
Production Photographer .... Joan Marcus

---

www.magicbirdbroadway.com

CREDITS
Donation of official NBA basketballs by Spalding, Inc. Historic video support from NCAA, USOC and USA Basketball. Scenery/automation by PRG Scenic Technologies and Proof Productions. Lighting equipment provided by PRG Lighting. Sound equipment by Masque Sound. Costumes by Sports Studio and Pimp My Kicks.

Magic/Bird rehearsed at Pearl Studios.

SPECIAL THANKS
National Basketball Association,

(L-R): Tug Coker and Kevin Daniels

Photo by Joan Marcus

Magic/Bird
SCRAPBOOK

Curtain call on opening night (L-R): Francois Battiste, *Yearbook* correspondent Tug Coker, Larry Bird, Earvin "Magic" Johnson, Kevin Daniels and Deirdre O'Connell.

multiple roles in the show. Didi and Francois played four. Rob and Peter each played five roles.

Who Has Done the Most Shows in Their Career: I'm guessing Peter Scolari here. He's been working hard since the 1970s.

Special Backstage Rituals: Everyone has their own rituals. At half-hour Kevin Daniels sings while taking a shower. Anything from show tunes to Adele to R Kelly. Stage management and I have our dressing rooms next to the shower and we always play Name That Tune. Didi O'Connell always stretches and warms up in the house before the show. Scolari does an improvisational two-minute phone call each night during the call for "places." Francois Battiste always has to be at the stage-right wing for "places" before I get there.

Favorite Moment During Each Performance: When we make our entrances for the top of the show, they announce our names like the starting lineup for a basketball game. It's really fun for us to give out some high-fives to each other, and it gets the crowd warmed up. I also make a quick costume and wig change in the third scene of the play and come out as the young Larry Bird. I can feel the audience's excitement when they see the flowing blond locks and mustache for the first time.

Favorite In-Theatre Gathering Place: Frankly, it's the stage. Our stage is also a functional basketball court so you can always find us shooting baskets before the show. Pretty fun.

Favorite Off-Site Hangout: We have two: Hurley's and The Glass House Tavern.

Favorite Snack Food: Donuts! I don't how we ended up with donuts, but we seemed to have donuts left in our greenroom all the time. Sometimes they're homemade, sometimes they're store-bought.

Mascot: The Longacre has its own mascot. It's the statue of a dog. For good luck, we stick it in the stage left locker we use during the show. Also, there's quite a bit of Boston Celtics and Los Angeles Lakers gear around the theatre.

Busiest Day at the Box Office: Whatever day it was we could've used a couple more of them.

Favorite Therapy: I personally put on some BenGay before or after the show. I'm not 22 anymore.

Memorable Ad-Lib: It rarely happens. During one particularly odd show, a glass of lemonade was spilled during the lunch. Didi: "Have you two boys prayed?" Me: "We Better." Kevin loved that.

Fastest Costume Change: We all do multiple quick costume changes in the show. Most of us do changes on stage. Kevin does a full costume change out of a Lakers uniform into a sports jacket and slacks while talking to the audience in about 20 seconds.

Cell Phone Rings, Cell Phone Photos or Texting Incidents During a Performance: Our audience has been pretty good, for the most part. We had a phone ring just when Magic announces he's HIV positive. That was unfortunate timing.

Memorable Press Encounter: Kevin and I did a piece in *Sports Illustrated* magazine. We also did a segment for "Sportscenter" on ESPN. To think that you're doing a play, yet talking to a sports channel, is beyond surreal. All my youth I wanted to be an athlete, and here I was on "SPORTSCENTER" at last...for being an actor!

Memorable Stage Door Fan Encounter: It's fun for us to see so many kids and sports fans coming to Broadway for the first time. A lot of people come with sports jerseys of the Lakers, Celtics, Indiana State, Michigan State, which are mentioned a lot in the show. Many times people have come up and said, "This is my first Broadway show." It's amazing to see how people come for the story, discover they love theatre and then want know what else is playing. That's really cool.

Latest Audience Arrival: The ushers tell me they once had arrivals 60 minutes into a 90 minute show. Not the best use of your money.

Catchphrases Only the Company Would Recognize: "Media Media Media." "Where's Peter?" "I love tapework." "Let me find out."

Memorable Directorial Note: Tommy is an amazing director and he is so articulate. To

mention one note wouldn't be fair. He's had hundreds. Plus, he'd always welcome ideas from us, let us try things, and say "Best idea wins." He's just a great person.

Company In-Jokes: "Where's Peter?" "Fourth Quarter!" "Thank you (insert last thing stage manager said)." "Put a dollar in the jar." Rob Manning Jr. laughing in the audience's place.

Company Legends: Peter Scolari has been in show business since he was a teenager. He's got thousands of stories and he loves to tell them. He's also a great impressionist and when he talks about working on previous jobs he loves to use these other voices. We'd just gather 'round and lap it up.

Who Wore the Heaviest/Hottest Costume: We all had to wear layers because of our quick changes. Francois, in particular, had a nice polyester suit with a butterfly collar that he got to rock every night.

Who Wore the Least: I had the pleasure of wearing short shorts through most of the show.

Understudy Anecdote: Our three understudies haven't been able to get on stage for the show, but they are three of the hardest-working actors that I've seen. They have incredible work ethic, great talent, and we appreciate them being ready at a moment's notice.

Nicknames: Francois Battiste is "Franky Bats." Robert Manning, Jr. is "Bobby Bones."

Sweethearts Within the Company: I think everyone is in love with Didi O'Connell.

Embarrassing Moments: Anytime a basketball went askew. Thankfully, that wasn't too often.

Ghostly Encounters Backstage: We've had a few gremlins. We're always grateful when they'd let us just have fun.

Coolest Thing About Being in This Show: Coming to work at the Longacre Theatre every night. Everyone involved with the show is a good egg, and it's been a pleasure to come to work. Broadway is an actor's dream. It's been a joy to make my Broadway debut with this show. The story of Magic Johnson and Larry Bird is a story that should be told, and we all feel very proud to be a part of this journey.

Mamma Mia!

First Preview: October 5, 2001. Opened: October 18, 2001.
Still running as of May 31, 2012.

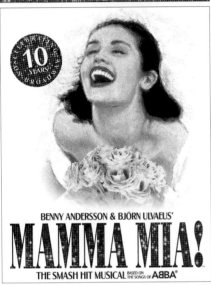

As her wedding approaches, Sophie decides to figure out which among three of her free-spirited mother's ex-lovers is her actual father. So she invites all three men to the wedding without telling mom. Set to the hits of the music group ABBA.

CAST
(in order of speaking)

Sophie Sheridan	LIANA HUNT
Ali	CATHERINE RICAFORT
Lisa	HALLE MORSE
Tanya	JUDY McLANE
Rosie	JENNIFER PERRY
Donna Sheridan	LISA BRESCIA
Sky	JORDAN DEAN
Pepper	JACOB PINION
Eddie	ANDREW CHAPPELLE
Harry Bright	DAVID BEACH
Bill Austin	PATRICK BOLL
Sam Carmichael	JOHN HEMPHILL
Father Alexandrios	BRYAN SCOTT JOHNSON

THE ENSEMBLE

DEANNA AGUINAGA, BRENT BLACK, TIMOTHY BOOTH, NATALIE BRADSHAW, ALLYSON CARR, FELICITY CLAIRE, MARK DANCEWICZ, STACIA FERNANDEZ, COREY GREENAN, BRYAN SCOTT JOHNSON, MONICA KAPOOR, CORINNE MELANÇON, PAUL HEESANG MILLER, GERARD SALVADOR, SHARONE SAYEGH, LAURIE WELLS

WINTER GARDEN

1634 Broadway
 A Shubert Organization Theatre

Philip J. Smith, *Chairman*   Robert E. Wankel, *President*

JUDY CRAYMER, RICHARD EAST AND BJÖRN ULVAEUS
FOR LITTLESTAR IN ASSOCIATION WITH UNIVERSAL

PRESENT

MAMMA MIA!

MUSIC AND LYRICS BY
BENNY ANDERSSON
BJÖRN ULVAEUS
AND SOME SONGS WITH STIG ANDERSON

BOOK BY CATHERINE JOHNSON

PRODUCTION DESIGNED BY
MARK THOMPSON

LIGHTING DESIGNED BY
HOWARD HARRISON

SOUND DESIGNED BY
ANDREW BRUCE &
BOBBY AITKEN

MUSICAL SUPERVISOR, ADDITIONAL MATERIAL
& ARRANGEMENTS
MARTIN KOCH

CHOREOGRAPHY
ANTHONY VAN LAAST

DIRECTED BY
PHYLLIDA LLOYD

2/13/12

(L-R): Judy McLane, Lisa Brescia, Jennifer Perry

Photo by Joan Marcus

Mamma Mia!

MUSICAL NUMBERS

(in alphabetical order)

CHIQUITITA
DANCING QUEEN
DOES YOUR MOTHER KNOW
GIMME! GIMME! GIMME!
HONEY, HONEY
I DO, I DO, I DO, I DO, I DO
I HAVE A DREAM
KNOWING ME, KNOWING YOU
LAY ALL YOUR LOVE ON ME
MAMMA MIA
MONEY, MONEY, MONEY
ONE OF US
OUR LAST SUMMER
SLIPPING THROUGH MY FINGERS
S.O.S.
SUPER TROUPER
TAKE A CHANCE ON ME
THANK YOU FOR THE MUSIC
THE NAME OF THE GAME
THE WINNER TAKES IT ALL
UNDER ATTACK
VOULEZ-VOUS

(L-R): Jacob Pinion, Judy McLane

Photo by Joan Marcus

Cast Continued

UNDERSTUDIES

For Sophie Sheridan:
NATALIE BRADSHAW, FELICITY CLAIRE
For Ali:
NATALIE BRADSHAW, MONICA KAPOOR,
SHARONE SAYEGH
For Lisa:
FELICITY CLAIRE, MONICA KAPOOR,
SHARONE SAYEGH
For Tanya:
STACIA FERNANDEZ,
CORINNE MELANÇON
For Rosie:
STACIA FERNANDEZ, LAURIE WELLS
For Donna Sheridan:
CORINNE MELANÇON, LAURIE WELLS
For Sky:
TONY GONZALEZ, COREY GREENAN
For Pepper:
MARK DANCEWICZ, GERARD SALVADOR
For Eddie:
JON-ERIK GOLDBERG, TONY GONZALEZ,
PAUL HEESANG MILLER
For Harry Bright:
TIMOTHY BOOTH,
BRYAN SCOTT JOHNSON
For Bill Austin:
BRENT BLACK, TIMOTHY BOOTH,
BRYAN SCOTT JOHNSON
For Sam Carmichael:
BRENT BLACK, TIMOTHY BOOTH
For Father Alexandrios:
BRENT BLACK, TIMOTHY BOOTH,
TONY GONZALEZ.

SWINGS

AJ FISHER, JON-ERIK GOLDBERG,
TONY GONZALEZ, LAUREN SAMBATARO,
LEAH ZEPEL

DANCE CAPTAINS

TONY GONZALEZ, JANET ROTHERMEL

PROLOGUE

Three months before the wedding

ACT ONE

The day before the wedding

ACT TWO

The day of the wedding

THE BAND

Music Director/Conductor/Keyboard 1:
ROB PREUSS

Associate Music Director/Keyboard 2:
STEVE MARZULLO

Keyboard 3:
SUE ANSCHUTZ

Keyboard 4:
MYLES CHASE

Guitar 1:
DOUG QUINN

Guitar 2:
JEFF CAMPBELL

Bass:
PAUL ADAMY

Drums:
RAY MARCHICA

Percussion:
DAVID NYBERG

Music Coordinator:
MICHAEL KELLER

Synthesizer Programmer:
NICHOLAS GILPIN

Lisa Brescia
Donna Sheridan

Liana Hunt
Sophie Sheridan

Judy McLane
Tanya

Jennifer Perry
Rosie

John Hemphill
Sam Carmichael

Patrick Boll
Bill Austin

David Beach
Harry Bright

Mamma Mia!

Jordan Dean
Sky

Catherine Ricafort
Ali

Halle Morse
Lisa

Jacob Pinion
Pepper

Andrew Chappelle
Eddie

Deanna Aguinaga
Ensemble

Brent Black
Ensemble

Timothy Booth
Ensemble

Natalie Bradshaw
Ensemble

Allyson Carr
Ensemble

Felicity Claire
Ensemble

Mark Dancewicz
Ensemble

Stacia Fernandez
Ensemble

AJ Fisher
Swing

Jon-Erik Goldberg
Swing

Tony Gonzalez
*Dance Captain,
Swing*

Corey Greenan
Ensemble

Bryan Scott Johnson
*Father Alexandrios,
Ensemble*

Monica Kapoor
Ensemble

Corinne Melançon
Ensemble

Paul HeeSang Miller
Ensemble

Janet Rothermel
Dance Captain

Gerard Salvador
Ensemble

Lauren Sambataro
Swing

Sharone Sayegh
Ensemble

Laurie Wells
Ensemble

Björn Ulvaeus
Music & Lyrics

Benny Andersson
Music & Lyrics

Catherine Johnson
Book

Phyllida Lloyd
Director

Anthony Van Laast,
MBE
Choreographer

Mark Thompson
Production Designer

Howard Harrison
Lighting Designer

Andrew Bruce
Sound Designer

Bobby Aitken
Sound Designer

Mamma Mia!

Martin Koch
*Musical Supervisor;
Additional Material;
Arrangements*

David Holcenberg
*Associate Music
Supervisor*

Nichola Treherne
*Associate
Choreographer*

Martha Banta
Resident Director

Tara Rubin Casting
Casting

David Grindrod
Casting Consultants

Arthur Siccardi
Theatrical Services,
Inc.
Production Manager

Judy Craymer
Producer

Richard East
Producer

Maggie Brohn
Bespoke Theatricals
*General
Management*

Amy Jacobs
Bespoke Theatricals
*General
Management*

Devin Keudell
Bespoke Theatricals
*General
Management*

Nina Lannan
Bespoke Theatricals
*General
Management*

Andrew Treagus
International
Executive Producer

ALUMNI
2011-2012

Meredith Akins
Ensemble

Michelle Dawson
Ensemble

John Dossett
Sam Carmichael

Annie Edgerton
Ensemble

Natalie Gallo
Ensemble

Albert Guerzon
Ensemble

Carol Linnea
Johnson
Ensemble

Alison Luff
Ensemble

Michael Mindlin
Pepper

Ryan Sander
Swing

Allison Strong
Ensemble

Clarke Thorell
Harry Bright

Blake Whyte
Ensemble

TRANSFER
STUDENTS
2011-2012

Annie Edgerton
Ensemble

Eric Giancola
Swing

Jennifer Noth
Ensemble

Ryan Sander
*Dance Captain,
Swing*

Leah Zepel
Swing

Mamma Mia!

Photos by Brian Mapp

COMPANY MANAGEMENT, STAGE MANAGEMENT, CREW

Front Row (L-R): Don Lawrence, Reginald Carter, Ryan Conway, Art Soyk, Tony Magner, Michael Maloney

Back Row (L-R): Dean R. Greer, Sherry Cohen, Michael Pule, Stephen Burns, Francis Lofgren, John Maloney

DOORMAN
Michael Bosch

WARDROBE & HAIR
Front Row (L-R): Carey Bertini, Irene L. Bunis, Rodd Sovar

Back Row (L-R): Art Soyk, Douglas Couture, Vickey Walker

Mamma Mia!

Photos by Brian Mapp

FRONT OF HOUSE
Bottom Step (L-R): Dennis Marion, Marc Bonanni

Second Step (L-R): Chris Gizzi, Rose Ann Cipriano

Third Step (L-R): Michael Cleary, Craig Dawson, Mike Lanza

Fourth Step (L-R): Pep Speed, David Christensen, Patrick Roberts

Top Step (L-R): Devin Elting, Elizabeth Reed, James Rees, unidentified

CAST
Front Row (L-R): John Hemphill, Lisa Brescia, Liana Hunt, Patrick Boll, Jennifer Perry

Second Row (L-R): Natalie Bradshaw, Gerard Salvador, David Beach, Jacob Pinion, Jon-Erik Goldberg, Judy McLane

Third Row (L-R): Laurie Wells, Paul HeeSang Miller, Felicity Claire, Bryan Scott Johnson, Corinne Melançon, AJ Fisher, Deanna Aguinaga

Back Row (L-R): Timothy Booth, Tony Gonzalez, Andrew Chappelle, Allyson Carr, Halle Morse, Lauren Sambataro, Catherine Ricafort

---

In loving memory of Daniel McDonald, a cast member of the *Mamma Mia!* Broadway Company 2004-2005.

LITTLESTAR SERVICES LIMITED

Directors ....Judy Craymer
Richard East
Benny Andersson
Björn Ulvaeus

International Executive Producer ....Andrew Treagus
Business & Finance Director ....Ashley Grisdale
Administrator....................................Peter Austin
PA to Judy Craymer ....Katie Wolfryd
Marketing & Communications Manager ....Claire Teare
Head of Accounts ....Jo Reedman
Accountant ....Sheila Egbujie
Administrative Assistant ....Matthew Willis

Receptionist ....Kimberley Wallwork
Legal Services.......................................Barry Shaw
Howard Jones at Sheridans
Production Insurance Services ....W & P Longreach
Business Manager for
Benny Andersson and
Björn Ulvaeus &
Scandinavian Press ....Görel Hanser

Mamma Mia!

ANDREW TREAGUS ASSOCIATES LIMITED

General Manager ....Philip Effemey
International Manager ....Mark Whittemore
PA to Andrew Treagus ....Jacki Harding
International Travel Manager ....Lindsay Jones
Production Coordinator ....Felicity White

EXECUTIVE PRODUCER ....**NINA LANNAN**

GENERAL MANAGEMENT
BESPOKE THEATRICALS
Devin Keudell
Maggie Brohn   Amy Jacobs   Nina Lannan

COMPANY MANAGER ......J. ANTHONY MAGNER
Associate Company Manager ....Ryan Conway

PRODUCTION TEAM
ASSOCIATE
    CHOREOGRAPHER ....NICHOLA TREHERNE
DANCE SUPERVISOR ....JANET ROTHERMEL
RESIDENT DIRECTOR ....MARTHA BANTA
ASSOCIATE
    MUSIC SUPERVISOR ......DAVID HOLCENBERG
ASSOCIATE
    SCENIC DESIGNER (US) ....NANCY THUN
ASSOCIATE
    SCENIC DESIGNER (UK) .....JONATHAN ALLEN
ASSOCIATE
    COSTUME DESIGNERS ....LUCY GAIGER
                                SCOTT TRAUGOTT
ASSOCIATE HAIR DESIGNER ...JOSH MARQUETTE
ASSOCIATE
    LIGHTING DESIGNERS ....DAVID HOLMES
                                ED MCCARTHY
                                ANDREW VOLLER
ASSOCIATE SOUND
    DESIGNERS ....BRIAN BUCHANAN
                                DAVID PATRIDGE
MUSICAL TRANSCRIPTION ......ANDERS NEGLIN
CASTING CONSULTANT ....DAVID GRINDROD

CASTING
TARA RUBIN CASTING
Tara Rubin CSA, Eric Woodall CSA,
Laura Schutzel CSA, Merri Sugarman CSA,
Dale Brown CSA,
Kaitlin Shaw, Lindsay Levine

PRESS REPRESENTATIVE
BONEAU/BRYAN-BROWN
Adrian Bryan-Brown   Joe Perrotta
Kelly Guiod

ADVERTISING AND MARKETING
SERINO COYNE INC.
Nancy Coyne   Greg Coradetti
Advertising ....Kim Hewski, Matt Upshaw,
                                Lauren Houlberg
Marketing ....Leslie Barrett, Diana Salameh,
                                Mike Rafael

**MUSIC PUBLISHED BY EMI GROVE PARK MUSIC, INC.
AND EMI WATERFORD MUSIC, INC.**

STAFF FOR MAMMA MIA!
PRODUCTION STAGE MANAGER SHERRY COHEN
Stage Managers ....Dean R. Greer, Michael Pule

PRODUCTION MANAGER .....ARTHUR SICCARDI

Head Carpenter ....Chris Nass
Assistant Carpenters ....Stephen Burns,
                                Clark Middleton
Production Electrician ....Rick Baxter
Head Electrician ....Don Lawrence
Assistant Electrician ....Andy Sather
Vari*Lite Programmer ....Andrew Voller
Production Sound ....David Patridge
Head Sound ....Craig Cassidy
Assistant Sound ....Colin Ahearn
Production Properties ....Simon E.R. Evans
Head Properties ....Gregory Martin
Wardrobe Supervisor ....Irene L. Bunis
Assistant Wardrobe ....Ron Glow
Dressers ....Carey Bertini, Jim Collum,
                                Lauren Kievit, Douglas Couture,
                                Jill Heller, Christine Richmond,
                                Rodd Sovar, I Wang
Hair Supervisor ....Sandy Schlender
Assistant Hair Supervisor ....Vickey Walker
Assistant Lighting Designer ....Jeffrey Lowney
Assistant Costume Designer ....Robert J. Martin
House Crew ....Richard Carney, Reginald Carter,
                                Holly Hanson, Mai-Linh Lofgren,
                                Meredith Kievit, Aarne Lofgren,
                                Francis Lofgren, John Maloney,
                                Michael Maloney, Glenn Russo,
                                Dennis Wiener
Rehearsal Pianist ....Sue Anschutz
Box Office ....Mary Cleary, Lee Cobb,
                                Steve Cobb, James Drury, Sue Giebler,
                                Bob McCaffrey, Ron Schroeder
Associates to Casting Consultant ....Stephen Crockett,
                                Will Burton
Legal Counsel (U.S.) ....Lazarus & Harris LLP
                                Scott Lazarus, Esq.
                                Robert Harris, Esq.
Immigration Counsel ....Mark D. Koestler/
                                Kramer Levin Naftalis & Frankel LLP
Accounting ....Rosenberg, Neuwirth and Kuchner/
                                Chris Cacace, In Woo
Interactive Marketing ....Situation Interactive/
                                Damian Bazadona, John Lanasa,
                                Maris Smith, Mollie Shapiro
Press Office Staff ....Chris Boneau, Jim Byk,
                                Jackie Green, Linnae Hodzic,
                                Jessica Johnson, Amy Kass, Holly Kinney,
                                Kevin Jones, Emily Meagher,
                                Aaron Meier, Christine Olver,
                                Matthew Polk, Heath Schwartz,
                                Michael Strassheim, Susanne Tighe
Production Photographer ....Joan Marcus
Merchandising ....Max Merchandise, LLC/
                                Randi Grossman, Meridith Maskara
                                Merchandising Manager: Marc Bonanni
Theater Displays ....King Display
Insurance ....Dewitt, Stern/
                                Walton & Parkinson Ltd.
Orthopedic Consultant ....Dr. Philip Bauman
Banking...............................City National Bank
Travel Agent ....Tzell Travel

Original Logo Design ....© Littlestar Services Limited

CREDITS AND ACKNOWLEDGMENTS
Scenery constructed and painted by Hudson Scenic Studio, Inc. and Hamilton Scenic Specialty. Computer motion control and automation by Feller Precision, Inc. SHOWTRAK computer motion control for scenery and rigging. Sound equipment supplied by Masque Sound. Lighting equipment supplied by Fourth Phase and Vari*Lite, Inc. Soft goods by I. Weiss and Sons. Costumes by Barbara Matera, Ltd., Tricorne New York City and Carelli Costumes, Inc. Additional costume work by Allan Alberts Productions. Millinery by Lynn Mackey. Wet suits by Aquatic Fabricators of South Florida. Custom men's shirts by Cego. Custom knitting by C.C. Wei. Custom fabric printing and dyeing by Dye-namix and Gene Mignola. Shoes by Native Leather, Rilleau Leather and T. O. Dey. Gloves by Cornelia James - London. Hair color by Redken. Properties by Paragon Theme and Prop Fabrication. Cough drops provided by Ricola U.S.A. Physical therapy provided by Sean Gallagher. Drums provided by Pearl. Cymbals provided by Zildjian. Drumsticks provided by Vic Firth. Drum heads provided by Remo.

Mamma Mia! was originally produced in London by LITTLESTAR SERVICES LIMITED on April 6, 1999.

Experience *Mamma Mia!* around the world:
London/Prince of Wales Theatre/mamma-mia.com
Broadway/Winter Garden Theatre/telecharge.com
North American Tour/ticketmaster.com
International Tour/mamma-mia.com
For more information on all our
global productions visit: www.mamma-mia.com

Energy-efficient washer/dryer courtesy of
LG Electronics.

 THE SHUBERT ORGANIZATION, INC.

Board of Directors

Philip J. Smith   **Robert E. Wankel**
Chairman   President

Wyche Fowler, Jr.   **Diana Phillips**

Lee J. Seidler   **Michael I. Sovern**

Stuart Subotnick

Chief Financial Officer ....Elliot Greene
Sr. Vice President, Ticketing ....David Andrews
Vice President, Finance ....Juan Calvo
Vice President, Human Resources ....Cathy Cozens
Vice President, Facilities ....John Darby
Vice President, Theatre Operations ....Peter Entin
Vice President, Marketing ....Charles Flateman
Vice President, Audit ....Anthony LaMattina
Vice President, Ticket Sales ....Brian Mahoney
Vice President, Creative Projects ............D.S. Moynihan
Vice President, Real Estate ....Julio Peterson

House Manager ....Patricia Berry

Mamma Mia!
SCRAPBOOK

Correspondent: Lisa Brescia, "Donna Sheridan"

Milestone Celebration: In October 2011, *Mamma Mia!* celebrated its tenth anniversary on Broadway. Mayor Bloomberg started things off by pronouncing October 18, 2011 "*Mamma Mia!* Day" in New York City. The performance itself felt like an opening night, without the pressures of pending reviews; the electrifying energy from the audience was palpable. After the performance, we invited the audience to join us outside, in front of the Winter Garden, where we performed an encore of the finale, complete with a laser light show and fireworks. I could sense how honored and proud we all felt to be a part of the *Mamma Mia!* company that night. The lavish party afterwards wasn't too shabby either. We all had a blast.

Memorable Fan Letter: Louise Pitre (the Tony-nominated actress who originated the role of Donna Sheridan in *Mamma Mia!*) saw the show on October 18, 2011, and sent a generous letter to the company afterwards. She was generously effusive and complimentary, and proved that her reputation as a very classy lady is spot-on.

Most Exciting Celebrity Visitors: Every December, there is a holiday door decorating competition at the theatre. Every dressing room door is decorated to the hilt, and it's taken very seriously. Celebrity judges come to judge the doors and present the prizes. In 2011, Patti LuPone and Mandy Patinkin showed up, and couldn't have been more generous, kind and down-to-earth. They were enthusiastic and ready for anything. At the end of the event, Mandy said: "I didn't know what I was walking into tonight, but after meeting all of you, I cannot wait to work with a company like yours again." And I understand his sentiment; this just might be the happiest bunch on Broadway.

Gypsy of the Year Skit: "_____!" written by the company.

Favorite Moment During Each Performance: "Money Money Money" in Act I. It's the first moment where the entire company is on stage where we can experience each other as an ensemble. Also the staging is fantastic, and I personally love the song.

Favorite In-Theatre Gathering Place: Birthdays and Happy Trails celebrations take place in the greenroom, where there has been much laughter and many tears shed.

Favorite Off-Site Hangout: Reflections Yoga on West 49th Street.

Favorite Therapy: Yoga. Without it, my body and my mind would be a collective hot mess.

Memorable Ad-Lib: John Hemphill (who plays Sam) got a little lost while saying a line during the wedding. We still don't know what he said, or if it made any sense. He was, however, heroic in his efforts to articulate something in the English language. Hilarious.

Memorable Stage Door Fan Encounter: I had a man propose to me. I flashed him my wedding ring, then when he pressed on, I laughingly said: "Back off Buster!" Buster? Who says "Buster"?

Fastest Costume Change: In the wedding, when I change from a pink dress to a white one, and a veil. It's lightning quick. No room for error.

Catchphrases Only the Company Would Recognize: "Go Team!" and "Doing it!"

Sweetheart of the Company: Jen Perry, who is a mommy at home and a natural caregiver. She lives and loves so expansively that one can't help but learn from her.

Coolest Thing About Being in This Show: The joy that we can see in the audience's faces during the finale, when we finally get to interact directly with them. They're beaming.

1. On hand to light the top of the Empire State Building Oct. 18, 2011 to mark the show's tenth anniversary (L-R): Jennifer Perry, Judy McLane and *Yearbook* correspondent Lisa Brescia.
2. Members of the cast perform as part of the "Broadway Belt-Off" competition.
3. Perry, Brescia and McLane.
4. Brescia at her make-up table prepares for an evening performance.

Man and Boy

First Preview: September 9, 2011. Opened: October 9, 2011.
Closed November 27 after 35 Previews and 57 Performances.

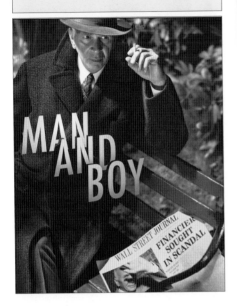

Timely revival of Rattigan's 1963 drama about an international financier who struggles to keep his longstanding Ponzi scheme from collapsing around him, while ignoring the effect his ruthless tactics are having on his wife and son.

CAST

(in order of appearance)

Carol Penn	Virginia Kull
Basil Anthony	Adam Driver
Sven Johnson	Michael Siberry
Gregor Antonescu	Frank Langella
Mark Herries	Zach Grenier
David Beeston	Brian Hutchison
Countess Antonescu	Francesca Faridany

Place: A basement apartment in
Greenwich Village, New York
Time: The time is continuous, roughly between
6 p.m. and 8:30 p.m. on an autumn night in 1934.

UNDERSTUDIES

For Sven Johnson and Mark Herries:
JOHN HICKOK
For Basil Anthony and David Beeston:
VAYU O'DONNELL
For Carol Penn and Countess Antonescu:
ALLISON JEAN WHITE

Production Stage Manager: NEVIN HEDLEY
Stage Manager: BRYCE McDONALD

AMERICAN AIRLINES THEATRE

ROUNDABOUTTHEATRECOMPANY

Todd Haimes, Artistic Director
Harold Wolpert, Managing Director
Julia C. Levy, Executive Director

Presents

Frank Langella

in

MAN AND BOY

By

Terence Rattigan

with

Adam Driver   Francesca Faridany   Zach Grenier
Brian Hutchison   Virginia Kull   Michael Siberry

Set Design	*Costume Design*	*Lighting Design*	*Original Music & Sound Design*
Derek McLane	Martin Pakledinaz	Kevin Adams	John Gromada

Hair & Wig Design	*Dialect Coach*	*Production Stage Manager*	*Production Management*
Paul Huntley	Stephen Gabis	Nevin Hedley	Aurora Productions

Casting by	*General Manager*	*Press Representative*
Jim Carnahan, C.S.A. & Kate Boka, C.S.A.	Denise Cooper	Boneau/Bryan-Brown

Associate Managing Director	*Director of Marketing & Sales Promotion*	*Director of Development*	*Founding Director*	*Associate Artistic Director*
Greg Backstrom	David B. Steffen	Lynne Gugenheim Gregory	Gene Feist	Scott Ellis

Directed by

Maria Aitken

Major support for *Man and Boy* provided by The Blanche and Irving Laurie Foundation.

Roundabout Theatre Company is a member of the League of Resident Theatres.
www.roundabouttheatre.org

10/3/11

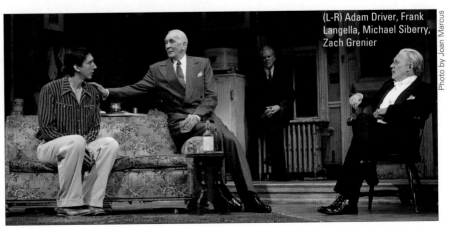

(L-R) Adam Driver, Frank Langella, Michael Siberry, Zach Grenier

Photo by Joan Marcus

225

Man and Boy

Frank Langella
Gregor Antonescu

Adam Driver
Basil Anthony

Francesca Faridany
Countess Antonescu

Zach Grenier
Mark Herries

Brian Hutchison
David Beeston

Virginia Kull
Carol Penn

Michael Siberry
Sven Johnson

John Hickok
Voice of Radio Announcer

Vayu O'Donnell
u/s Basil Anthony, David Beeston

Allison Jean White
u/s Carol Penn, Countess Antonescu

Terence Rattigan
Playwright

Maria Aitken
Director

Derek McLane
Set Design

Martin Pakledinaz
Costume Design

Kevin Adams
Lighting Design

John Gromada
Original Music and Sound Design

Stephen Gabis
Dialect Coach

Paul Huntley
Hair and Wig Designer

Joe Dulude II
Makeup Designer

Jim Carnahan
Casting

Gene Feist
Roundabout Theatre Company
Founding Director

Todd Haimes
Roundabout Theatre Company
Artistic Director

Photos by Brian Mapp

CREW
(L-R): Brian Maiuri, Dann Wojnar, Hannah Overton, Glenn Merwede, Robert Dowling II

BOX OFFICE
(L-R): Ted Osborne, Mead Margulies

Man and Boy

WARDROBE
(L-R): Susan Fallon, Dale Carman, Kat Martin, Vangeli Kaseluris

Photos by Brian Mapp

FRONT OF HOUSE
(L-R): Alvin Vega, Maria Graves, Christopher Busch, Crystal Suarez

MANAGEMENT
(L-R): Nevin Hedley, Carly DiFulvio, Bryce McDonald, Kristen Torgrimson

HAIR
Manuela LaPorte

ROUNDABOUT THEATRE COMPANY STAFF
ARTISTIC DIRECTOR ....TODD HAIMES
MANAGING DIRECTOR ....HAROLD WOLPERT
EXECUTIVE DIRECTOR ....JULIA C. LEVY
ASSOCIATE ARTISTIC DIRECTOR ...SCOTT ELLIS

ARTISTIC STAFF
DIRECTOR OF ARTISTIC DEVELOPMENT/
  DIRECTOR OF CASTING ....Jim Carnahan
Artistic Consultant ....Robyn Goodman
Resident Director ....Doug Hughes
Associate Artists ....Mark Brokaw, Scott Elliott, Sam Gold,
  Bill Irwin, Joe Mantello, Kathleen Marshall, Theresa Rebeck
Literary Manager ....Jill Rafson
Senior Casting Director......................Carrie Gardner
Casting Director ....Stephen Kopel
Casting Associate ....Jillian Cimini
Casting Assistant ....Michael Morlani
Artistic Assistant ....Amy Ashton
Literary Associate ....Josh Fiedler
The Blanche and Irving Laurie Foundation
  Theatre Visions Fund Commissions ...David West Read,
                                      Nathan Louis Jackson
Educational Foundation of
  America Commissions ....Bekah Brunstetter,
                          Lydia Diamond, Diana Fithian,
                                      Julie Marie Myatt

New York State Council
  on the Arts Commission ....Nathan Louis Jackson
Roundabout Commissions ....Steven Levenson,
                          Matthew Lopez, Kim Rosenstock
Casting Interns ....Nick Gereffi, Rebecca Henning,
                          Nathan Lehman, Krystal Rowley
Script Readers ....Jay Cohen, Ben Izzo,
                          Alexis Roblan, Nicholas Stimler
Artistic Apprentice ....Joshua M. Feder

EDUCATION STAFF
EDUCATION DIRECTOR ....Greg McCaslin
Associate Education Director ....Jennifer DiBella
Education Program Manager ....Aliza Greenberg
Education Program Associate ....Sarah Malone
Education Assistant ....Holly Sansom
Education Dramaturg ....Ted Sod
Teaching Artists ....Josh Allen, Cynthia Babak,
                          Victor Barbella, LaTonya Borsay,
                  Mark Bruckner, Eric C. Dente, Joe Doran,
              Elizabeth Dunn-Ruiz, Carrie Ellman-Larsen,
          Deanna Frieman, Sheri Graubert, Melissa Gregus,
              Adam Gwon, Devin Haqq, Carrie Heitman,
              Karla Hendrick, Jason Jacobs, Alana Jacoby,
          Lisa Renee Jordan, Jamie Kalama, Alvin Keith,
          Erin McCready, James Miles, Nick Moore,
          Meghan O'Neil, Nicole Press, Leah Reddy,

Amanda Rehbein, Nick Simone, Joe Skowronski,
              Heidi Stallings, Daniel Sullivan, Carl Tallent,
          Vickie Tanner, Laurine Towler, Jennifer Varbalow, Leese
                  Walker, Gail Winar, Chad Yarborough
Teaching Artist Emeritus ....Reneé Flemings
Education Apprentice ....Kimberley Oria

EXECUTIVE ADMINISTRATIVE STAFF
ASSOCIATE MANAGING
  DIRECTOR...........................Greg Backstrom
Assistant Managing Director ....Katharine Croke
Assistant to the Managing Director ....Zachary Baer
Assistant to the Executive Director ....Nicole Tingir

MANAGEMENT/ADMINISTRATIVE STAFF
GENERAL MANAGER ....Sydney Beers
General Manager,
  American Airlines Theatre ....Denise Cooper
General Manager, Steinberg Center ....Rachel E. Ayers
Human Resources Director ....Stephen Deutsch
Operations Manager ....Valerie D. Simmons
Associate General Manager ....Maggie Cantrick
Office Manager ....Scott Kelly
Archivist ....Tiffany Nixon
Receptionists ....Dee Beider, Emily Frohnhoefer,
                          Elisa Papa, Allison Patrick
Messenger ....Darnell Franklin

Man and Boy

Management Apprentice ....Christine Pezzello

FINANCE STAFF

DIRECTOR OF FINANCE.................Susan Neiman
Payroll Director ....John LaBarbera
Accounts Payable Manager ....Frank Surdi
Payroll Benefits Administrator ....Yonit Kafka
Manager Financial Reporting ....Joshua Cohen
Business Office Assistant ....Jackie Verbitski

DEVELOPMENT STAFF

DIRECTOR OF
  DEVELOPMENT ....Lynne Gugenheim Gregory
Assistant to the
  Director of Development ....Liz Malta
Director, Institutional Giving ....Liz S. Alsina
Director, Individual Giving ....Christopher Nave
Director, Special Events ....Steve Schaeffer
Associate Director, Individual Giving ....Tyler Ennis
Manager, Telefundraising ....Gavin Brown
Manager, Corporate Relations.................Sohyun Kim
Manager, Friends of Roundabout ....Marisa Perry
Manager, Donor Information Systems ....Lise Speidel
Special Events Associate ....Natalie Corr
Individual Giving Officer.....................Joseph Foster
Individual Giving Officer.............Sophia Hinshelwood
Institutional Giving Assistant ....Brett Barbour
Development Assistant ....Martin Giannini
Special Events Assistant ....Amy Rosenfield
Development Apprentice ....Julie Erhart
Special Events Apprentice.................Genevieve Carroll

INFORMATION TECHNOLOGY STAFF

IT DIRECTOR ....Antonio Palumbo
IT Associates ....Jim Roma, Cary Kim
DIRECTOR DATABASE
  OPERATIONS.........................Wendy Hutton
Database Administrator/Programmer ....Revanth Anne

MARKETING STAFF

DIRECTOR OF MARKETING
  AND SALES PROMOTION ....David B. Steffen
Associate Director of Marketing ....Tom O'Connor
Senior Marketing Manager ....Shannon Marcotte
Marketing Associate ....Eric Emch
Marketing Assistant ....Bradley Sanchez
Web Producer ....Mark Cajigao
Website Consultant ....Keith Powell Beyland
Director of Telesales
  Special Promotions.........................Marco Frezza
Telesales Manager ....Patrick Pastor
Marketing Apprentices.........................Julie Boor,
    Bethany Nothstein

TICKET SERVICES STAFF

DIRECTOR OF
  SALES OPERATIONS ....Charlie Garbowski, Jr.
Ticket Services Manager ....Ellen Holt
Subscription Manager ....Bill Klemm
Box Office Managers ....Edward P. Osborne,
    Jaime Perlman, Krystin MacRitchie,
    Nicole Nicholson
Group Sales Manager ....Jeff Monteith
Assistant Box Office Managers ....Robert Morgan,
    Joseph Clark, Andrew Clements,
    Catherine Fitzpatrick
Assistant Ticket Services Managers ....Robert Kane,

Lindsay Ericson,
    Jessica Pruett-Barnett
Customer Services Coordinator ....Thomas Walsh
Ticket Services ....Solangel Bido, Arianna Boykins,
    Michael Bultman, Lauren Cartelli,
    Adam Elsberry, Joe Gallina,
    James Graham, Kara Harrington,
    Lindsay Hoffman, Nicki Ishmael,
    Kiah Johnson, Kate Longosky,
    Michelle Maccarone, Mead Margulies,
    Laura Marshall, Kenneth Martinez,
    Chuck Migliaccio, Carlos Morris,
    Kaia Rafoss, Josh Rozett,
    Ben Schneider, Heather Siebert,
    Nalane Singh, Lillian Soto, Ron Tobia,
    Michael Valentine, Paula Weaver,
    Hannah Weitzman, Devon Yates
Ticket Services Apprentice ....Jennifer Almgreen

SERVICES

Counsel ....Paul, Weiss,
    Rifkind, Wharton and Garrison LLP,
    Charles H. Googe Jr., Carol M. Kaplan
Counsel ....Rosenberg & Estis
Counsel ....Andrew Lance,
    Gibson, Dunn, & Crutcher, LLP
Counsel ....Harry H. Weintraub,
    Glick and Weintraub, P.C.
Counsel ....Stroock & Stroock & Lavan LLP
Counsel ....Daniel S. Dokos
    Weil, Gotshal & Manges LLP
Counsel ....Claudia Wagner/
    Manatt, Phelps & Phillips, LLP
Immigration Counsel ....Mark D. Koestler and
    Theodore Ruthizer
House Physicians ....Dr. Theodore Tyberg,
    Dr. Lawrence Katz
House Dentist ....Neil Kanner, D.M.D.
Insurance ....DeWitt Stern Group, Inc.
Accountant ....Lutz & Carr CPAs, LLP
Advertising ....Spotco/
    Drew Hodges, Jim Edwards,
    Tom Greenwald, Kyle Hall, Josh Fraenkel
Interactive Marketing ....Situation Interactive/
    Damian Bazadona, John Lanasa,
    Eric Bornemann, Mollie Shapiro
Events Photography ....Anita and Steve Shevett
Production Photographer ....Joan Marcus
Theatre Displays ....King Displays, Wayne Sapper
Lobby Refreshments.....................Sweet Concessions
Merchandising ....Spotco Merch/
    James Decker

MANAGING DIRECTOR
  EMERITUS ....Ellen Richard

Roundabout Theatre Company
231 West 39th Street, New York, NY 10018
(212) 719-9393.

GENERAL PRESS REPRESENTATIVE

BONEAU/BRYAN-BROWN
Adrian Bryan-Brown
Matt Polk   Jessica Johnson   Amy Kass

STAFF FOR *MAN AND BOY*

Company Manager ....Carly DiFulvio

Production Stage Manager ....Nevin Hedley
Stage Manager ....Bryce McDonald
Production Management by ...... Aurora Productions Inc./
    Gene O'Donovan, Ben Heller,
    Stephanie Sherline, Jarid Sumner,
    Liza Luxenberg, Anita Shah, Rebecca Zuber,
    Steven Dalton, Eugenio Saenz Flores,
    Isaac Katzanek, Melissa Mazdra
Assistant Director ...........................G.D. Kimble
Make-Up Designer ....Joe Dulude II
Associate Scenic Designer ....Shoko Kambara
Assistant Scenic Designer ....Erica Hemminger
Associate Costume Designer ....Matthew Pachtman
Assistant Lighting Designer ....Pete Bragg
Assistant Sound Designer ....Matthew Walsh
Production Properties Supervisor ....Peter Sarafin
Assistant Production Properties ....Matt Hodges
Production Carpenter ....Glenn Merwede
Production Electrician ....Brian Maiuri
Running Properties ....Robert W. Dowling II
Sound Operator ....Dann Wojnar
Wardrobe Supervisor ....Susan J. Fallon
Dressers ....Vangeli Kaseluris, Kat Martin
Wardrobe Dayworker ....Dale Carman
Hair and Wig Supervisor ....Manuela Laporte
Production Assistant ....Kristen Torgrimson
Assistant to Mr. Langella ....Joshua Pilote

CREDITS

Scenery fabrication by Hudson Scenic Studio, Inc. Lighting
equipment by PRG Lighting. Sound equipment by Sound
Associates. Menswear by Artur & Tailors, Ltd. Women's
clothing by Tricorne, Inc. Custom footwear by LaDuca
Shoes. Additional fabrication by Daedalus Design and
Production. Custom jewelry by Larry Vrba. Special thanks
to Early Halloween Vintage, Helen Uffner Vintage Clothing
LLC, Alissa Vintage Clothing and Barbara Kennedy
Vintage. Special thanks to Bra*Tenders for hosiery and
undergarments.

M•A•C Cosmetics
Official Makeup of Roundabout Theatre Company

AMERICAN AIRLINES THEATRE STAFF

Company Manager ....Carly DiFulvio
House Carpenter ....Glenn Merwede
House Electrician ....Brian Maiuri
House Properties.....................Robert W. Dowling II
House Sound ....Dann Wojnar
IA Apprentice ....Hannah Overton
Wardrobe Supervisor ....Susan J. Fallon
Box Office Manager ....Ted Osborne
Assistant Box Office Manager ....Robert Morgan
House Manager ....Stephen Ryan
Associate House Manager ....Zipporah Aguasvivas
Head Usher ....Crystal Suarez
House Staff ....Lance Andrade, Christopher Busch,
    Jeanne Coutant, Anne Ezell,
    Denise Furbert, Maria Graves, Lee Henry,
    Rebecca Knell, Taylor Martin, Enrika Nicholas,
    Jazmine Perez, Celia Torres
Security ....Julious Russell
Additional Security provided by ....Gotham Security
Maintenance ....Jerry Hobbs, Daniel Pellew,
    Magali Western
Lobby Refreshments ....Sweet Concessions

Man and Boy
SCRAPBOOK

Bows on opening night (L-R): Brian Hutchison, Francesca Faridany, Adam Driver, Frank Langella, Michael Siberry, *Yearbook* Correspondent Zach Grenier and Virginia Kull.

Correspondent: Zach Grenier, "Mark Herries"

Life Backstage: Our play took place in the 1930s. We did several things to set the scene, not just for the audience, but for the actors as well. John Gromada's original music put the play in the '30s context and helped the actors get inside the heads of the characters. That was very important. We also had a marvelous stage manager, Nevin Hedley, whose loudspeaker announcements sounded like they came from way back when: "Ladies and gentlemen, it's come to this: It's half hour!" When we got to "places," we'd hear, "First Act beginners - to your places...." You felt like you were at a Manhattan dance hall in 1933. Something very charming about that. It fit the style and time of the play. Nevin is a wonderful ringmaster. The company consisted of professional, skilled, talented and congenial people. We had a lot of fun together.

Memorable Opening Night Note: There were so many people at the opening night party, and I saw only a few. I hunkered down at a table with my wife and a couple we're very close to, who often attend my openings. I found out that Bill Irwin was there—I think very highly of him. He sent a note the next week. He's a class act. Next opening, I'll try to mix more.

Opening Night Gifts: The traditional bottle of champagne from my agents. Frank Langella gave me a wallet—a fitting gift from his character, Gregor Antonescu. Frank said, "Perhaps I should have put a dollar in there." No need, Frank. Awfully nice wallet.

Who Has Done the Most Shows in Their Career: Frank, probably. Michael Siberry has performed all over the world; he has an extraordinary resume that includes the title role in the revival of *Nicholas Nickleby*. He's one of the great Broadway stalwarts.

Special Backstage Rituals: Brian Hutchison and I knocked fists before each and every performance. Adam had a banshee cry that he howled when places were called—you heard it up the stairs as he came tumbling down. Youthful glee coursing through his veins, it put us in the right mood.

Favorite Moment During Each Performance: My one scene in Act I with Frank. It's sort of a one-act play nestled into the action, with its own exposition and arc. It changed each night, as the audience is always a little different. Sometimes they responded to one aspect of it, sometimes another. I've never played a character who is only in the First Act. What do you do with yourself for the Second Act? There were three of us in the same boat: Brian Hutchison, Virginia Kull and myself. We played cards, sometimes had in-depth discussions about this or that. Frank was always pretending to shoo us away: "Now all of you First Act people go away, we have a Second Act to do!" At least I *think* he was pretending.

Favorite In-Theatre Gathering Place: The Roundabout has this tradition: in the greenroom before the Sunday matinees, when a show is up and running, Susan Fallon, our wardrobe mistress, acts as the master of ceremonies, and makes incredible breakfasts. It's like a family brunch.

Favorite Off-Site Hangout: I was always ripping my costume off to make the train to New Jersey, but there was a standing invite on the call board for "Thirsty Thursdays" at the Rosie O'Grady's on 46th Street.

Favorite Snack Food: The Roundabout often shared goodies from the functions upstairs. Frank was very generous. All through rehearsals and performances, he'd have his driver stop and get bagels, or tiny pizzas, or lavender shortbread and lay it out for us in the greenroom area.

Mascot: I'll say Company Manager Carly DiFulvio's miniature Australian shepherd.

Favorite Therapy: Francesca Faridany, who played Countess Antonescu, turned me on to Green Symphony, a health food shop just across from the stage door on 43rd Street, run by an absolute wizard—the Medicine Man of Broadway. He has all these concoctions. Tell him your malady and he'll make you the proper healthy shake. I'd been building a deck at my house and had a bit of heat stroke. He made me an oregano oil and honey mixture that helped set me right.

Understudy Anecdotes: Adam Driver went off to do the film *Lincoln* for a few days. His cover, Vayu O'Donnell, did a fantastic job. I was out for a couple of days, and John Hickok covered. I heard he was splendid. Allison Jean White covered the women. These were all tough roles, and they knew them all, ready to perform in a pinch. Covers and swings are unsung heroes in our business.

Cell Phone Rings, Cell Phone Photos or Texting Incidents During a Performance: It's always terrible, and it will never end. There's nothing to do but confiscate all phones before people enter the theatre, but that will never happen. So it's just something you have to live with. The worst times are when people answer the phone and start to have conversations while the show is going on, which proves that true dunderheads attend the theatre. You might hear, "Yes, I'm in the theatre now!" Thanks for the update! It happens so often it's become just another thing to deal with, like learning your lines. Luckily there was nothing so bad as to stop the show.

Memorable Stage Door Fan Encounters: Autograph hunters are often very nice to us, but mostly they are waiting for Frank.

Catchphrase Only the Company Would Recognize: "The man is still the man," I suppose.

Memorable Directorial Note: Maria Aitken loves language and hates to see it mangled. "When discussing Beeston, you got a bit out of puff and gabbled the second line," she wrote me. Out of puff, of course. But gabbled? I looked it up: "gabbled" actually means "To make gruff, unintelligible sounds."

Ghostly Encounters Backstage: Susan Fallon posts snapshots of previous shows on the wall, and one of them was a picture of myself (or the ghost of my former self) when I played here in *A Man for All Seasons*. I looked at that picture and thought, "Jeez, how you've aged in three years."

Superstitions That Turned Out To Be True: I will not go on stage without knocking fists with Brian. I just won't.

Coolest Thing About Being in This Show: Meeting all these great people—actors and crew I know I'm going to meet again down the road. And, in a word, Roundabout—a great place to work.

Mary Poppins

First Preview: October 14, 2006. Opened: November 16, 2006.
Still running as of May 31, 2012.

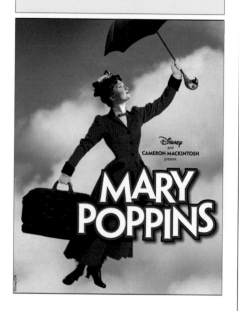

Into the lives of the dysfunctional Banks family of 17 Cherry Tree Lane, London, floats the magical nanny Mary Poppins, who uses her supercalifragilisticexpialidocious powers to escort them on a series of marvelous adventures, accompanied by a friendly chimney sweep named Bert. Along the way she teaches the Bankses the meaning and value of family togetherness. Based on both original P.L. Travers stories and the Disney film musical, with several new songs.

CAST OF CHARACTERS

(in order of appearance)

Bert .... GAVIN LEE
George Banks .... KARL KENZLER
Winifred Banks .... MEGAN OSTERHAUS
Jane Banks .... ANNIE BALTIC,
                                                CAMILLE MANCUSO
                                                or KARA OATES
Michael Banks .... REESE SEBASTIAN DIAZ,
                                                NOAH MARLOWE
                                                or TYLER MERNA
Katie Nanna .... KRISTIN CARBONE
Policeman .... COREY SKAGGS
Miss Lark .... EMILY HARVEY
Admiral Boom .... ED DIXON
Mrs. Brill .... VALERIE BOYLE
Robertson Ay .... DENNIS MOENCH
Mary Poppins .... STEFFANIE LEIGH
Park Keeper .... JAMES HINDMAN
Neleus .... JOSH ASSOR
Queen Victoria .... RUTH GOTTSCHALL

Continued on next page

Continued on next page

NEW AMSTERDAM THEATRE

Disney
and
CAMERON MACKINTOSH
present

MARY POPPINS

A MUSICAL BASED ON THE STORIES OF P.L. TRAVERS AND THE WALT DISNEY FILM

With

STEFFANIE LEIGH   GAVIN LEE

KARL KENZLER   MEGAN OSTERHAUS

ANN ARVIA   RUTH GOTTSCHALL   DENNIS MOENCH   ED DIXON

and

VALERIE BOYLE

ANNIE BALTIC   REESE SEBASTIAN DIAZ   CAMILLE MANCUSO   NOAH MARLOWE   TYLER MERNA   KARA OATES
JOSH ASSOR   EMILY HARVEY   JAMES HINDMAN   JANELLE ANNE ROBINSON   CHAD SEIB   COREY SKAGGS   TOM SOUHRADA

TIA ALTINAY   PAM BRADLEY   CATHERINE BRUNELL   KATHY CALAHAN   KRISTIN CARBONE   BRIAN COLLIER   BARRETT DAVIS
ELIZABETH DeROSA   GEOFFREY GOLDBERG   SUZANNE HYLENSKI   KELLY JACOBS   KOH MOCHIZUKI   KATHLEEN NANNI   BRIAN OGILVIE   AMBER OWENS
CHUCK REA   ROMMY SANDHU   LAURA SCHUTTER   CHRISTOPHER SHIN   JESSE SWIMM   JAMES TABEEK   JEN TAYLOR   NIC THOMPSON

Original Music and Lyrics by
RICHARD M. SHERMAN and ROBERT B. SHERMAN

Book by
JULIAN FELLOWES

New Songs and Additional Music and Lyrics by
GEORGE STILES and ANTHONY DREWE

Co-created by
CAMERON MACKINTOSH

Produced for Disney Theatrical Productions by
THOMAS SCHUMACHER

Music Supervisor   Music Director
DAVID CADDICK   BRAD HAAK

Orchestrations by
WILLIAM DAVID BROHN

Broadway Sound Design   Dance and Vocal Arrangements
STEVE CANYON KENNEDY   GEORGE STILES

Associate Choreographer   Associate Director   Associate Producer   Makeup Design
GEOFFREY GARRATT   ANTHONY LYN   ANNE QUART   NAOMI DONNE

Technical Director   Production Stage Manager   Casting
DAVID BENKEN   JIMMIE LEE SMITH   TARA RUBIN CASTING

Co-choreographer   Lighting Design
STEPHEN MEAR   HOWARD HARRISON

Scenic and Costume Design
BOB CROWLEY

Co-direction and Choreography
MATTHEW BOURNE

Directed by
RICHARD EYRE

2/27/12

(L-R): Steffanie Leigh, Gavin Lee

Photo by Joan Marcus

Mary Poppins

MUSICAL NUMBERS

Mary Poppins takes place in and around the Banks' household somewhere in London at the turn of the last century.

ACT I

"Chim Chim Cher-ee" † ....Bert
"Cherry Tree Lane" (Part 1)* ....George and Winifred Banks, Jane and Michael, Mrs. Brill, and Robertson Ay
"The Perfect Nanny" ....Jane and Michael
"Cherry Tree Lane" (Part 2) ....George and Winifred Banks, Jane, and Michael, Mrs. Brill, and Robertson Ay
"Practically Perfect"* ....Mary Poppins, Jane, and Michael
"Jolly Holiday" † ....Bert, Mary Poppins, Jane, Michael, Neleus, and the Statues
"Cherry Tree Lane" (Reprise),
   "Being Mrs. Banks,"*
   "Jolly Holiday" (Reprise) ....George, Winifred, Jane, and Michael
"A Spoonful of Sugar" ....Mary Poppins, Jane, Michael, Robertson Ay, and Winifred
"Precision and Order"* ....Bank Chairman and the Bank Clerks
"A Man Has Dreams" † ....George Banks
"Feed the Birds" ....Bird Woman and Mary Poppins
"Supercalifragilisticexpialidocious" † ....Mary Poppins, Mrs. Corry, Bert, Jane, Michael, Fannie, Annie, and Customers
"Playing the Game"* ....Mary Poppins, Valentine and other Toys
"Chim Chim Cher-ee" (Reprise) ....Bert and Mary Poppins

ACT II

"Cherry Tree Lane" (Reprise) ....Mrs. Brill, Michael, Jane, Winifred, Robertson Ay, and George
"Brimstone and Treacle" (Part 1)* ....Miss Andrew
"Let's Go Fly a Kite" ....Bert, Park Keeper, Jane, and Michael
"Cherry Tree Lane" (Reprise),
   "Being Mrs. Banks" (Reprise) ....George and Winifred
"Brimstone and Treacle" (Part 2) ....Mary Poppins and Miss Andrew
"Practically Perfect" (Reprise) ....Jane, Michael, and Mary Poppins
"Chim Chim Cher-ee" (Reprise) ....Bert
"Step in Time" † ....Bert, Mary Poppins, Jane, Michael, and the Sweeps
"A Man Has Dreams,"
   "A Spoonful of Sugar" (Reprise) ....George and Bert
"Anything Can Happen"* ....Jane, Michael, Mary Poppins, and the Company
"A Spoonful of Sugar" (Reprise) ....Mary Poppins
"A Shooting Star" † ....Orchestra

* New Songs   † Adapted Songs

SONG CREDITS

"The Perfect Nanny," "A Spoonful of Sugar," "Feed the Birds," "Let's Go Fly a Kite"
written by Richard M. Sherman and Robert B. Sherman.

"Chim Chim Cher-ee," "Jolly Holiday," "A Man Has Dreams," "Supercalifragilisticexpialidocious," "Step in Time" written by Richard M. Sherman and Robert B. Sherman,
with new material by George Stiles and Anthony Drewe.

"Cherry Tree Lane," "Practically Perfect," "Being Mrs. Banks," "Precision and Order," "Playing the Game,"
"Brimstone and Treacle," "Anything Can Happen" written by George Stiles and Anthony Drewe.

Cast Continued

Bank Chairman ....ED DIXON
Miss Smythe ....RUTH GOTTSCHALL
Von Hussler......................TOM SOUHRADA
Northbrook ....CHAD SEIB
Bird Woman ....ANN ARVIA
Mrs. Corry ....JANELLE ANNE ROBINSON
Fannie ....AMBER OWENS
Annie ....CATHERINE BRUNELL
Valentine ....BARRETT DAVIS
Miss Andrew ....RUTH GOTTSCHALL

ENSEMBLE

TIA ALTINAY, JOSH ASSOR,
CATHERINE BRUNELL,
KRISTIN CARBONE, BARRETT DAVIS,
ELIZABETH DeROSA, EMILY HARVEY,
JAMES HINDMAN, KOH MOCHIZUKI,
KATHLEEN NANNI, BRIAN OGILVIE,
AMBER OWENS, CHUCK REA,
JANELLE ANNE ROBINSON, CHAD SEIB,
LAURA SCHUTTER, CHRISTOPHER SHIN,
COREY SKAGGS, TOM SOUHRADA,
JESSE SWIMM, NIC THOMPSON

SWINGS

PAM BRADLEY, KATHY CALAHAN,
BRIAN COLLIER, GEOFFREY GOLDBERG,
SUZANNE HYLENSKI, KELLY JACOBS,
ROMMY SANDHU, JAMES TABEEK,
JEN TAYLOR

Statues, bank clerks, customers, toys, chimney sweeps, lamp lighters and inhabitants of Cherry Tree Lane played by members of the company.

UNDERSTUDIES

Mary Poppins: CATHERINE BRUNELL,
   ELIZABETH DeROSA
Bert: BRIAN COLLIER, CHUCK REA,
   JESSE SWIMM
George Banks: JAMES HINDMAN,
   COREY SKAGGS, TOM SOUHRADA
Winifred Banks: KRISTIN CARBONE,
   LAURA SCHUTTER
Mrs. Brill: ANN ARVIA,
   PAM BRADLEY, EMILY HARVEY
Robertson Ay: BRIAN COLLIER,
   BARRETT DAVIS, BRIAN OGILVIE
Bird Woman: KRISTIN CARBONE,
   JANELLE ANNE ROBINSON
Miss Andrew/Queen Victoria/
   Miss Smythe: ANN ARVIA, EMILY HARVEY,
   JANELLE ANNE ROBINSON

Mary Poppins

Cast Continued

Admiral Boom/Bank Chairman:
    JAMES HINDMAN, COREY SKAGGS,
    TOM SOUHRADA
Mrs. Corry: TIA ALTINAY, PAM BRADLEY,
    KATHY CALAHAN, KELLY JACOBS,
    JEN TAYLOR
Katie Nanna: PAM BRADLEY,
    KATHY CALAHAN, SUZANNE HYLENSKI,
    KELLY JACOBS, JEN TAYLOR
Miss Lark: PAM BRADLEY, KATHY CALAHAN,
    KELLY JACOBS, LAURA SCHUTTER,
    JEN TAYLOR
Neleus: BRIAN COLLIER, BARRETT DAVIS,
    GEOFFREY GOLDBERG, JAMES TABEEK
Von Hussler: ROMMY SANDHU,
    COREY SKAGGS
Northbrook: GEOFFREY GOLDBERG,
    COREY SKAGGS, JESSE SWIMM
Policeman: ROMMY SANDHU,
    TOM SOUHRADA
Park Keeper: ROMMY SANDHU, CHAD SEIB,
    COREY SKAGGS
Valentine: BRIAN COLLIER,
    GEOFFREY GOLDBERG, BRIAN OGILVIE

DANCE CAPTAINS

Brian Collier, Geoffrey Goldberg, Kelly Jacobs

ORCHESTRA

Conductor: BRAD HAAK
Associate Conductor/2nd Keyboard:
    DALE RIELING
Assistant Conductor/Piano: MILTON GRANGER
Bass: PETER DONOVAN
Drums: DAVE RATAJCZAK
Percussion: DANIEL HASKINS
Guitar/Banjo/E-Bow: NATE BROWN
Horns: RUSSELL RIZNER, SHELAGH ABATE
Trumpets: JASON COVEY, JOHN SHEPPARD
Trombone/Euphonium: MARC DONATELLE
Bass Trombone/Tuba: JEFF CASWELL
Clarinet: MERYL ABT
Oboe/English Horn: ALEXANDRA KNOLL
Flutes: BRIAN MILLER
Cello: STEPHANIE CUMMINS
Music Contractor: DAVID LAI

Steffanie Leigh
Mary Poppins

Gavin Lee
Bert

Karl Kenzler
George Banks

Megan Osterhaus
Winifred Banks

Valerie Boyle
Mrs. Brill

Ann Arvia
Bird Woman

Ruth Gottschall
*Miss Andrew,
Queen Victoria,
Miss Smythe*

Dennis Moench
Robertson Ay

Ed Dixon
*Admiral Boom,
Bank Chairman*

Annie Baltic
*Jane Banks at
certain
performances*

Reese Sebastian
Diaz
*Michael Banks
at certain
performances*

Camille Mancuso
*Jane Banks at
certain
performances*

Noah Marlowe
*Michael Banks at
certain
performances*

Tyler Merna
*Michael Banks at
certain
performances*

Kara Oates
*Jane Banks at
certain
performances*

Emily Harvey
Miss Lark, Ensemble

James Hindman
*Park Keeper,
Ensemble*

Josh Assor
Neleus, Ensemble

Janelle Anne
Robinson
Mrs. Corry

Chad Seib
*Northbrook,
Ensemble*

Mary Poppins

Corey Skaggs
*Policeman,
Ensemble*

Tom Souhrada
*Von Hussler,
Ensemble*

Tia Altinay
Ensemble

Pam Bradley
Swing

Catherine Brunell
Annie, Ensemble

Kathy Calahan
Swing

Kristin Carbone
*Katie Nanna,
Ensemble*

Brian Collier
*Swing,
Dance Captain*

Barrett Davis
Valentine, Ensemble

Elizabeth DeRosa
Ensemble

Geoffrey Goldberg
*Swing, Dance
Captain*

Suzanne Hylenski
Swing

Kelly Jacobs
*Swing, Dance
Captain*

Koh Mochizuki
Ensemble

Kathleen Nanni
Ensemble

Brian Ogilvie
Ensemble

Amber Owens
Fannie, Ensemble

Chuck Rea
Ensemble

Rommy Sandhu
Swing

Laura Schutter
Ensemble

Christopher Shin
Ensemble

Jesse Swimm
Ensemble

James Tabeek
Swing

Jen Taylor
Swing

Nic Thompson
Ensemble

P.L. Travers
*Author of the
Mary Poppins stories*

Thomas Schumacher
*Producer
and President,
Disney Theatrical
Productions*

Cameron Mackintosh
*Producer and
Co-Creator*

Richard M. Sherman and Robert B. Sherman
Original Music & Lyrics

Julian Fellowes
Book

George Stiles
*New Songs,
Additional Music,
Dance & Vocal
Arrangements*

Anthony Drewe
*New Songs &
Additional Lyrics*

Richard Eyre
Director

Matthew Bourne
*Co-Director &
Choreographer*

Mary Poppins

Bob Crowley
Scenic and Costume Design

Stephen Mear
Co-Choreographer

Howard Harrison
Lighting Designer

Steve Canyon Kennedy
Broadway Sound Designer

William David Brohn
Orchestrations

David Caddick
Music Supervisor

Brad Haak
Music Director

Naomi Donne
Makeup Designer

Angela Cobbin
Wig Creator

Geoffrey Garratt
Associate Choreographer

Anthony Lyn
Associate Director

David Benken
Technical Director

Tara Rubin Casting
Casting

ALUMNI
2011-2012

Rozi Baker
Jane Banks

Julie Barnes
Swing

David Baum
Ensemble

Ashley Brown
Mary Poppins

Case Dillard
Ensemble

Jonathan Freeman
Admiral Boom, Bank Chairman

Lewis Grosso
Michael Banks

Brigid Harrington
Jane Banks

Garett Hawe
Neleus, Ensemble

Rachel Izen
Mrs. Brill

Andrew Keenan-Bolger
Robertson Ay

Laura Michelle Kelly
Mary Poppins

Nick Kepley
Neleus, Ensemble

Sam Kiernan
Ensemble

David Gabriel Lerner
Michael Banks

Tyler Maynard
Ensemble

Shua Potter
Robertson Ay

T. Oliver Reid
Ensemble

Rachel Resheff
Jane Banks

Dominic Roberts
Ensemble

Mary Poppins

Anthony Scarpone-
Lambert
Michael Banks

Jessica Sheridan
*Miss Andrew,
Queen Victoria,
Miss Smythe,
Miss Lark, Ensemble*

Blythe Wilson
Winifred Banks

Kevin Samual Yee
Ensemble

Jonathan Freeman
*Admiral Boom,
Bank Chairman*

Eric Hatch
Valentine

THE ORIGINAL FILM SCREENPLAY
FOR WALT DISNEY'S *MARY POPPINS*
BY BILL WALSH * DON DA GRADI

DESIGN CONSULTANT
TONY WALTON

STAFF FOR *MARY POPPINS*

COMPANY MANAGER ....DAVE EHLE
Assistant Company Manager ....Laura Eichholz
Production Stage Manager...............Jimmie Lee Smith
Stage Manager ....David Sugarman
Assistant Stage
    Managers ....Terence Orleans Alexander,
        Alexis R. Prussack, Liza Vest
Dance Supervisor ....Brian Collier
Dance Captains ....Geoffrey Goldberg, Kelly Jacobs
Production Coordinator ....Kerry McGrath

DISNEY ON BROADWAY PUBLICITY

Senior Publicist............................Dennis Crowley
Associate Publicist ....Michelle Bergmann

Associate Scenic Designer ....Bryan Johnson
Scenic Design Associate .... Rosalind Coombes
US Scenic Assistants ....Dan Kuchar,
        Rachel Short Janocko,
        Frank McCullough
UK Scenic Assistants ....Al Turner,
        Charles Quiggin, Adam Wiltshire
Associate Costume Designer ....Christine Rowland
Associate Costume Designer ....Mitchell Bloom
Assistant Costume Designer ....Patrick Wiley
Assistant Costume Designer ....Rick Kelly
Associate Lighting Designer ....Daniel Walker
Assistant Lighting Designer ....Kristina Kloss
Lighting Programmer ....Rob Halliday
Associate Sound Designer ....John Shivers
Wig Creator ....Angela Cobbin
Illusions Designer ....Jim Steinmeyer
Technical Director ....David Benken
Scenic Production Supervisor ....Patrick Eviston
Assistant Technical Supervisor ....Rosemarie Palombo
Production Carpenter ....Drew Siccardi
Production Flyman ....Michael Corbett
Foy Flying Operator ....Raymond King
Automation ....Steve Stackle, David Helck
Carpenters...................Eddie Ackerman, Frank Alter,
        Brett Daley, Tony Goncalves,
        Gary Matarazzo

Production Electrician ....James Maloney
Key Spot Operator ....Joseph P. Garvey
Lighting Console Operator ....Carlos Martinez
Pyro Operator ....Kevin Strohmeyer
Automated Lighting Technician .... Andy Catron
Assistant Electricians ....Gregory Dunkin,
        Al Manganaro, Chris Passalacqua
Production Propman ....Victor Amerling
Assistant Propman .... Tim Abel
Props..........................Alan Cabrera, Dave Hogan,
        John Saye, John Taccone
Production Sound Engineer .... Andrew Keister
Sound Engineer .... Kurt Fischer
Sound Engineer......................Marie Renee Foucher
Sound Assistant ....Bill Romanello, Karen Zabinski
Production Wardrobe Supervisor ....Helen Toth
Assistant Wardrobe Supervisor ....Abbey Rayburn
Dressers ....Richard Byron, Vivienne Crawford,
        Marjorie Denton, Russell Easley,
        Steven Epstein, Maya Hardin,
        Carly Hirschberg, Barbara Hladsky,
        Larry Kleinstein, Chris Lavin,
        Janet Netzke, Tom Reiter,
        Wendy Samland, Gary Seibert
Production Hair Supervisor ....Gary Martori
Hair Dept Assistants ....Chris Calabrese,
        Mitch Ely, Paula Schaffer
Production Makeup Supervisor ....Amy Porter
Child Guardian ....Christina Huschle
UK Prop Coordinators ....Kathy Anders, Lisa Buckley
UK Wig Shop Assistant ....Beatrix Archer

Music Copyist ....Emily Grishman Music Preparation –
        Emily Grishman/
        Katharine Edmonds
Keyboard Programming ....Stuart Andrews

MUSIC COORDINATOR ....DAVID LAI

DIALECT & VOCAL COACH ....DEBORAH HECHT

Resident Dialect Coach ....Shane Ann Younts
Associate General Manager ....Alan Wasser
Production Co-Counsel ....F. Richard Pappas
Casting Directors ....Tara Rubin, Eric Woodall
Children's Tutoring ....On Location Education,
        Muriel Kester
Physical Therapy ....Physioarts
Advertising ....Serino Coyne, Inc
Interactive Marketing ....Situation Marketing
Web Design Consultant ....Joshua Noah
Production Photography ....Joan Marcus

Production Travel ....Jill L. Citron
Payroll Managers ....Anthony DeLuca, Cathy Guerra
Corporate Counsel ....Michael Rosenfeld

CREDITS

Scenery by Hudson Scenic, Inc.; Adirondack Studios, Inc.;
Proof Productions, Inc.; Scenic Technologies, a division of
Production Resource Group, LLC, New Windsor NY.
Drops by Scenic Arts. Automation by Hudson Scenic, Inc.
Lighting equipment by Hudson Sound & Light, LLC.
Lighting truss by Showman Fabricators, Inc. Sound
equipment by Masque Sound. Projection equipment by
Sound Associates Inc. Magic props by William Kennedy of
Magic Effects. Props by The Spoon Group, LLC;
Moonboots Productions Inc.; Russell Beck Studio Ltd.
Costumes by Barbara Matera Ltd.; Parsons-Meares, Ltd.;
Eric Winterling; Werner Russold; Studio Rouge; Seamless
Costumes. Millinery by Rodney Gordon, Arnold Levine,
Lynne Mackey Studio. Shoes by T.O. Dey. Shirts by Cego.
Puppets by Puppet Heap. Flying by Foy. Ricola cough drops
courtesy of Ricola USA, Inc. Emergen-C super energy
booster provided by Alacer Corp. Makeup provided by
M•A•C.

MARY POPPINS rehearsed at the
New 42nd Street Studios.

THANKS

Thanks to Marcus Hall Props, Claire Sanderson, James Ince
and Sons, Great British Lighting, Bed Bazaar, The Wakefield
Brush Company, Heron and Driver, Ivo and Kay Coveney,
Mike and Rosi Compton, Bebe Barrett, Charles Quiggin,
Nicola Kileen Textiles, Carl Roberts Shaw, David Scotcher
Interiors, Original Club Fenders Ltd., Lauren Pattison,
Robert Tatad.

Mary Poppins is a proud member of the Broadway Green
Alliance.

FOR CAMERON MACKINTOSH LIMITED

Directors ....Nicholas Allott, Richard Johnston
Deputy Managing Director ....Robert Noble
Executive Producer &
    Casting Director ....Trevor Jackson
Technical Director ....Nicolas Harris
Financial Controller ....Richard Knibb
Associate Producer ....Darinka Nenadovic
Sales & Marketing Manager ....David Dolman
Head of Musical Development ....Stephen Metcalfe
Production Associate ....Shidan Majidi

Mary Poppins
Scrapbook

Correspondent: Jesse Swimm, Ensemble and Understudy for "Bert"

Memorable Note, Fax or Fan Letter: I actually got my very first fan letter this year from a woman in Afton, Minnesota. She had seen me go on for the role of Bert and she brought along a student of hers who speaks very limited English. It was her student's first time seeing a Broadway show and after she saw me tap dance on the ceiling in "Step in Time" she kept saying, "How did he do that, how did he do that???" I guess I made a good impression on them.

Anniversary Parties and/or Gifts: I was very lucky to join the show a few months before its fifth anniversary :) It was such a magical night being part of a show that has had such a long and successful run. Also seeing all the people who have worked on the show and are still working on the show coming together to celebrate the show's success was a very special experience.

Most Exciting Celebrity Visitor: I happened to be on for Bert, again, and this time Paul McCartney was in the audience. He came backstage afterwards with his family and we talked about the show, his family and we all congratulated him on the Grammy Award that he had just won.

"Easter Bonnet" Sketch: Jim Hindman, our Park Keeper and Tom Souhrada, who plays Von Hussler created it together. They were both in it, as well as kids from our show, Camille Mancuso, Tyler Merna, Annie Baltic, Noah Marlowe, and Kara Oates. It dealt with the kids recreating classic (and bloody) scenes from *Medea, Sweeney Todd* and The Scottish Play. We won runner-up for best bonnet presentation.

Actors Who Performed the Most Roles in This Show: I would have to say the Swings. They are the hardest-working performers on Broadway. I myself was a Swing first when I joined *Mary Poppins* and of the 12 ensemble tracks I covered, I went on for 11 of them in four months.

Who Has Done the Show the Most Times: I'd have to say it is our remaining original company members. Katie Nanni, Jim Hindman, Janelle Robinson, Kristin Carbone, Megan Osterhaus, and of course Gavin Lee who has been doing the show since it first started in England back in 2004. As of April 26, 2012 we will have given 2,269 performances.

Special Backstage Rituals: There are two. Katie Nanni leads a group of us in a ballet bar warm-up before the show and we call ourselves Bar-Tinis. Also right before "Step in Time" it is our little ritual to bump sweep brushes as a form of good luck.

Favorite Moment During Each Performance: I really love dancing in "Step in Time." It is such an incredible rush—plus I get to have a little tap trio with Gavin Lee, so that makes it extra special.

Favorite In-Theatre Gathering Places: On Wednesday nights at intermission we gather in Mary Poppins' (Steffanie Leigh's) dressing room for Tea Time. Sunday Matinee at intermission we gather in Mrs. Brill's (Valerie Boyle's) dressing room for Tea Time. It's basically an excuse to eat really good pastries.

Favorite Off-Site Hangouts: We have a couple. We like Reunion Bar on 44th Street and Ninth Avenue—lots of fun and it's great in the winter cause it's a surf bar and it makes you forget that it is cold outside. The Long Room is also a great place for us to have parties for cast members who are leaving or making their debuts with us.

DISNEY THEATRICAL PRODUCTIONS

President	Thomas Schumacher
EVP & Managing Director	David Schrader
Senior Vice President, International	Ron Kollen
Vice President, International, Europe	Fiona Thomas
Vice President, International, Australia	James Thane
Vice President, Operations	Dana Amendola
Vice President, Publicity	Joe Quenqua
Vice President, Domestic	Jack Eldon
Vice President, Human Resources	June Heindel
Director, Domestic Touring	Michael Buchanan
Director, Worldwide Publicity	Michael Cohen
Director, Regional Engagements	Scott A. Hemerling
Director, Regional Engagements	Kelli Palan
Director, Regional Engagements	Deborah Warren
Manager, Domestic Touring & Planning	Liz Botros
Manager, Human Resources	Jewel Neal
Manager, Publicity	Lindsay Braverman
Project Manager	Ryan Pears
Senior Computer Support Analyst	Kevin A. McGuire
IT/Business Analyst	William Boudiette

Creative & Production

Executive Music Producer	Chris Montan
VP, Creative Development	Steve Fickinger
VP, Production	Anne Quart
Director, International Production	Felipe Gamba
Director, Labor Relations	Edward Lieber
Associate Director	Jeff Lee
Production Supervisor	Clifford Schwartz
Production Manager	Eduardo Castro
Manager, Labor Relations	Stephanie Cheek
Manager, Physical Production	Karl Chmielewski
Manager, Creative Development	Jane Abramson
Manager, Theatrical Licensing	David R. Scott
Dramaturg & Literary Manager	Ken Cerniglia
Manager, Education Outreach	Lisa Mitchell

Marketing

Senior Vice President	Andrew Flatt
Director, Creative Resources	Victor Adams
Director, Synergy & Partnership	Kevin Banks
Director, Digital Marketing	Kyle Young
Design Manager	James Anderer
Manager, Media & Strategy	Jared Comess
Manager, Creative Services	Lauren Daghini
Manager, Synergy & Partnership	Sarah Schlesinger
Manager, Consumer Insights	Craig Trachtenberg
Manager, Digital Marketing	Peter Tulba

Sales

Vice President, National Sales	Bryan Dockett
National Sales Manager	Victoria Cairl
Sr. Manager, Sales & Ticketing	Nick Falzon
Manager, Group Sales	Hunter Robertson

Business and Legal Affairs

Senior Vice President	Jonathan Olson
Director	Daniel M. Posener
Director	Seth Stuhl
Paralegal	Jessica White

Finance

VP, Finance/Bus. Development	Mario Iannetta
Director, Finance	Joe McClafferty
Director, Business Development	Michael Barra
Director, Accounting	Leena Mathew
Manager, Finance	Liz Jurist Schwarzwalder
Manager, Production Accounting	Nick Judge
Manager, Accounting	Adrineh Ghoukassian
Senior Business Analyst	Sven Rittershaus
Senior Financial Analyst	Mikhail Medvedev
Senior Financial Analyst	Jason Ve
Senior Business Planner	Jennifer August
Production Accountant	Joy Sims Brown
Production Accountant	Angela DiSanti
Assistant Production Accountant	Isander Rojas

Administrative Staff

Brian Bahr, Sarah Bills, Elizabeth Boulger, Whitney Britt, Jonelle Brown, Amy Caldamone, Michael Dei Cas, Preston Copley, Alanna Degner, Brittany Dobbs, Cara Epstein, Nicholas Faranda, Cristi Finn, Phil Grippe, Greg Josken, Cyntia Leo, Colleen McCormack, Brendan Padgett, Matt Quinones, Jillian Robbins, Kattia Soriano, Lee Taglin, Anji Taylor

DISNEY THEATRICAL MERCHANDISE

Vice President	Steven Downing
Merchandise Manager	Neil Markman
District Manager	Alyssa Somers
Associate Buyer	Violet Burlaza
Assistant Manager, Inventory	Suzanne Jakel
On-Site Retail Manager	Scott Koonce
On-Site Assistant Retail Manager	Thad Wilkes
On-Site Retail Manager	Jeff Knizer
On-Site Assistant Retail Manager	Jana Cristiano

Disney Theatrical Productions
guestmail@disneytheatrical.com

Staff for the New Amsterdam Theatre

Theatre Manager	John M. Loiacono
Guest Services Manager	Kenneth Miller
Box Office Treasurer	Andrew Grennan
Assistant Treasurer	Anthony Oliva
Chief Engineer	Frank Gibbons
Engineer	Dan Milan
Security Manager	Carl Lembo
Head Usher	Jeryl Costello
Lobby Refreshments	Sweet Concessions
Special thanks	Sgt. Arthur J. Smarsch, Det. Adam D'Amico

Mary Poppins
SCRAPBOOK

Favorite Snack Foods: Whatever is in the snack box down in the bunker where we change.

Mascot: In the bunker in my wardrobe pod we have a little stuffed gnome named Henry the Gnome. You press on his foot, record something silly, and then he plays back at much higher pitch. Yes kids, Broadway is this exciting!!!

Favorite Therapy: Physio Arts on 38th Street. I don't know what I would do without them.

Memorable Ad-Lib: One time Mary didn't come out of the chimney at the top of "Step in Time" and one of our Michael Banks turned to Gavin and said "sing something Bert." To which he replied, "No." It was very dry and very funny.

Record Number of Cell Phone Rings, Cell Phone Photos or Texting Incidents During a Performance: Too many to count. It's like a sea of glowing faces out there sometimes.

Memorable Press Encounter: We recently got to perform "Supercal" on "The Chew" for ABC. I was lucky enough to get asked to be Bert for this, plus I got to meet Carla Hall who I was a big fan of when she was on "Top Chef." She is just as sweet in person as she is in TV.

Memorable Stage Door Fan Encounter: When I came out of the stage door to see my mom and dad waiting for me when I made my Broadway debut as Bert.

Latest Audience Arrival: I would have to say during "Supercal." It usually happens when we have an odd Sunday matinee and people think the show starts later than it does. Usually by an hour. Always look at your tickets, kids, always look at your tickets.

Fastest Costume Change: In "Jolly Holiday" as Bert, going from the opening outfit to the "colorful" outfit. I have probably about 30 seconds. But we have the best dresser on Broadway ever, Gary Seibert, who makes it all run smoothly.

Who Wore the Heaviest/Hottest Costume: Every actress who has had to play Miss Lark.

Who Wore the Least: All the ensemble members who play statues in the show. We wear one-piece unitards in "Jolly Holiday" painted to look like statues.

Catchphrases Only the Company Would Recognize: "Gorg!!!, Going for it!!!"

Sweethearts Within the Company: Gavin Lee (our Bert) and his wife Emily Harvey (our Miss Lark).

Memorable Directorial Note: My favorite one is from our resident director, Anthony Lyn. "There is someone out there who is seeing their first Broadway show and there is someone out there seeing their last Broadway show."

Company In-Jokes: In the men's ensemble dressing room we have a special award for the male ensemble member who comes up with the best one-liner backstage. We call it the "Peach in the Pudding." The reason being, a

Anthony Scarpone-Lambert and Brigid Harrington perform a scene from *Who's Afraid of Virginia Woolf?* on the *Mary Poppins* set in the annual "Gypsy of the Year" competition

Photo by Monica Simoes

former cast member said they were going to be a "peach in the put-in" tomorrow and someone thought they said "peach in the pudding." After that, another ensemble member brought in a really bad football trophy and the rest is history. It has made the rounds in the male dressing rooms many times over.

Tales from the Put-In: I actually had two put-ins when I joined the company. One for my own ensemble track and then, the following day, I had my put-in as Bert with Laura Michelle Kelly, the original London Mary Poppins, because she was going back into the show after a leave of absence. That was pretty much one of the coolest experiences I have had in my career.

Understudy Anecdote: Don't put off learning your part till the last minute. You will most likely be the first one to go on if you do.

Embarrassing Moment: It was embarrassing only to me, but one time I put on the wrong shoes for "Step in Time." It wasn't until I had stepped out on stage to get ready for the number that I realized I had to do the whole number without tap shoes.

Ghostly Encounters Backstage: Nothing has happened to me, but we do have a ghost in The New Amsterdam: Olive Thomas. She was one of Ziegfeld's original dancers. There is a picture of her as you first enter the stage door and I know all the crew guys make sure to say hello to her every day.

Coolest Thing About Being in This Show: Aside from getting to be on Broadway every night. I would have to say that when I get to go on for Bert it is pretty spectacular tap dancing 30 feet in the air and upside down!

Also: It has been such a whirlwind. Ever since I joined the Broadway Company I have been fortunate enough to be a part of almost every benefit and special event that Broadway has to offer. I got to sing with Broadway in Bryant Park, did the opening numbers for Gypsy of the Year and Easter Bonnet, and I look forward to being a part of Broadway Bares. I still remember going on for my first night on Broadway. Amber Owens, who is in our show, told me that when I go to bow, "Remember to look up and take it all in." I have to say the sight of an entire Broadway house filled with cheering audience members still gets me pumped every time.

Master Class

First Preview: June 14, 2011. Opened: July 7, 2011.
Closed September 4, 2011 after 26 Previews and 67 Performances.

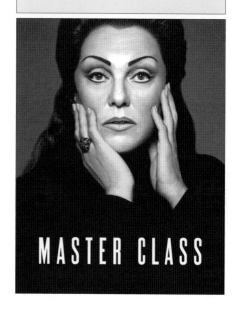

As opera diva Maria Callas conducts a master class in singing (with the audience as her "students"), her memory keeps taking her back to relive her moments of greatest triumph and heartbreak.

CAST
(in alphabetical order)

Sharon Graham ....SIERRA BOGGESS
Stagehand ....CLINTON BRANDHAGEN
Emmanuel Weinstock ....JEREMY COHEN
Maria Callas...............................TYNE DALY
Sophie De Palma.............ALEXANDRA SILBER
Anthony Candolino ....GARRETT SORENSON

Stage Manager ....ALLISON SOMMERS

UNDERSTUDIES
For Maria Callas:
JACQUELINE ANTARAMIAN
For Stagehand/Anthony Candolino:
BRIAN CALÌ
For Sharon Graham/Sophie De Palma:
LEAH EDWARDS
For Emmanuel Weinstock:
DAN K. KURLAND

MANHATTAN THEATRE CLUB
SAMUEL J. FRIEDMAN THEATRE

ARTISTIC DIRECTOR
LYNNE MEADOW

EXECUTIVE PRODUCER
BARRY GROVE

BY SPECIAL ARRANGEMENT WITH

MAX
COOPER

MABERRY
THEATRICALS

MARKS-MOORE-TURNBULL
GROUP

TED
SNOWDON

PRESENTS

MASTER CLASS

BY
TERRENCE McNALLY

WITH

SIERRA BOGGESS   CLINTON BRANDHAGEN   JEREMY COHEN
TYNE DALY   ALEXANDRA SILBER   GARRETT SORENSON

SCENIC DESIGN
THOMAS LYNCH

COSTUME DESIGN
MARTIN PAKLEDINAZ

LIGHTING DESIGN
DAVID LANDER

SOUND DESIGN
JON GOTTLIEB

WIG DESIGN
PAUL HUNTLEY

PRODUCTION STAGE MANAGER
SUSIE CORDON

DIRECTED BY
STEPHEN WADSWORTH

ARTISTIC PRODUCER
MANDY GREENFIELD

GENERAL MANAGER
FLORIE SEERY

DIRECTOR OF ARTISTIC DEVELOPMENT
JERRY PATCH

DIRECTOR OF MARKETING
DEBRA WAXMAN-PILLA

PRESS REPRESENTATIVE
BONEAU/BRYAN-BROWN

PRODUCTION MANAGER
JOSHUA HELMAN

DIRECTOR OF CASTING
NANCY PICCIONE

ARTISTIC LINE PRODUCER
LISA McNULTY

DIRECTOR OF DEVELOPMENT
LYNNE RANDALL

MASTER CLASS was produced on Broadway by Robert Whitehead, Lewis Allen and Spring Sirkin.
Originally commissioned by Circle Repertory Company.
MASTER CLASS was produced by the Kennedy Center from March 25–April 18, 2010.
Kennedy Center casting by Laura Stanczyk.
Corporate Sponsorship for MASTER CLASS provided by JPMorgan Chase & Co.
Manhattan Theatre Club wishes to express its appreciation to Theatre Development Fund for its support of this production.

7/7/11

(L-R): Sierra Boggess and Tyne Daly

Photo by Joan Marcus

Master Class

Sierra Boggess
Sharon Graham

Clinton Brandhagen
Stagehand

Jeremy Cohen
Emmanuel Weinstock

Tyne Daly
Maria Callas

Alexandra Silber
Sophie De Palma

Garrett Sorenson
Anthony Candolino

Jacqueline Antaramian
u/s Maria Callas

Brian Calì
u/s Stagehand/ Anthony Candolino

Leah Edwards
u/s Sharon Graham/ Sophie De Palma

Dan K. Kurland
u/s Emmanuel Weinstock

Terrence McNally
Playwright

Stephen Wadsworth
Director

Thomas Lynch
Scenic Design

Martin Pakledinaz
Costume Design

David Lander
Lighting Design

Jon Gottlieb
Sound Design

Paul Huntley
Wig Design

Kate Wilson
Voice Coach

Lynne Meadow
Artistic Director, Manhattan Theatre Club, Inc.

Barry Grove
Executive Producer, Manhattan Theatre Club, Inc.

Max Cooper
Co-Producer

Tom Kirdahy
Maberry Theatricals
Producer

Ted Snowdon
Co-Producer

David M. Rubenstein
Chairman,
The John F. Kennedy
Center for the
Performing Arts

Michael M. Kaiser
President,
The John F. Kennedy
Center for the
Performing Arts

Photo by Joan Marcus

(L-R): Jeremy Cohen
and Alexandra Silber

Master Class

Photo by Joan Marcus

(L-R): Garrett Sorenson and Tyne Daly

Master Class
SCRAPBOOK

Photos by Joseph Marzullo/WENN

1. At the opening night party at B.B. King's (L-R): Alexandra Silber, Tyne Daly, Sierra Boggess and playwright Terrence McNally.
2. Daly and Garrett Sorenson.
3. (L-R): Stephen Wadsworth, Alexandra Silber, Sierra Boggess, Tyne Daly, Clinton Brandhagen and *Yearbook* correspondent Jeremy Cohen.
4. Daly's curtain call on opening night.

Correspondent: Jeremy Cohen, "Manny"

Opening Night Gifts: Many creative presents were exchanged based on the themes of oranges, pencils, music and MUT!

Most Exciting Celebrity Visitors: One evening in July, several cast members from the original production of *Master Class* attended the performance. Zoe Caldwell, Audra McDonald and David Loud joined us backstage after the show. They were thrilled to support the play's continuing journey. That was an exciting night for everyone involved.

Actor Who Has Done the Most Shows: The one, the only, the incomparable...Tyne Daly.

Special Backstage Ritual: We listen to some killer 1980's tunes before every matinee. Nothing gets us ready for the day quite like Huey Lewis' "The Power of Love." Or MJ's "Man in the Mirror." Or "Highway to the Danger Zone" from *Top Gun*.

Favorite Moment During Each Performance (On Stage or Off): I have a soft spot for our trio in Act I. I love playing "Ah Non Credea" from Bellini's *Sonnambula*. Tyne is reciting the words. Al sings a few phrases and has a transformative emotional experience. It's a very special few minutes for the three of us.

Favorite In-Theatre Gathering Place: The Men's Dressing Room is the place to be for card games, company hangouts and general mischief.

Favorite Off-Site Hangouts: Sombrero for margaritas and the Glass House Tavern for a nice post-show brew with friends.

Favorite Snack Food: Anything that Tyne bakes.

Mascot: The Honey Badger

Favorite Therapy: Sierra and I are serious practitioners of Bikram Yoga. Namaste.

Memorable Stage Door Fan Encounter: One evening, Sierra met a teenage girl at the stage door who had drawn her a picture. It features Sierra in full *Little Mermaid* attire, a tribute to her Disney days. It hangs proudly backstage.

Catchphrase Only the Company Would Recognize: "Deeper, Richer, Fuller, Better."

Memorable Directorial Note: Too many to mention. Our director, Stephen Wadsworth, is a brilliant artist and an extraordinary person. Between him and Tyne, we had some awesome company leaders.

Company In-Joke: "Goodbye, My Love!" Thank you, Jim Carrey.

Company Legend: Callas! La Divina!

Nicknames: Sea-Bull, Honey Badger, B-Cal, Cobra, Grumpy, among others.

Coolest Thing About Being in This Show: Working with and getting to know Tyne. I know my colleagues feel the same way. This whole experience has been such a gift for all of us.

Memphis

First Preview: September 23, 2009. Opened: October 19, 2009.
Still running as of May 31, 2012.

At the dawn of the rock 'n' roll era a white deejay in Memphis, Tennessee falls in love with "black" music, and then falls in love with a beautiful black singer. The two become pioneers in promoting the new musical sound, and become pioneers in interracial romance in a deeply racist society. When things go better for the music than for the romance, the two have to make some soul-shaking choices.

CAST

(in order of appearance)

White DJ/Mr. Collins/White Father/ Gordon Grant/Ensemble	DAVID McDONALD
Black DJ/Ensemble	ANTOINE L. SMITH
Delray	J. BERNARD CALLOWAY
Gator	DERRICK BASKIN
Bobby	JAMES MONROE IGLEHART
Ensemble/Wailin' Joe/ Reverend Hobson	ROBERT HARTWELL
Ensemble/Someday Backup Singer	ASHLEY BLANCHET
Ensemble/Someday Backup Singer/Double Dutch Girl	TIFFANY JANENE HOWARD
Ensemble	BAHIYAH SAYYED GAINES
Ensemble/Ethel	MONETTE McKAY
Ensemble/Be Black Trio	DARIUS BARNES
Ensemble/Be Black Trio	SAM J CAHN
Ensemble/ Be Black Trio	PRESTON W. DUGGER III
Ensemble/Someday Backup Singer	DAN'YELLE WILLIAMSON
Felicia	MONTEGO GLOVER
Huey	ADAM PASCAL

Continued on next page

Adam Pascal (third from left) with Montego Glover (at microphone) and the Company.

Photo by Joan Marcus

SAM S. SHUBERT THEATRE

225 West 44th Street
A Shubert Organization Theatre

Philip J. Smith, *Chairman*   Robert E. Wankel, *President*

JUNKYARD DOG PRODUCTIONS   BARBARA AND BUDDY FREITAG   MARLEEN AND KENNY ALHADEFF
LATITUDE LINK   JIM AND SUSAN BLAIR   DEMOS BIZAR ENTERTAINMENT   LAND LINE PRODUCTIONS
APPLES AND ORANGES PRODUCTIONS   DAVE COPLEY   DANCAP PRODUCTIONS, INC.   ALEX AND KATYA LUKIANOV   TONY PONTURO   2 GUYS PRODUCTIONS   RICHARD WINKLER

IN ASSOCIATION WITH

LAUREN DOLL   ERIC AND MARSI GARDINER   LINDA AND BILL POTTER   BROADWAY ACROSS AMERICA   JOCKO PRODUCTIONS   PATTY BAKER   DAN FRISHWASSER
BOB BARTNER/SCOTT AND KAYLIN UNION   LORAINE BOYLE/CHASE MISHKIN   REMMEL T. DICKINSON/MEMPHIS ORPHEUM GROUP   SHADOWCATCHER ENTERTAINMENT/VIJAY AND SITA VASHEE

PRESENT

MEMPHIS

BOOK AND LYRICS BY
JOE DiPIETRO

MUSIC AND LYRICS BY
DAVID BRYAN

BASED ON A CONCEPT BY
GEORGE W. GEORGE

STARRING

ADAM PASCAL   **MONTEGO GLOVER**

WITH

DERRICK BASKIN   J. BERNARD CALLOWAY   JAMES MONROE IGLEHART   JOHN JELLISON   NANCY OPEL

DARIUS BARNES   ASHLEY BLANCHET   SAM J CAHN   PRESTON W. DUGGER III   HILLARY ELK   BAHIYAH SAYYED GAINES
ROBERT HARTWELL   TIFFANY JANENE HOWARD   TYRONE JACKSON   ELIZABETH WARD LAND   BRYAN LANGLITZ
KEVIN MASSEY   CANDICE MONET McCALL   DAVID McDONALD   PAUL McGILL   MONETTE McKAY   ANDY MILLS   SYDNEY MORTON
JUSTIN PATTERSON   JERMAINE R. REMBERT   JAMISON SCOTT   ANTOINE L. SMITH   BETSY STRUXNESS   DAN'YELLE WILLIAMSON

SCENIC DESIGN	COSTUME DESIGN	LIGHTING DESIGN	SOUND DESIGN
DAVID GALLO	PAUL TAZEWELL	HOWELL BINKLEY	KEN TRAVIS

PROJECTION DESIGN	HAIR & WIG DESIGN	FIGHT DIRECTOR	CASTING	ASSOCIATE CHOREOGRAPHER
DAVID GALLO & SHAWN SAGADY	CHARLES G. LaPOINTE	STEVE RANKIN	TELSEY + COMPANY	KELLY DEVINE

ORCHESTRATIONS	MUSICAL DIRECTOR	DANCE ARRANGEMENTS	MUSIC CONTRACTOR	PRODUCTION STAGE MANAGER
DARYL WATERS & DAVID BRYAN	KENNY J. SEYMOUR	AUGUST ERIKSMOEN	MICHAEL KELLER	ARTURO E. PORAZZI

GENERAL MANAGER	PRODUCTION MANAGEMENT	PRESS AGENT	ADVERTISING/MARKETING
ALCHEMY PRODUCTION GROUP CARL PASBJERG & FRANK SCARDINO	JUNIPER STREET PRODUCTIONS, INC.	THE HARTMAN GROUP	aka

ASSOCIATE PRODUCERS
EMILY AND AARON ALHADEFF   ALISON AND ANDI ALHADEFF   KEN CLAY   JOSEPH CRAIG   RON AND MARJORIE DANZ   CYRENA ESPOSITO   BRUCE AND JOANNE GLANT   MATT MURPHY

MUSIC PRODUCER/MUSIC SUPERVISOR
CHRISTOPHER JAHNKE

CHOREOGRAPHER
SERGIO TRUJILLO

DIRECTOR
CHRISTOPHER ASHLEY

THIS PRODUCTION OF *MEMPHIS* ORIGINALLY CO-PRODUCED BY LA JOLLA PLAYHOUSE, CHRISTOPHER ASHLEY, ARTISTIC DIRECTOR, MICHAEL S. ROSENBERG, MANAGING DIRECTOR
AND 5TH AVENUE THEATRE, SEATTLE, WA, DAVID ARMSTRONG, PRODUCING ARTISTIC DIRECTOR, BERNADINE GRIFFIN, MANAGING DIRECTOR, AND BILL BERRY, PRODUCING DIRECTOR
ORIGINALLY PRODUCED AS A JOINT WORLD PREMIERE AT NORTH SHORE MUSIC THEATRE, JON KIMBELL, EXECUTIVE PRODUCER
AND THEATREWORKS, ROBERT KELLEY, ARTISTIC DIRECTOR AND PHIL SANTORA, MANAGING DIRECTOR

10/24/11

Memphis

MUSICAL NUMBERS

ACT I

"Underground" ....Delray, Felicia and Company
"The Music of My Soul" ....Huey, Felicia and Company
"Scratch My Itch" ....Wailin' Joe and Company
"Ain't Nothin' But a Kiss" ....Felicia and Huey
"Hello, My Name Is Huey" ....Huey
"Everybody Wants to Be Black on a Saturday Night" ....Company
"Make Me Stronger" ....Huey, Mama, Felicia and Company
"Colored Woman" ....Felicia
"Someday" ....Felicia and Company
"She's My Sister" ....Delray and Huey
"Radio" ....Huey and Company
"Say a Prayer" ....Gator and Company

ACT II

"Crazy Little Huey" ....Huey and Company
"Big Love" ....Bobby
"Love Will Stand When All Else Falls" ....Felicia and Company
"Stand Up" ....Delray, Felicia, Huey, Gator, Bobby and Company
"Change Don't Come Easy" ....Mama, Delray, Gator and Bobby
"Tear Down the House" ....Huey and Company
"Love Will Stand/Ain't Nothin' But a Kiss" (Reprise) ....Felicia and Huey
"Memphis Lives in Me" ....Huey and Company
"Steal Your Rock 'n' Roll" ....Huey, Felicia and Company

(L-R): Adam Pascal,
Montego Glover,
J. Bernard Calloway

Photo by Joan Marcus

Cast Continued

Mr. Simmons ....JOHN JELLISON
Clara/White Mother/
    Ensemble ....ELIZABETH WARD LAND
Buck Wiley/Ensemble/
    Martin Holton ....JUSTIN PATTERSON
Ensemble/Teenager ....HILLARY ELK
Ensemble ....KEVIN MASSEY
Ensemble/
    Double Dutch Girl ....BETSY STRUXNESS
Ensemble ....PAUL McGILL
Ensemble ....ANDY MILLS
Perry Como/Ensemble/
    Frank Dryer ....JAMISON SCOTT
Ensemble ....BRYAN LANGLITZ
Mama ....NANCY OPEL

SWINGS
TYRONE JACKSON,
CANDICE MONET McCALL,
SYDNEY MORTON, JERMAINE R. REMBERT

UNDERSTUDIES
For Mama: ELIZABETH WARD LAND,
    BETSY STRUXNESS
For Huey: KEVIN MASSEY,
    JUSTIN PATTERSON
For Felicia: ASHLEY BLANCHET,
    DAN'YELLE WILLIAMSON
For Gator: ROBERT HARTWELL,
    JERMAINE R. REMBERT,
    ANTOINE L. SMITH
For Bobby: ROBERT HARTWELL,
    ANTOINE L. SMITH
For Delray: ROBERT HARTWELL,
    ANTOINE L. SMITH
For Mr. Simmons: DAVID McDONALD,
    JUSTIN PATTERSON

DANCE CAPTAIN
JERMAINE R. REMBERT

TIME
The 1950s

BAND
Conductor: KENNY J. SEYMOUR
Associate Conductor: JASON MICHAEL WEBB
Keyboard 1: KENNY J. SEYMOUR
Keyboard 2: JASON MICHAEL WEBB
Guitars: JOHN PUTNAM
Bass: GEORGE FARMER
Drums: CLAYTON CRADDOCK
Trumpet: JOHN WALSH
Trombone: BIRCH JOHNSON
Reeds: KEN HITCHCOCK, SCOTT KREITZER
Music Coordinator: MICHAEL KELLER

Memphis

Adam Pascal
Huey

Montego Glover
Felicia

Derrick Baskin
Gator

J. Bernard Calloway
Delray

James Monroe
Iglehart
Bobby

John Jellison
Mr. Simmons

Nancy Opel
Mama

Darius Barnes
Ensemble

Ashley Blanchet
Ensemble

Sam J Cahn
Ensemble

Preston W.
Dugger III
Ensemble

Hillary Elk
Ensemble

Bahiyah Sayyed
Gaines
Ensemble

Robert Hartwell
Ensemble

Tiffany Janene
Howard
Ensemble

Tyrone Jackson
Swing

Elizabeth Ward Land
Ensemble

Bryan Langlitz
Ensemble

Kevin Massey
Ensemble

Candice Monet
McCall
*Swing, Assistant
Dance Captain*

David McDonald
Ensemble

Paul McGill
Ensemble

Monette McKay
Ensemble

Andy Mills
Ensemble

Sydney Morton
Swing

Justin Patterson
Ensemble

Jermaine R. Rembert
*Swing, Dance
Captain, Fight
Captain*

Jamison Scott
Ensemble

Antoine L. Smith
Ensemble

Betsy Struxness
Ensemble

Dan'yelle Williamson
Ensemble

Joe DiPietro
Book and Co-Lyrics

David Bryan
Music, Co-Lyrics

Christopher Ashley
Director

Sergio Trujillo
Choreographer

Memphis

Christopher Jahnke
Music Producer/
Music Supervisor

David Gallo
Set and Co-
Projections Design

Howell Binkley
Lighting Design

Paul Tazewell
Costume Design

Ken Travis
Sound Design

Charles G. LaPointe
Hair and Wig Design

Steve Rankin
Fight Director

Bernard Telsey
Telsey + Company
Casting

Kelly Devine
Associate
Choreographer

Daryl Waters
Co-Orchestrator

Kenny J. Seymour
Music Director/
Conductor

August Eriksmoen
Dance Arranger

Michael Keller
Music Coordinator

Carl Pasbjerg
Alchemy Production
Group LLC
General
Management

Ana Rose Greene, Guy Kwan, Joe DeLuise,
Hillary Blanken
Juniper Street Production
Production Manager

Beatrice Terry
Associate Director

Edgar Godineaux
Associate
Choreographer

Randy Adams
Junkyard Dog
Productions
Producer

Kenny Alhadeff
Junkyard Dog
Productions
Producer

Marleen Alhadeff
Junkyard Dog
Productions
Producer

Sue Frost
Junkyard Dog
Productions
Producer

Barbara Freitag
Producer

Buddy Freitag
Producer

Jim Blair
Producer

Susan Blair
Producer

Nick Demos
Demos Bizar
Entertainment
Producer

Tim Kashani
Apples and Oranges
Productions
Producer

Pamela Winslow
Kashani
Apples and Oranges
Productions
Producer

Aubrey Dan
Dancap Productions
Inc.
Producer

Alex Lukianov
Producer

Tony Ponturo
Producer

Richard Winkler
Producer

Lauren Doll
Producer

John Gore
CEO,
Broadway Across
America
Producer

Memphis

Linda and Bill Potter
Producers

Thomas B. McGrath
Chairman,
Broadway Across
America
Producer

Patty Baker,
Good Productions
Producer

Scott & Kaylin Union
Producers

Loraine Alterman
Boyle
Producer

Chase Mishkin
Producer

Remmel T. Dickinson
Producer

Pat Halloran
Memphis Orpheum
Group
Producer

Vijay Vashee
Producer

Sita Vashee
Producer

Ken Clay
Associate Producer

David Armstrong,
Executive Producer/
Artistic Director
The 5th Avenue
Theatre

Bernadine Griffin,
Managing Director,
The 5th Avenue
Theatre

Bill Berry
Producing Director,
The 5th Avenue
Theatre

Christopher Ashley,
Artistic Director,
La Jolla Playhouse

Robert Kelley
Artistic Director
TheatreWorks

Phil Santora
Managing Director,
TheatreWorks

Felicia Boswell
*Ensemble, Someday
Backup Singer*

Bryan Fenkart
Standby Huey

Rhett George
*Black DJ, Be Black
Trio, Ensemble*

Gregory Haney
*Be Black Trio,
Ensemble*

Chad Kimball
Huey

Kyle Leland
*Be Black Trio,
Ensemble*

Will Mann
Bobby

Ephraim M. Sykes
Ensemble

Carmen Shavone
Borders
Ensemble

Angela C. Brydon
*Double Dutch Girl,
Ensemble*

Sasha Hutchings
Swing

Christopher Jackson
Delray

Lauren Lim Jackson
*Double Dutch Girl,
Someday Backup
Singer, Ensemble*

Cass Morgan
Mama

Memphis

Ken Robinson
Black DJ, Ensemble

Cary Tedder
Ensemble

WARDROBE
Front Row (L-R): Dora Bonilla, (Sitting) Doug Earl, (Sitting) Tasha Cowd, Rory Powers
Back Row (L-R): Rick Ortiz, Billy Hipkins, Kim Kaldenberg, Lizz Hirons, Charles van de Craats

CREW
Front Row (L-R): Joe Pearson, Karen Hyman
Second Row (L-R): (Standing) Tommy Manoy, (Sitting) Erik Yans, Joe Manoy, Mike Pilipski, Randy Morrison, AJ Giegerich, Ralph Sanford, (Standing) Hank Hal"
Back Row (L-R): (on platform) Greg Freedman, TJ Manoy, Mike Maher, Cassandra Givens, Ron Vitelli, Eric "Speed" Smith, James Spradling

HAIR
Front: Mary Kay Yezerski-Bondoc
Back Row (L-R): Michele Rutter, Jameson Eaton, Charlene Belmond

STAGE MANAGEMENT
(L-R): Arturo E. Porazzi, Gary Mickelson, Janet Takami, Alexis Shorter

Photos by Brian Mapp

Memphis

STAFF for MEMPHIS

GENERAL MANAGEMENT
ALCHEMY PRODUCTION GROUP
Carl Pasbjerg   Frank P. Scardino

COMPANY MANAGER
Jim Brandeberry

PRODUCTION MANAGEMENT
JUNIPER STREET PRODUCTIONS
Hillary Blanken   Guy Kwan
Kevin Broomell   Ana Rose Greene

GENERAL PRESS REPRESENTATIVE
THE HARTMAN GROUP
Michael Hartman
Juliana Hannett   Emily McGill

CASTING
TELSEY + COMPANY
Bernie Telsey CSA, Will Cantler CSA, David Vaccari CSA,
Bethany Knox CSA, Craig Burns CSA,
Tiffany Little Canfield CSA, Rachel Hoffman CSA,
Justin Huff CSA, Patrick Goodwin CSA,
Abby Brady-Dalton, David Morris, Cesar A. Rocha

DOORWOMAN
Rose Alaio

ADVERTISING/MARKETING
aka
Liz Furze   Scott A. Moore   Clint Bond, Jr.
Elizabeth Findlay   Joshua Lee Poole
Adam Jay   Janette Roush
Erik Alden   Meghan Bartley

ASSOCIATE DIRECTOR
Beatrice Terry

ASSOCIATE CHOREOGRAPHER
Edgar Godineaux

Production Stage Manager ....Arturo E. Porazzi
Stage Manager ....Gary Mickelson
Assistant Stage Manager ....Christine Viega
Assistant Stage Manager ....Alexis Shorter
Associate Company Manager ....Michelle Tamagawa
Junkyard Dog Associate ....Kristel J. Brown
Associate to the General Managers ......Amanda Coleman
Dance Captain ....Jermaine R. Rembert
Assistant Dance Captain ....Candice Monet McCall
Assistant Fight Director ....Shad Ramsey
Fight Captain ....Jermaine R. Rembert
Dramaturg ....Gabriel Greene
Dialect Coach ....Stephen Gabis
Make-Up Designer ....Angelina Avallone
Associate Scenic Designer ....Steven C. Kemp
Associate Costume Designer ....Rory Powers
Associate Lighting Designer ....Mark Simpson
Associate Hair Designer ....Leah Loukas
Assistant Costume Designer ....Maria Zamansky
Assistant to the Costume Designer ....Kara Harmon
Assistant to the Lighting Designer ....Amanda Zieve
Assistant Sound Designer ....Alex Hawthorn
Assistant Projection Designer ....Steve Channon
Moving Light Programmer ....David Arch
Projections Programmer ....Florian Mosleh
Production/Head Carpenter ....Hank Hale
Flyman ....Erik Yans
Assistant Carpenter
    (Automation) ....Eric "Speed" Smith
Production Electrician ....James Fedigan
Head Electrician ....Joe Pearson
Production Property Master ....Mike Pilipski
Head Property Master ....John Paull
Assistant Property Master ....Peter Drummond

Production Sound Engineer ....Phillip Lojo
FOH Sound Engineer ....Greg Freedman
Assistant Sound Engineer ....Cassandra Givens
Wardrobe Supervisor ....Kyle Wesson
Associate Wardrobe Supervisor ....Shana Albery
Dressers ....Dora Bonilla, Tasha Cowd,
                            Douglas Earl, Maureen George,
        Betty Gillispie, Billy Hipkins, Lizz Hirons,
                James Hodun, Kim Kaldenberg
Hair Supervisor ....Michele Rutter
Assistant Hair Supervisor ....Mary Kay Yezerski-Bondoc
Hair Stylists ....Charlene Belmond, Lisa Weiss
Music Copying ....Christopher Deschene
Keyboard Programmer ....Kenny J. Seymour
Music Assistant ....Clare Cooper
Rehearsal Drummer ....Clayton Craddock
Technical Assistant ....Alexandra Paull
Production Assistants ....Megan J. Alvord,
                                        Meg Friedman
Scenic/Projection Studio Manager ....Sarah Zeitler
Production Intern ....Kendra Stockton
Lighting Interns ....Avery Lewis, Jeff Kastenbaum
Scenic Design Interns ....Tiffany Dalian, Caite Hevner
Projection Design Intern ....Wolfram Ott
Sound Interns ....Stephanie Celustka, Cynthia Hannon
Physical Therapy ....Performing Arts Physical Therapy
Digital/Internet Marketing 87AM/
                            Adam Cunningham, Alex Bisker,
                        Ximena Sanchez, Nick Shylo
Social Media Director ....Carolyn D. Miller
Multicultural Marketing ....Full House Theater Tickets
Production Photographer ....Joan Marcus
Accountant ....Fried & Kowgios LLC
Controller ....Joe Kabula
Legal Counsel ....Beigelman Feldman & Associates PC
Payroll Services ....Castellana Services, Inc.
Banking ....Signature Bank
Insurance ..........D.R. Rieff & Associates/Sonny Everett
Hotel Broker ....Road Concierge/Lisa Morris
Air Travel Broker ....Tzell Travel/Andi Henig
Opening Night
    Coordination ....The Lawrence Company Events
Merchandising ....Marquee Merchandise, LLC/
                                        Matt Murphy
Theatre Displays ....King Displays Inc.

FRONT OF HOUSE
Front Row (L-R): Susan Maxwell, Brian Gaynair, John Barbaretti, Joanne Blessington, Maura Gaynor, Erin O'Donnell, Stephen Ivelja,
Martin Cooper, Alexis Stewart
Back Row (L-R): Stephanie Lopez, Paul Rodriguez, Tomas Ortiz, Jamie Wilhelm-Jacobs, Leonardo Ruiz, Delia Pozo, Jason Weixelman, Elvis Caban

Memphis
SCRAPBOOK

Correspondent: Bryan Langlitz, "Ensemble"
Most Exciting Celebrity Visitor: Seeing Steve Young dancing in his seat during "Steal Your Rock 'n' Roll." We have a football-friendly cast; Imagine lots of guys dancing onstage trying to get each other's attention shouting, "That's Steve Young! Do you see Steve Young!? He's a Hall of Famer!"
Special Backstage Rituals: Prayer Circle before every single performance. All religions, all beliefs. Many cast members coming together to pray for well-being, safety, success, and graciously praising. It's a wonderful moment to center yourself.
Favorite At-Theatre Gathering Place: The Beach! "The Beach" is the name for the big fire escape attached to the men's dressing room. It's brilliant in the summertime. Especially for the swings…and hammocks!
Favorite Off-Site Hangouts: Swanky? Glass House Tavern. Grungy? Reunion Bar! Someone's birthday? Ember Room.
Favorite Snack Foods: Whole Wheat Pretzels from Stage Management and York Peppermint Patties.
Mascot: Samson The Dog.
Favorite Therapy: Sore No More! A gift from one of our producers.
Memorable Ad-Lib: Montego saying "Bless You" after Adam sneezed 30 seconds into his entrance as Huey. She didn't miss a beat.
Memorable Press Encounter: 2011 Thanksgiving Day Parade music video with Adam Pascal. Shooting it surrounded by real New Yorkers and their kids on a beautiful playground.
Memorable Stage Door Fan Encounter: We have amazing fans! But it's more fun to see them in the front row grooving to the show! Some of them know every single word of dialogue and mouth it along with us. That's…special.

Members of the ensemble gather at Glass House Tavern October 19, 2011 to celebrate the show's second anniversary.

Web Buzz: I'll go ahead and Tweet this answer: @MemphisonBroadway is nailing it. #hockadoo.
Fastest Costume Change: Huey takes the cake. 21 seconds?
Catchphrases Only the Company Would Recognize: "So Fiercely." "Not Making It."
Understudy Anecdote: This isn't so much an anecdote as a proclamation of their insane talents. Our understudies are scary at how well they perform at the drop of a hat. Y'all better watch out! It's AMAZING what kind of talent hides in a Broadway Ensemble.
Nicknames: The men's dressing room renamed each other for an entire month. A sampling: "Goober," "Ping Ping," and "Precious, Based on the Novel Push, by Sapphire."
Embarrassing Moments: Every cast member in every show every night on Broadway risks a fair amount of embarrassment, and has found themselves blushing at least once a week. Recent example? My first time "going up" on the very first line of the show. Light up…face blank…fear…rambling…hoping something I say makes sense. It was awful. But then it was over!
Coolest Thing About Being in This Show: Turning left onto 44th street as I walk up Seventh Avenue and seeing the famous Shubert Theatre lit up. That little voice in the back of my head that still says, "You did it. This is where you work." It's magical.

CREDITS

Scenery constructed by Showman Fabricators, Inc., Long Island City, NY. Show control and scenic motion control featuring Stage Command® Systems by PRG Scenic Technologies, New Windsor, NY. Additional scenery painted by Scenic Arts Studios, Cornwall, NY. Soft goods built by I. Weiss and Sons, Inc., Long Island City, NY. Lighting equipment provided by PRG Lighting, North Bergen, NJ. Sound equipment provided by Masque Sound, East Rutherford, NJ. Projection equipment provided by Scharff Weisberg Inc., Long Island City, NY. Props built by the Spoon Group, Rahway, NJ. Ms. Glover and Ms. Morgan's costumes by Donna Langman. Additional ladies costumes by Euro Co Costumes, Inc.; D. Barak Stribling; Tricorne, Inc.; and Eric Winterling, Inc. Mr. Kimball, Mr. Calloway, and Mr. Iglehart's tailoring by Brian Hemesath. Additional men's tailoring by Jennifer Love Costumes, Inc.; Scafati, Inc.; and D. L. Cerney. Men's finale suits by Top Hat Imagewear. Custom shirts by Cego. Dance shoes by Worldtone Dance. 'Gator' head by Rodney Gordon, Inc. Makeup provided by M•A•C. ©Ernest C. Withers Estate, courtesy Panopticon Gallery, Boston, MA: Dewey Phillips of WHQB, Red Hot and Blue Program, The Hippodrome, Beale Street, Memphis, early 1950s #LV61C. Clarence Gatemouth Brown at Club Handy, Memphis, TN. Count Basie, Ruth Brown, Billy Eckstine, The Hippodrome, 1950s. Percy Mayfield (with drumsticks) and band, The Hippodrome, 1951. Special thanks to Edgar Godineaux, Gabriel Barre, Sarah Nashman, Kent Nicholson, Marilynn Sheldon, TeamTastic, Adam Arian, Mo Brady, Michael Finkle, Debra Hatch, Sue Makkoo, Michael Clark and the many folks that made it happen at NSMT, TheatreWorks, La Jolla Playhouse and the Fifth Avenue Theatre.

Energy-efficient washer/dryer courtesy of LG Electronics.

THE SHUBERT ORGANIZATION, INC.
Board of Directors

Philip J. Smith	**Robert E. Wankel**
Chairman	President
Wyche Fowler, Jr.	**Diana Phillips**
Lee J. Seidler	**Michael I. Sovern**
Stuart Subotnick	

Elliot Greene	**David Andrews**
Chief Financial Officer	Senior Vice President Shubert Ticketing
Juan Calvo	**John Darby**
Vice President – Finance	Vice President – Facilities
Peter Entin	**Charles Flateman**
Vice President – Theatre Operations	Vice President – Marketing
Anthony LaMattina	**Brian Mahoney**
Vice President – Audit & Production Finance	Vice President – Ticket Sales

D.S. Moynihan
Vice President – Creative Projects

House Manager ....Brian Gaynair

The Mountaintop

First Preview: September 22, 2011. Opened: October 13, 2011.
Closed January 22, 2012 after 24 Previews and 117 Performances.

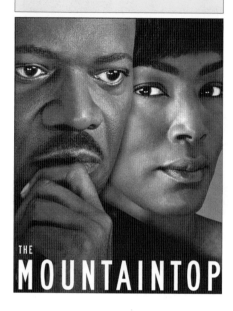

PLAYBILL®

THE MOUNTAINTOP

On the night before Dr. Martin Luther King's assassination, the civil rights leader encounters a maid at his hotel who turns out to be the Angel of Death, offering him a vision of the future before she escorts him to the next world.

CAST
(in order of appearance)

Dr. Martin Luther
King, Jr. ....SAMUEL L. JACKSON
Camae ....ANGELA BASSETT

STANDBYS
Standby for Dr. Martin Luther King, Jr.:
BILLY EUGENE JONES

Standby for Camae:
ROSALYN COLEMAN

The action takes place on April 3, 1968.
Room 306, Lorraine Motel
Memphis, Tennessee

---

⑤ BERNARD B. JACOBS THEATRE
242 West 45th Street
A Shubert Organization Theatre

Philip J. Smith, *Chairman*   Robert E. Wankel, *President*

JEAN DOUMANIAN   SONIA FRIEDMAN PRODUCTIONS   AMBASSADOR THEATRE GROUP
RAISE THE ROOF 7   TED SNOWDON   ALHADEFF PRODUCTIONS/LAUREN DOLL
B SQUARE · 4 PRODUCTIONS/BROADWAY ACROSS AMERICA
JACKI BARLIA FLORIN/COOPER FEDERMAN   RONNIE PLANALP/MOELLENBERG TAYLOR
MARLA RUBIN PRODUCTIONS/BLUMENTHAL PERFORMING ARTS

PRESENT

SAMUEL L. JACKSON   ANGELA BASSETT

IN

THE MOUNTAINTOP

BY
KATORI HALL

ORIGINAL MUSIC
BRANFORD MARSALIS

SET & PROJECTION DESIGN   COSTUME DESIGN   LIGHTING DESIGN   SOUND DESIGN
DAVID GALLO   CONSTANZA ROMERO   BRIAN MacDEVITT   DAN MOSES SCHREIER

HAIR & WIG DESIGN   CASTING   PRODUCTION MANAGEMENT
CHARLES G. LaPOINTE   JIM CARNAHAN, C.S.A.   AURORA PRODUCTIONS

PRODUCTION STAGE MANAGER   PRESS REPRESENTATIVE   ADVERTISING
JIMMIE LEE SMITH   O&M CO.   SPOTCO

ASSOCIATE PRODUCER   COMPANY MANAGER   GENERAL MANAGER
PATRICK DALY   BRIG BERNEY   RICHARDS/CLIMAN, INC.

Produced in association with SCOTT DELMAN

DIRECTED BY
KENNY LEON

The Mountaintop was developed at the Lark Play Development Center, New York City and was first produced by Theatre503, London in June 2009. The production was transferred to Trafalgar Studios One in July 2009 where it was produced by Sonia Friedman Productions and Jean Doumanian, Tali Pelman for Ambassador Theatre Group, Bob Bartner, Freddy DeMann, Jerry Frankel, Ted Snowdon and Marla Rubin Productions Ltd.

The Mountaintop was developed at the 2008 Bay Area Playwrights Festival, a program of the Playwrights Foundation. Amy L. Mueller, Artistic Director.

The producers wish to express their appreciation to Theatre Development Fund for its support of this production.

10/13/11

(L-R): Samuel L. Jackson, Angela Bassett

Photo by Joan Marcus

The Mountaintop

Samuel L. Jackson
Dr. Martin Luther King, Jr.

Angela Bassett
Camae

Rosalyn Coleman
Standby for Camae

Billy Eugene Jones
Standby for Dr. Martin Luther King, Jr.

Katori Hall
Playwright

Kenny Leon
Director

Branford Marsalis
Original Music

David Gallo
Set and Projection Design

Constanza Romero
Costume Design

Brian MacDevitt
Lighting Design

Dan Moses Schreier
Sound Design

Charles G. LaPointe
Hair & Wig Design

Kate Wilson
Dialect Coach

Jim Carnahan
Casting

David R. Richards and Tamar Haimes
Richards/Climan, Inc.
General Manager

Brig Berney
Company Manager

Jean Doumanian
Producer

Sonia Friedman,
Sonia Friedman Productions
Producer

Howard Panter
Ambassador Theatre Group
Producer

Rosemary Squire
Ambassador Theatre Group
Producer

Elaine Krauss
Raise The Roof 7
Producer

Harriet Leve
Raise The Roof 7
Producer

Jennifer Manocherian
Raise The Roof 7
Producer

Ted Snowdon
Producer

Marleen Alhadeff
Alhadeff Productions
Producer

Kenny Alhadeff
Alhadeff Productions
Producer

Lauren Doll
Producer

Barbara Freitag
B Square +4 Productions
Producer

Buddy Freitag
B Square +4 Productions
Producer

John Gore
Broadway Across America
Producer

Thomas B. McGrath
Broadway Across America
Producer

Jacki Barlia Florin
Producer

Max Cooper
Cooper Federman
Producer

Wendy Federman
Cooper Federman
Producer

The Mountaintop

Ronnie Planalp
Ronnie Planalp/
Moellenberg Taylor
Producer

Carl Moellenberg
Ronnie Planalp/
Moellenberg Taylor
Producer

Deborah Taylor
Ronnie Planalp/
Moellenberg Taylor
Producer

Tom Gabbard
Blumenthal
Performing Arts
Producer

SCRAPBOOK

Photos by Joseph Marzullo/WENN

Correspondent: Rosalyn Coleman, understudy for Camae.

Opening Night Gifts: Batons. Sam gave everyone really cool knage hats.

Most Exciting Celebrity Visitors: Oprah. Aretha. I just stared at them. My husband told Oprah that I am the understudy.

Actor Who Has Done the Most Shows in Their Career: Sam is a billion-dollar actor. I guess he did. I saw him back in the day when he was at NEC. He was in Charles Fuller's plays. He was really good then too.

Favorite Moment During Each Performance (On Stage or Off): Word Bridge.

Favorite In-Theatre Gathering Place: Sam's dressing room is tricked out.

Favorite Off-Site Hangout: Uh...I am not that cool.

Favorite Snack Food: Chocolate.

Internet Buzz on the Show: Folks love it. I love it. My Facebook page and Twitter are filled with accolades.

Latest Audience Arrival: Gotta be 8:40 p.m.

Heaviest/Hottest Costume: Sam has a wig and nose vs. A.B. has a glam dress.

Understudy Anecdote: The audience would kill us if we went on.

Embarrassing Moment: My phone went off during a preview.

Coolest Thing About Being in This Show: Working with the Prince of Peace and God, so I guess that's Katori Hall's imagination. Living in her imagination.

1. Angela Bassett and Samuel L. Jackson unveil their portraits at Sardi's restaurant January 12, 2012.
2. A surprise visit to Brooklyn High School of the Arts September 19, 2011. (L-R): Director Kenny Leon, Bassett, NY Schools Chancellor Dennis M. Walcott, Katori Hall and Jackson.
3. (L-R): Jackson and Leon with backstage visitor Denzel Washington.
4. Celebrating Jackson's 63rd birthday December 21, 2011 (L-R): Rev. Al Sharpton, Jackson and Bassett.

The Mountaintop

Photos by Brian Mapp

COMPANY AND STAGE MANAGEMENT
(L-R): Brig Berney (Company Manager), Jimmie Lee Smith (Production Stage Manager), Ken McGee (Assistant Stage Manager), Paula Wise (Production Assistant)

DOORMEN
(L-R): Rick Ramos, Elvin Ventura

FRONT OF HOUSE
Standing (L-R): Billy Mitchell, Kathleen Spock, John Minore, Al Peay, Al Nazario, Rosa Pesante
Sitting (L-R): Martha Rodriguez, Eva Laskow, John Seid

BOX OFFICE
(L-R): Karen Coscia, Michael Kolbrenner

CREW
(L-R): Edward Ruggiero (Flyman), Carole Morales (Hair/Makeup Supervisor), Moira Conrad (Wardrobe Supervisor), Alfred Ricci (House Props), Volney McFarlin (Asst. to Mr. Jackson), Will King (Sub Production Electrician), Michael Van Praag (House Carpenter), Rebecca O'Neill (Production Carpenter), Brian Munroe (Production Carpenter), John Dory (Production Sound), Askia Jacob (Dresser), Herb Messing (House Electrician)

The Mountaintop

STAFF FOR *THE MOUNTAINTOP*

GENERAL MANAGEMENT
RICHARDS/CLIMAN, INC.
David R. Richards   Tamar Haimes
Michael Sag   Kyle Bonder
Jessica Fried   Jaqueline Kolek

COMPANY MANAGER
Brig Berney

PRODUCTION MANAGEMENT
AURORA PRODUCTIONS
Gene O'Donovan   W. Benjamin Heller II
Stephanie Sherline   Jarid Sumner   Liza Luxenberg
Anita Shah   Rebecca Zuber   Steven Dalton
Eugenio Saenz Flores   Isaac Katzanek
Melissa Mazdra

PRESS REPRESENTATIVE
O&M Co.
Rick Miramontez   Philip Carrubba
Molly Barnett   Sam Corbett   Andy Snyder

CASTING
Jim Carnahan, CSA
Kate Boka, CSA
Carrie Gardner, CSA   Stephen Kopel
Jillian Cimini   Michael Morlani

PRODUCTION STAGE
  MANAGER ....Jimmie Lee Smith
Stage Manager ....Kenneth J. McGee
Assistant Director ....Kamilah Forbes
Dialect Coach ....Kate Wilson
Special Effects ....Jeremy Chernick
Associate Scenic Designer ....Evan F. Adamson
Associate Projection Design/
  Animation ....Steve Channon
Design Studio Manager ....Sarah Zeitler
Projection Research Director ....Jan Price Frazier
Set Design Interns ....Pamela Lee, Ga Hyun Bae
Projection Design Interns ....Samantha Shoffner,
                                      Tess James
Assistant Costume Designer ....Angela M. Kahler
Associate Lighting Designer ....Jennifer Schriever
Assistant Lighting Designer ....Peter Hoerburger
Associate Sound Designer ....David Bullard
Prosthetic Design ....Adam Bailey
Production Carpenter ....Brian Munroe
Production Electrician ....Dan Coey
Production Sound Engineer ....John Dory
Production Properties Coordinator ....Peter Sarafin
Assistant Production Properties
  Coordinator ....Buist Bickley
Wardrobe Supervisor ....Moira MacGregor Conrad
Dresser ....Askia Won Ling Jacob
Hair Supervisor ....Carole Morales
Assistant to Mr. Jackson ....Volney McFarlin
Assistant to Ms. Bassett ....Alex Van Praag
Assistant to Ms. Hall ....JaMeeka Holloway
Assistant to Mr. Leon ....Victoria Dunn
Production Assistant ....Paula Wise
Advertising ....SpotCo/
        Drew Hodges, Jim Edwards,
      Tom Greenwald, Vinny Sinato,
        Jim Aquino, Laura Ellis

Website Design/Online Marketing ....SpotCo/
        Sara Fitzpatrick, Kristen Bardwil
Marketing ....SpotCo/
      Nick Pramik, Caroline Newhouse,
       Kristen Rathbun, Julie Wechsler
Press Associates ....Jaron Caldwell, Jon Dimond,
        Richard Hillman, Yufen Kung,
     Chelsea Nachman, Elizabeth Wagner
Press Interns ....Sarah Babin, Michael Jorgensen
Merchandising ....Randi Grossman/
              Max Merchandising LLC
Banking ....City National Bank/Michele Gibbons
Insurance ....DeWitt Stern Group
        Peter Shoemaker, Anthony Pittari
Accountants ....Fried & Kowgios CPAs LLP/
        Robert Fried, Anthony Moore
Comptroller ....Elliott Aronstam
Legal Counsel ....Lazarus and Harris LLP/
            Scott Lazarus, Esq.,
          Robert C. Harris, Esq.
Payroll ....Castellana Services
Opening Night Coordination ....Michael Lawrence
Production Photographer ....Joan Marcus

JEAN DOUMANIAN PRODUCTIONS
Vice President Production/
  Development ....Patrick Daly
Director Production/
  Development ....Mirella Cheeseman
Executive Assistant ....Elizabeth Grobel
Assistant ....Saul Nathan-Kazis

SONIA FRIEDMAN PRODUCTIONS
General Manager ....Diane Benjamin
Head of Production ....Pam Skinner
Literary Associate ....Jack Bradley
Associate Producer
  (Development & Marketing) ....Lucie Lovatt
Production Coordinator ....Fiona Stewart
Associate General Manager ....Emma Laugier
General Management Assistant ....Ben Canning
Assistant to Sonia Friedman ....Sarah Hammond
Production Assistant ....Pelé Ling
Production Assistant
  (funded by Stage One) ....Sarah Brocklehurst
Production Accountant ....Melissa Hay
Chief Executive Officer – New York...........David Lazar
New York Assistant ....Valerie Steinberg
SFP Board ....Helen Enright, Howard Panter,
                      Rosemary Squire

THE AMBASSADOR THEATRE GROUP LTD.
Life President ....Sir Eddie Kulukundis OBE
Executive Chairman ....Greg Dyke
Joint Chief Executive &
  Creative Director ....Howard Panter
Joint Chief Executive ....Rosemary Squire OBE
Chief Financial Officer ....Helen Enright
Managing Director (Content) ....Michael Lynas
Property Director ....David Blyth
Business Affairs Director ....Peter Kavanagh
Managing Director (Venues) ....Nick Potter
Managing Director (Ticketing) ....Simon Palethorpe
Directors ....Peter Beckwith OBE, Bill Benjamin,
        Simon Davidson, Chris Graham,
                 Richard Lenane
Producer ....Tali Pelman

AMBASSADOR THEATRE GROUP – NEW YORK
Chief Executive Officer ....David Lazar

CREDITS
Scenery automation and show control by Show Motion Inc,
Milford, CT, using the AC2 Computerized Motion Control
System. Projection, lighting and sound equipment from
Production Resource Group. Rehearsal furniture by
Sightline Fabrication. Prop upholstery by Anna Light.
Fabric dyed by Staf Maus. Soft goods by R-Ramos
Upholstery. Some furniture by SFDS Fabrication & Design
Shop. Special effects by Lydic Design, Jerard Studio,
Showman Fabricators and J&M Special Effects. Costumes
built by Tricorne Studios and Artur & Tailors, Ltd. Prop
fabrication by Jeremy Lydic, Bobby Dowling, Glenn
Merwede and Daedalus Scene Shop.

SPECIAL THANKS AND ACKNOWLEDGEMENTS
Southern Poverty Law Center

THE MOUNTAINTOP
rehearsed at New 42nd Street Studios

Newsies

First Preview: March 15, 2012. Opened: March 29, 2012.
Still running as of May 31, 2012.

A musical based on the cult 1992 Disney film about the real-life 1899 New York City newsboy strike. Street-wise "newsie" Jack Kelly reaches his limit when wealthy publisher Joseph Pulitzer tries to squeeze a few more precious pennies out of the hardworking street-hawkers. With help from a crusading journalist, the plucky Jack organizes the newsboys of all the papers in all the boroughs into a union, and manages—despite a series of setbacks—to push the city's publishers into an unexpected corner. But what of Jack's dream to chuck it all and move to a better life in Santa Fe?

CAST
(in order of appearance)

Jack Kelly	JEREMY JORDAN
Crutchie	ANDREW KEENAN-BOLGER
Race	RYAN BRESLIN
Albert	GARETT HAWE
Specs	RYAN STEELE
Henry	KYLE COFFMAN
Finch	AARON J. ALBANO
Elmer	EVAN KASPRZAK
Romeo	ANDY RICHARDSON
Mush	EPHRAIM SYKES
Katherine	KARA LINDSAY
Darcy	THAYNE JASPERSON
Nuns	JULIE FOLDESI, CAPATHIA JENKINS, LAURIE VELDHEER
Morris Delancey	MIKE FAIST
Oscar Delancey	BRENDON STIMSON
Wiesel	JOHN E. BRADY
Davey	BEN FANKHAUSER

Continued on next page

The Playbill Broadway Yearbook 2011-2012

≈N≈ NEDERLANDER THEATRE
UNDER THE DIRECTION OF
JAMES M. NEDERLANDER AND JAMES L. NEDERLANDER

Disney Theatrical Productions
under the direction of
Thomas Schumacher
Presents

DISNEY NEWSIES
THE MUSICAL

Music by | *Lyrics by* | *Book by*
ALAN MENKEN | **JACK FELDMAN** | **HARVEY FIERSTEIN**

Based on the Disney film written by BOB TZUDIKER and NONI WHITE

Starring
JEREMY JORDAN

JOHN DOSSETT KARA LINDSAY CAPATHIA JENKINS BEN FANKHAUSER
ANDREW KEENAN-BOLGER LEWIS GROSSO MATTHEW J. SCHECHTER

AARON J. ALBANO   MARK ALDRICH   TOMMY BRACCO   JOHN E. BRADY   RYAN BRESLIN
KEVIN CAROLAN   CAITLYN CAUGHELL   KYLE COFFMAN   MIKE FAIST   MICHAEL FATICA
JULIE FOLDESI   GARETT HAWE   THAYNE JASPERSON   EVAN KASPRZAK   JESS LePROTTO
STUART MARLAND   ANDY RICHARDSON   JACK SCOTT   RYAN STEELE   BRENDON STIMSON
NICK SULLIVAN   EPHRAIM SYKES   LAURIE VELDHEER   ALEX WONG   STUART ZAGNIT

Scenic Design	*Costume Design*	*Lighting Design*	*Sound Design*
TOBIN OST	**JESS GOLDSTEIN**	**JEFF CROITER**	**KEN TRAVIS**

Projection Design	*Hair & Wig Design*	*Fight Direction*	*Casting*
SVEN ORTEL	**CHARLES G. LAPOINTE**	**J. ALLEN SUDDETH**	**TELSEY + COMPANY JUSTIN HUFF, CSA**

Associate Producer	*Technical Supervision*	*Production Manager*	*Production Stage Manager*
ANNE QUART	**NEIL MAZZELLA & GEOFFREY QUART**	**EDUARDO CASTRO**	**THOMAS J. GATES**

Music Director/ Dance Music Arrangements	*Music Coordinator*	*Associate Director*	*Associate Choreographer*
MARK HUMMEL	**JOHN MILLER**	**RICHARD J. HINDS**	**LOU CASTRO**

Orchestrations by
DANNY TROOB

Music Supervision/ Incidental Music & Vocal Arrangements by
MICHAEL KOSARIN

Choreographed by
CHRISTOPHER GATTELLI

Directed by
JEFF CALHOUN

World Premiere, Paper Mill Playhouse, in Millburn, New Jersey on September 25, 2011.   Mark S. Hoebee, Producing Artistic Director, Todd Schmidt, Managing Director

3/29/12

Ben Fankhauser and Jeremy Jordan (center) with the cast

Photo by Deen van Meer

Newsies

MUSICAL NUMBERS

ACT I

Prologue: Rooftop, Dawn
"Santa Fe" (Prologue) ....Jack, Crutchie
Scene 1: Newsie Square
"Carrying the Banner" ....Jack, Newsies
Scene 2: Pulitzer's Office, Afternoon
"The Bottom Line" ....Pulitzer, Seitz, Bunsen, Hannah
Scene 3: A Street Corner
Scene 4: Medda's Theater
"That's Rich" ....Medda
"I Never Planned on You/Don't Come a-Knocking" ....Jack, Bowery Beauties
Scene 5: Newsie Square, Next Morning
"The World Will Know" ....Jack, Davey, Les, Newsies
Scene 6: Jacobi's Deli and Street, Afternoon
"The World Will Know" (Reprise) ....Newsies
Scene 7: Katherine's Office
"Watch What Happens" ....Katherine
Scene 8: Newsie Square, Next Morning
"Seize the Day" ....Davey, Jack, Newsies
Scene 9: Rooftop
"Santa Fe" ....Jack

ACT II

Entre'acte
Scene 1: Jacobi's Deli, Next Morning
"King of New York" ....Davey, Katherine, Les, Newsies
Scene 2: Medda's Theater
"Watch What Happens" (Reprise) ....Davey, Jack, Katherine, Les
Scene 3: Pulitzer's Office and Cellar, Afternoon
"The Bottom Line" (Reprise) ....Pulitzer, Seitz and Mayor
Scene 4: Brooklyn Bridge and Medda's Theater
"Brooklyn's Here" ....Spot Conlon and Newsies
Scene 5: Rooftop
"Something to Believe In" ....Katherine, Jack
Scene 6: Pulitzer's Cellar
"Seize the Day" (Reprise) ....Newsies
"Once and for All" ....Jack, Davey, Katherine, Newsies
Scene 7: Pulitzer's Office, Next Morning
"Seize the Day" (Reprise) ....Newsies
Scene 8: Newsie Square
"Finale" ....Jack, Newsies

The Ensemble

Photo by Deen van Meer

Cast Continued

Les ....LEWIS GROSSO and
MATTHEW J. SCHECHTER
Joseph Pulitzer ....JOHN DOSSETT
Seitz ....MARK ALDRICH
Bunsen ....NICK SULLIVAN
Hannah ....LAURIE VELDHEER
Snyder ....STUART MARLAND
Medda Larkin ....CAPATHIA JENKINS
Stage Manager ....JOHN E. BRADY
Mr. Jacobi ....JOHN E. BRADY
Scabs ....TOMMY BRACCO,
JESS LePROTTO, ALEX WONG
Mayor ....JOHN E. BRADY
Spot Conlon ....TOMMY BRACCO
Bill ....GARETT HAWE
Governor Roosevelt ....KEVIN CAROLAN
Citizens of New York ....AARON J. ALBANO,
MARK ALDRICH, TOMMY BRACCO,
JOHN E. BRADY, RYAN BRESLIN,
KEVIN CAROLAN, KYLE COFFMAN,
MIKE FAIST, JULIE FOLDESI,
GARETT HAWE, THAYNE JASPERSON,
EVAN KASPRZAK, JESS LePROTTO,
STUART MARLAND, ANDY RICHARDSON,
RYAN STEELE, BRENDON STIMSON,
NICK SULLIVAN, EPHRAIM SYKES,
LAURIE VELDHEER, ALEX WONG

SWINGS

CAITLYN CAUGHELL, MICHAEL FATICA,
JACK SCOTT, STUART ZAGNIT

Dance Captain:
RYAN STEELE
Assistant Dance Captain:
MICHAEL FATICA
Fight Captain:
KEVIN CAROLAN

UNDERSTUDIES

For Jack Kelly:
MIKE FAIST, BRENDON STIMSON
For Katherine:
CAITLYN CAUGHELL, LAURIE VELDHEER
For Davey:
RYAN BRESLIN, GARETT HAWE
For Crutchie:
GARETT HAWE, ANDY RICHARDSON
For Medda:
CAITLYN CAUGHELL, JULIE FOLDESI
For Pulitzer:
JOHN E. BRADY, STUART MARLAND

Newsies

Cast Continued

For Roosevelt:
MARK ALDRICH, STUART ZAGNIT
For Seitz/Bunsen:
EVAN KASPRZAK, STUART ZAGNIT
For Snyder:
NICK SULLIVAN, STUART ZAGNIT
For Wiesel/Stage Manager/Jacobi/Mayor:
NICK SULLIVAN, STUART ZAGNIT

TIME:

Summer, 1899

PLACE:

Lower Manhattan

ORCHESTRA

Conductor:
MARK HUMMEL
Associate Conductor:
STEVEN MALONE
Assistant Conductor:
MAT EISENSTEIN
Woodwinds:
TOM MURRAY, MARK THRASHER
Trumpet/Flugel:
TREVOR D. NEUMANN
Trombone:
DAN LEVINE
Guitar:
BRIAN KOONIN
Bass:
RAY KILDAY
Drums:
PAUL DAVIS
Percussion:
ED SHEA
Keyboards:
MAT EISENSTEIN, STEVEN MALONE
Violin:
MARY ROWELL
Cello:
DEBORAH ASSAEL-MIGLIORE

Electronic Music Programmer:
JEFF MARDER
Music Coordinator:
JOHN MILLER

Jeremy Jordan
Jack Kelly

John Dossett
Joseph Pulitzer

Kara Lindsay
Katherine

Capathia Jenkins
Medda Larkin

Ben Fankhauser
Davey

Andrew Keenan-Bolger
Crutchie

Lewis Grosso
Les

Matthew J. Schechter
Les

Aaron J. Albano
Finch, Ensemble

Mark Aldrich
Seitz, Ensemble

Tommy Bracco
Spot Conlon, Scab, Ensemble

John E. Brady
Wiesel, Stage Manager, Mr. Jacobi, Mayor, Ensemble

Ryan Breslin
Race, Ensemble

Kevin Carolan
Roosevelt, Ensemble

Caitlyn Caughell
Swing

Kyle Coffman
Henry, Ensemble

Mike Faist
Morris Delancey, Ensemble

Michael Fatica
Swing

Julie Foldesi
Nun, Ensemble

Garett Hawe
Albert, Bill, Ensemble

Newsies

Thayne Jasperson
Darcy, Ensemble

Evan Kasprzak
Elmer, Ensemble

Jess LeProtto
Scab, Ensemble

Stuart Marland
Snyder, Ensemble

Andy Richardson
Romeo, Ensemble

Jack Scott
Swing

Ryan Steele
Specs, Ensemble, Dance Captain

Brendon Stimson
Oscar Delancey, Ensemble

Nick Sullivan
Bunsen, Ensemble

Ephraim Sykes
Mush, Ensemble

Laurie Veldheer
Hannah, Ensemble

Alex Wong
Scab, Ensemble

Stuart Zagnit
Swing

Alan Menken
Music

Jack Feldman
Lyrics

Harvey Fierstein
Book

Bob Tzudiker
Original Screenplay

Noni White
Original Screenplay

Jeff Calhoun
Director

Christopher Gattelli
Choreographer

Tobin Ost
Scenic Design

Jess Goldstein
Costume Design

Jeff Croiter
Lighting Design

Ken Travis
Sound Design

Sven Ortel
Projection Design

Michael Kosarin
Music Supervisor, Vocal and Incidental Music Arrangements

Danny Troob
Orchestrations

Mark Hummel
Music Director, Dance Music Arrangements

John Miller
Music Coordinator

Charles LaPointe
Hair & Wig Design

J. Allen Suddeth
Fight Director

Bernard Telsey
Telsey + Company
Casting

Richard J. Hinds
Associate Director

Lou Castro
Associate Choreographer

Neil Mazzella
Technical Supervisor

Newsies

Thomas Schumacher
Disney Theatrical
Productions
Producer

Madeline Trumble
Standby Katherine

STAFF FOR *NEWSIES*

COMPANY MANAGER ....EDUARDO CASTRO
Production Stage Manager ....Thomas J. Gates
Assistant Company Manager ....Emily Powell
Stage Manager ....Timothy Eaker
Assistant Stage Manager ....Becky Fleming
Production Coordinator ....Kerry McGrath
Dance Captain ....Ryan Steele
Assistant Dance Captain ....Michael Fatica
Fight Captain ....Kevin Carolan
Production Assistants ....Bryan Bradford, Patrick Egan,
Aaron Elgart, Mark A. Stys, Amanda Tamny

DISNEY ON BROADWAY PUBLICITY

Senior Publicist ....Dennis Crowley
Associate Publicist ....Michelle Bergmann

Associate Scenic Designer ....Christine Peters
Assistant Scenic Designer ....Jerome Martin
Assistant Set Designer ....John Raley
Associate Costume Designer ....Mike Floyd
Associate Costume Designer ....China Lee
Associate Lighting Designer ....Cory Pattak
Assistant Lighting Designer ....Wilburn Bonnell
Associate Sound Designer ....Alex Hawthorne
Moving Light Programmer ....Victor Seastone
Assistant Projection Designer ....Lucy Mackinnon
Assistant to the
Projection Designer ....Gabe Rives-Corbett
Projection Programmer ....Florian Mosleh
Assistant Hair and Wig Designer ....Leah Loukas
Assistant Fight Director ....Ted Sharon
Technical Supervision ....Neil Mazzella
Technical Supervision ....Troika Entertainment
Technical Associates ....Irene Wang, Sam Ellis
Technical Production Assistant ....Canara Price
Advance Carpenter ....Sam Mahan
Head Carpenter ....Eddie Bash
Automation ....Karl Schuberth
Carpenter ....Michael Allen
Production Electrician ....James Maloney
Associate Production Electrician ....Brad Robertson
Production Properties ....Emiliano Pares
Head Properties ....Brian Schweppe
Assistant Properties ....Michael Critchlow
Production Sound ....Phil Lojo, Paul Delcioppo
Head Sound ....Cassy Givens
Sound Assistant ....Gabe Wood
Wardrobe Supervisor ....Rick Kelly
Dressers ....Jenny Barnes, Gary Biangone,
Franklin Hollenbeck, Phillip Rolfe,
Keith Shaw, Franc Weinperl
Hair Supervisor ....Frederick Waggoner
Hairdresser ....Amanda Duffy
Associate Music Director ....Steven Malone
Additional Orchestrations ....Steve Margoshes, Dave Siegel
Music Preparation ....Anixter Rice Music Services
Electronic Music Programming ....Jeff Marder
Associate to Mr. Menken ....Rick Kunis
Assistant to John Miller ....Jennifer Coolbaugh
Rehearsal Musicians ....Paul Davis, Mat Eisenstein
Music Production Assistant ....Brendan Whiting
Dialect & Vocal Coach ....Shane Ann Younts
Assistant to Mr. Calhoun ....Derek Hersey
Children's Guardian ....Vanessa Brown
Children's Tutoring ....On Location Education/
Nancy Van Ness, Beverly Brennan
Physical Therapy ....PhysioArts

CASTING
TELSEY + COMPANY
Bernie Telsey CSA, Will Cantler CSA,
David Vaccari CSA, Bethany Knox CSA,
Craig Burns CSA, Tiffany Little Canfield CSA,
Rachel Hoffman CSA, Justin Huff CSA,
Patrick Goodwin CSA, Abbie Brady-Dalton CSA,
David Morris, Cesar A. Rocha, Andrew Femenella,
Karyn Casl, Kristina Bramhall, Jessie Malone

Advertising ....Serino Coyne, Inc.
Production Photography ....Deen Van Meer
Production Travel ....Jill L. Citron
Payroll Managers ....Anthony DeLuca, Cathy Guerra
Counsel–Immigration ....Michael Rosenfeld

CREDITS
Custom scenery and automation by Hudson Scenic Studio,
Inc. Lighting equipment by Production Resource Group,
LLC. Sound equipment by Masque Sound. Video
projection system provided by Scharff Weisberg, Inc. Soft
goods by iWeiss. Costumes by Carelli Costumes, Jennifer
Love Studios, Claudia Diaz Costumes. Millinery by Rodney
Gordon. Shoes by JC Theatrical & Custom Footwear Inc.;
T.O. Dey; Capezio. Rehearsal sets by Proof Productions,
Inc. Smoke effect by Jauchem & Meeh, NYC. Ricola cough
drops courtesy of Ricola USA, Inc.

NEWSIES rehearsed at the
New 42nd Street Studios & Ripley Grier Studios

THANKS
Thanks to the TDF Costume Collection; Paper Mill
Playhouse; Prop N Spoon; Jake Zerrer

NEDERLANDER

Chairman ....**James M. Nederlander**
President ....**James L. Nederlander**

Executive Vice President
Nick Scandalios

Vice President
Corporate Development
Charlene S. Nederlander

Senior Vice President
Labor Relations
Herschel Waxman

Vice President
Jim Boese

Chief Financial Officer
Freida Sawyer Belviso

STAFF FOR THE NEDERLANDER THEATRE
House Manager ....Dixon Rosario
Treasurer ....Anthony Giannone
Assistant Treasurer ....Richard Loiacono
House Carpenter ....Joseph Ferreri Sr.
Flyman ....Joseph Ferreri Jr.
House Electrician ....Rick Poulin
House Properties ....William Wright
Head Usher ....Trish Ryan

Kara Lindsay and
Jeremy Jordan

Photo by Deen van Meer

Newsies

Jeremy Jordan and the Newsies

Photo by Deen van Meer

DISNEY THEATRICAL PRODUCTIONS

President ....Thomas Schumacher
EVP & Managing Director ....David Schrader
Senior Vice President, International ....Ron Kollen
Vice President, International,
    Europe ....Fiona Thomas
Vice President, International,
    Australia ....James Thane
Vice President, Operations ....Dana Amendola
Vice President, Publicity ....Joe Quenqua
Vice President, Domestic ....Jack Eldon
Vice President, Human Resources ....June Heindel
Director, Domestic Touring.............Michael Buchanan
Director, Worldwide Publicity ....Michael Cohen
Director, Regional Engagements ....Scott A. Hemerling
Director, Regional Engagements ....Kelli Palan
Director, Regional Engagements ....Deborah Warren
Manager, Domestic Touring & Planning ....Liz Botros
Manager, Human Resources ....Jewel Neal
Manager, Publicity ....Lindsay Braverman
Project Manager ....Ryan Pears
Senior Computer Support Analyst ....Kevin A. McGuire
IT/Business Analyst ....William Boudiette

Creative & Production

Executive Music Producer ....Chris Montan
VP, Creative Development ....Steve Fickinger
VP, Production ....Anne Quart
Director, International Production ....Felipe Gamba
Director, Labor Relations...................Edward Lieber
Associate Director ....Jeff Lee
Production Supervisor ....Clifford Schwartz
Production Manager ....Eduardo Castro
Manager, Labor Relations..................Stephanie Cheek

Manager, Physical Production ....Karl Chmielewski
Manager, Creative Development ....Jane Abramson
Manager, Theatrical Licensing ....David R. Scott
Dramaturg & Literary Manager ....Ken Cerniglia
Manager, Education & Outreach ....Lisa Mitchell

Marketing

Senior Vice President..........................Andrew Flatt
Director, Creative Resources ....Victor Adams
Director, Synergy & Partnership ....Kevin Banks
Director, Digital Marketing.....................Kyle Young
Design Manager ....James Anderer
Manager, Media & Strategy ....Jared Comess
Manager, Creative Services ....Lauren Daghini
Manager, Synergy & Partnership ....Sarah Schlesinger
Manager, Consumer Insights ....Craig Trachtenberg
Manager, Digital Marketing ....Peter Tulba

Sales

Vice President, National Sales ....Bryan Dockett
National Sales Manager ....Victoria Cairl
Sr. Manager, Sales & Ticketing ....Nick Falzon
Manager, Group Sales ....Hunter Robertson

Business and Legal Affairs

Senior Vice President.........................Jonathan Olson
Director...................................Daniel M. Posener
Director...Seth Stuhl
Sr. Paralegal ....Jessica White

Finance

VP, Finance/Business Development ....Mario Iannetta
Director, Finance ....Joe McClafferty
Director, Business Development ....Michael Barra

Director, Accounting ....Leena Mathew
Manager, Finance ....Liz Jurist Schwarzwalder
Manager, Production Accounting ....Nick Judge
Manager, Accounting ....Adrineh Ghoukassian
Senior Business Analyst ....Sven Rittershaus
Senior Financial Analyst ....Mikhail Medvedev
Senior Financial Analyst............................Jason Ve
Senior Business Planner ....Jennifer August
Production Accountant ....Joy Sims Brown
Production Accountant ....Angela DiSanti
Assistant Production Accountant ....Isander Rojas

Administrative Staff

Kelly Archer, Brian Bahr, Sarah Bills, Elizabeth Boulger, Whitney Britt, Jonelle Brown, Amy Caldamone, Michael Dei Cas, Preston Copley, Brittany Dobbs, Tara Engler, , Nicholas Faranda, Phil Grippe, Greg Josken, Cyntia Leo, Colleen McCormack, Kerry McGrath, Brendan Padgett, Matt Quinones, Jillian Robbins, Kattia Soriano, Lee Taglin, Anji Taylor

DISNEY THEATRICAL MERCHANDISE

Vice President ....Steven Downing
District Manager ....Alyssa Somers
Merchandise Manager ....Neil Markman
Associate Buyer ....Violet Burlaza
Assistant Manager, Inventory ....Suzanne Jakel
On-Site Retail Manager ....James Thad Wilkes
Senior Lead Sales Associates ....Georgia Nikki Dillon,
    Anna Lewgood

Disney Theatrical Productions
guestmail@disneytheatrical.com

Newsies
SCRAPBOOK

Correspondent: Tommy Bracco, "Spot Conlon"

Memorable Fan Letter: The most memorable "fan letter" I ever got was the fake one I received from the boys on April Fool's Day. It wasn't until after I read the wildly inappropriate fan mail out loud in the dressing room that the boys revealed it was all a prank.

Most Exciting Celebrity Visitor: I can't decide between Sting, the Jonas Brothers, Darren Criss, Susan Lucci, Katie Holmes, Tommy Tune, Anna Wintour and Joseph Pulitzer's great grandson. But I will say it was extremely awesome when Sting squeezed my muscle and nodded in approval.

Actor Who Performed the Most Roles in This Show: Kevin Carolan. He plays a total of seven roles in the show, all of which are very different and have very detailed and imaginative backstories. Let's see, there's Blue Collar Man (Jean Claude), Nunzio the Barber, Bruce Lewsnewski the Security Guard, Patron at Medda's, Sergei Eisenstein the Cameraman,

Jeremy Jordan and Kara Lindsay take curtain call on opening night

Capathia Jenkins and John Dossett at the premiere

O'Leary the Cop, and Governor Teddy Roosevelt, of course.

Special Backstage Rituals: Before the show you will find the Newsies doing their own warmups. Each person's warmup is very individual and...special. Just to name a few, you will find Jess LeProtto doing continuous *battements*, Andy Richardson practicing his scarily flexible back contortions, Mike Faist doing a full body

workout, me (Tommy Bracco) enthusiastically dancing to Britney Spears, Ephraim Sykes steaming his voice with his abnormally large steamer, and Ryan Breslin eating McDonald's in the dressing room. Every day John Dossett comes into the boys' dressing room at ten minutes before "places" and belts the word "Gentlemen" as loud as he can. And every day he manages to startle me when he does. At five to "places" we all huddle backstage, hold hands, and Ephraim Sykes leads us in a group prayer. Of all the rituals, that is my favorite. It gives us a chance to connect as a cast and feel each other's energy before going on stage!!

Favorite Moment of the Show: "The World Will Know." It is the first moment of the show that the boys realize how strong they are when they stand together. As an actor it is very rewarding to re-live that every night.

Favorite Off-Site Hangout: Schnipper's!!!!! ...and Patron.

Favorite Snack Foods: Some of the best are the practically endless supply of Biscoff cookies provided by the lovely Capathia Jenkins, the enormous life-size chocolate legs provided by none other then Harvey Fierstein (they usually come with a note that reads "Break-a-leg." Clever man.), scrumptious lemon squares baked by our dresser Franklin Hollenbeck and Flamin' Hot Cheetos delivered to Andrew Keenan-

Bolger from his awesome fansies! And of course you can't forget the obvious Hershey kisses, airheads, lollipops, gummy bears, etc. We've managed to turn the backstage of the Nederlander into our very own Candy Land.

Mascot: Aaron Albano's puppy, Bandit!!!

Memorable Ad-Libs: "Bring 'em here!!!" and "Bye bye, Snidey."

Memorable Stage Door Fan Encounter: I'm trying to think of one that stuck out as particularly memorable but after being asked to sign arms, legs and other body parts I'm pretty sure nothing can surprise me.

Heaviest Costume: Goes to Capathia Jenkins. She has three dresses that look like they weigh more than I do.

Who Wore the Least: Kyle Coffman. Shirtless two scenes and the audience surely doesn't mind.

Catchphrases Only the Company Would Recognize: "Liiiiike." "You must be joking." "Koiiii." "Ooooooop." "Not to be believed."

Andrew Keenan-Bolger acknowledges the applause

Photos by Monica Simoes

"Gorgggg." "That's Rich" (which we used to say BEFORE it was a song title in the show).

Company Legends: When we had a fight call in our underwear. Equally disturbing and hilarious. Also, Kevin Carolan is legend for forgetting his lines on stage. We love him.

Nicknames: Aaron Albano: "Cookie." Kyle Coffman: "Kylie." Ryan Breslin: "Bresibelle." Jeremy Jordan: "Jorgan." Christopher Gattelli: "Gorgelli." Kara Lindsay: "Kare Bear."

Embarrassing Moment: At Twittah (Twitter).

Coolest Thing About Being in This Show: The camaraderie we share on stage and off. Through this journey we've all become a family much like the News Boys of 1899. The Newsie boys AND girls love each other very much and the audience can feel that when they see the show!!

The Newsies take their bow

Nice Work If You Can Get It

First Preview: March 29, 2012. Opened: April 24, 2012.
Still running as of May 31, 2012.

PLAYBILL

Traditional-style screwball Broadway musical comedy loosely based on the 1926 show Oh, Kay! *with a completely new libretto, drawing liberally on the Gershwin songbook. Three bootleggers, including the pretty Billie Bendix, hide their illegal booze in the basement of a Long Island summer house owned by wealthy playboy Jimmy Winter, who is about to marry for the fourth time. But the nuptials are complicated when the wedding party arrives at the house and Jimmy falls for Billie instead.*

CAST

(in order of appearance)

Jeannie Muldoon	ROBYN HURDER
Jimmy Winter	MATTHEW BRODERICK
Billie Bendix	KELLI O'HARA
Duke Mahoney	CHRIS SULLIVAN
Cookie McGee	MICHAEL McGRATH
Chief Berry	STANLEY WAYNE MATHIS
Senator Max Evergreen	TERRY BEAVER
Duchess Estonia Dulworth	JUDY KAYE
Eileen Evergreen	JENNIFER LAURA THOMPSON
Millicent Winter	ESTELLE PARSONS

The Chorus Girls

Olive	CAMERON ADAMS
Dottie	KIMBERLY FAURÉ
Midge	STEPHANIE MARTIGNETTI
Alice	SAMANTHA STURM
Rosie	KRISTEN BETH WILLIAMS
Flo	CANDICE MARIE WOODS

Continued on next page

---

⑤ IMPERIAL THEATRE

249 West 45th Street
A Shubert Organization Theatre

Philip J. Smith, *Chairman*   **Robert E. Wankel,** *President*

Scott Landis, Roger Berlind, Sonia Friedman Productions, Roy Furman
Standing CO Vation, Candy Spelling, Freddy DeMann, Ronald Frankel, Harold Newman, Jon B. Platt,
Raise the Roof 8, Takonkiet Viravan, William Berlind/Ed Burke, Carole L. Haber/Susan Carusi,
Buddy and Barbara Freitag/Sanford Robertson, Jim Herbert/Under the Wire,
Emanuel Azenberg, The Shubert Organization

PRESENT

**Matthew
Broderick**   **Kelli
O'Hara**

STARRING IN

NICE WORK
If You Can Get It

A New Musical Comedy

MUSIC & LYRICS BY

George Gershwin and Ira Gershwin

BOOK BY

Joe DiPietro

Inspired by material by Guy Bolton and P.G. Wodehouse

ALSO STARRING

**Michael McGrath   Jennifer Laura Thompson   Chris Sullivan
Robyn Hurder   Stanley Wayne Mathis   Terry Beaver**

WITH

Judy Kaye

AND

Estelle Parsons

Cameron Adams   Clyde Alves   Kaitlyn Davidson   Jason DePinto   Kimberly Fauré
Robert Hartwell   Stephanie Martignetti   Barrett Martin   Michael X. Martin   Adam Perry   Jeffrey Schecter
Jennifer Smith   Joey Sorge   Samantha Sturm   Kristen Beth Williams   Candice Marie Woods

SCENIC DESIGN **Derek McLane**	COSTUME DESIGN **Martin Pakledinaz**	LIGHTING DESIGN **Peter Kaczorowski**	SOUND DESIGN **Brian Ronan**
HAIR & WIG DESIGN **Paul Huntley**	MAKE-UP DESIGN **Angelina Avallone**	PROJECTION DESIGN **Alexander V. Nichols**	CASTING BY **Binder Casting** **Jay Binder/Jack Bowdan**
ORCHESTRATOR **Bill Elliott**	MUSIC DIRECTOR **Tom Murray**	MUSIC COORDINATOR **Seymour Red Press**	ASSOCIATE DIRECTOR **Marc Bruni**

ASSOCIATE CHOREOGRAPHER
David Eggers

PRESS REPRESENTATIVE **Boneau/Bryan-Brown**	ADVERTISING & MARKETING **Serino/Coyne**	TECHNICAL DIRECTOR **Neil Mazzella**	PRODUCTION STAGE MANAGER **Bonnie L. Becker**	GENERAL MANAGEMENT **101 Productions, Ltd.**

MUSIC SUPERVISION AND ARRANGEMENTS
David Chase

DIRECTED AND CHOREOGRAPHED BY

Kathleen Marshall

The worldwide copyrights in the works of George Gershwin and Ira Gershwin for this presentation are licensed by the Gershwin Family.

4/24/2012

Matthew Broderick with
The Chorus Girls

Photo by Joan Marcus

Nice Work If You Can Get It

SCENES AND MUSICAL NUMBERS

ACT ONE

Overture .... Orchestra

SCENE 1: A Speakeasy
"Sweet and Lowdown" .... Jimmy, Jeannie, Chorus Girls, Society Guys

SCENE 2: Outside the Speakeasy, a Dimly Lit Dock
"Nice Work If You Can Get It" .... Jimmy, Billie
"Nice Work If You Can Get It" (Reprise) .... Billie
"Demon Rum" .... Duchess, Chief Berry, Senator, Vice Squad

SCENE 3: The Ritzy Front Lawn of Jimmy's Beach House
"Someone to Watch Over Me" .... Billie

SCENE 4: The Ritzy Bathroom
"Delishious" .... Eileen, Bubble Girls & Boys

SCENE 5: The Ritzy Living Room
"I've Got to Be There" .... Jimmy, Jeannie, Chorus Girls
"I've Got to Be There" (Reprise) .... Jeannie, Chorus Girls

SCENE 6: Jimmy's Ritzy Bedroom
"Treat Me Rough" .... Billie
"Let's Call the Whole Thing Off" .... Jimmy, Billie, Chief Berry

SCENE 7: The Ritzy Front Lawn
"Do It Again"* .... Jeannie, Duke

SCENE 8: The Ritzy Living Room
"'S Wonderful" .... Jimmy, Billie
"Fascinating Rhythm" .... Jimmy, Cookie & Company

ACT TWO

SCENE 1: The Ritzy Veranda
"Lady Be Good" .... Orchestra
"But Not for Me" .... Billie
"By Strauss" .... Duchess
"Sweet and Lowdown" (Reprise) .... Cookie

SCENE 2: The Ritzy Dining Room
"Do, Do, Do" .... Jimmy, Elliot, Vic, Floyd
"Hangin' Around With You" .... Billie
"Looking for a Boy" .... Duchess, Cookie
"Blah, Blah, Blah" .... Duke, Jeannie

SCENE 3: Jimmy's Ritzy Bedroom
"Let's Call the Whole Thing Off" (Reprise) .... Billie, Jimmy
"Will You Remember Me?" .... Billie, Jimmy

SCENE 4: The Ritzy Living Room
"I've Got to Be There" (Reprise) .... Chorus Girls, Vice Squad
"I've Got a Crush on You" .... Eileen, Chorus Girls, Vice Squad
"Blah, Blah, Blah" (Reprise) .... Jeannie, Duke
"Looking for a Boy" (Reprise) .... Cookie, Duchess
"Delishious" (Reprise) .... Chief Berry, Eileen

SCENE 5: The Boat House
"Someone to Watch Over Me" (Reprise) .... Jimmy, Billie

SCENE 6: The Ritzy Veranda
"They All Laughed" .... Full Company

* "Do It Again," music by George Gershwin, lyrics by Buddy DeSylva
GERSHWIN INSTRUMENTAL COMPOSITIONS
Excerpts from Rialto Ripples (1916), Novelette in Fourths (ca. 1919), Rhapsody in Blue (1924),
Impromptu in Two Keys (ca. 1924), Prelude I (1926), Prelude II: Blue Lullaby (1926), Prelude III:
Spanish Prelude (1926), The Three Note Waltz (ca. 1926), Prelude: Sleepless Night (ca. 1926),
Concerto in F (1927), Second Rhapsody (1932), Cuban Overture (1933),
Promenade (Walking the Dog) (1937).

Cast Continued

The Vice Squad
Elliot .... CLYDE ALVES
Slim .... ROBERT HARTWELL
Fletcher .... BARRETT MARTIN
Edgar .... ADAM PERRY
Floyd .... JEFFREY SCHECTER
Vic .... JOEY SORGE

SWINGS
KAITLYN DAVIDSON, JASON DePINTO

UNDERSTUDIES
Standby for Duke, Cookie, Chief Berry, Senator:
MICHAEL X. MARTIN
Standby for Duchess, Millicent:
JENNIFER SMITH
For Jeannie:
KIMBERLY FAURÉ,
KRISTEN BETH WILLIAMS
For Jimmy:
JOEY SORGE
For Billie:
CAMERON ADAMS,
STEPHANIE MARTIGNETTI
For Cookie and Chief Berry:
JEFFREY SCHECTER
For Duchess:
KRISTEN BETH WILLIAMS
For Eileen:
KIMBERLY FAURÉ,
KRISTEN BETH WILLIAMS

DANCE CAPTAIN
JASON DePINTO

ASSISTANT DANCE CAPTAIN
KAITLYN DAVIDSON

TIME
July, 1927
PLACE
Long Island, New York

ORCHESTRA
Conductor:
TOM MURRAY
Associate Conductor:
SHAWN GOUGH
Assistant Conductor:
JOSEPH JOUBERT
Music Coordinator:
SEYMOUR RED PRESS
Violin:
PAUL WOODIEL
Woodwinds:
RALPH OLSEN, TODD GROVES,
RICHARD HECKMAN, JAY BRANDFORD

Nice Work If You Can Get It

Orchestra Continued

Trumpets:
ROBERT MILLIKAN, BRIAN PARESHI,
SHAWN EDMONDS
Trombones:
CLINT SHARMAN, JASON JACKSON,
JACK SCHATZ
Piano/Accordion:
SHAWN GOUGH
Piano/Keyboards:
JOSEPH JOUBERT
Drums:
ERIC POLAND
Percussion:
ANDREW BLANCO
Guitar:
JAMES HERSHMAN
Bass:
RICHARD SARPOLA

2011-2012 AWARDS

TONY AWARDS
Best Performance by an Actor in a
Featured Role in a Musical
(Michael McGrath)
Best Performance by an Actress in a
Featured Role in a Musical
(Judy Kaye)

DRAMA DESK AWARDS
Outstanding Featured Actor in a Musical
(Michael McGrath)
Outstanding Featured Actress in a Musical
(Judy Kaye)
Outstanding Book in a Musical
(Joe DiPietro)

OUTER CRITICS CIRCLE AWARDS
Outstanding Featured Actor in a Musical
(Michael McGrath)
Outstanding Featured Actress in a Musical
(Judy Kaye)

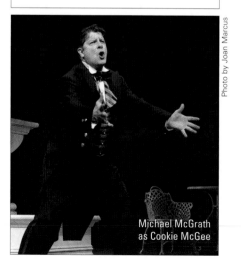

Photo by Joan Marcus

Michael McGrath
as Cookie McGee

Matthew Broderick
Jimmy Winter

Kelli O'Hara
Billie Bendix

Estelle Parsons
Millicent Winter

Judy Kaye
Duchess Estonia Dulworth

Michael McGrath
Cookie McGee

Jennifer Laura
Thompson
Eileen Evergreen

Chris Sullivan
Duke Mahoney

Robyn Hurder
Jeannie Muldoon

Stanley Wayne
Mathis
Chief Berry

Terry Beaver
Senator Max Evergreen

Cameron Adams
Olive

Clyde Alves
Elliot

Kaitlyn Davidson
Swing, Asst. Dance Captain

Jason DePinto
Swing, Dance Captain

Kimberly Fauré
Dottie

Robert Hartwell
Slim

Stephanie
Martignetti
Midge

Barrett Martin
Fletcher

Michael X. Martin
Standby

Adam Perry
Edgar

Nice Work If You Can Get It

Jeffrey Schecter
Floyd

Jennifer Smith
Standby

Joey Sorge
Vic

Samantha Sturm
Alice

Kristen Beth
Williams
Rosie

Candice Marie
Woods
Flo

George Gershwin
Composer

Ira Gershwin
Lyricist

Joe DiPietro
Book

Guy Bolton
Source Material

P.G. Wodehouse
Source Material

Kathleen Marshall
*Director &
Choreographer*

David Chase
*Music Supervisor
and Arrangements*

Derek McLane
Scenic Design

Martin Pakledinaz
Costume Design

Peter Kaczorowski
Lighting Design

Brian Ronan
Sound Design

Paul Huntley
Hair & Wig Design

Alexander V. Nichols
Projection Design

Kathy Fabian/
Propstar
*Properties
Coordinator*

Angelina Avallone
Makeup Design

Bill Elliott
Orchestrations

Seymour Red Press
Music Coordinator

Marc Bruni
Associate Director

David Eggers
*Associate
Choreographer*

Jay Binder, CSA
Binder Casting
Casting

Jack Bowdan, CSA
Binder Casting
Casting

Mark Brandon, CSA
Binder Casting
Casting

Wendy Orshan
101 Productions, Ltd
*General
Management*

Scott Landis
Producer

Roger Berlind
Producer

Sonia Friedman
Productions
Producer

Roy Furman
Producer

Chris Bensinger
Standing Co Vation
Producer

Richard Winkler
Standing Co Vation
Producer

Nice Work If You Can Get It

Bows on opening night (front L-R): Chris Sullivan, Estelle Parsons, Judy Kaye, Matthew Broderick, Kelli O'Hara, Michael McGrath and Jennifer Laura Thompson, with members of the ensemble.

Jamie deRoy
Standing Co Vation
Producer

Michael Filerman
Standing Co Vation
Producer

Remmel T. Dickinson
Standing Co Vation
Producer

Bruce Robert Harris
Standing Co Vation
Producer

Jack W. Batman
Standing Co Vation
Producer

Candy Spelling
Producer

Freddy DeMann
Producer

Jon B. Platt
Producer

Jennifer
Manocherian
Raise The Roof 8
Producer

Elaine Krauss
Raise The Roof 8
Producer

Jean Doumanian
Raise The Roof 8
Producer

Harriet Newman
Leve
Raise The Roof 8
Producer

Buddy Freitag
Producer

Barbara Freitag
Producer

Jacki Barlia Florin
Under The Wire
Producer

Douglas Denoff
Under The Wire
Producer

Margot Astrachan
Producer

Emanuel Azenberg
Producer

Philip J. Smith
Chairman
The Shubert
Organization
Producer

Robert E. Wankel
President
The Shubert
Organization
Producer

Nice Work If You Can Get It

(L-R): Matthew Broderick, Kelli O'Hara

Photo by Joan Marcus

On a Clear Day You Can See Forever

First Preview: November 12, 2011. Opened: December 11, 2011.
Closed January 29, 2012 after 29 Previews and 57 Performances.

PLAYBILL®

A psychiatrist finds himself in a unique professional and personal quandary. One of his patients, David Gamble, a gay man who works in a flower shop, wants help to quit smoking. But, when hypnotized, the shy David regresses into a previous life as a beautiful female World War II-era Big Band singer named Melinda. The psychiatrist finds himself falling in love with Melinda, leaving poor David fighting a romantic rivalry with his own previous self.

CAST
(in order of appearance)

Dr. Mark Bruckner	HARRY CONNICK, JR.
David Gamble	DAVID TURNER
Anton	PAUL O'BRIEN
Vera	LORI WILNER
Muriel Bunson	SARAH STILES
Hannah	ALEX ELLIS
Paula	ALYSHA UMPHRESS
Roger	TYLER MAYNARD
Alan	ZACHARY PRINCE
Preston	BENJAMIN EAKELEY
Dr. Sharone Stein	KERRY O'MALLEY
Leora Kahn	HEATHER AYERS
Mrs. Hatch	LORI WILNER
Dr. Leo Kravis	PAUL O'BRIEN
Melinda Wells	JESSIE MUELLER
Club Vedado Singer	HEATHER AYERS
Sawyer	TYLER MAYNARD
Maurice	PAUL O'BRIEN
Warren Smith	DREW GEHLING
Wesley Porter (1944)	ZACHARY PRINCE

Continued on next page

Continued on next page

♪ ST. JAMES THEATRE
A JUJAMCYN THEATRE

JORDAN ROTH
President

PAUL LIBIN
Executive Vice President

JACK VIERTEL
Senior Vice President

TOM HULCE & IRA PITTELMAN   LIZA LERNER   BROADWAY ACROSS AMERICA
JOSEPH SMITH   MICHAEL McCABE
BERNIE ABRAMS/MICHAEL SPEYER   TAKONKIET VIRAVAN/SCENARIO THAILAND   MICHAEL WATT
JACKI BARLIA FLORIN-ADAM BLANSHAY/CHAUSPECIALE/ASTRACHAN&JUPIN
PAUL BOSKIND AND MARTIAN ENTERTAINMENT   BRANNON WILES
CARLOS ARANA/CHRISTOPHER MARING

present

HARRY CONNICK, JR.

in

ON A CLEAR DAY
YOU CAN SEE FOREVER

Music by
BURTON LANE

Lyrics by
ALAN JAY LERNER

New Book by
PETER PARNELL

Based on the Original Book by
ALAN JAY LERNER

Starring

DAVID TURNER   JESSIE MUELLER

DREW GEHLING   SARAH STILES   PAUL O'BRIEN   HEATHER AYERS   LORI WILNER

BENJAMIN EAKELEY   ALEX ELLIS   KENDAL HARTSE   GRASAN KINGSBERRY   TYLER MAYNARD   ZACHARY PRINCE   ALYSHA UMPHRESS
PHILIP HOFFMAN   SEAN ALLAN KRILL   PATRICK O'NEILL   CHRISTIANNE TISDALE

and

KERRY O'MALLEY

Scenic Design	Costume Design	Lighting Design	Sound Design
CHRISTINE JONES	CATHERINE ZUBER	KEVIN ADAMS	PETER HYLENSKI

Wig & Hair Design	Casting by		Music Coordinator
TOM WATSON	JIM CARNAHAN, C.S.A./STEPHEN KOPEL		JOHN MILLER

Associate Producers	Associate Director	Associate Choreographer	Production Stage Manager
STAGE VENTURES 2011 LIMITED PARTNERSHIP	AUSTIN REGAN	SCOTT TAYLOR	LISA IACUCCI

Press Representative	Marketing	Technical Supervision	General Manager
THE HARTMAN GROUP	TYPE A MARKETING/ANNE RIPPEY	HUDSON THEATRICAL ASSOCIATES	THE CHARLOTTE WILCOX COMPANY

Orchestrations
DOUG BESTERMAN

Music Director, Vocal & Instrumental Music Arrangements
LAWRENCE YURMAN

Choreographed by
JOANN M. HUNTER

Re-conceived & Directed by
MICHAEL MAYER

Originally presented by New York Stage and Film Company & The Powerhouse Theater at Vassar, July 2010,
ON A CLEAR DAY YOU CAN SEE FOREVER received a developmental lab production at the Vineyard Theatre in 2011.

12/11/11

(L-R): David Turner, Jessie Mueller, Harry Connick, Jr.

Photo by Nicole Rivelli

On a Clear Day You Can See Forever

MUSICAL NUMBERS

ACT I	
OVERTURE	
"Hurry! It's Lovely Up Here"	David
"She Isn't You"	Mark
"Open Your Eyes"	Club Singer
"Open Your Eyes" (Reprise)	Melinda
"Hurry! It's Lovely Up Here" (Reprise)	David
"Wait 'Til We're Sixty-Five"	Warren, David, Muriel, Alan, Hannah, Paula, Preston, Roger
"Wait 'Til We're Sixty-Five" (Reprise)	Warren
"You're All the World to Me"	Melinda, Mark, David
"Who Is There Among Us Who Knows"	Mark, Sharone
"Who Is There Among Us Who Knows" (Reprise)	Mark, Melinda
"On the S.S. Bernard Cohn"	Mark, David, Muriel, Melinda, Alan, Hannah, Paula, Preston, Roger
"Love With All the Trimmings"	Warren
"Open Your Eyes" (Reprise)	Mark, Sharone, Muriel, Mrs. Hatch, Kravis, Cynthia, Alan, Hannah, Paula, Preston, Roger
"Melinda"	Mark, Melinda, David

ACT II	
ENTR'ACTE	
"Go to Sleep"	Muriel, David
"Ev'ry Night at Seven"	Melinda, Radio Singers
"Too Late Now"	Mark, Melinda
"Love With All the Trimmings" (Reprise)	Warren
"When I'm Being Born Again"	Muriel, Mark, Alan, Hannah, Paula, Preston, Roger
"(S)he Wasn't You"	Sharone, Warren, David, Mark
"What Did I Have That I Don't Have?"	David
"Come Back to Me"	Mark, Warren
"Too Late Now" (Reprise)	Mark, Melinda
"On a Clear Day You Can See Forever"	Mark
"Finale"	Full Company

ORCHESTRA

Conductor:
LAWRENCE YURMAN
Associate Conductor:
DAVID J. HAHN
Woodwinds:
TOM MURRAY, CHARLIE PILLOW, DON McGEEN
Trumpets:
GREG GISBERT, KEVIN BRYAN
Trombones:
DION TUCKER, JOE BARATI
French Horn: PATRICK PRIDEMORE
Guitar: JACK CAVARI
Bass: NEAL CAINE
Drums: PAUL PIZZUTI
Percussion: JAVIER DIAZ
Keyboards: DAVID J. HAHN, KARL MANSFIELD
Harp: ANNA REINERSMAN

Violins: SYLVIA D'AVANZO, LOUISE OWEN
Cello: AMY RALSKE
Music Coordinator: JOHN MILLER

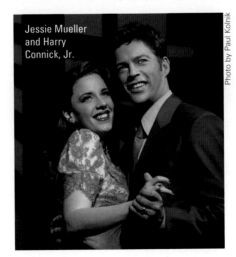
Jessie Mueller and Harry Connick, Jr.

Photo by Paul Kolnik

2011-2012 AWARD

THEATRE WORLD AWARD
For Outstanding Broadway
or Off-Broadway Debut
(Jessie Mueller)

On a Clear Day Day You Can See Forever

Harry Connick, Jr.
Dr. Mark Bruckner

David Turner
David Gamble

Jessie Mueller
Melinda Wells

Kerry O'Malley
Dr. Sharone Stein

Drew Gehling
Warren Smith

Sarah Stiles
Muriel Bunson

Paul O'Brien
Anton, Leo Kravis, Gene Miller, Wesley Porter 1974, Maurice, Mr. Van Deusen

Heather Ayers
Cynthia Roland, Leora Kahn, Club Vedado Singer, Betsy Rappaport, Radio Singer

Lori Wilner
Vera, Mrs. Hatch, Mrs. Lloyd

Benjamin Eakeley
Preston, Announcer, Radio Singer, Stage Manager, Ensemble

Alex Ellis
Hannah, Ensemble

Kendal Hartse
Ensemble

Grasan Kingsberry
Ensemble

Tyler Maynard
Roger, Sawyer, Radio Singer, Ensemble

Zachary Prince
Alan, Wesley Porter 1944, Ensemble

Alysha Umphress
Paula, Ensemble

Philip Hoffman
Standby for Anton/Leo/Gene/Wesley

Sean Allan Krill
Standby for Dr. Mark Bruckner

Patrick O'Neill
Swing, Dance Captain

Christianne Tisdale
Swing

Burton Lane
Music

Alan Jay Lerner
Original Book/Lyrics

Peter Parnell
New Book

Michael Mayer
Re-Conceiver and Director

Joann M. Hunter
Choreographer

Christine Jones
Scenic Design

Catherine Zuber
Costume Design

Kevin Adams
Lighting Design

Peter Hylenski
Sound Design

Tom Watson
Hair Design

Doug Besterman
Orchestrator

Jim Carnahan
Casting

John Miller
Music Coordinator

Austin Regan
Associate Director

Scott Taylor
Associate Choreographer

On a Clear Day You Can See Forever

Neil A. Mazzella
Hudson Theatrical
Associates
*Technical
Supervision*

The Charlotte Wilcox
Company
General Manager

Tom Hulce
Producer

Ira Pittelman
Producer

Liza Lerner
Producer

John Gore
Broadway Across
America
Producer

Thomas B. McGrath
Broadway Across
America
Producer

Beth Williams
Broadway Across
America
Producer

Joseph Smith
Producer

Michael McCabe
Producer

Bernard Abrams
Producer

Michael Speyer
Producer

Jacki Barlia Florin
Producer

Adam Blanshay
Producer

Paul Chau
Producer

Paul Boskind
Martian
Entertainment
Producer

David Turner sings "Hurry! It's Lovely Up Here."
Photo by Paul Kolnik

PLAYBILL Cover - November 2011

Carlos Arana
Producer

Douglas Aibel
Artistic Director
Vineyard Theatre

STAFF FOR
ON A CLEAR DAY YOU CAN SEE FOREVER

GENERAL MANAGEMENT
CHARLOTTE WILCOX COMPANY
Charlotte W. Wilcox
Seth Marquette
Dina S. Friedler   Matthew W. Krawiec
Regina Mancha   Margaret Wilcox
Chantel Hopper   Ryan Smillie   Stephen Donovan

COMPANY MANAGER
James Lawson

ASSISTANT COMPANY MANAGER
Francesca De La Vega

GENERAL PRESS REPRESENTATIVE
THE HARTMAN GROUP
Michael Hartman
Leslie Papa   Whitney Holden Gore

CASTING
CARNAHAN CASTING
Jim Carnahan, CSA
Stephen Kopel
Carrie Gardner, CSA   Jillian Cimini
Michael Morlani   Lexie Pregosin

OFFICE OF IRA PITTELMAN & TOM HULCE
Producing Associate ....Christopher Maring
Executive Assistant to Mr. Pittelman ....Dorothy Evins

Production Stage Manager ....Lisa Iacucci
Stage Manager ....Rachel A. Wolff
Assistant Stage Manager ....Steve Henry
Assistant Choreographer ....Patrick O'Neill
Associate Set Designer ....Ed Coco
Assistant Set Designers ....Brett Banakis,
Jonathan Collins, Michael Riha
Associate Costume Designer ....Ryan Park
Assistant Costume Designers ....Patrick Bevilacqua,
David Newell

On a Clear Day You Can See Forever

Personal Assistant to the
   Costume Designer . . . . .Leon Dobkowski
Associate Lighting Designer . . . . .Joel E. Silver
Assistant Lighting Designer .Paul Toben
Moving Light Programmer . . . . .Victor Seastone
Associate Sound Designer . . . . .Keith Caggiano
Makeup Designer . . . . .Ashley Ryan
Head Carpenter . . . . .Todd Frank
Deck Carpenter . . . . .Chris Pravata
Deck Automation . . . . .Robert N. Valli
Production Electrician .Greg Husinko
Head Electrician . . . . .Nicholas Keslake
Production Properties Coordinator . . . . .PropStar/
                                         Kathy Fabian
Head Propmaster . . . . .Eric Castaldo
Production Sound . . . . .Phil Lojo, Paul Delcioppo
Sound Engineer . . . . .Jesse Stevens
Assistant Sound Engineer . . . . .Bill Ruger
Wardrobe Supervisor . . . . .Patrick Bevilacqua
Assistant Wardrobe Supervisor . . . . .Tom Bertsch
Dressers . . . . .Sara Darneille, Joe Hickey,
               Savana Leveille, Kimberly Mark,
                Del Miskie, Derek Moreno,
         Claire Verlaet, Libby Villanova, Sandy Vojta
Harry Connick, Jr.'s Dresser . . . . .Victoria Grecki
Hair Supervisor . . . . .Joshua Gericke
Assistant Hair Supervisor . . . . .Kevin Maybee
Additional Orchestrations . . . . .Larry Blank
Keyboard Programmer . . . . .Karl Mansfield
Music Preparation Services . . . . .Anxiter Rice Music Services
Rehearsal Musicians . . . . .David Hahn, Paul Pizzuti
Production Assistants . . . . .Samantha Preiss,
                                      Taylor Michael
Assistant to John Miller . . . . .Jennifer Coolbaugh
Legal Counsel .Lazarus & Harris LLP/
                              Scott Lazarus, Esq.;
                         Robert C. Harris, Esq.
Accountant . . . . .FK Partners, LLP/Robert Fried
Comptroller . . . . .Galbraith & Company/Heather Allen
Advertising . . . . .Serino/Coyne/
                Sandy Block, Scott Johnson,
              Tom Callahan, Robert Jones,
            Ryan Cunningham, Jamie Caplan
Digital Outreach & Website . . . . .Serino/Coyne/
               Jim Glaub, Chip Meyrelles,
             Laurie Connor, Kevin Keating,
           Ryan Greer, Whitney Creighton,
                        Crystal Chase
Marketing . . . . .Type A Marketing/
              Anne Rippey, Elyce Henkin,
                        Sarah Ziering
Payroll Services . . . . .Checks and Balances, Inc.
Production Photographer .Paul Kolnik
Press Representative Staff .Katie Britton,
          Nicole Capatasto, Tom D'Ambrosio,
          Juliana Hannett, Bethany Larsen,
            Emily McGill, Matt Ross,
           Frances White, Wayne Wolfe
Opening Night
   Coordination . . . . .The Lawrence Company/
                     Michael P. Lawrence
Banking .JP Morgan Chase Bank, N.A./
                            Grace J. Correa
Insurance Broker . . . . .Ventura Insurance/
                           Jessica Martinez
Group Sales . . . . .Broadway Inbound
Merchandise . . . . .Creative Goods/Pete Milano

Information Management
   Services . . . . .Marion Finkler Taylor
Travel Services .Tzell Travel/Andi Henig

CREDITS

Scenery and automation by Hudson Scenic Studio, Inc.
Audio equipment from PRG Audio. Lighting equipment
from PRG Lighting. Costumes executed by Brian
Hemeseth, Edward Dawson, EuroCo Costumes, KD
Studios, Parsons-Meares. Footwear executed by JC
Theatrical, T.O. Dey, Worldtone Dance. Millinery by
Rodney Gordon. Jewelry by Larry V'rba. Makeup provided
by M•A•C. Hair products provided by Pravana
Naturceuticals.

SPECIAL THANKS

Rebecca Hengstenberg, David B. Stern, Esq., Craig Levine,
Esq., Bob Tarantino, Esq., The Alan Jay Lerner Estate, The
Burton Lane Estate, Charles Ortner, Brian Siberell, Roy
Latham, Ann Marie Wilkins

The Vineyard Theatre Lab Production was made possible
in part by a grant from The National Endowment for the
Arts and the Blanche and Irving Laurie Foundation.

To learn more about the production, please visit
ONACLEARDAYBROADWAY.COM

Rehearsed at New 42nd Street Studios

JUJAMCYN THEATERS

JORDAN ROTH
President

PAUL LIBIN
Executive Vice President

JACK VIERTEL
Senior Vice President

MEREDITH VILLATORE
Chief Financial Officer

JENNIFER HERSHEY
Vice President,
Building Operations

MICAH HOLLINGWORTH
Vice President,
Company Operations

HAL GOLDBERG
Vice President,
Theatre Operations

Director of Business Affairs . . . . .Albert T. Kim
Director of Ticketing Services . . . . .Justin Karr
Theatre Operations Managers . . . . .Willa Burke,
               Susan Elrod, Emily Hare,
          Jeff Hubbard, Albert T. Kim
Theatre Operations Associates . . . . .Carrie Jo Brinker,
                    Michael Composto,
                    Anah Jyoti Klate
Accounting .Cathy Cerge, Erin Dooley,
                       Christian Sislian
Executive Producer, Red Awning . . . . .Nicole Kastrinos
Director of Marketing, Givenik.com . . . . .Joe Tropia
Marketing Associate, Givenik.com . . . . .Ben Cohen
Building Operations Associate . . . . .Erich Bussing
Executive Coordinator . . . . .Ed Lefferson
Executive Assistants .Clark Mims Tedesco,
                   Julia Kraus, Beth Given
Receptionist . . . . .Kate Garst
Maintenance . . . . .Ralph Santos, Ramon Zapata
Security . . . . .Rasim Hodzic, John Acero
Interns . . . . .Jason Blackwell, Stephanie Ditman,
     Burton Frey, Sam Chapin, Emily Petrain, Lisa Perchinske,
         Kate Siegel, Mark Smith, Kelsey Wehde

Staff for the St. James Theatre for
On a Clear Day You Can See Forever

Manager . . . . .Jeff Hubbard
Associate Manager . . . . .Michael Composto
Treasurer . . . . .Vincent Sclafani
Head Carpenter . . . . .Timothy McDonough, Jr.
Head Propertyman . . . . .Timothy McDonough, Sr.
Head Electrician . . . . .Albert Sayers
Flyman . . . . .David Brown
Engineer . . . . .Zaim Hodzic
Assistant Treasurers .Carmine Loiacono,
        Thomas Motylenski, Vincent Siniscalchi
Propertymen . . . . .Justine Borowinski, Joseph Ferreri
Electricians . . . . .Tom Maloney, Bob Miller,
                        Sue Pelkofer
Carpenter . . . . .Chris Riggins
Head Usher . . . . .Cynthia Lopiano
Ticket-takers/Directors/Ushers . . . . .Leonard Baron,
           Jim Barry, Murray Bradley,
           Barbara Carroll, Julia Furay,
          Heather Jewels, Barbara Kagan,
        Andrew Mackay, Kendra McDuffie,
       Margaret McElroy, Katie Schmidt,
       Kathryn Siegmund, Jessica Theisen,
                    Donna Vanderlinden
Doormen . . . . .Russell Buenteo, Adam Hodzic
Head Porter . . . . .Jacobo Medrano
Porters . . . . .Rafael Liriano, Francisco Medina,
                           Donnette Niles
Head Cleaner . . . . .Carmela Tenebruso
Cleaners . . . . .Juana Medrano, Antonia Moreno

Lobby refreshments by Sweet Concessions.

Security provided by P and P Security.

Harry Connick, Jr.

On a Clear Day You Can See Forever
SCRAPBOOK

Correspondent: Sarah Stiles, "Muriel"

Coolest Opening Night Gift: A colorful illustration of a Rorschach, from Peter Parnell.

Sassiest Gift: An original card using a internet photo of a barely-clothed Harry Connick, Jr. in a bathtub wishing us all a warm hand on our opening, from Zachary Prince.

Most Creative Opening Night Gift: A paper cut-out poster based on the *Clear Day* window card. Created by our hugely talented night doorman, Russ.

Memories of the Opening Night Party: Walking from one giant room at the Plaza Hotel to the next, only to find a grandiose staircase that led to an even more enormous room that was connected to three more rooms that was....hey—where IS everybody?!?

Most Exciting Celebrity Visitor: Seth MacFarlane. When I saw him, I was yammering on about my brand new owl slippers in a voice much louder and higher-pitched than I normally...OK, who am I kidding? I always sound like that. I saw him, I froze, I ran away. I wish I was cooler. Sigh.

Actor Who Performed the Most Roles in This Show: Paul O'Brien—SIX characters! Anton, Leo Kravis, Maurice, Mr. Van Deusen, Wesley and that dude that yells "Dames!" right before Jessie wails her face off in Act II.

Actor Who Has Done the Most Shows in His Career: I believe it's Philip Hoffman, because when I ask him how many, he can't remember all of them.

Special Backstage Ritual: My favorite ritual happens at intermission: My dresser Claire zips up my pajamas at Five in our quick change booth stage left. I dance to Bonnie Raitt with Bill, the backstage sound guy, while he tests the speaker in the desk. Then I climb into Muriel's bed, which on any given day has been turned down and a chocolate hidden under the heart-shaped "M" pillow, by a "mysterious elf," the crew tells me.

Favorite Moments During Each Performance (On Stage or Off): On: Jessie Mueller blowing people's minds when she sings "Every Night at Seven." Counting how many laughs Lori Wilner can get from one line at the Mrs. Hatch desk. David Turner's line "Where are Peter and Paul, Mary?" Pretty much that entire scene with Davey and Drew! Everyone singing together at the end in front of the gorgeous finale backdrop.

Off: Tyler Maynard's "J. Lo" impression. Harry's constant interpretive dancing in the wings and behind the drops. Kerry O'Malley's foot massager and water mint candle.

Favorite In-Theatre Gathering Place: St. Timmy's Place, a.k.a. the crew room. Constantly stocked with coffee, snacks and dudes ready to make you laugh!

Favorite Snack Food: There is more chocolate in this building than the candy aisle in a Duane Reade at Easter! So, by sheer availability—chocolate!

Mascots: Harry Connick, Jr.'s daughters Kate

1. (L-R): Drew Gehling, Lori Wilner, Jessie Mueller and Paul O'Brien relax in a dressing room.

2. *Yearbook* correspondent Sarah Stiles in her dressing room, playing paparazzo with the mirror.

3. Kerry O'Malley in her dressing room, in full Red Sox gear.

and Charlotte. Always around and cheering us on.

Favorite Therapy: Vitamin D. Harry is adamant that if taken every day, it will prevent and at the very least lessen symptoms. So far, so good! My personal favorite is greens—raw, cooked, juiced… as many and as often as you can! We have a lot of Neti Potters and Emergen-C lovers as well.

Record Number of Technological Interruptions During a Performance: The most distracting thing so far has been a particularly shiny sequined Christmas sweater worn by an exuberant older gentleman who attended the show in December. One must applaud his courage!

Fastest Costume Change: Ben Eakeley's change from Preston to the Stage Manager. It takes 4 people—2 dressers, hair and sound. I get to watch it every night. It's completely choreographed and quite entertaining.

Catchphrases Only the Company Would Recognize: "Just a scouch." (JoAnn Hunter) and "Eeeeuuuwwwwweee" (Alex Ellis).

Memorable Stage Door Fan Encounter: "You are 10 shades of fabulous, Mr. Connick!"

Orchestra Member Who Played the Most Instruments: Javier Diaz on percussion: the timpani, triangle, tambourine and 7 other ones that don't start with T.

Memorable Directorial Note: "We have 50 new pages and they're going in tonight. Don't

On a Clear Day You Can See Forever
SCRAPBOOK

1. Liza Lerner, daughter of original lyricist Alan Jay Lerner, attends opening night.
2. Curtain call at the premiere.
3. Marquee of the St. James Theatre.
4. Harry Connick, Jr. with wife Jill Goodacre (R) and their daughters at the opening.
5. "Smash" stars Debra Messing and Megan Hilty.
6. (L-R): Director Michael Mayer, choreographer JoAnn M. Hunter and librettist Peter Parnell.

panic." —Michael Mayer. Not necessarily a note, more of a statement—but either way, definitely memorable!

Embarrassing Moment: Heather Ayers tripping on her Palazzo pants and sprawling flat out on the floor right after her bow, only to drag herself far enough stage right to have our stage manager Rachel pull her off. "In all my years in this business, I have never seen anyone crawl off the stage."—Michael Mayer

Fun Behind-The-Scenes *Clear Day* Facts:
• We had three Broadway debuts in our show: Jessie Mueller (Melinda), Kendal Hartse (swing), and Patrick O'Neill (swing/dance captain).
• The most elaborate costumes are the Melinda dresses. They are all couture-made in luxurious fabrics and a vintage style to fit her body perfectly.
• If you added the platform/ heel height of all our shoes in the show you would get a 12-feet-tall heel. That number also includes the 6-inch platform our PSM Lisa Iacucci has to stand on to reach all the buttons when she calls the show.
• Harry isn't the only amazing pianist in our cast. That list includes David Turner, Lori Wilner and Ben Eakeley. During lunch break in our rehearsal studio at New 42nd Street, you would often get a concert from one of these multi-talented people.
• Jessie Mueller is an amazing manicurist, and between shows you can schedule an ap-

pointment to get one!
• Kerry O'Malley wears nothing but Boston sports teams fleece onesies backstage. She has four total, with matching slippers. (See photo on previous page.)
• Drew had to learn how to play the guitar for his role; Ben and Zach also had to learn, in order to cover him. Needless to say, they all play one song really well—"Love With All the Trimmings"!
• Alysha Umphress is in the exact same dressing room spot that she had for *American Idiot*.

Coolest Things About Being in This Show: Platforms, beautiful spacious dressing rooms, and the coolest celebrity out there! Who's cooler than Harry?

Once

First Preview: February 28, 2012. Opened: March 18, 2012.
Still running as of May 31, 2012.

PLAYBILL

Bittersweet romantic musical based on the 2006 Oscar-winning film of the same title, about an Irish street musician who gains new inspiration when he meets a Czech woman who reawakens his musical muse—and his heart. Staged with a company of actors who also function as the onstage orchestra.

CAST

(in alphabetical order)

Eamon .... DAVID ABELES
    Guitar, Piano, Melodica, Harmonica
Andrej .... WILL CONNOLLY
    Electric Bass, Ukulele, Tambourine, Cajon, Guitar
Réza .... ELIZABETH A. DAVIS
    Violin
Guy .... STEVE KAZEE
    Guitar
Da .... DAVID PATRICK KELLY
    Mandolin
Girl .... CRISTIN MILIOTI
    Piano
Baruška .... ANNE L. NATHAN
    Piano, Accordion, Tambourine, Melodica
Švec .... LUCAS PAPAELIAS
    Banjo, Guitar, Mandolin, Drum Set
* Ivanka .... RIPLEY SOBO
Bank Manager .... ANDY TAYLOR
    Violin, Accordion, Cello, Guitar, Mandolin
* Ivanka .... MCKAYLA TWIGGS
Ex-Girlfriend .... ERIKKA WALSH
    Violin
Billy .... PAUL WHITTY
    Guitar, Ukulele, Cajon, Snare Drum

Continued on next page

---

⑤ BERNARD B. JACOBS THEATRE

242 West 45th Street
A Shubert Organization Theatre

Philip J. Smith, *Chairman*   Robert E. Wankel, *President*

BARBARA BROCCOLI   JOHN N. HART JR.   PATRICK MILLING SMITH   FREDERICK ZOLLO
BRIAN CARMODY   MICHAEL G. WILSON   ORIN WOLF   THE SHUBERT ORGANIZATION
ROBERT COLE, EXECUTIVE PRODUCER

in association with

NEW YORK THEATRE WORKSHOP

present

Once

book   music and lyrics
ENDA WALSH   **GLEN HANSARD & MARKÉTA IRGLOVÁ**

based on the motion picture written and directed by

JOHN CARNEY

starring

STEVE KAZEE   **CRISTIN MILIOTI**

DAVID ABELES   WILL CONNOLLY   ELIZABETH A. DAVIS   DAVID PATRICK KELLY
ANNE L. NATHAN   LUCAS PAPAELIAS   RIPLEY SOBO   ANDY TAYLOR
MCKAYLA TWIGGS   ERIKKA WALSH   PAUL WHITTY   J. MICHAEL ZYGO

scenic and costume design   lighting design
BOB CROWLEY   **NATASHA KATZ**

sound design   dialect coach   casting
CLIVE GOODWIN   **STEPHEN GABIS**   **JIM CARNAHAN, CSA/STEPHEN KOPEL**

production stage manager   production manager   press representative   company manager
BESS MARIE GLORIOSO   **AURORA PRODUCTIONS**   **BONEAU/BRYAN-BROWN**   **LISA M. POYER**

music supervisor and orchestrations

MARTIN LOWE

movement by

STEVEN HOGGETT

directed by

JOHN TIFFANY

Once was originally developed at the American Repertory Theater, Cambridge, Massachusetts, in April 2011,
Diane Paulus, Artistic Director, Diane Borger, Producer
The producers wish to express their appreciation to Theatre Development Fund for its support of this production.

3/18/12

Steve Kazee and Cristin Milioti
sing "Falling Slowly"

Photo by Joan Marcus

Once

MUSICAL NUMBERS

ACT ONE

"Leave" ....Guy
"Falling Slowly" ....Guy & Girl
"North Strand" ....Ensemble
"The Moon" ....Andrej (as Ensemble)
"Ej, Pada, Pada, Rosicka" ....Ensemble
"If You Want Me"...Guy, Girl, Ensemble
"Broken Hearted Hoover Fixer Sucker Guy" ....Guy
"Say It to Me Now" ....Guy
"Abandoned in Bandon" ....Bank Manager
"Gold" ....Guy & Ensemble

ACT TWO

"Sleeping" ....Guy
"When Your Mind's Made Up" ....Guy, Girl, Ensemble
"The Hill" ....Girl
"Gold" (A capella) ....Company
"The Moon" ....Company
"Falling Slowly" (Reprise) ....Guy, Girl, Ensemble

(L-R): Cristin Milioti, Steve Kazee

Photo by Joan Marcus

Cast Continued

Emcee ....J. MICHAEL ZYGO
Guitar
* Ripley Sobo and Mckayla Twiggs alternate in the
role of Ivanka.

Dance Captain: J. MICHAEL ZYGO

UNDERSTUDIES

For Eamon:
SAMUEL COHEN, BRANDON ELLIS
For Andrej:
BRANDON ELLIS, BEN HOPE
For Réza:
ANDREA GOSS, ERIKKA WALSH
For Guy:
BEN HOPE, J. MICHAEL ZYGO
For Da:
SAMUEL COHEN
For Girl:
ANDREA GOSS, ERIKKA WALSH
For Baruška:
JOANNE BORTS
For Švec:
BRANDON ELLIS, BEN HOPE
For Bank Manager:
BRANDON ELLIS
For Ex-Girlfriend:
ANDREA GOSS
For Billy:
BRANDON ELLIS, J. MICHAEL ZYGO
For Emcee:
SAMUEL COHEN, BEN HOPE

2011-2012 AWARDS

TONY AWARDS
Best Musical
Best Direction of a Musical
(John Tiffany)
Best Book of a Musical
(Enda Walsh)
Best Performance by an Actor
in Leading Role in a Musical
(Steve Kazee)
Best Lighting Design of a Musical
(Natasha Katz)
Best Scenic Design of a Musical
(Bob Crowley)

Best Sound Design of a Musical
(Clive Goodwin)
Best Orchestrations
(Martin Lowe)

DRAMA DESK AWARDS
Outstanding Musical
Outstanding Director of a Musical
(John Tiffany)
Outstanding Lyrics
(Glen Hansard and Markéta Irglová)
Outstanding Orchestrations
(Martin Lowe)

NEW YORK DRAMA CRITICS' CIRCLE AWARD
Best Musical

OUTER CRITICS CIRCLE AWARDS
Outstanding New Broadway Musical
Outstanding Book of a Musical
Broadway or Off Broadway
(Enda Walsh)
Outstanding Director of a Musical
(John Tiffany)

DRAMA LEAGUE AWARD
Distinguished Production of a Musical

Once

Steve Kazee
Guy

Cristin Milioti
Girl

David Abeles
Eamon

Will Connolly
Andrej

Elizabeth A. Davis
Réza

David Patrick Kelly
Da

Anne L. Nathan
Baruška

Lucas Papaelias
Švec

Ripley Sobo
Ivanka

Andy Taylor
Bank Manager

Mckayla Twiggs
Ivanka

Erikka Walsh
Ex-Girlfriend

Paul Whitty
Billy

J. Michael Zygo
Emcee, Dance Captain

Joanne Borts
u/s Baruška

Samuel Cohen
u/s Da, Eamon, Emcee

Brandon Ellis
u/s Bank Manager, Billy, Andrej, Švec, Eamon

Andrea Goss
u/s Girl, Réza, Ex-Girlfriend

Ben Hope
u/s Guy, Andrej, Švec, Emcee

Enda Walsh
Playwright

Glen Hansard
Music and Lyrics

Markéta Irglová
Music and Lyrics

John Carney
Writer and Director of the Film Once

John Tiffany
Director

Steven Hoggett
Movement

Martin Lowe
Musical Supervisor, Orchestrations and Additional Material

Bob Crowley
Scenic and Costume Design

Natasha Katz
Lighting Design

Clive Goodwin
Sound Design

Stephen Gabis
Dialect Coach

Liz Caplan
Vocal Studios, LLC
Vocal Supervisor

Jim Carnahan
Casting

Gene O'Donovan
Aurora Productions
Production Management

Ben Heller
Aurora Productions
Production Management

John N. Hart Jr.
Producer

Once

Patrick Milling Smith
Producer

Frederick Zollo
Producer

Orin Wolf
Productions
Producer

Philip J. Smith
The Shubert
Organization
Producer

Robert E. Wankel
The Shubert
Organization
Producer

Robert Cole
Executive Producer

James C. Nicola,
Artistic Director
NYTW
Producer

Diane C. Paulus,
Artistic Director
A.R.T.
Workshop Producer

Charles Stone
Associate Producer

COMPANY AND STAGE MANAGERS
(L-R): Lisa M. Poyer, Ana M. Garcia, Bess Glorioso, Katherine Shea, Susan Keappock

WARDROBE
(L-R): Kathleen Gallagher, Cailin Anderson, Katie Chihaby

CREW
Front Row (L-R): Reid Hall (on stool), Bill Grady, Dan Hochstine
Back Row (L-R): Danny Carpio, Brien Brannigan, Herb Messing, Reg Vessey, Rebecca O'Neill, Mike Van Praagh, Eric Norris, Eddie Ruggiero

Photos by Brian Mapp

Once

The Girl and her immigrant Czech family (L-R): Anne L. Nathan, Will Connolly, Cristin Milioti, Elizabeth A. Davis and Lucas Papaelias

GENERAL PRESS REPRESENTATIVE
BONEAU/BRYAN-BROWN
Adrian Bryan-Brown   Matt Polk   Christine Olver

PRODUCTION MANAGEMENT
AURORA PRODUCTIONS INC.
Gene O'Donovan, Ben Heller,
Stephanie Sherline, Jarid Sumner, Liza Luxenberg,
Anita Shah, Anthony Jusino, Steven Dalton,
Eugenio Saenz Flores, Isaac Katzanek,
Aneta Feld, Melissa Mazdra

CASTING
Jim Carnahan, C.S.A
Stephen Kopel
Carrie Gardner, C.S.A.   Jillian Cimini
Michael Morlani   Rachel Reichblum

MUSIC COORDINATOR
John Miller

Company Manager .... Lisa M. Poyer
Associate Company Manager .... Susan Keappock

Production Stage Manager .... Bess Marie Glorioso
Stage Manager .... Ana M. Garcia
Assistant Stage Manager .... Katherine Shea

Associate Producer .... Charles Stone
Associate Producer .... Ben Limberg
Movement Associate .... Yasmine Lee
Associate Music Supervisor .... Rob Preuss
Music Captain .... David Abeles
Assistant Scenic Designer .... Frank McCullough
Assistant Lighting Designers .... Peter Hoerburger,
                                            Yael Lubetzky
Assistant Sound Designer/
    Advance Audio .... Brian Walters
Czech Diction and Translation .... Suzanna Halsey

Assistant to John N. Hart, Jr .... Maximillian Traber
Assistant to Patrick Milling Smith .... Catherine Waage
Assistant to Robert Cole &
    Frederick Zollo .... Timothy Flateman

Production Carpenter .... Rebecca O'Neill
Production Electrician .... Michael Pitzer
Production Props .... Reg Vessey
Production Sound Engineer .... Phillip Lojo/
                                            Paul Delcioppo
Head Electrician .... Eric Norris
Sound Engineer .... Dan Hochstine
Instrument Technician .... Reid Hall
Props Supervisor .... Matt Hodges

UK Props .... Lisa Buckley
Lighting Programmer .... Sean Beach
Advance Production Sound .... Jason Choquette
NYTW Costume Liaison .... Jeffrey Wallach
Wardrobe Supervisor .... Kathleen Gallagher
Dressers .... Cailin Anderson, Katie Chihaby
Child Actor Guardian .... Lisa Schwartz
Tutoring .... On Location Education/Muriel Kester
Production Assistants .... Brandon Bart, Amanda Hutt,
                                Eric Love, Ryan McCurdy,
                                Danese C. Smalls

Advertising .... SpotCo/
                        Drew Hodges, Jim Edwards,
                Tom Greenwald, Tom McCann, Laura Ellis
Website and Online Marketing .... SpotCo/
                        Sara Fitzpatrick, Marc Mettler,
                    Michael Crowley, Meghan Ownbey
Marketing and Promotions .... SpotCo/
                        Nick Pramik, Kristen Rathbun,
                Julie Wechsler, Caroline Newhouse
Legal
    Counsel ..... Franklin, Weinrib, Rudell & Vassallo, P.C./
                        Jonathan Lonner, Heather Reid
Additional Legal
    Counsel .... Frankfurt, Kurnit, Klein & Selz, P.C./
                                        Mark Merriman
Immigration Counsel .... Shannon K. Such
Accountant .... Fried & Kowgios CPAs LLP/
                                        Robert Fried, CPA
Comptroller .... Anne Stewart FitzRoy, CPA
Banking .... City National Bank/
                            Anne McSweeney, Michael Tynan
Insurance .... Dewitt Stern Group/
                        Peter Shoemaker, Rebecca LaFazia
Payroll Service .... Castellana Payroll Services, Inc./
                        Lance Castellana, James Castellana,
                                        Norman Sewell
Travel .... Kristine Ljungdahl, Manifest Travel
Production Photographer .... Joan Marcus
Opening Night
    Coordination ...... The Lawrence Company Events, Inc./
                                        Michael P. Lawrence
Theatre Displays .... King Displays, Inc.
Group Sales .... Telecharge.com Group Sales/
                        212-239-6262, 1-800-432-7780,
                        www.telecharge.com/groups

CREDITS

Scenery and scenic effects built, painted, electrified and automated by Show Motion, Inc., Milford, CT. Automation and show control by Show Motion, Inc., Milford, CT, using the AC2 Computerized Motion Control System. Lighting equipment from PRG Lighting. Video equipment from PRG Video. Sound equipment by Masque Sound™. Banjo built by Nechville Musical Products. Mandolins supplied by Sound to Earth, Ltd. Drum kit supplied by Carroll Musical Instrument Rentals, LLC. Hosiery and undergarments supplied by Bra*Tenders.

MUSIC CREDITS

"On Raglan Road" by Patrick Kavanagh is performed by kind permission of the Trustees of the Estate of the late Katherine B. Kavanagh, through the Jonathan Williams Literary Agency. "Gold" composed by Fergus O'Farrell, published by Yell Music Ltd. "Abandoned in Bandon" composed by Martin Lowe, Andy Taylor and Enda Walsh.

Souvenir merchandise designed and created by:
The Araca Group

Original Broadway cast recording
available on Sony Masterworks

SPECIAL THANKS

C.F. Martin and Company is the official guitar of the Broadway musical *Once*.

www.oncemusical.com

 THE SHUBERT ORGANIZATION, INC.

Board of Directors

Philip J. Smith	**Robert E. Wankel**
Chairman	President
Wyche Fowler, Jr.	**Diana Phillips**
Lee J. Seidler	**Michael I. Sovern**

Stuart Subotnick

Chief Financial Officer .... Elliot Greene
Sr. Vice President, Ticketing .... David Andrews
Vice President, Finance .... Juan Calvo
Vice President, Human Resources .... Cathy Cozens
Vice President, Facilities .... John Darby
Vice President, Theatre Operations .... Peter Entin
Vice President, Marketing .... Charles Flateman
Vice President, Audit .... Anthony LaMattina
Vice President, Ticket Sales .... Brian Mahoney
Vice President, Creative Projects .... D.S. Moynihan
Vice President, Real Estate .... Julio Peterson

House Manager .... William Mitchell

Once
SCRAPBOOK

Correspondent: Andy Taylor, "Bank Manager," Cellist

Memorable Opening Night Note: Since the show has started I have heard from many old friends in the biz who loved the show. One was my old college housemate Judy Kuhn who was a voice major at Oberlin when I was a double major in cello and theatre. I actually played cello on her senior recital and will take credit for coaching her before her first acting audition for *The House of Bernarda Alba*. Needless to say she got the part, so the three-time Tony nominee really owes it all to me.

Memorable Party: The best party we've had so far was when Glen Hansard came to Boston to watch the workshop. That weekend we had a musical evening planned and Paul Whitty said it was a shame he wasn't going to be there for it. He said, "Why don't we just play now?" We were all hanging out on stage at the Oberon Theatre at ART and we just grabbed our instruments and started jamming with Glen. He was uber-cool and we had a good old Irish sesh, swilling Sam Adams, alternating one of his tunes with a chorus of "Take a Load Off Fannie," et cetera, on into the wee hours.

Memorable Celebrity Encounters: Meeting Sting was pretty darn cool. He uncannily remembered Elizabeth's, Erikka's, and Cristin's names but seemed to struggle retaining the fellas'—but then you don't have to be a mega icon rock star to notice the charms of the women in our cast.

Understudy Anecdote: One of our covers, Andrea Goss must have made some kind of Broadway history by going on for Cristin at a matinee, brilliantly playing the Girl (with piano) and then when Cristin got back that night and Elizabeth was ill, Andrea also brilliantly played Réza (with violin). A ridiculous display of chops and professionalism.

Special Backstage Ritual: Since Paul Whitty and I play adversaries in the show, the last moment before we enter onstage we always exchange gestures and I indicate to Paul that I would like him to perform an anatomically impossible act upon himself.

Favorite Moment During Each Performance: There are many. I like doing the preshow because the set list changes, we get to play different instruments, and a great vibe is created in the house where the audience can already tell we can flat-out shred before the play even starts. Also, I see Cristin Milioti for only about one minute a night right before places for Act II and that's always a pleasure.

Favorite In-Theatre Gathering Place: We have a greenroom downstairs where we convene but I like hanging in the dressing room I share with David Abeles. He's smarter than he looks, with a heart like a lump of coal—just my type.

Favorite Off-Site Gathering Place: We've started doing a little music session on Sundays at O'Flaherty's. That's cool. They always treat us well and now that we are a hot ticket we are

1. The original cast musicians with musical director Martin Lowe (front, center) ready to record the cast album at Avatar Studios.
2. Cast members Ripley Sobo and Mckayla Twiggs dressed up for the opening night party.
3. Songwriters and original film stars Glen Hansard and Markéta Irglová at the Broadway premiere.

welcome at Bar Centrale as well, where you get to hang with the groovy kids like Mel Brooks.

Favorite Snack Foods: I eat candy during the show. I've tried Jolly Ranchers cuz they keep me busy for awhile but the wardrobe department got tired of getting the sticky stuff off the inside of my pockets. Chocolates melt too fast, Hot Tamales just dissolve too quickly, so lately it's been Starbursts cuz the wrapper doesn't crinkle when I undo it.

Mascot: Paul Whitty

Favorite Therapy: Steven Hoggett prepared a voluntary warm-up for us that our dance captain Mike Zygo leads every night before half hour. Though I don't have perfect attendance, it really does help me stay in shape for the long run.

Memorable Ad-Libs: We've broken some strings occasionally so there have been a few ad-libs about that, but we tend to stick to the script. It's a fairly naturalistic acting style that doesn't really lend itself to duct-taping the fourth wall back up.

Technological Interruptions: Like most shows we've had our share of cell phones going off, people texting, unwrapping cellophane Christmas gifts and taking pictures from the front row DURING the show. The regularity of the interruptions is a troubling trend.

Embarrassing Incident: No biggie, but when the first broken string occurred in a critical point as Steve Kazee sang "Say It to Me Now" we hadn't practiced a contingency plan that we have now. Will Connolly, who had fortunately learned the song just goofing around and with his ukulele in his lap, just started to play the back-up while Steve continued to sing. It was different but very cool.

Memorable Press Encounter: Our coolest press event probably had to be our *Vogue* shoot. My joy at the shoot turned to disappointment when the magazine came out and Erikka and I are not in the shots they chose. Well my right arm is. I try to look at it as an object lesson in not getting too drunk with your own perfume

Once

Scrapbook

1. David Patrick Kelly preps for the cast's April 6, 2012 appearance on TV's "The Today Show."
2. The cast performs on "The Today Show."
3. Anne Nathan recording the cast album.
4. *Yearbook* correspondent Andy Taylor recording the cast album.
5. Cristin Milioti on opening night.

but it was bittersweet to see all my pals in the mag and not be beaming alongside.

Memorable Stage Door Fan Encounter: At the stage door my old pal J.K. Simmons surprised me. We've known each other since summer stock in Montana. It's lovely to see how his extraordinary career has not changed him a bit, just a swell guy, father, and husband, and great actor.

Web Buzz on the Show: Must say I don't read the buzz on the web too much. I do read reviews since I made a decision many years ago. I often overheard what reviewers said anyway and I wanted to be able to maintain and trust my performances with other critical voices in my head. Sometimes I agree, sometimes I disagree. I understand their function and try to keep an even keel. As for the web bloggers, it seems they are more personal, quite often vociferous. For *Once* the buzz seems very good and I hope it continues and reaches others interested in checking it out. I just find that once I start following online threads, I look up and an hour has gone by that I could have spent watching Mexican wrestling.

Latest Audience Arrival: We had two busloads of people arrive late and they were allowed to be (noisily) seated during a delicate part of the beginning of the show. It almost seemed appropriate to stop and wait for everyone to sit, or to rewind and take it from the top but what do you do? You owe it to the other 800 patrons who paid a significant amount of money and arrived on time to continue as best you can.

Fastest Costume Change: It occurs on stage when Steve puts on his lamé suit. We all have basically one outfit that's pretty comfortable. We are thankfully not doing a period piece or anything seasonal. Elizabeth Davis wears the most revealing outfit, but it's relatively modest, i.e. my wife would let my 10-year-old daughter wear it.

Sweethearts Among the Cast: We are fortunate to have a company made mostly of sweethearts who will now mock me mercilessly for admitting that.

Catchphrases Only the Cast Would Understand: We call the program of songs

selected to be that night's pre-show "Bull****," and that's to take the p*** out of David Abeles whose job it is to choose them, since someone always gets their favorites cut. We also say "Yeah bud" a lot.

Orchestra Member Who Plays the Most Instruments: Many of us play multiple instruments, not sure who plays the most. I play five: the cello, violin, guitar, accordion, and mandolin. My understudy Brandon has to learn about ten, I think, though some of those would be various percussion instruments. But a herculean effort nonetheless.

Company In-Joke: We like to play a game called major/minor where we basically take each song in the show and by changing the key signatures from major to minor or vice versa, create the sort of yin yang happy-clown/sad-clown version of the tunes. Lucas, a.k.a. L.P. Funk has elevated it to an art form and now has a respectable 12 minute rock-opera version

done on solo guitar with wailing that is hilarious, but possibly only to the fourteen of us.

Memorable Directorial Note: We had just opened off-Broadway and we knew we had something special. John Tiffany perhaps foreseeing a long run simply said don't turn on one another.

Best Thing About Working on This Show: I believe if you are lucky you have a few shows in your career that are truly magical. The reasons vary, maybe you get to play a role of a lifetime, or work with a legend, or recover from something that seemed unsurmountable. This is such a show, a culmination of a whole life's experience; forty years playing cello, dialect work, singing lessons, dance training, comic chops honed, blending gracefully with others to create a whole greater than the sum of its parts. It is art. The feeling I get from playing *Once* and from these audiences will continue to fill my soul long into my dotage.

One Man, Two Guvnors

First Preview: April 6, 2012. Opened: April 18, 2012.
Still running as of May 31, 2012.

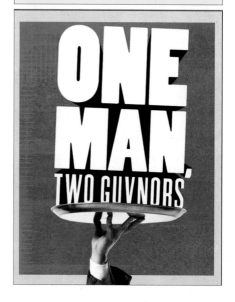

British farce (based on Carlo Goldoni's commedia dell'arte masterpiece The Servant of Two Masters*) about a man who finds himself in the employ of two tough characters on the run from the law. His efforts to serve them both simultaneously without one finding out about the other (and without any of them winding up in the hands of the constabulary) provides the ever-escalating action. The production's centerpiece is James Corden's manic performance as the overworked and underfed employee, Francis Henshall.*

CAST

(in order of appearance)

Harry Dangle	MARTYN ELLIS
Dolly	SUZIE TOASE
Lloyd Boateng	TREVOR LAIRD
Charlie "the Duck" Clench	FRED RIDGEWAY
Pauline Clench	CLAIRE LAMS
Alan Dangle	DANIEL RIGBY
Francis Henshall	JAMES CORDEN
Rachel Crabbe	JEMIMA ROOPER
Stanley Stubbers	OLIVER CHRIS
Gareth	BEN LIVINGSTON
Alfie	TOM EDDEN

Ensemble ....ELI JAMES, BEN LIVINGSTON, SARAH MANTON, STEPHEN PILKINGTON, DAVID RYAN SMITH, NATALIE SMITH

Continued on next page

☕ THE MUSIC BOX

239 W. 45th Street
A Shubert Organization Theatre

Philip J. Smith, *Chairman*   **Robert E. Wankel,** *President*

NATIONAL THEATRE OF GREAT BRITAIN
under the direction of
NICHOLAS HYTNER and NICK STARR
and
BOB BOYETT

NATIONAL ANGELS · CHRIS HARPER · TIM LEVY

SCOTT RUDIN · ROGER BERLIND · HARRIET NEWMAN LEVE · STEPHANIE P. McCLELLAND
BROADWAY ACROSS AMERICA · JAM THEATRICALS · DARYL ROTH
SONIA FRIEDMAN · HARRIS KARMA PRODUCTIONS · DEBORAH TAYLOR · RICHARD WILLIS

Present

JAMES CORDEN

In

ONE MAN, TWO GUVNORS

By RICHARD BEAN

Based on *THE SERVANT OF TWO MASTERS* by CARLO GOLDONI

With songs by GRANT OLDING

With

OLIVER CHRIS   JEMIMA ROOPER

TOM EDDEN   MARTYN ELLIS   TREVOR LAIRD   CLAIRE LAMS
FRED RIDGEWAY   DANIEL RIGBY   SUZIE TOASE
BRIAN GONZALES   ELI JAMES   BEN LIVINGSTON   SARAH MANTON
STEPHEN PILKINGTON   DAVID RYAN SMITH   NATALIE SMITH
JACOB COLIN COHEN   AUSTIN MOORHEAD   JASON RABINOWITZ   CHARLIE ROSEN

Director NICHOLAS HYTNER

Physical Comedy Director CAL McCRYSTAL

Designer MARK THOMPSON

Lighting Designer MARK HENDERSON

Sound Designer PAUL ARDITTI

Associate Director and Choreographer **ADAM PENFORD**	Original UK Casting **ALASTAIR COOMER CDG**	US Casting **TARA RUBIN CASTNG, CSA**	Music Director **CHARLIE ROSEN**
Production Stage Manager **WILLIAM JOSEPH BARNES**	Technical Supervisor **DAVID BENKEN**	NT Technical Producer **KATRINA GILROY**	NT Administrative Producer **ROBIN HAWKES**
Press Representative **BONEAU/BRYAN-BROWN**	Advertising & Marketing **SPOTCO**	General Management **JAMES TRINER**	

National Theatre is supported by Arts Council England
The Producers wish to express their appreciation to Theatre Development Fund for its support of this production.

4/18/12

(L-R): Suzie Toase, Claire Lams, Daniel Rigby, James Corden, Oliver Chris, Jemima Rooper, Fred Ridgeway, Martyn Ellis, Trevor Laird

Photo by Johan Persson

One Man, Two Guvnors

Cast Continued

THE CRAZE
JASON RABINOWITZ (Lead Vocals)
AUSTIN MOORHEAD (Lead Guitar)
CHARLIE ROSEN (Music Director/Bass)
JACOB COLIN COHEN (Drums/Percussion)

UNDERSTUDIES
For Francis:
BRIAN GONZALES
For Stanley:
ELI JAMES
For Rachel:
NATALIE SMITH
For Charlie, Harry:
BEN LIVINGSTON
for Dolly, Pauline:
SARAH MANTON
For Alan, Alfie:
STEPHEN PILKINGTON
For Lloyd, Gareth:
DAVID RYAN SMITH
For Female Ensemble:
LIZ BALTES
For Lead Guitar, Drums, Lead Singer:
CHARLIE ROSEN
For Bass, Lead Singer:
MATT CUSACK
For Lead Singer, Drums:
ZACH JONES

James Corden is appearing with the permission of
Actors' Equity Association. Oliver Chris, Jemima
Rooper, Tom Edden, Martyn Ellis, Trevor Laird,
Claire Lams, Fred Ridgeway, Daniel Rigby and Suzie
Toase are appearing with the support of Actors'
Equity Association pursuant to an exchange program
between American Equity and UK Equity.

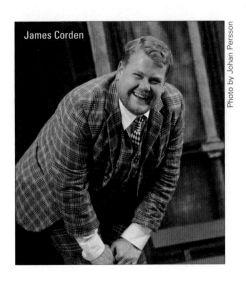

James Corden

Photo by Johan Persson

James Corden
Francis Henshall

Oliver Chris
Stanley Stubbers

Jemima Rooper
Rachel Crabbe

Tom Edden
Alfie

Martyn Ellis
Harry Dangle

Trevor Laird
Lloyd Boateng

Claire Lams
Pauline Clench

Fred Ridgeway
Charlie Clench

Daniel Rigby
Alan

Suzie Toase
Dolly

Brian Gonzales
Ensemble

Eli James
Ensemble

Ben Livingston
Gareth/Ensemble

Sarah Manton
Ensemble

Stephen Pilkington
Ensemble

David Ryan Smith
Ensemble

Natalie Smith
Ensemble

Jacob Colin Cohen
Drums/Percussion

Austin Moorhead
Lead Guitar

Jason Rabinowitz
Lead Vocals

One Man, Two Guvnors

Charlie Rosen
Music Director/Bass

Matt Cusack
u/s Bass, Lead Singer

Zach Jones
u/s Lead Singer, Percussion

Richard Bean
Author

Nicholas Hytner
Director

Cal McCrystal
Physical Comedy Director

Mark Thompson
Set and Costume Design

Mark Henderson
Lighting Design

Paul Arditti
Sound Design

Grant Olding
Composer

Adam Penford
Associate Director/ Choreographer

Tara Rubin Casting
US Casting

David Benken
Technical Supervisor

James Triner
General Manager

Bob Boyett
Producer

Roger Berlind
Producer

Harriet Newman Leve
Producer

Stephanie P. McClelland
Producer

John Gore
CEO Broadway Across America
Producer

Thomas B. McGrath
Chairman Broadway Across America
Producer

Arny Granat
Jam Theatricals
Producer

Steve Traxler
Jam Theatricals
Producer

Daryl Roth
Producer

Sonia Friedman Productions
Producer

Dede Harris
Producer

Sharon Karmazin
Producer

Deborah Taylor
Producer

Richard Willis
Producer

One Man, Two Guvnors

STAGE MANAGEMENT
Front: Billy Barnes
Back (L-R): Liz Baltes,
Chris Zaccardi

Photos by Brian Mapp

BOX OFFICE
(L-R): Robert Kelly,
Tracie Giebler

CREW
Seated (L-R): Kyle Garnett, Kim Garnett
Standing (L-R): Brian Maher, Lucas Indelicato, John McPherson, Dana Gracey

WARDROBE
(L-R): Raymond Panelli,
Sue Cerceo,
Chip White

HAIR
(L-R): Kevin Maybee,
Carmel Vargyas

One Man, Two Guvnors

Photo by Brian Mapp

FRONT OF HOUSE
Front Row (L-R): Edith Rosado, Lottie Dennis, Kenny Kelly, Thomas Murdoch, Michael Concepcion
Back Row (L-R): John Himmel, Nick Fusco, Dennis Scanlon, Joe Amato, John Seid, Laura Scanlon

---

STAFF FOR *ONE MAN, TWO GUVNORS*

GENERAL MANAGEMENT
James Triner

PRESS REPRESENTATIVE
BONEAU/BRYAN-BROWN
Adrian Bryan-Brown
Jessica Johnson   Christine Olver

CASTING
TARA RUBIN CASTING
Tara Rubin, CSA; Lindsay Levine;
Eric Woodall, CSA; Merri Sugarman, CSA;
Dale Brown, CSA; Stephanie Yankwitt, CSA;
Kaitlin Shaw

PRODUCTION MANAGEMENT
David Benken   Rose Palombo

COMPANY MANAGER
Elizabeth M. Talmadge

Production Stage Manager	William Joseph Barnes
Stage Manager	Chris Zaccardi
Assistant Stage Manager	Liz Baltes
Music Director	Charlie Rosen
UK Production Manager	Anna Anderson
Associate Scenic Designer	Peter Eastman
Associate Costume Designer	Daryl Stone
UK Associate Lighting Designer	Tom Snell
US Associate Lighting Designer	Michael Jones
Moving Light Programmer	Marc Polimeni
UK Associate Sound Designer	John Owens
US Associate Sound Designer	Drew Levy
Hair Coordinator	Campbell Young Associates
Head Carpenter	John McPherson
Advance Rigger	Michael Shepp
Production Electrician	Jon Lawson
Head Sound Engineer	Lucas Indelicato
Production Properties Coordinator	Denise J. Grillo
Assistant Props	Kevin Crawford
Wardrobe Supervisor	Raymond Panelli
Assistant Wardrobe Supervisor	Susan Cerceo
Dressers	Karen Gilbert, Chip White
Stitcher/Laundry	Kathryn Guida, Scott Tucker
Hair Supervisor	Carmel Vargyas
Hairdresser	Kevin R. Maybee

Production Assistants	Morgan Holbrook, Katie McKee, James C. Steele, Michael Tosto
General Management Assistant	Megan Bowers
Banking	JPMorgan/Chase
Payroll	Castellana Services, Inc.
Production Accountant	Rosenberg, Neuwirth & Kuchner/ Chris Cacace
Insurance	DeWitt Stern Group
Legal Counsel	Lazarus & Harris LLP/ Scott Lazarus, Esq., Robert C. Harris, Esq.
Merchandising	Encore Merchandising
Advertising	SPOTCO/ Drew Hodges, Jim Edwards, Tom Greenwald, Jim Aquino, Laura Ellis
Website Design	SPOTCO/ Sara Fitzpatrick, Marc Mettler, Kristen Bardwil, Michelle Haines, Cory Spinney
Marketing	SPOTCO/ Nick Pramik, Kristen Rathbun, Julie Wechsler, Caroline Newhouse
Theatre Displays	BAM Signs/Adam Miller
Group Sales	Shubert Group Sales
Housing Accommodations	Gregory Diaz/ Premier Furnished Solutions
Flight/Hotel Arrangements	Andi Henig/Tzell Travel

FOR BOYETT THEATRICALS
Executive Assistant	Diane Murphy
Office Assistants	Michael Mandell, Kiefer Mansfield

FOR THE NATIONAL THEATRE OF GREAT BRITAIN
Chairman of the NT Board	John Makinson
Director of the National Theatre	Nicholas Hytner
Executive Director	Nick Starr
Chief Operating Officer	Lisa Burger
NT Associate Producer	Pádraig Cusack
Producer	Chris Harper
Technical Producer	Katrina Gilroy
Administrative Producer	Robin Hawkes
Assistant Producer	Marianne Dicker
Producing Assistant	Hetty Wooding
Head of Music	Matthew Scott
Casting	Alastair Coomer

Production Accountant	Michelle Woods
Assistant Production Accountant	Akos Koranteng
General Counsel	Peter Taylor

CREDITS
Scenery constructed by the National Theatre Carpentry and Paintframe Departments, and Hudson Scenic Studio, Inc. Technical drawings by the National Theatre Digital Design and Drawing Department. Properties constructed by the National Theatre Props Department. Costumes constructed by the National Theatre Costume Department. Lighting equipment from PRG Lighting. Sound equipment from Sound Associates, Inc. Special thanks to Bra*Tenders for hosiery and undergarments.

Rehearsed at the New 42nd Street Studios

SPECIAL THANKS
Special thanks to the National Theatre's Digital, Finance, Graphics, Marketing and Press Departments; the West End team of *One Man, Two Guvnors*.

THE SHUBERT ORGANIZATION, INC.
Board of Directors

Philip J. Smith	**Robert E. Wankel**
Chairman	President
Wyche Fowler, Jr.	**Diana Phillips**
Lee J. Seidler	**Michael I. Sovern**

Stuart Subotnick

Chief Financial Officer	Elliot Greene
Sr. Vice President, Ticketing	David Andrews
Vice President, Finance	Juan Calvo
Vice President, Human Resources	Cathy Cozens
Vice President, Facilities	John Darby
Vice President, Theatre Operations	Peter Entin
Vice President, Marketing	Charles Flateman
Vice President, Audit	Anthony LaMattina
Vice President, Ticket Sales	Brian Mahoney
Vice President, Creative Projects	D.S. Moynihan
Vice President, Real Estate	Julio Peterson

House Manager	Jonathan Shulman

One Man, Two Guvnors
SCRAPBOOK

Photos by Joseph Marzullo/WENN

1. James Corden accepts applause from the audience and fellow cast member (and Yearbook correspondent) Jemima Rooper on opening night.
2. Suzie Toase and Fred Ridgeway take curtain call at the premiere.
3. Corden (C) with his "two guvnors," Rooper and Oliver Chris at the Liberty Theatre for the cast party.
4. House band The Craze (L-R): Charlie Rosen, Jacob Colin Cohen, Jason Rabinowitz, Austin Moorhead.
5. Corden shakes the hand of an audience member on opening night.

Correspondent: Jemima Rooper, "Rachel Crabbe"

Memorable Opening Night Message: The new London cast of *One Man, Two Guvnors* sent us all a photograph of them in our costumes pulling hideous faces to make fun of a photo shoot we all did for Vogue. The painstaking accuracy of recreating the photo was pretty touching and very funny.

Opening Night Gifts: I love giving gifts but usually bankrupt myself in the process. The loveliest gift I've ever received was a hand-painted mug from an actress for my dressing room and I take it everywhere.

Most Exciting Celebrity Visitor: Joan Rivers. It was a few days before opening and she said, "If they don't like it they're ASSHOLES!"

Who Has Done the Most Shows in Their Career: Probably me. I'm actually 80 but have spent a lot on plastic surgery.

Special Backstage Ritual: We do a lot of dancing in the wings. Very special choreographed moments which stretch to bull fighting mimes on matinee days.

Favorite Moments During Each Performance: I really weirdly enjoy my quick-changes. I feel like a sweaty rock star. Chip, one of the dressers, sings me a little sweaty rock star song to help me be quick.

Favorite In-Theatre Gathering Place: Too easy. Boys' dressing room! I often "accidentally" burst in. Just to catch a glimpse.

Favorite Off-Site Hangout: There are too many...and we've only been here a few weeks....

Favorite Snack Food: Popcorn. And the U.S. is the popcorn king. I'm in heaven.

Mascot: Trunklestiltslug. Don't ask.

Most Memorable Ad-Lib: James Corden was being mischievous and in trying to make him laugh myself I forgot my line and panicked and blurted out "I've got a stinky shirt," which was along the right lines but took us all slightly by surprise and started the worst giggling epidemic theatre had ever seen.

Memorable Press Encounter: Pulling a ridiculous face at my first red-carpet event. Never again. Me and photos do not mix.

Internet Buzz on Your Show: I get a bit scared that I'll read something horrible so don't look at that stuff but am so thrilled if there is a buzz!

Fastest Costume Change: Going from East End gangster man into 1960's Andrews Sister-style singer in 45 seconds.

Who Wore the Least: Oliver Chris. But by choice. His not ours.

Catchphrases Only the Company Would Recognize: Rigbones.

Memorable Directorial Note: "Don't do that. It's an abomination." Sir Nicholas Hytner to Jemima Rooper, April 2012.

Company In-Jokes: Naughty photographs hidden in props. And by "naughty" I mean "disgusting."

Company Legends: Our New York crew! They make every day fun and wonderful. I adore them.

Embarrassing Moments: Showing very colorful underwear to half the band and half the audience unknowingly and innocently. I apologize.

Ghostly Encounters Backstage: While we were doing the play in London a ghost used to knock on my dressing room door and run away. With heavy footsteps and a masculine chuckle.

Superstitions That Turned Out To Be True: Break a leg? Daniel Rigby has broken his wrist. And Oliver Chris lost his voice after saying the title of The Scottish Play.

Nicknames: Scoops. Pooper. Trooper. Scooper Trooper. Pooper Scooper.

Coolest Thing About Being in This Show: The audience. Every night they make it special and different and a pleasure. And being able to be in New York. I never want to leave. They're going to have to throw me out.

Other Desert Cities

First Preview: October 12, 2011. Opened: November 3, 2011.
Still running as of May 31, 2012.

Author Brooke Wyeth plans a tell-all book to blow the lid off the secrets of her conservative showbiz parents, whose neglect she believes led to her brother's untimely death. But she soon discovers that even she doesn't know all *the family secrets.*

CAST
(in order of speaking)

Polly Wyeth .... STOCKARD CHANNING
Brooke Wyeth .... RACHEL GRIFFITHS
Lyman Wyeth .... STACY KEACH
Trip Wyeth .... THOMAS SADOSKI
Silda Grauman .... JUDITH LIGHT

TIME: Christmas 2004
and the last scene – March 2010

PLACE: The Wyeth home,
Palm Springs, California

Assistant Stage Manager .... Jenn McNeil

Rachel Griffiths is appearing with the permission of Actors' Equity Association.

UNDERSTUDIES
For Polly Wyeth and Silda Grauman:
LAUREN KLEIN
for Lyman Wyeth:
JACK DAVIDSON
for Brooke Wyeth:
LIZ WISAN
for Trip Wyeth:
MATTHEW RISCH

⑥ BOOTH THEATRE
222 West 45th Street
A Shubert Organization Theatre
Philip J. Smith, *Chairman*   **Robert E. Wankel,** *President*

LINCOLN CENTER THEATER
under the direction of
André Bishop and **Bernard Gersten**
in association with
Bob Boyett
presents

**Stockard Channing   Rachel Griffiths   Stacy Keach
Judith Light   Thomas Sadoski**
in

OTHER DESERT CITIES

A Play by
Jon Robin Baitz

Sets	Costumes	Lighting
John Lee Beatty	**David Zinn**	**Kenneth Posner**

Sound		Original Music
Jill BC DuBoff		**Justin Ellington**

Production Stage Manager	Casting	General Press Agent
James FitzSimmons	**Daniel Swee**	**Philip Rinaldi**

Executive Director
of Development & Planning
Hattie K. Jutagir

Director of Marketing
Linda Mason Ross

Managing Director
Adam Siegel

Production Manager
Jeff Hamlin

Directed by
Joe Mantello

LCT gratefully acknowledges a gift from the Estate of Edith K. Ehrman.

Special thanks to The Harold and Mimi Steinberg Charitable Trust
for supporting new American plays at LCT.

American Airlines is the official airline of Lincoln Center Theater.

10/31/11

(L-R): Rachel Griffiths, Thomas Sadoski, Judith Light, Stacy Keach, Stockard Channing

Photo by Joan Marcus

Other Desert Cities

Stockard Channing
Polly Wyeth

Stacy Keach
Lyman Wyeth

Rachel Griffiths
Brooke Wyeth

Judith Light
Silda Grauman

Thomas Sadoski
Trip Wyeth

Jack Davidson
Understudy

Lauren Klein
Understudy

Matthew Risch
Understudy

Liz Wisan
Understudy

Jon Robin Baitz
Playwright

Joe Mantello
Director

John Lee Beatty
Sets

David Zinn
Costumes

Kenneth Posner
Lighting

Jill BC DuBoff
Sound

Justin Ellington
Original Music

Paul Huntley
Hair and Wig Designer

Bob Boyett
Producer

André Bishop
Lincoln Center Theater, Producer

Bernard Gersten
Lincoln Center Theater, Producer

TRANSFER STUDENTS 2011-2012

Jennifer Harmon
Understudy

Justin Kirk
Trip Wyeth

Elizabeth Marvel
Brooke Wyeth

Jed Orlemann
u/s Trip Wyeth

Robbie Collier Sublett
u/s Trip Wyeth

Karen Walsh
Understudy

Judith Light as Silda Grauman

Photo by Joan Marcus

Other Desert Cities

Photos by Amanda Dekker

WARDROBE
(L-R): John McNulty, Ryan Rossetto (Wardrobe Supervisor), Mary Ann Oberpriller, Betsy Waddell, Catherine Goetschius
Not pictured: Charlie Catanese

FRONT OF HOUSE STAFF
(L-R): Daniel Rosario, Marjorie Glover, Reginald Browne, Chrissie Collins, Timothy Wilhelm (Head Usher)
Not Pictured: Bernadette Bokun, Marco Malgiolio, Nirmala Sharma, Nadine Space, and Laurel Ann Wilson (House Manager).

STAGE MANAGEMENT
(L-R): James FitzSimmons, Jenn McNeil

CREW
(L-R): David Karlson, Beth Berkeley, Susan Goulet

(L-R): Rachel Griffiths, Stockard Channing
Stacy Keach, Thomas Sadoski

Photo by Joan Marcus

Other Desert Cities

2011-2012 AWARDS

TONY AWARD
Best Performance by an Actress
in a Featured Role in a Play
(Judith Light)

DRAMA LEAGUE AWARD
Distinguished Production of a Play

DRAMA DESK AWARD
Outstanding Featured Actress in a Play
(Judith Light)

(L-R): Stockard Channing,
Rachel Griffiths,
Stacy Keach

Photo by Joan Marcus

Other Desert Cities
SCRAPBOOK

Photos by Joseph Marzullo/WENN

1. (L-R): Thomas Sadoski, Judith Light, Jon Robin Baitz, Stockard Channing and Rachel Griffiths at the Mariott Marquis Hotel for the debut party.
2. Co-stars Stacy Keach and Thomas Sadoski at the Marriott Marquis opening night.
3. Director Joe Mantello and playwright Jon Robin Baitz at the premiere.
4. Stockard Channing.

Correspondents: James FitzSimmons, Production Stage Manager, and Jenn McNeil, Assistant Stage Manager

Memorable Opening Night Notes: We got so many—though the one from Hugh Jackman was pretty sweet. (He and Rachel being fellow Aussies).

Opening Night Gifts: As we take place in Palm Springs, Rachel gave everyone items found in a desert, such as a sun-bleached animal skull or the large tarantula paperweight she gave me. (Me being especially arachnophobic.)

Most Exciting Celebrity Visitors: It was fun keeping track of all the cast members of "Brothers and Sisters" stopping back. But there's been a lot.

Who Has Done the Most Shows in Their Career: With this cast—between Stockard, Stacy and Judith, it's a history of theatre.

Special Backstage Rituals: At "places" the company gathers and does a very special salute. It started back at the Mitzi Newhouse Theatre and they've continued with it every show. The salute involves a particular unprintable word and the raising of tennis racquets....

Favorite Moments: My personal favorite is the first big laugh line for the show—which is the word "Jews." That laugh will tell us how the house is going behave. My second favorite is watching Stacy Keach fake "die"—it's hysterical for us, even if the house doesn't always laugh!

Favorite In-Theatre Gathering Place: Judith Light's dressing room

Favorite Snack Food: Peanut butter filled pretzels are a must!

Mascot: We had this stuffed dog from rehearsals in the beginning that had its own table and chair—he now resides in the stage management office

Favorite Therapy: Our special Lemon–Ginger honey tea and smashed ricola nubs.

Record Number of Cell Phone Rings, Cell Phone Photos or Texting Incidents During a Performance: Nine that we counted in Act II – and at our BC/EFA speech that night Rachel asked that everyone whose cell phone went off must make a $100 donation or risk going to theatre hell. She got a huge round of applause!

Latest Audience Arrival: End of Act I—one hour into the show.

Catchphrases Only the Company Would Recognize: "Kill the kitty" which might also apply to the most memorable directorial note.

Nicknames: We have a rash of bad knees in this cast and crew—so Stacy nicknamed us "Wounded Knee"

Ghostly Encounters Backstage: Not ghostly but my maternal great-grandmother was a relative of Edwin Booth so it's a thrill to be able to finally work at the Booth Theater.

Coolest Thing About Being in This Show: Working with this amazing cast and crew.

Peter and the Starcatcher

First Preview: March 28, 2012. Opened: April 15, 2012.
Still running as of May 31, 2012.

Rick Elice's adaptation of the book by syndicated humor columnist Dave Barry and novelist Ridley Pearson, which offers a swashbuckling prequel to Peter Pan. It explains not only how Pan, Tinkerbell, Captain Hook and the Lost Boys came to Neverland, but reveals the origin of magic itself in the precious extraterrestrial substance known as "Starstuff" (a.k.a. Fairy Dust) and the organization (the Starcatchers) that has formed to gather it as it falls from the heavens. A distinctive feature of this production is Roger Rees' and Alex Timbers' staging, which makes innovative use of lowest-tech traditional stagecraft to stimulate the imagination.

CAST
(in alphabetical order)

Fighting Prawn	TEDDY BERGMAN
Black Stache	CHRISTIAN BORLE
Mrs. Bumbrake	ARNIE BURTON
Boy	ADAM CHANLER-BERAT
Slank/Hawking Clam	MATT D'AMICO
Smee	KEVIN DEL AGUILA
Prentiss	CARSON ELROD
Alf	GREG HILDRETH
Lord Aster	RICK HOLMES
Captain Scott	ISAIAH JOHNSON
Molly	CELIA KEENAN-BOLGER
Ted	DAVID ROSSMER

Continued on next page

The Playbill Broadway Yearbook 2011-2012

⫷N⫸ BROOKS ATKINSON THEATRE
UNDER THE DIRECTION OF JAMES M. NEDERLANDER AND JAMES L. NEDERLANDER

Nancy Nagel Gibbs   Greg Schaffert   Eva Price   Tom Smedes   Disney Theatrical Productions

Suzan & Ken Wirth/DeBartolo Miggs   Catherine Schreiber/Daveed Frazier & Mark Thompson
Jack Lane   Jane Dubin   Allan S. Gordon/Adam S. Gordon   Baer & Casserly/Nathan Vernon
Rich Affannato/Peter Stern   Brunish & Trinchero/Laura Little Productions   Larry Hirschhorn/Hummel & Greene
Jamie deRoy & Probo Prods./Radio Mouse Ent.   Hugh Hysell/Freedberg & Dale

New York Theatre Workshop

Present

PETER AND THE ST★RCATCHER

A New Play By
Rick Elice

Based Upon the Novel by Dave Barry and Ridley Pearson

Starring

Christian Borle   Celia Keenan-Bolger   and   Adam Chanler-Berat

Teddy Bergman   Arnie Burton   Matt D'Amico
Kevin Del Aguila   Carson Elrod   Greg Hildreth
Rick Holmes   Isaiah Johnson   David Rossmer

Betsy Hogg   Orville Mendoza   Jason Ralph   John Sanders

Scenic Design	Costume Design	Lighting Design	Sound Design
Donyale Werle	Paloma Young	Jeff Croiter	Darron L West

Music Direction	Technical Supervisor	Production Supervisor
Marco Paguia	David Benken	Clifford Schwartz

Casting	Press	General Management
Jim Carnahan, CSA	O&M Co.	321 Theatrical Management
Jack Doulin, CSA		
Tara Rubin, CSA		

Music By
Wayne Barker

Movement
Steven Hoggett

Directed By
Roger Rees and Alex Timbers

Originally Presented as a "Page to Stage" Workshop Production by La Jolla Playhouse, 2009
Christopher Ashley, Artistic Director & Michael S. Rosenberg, Managing Director

We wish to express our appreciation to Theatre Development Fund for its support of this production.

4/15/12

(Center L-R): David Rossmer, Adam Chanler-Berat (as Boy), Carson Elrod and Cast

Photo courtesy O&M Co.

Peter and the Starcatcher

Cast Continued

UNDERSTUDIES

Understudy for Molly/Ted/Mrs. Bumbrake:
BETSY HOGG
For Smee/Alf/Fighting Prawn/Slank/
    Hawking Clam/Mrs. Bumbrake:
ORVILLE MENDOZA
For Boy/Prentiss/Ted/Fighting Prawn/
    Captain Scott:
JASON RALPH
For Black Stache/Lord Aster/Captain Scott/
    Mrs. Bumbrake/Smee:
JOHN SANDERS
For Black Stache:
CARSON ELROD
For Lord Aster/Slank/Hawking Clam/Alf:
ISAIAH JOHNSON

MUSICIANS

Conductor: MARCO PAGUIA
Drums/Percussion: DEANE PROUTY
Keyboard and Electronic
    Percussion Programmer: RANDY COHEN
Arrangements by: WAYNE BARKER
Additional Arrangements by: MARCO PAGUIA

(L-R): Kevin Del Aguila as Smee
and Christian Borle
as Black Stache

Photo courtesy O&M Co.

Christian Borle
Black Stache

Celia Keenan-Bolger
Molly

Adam Chanler-Berat
Boy

Teddy Bergman
Fighting Prawn

Arnie Burton
Mrs. Bumbrake

Matt D'Amico
Slank/Hawking Clam

Kevin Del Aguila
Smee

Carson Elrod
Prentiss

Greg Hildreth
Alf

Rick Holmes
Lord Aster

Isaiah Johnson
Captain Scott

David Rossmer
Ted

Betsy Hogg
*u/s Molly/Ted/
Mrs. Bumbrake*

Orville Mendoza
*u/s Smee/Alf/
Fighting Prawn/
Slank/
Mrs. Bumbrake*

Jason Ralph
*u/s Boy/Prentiss/Ted/
Fighting Prawn/
Captain Scott*

John Sanders
*u/s Black Stache/
Lord Aster/
Captain Scott/
Mrs. Bumbrake/
Smee*

Rick Elice
Playwright

Roger Rees
Director

Alex Timbers
Director

Wayne Barker
Composer

Peter and the Starcatcher

Steven Hoggett
Movement

Donyale Werle
Set Designer

Paloma H. Young
Costume Designer

Jeff Croiter
Lighting Design

Darron L. West
Sound Designer

Marco Paguia
Musical Director

Patrick McCollum
Movement Associate

Clifford Schwartz
*Production
Supervisor*

Marcia Goldberg, Nancy Nagel Gibbs,
Nina Essman
321 Theatrical Management
General Management

David Benken
Technical Supervisor

Dave Barry
Original Novel

Ridley Pearson
Original Novel

Nancy Nagel Gibbs
Producer

Greg Schaffert
Producer

Eva Price
Producer

Tom Smedes
Producer

Suzan Wirth
Co-Producer

Ken Wirth
Co-Producer

Lisa DeBartolo
DeBartolo Miggs
Co-Producer

Don Miggs
DeBartolo Miggs
Co-Producer

Catherine Schreiber
Co-Producer

Daveed Frazier
Co-Producer

Mark Thompson
Co-Producer

Jack Lane
Co-Producer

Jane Dubin
Co-Producer

Allan S. Gordon
Co-Producer

Adam S. Gordon
Co-Producer

Zachary Baer
Baer & Casserly/
Nathan Vernon
Co-Producer

Tom Casserly
Baer & Casserly/
Nathan Vernon
Co-Producer

Nathan Vernon
Baer & Casserly/
Nathan Vernon
Co-Producer

Rich Affannato
Co-Producer

Peter Stern
Co-Producer

Corey Brunish
Brunish & Trinchero/
Laura Little
Productions
Co-Producer

Brisa Trinchero
Brunish & Trinchero/
Laura Little
Productions
Co-Producer

Peter and the Starcatcher

Laura Little
Brunish & Trinchero/
Laura Little
Productions
Co-Producer

Larry Hirschhorn
Larry Hirschhorn/
Hummel & Greene
Co-Producer

Martin Hummel
Larry Hirschhorn/
Hummel & Greene
Co-Producer

R.K. Greene
Larry Hirschhorn/
Hummel & Greene
Co-Producer

Jamie deRoy
deRoy/Probo Prods/
Radio Mouse
Co-Producer

M. Kilburg Reedy
deRoy/Probo Prods/
Radio Mouse
Co-Producer

Jason E. Grossman
deRoy/Probo Prods/
Radio Mouse
Co-Producer

Hugh Hysell
Hugh Hysell/
Freedberg & Dale
Co-Producer

Avram Freedberg
Hugh Hysell/
Freedberg & Dale
Co-Producer

Marybeth Dale
Hugh Hysell/
Freedberg & Dale
Co-Producer

James C. Nicola
Artistic Director
New York Theatre
Workshop
Producer

Christopher Ashley
Artistic Director
La Jolla Playhouse
Producer

Michael S.
Rosenberg
Managing Director
La Jolla Playhouse
Producer

Photos by Brian Mapp

CREW

Front Row (L-R): Jerry Marshall (Production Props), Tommy Grasso (Sound), Bill Smith (Engineer), Jamie Englehart (Wardrobe), Jessica Dermody (Wardrobe), Marc Schmittroth (Spot Operator), Joe Maher (House Flyman), Joe DePaulo (House Props)

Back Row (L-R): Rob Bass (Production Sound), Patrick Eviston (Production Carpenter), Manny Becker (House Electrician), Tommy Lavaia (House Carpenter), Mike Attianese (Flyman), Bill Staples (Spot Operator), Brian McGarity (House Electrician) John Senter (Sound)

Peter and the Starcatcher

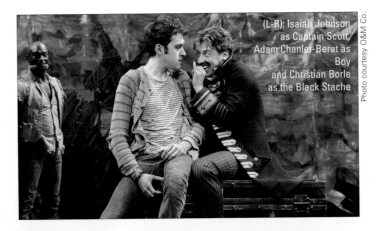

(L-R): Isaiah Johnson as Captain Scott, Adam Chanler-Berat as Boy and Christian Borle as the Black Stache

Photo courtesy O&M Co.

COMPANY AND STAGE MANAGEMENT
(L-R): Brent McCreary (Company Management) Tracy Geltman (Company Management),
McKenzie Murphy, Clifford Schwartz, Kristen Harris, Katherine Wallace (All Stage Management)

Photos by Brian Mapp

BOX OFFICE
(L-R): Richard Aubrey, William O'Brien

FRONT OF HOUSE STAFF
Front Row (L-R): Ilona Figueroa, Megan Frazier, Tara McCormack, Marie Gonzalez, Kaitlin Dato, Marion Danton

Back Row (L-R): Austin Branda, Hector Aguilar, Sam Figert, James Holley, Roberto Rivera, Kimberlee Imperato

Peter and the Starcatcher

(C): Celia Keenan-Bolger as Molly, Adam Chanler-Berat (upside down) as Peter, with members of the cast

Photo courtesy O&M Co.

STAFF FOR *PETER AND THE STARCATCHER*

GENERAL MANAGEMENT
321 THEATRICAL MANAGEMENT
Nina Essman   Marcia Goldberg

CASTING
JIM CARNAHAN, CSA
Carrie Gardner, CSA   Stephen Kopel
Jillian Cimini   Michael Morlani   Rachel Reichblum

GENERAL PRESS REPRESENTATIVE
O&M CO.
Rick Miramontez   Molly Barnett
Ryan Ratelle   Chelsea Nachman

PRODUCTION MANAGEMENT
David Benken   Rose Palombo

COMPANY MANAGER:
Tracy Geltman

PRODUCTION STAGE MANAGER ..Clifford Schwartz
Assistant Stage Manager ....Katherine Wallace
Assistant Company Manager ....Brent McCreary
Dramaturg ....Ken Cerniglia
For Disney Theatrical ....Daniel Posener
Assistant Director.................................Lillian King
Movement Associate ....Patrick McCollum
Associate Scenic Designer ....Michael Carnahan
Assistant to Prop Sculptor ....Craig Napoliello
Assistant to Scenic Designer ....Stephen Dobay
Rendering Painter ....Hannah Davis
Associate Costume Designer ....Matthew Pachtman
Assistant to Costumer Designer ....David Mendizabal
Associate Lighting Designer ....Joel Silver
Assistant Lighting Designer ......Cory Pattak, Andy Fritsch
Assistant to Lighting Designer ....Grant Yeager
Associate Sound Designer ....Charles Coes
Fight Director ....Jacob Grigolia-Rosenbaum
Production Carpenter ....Patrick Eviston
Advance Carpenter ....Michael Muery

Production Electrician ....Brian GF McGarity
Production Props ....Jerry Marshall
Sound Engineer ....Rob Bass
Vari Light Programmer ....Timothy Rogers
Wardrobe Supervisor ....Jessica Dermody
Dressers ....Jim Hodun, Jamie Englehart
Hair Stylist.................................Brandon Dailey
Hair Consultant ....J. Jared Janas
Production Assistants ....McKenzie Murphy,
                                      Samantha Preiss
Advertising ....Serino/Coyne/
                            Greg Corradetti, Robert Jones,
               Ryan Cunningham, Vanessa Javier, David Barrineau
Digital Outreach & Website ....Serino/Coyne/
                       Jim Glaub, Chip Meyrelles, Laurie Connor,
               Kevin Keating, Whitney Creighton, Crystal Chase
Marketing ....Serino/Coyne/
                       Leslie Barrett, Abby Wolbe, Diana Salameh
Merchandise ....Broadway Merchandising, Inc.
Special Promotions ....Jeffrey Solis
Group Sales ....Nathan Vernon (877-321-0020)
Banking ....City National Bank/Michele Gibbons
Payroll ....Checks and Balances
Director of Finance ....John DiMeglio
Accountant ....FK Partners CPAs LLP/Robert Fried
Insurance ....AON/Albert G. Ruben Insurance
Legal Counsel ....Brooks & Distler/Tom Distler, Esq.

321 THEATRICAL MANAGEMENT
Bob Brinkerhoff, Susan Brumley, Mattea Cogliano-
Benedict, Eric Cornell, Tara Geesaman, Jason Haft,
Andrew Hartman, Adam Jackson, Alex Owen, Rebecca
Peterson, Susan Sampliner, Ken Silverman, Haley Ward

www.peterandthestarcatcher.com

SPECIAL THANKS
Michael Keller, Wendy Lefkon, Kaitlin Conci, Aaron Glick,
Broadway Green Alliance, Kids Night on Broadway, Build it
Green, Recycle-a-Bicycle, Salvation Army, Housing Works,
Paper Mache Monkey, Paul Jepson, Chris Ashley, Dana
Harrel, Gabriel Greene, Jim Nicola, Bill Darger, Kris Kukul,

Amanda Charlton, Williamstown Theatre Festival, Michele
Steckler, Neil Patel, Joe Huppert, Eric Stahlhammer, Kelly
Devine, Adrienne Campbell-Holt, Amy Groeschel, Steve
Rosen, Eric Love, Adam Green, Danny Deferarri, Rob
O'Hare, all the actors who helped us along the way.

CREDITS
Computer motion control and automation of scenery and
rigging by Showman Fabricators, Inc. Sound by Masque
Sound. Lighting by PRG Lighting. Costumes by Artur &
Tailors, Inc., Giliberto Designs, Inc., Katrina Patterns,
Marie Stair, Melissa Crawford. Custom leatherwear by
David Menkes. Custom knitwear by Knit Illustrated.
Millinery by Jeffrey Wallach and Rodney Gordon, Inc.
Fabric dyeing and painting by Jeff Fender Studios and
Juliann Kroboth. Custom tattoos by TEMPTU. Props by
Kathy Fabian and Jerard Studios.

NEDERLANDER

Chairman ....**James M. Nederlander**	
President ....**James L. Nederlander**	

Executive Vice President
Nick Scandalios

Vice President	Senior Vice President
Corporate Development	Labor Relations
Charlene S. Nederlander	**Herschel Waxman**

Vice President	Chief Financial Officer
Jim Boese	**Freida Sawyer Belviso**

STAFF FOR THE BROOKS ATKINSON THEATRE
Theatre Manager ....Susan Martin
Treasurer ....Peter Attanasio
Associate Treasurer ....Elaine Amplo
House Carpenter ....Thomas Lavaia
Flyman ....Joe Maher
House Electrician ....Manuel Becker
House Propman ....Joseph P. DePaulo
House Engineer ....Reynold Barriteau

Peter and the Starcatcher
SCRAPBOOK

Correspondents: Celia Keenan-Bolger, "Molly"; Greg Hildreth, "Alf"; and Teddy Bergman, "Fighting Prawn."

Opening Night Gifts: Presents: Fighting Prawn Spicy Puttanesca Sauce from Teddy and a meteorite from Rick and Roger. Party: Pizza on a hook. (Say what?)

Most Exciting Celebrity Visitors: The super gorgeous Emily Blunt and the super tall John Krasinski.

Who Wrote the "Easter Bonnet" Sketch: Future Rossmer.

Actor Who Performed the Most Roles in This Show: Teddy Bergman (Fighting Prawn, Gremkin, pirate, Sanchez, directionally challenged seaman, door, ocean, jungle, British sailor.)

Actor Who Has Done the Most Shows in Their Career: Rick Holmes—67 (this number includes when he played "Broccoli" in an elementary school play).

Special Backstage Rituals: Kevin and Christian do a bit every night before "Coming Down the Mountain," and Teddy snaps Christian into his mermaid tail every day (this started downtown).

Favorite Moment During Each Performance: Cats and amulets.

Favorite In-Theatre Gathering Place: The bar in Christian's room.

Favorite Off-Site Hangout: Glass House Tavern.

Favorite Snack Food: Momofuku Cookies.

Mascot: Spiggy Pokesman.

Favorite Therapy: Honey Loquat.

Most Memorable Ad-Libs: We've had a few: "Is there a vegetarian ensemble?" "You know what this is, Amulet. And how to use it if you're ever in trouble." "I may not have been born in a silver spoon with me bum."

Web Buzz on the Show: Stache-tastic.

Memorable Press Encounter: Teddy and Greg hosting Broadway Hour on the aircraft carrier Intrepid for Fleet Week May 25th. Be there!

Memorable Stage Door Fan Encounter: Teddy Bergman (who has a beard) is often mistaken for Adam who plays Peter. And Rick Holmes (because of his mustache) is often mistaken for Christian who plays Stache.

Fastest Costume Change: Mr. Grin becoming Giant Mister Grin. A feat of dentistry.

Heaviest/Hottest Costume: Kevin wears a mop as a wig. Greg wears a thermal and a half-sweater and a knit cap!! Phew!

Who Wore the Least: Tinkerbell.

Catchphrase Only the Company Would Recognize: "Shabongulay."

Orchestra Member Who Played the Most Instruments: MARCO many noises.

Best In-House Parody Lyrics: "I got a bus, it's covered in dust, that's what it does. It's a bus!"

Memorable Directorial Note: "Can you make your bird sound more Mexican?" "Can you be physically smaller in that moment?"

Company In-Jokes: The oft used "I'm gonna take off" from Rick Holmes.

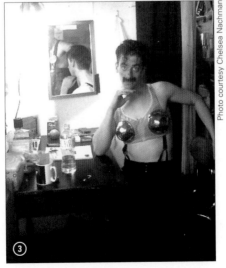

1. The "Family Portrait" of the show's cast and creators in the rehearsal studio.
2. (L-R): Hat-wearing co-directors Roger Rees and Alex Timbers with writers Rick Elice, Dave Barry and Ridley Pearson at the McKittrick Hotel for the cast party.
3. Christian Borle in his dressing room during intermission, getting into costume for Act II.
4. Opening-night audience applause washes over (L-R): Rick Holmes, Adam Chanler-Berat, Celia Keenan-Bolger and Christian Borle.

Company Legends: Ron Cherlutain (this man IS Smee), and Jim the orphan we left in La Jolla.

Understudy Anecdote: The four-person understudy version of PATSC (or *Four "Men," Twelve Guvnors*) is a sight to behold. It involves rope, rubber gloves, mild schizophrenia, and usually always includes the question: "Teddy Bergman does what on his back in the dark?!?!"

Nicknames: Greg and Teddy came up with their *Newsies* character names: Starchie and Jewbags.

Sweethearts Within the Company: Greg Hildreth and the plunger prop? Rick Holmes and his reflection?

Coolest Thing About Being in This Show: Working with your friends!!!

The Phantom of the Opera

First Preview: January 9, 1988. Opened: January 26, 1988.
Still running as of May 31, 2012.

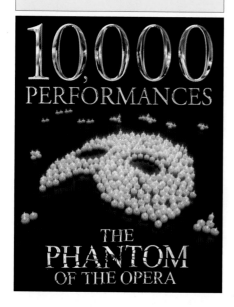

The dashing Raoul is in love with Christine Daaé, a pretty soprano in the chorus of the Paris Opera. But Raoul discovers that she is under the spell of the legendary Phantom of the Opera, a disfigured musical genius who haunts the endless grottos beneath the ancient opera house. The obsessed Phantom demands that Christine be elevated to star and that the company produce an unplayable opera he has written. When his commands are not obeyed the Phantom becomes violent, even murderous. Raoul strives ever more desperately to free Christine from his clutches. As a torch-wielding mob closes in on his lair, the Phantom makes one last bid for Christine's love.

CAST

The Phantom of the Opera ....HUGH PANARO
Christine Daaé ....TRISTA MOLDOVAN
Christine Daaé
    (Mon. & Wed. mat. perfs) ....MARNI RAAB
Raoul, Vicomte de Chagny ....KYLE BARISICH
Carlotta Giudicelli ......MICHELE McCONNELL
Monsieur André ... AARON GALLIGAN-STIERLE
Monsieur Firmin ....KEVIN LIGON
Madame Giry ....CRISTIN J. HUBBARD
Ubaldo Piangi ....CHRISTIAN ŠEBEK
Meg Giry ....HEATHER McFADDEN
Monsieur Reyer/
    Hairdresser ("Il Muto") ....JIM WEITZER
Auctioneer/Don Attilio
    ("Il Muto") ....JOHN KUETHER
Jeweler ("Il Muto") ....FRANK MASTRONE
Monsieur Lefèvre/Firechief ..KENNETH KANTOR

Joseph Buquet ....RICHARD POOLE
Passarino ("Don Juan
    Triumphant") ....JEREMY STOLLE
Slave Master ("Hannibal") ....JUSTIN PECK
Slave Master ("Hannibal") (Sat. mat.
    performance) .....NICHOLAS CUNNINGHAM
Solo Dancer
    ("Il Muto") ....NICHOLAS CUNNINGHAM
Page ("Don Juan Triumphant") ......SUSAN OWEN
Porter/Fireman ....STEPHEN TEWKSBURY
Spanish Lady
    ("Don Juan Triumphant") ...KIMILEE BRYANT
Wardrobe Mistress/
    Confidante ("Il Muto") ...SATOMI HOFMANN

Continued on next page

Continued on next page

⊕ MAJESTIC THEATRE
247 West 44th Street
A Shubert Organization Theatre

Philip J. Smith, *Chairman*   Robert E. Wankel, *President*

CAMERON MACKINTOSH and
THE REALLY USEFUL THEATRE COMPANY, INC.

present

THE PHANTOM OF THE OPERA

Starring

HUGH PANARO
TRISTA MOLDOVAN
KYLE BARISICH

AARON GALLIGAN-STIERLE   KEVIN LIGON   MICHELE McCONNELL
CRISTIN J. HUBBARD   CHRISTIAN ŠEBEK   HEATHER McFADDEN

At certain performances
MARNI RAAB
plays the role of "Christine"

Music by
ANDREW LLOYD WEBBER
Lyrics by ## CHARLES HART

Additional Lyrics by RICHARD STILGOE

Book by RICHARD STILGOE & ANDREW LLOYD WEBBER

Based on the novel "Le Fantôme de L'Opéra" by GASTON LEROUX

Production Design by MARIA BJÖRNSON   Lighting by ANDREW BRIDGE

Sound Design by MICK POTTER   Original Sound Design by MARTIN LEVAN

Musical Supervision & Direction DAVID CADDICK   Conductor PAUL SCHWARTZ

Production Supervisor PETER von MAYRHAUSER

Orchestrations by DAVID CULLEN & ANDREW LLOYD WEBBER

Casting by TARA RUBIN CASTING   Original Casting by JOHNSON-LIFF ASSOCIATES

General Management ALAN WASSER ASSOCIATES

Musical Staging & Choreography by GILLIAN LYNNE

Directed by ## HAROLD PRINCE

3/5/12

(L-R): Hugh Panaro, Marni Raab

Photo by Joan Marcus

The Phantom of the Opera

MUSICAL NUMBERS

PROLOGUE
The stage of the Paris Opéra House, 1911

OVERTURE

ACT ONE—PARIS, LATE NINETEENTH CENTURY

Scene 1—The dress rehearsal of "Hannibal"
"Think of Me" .... Carlotta, Christine, Raoul
Scene 2—After the Gala
"Angel of Music" .... Christine and Meg
Scene 3—Christine's dressing room
"Little Lotte/The Mirror" (Angel of Music) .... Raoul, Christine, Phantom
Scene 4—The Labyrinth underground
"The Phantom of the Opera" .... Phantom and Christine
Scene 5—Beyond the lake
"The Music of the Night" .... Phantom
Scene 6—Beyond the lake, the next morning
"I Remember/Stranger Than You Dreamt It" .... Christine and Phantom
Scene 7—Backstage
"Magical Lasso" .... Buquet, Meg, Madame Giry and Ballet Girls
Scene 8—The Managers' office
"Notes/Prima Donna" .... Firmin, André, Raoul, Carlotta, Giry, Meg,
Piangi and Phantom
Scene 9—A performance of "Il Muto"
"Poor Fool, He Makes Me Laugh" .... Carlotta and Company
Scene 10—The roof of the Opéra House
"Why Have You Brought Me Here/Raoul, I've Been There" .... Raoul and Christine
"All I Ask of You" .... Raoul and Christine
"All I Ask of You" (Reprise) .... Phantom

ENTR'ACTE

ACT TWO—SIX MONTHS LATER

Scene 1—The staircase of the Opéra House, New Year's Eve
"Masquerade/Why So Silent" .... Full Company
Scene 2—Backstage
Scene 3—The Managers' office
"Notes/Twisted Every Way" .... André, Firmin, Carlotta, Piangi, Raoul,
Christine, Giry and Phantom
Scene 4—A rehearsal for "Don Juan Triumphant"
Scene 5—A graveyard in Perros
"Wishing You Were Somehow Here Again" .... Christine
"Wandering Child/Bravo, Bravo" .... Phantom, Christine and Raoul
Scene 6—The Opéra House stage before the Premiere
Scene 7—"Don Juan Triumphant"
"The Point of No Return" .... Phantom and Christine
Scene 8—The Labyrinth underground
"Down Once More/Track Down This Murderer" .... Full Company
Scene 9—Beyond the lake

Princess ("Hannibal") .... ELIZABETH WELCH
Madame Firmin .... KRIS KOOP
Innkeeper's Wife
("Don Juan Triumphant") .... MARY ILLES
Marksman .... PAUL A. SCHAEFER
The Ballet Chorus of
the Opéra Populaire .... AMANDA EDGE,
KARA KLEIN, GIANNA LOUNGWAY,
AUBREY MORGAN, JESSICA RADETSKY,
CARLY BLAKE SEBOUHIAN
Ballet Swing .... LAURIE V. LANGDON
Swings .... SCOTT MIKITA,
JAMES ROMICK, JANET SAIA,
JIM WEITZER

UNDERSTUDIES

For the Phantom: JAMES ROMICK,
PAUL A. SCHAEFER, JEREMY STOLLE,
STEPHEN TEWKSBURY
For Christine: KIMILEE BRYANT,
SUSAN OWEN, ELIZABETH WELCH
For Raoul: JAMES ROMICK,
PAUL A. SCHAEFER, JEREMY STOLLE,
JIM WEITZER
For Firmin: KENNETH KANTOR,
JOHN KUETHER, JAMES ROMICK
For André: FRANK MASTRONE,
SCOTT MIKITA, RICHARD POOLE,
JAMES ROMICK
For Carlotta: KIMILEE BRYANT,
SATOMI HOFMANN, KRIS KOOP,
JANET SAIA
For Mme. Giry: KIMILEE BRYANT,
SATOMI HOFMANN, MARY ILLES,
KRIS KOOP, JANET SAIA
For Piangi: FRANK MASTRONE,
JEREMY STOLLE, STEPHEN TEWKSBURY
For Meg Giry: AMANDA EDGE, KARA KLEIN,
CARLY BLAKE SEBOUHIAN
For Slave Master: NICHOLAS CUNNINGHAM,
JUSTIN PECK
For Solo Dancer ("Il Muto"):
NICHOLAS CUNNINGHAM, JUSTIN PECK
Dance Captain: LAURIE V. LANGDON
Assistant Dance Captain: HEATHER McFADDEN

ORCHESTRA

Conductors: DAVID CADDICK,
KRISTEN BLODGETTE, DAVID LAI,
PAUL SCHWARTZ, TIM STELLA,
NORMAN WEISS
Violins: JOYCE HAMMANN (Concert Master),
CLAIRE CHAN, KURT COBLE,
JAN MULLEN, KAREN MILNE,

The Phantom of the Opera

Orchestra Continued

SUZANNE GILMAN
Violas: VERONICA SALAS,
    DEBRA SHUFELT-DINE
Cellos: TED ACKERMAN, KARL BENNION
Bass: MELISSA SLOCUM
Harp: HENRY FANELLI
Flute: SHERYL HENZE
Flute/Clarinet: ED MATTHEW
Oboe: MELANIE FELD
Clarinet: MATTHEW GOODMAN
Bassoon: ATSUKO SATO
Trumpets: LOWELL HERSHEY,
    FRANCIS BONNY
Bass Trombone: WILLIAM WHITAKER
French Horns: DANIEL CULPEPPER,
    PETER REIT, DAVID SMITH
Percussion: ERIC COHEN, JAN HAGIWARA
Keyboards: TIM STELLA, NORMAN WEISS

(L-R): Kyle Barisich
and Marni Raab

Photo by Joan Marcus

Hugh Panaro
The Phantom of the Opera

Trista Moldovan
Christine Daaé

Kyle Barisich
Raoul, Vicomte de Chagny

Aaron Galligan-Stierle
Monsieur André

Kevin Ligon
Monsieur Firmin

Michele McConnell
Carlotta Giudicelli

Cristin J. Hubbard
Madame Giry

Christian Šebek
Ubaldo Piangi

Heather McFadden
Meg Giry/ Assistant Dance Captain

Marni Raab
Christine Daaé at certain performances

Kimilee Bryant
Spanish Lady

Nicholas Cunningham
Solo Dancer & Slave Master at certain performances

Amanda Edge
Ballet Chorus

Satomi Hofmann
Wardrobe Mistress/ Confidante

Mary Illes
Innkeeper's Wife

Kenneth Kantor
Monsieur Lefèvre/Firechief

Kara Klein
Ballet Chorus

Kris Koop
Madame Firmin

John Kuether
Auctioneer/ Don Attilio

Laurie V. Langdon
Dance Captain/ Ballet Swing

The Phantom of the Opera

Gianna Loungway
Ballet Chorus

Frank Mastrone
Jeweler

Scott Mikita
Swing

Aubrey Morgan
Ballet Chorus

Susan Owen
Page

Justin Peck
Slave Master

Richard Poole
Joseph Buquet

Jessica Radetsky
Ballet Chorus

James Romick
Swing

Janet Saia
Swing

Paul A. Schaefer
Marksman

Carly Blake
Sebouhian
Ballet Chorus

Jeremy Stolle
Passarino

Stephen Tewksbury
Porter/Fireman

Jim Weitzer
*Monsieur Reyer/
Hairdresser*

Elizabeth Welch
Princess

Andrew Lloyd
Webber
*Composer/Book/
Co-Orchestrator*

Harold Prince
Director

Charles Hart
Lyrics

Richard Stilgoe
*Book and Additional
Lyrics*

Gillian Lynne
*Musical Staging and
Choreography*

Maria Björnson
Production Design

Andrew Bridge
Lighting Designer

Mick Potter
Sound Designer

Martin Levan
*Original Sound
Designer*

David Cullen
Co-Orchestrator

David Caddick
*Musical Supervision
and Direction*

Kristen Blodgette
*Associate Musical
Supervisor*

Peter von
Mayrhauser
*Production
Supervisor*

Denny Berry
*Production Dance
Supervisor*

Jake Bell
*Technical Production
Manager*

Craig Jacobs
*Production Stage
Manager*

Bethe Ward
*Stage Manager from
the beginning*

Paul Schwartz
Conductor

David Lai
Conductor

The Phantom of the Opera

Tara Rubin Casting
Casting

Alan Wasser
Associates
*General
Management*

Cameron Mackintosh
Producer

Dara Adler
*Ballet Chorus,
Dance Captain,
Ballet Swing*

George Lee Andrews
Monsieur André

Polly Baird
Ballet Chorus

Harlan Bengel
*Slave Master, Solo
Dancer*

Jessica Bishop
*Meg Giry, Ballet
Chorus*

Chris Bohannon
Porter/Fireman

Marilyn Caskey
Madame Giry

Darius Crenshaw
*Slave Master, Solo
Dancer*

David Cryer
Monsieur Firmin

Andrew Drost
*Porter/Fireman,
Ubaldo Piangi
(at certain
performances)*

Sara Jean Ford
Christine Daaé

Paloma Garcia-Lee
*Meg Giry (at certain
performances),
Ballet Chorus*

David Gaschen
Ubaldo Piangi

Kelly Jeanne Grant
*Innkeeper's Wife,
Madame Firmin,
OPage, Spanish
Lady, Wardrobe
Mistress/Confidante*

Evan Harrington
Ubaldo Piangi

Kfir
*Slave Master, Solo
Dancer*

Sean MacLaughlin
*Raoul, Vicomte de
Chagny*

Greg Mills
*Raoul, Vicomte de
Chagny, Passarino,
Monsieur Reyer/
Hairdresser, Swing*

Mabel Modrono
Ballet Chorus

Carrington Vilmont
*Auctioneer/Don
Attilio, Jeweler,
Marksman, Monsieur
Reyer/ Hairdresser,
Passarino, Swing*

James Zander
*Slave Master, Solo
Dancer*

Dara Adler
Ballet Chorus

Jessica Bishop
*Meg Giry (at certain
performances),
Ballet Chorus, Swing*

DOORMAN
Wally Carroll

Not pictured:
Jim Cucinell

Photo by Brian Mapp

The Phantom of the Opera

CREW
Kneeling (L-R): Alan Lampel, Frank Dwyer, Jr., Terrence Miller, Raoul Sanchez, Annie Miller

Standing (L-R): Matt Mezick, Frank Dwyer, Michael Girman, Daryl Miller, Bill Kazden, John Alban

Not pictured: "Innumerable and all working!"

ORCHESTRA
Front Row (L-R): Lowell Hershey, Claire Chan, Suzanne Gilman, Melanie Feld, Rick Walburn, Henry Fanelli, Jan Hagiwara, Karl Bennion

Back Row (L-R) Ian Donald, Rheagan Osteen; Sheryl Henze; Ted Ackerman; Matt Goodman, Norman Weiss, William Whitaker, Caryn Briskin

Not pictured: Kristen Blodgette, David Lai, Paul Schwartz, Tim Stella, Joyce Hammann, Kurt Coble, Jan Mullen, Karen Milne, Veronica Salas, Debra Shufelt-Dine, Melissa Slocum, Ed Matthew, Atsuko Sato, Francis Bonny, Daniel Culpepper, Peter Reit, David Smith, Eric Cohen

MANAGEMENT
(L-R): Shaun Colledge (Assistant Stage Manager), Seth Sklar-Heyn (Production Supervisor), Craig Jacobs (Production Stage Manager), Andrew Glant-Linden (Assistant Stage Manager), Katherine McNamee (Assistant Company Manager), Michael Borowski (Press Agent), Brendan Smith (Stage Manager), on stage all in front of Herself: the chandelier!

Not pictured: Denny Berry (Production Dance Supervisor), Bethe Ward (Stage Manager), Steve Greer (Company Manager)

The Phantom of the Opera

FRONT OF HOUSE

Front Row (L-R): Georgina Villacort, Matt Kuehl, Marcia Rodriguez, Deanna Sorenson, Dorothy Curich, Theresa Aceves, Hannah Owens, Casey Hunsader

Second Row (L-R): Jonah Bamel, Beth Kovarik, Lawrence Darden

Back Row (L-R): Heather Cooper, Cynthia Carlin, Lisa Bruno, Joan Thorn, Perry DellAquila, Tony Stovick, Grace Jones, Diona Woodward, Ahyan Sahin, Ina Biggs Devonish, Lori Prager

Standing: Lucia Cappelletti

HAIR/WARDROBE

Front Row (L-R): Pearleta N. Price, Erna Dias, Thelma Pollard (Hair/Make-up Supervisor), Paula Cohen, Julie Ratcliffe (Wardrobe Supervisor)

Middle Row (L-R): Eileen Casey, Rosemary Taylor, Alexa Burt, Mary Lou Rios, Aaron Carlson

Back Row (L-R): Ron Blakely, Andrew Nelson, Annette Lovece, Jenna Barrios, Tiffany Bolick, Michael Jacobs

Not Pictured: Leone Gagliardi (Hair Supervisor), Jennifer Arnold, Jennifer Caruso, Terence Doherty, Margie Marchionni, Ann McDaniel, Peter McIver, Ellen Pellicciaro, George Sheer, Charise Champion, Karen Dickenson, Magdalena Kolodziej, Shazia J. Saleem

The Phantom of the Opera

The Phantom of the Opera

SCRAPBOOK

Correspondent: Kris Koop Ouellette, "Mme. Firmin," understudy for "Carlotta" and "Mme. Giry"

Favorite Memories From a Year of Tremendous Change and Remarkable Celebrations: 2011-early 2012 was HUGE!

Phantom's **Emotional Farewell to Beloved Cast Mates, George Lee Andrews and David Cryer:** We were all stunned to learn that two of the hearts of our company, original company member, George Lee Andrews, and his on-stage "business partner," David Cryer, would be leaving the company in tandem. It took months for us all to wrap our heads around what we could only perceive as a tremendous loss. But the boys…(both grandparents, but truly still BOYS at heart…) gently coaxed the company into acceptance. When the announcement was made that their replacements had been cast, this loving company began to heal, because both of the new hires were well-loved in the business. As our new Monsieur Firmin, Kevin Ligon was cast, leaving a spot open in *Sister Act* (only to be snatched up by *Phantom* cast member, Chris Bohannon, creating a win-win situation!) Joining him, as Monsieur André, would be none other than George Lee Andrews' son-in-law, Aaron Galligan-Stierle, a double blessing because the Lee and Galligan-Stierle family had just learned that the Galligan-Stierles were expecting a baby!

The final weeks leading up to departure of "the boys" were filled with rehearsal, rehearsal, rehearsal. We actually did 24 hours of rehearsal within a two-week period, in addition to performing 16 shows.

But that's no excuse not to plan a great party with fabulous parting gifts! The entire company, from cast to crew to management and front of house posed for photos, taken on my iPhone, holding the walking sticks that George and David used as personal props in the show. Over 850 photos were taken, yet the reason for their poor quality wasn't discovered until after Jeremy Stolle filtered through them all. Only THEN was it was revealed that I had never removed the clear cellophane cover from the back of my phone. The smudged cellophane had created a distorted effect in nearly 100 percent of the photos (OOPS!), but Jeremy used his creative genius and further treated the photos until they looked like great comic book art. He then created a red-leather-bound comic book for each of the departing actors, made to look identical to the prop Don Juan score the Phantom tosses to the Managers at the base of the Masquerade Staircase. To recall the humidor prop on the manager's desk, I shopped for fancy cigars, which were wrapped in custom-made labels, created by Jeremy, featuring the visage of the handles of the walking sticks. A collection of postcards with hand-written messages from everyone in the company for George, was lovingly bound into a book by George's daughter, Shannon. A journal was passed throughout the company with a page for everyone to write a personal memory

A special cake brought onstage after the 10,000th Broadway performance January 26, 2012. (L-R): Michele McConnell, Gillian Lynne, Kyle Barisich, Trista Moldovan and Hugh Panaro, Aaron Galligan-Stierle, Kevin Ligon

for David as a gift from his Stage Wife. Finally, so that our boys could take home a piece of the show that had accompanied them onstage in every performance, the walking sticks were retired into their hands to take home!

As a reward for our effort, Jeremy and I were named emcees of the beautiful party held at Sardi's, following George and David's final performance. The gifts were presented following a company tribute to ten of the thousands of silly names George Lee made up as special "guests" in our audience. To name a few: Calliope Krapschprinkle; Skillibutt Bibity Bibity Billikinkinkin; Miss Ogenation Sexpotte; and the unforgettable Tipitipi Tuppermann Galligan-Stierle and his child Tonto!) Topping off the food and drink and festivities, Hal Prince toasted the boys, who "roasted" themselves a bit, then sang and danced for all in this grateful company. Our huge thanks to Alan Wasser and the entire company for creating an unforgettable tribute to two unforgettable men.

24th Anniversary Performance (1/26/2012) and 10,000th Performance on Broadway (2/11/2012): These two remarkable events happened so closely together, they became one giant celebration. There were tons of press events leading up to these unparalleled Broadway achievements. A *New York Times* photographer visited backstage to snap our show from behind the scenes; an on-camera makeup demonstration transformed a local TV broadcaster into a Phantom look-alike; the original production team, Hal Prince, Gillian Lynne and David Caddick visited and gave notes; the company received a gift of the 25th Anniversary Concert performance of *Phantom* in London, as well as a filmed tribute from the London Company of *Phantom* followed by a fond greeting from Lord Andrew Lloyd Webber. Our record-shattering run and our many celebrations always warrant a stunning cake, presented onstage before the audience (whom we thank for always making us feel like rock stars), accompanied by a brief speech made by the charming Hugh Panaro. Souvenir PLAYBILLS were printed for each of these triumphs (see the first page of this chapter).

We reached the 10,000 mark on a matinee performance and then did another show that night. But you know what they say: "The first 10,000 performances are the hardest. Piece of cake from here…."

We celebrated all together at Bond 45, a truly GREAT space to eat, drink and be merry. The only brief pause in the celebration was to extinguish the tresses of swing dresser, Linda Roots, who briefly caught fire when she brushed past a votive candle. From the size of the flames, it was a tremendous relief to see that only her hair was damaged.

Most Exciting Celebrity Visitors: The legendary portrait photographer Annie Leibovitz, along with her amazing team of assistants, swept into the Majestic Theatre to photograph the legendary theatrical director Harold Prince for *Vanity Fair* magazine. I, Koopie, had the honor to act as an assistant to Publicist Michael Borowski (I totally begged).

To stand in the presence of Ms. Leibovitz and Mr. Prince, breathing the same air as these artistic geniuses, allowed me to sit in on some really provocative conversation in between shots. When Hal and Annie name-drop, consider that they are of equal or greater stature than most of the people they are mentioning in casual conversation. "I was just doing a shoot with Brad and Angelina…." led politely into politics, which led to inspiration gained at an Obama presidential dinner at which Prince was an honoree. That inspiration provided a solution to a problem slowing the creation of *Prince of Broadway*, a forthcoming new Broadway show designated to celebrate Mr. Prince's stellar career. I heard them speak of "aha" moments in their own lives and I realized that they deserve to be the superstars they are. Annie spoke so lovingly of her kids. Hal spoke so lovingly of his wife. They talked shop. They downplayed their success. Sweet! Then these two cultural icons traded autographs (come on, that's awesome), hugged it out and parted friends. As of this deadline, the portrait has not yet been published in Vanity Fair, but I will keep that issue forever when it finally is.

"Carols for a Cure" Song: "I Wonder As I

The Phantom of the Opera
Scrapbook

Wander," beautifully arranged by T. O. Sterrett; gorgeously played by volunteers from our *Phantom* orchestra and orchestra subs; sung brilliantly by Hugh Panaro as soloist; backing vocals sung angelically by a group of volunteers from every department in the theatre, and even a few people who don't work here…yet!

"Easter Bonnet" Skit: Ours was a celebration of LIFE! Elizabeth Welch (Mirror Bride/Christine understudy) stood beside her daughter who was dressed in a miniature Christine Daáe wedding dress (created by Liz McCartney). Seven-year-old Vivian Welch's honeyed voice touched every heart in the building with her solo, "Heal the World," backed by Mommy and Dad, Tim, (who served as music director and also played guitar). On the chorus, a black drop lifted to reveal a huge ensemble of *Phantom* mommies, daddies, little kids and teeny babies. (Polly Baird brought her dog, Lexie!) The humans were all dressed in blue jeans and white tops, carrying vibrant flowers. They circled the "Welch Family Singers" and finished the number together. Jeremy Stolle and Ashlee Fife Stolle carried their son, Lincoln, who was dressed as a mini Phantom, including a tiny tux with tails and a real Phantom mask. Jeremy toasted Phantom's dedication to fundraising, our pet adoption, and our repopulation of the planet "with like, a MILLION babies…." The button of the number revealed Cristin Hubbard and Kara Klein, both visibly pregnant, while the cast shouted "…AND COUNTING!!!!" Maybe too cute for words. Jeremy's Bonnet was an enormous tri-corn hat filled with roses, designed and created by Bob Miller.

Special Backstage Rituals: Boat Driver, Captain Joe Caruso gives my aching shoulders some much-needed TLC while the overture crescendos to its end; Satomi Hofmann tingles the back of any person standing still by tracing her fingertips across their skin; Jeremy Stolle personalizes each of his white t-shirts with a distinct hand-drawn or hand-written design (in Sharpie, to be exact); Elizabeth Welch searches for Baby Ruth mini candy bars in all the secret hiding places (hidden from mice, not humans). She also "moisturizes" with a neatly hidden bottle of hand lotion. (There is a theme there…); Craig Jacobs pages Susan Owen to his office to talk about their beautiful dogs, and to look at puppy adoption sites online; The Orchestra members assemble in the tiny Green Room for a cup of pre-show jazz in the form of coffee (thank you Debra Shufelt-Dine for the Keurig, and thank you Karl Bennion for supplying filtered water). George Lee Andrews recites an Irish poem over the PA system on Saint Patrick's Day each year, from memory. (Even after our dear Georgie left us in September, 2011, he stopped by and kept his tradition alive…and then scooted off to perform in a preview performance of *Evita*, right down the street.); Kyle Barisich, Kevin Ligon, Aaron Galligan-Stierle and Jim Weitzer

The Majestic Theatre erupts in streamers after the 10,000th performance

Photo by Monica Simoes

form a tight circle off-stage left prior to a cross, to quietly, humorously discuss theatre, television and other pop culture and sort of perform a brilliant riff on whatever topic makes them giggle most. And EVERYONE in the building denies ever being sick. "It's allergies"… to the point that when a dancer sprained his ankle, I told him not to worry. It's only allergies.

Awkward Moments: 1) While seated in Box Five to watch the *Il Muto* scene, Kyle Barisich (Raoul) heard a faint hissing sound above him, like a "giant rain-stick." A moment later, he felt a stream of cold sand pouring down the back of his neck. A sandbag above him had sprung a not-so-insignificant leak. Even slightly adjusting his chair couldn't take him out of range of the falling sand, so he just played the scene as if all was well…and then we all laughed our asses off when he was able to share his story offstage.

2) For the second year in a row, we have had a sudden guest appearance by Richard Poole's (Buquet) two front teeth-veneers, which landed at the feet of Carlotta in HANNIBAL, and on a separate occasion, at the feet of the ballerinas during his PUNJAB LASSO scene! It's impossible not to laugh when such a thing happens, so everyone generally just looks away and tries to keep it together. Richard assures us he is finding a new dentist to repair the damage that was originally caused to his teeth when he collided with a set piece in the dark, backstage. This theatre stuff is DANGEROUS.

3) I myself missed a week of shows after being thrown from a malfunctioning set piece and breaking my fall with my head. Exiting the manager's box as directed, Kevin Ligon had just cleared the stair unit as I had just stepped on, and the stairs "hiccupped" and began to fold back up into a ladder. My feet were trapped behind a stair so the only way out was down. Though I was gripping the handrails, I was

wearing velvet gloves, so I couldn't hold on. A little skull fracture, a shattered fingertip and a big bone chip out of my shin wouldn't keep me from coming back to work, though. It was "hamburger neck"—my skin was torn up badly by the fancy jewelry my character wears. I keep saying they should give me real diamonds…this costume jewelry is for suckers!

4) The opening scene of Act II was going so well. Mssr. André (Aaron Galligan-Stierle) and Mssr. Firmin (Kevin Ligon) had crept around the stage in heavy cloaks, peering around corners and nervously checking to be sure the Paris Opéra House was Phantom-free before the big party. They bumped into each other, back to back, as directed, and tried to determine the identity of the stranger in the dark. But Aaron accidentally asked if the stranger behind him was… "Mssr. André??" (his own character name). Kevin gamely answered him with a second "Mssr. André?????" And though the ensemble giggled their way through the beginning of "Masquerade," the show went on. Quite frankly, we LOVE when little things like that happen!

Favorite Moment During Each Performance: Ballerina Paloma Garcia-Lee LOVES the overture. "After such an interesting Prologue to the show you are given the theme song and it completely jazzes me up every show—even the nights I have a headache or my pointe shoes are killing me, that song always gets me into my body and ready for the show." Conductor Paul Schwartz recently noted how thrilling it is to resume the helm of our magnificent orchestra— at least 50 percent of whom are original company members. He commented that the mutual dedication of everyone in that pit is to making truly beautiful music and relishing the LIVE aspect of it all. The audience really gets the difference…Help us keep our orchestras LIVE on Broadway.

Priscilla Queen of the Desert

First Preview: February 28, 2011. Opened: March 20, 2011.
Still running as of May 31, 2012.

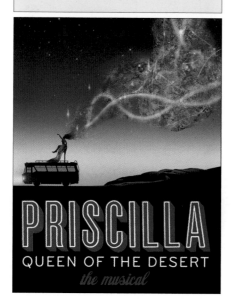

Three drag queens go on an epic adventure through the dusty Outback of Australia in a tricked-out bus named Priscilla. They believe they are headed to do a show in a distant city, but one of them has a hidden goal—to be reunited with his son. Based on a popular film, this musical uses pop songs of the 1970s and 1980s to tell its story.

CAST

(in order of appearance)

Divas .... JACQUELINE B. ARNOLD
ANASTACIA McCLESKEY
ASHLEY SPENCER
Tick (Mitzi) .... WILL SWENSON
Miss Understanding .... NATHAN LEE GRAHAM
Marion .... JESSICA PHILLIPS
Benji .... LUKE KOLBE MANNIKUS
(Mon., Thurs., Sat. mat. & eve.)
Benji .... GATEN MATARAZZO
(Tues., Fri., Sun. mat & eve.)
Farrah/Young Bernadette .... STEVE SCHEPIS
Bernadette .... TONY SHELDON
Adam (Felicia) .... NICK ADAMS
Shirley .... KEALA SETTLE
Jimmy .... JAMES BROWN III
Bob .... C. DAVID JOHNSON
Cynthia .... J. ELAINE MARCOS
Frank .... MIKE McGOWAN
Ensemble .... THOM ALLISON
JACQUELINE B. ARNOLD
JAMES BROWN III, KYLE BROWN,
NATHAN LEE GRAHAM, J. ELAINE
MARCOS, ANASTACIA McCLESKEY,

Continued on next page

Bette Midler; James L. Nederlander; Garry McQuinn; Liz Koops; Michael Hamlyn; Allan Scott; Roy Furman/Richard Willis; Terry Allen Kramer; Terri and Timothy Childs; Ken Greiner; Ruth Hendel; Chugg Entertainment; Michael Buckley; Stewart F. Lane/Bonnie Comley; Bruce Davey; Thierry Suc /TS3; Bartner/Jenkins; Broadway Across America/H. Koenigsberg; M. Lerner/D. Bisno/K. Seidel/R. Gold; Paul Boskind and Martian Entertainment/Spiritas-Mauro Productions/MAS Music Arts & Show; and David Mirvish

In association with **MGM ON STAGE**
Darcie Denkert and Dean Stolber
Present

PRISCILLA
QUEEN OF THE DESERT
the musical

Book by
STEPHAN ELLIOTT & ALLAN SCOTT
Based on the Latent Image/ Specific Films Motion Picture
Distributed by Metro-Goldwyn-Mayer Inc.
Starring

WILL SWENSON   **TONY SHELDON**   **NICK ADAMS**   **C. DAVID JOHNSON**

with
JAMES BROWN III   NATHAN LEE GRAHAM   J. ELAINE MARCOS   MIKE McGOWAN   JESSICA PHILLIPS   STEVE SCHEPIS   KEALA SETTLE
and
JACQUELINE B. ARNOLD   ANASTACIA MCCLESKEY   ASHLEY SPENCER

THOM ALLISON   KYLE BROWN   JOSHUA BUSCHER   LUKE KOLBE MANNIKUS   ELLYN MARIE MARSH   GATEN MATARAZZO   JEFF METZLER
ERIC SCIOTTO   AMAKER SMITH   ESTHER STILWELL   BRYAN WEST   WAYNE ALAN WILCOX   TAD WILSON

Bus Concept & Production Design BRIAN THOMSON	*Costume Design* TIM CHAPPEL & LIZZY GARDINER	*Lighting Design* NICK SCHLIEPER	*Sound Design* JONATHAN DEANS & PETER FITZGERALD
Orchestrations STEPHEN "SPUD" MURPHY & CHARLIE HULL	*Music Director* JEFFREY KLITZ	*Musical Coordinator* JOHN MILLER	*Developed for the Stage By* SIMON PHILLIPS
Casting TELSEY + COMPANY	*Press Representative* BONEAU/BRYAN-BROWN	*Advertising* SPOTCO	*Director of Marketing* NICK PRAMIK
Technical Supervisor DAVID BENKEN	*Production Stage Manager* DAVID HYSLOP	*Flying By* FOY	*Makeup Design* CASSIE HANLON
Associate Director DEAN BRYANT	*Associate Choreographer* ANDREW HALLSWORTH		*Associate Producer* KEN SUNSHINE
	General Manager B.J. HOLT	*Executive Producer* ALECIA PARKER	

Production Supervised by
JERRY MITCHELL

Music Supervision & Arrangements
STEPHEN "SPUD" MURPHY

Choreographer
ROSS COLEMAN

Director
SIMON PHILLIPS

The original motion picture was written by Stephan Elliott, produced by Al Clark and Michael Hamlyn, executive producer Rebel Penfold-Russell and was financed with the assistance of the Film Finance Corporation of Australia Limited and the New South Wales Film and Television Office.

10/3/11

(L-R): Will Swenson, Tony Sheldon, Nick Adams and the Company

Photo by Joan Marcus

Priscilla Queen of the Desert

MUSICAL NUMBERS

Music composer and publisher information at www.PriscillaOnBroadway.com.

ACT I

The Overture

DOWNTOWN SYDNEY

"It's Raining Men" .... The Divas, Tick and Company
"What's Love Got to Do With It?" .... Miss Understanding
"I Say a Little Prayer" .... Tick
"Don't Leave Me This Way" .... Bernadette, Tick and Company
"Material Girl" .... Felicia and the Boys
"Go West" .... Bernadette, Tick, Adam and Company

THE BLACK STUMP

"Holiday/Like a Virgin" .... Adam, Tick, Bernadette
"I Say a Little Prayer" (reprise) .... Tick and the Divas

BROKEN HILL

"I Love the Nightlife" .... Shirley, Bernadette, Mitzi, Felicia and Company
"True Colors" .... Bernadette, Mitzi, Felicia

THE ROAD TO NOWHERE

"Sempre Libera" .... Felicia and the Divas

THE MIDDLE OF NOWHERE

"Colour My World" .... Adam, Tick, Bernadette and Company
"I Will Survive" .... Bernadette, Felicia, Mitzi, Jimmy and Company

ACT II

WOOP WOOP

"Thank God I'm a Country Boy" .... The Company
"A Fine Romance" .... Young Bernadette and Les Girls
"Thank God I'm a Country Boy" (reprise) .... The Company
"Shake Your Groove Thing" .... Mitzi, Bernadette, Felicia and the Divas
"Pop Muzik" .... Cynthia and Company
"A Fine Romance" (reprise) .... Bob

THE BACK OF BEYOND

"Girls Just Wanna Have Fun" .... Adam and the Divas

COOBER PEDY

"Hot Stuff" .... Felicia, the Divas and Bernadette
"MacArthur Park" .... Bernadette, Tick, the Divas and Company

ALICE SPRINGS

"Boogie Wonderland" .... The Company
"The Floor Show" .... Mitzi, Bernadette, Felicia and Company
"Always on My Mind" .... Tick, Benji
"Like a Prayer" .... Felicia and Company
"We Belong" .... Felicia, Mitzi, Bernadette and Company
"Finally Medley" .... The Company

The Company

Photo by Joan Marcus

Priscilla Queen of the Desert

Will Swenson
Tick/Mitzi

Tony Sheldon
Bernadette

Nick Adams
Adam/Felicia

C. David Johnson
Bob

Jacqueline B. Arnold
Diva

Anastacia McCleskey
Diva

Ashley Spencer
Diva

James Brown III
Jimmy

Nathan Lee Graham
Miss Understanding

J. Elaine Marcos
Cynthia

Mike McGowan
Frank

Jessica Phillips
Marion

Steve Schepis
Farrah/Young Bernadette

Keala Settle
Shirley

Thom Allison
Ensemble

Kyle Brown
Ensemble

Joshua Buscher
Swing, Asst. Dance Captain

Luke Kolbe Mannikus
Benji

Ellyn Marie Marsh
Swing

Gaten Matarazzo
Benji

Jeff Metzler
Ensemble

Eric Sciotto
Swing, Dance Captain

Amaker Smith
Swing

Esther Stilwell
Swing

Bryan West
Ensemble

Wayne Alan Wilcox
Ensemble

Tad Wilson
Ensemble

Stephan Elliott
Book

Simon Phillips
Director

Ross Coleman
Choreographer

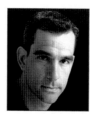
Jerry Mitchell
Production Supervisor

Tim Chappel
Costume Design

Lizzy Gardiner
Costume Design

Jonathan Deans
Sound Design

Jeffrey Klitz
Music Director

312

Priscilla Queen of the Desert

John Miller
Music Coordinator

Bernard Telsey
Telsey + Company
Casting

Dean Bryant
Associate Director

David Benken
Technical Supervisor

Alecia Parker
Executive Producer

Ken Sunshine
Associate Producer

Bette Midler
Producer

James L.
Nederlander
Producer

Garry McQuinn
Producer

Liz Koops
Producer

Roy Furman
Producer

Richard Willis
Producer

Terry Allen Kramer
Producer

Timothy Childs
Producer

Ken Greiner
Producer

Ruth Hendel
Producer

Michael Chugg
Producer

Stewart F. Lane/Bonnie Comley
Producers

Michael Jenkins
Bartner/Jenkins
Producer

John Gore
Broadway Across
America
Producer

Thomas B. McGrath
Broadway Across
America
Producer

Myla Lerner
Producer

Debbie Bisno
Producer

Kit Seidel
Producer

Rebecca Gold
Producer

Paul Boskind and
Martian
Entertainment
Producer

Kevin Spirtas
Spirtas-Mauro
Productions
Producer

Scott Mauro
Spirtas-Mauro
Productions
Producer

David Mirvish, C.M.
Producer

ALUMNI
2011-2012

Gavin Lodge
Ensemble

Julie Reiber
Marion, Ensemble

Ashton Woerz
Benji

Priscilla Queen of the Desert

Todd A. Horman
Ensemble

Lisa Howard
Diva, Ensemble

Adam LeFevre
Bob

Gavin Lodge
Ensemble

Sebastian Thomas
Benji

Alysha Umphress
Shirley, Ensemble

Anthony Wayne
Jimmy, Ensemble

Branch Woodman
Ensemble

HAIR/MAKEUP
Front Row (L-R): Hagen Linss, Jack Curtin

Back Row (L-R): Josh Schwartz, Isabelle Decauwert

EVENING DOORMAN
Freddy Quionest

STAGE MANAGERS
(L-R): David Hyslop, Mary Kathryn Flynt, Chad Lewis, Mahlon Kruse

Priscilla Queen of The Desert

Photo by Brian Mapp

WARDROBE
Front Row (L-R): Herb Ouellette, Emily Ockenfels, Dan Foss, Dawn Marcoccia
Back Row (L-R): Megan Bowers, Sara Foster, Laura Ellington, David Thompson, Renee Borys, Laura Horner, Ricardo Fernandez, Pam Hughes, Meghan Carsella, Thomas Sharkey.

STAFF FOR
PRISCILLA QUEEN OF THE DESERT
THE MUSICAL

CASTING

TELSEY + COMPANY
Bernie Telsey CSA, Will Cantler CSA, David Vaccari CSA,
Bethany Knox CSA, Craig Burns CSA,
Tiffany Little Canfield CSA, Rachel Hoffman CSA
Justin Huff CSA, Patrick Goodwin CSA,
Abbie Brady-Dalton, David Morris, Cesar A. Rocha

COMPANY MANAGER
Shaun Moorman

PRESS REPRESENTATIVE
BONEAU/BRYAN-BROWN
Adrian Bryan-Brown Joe Perrotta Michael Strassheim

North America/
    International Associate Producer ....Clare Rainbow
International Associate Producer ....Kirsten Hann
Script Consultant ....Phil Scott
Associate Technical Supervisor ....Rose Palombo
Production Stage Manager ....David Hyslop
Stage Manager ....Mahlon Kruse
Assistant Stage Manager ....Glynn David Turner
Assistant Stage Manager ....Mary Kathryn Flynt
Associate General Manager ....Hilary Hamilton
General Management Associate ....Stephen Spadaro
Assistant Company Manager ....Jeremy Davis
Assistant to Alecia Parker ....Marilyn Stout
Assistant to BJ Holt ....Katharine Hayes
Associate Scenic Designer ....Bryan Johnson
Associate Costume Designer ....Brian J. Bustos
Assistant Costume Designers ......Katie Irish, Mike Floyd
Associate Lighting Designer ....Michael P. Jones
Assistant Lighting Designer ....Carolyn Wong
Bus Visual Animation
    Sequences Design ....Brian Thomson
Animators ....Jamie Clennett, Kenji Oates
Photoshoppers ....Pip Runciman, Micka Agosta
Head Carpenter ....Patrick Eviston
Automation ....Michael Shepp Jr.
Assistant Carpenter ....Jeff Zink
Production Electrician ....Jon Lawson
Head Electrician ....Patrick Ainge

Assistant Electrician ....Jesse Hancox
Moving Lights and Video Programmer ......Chris Herman
Production Sound ....Garth Helm
Head Sound ....Steve Henshaw
Additional Synthesizer Programmer ....Jeff Marder
Production Props ....Jerry Marshall
Assistant Props ....James Cariot
Wardrobe Supervisor ....Meghan Carsella
Assistant Wardrobe Supervisor ....Megan Bowers
Dressers ....Sara Darneille, Laura Ellington,
                    Danny Foss, Jacob Fry, Laura Horner,
            Pam Hughes, Kurt Kielmann, Del Miskie,
        Herb Ouellette, Thomas Sharkey, Keith Shaw
Associate Wig Designer ....Richard Mawbey
Assistant Make Up Designer ....Benjamin Moir
Australian Sound Designer ....Michael Waters
Hair & Make Up Supervisor ....John "Jack" Curtin
Production Assistants ....Nathan K. Claus,
                    Amanda Gwin, Kevin MacLeod,
                    Carly J. Price, Willie Ruiz
Advertising..SpotCo/
                    Drew Hodges, Jim Edwards,
            Tom Greenwald, Vinny Sainato,
                    Jim Aquino, Stacey Maya
Website Design/
    Online Marketing ....SpotCo/
            Sara Fitzpatrick, Matt Wilstein,
                Marc Mettler, Christine Sees
Sales Dude..................................Stephen Santore
Children's Supervisor ....Jill Valentine
Children's Teachers ....On Location Education
Dialect Coach ....Gillian Lane-Plescia
Production Photography ....Joan Marcus
Music Copyist ....Martine Monroe
Legal Counsel ....Loeb & Loeb/Seth Gelblum
Music Rights Consultant ....Jill Meyers Music
Insurance ....Stockbridge Risk Management/
                                        Neil Goldstein
Accounting ....Rosenberg, Neuwirth & Kuchner/
                    Mark D'Ambrosi, Marina Flom
Business Affairs Consultant ....Daniel M. Posener
Banking ....City National Bank/Michele Gibbons
Travel Services ....Tzell Travel/Andi Henig
Payroll Service ....Castellana Services, Inc.

CREDITS
Scenery and automation by Hudson Scenic Studio. Lighting

by Hudson Sound & Light. Sound by Sound Associates. Props by Proof Production, The Rabbit's Choice. Masks manufactured by Den Design Studio. Wigs made by Wig Specialties London. Custom costumes by Tricorne, Inc., Seamless Costumes, Phil Reynolds, John Sheward, Lorraine Richards, Jill Paskin, Character Costumes, Amanda Barrow, Fay Fullerton, Mein Roberts, Leigh Cranston, Paragon, Eric Winterling, Inc. Custom millinery by Lynne Mackey, Rodney Gordon, Sean Barrett, Monica Vianni, Marian Jean Hose, LLC. Custom shoes by LaDuca Shoes, Jitterbug Boy Footwear. Custom knitwear by Maria Ficalora. Special thanks to Bra*Tenders for undergarments and hosiery. Custom painting by Jeff Fender. Makeup provided by M*A*C Cosmetics. Costume sponsor: Swarovski Elements. Special thanks Manolo Blahnik, Magnolia Bakery, Tristan Tidswell. Housing provided by Elizabeth Helke, ABA.

Village People characters and choreography are used with permission of their trademark owner,
Can't Stop Productions, Inc.

⊁N⊱
NEDERLANDER

Chairman	**James M. Nederlander**
President	**James L. Nederlander**

Executive Vice President
Nick Scandalios

Vice President Corporate Development **Charlene S. Nederlander**	Senior Vice President Labor Relations **Herschel Waxman**
Vice President **Jim Boese**	Chief Financial Officer **Freida Sawyer Belviso**

STAFF FOR THE PALACE THEATRE
Theatre Manager ....Austin Nathaniel
Treasurer ....Cissy Caspare
Assistant Treasurer ....Anne T. Wilson
Carpenter ....Thomas K. Phillips
Flyman ....Robert W. Kelly
Electrician ....Eddie Webber
Propertymaster ....Steve Camus
Engineer ....Rob O'Connor
Chief Usher ....Gloria Hill

Priscilla Queen of the Desert
SCRAPBOOK

Correspondent: Tony Sheldon, "Bernadette"

Memorable Fan Appreciation: Our devoted followers have moved well beyond fan mail. They draw pictures of us, send fabulous gifts, dress up as our characters, attend our publicity appearances, make cupcakes for us, buy our memorabilia at the Broadway Flea Market, read our blogs, Tweet us, donate huge sums of money to Broadway Cares so that they can tour backstage, drink champagne or have supper with the cast, get engaged during the curtain call, walk-on during performances or even just say hello at the stage door. *Priscilla* fans are the best EVER!

Milestone Celebrations: Our wardrobe department occasionally gets crazy on a Tuesday night and puts on a post-show spread. We've had a couple of Hawaiian themed soirees and Dip Night was hugely popular. Who knew cream cheese was so versatile? We always celebrate birthdays in the greenroom at intermission with a cake from Amy's Bread, and now that so many people are moving on to other projects we have a "Happy Trails" cake as well. Any excuse for an Amy's cake, really. I like to celebrate my personal *Priscilla* milestones (1700 performances and counting) by force-feeding the company with glazed yeasty goodies from The Doughnut Plant. Of course, our sylph-like figures are totally doomed now that Pie Face has opened up the street because they're an Australian company and they make a killer version of the Aussie national cake, the Lamington. Every home should have one.

Most Exciting Celebrity Visitors: Cloris Leachman was chased around backstage by her son who tickled her until she became hysterical. Kirstie Alley disco danced in Nick Adams' dressing room. Billie Jean King signed a tennis racquet for Will Swenson's kids. Joan and Melissa Rivers filmed a sequence of their TV series in my dressing room. Patti LaBelle caused great excitement, especially amongst the Divas. She hugged us all and whispered "You better WERK!" which, in my paranoia, I thought meant I should immediately enroll in a drama school to improve my performance. I have since been reassured that it was a compliment. There's a more complete list of celebrity visitors on our website.

Actor Who Performed the Most Roles in This Show: I think most of the company play around 8 or 9 roles. We have approximately 300 costumes so SOMEONE must be wearing them.

Actor Who Has Done the Most Shows: Tony Sheldon. He began his stage career in Australia as a small child and is now older than dirt.

Special Backstage Rituals: Push-ups for the girls, push-up bras for the guys.

Favorite Moment During Each Performance: I personally love catching glimpses of our company interacting backstage with the little boys who play Benji. To see those kids bopping with Kyle Brown during "Boogie Wonderland" or performing intricate secret handshakes with

1. Members of the men's ensemble cool off backstage.
2. Jeff Metzler, an exhausted paintbrush.
3. Shirley MacLaine visits backstage with (L-R): Nick Adams, *Yearbook* correspondent Tony Sheldon and Tad Wilson.

Ashley Spencer or just being enveloped in enormous hugs from Lisa Howard warms this crusty old heart.

Favorite In-Theatre Gathering Place: The "adult male" dressing room. Thom Allison took charge of the Christmas decorations last December and turned it into a veritable Aladdin's cave which everyone was most reluctant to dismantle. With the gourmet cupcakes he baked several times a week, show tunes playing softly in the background and extremely flattering lighting it was a magnet for anyone passing by, much to the annoyance of the actors trying to get ready for their performance.

Favorite Off-Site Hangout: Rum House, Industry, The R Room (commonly known as the Womb Room) at the Renaissance Hotel.

Favorite Snack Foods: Anything that isn't nailed down.

Mascot: George De Witt

Favorite Therapy: Physical therapy, Ice, Ricola, Throat Coat Tea, Entertainer's Secret, Thom Allison's cupcakes.

Memorable Ad-Lib: Will Swenson still wins with "Go suck the toes off a pop star" (instead of "Go suck the chrome off a tow bar") but Tony Sheldon did amuse the natives when he forgot the line "Stop flexing your sweaty old muscles" and substituted "Stop sweating your sweaty old arse off."

Record Number of Cell Phone Rings, Cell Phone Photos or Texting Incidents During a Performance: At every performance we have audience members who simply ignore the pre-show announcement and take photos or video of the show. It's terribly distracting, it pulls our focus and can be very dangerous. The latest fad is filming us on iPads. Do these people seriously think we can't see them? They might just as well set up a tripod in the aisle, hold up a clapper board, call out "action" and hold a wrap party.

Memorable Press Encounter: Singing at Gracie Mansion was pretty cool, as was performing "New York, New York" in Duffy Square with the other Broadway casts on the anniversary of 9/11. The Macy's Thanksgiving Parade is one for the Bucket List. The details of our press appearance

Priscilla Queen of the Desert
SCRAPBOOK

1. Nick Adams, Guy Pearce, Tony Sheldon and Will Swenson.
2. Tony Sheldon on Rosie O'Donnell's TV show.
3. Lisa Howard takes wing.

at Bette Midler's Hulaween Party at the Waldorf can only be divulged to the general public after all the participants are dead.

Memorable Stage Door Fan Encounters: One young man drove us crazy by taking photos all the way through the show then waited at the stage door and asked us to pose for pictures! Nick Adams, who is never less than charming, was shocked enough to blurt out "Haven't you got enough by now?" Then there is the woman who had Nick's signature tattooed on her shoulder. She sat in the front row that night so most of the cast copied Nick's signature onto some part of their body where only Nick could see it and spent the entire performance flashing him. The poor boy was a wreck by the curtain call.

Web Buzz: I have noticed that the chat rooms are inching their way from dismissive contempt towards grudging acceptance.

Latest Audience Arrival: Latecomers are ushered in after "It's Raining Men" so that Nathan Lee Graham can single them out, publicly humiliate them and unite the entire audience in derisive laughter. It's a bonding thing.

Fastest Costume Change: Almost everyone has a ridiculously fast change at some point with up to five people at once ripping their clothes off. It's certainly never dull.

Who Wore the Least: The "Material Girl" boys. They are naked boys singing.

Catchphrases Only the Company Would Recognize: "Tommy's in again." "BORE IT UP 'EM!" "Stuuuuuupid." "P-WU." "You better WERK!"

Sweethearts Within the Company: Three couples that I'm aware of but I might not be paying close enough attention.

Best In-House Parody Lyrics: There is a secret list of "cut songs" including "Funny Ha Ha," "Mitzi's Got A Minor" and "Don't Worry, It Happens To Everybody." The Divas can sometimes be heard singing "Solid Gold" on the last three notes of the finale. And after Bernadette's reprise of "Hot Stuff," the final notes are usually signaled by an offstage rendition of "She's Kicked Him in the Nuts."

Company In-Jokes: During the "Material Girl" scene, Will and I give a different name to the nightclub we're supposedly in at each performance, such as "Nickersniffers" or "Penis in Fur." Sadly, 99.9 percent of the names are too filthy to repeat.

Company Legends: Our dressers, without whom the show would be very drab indeed. And Mr. Eric Sciotto, our indefatigable Dance Captain who somehow manages to keep our stage energetically peopled with paint brushes and lizards even as the cast dwindles with flu and fatigue, whilst also auditioning cast replacements, raising a child, making our *Priscilla* patch for the Gypsy Robe, understudying Will Swenson and occasionally unleashing his alter ego Miss Lavender Shortbread during "Country Boy."

Understudy Anecdote: The role of Jimmy has been played by the very blonde Joshua Buscher who looked more like a Malibu surfer dude than an Australian aboriginal. We decided that he was an albino.

Embarrassing Moments: My personal day from hell was the matinee when I knocked my dresser's glasses off during the change into "Go West." That made me late for my entrance into the number, and in my haste I tripped and fell, skidding the length of the stage behind the black flitter curtain. I only had time to pick myself up and dance on with badly scraped knees, ripped stockings, my wig knocked askew and blood everywhere. I figured if I took dainty little steps my skirt would cover the damage so I'm afraid the choreography went completely out the window. I couldn't leave the stage until "Nightlife" so I couldn't even see what I looked like. Then I got on to the bus to change for "Color My World" and my poor distracted dresser had forgotten to set my leopard skin leotard, so I had to wrap a skirt over my corset, gulp hard and do the rest of Act I in my underwear. Strangely, I didn't get any laughs that day. The audience must have been transfixed by my painted-on breasts which were now clearly visible to all. I don't remember the gory details of the rest of the show, although I did Act II with my legs covered in bandages. Bob surely didn't fall in love with Bernadette's shapely gams that day! During the curtain call I was too ashamed to even look at the audience and I was wishing myself a million miles away when I noticed the excited murmuring from the cast behind me and the awe-struck looks on their faces. That was when Tad Wilson, remembering that I'm blind as a bat without my glasses, hissed in my ear, "Look in the third row! It's Shirley MacLaine!!" My humiliation was complete. But we were auctioning off backstage tours for Broadway Cares at the time and astonishingly Ms. MacLaine paid $700 so she could come back and meet the cast. She was incredibly complimentary and I'm told that she has since been heard to say that *Priscilla* is a very important show for Broadway. So in my eyes she can do no wrong.

Private Lives

First Preview: November 6, 2011. Opened: November 17, 2011.
Closed December 31, 2011 after 12 Previews and 53 Performances.

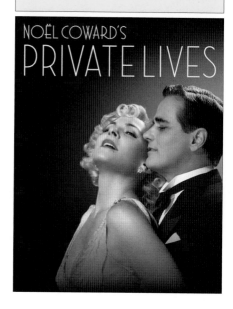

PLAYBILL

NOËL COWARD'S
PRIVATE LIVES

Revival of Noël Coward's high comedy about a divorced couple who find themselves falling back in love when they are booked into adjoining hotel rooms while on their respective honeymoons with new spouses.

CAST

(in order of appearance)

Sybil .... ANNA MADELEY
Elyot .... PAUL GROSS
Victor .... SIMON PAISLEY DAY
Amanda .... KIM CATTRALL
Louise .... CAROLINE LENA OLSSON

UNDERSTUDIES

For Sybil, Amanda, Louise:
CHRISTY BRUCE
for Elyot, Victor:
DYLAN SCOTT SMITH

ACT 1

A hotel terrace in Deauville, France

ACT 2

Amanda's apartment in Paris —
late in the evening a few days later

ACT 3

Amanda's apartment in Paris — next morning

Continued on next page

THE MUSIC BOX
239 W. 45th Street
A Shubert Organization Theatre

Philip J. Smith, *Chairman*   **Robert E. Wankel,** *President*

DUNCAN C. WELDON   THEATRE ROYAL   TERRI & TIMOTHY   SONIA FRIEDMAN
& PAUL ELLIOTT   BATH   CHILDS   PRODUCTIONS

BILL   &   DAVID
BALLARD   MIRVISH

PRESENT

KIM CATTRALL   PAUL GROSS

NOËL COWARD'S
PRIVATE LIVES

SIMON PAISLEY DAY   ANNA MADELEY

CAROLINE LENA OLSSON

DIRECTED BY RICHARD EYRE

SET AND COSTUME DESIGN BY ROB HOWELL

LIGHTING DESIGN BY DAVID HOWE

MUSIC SUPERVISOR/COMPOSER   ASSOCIATE DIRECTOR   SOUND DESIGNER UK   SOUND DESIGNER US
MATTHEW SCOTT   ANNA LEDWICH   JASON BARNES   CHRIS CRONIN

FIGHT DIRECTOR   MOVEMENT DIRECTOR   PRODUCTION MANAGER
ALISON DE BURGH   SCARLETT MACKMIN   PATRICK MOLONY

TECHNICAL SUPERVISOR   PRESS REPRESENTATION   GENERAL MANAGEMENT
JUNIPER STREET   BONEAU/BRYAN-BROWN   ALAN WASSER · ALLAN WILLIAMS
PRODUCTIONS   MARK SHACKET

The Producers wish to express their appreciation to Theatre Development Fund for its support of this production.

11/17/11

(L-R): Paul Gross,
Kim Cattrall

Private Lives

Kim Cattrall
Amanda

Paul Gross
Elyot

Simon Paisley Day
Victor

Anna Madeley
Sybil

Caroline Lena Olsson
Louise

Christy Bruce
*u/s Sybil, Amanda,
Louise the Maid*

Dylan Scott Smith
u/s Elyot, Victor

Noël Coward
Playwright

Richard Eyre
Director

Rob Howell
*Scenic & Costume
Designer*

David Howe
Lighting Designer

Anna Ledwich
Associate Director

Chris Cronin
Sound Designer U.S.

Alison De Burgh
Fight Director

Scarlett Mackmin
Movement Director

Ana Rose Greene, Guy Kwan, Joe DeLuise,
Hillary Blanken
Juniper Street Productions
Technical Supervisor

Alan Wasser
General Manager

BOX OFFICE
(L-R): Robert Kelly, Gerard O'Brien
Not Pictured: Brendan Berberich, Tracie Giebler

CREW
Back Row (L-R): Kim Garnett, Howard Jepson, Deirdre LaBarre, Kyle Garnett, Doug McNeill
Front Row (L-R): Olivia Roberts, Laura Beattie, Jill Johnson, Douglas Petitjean, Bobby Hentze

Photos by Brian Mapp

Private Lives

FRONT OF HOUSE
Back Row (L-R): Jenna Scanlon, Dennis Scanlon, Francis T. Sanabria, John Seid, Jonathan Shulman
Front Row (L-R): Lottie Dennis, Joseph Spezzano, Michael Concepcion, Kenneth Kelly
Not Pictured: Joe Amato, Nick Fusco, John Himmel, Thomas Murdoch, Edith Rosado

STAFF FOR *PRIVATE LIVES*

GENERAL MANAGEMENT
ALAN WASSER ASSOCIATES
Alan Wasser   Allan Williams
Mark Shacket   Aaron Lustbader

GENERAL PRESS REPRESENTATIVE
BONEAU/BRYAN-BROWN
Adrian Bryan-Brown   Jackie Green   Kelly Guiod

COMPANY MANAGER
Cathy Kwon

PRODUCTION STAGE MANAGER
Howard Jepson

UK PRODUCTION MANAGER
Patrick Molony

U.S. PRODUCTION MANAGEMENT
JUNIPER STREET PRODUCTIONS
Hillary Blanken   Guy Kwan
Joseph DeLuise   Ana Rose Greene

HAIR DESIGN
CAMPBELL YOUNG ASSOCIATES
Luc Verschueren

Stage Manager	Olivia Roberts
Dialect Coach	Jill McCulloch
Fight Director	Alison De Burgh
Movement Director	Scarlett Mackmin
Associate Lighting Designer	Vivien Leone
Production Carpenter	Bobby Hentze
Production Electrician	Jon Lawson
Production Props	Jill Johnson
Production Sound	Rafe Carlotto
Wardrobe Supervisor	Doug Petitjean
Star Dresser	Laura Beattie
Dresser	Julie Tobia
Hair Supervisor	Rick Carato
House Carpenter	Dennis Maher
House Electrician	William K. Rowland
House Props	Kim Garnett
House Flyman	Brian Maher

Cover Photography	Hugo Glendenning
Advertising & Marketing	aka/ Clint Bond, Jr., Andrew Damer, Pippa Bexon, Kevin Hirst, Adam Jay, Janette Roush, Meghan Bartley, Sara Rosenzweig, Trevor Sponseller
Digital & Interactive	aka/Erin Rech, Jen Taylor
Theatre Displays	King Displays
Legal Counsel	NLS Law/Noel Silverman
Immigration Attorney	Shannon K. Such
Accounting	Rosenberg, Neuwirth & Kuchner/ Chris Cacace

For Triumph Entertainment

Producers	Paul Elliott, Duncan C. Weldon
UK Finance Director	Dinesh Khanderia
Production Associate	Simon Friend

For Theatre Royal Bath Productions

Chairman	Stephen Ross
Board of Directors	Sir Robert Hill, Greg Ingham, Paul Heal
Managing Director	Danny Moar
Finance Director	Simon Payne
General Manager	Eugene Hibbert
Production Administrator	Nicky Palmer
Finance Supervisor	Cheryl Hardy
Assistant to the General Manager	Katharine Wojcik
General Management Associates	Lane Marsh, Thom Mitchell
General Management Office	Hilary Ackerman, Mark Barna, Christopher D'Angelo, Jake Hirzel, Nina Lutwick, Jennifer O'Connor
Press Office Staff	Chris Boneau, Jim Byk, Linnae Hodzic, Jessica Johnson, Kevin Jones, Amy Kass, Holly Kinney, Emily Meagher, Aaron Meier, Christine Olver, Joe Perrotta, Matt Polk, Heath Schwartz, Michael Strassheim, Susanne Tighe
Insurance	Ventura Insurance Brokerage/ Christine Sadofsky
Banking	Signature Bank/ Barbara von Borstel, Margaret Monigan, Mary Ann Fanelli, Janett Urena
Payroll	Castellana Services, Inc.
Housing Services	Road Concierge, Inc.

Group Sales	Shubert Group Sales (212) 239-6200
Transportation	BLS Limo

www.privatelivesbroadway.com

CREDITS AND ACKNOWLEDGEMENTS
Show control and scenic motion control featuring Stage Command® Systems by PRG Scenic Technologies, a division of Production Resources Group, LLC. Lighting equipment provided by PRG Lighting. Sound equipment provided by Sound Associates Inc. Additional softgoods provided by I. Weiss and Sons, Inc. Special thanks to Philip Large.

 THE SHUBERT ORGANIZATION, INC.
Board of Directors

Philip J. Smith Chairman	**Robert E. Wankel** President
Wyche Fowler, Jr. **Lee J. Seidler**	**Diana Phillips** **Michael I. Sovern**
Stuart Subotnick	

Elliot Greene Chief Financial Officer	**David Andrews** Senior Vice President – Shubert Ticketing
Juan Calvo Vice President – Finance	**John Darby** Vice President – Facilities
Peter Entin Vice President – Theatre Operations	**Charles Flateman** Vice President – Marketing
Anthony LaMattina Vice President – Audit & Production Finance	**Brian Mahoney** Vice President – Ticket Sales

D.S. Moynihan
Vice President – Creative Projects

House Manager	Jonathan Shulman

Private Lives
SCRAPBOOK

Photos by Joseph Marzullo/WENN

1. Kim Cattrall accepts a bouquet on opening night.
2. The company takes a curtain call at the premiere (L-R) Caroline Lena Olsson, Paul Gross, Simon Paisley Day and Anna Madeley.
3. Cattrall welcomes actress Tammy Grimes, who won a Tony Award for playing Amanda in the 1969 Broadway revival.
4. Madeley at at a press event.
5. The company greets the press at the Paramount Hotel, along with director Richard Eyre (second from right).
6. The Music Box Theatre gets a facelift during the run.

Rain: A Tribute to The Beatles on Broadway

First Preview: October 19, 2010. Opened: October 26, 2010 at the Neil Simon Theatre.
Moved to the Brooks Atkinson Theatre February 8, 2011. Closed July 31, 2011 after 8 Previews and 300 Performances.

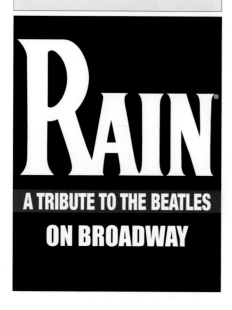

The Fab Four live again in a never-never concert featuring many of the band's greatest hits.

MUSICIANS

STEVE LANDES .....Vocals, Rhythm Guitar, Piano, Harmonica
JOEY CURATOLO ....Vocals, Bass, Piano, Guitar
JOE BITHORN ....Vocals, Lead Guitar, Guitar Synth, Sitar
RALPH CASTELLI ....Drums, Percussion, Vocals
JOHN KORBA ....Keyboard, Percussion

AT CERTAIN PERFORMANCES

GRAHAM ALEXANDER........Vocals, Bass, Piano, Guitar
MARK BEYER ....Keyboard, Percussion
JOE BOLOGNA ....Drums, Percussion, Vocals
DOUGLAS COX ....Drums, Percussion, Vocals
JIM IRIZARRY ....Vocals, Rhythm Guitar, Piano, Harmonica
ALAN LeBOEUF ....Vocals, Bass, Piano, Guitar
DAVID LEON ....Vocals, Rhythm Guitar, Piano, Harmonica
MARK LEWIS ....Keyboard, Percussion
JIMMY POU ......Vocals, Lead Guitar, Guitar Synth
MAC RUFFING ....Vocals, Bass, Piano, Guitar
ARDY SARRAF ....Vocals, Bass, Piano, Guitar
CHRIS SMALLWOOD ....Keyboard, Percussion
TOM TEELEY ....Vocals, Lead Guitar, Guitar Synth, Sitar
DANIEL A. WEISS ....Keyboard, Percussion

BROOKS ATKINSON THEATRE
UNDER THE DIRECTION OF JAMES M. NEDERLANDER AND JAMES L. NEDERLANDER

Annerin Productions, MagicSpace Entertainment
Nederlander Presentations, Inc., Sony/ATV and RAIN

Present

Starring

STEVE LANDES
JOEY CURATOLO
JOE BITHORN
RALPH CASTELLI

Scenic Design	Video Design	Lighting Design	Sound Design
Scott Christensen	Darren McCaulley	Stephan Gotschel	Abe Jacob
Todd Skinner	Mathieu St-Arnaud		

Talent Coordinator	Production Stage Manager	Production Supervisor	Band Management
Dave Clemmons	Lurie Horns Pfeffer	Theatrical Services, Inc.	Mark Lewis
		Artie Siccardi	
		Pat Sullivan	

General Management	Press Representative	Marketing Director
NIKO Companies	The Hartman Group	Bruce Granath
& Steve Boulay		

7/25/11

(L-R): Joey Curatolo, Joe Bithorn, Ralph Castelli, Steve Landes

Photo by Cylla von Tiedemann

Rain: A Tribute to The Beatles on Broadway

Steve Landes
Vocals, Rhythm Guitar, Harmonica, Piano

Joey Curatolo
Vocals, Bass, Piano, Guitar

Joe Bithorn
Vocals, Lead Guitar, Guitar Synth, Sitar

Ralph Castelli
Drums, Percussion, Vocals

Mark Lewis
Founder, Manager, Original Keyboardist

Graham Alexander
Vocals, Bass, Piano, Guitar

Mark Beyer
Keyboards, Percussion

Joe Bologna
Drums, Percussion, Vocals

Douglas Cox
Drums, Percussion, Vocals

Jim Irizarry
Vocals, Rhythm Guitar, Piano, Harmonica

John Korba
Keyboards, Percussion

Alan LeBoeuf
Vocals, Bass, Piano, Guitar

David Leon
Vocals, Rhythm Guitar, Piano, Harmonica

Jimmy Pou
Vocals, Lead Guitar, Guitar Synth

Mac Ruffing
Vocals, Bass, Piano, Guitar

Ardy Sarraf
Bass, Guitar, Piano, Vocals

Chris Smallwood
Keyboard, Percussion

Tom Teeley
Vocals, Lead Guitar, Guitar Synth, Sitar

Daniel A. Weiss
Keyboards, Percussion

Dave Clemmons –
Clemmons/Dewing Casting
Talent Coordinator

James M. Nederlander,
Nederlander Presentations, Inc.
Producer

James L. Nederlander,
Nederlander Presentations, Inc.
Producer

Manny Kladitis
Niko Companies, Ltd.
General Management

Arthur Siccardi
Theatrical Services,
Production Supervisor

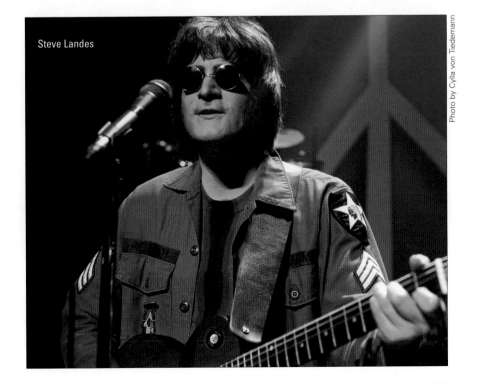

Steve Landes

Photo by Cylla von Tiedemann

Rain: A Tribute to The Beatles on Broadway

BOX OFFICE
(L-R): Guy Bentley, Erich Stollberger

Photos by Brian Mapp

STAGE DOOR STAFF
(L-R): Errolyn Rosa (Stage Door), Roxanne Mosaphir (Stage Door), Dawn Edmonds (Elevator Operator)

FRONT OF HOUSE STAFF
Front Row (L-R): Michelle Schechter (Usher), Dana Diaz (Ticket Taker), Joanne DeCicco, Megan Frazier, Grace Darbasie, Marilyn Christie (Ushers), Christopher Langdon (Ticket Taker)

Middle Row (L-R): Eshautine King, Michelle Smith, Maria Collado, Jean Manso, Deborah Ryan, Eddie Cuevas, Kaitlyn Spillane, Christine Bentley, Frank Clark (Ushers)

Back Row (L-R): Ryan Goodale, Jen King, Mike D'Arcy (Merchandise), Jose Lopez (Porter), Steven Ouellette (House Manager), Angel Diaz (Head Usher), Jane Publik, Evelyn Gutierrez, Marisol Olavarria, Evelyn Olivero, Kim Raccioppi (Ushers)

CREW
Kneeling (L-R): Sean Farrugia (Carpenter), Bill Teeley (Guitar Tech), Mitchell Christenson (Electrics), Stephen Vessa (Electrics), John Kelly (Electrics), Arthur Lutz (Electrics)

Standing (L-R): Jim van Bergen (Production Sound Operator), Max Reed (Carpenter), John Gordon (House Carpenter), Sean McGrath (Carpenter), Doug McNeill (Flyman), Mike Bennet (Carpenter), Brandon Epperson (Video Technician), Jens McVoy (Electrics), Danny Viscardo (House Propman), Michael Cornell (Show Electrician), James Travers, Sr. (House Electrician), Craig Van Tassel (Monitor Mixer)

Drums: Lurie Horns Pfeffer (PSM)

Rain: A Tribute to The Beatles on Broadway

Joe Bithorn

Photo by Cylla von Tiedemann

Relatively Speaking

First Preview: September 20, 2011. Opened: October 20, 2011.
Closed January 29, 2012 after 35 Previews and 117 Performances.

A triple-bill of one-act comedies about families. Talking Cure shows a mental patient who deftly outmaneuvers his psychologist. George Is Dead depicts a spoiled wealthy woman who still relies on her childhood nanny—much to the displeasure of the nanny's grown daughter. Honeymoon Hotel is a farce about a man who runs off with his own son's would-be bride on their wedding day—only to have the entire wedding party track them down and crash their love nest.

CAST

(in order of appearance)

Talking Cure

Doctor	JASON KRAVITS
Patient	DANNY HOCH
Attendant	MAX GORDON MOORE
Father	ALLEN LEWIS RICKMAN
Mother	KATHERINE BOROWITZ

George Is Dead

Carla	LISA EMERY
Doreen	MARLO THOMAS
Michael	GRANT SHAUD
Nanny	PATRICIA O'CONNELL
Funeral Director	ALLEN LEWIS RICKMAN
Assistant Funeral Director	MAX GORDON MOORE

Honeymoon Motel

Jerry Spector	STEVE GUTTENBERG
Nina Roth	ARI GRAYNOR

Continued on next page

⇥N⇤ BROOKS ATKINSON THEATRE
UNDER THE DIRECTION OF JAMES M. NEDERLANDER AND JAMES L. NEDERLANDER

Julian Schlossberg   Letty Aronson

Edward Walson   LeRoy Schecter   Tom Sherak   Daveed D. Frazier
and Roy Furman

present

RELATIVELY SPEAKING
3 ONE-ACT COMEDIES

Talking Cure	**George is Dead**	**Honeymoon Motel**
by	by	by
Ethan Coen	**Elaine May**	**Woody Allen**

with

Caroline Aaron   Bill Army   Katherine Borowitz   Lisa Emery
Ari Graynor   Steve Guttenberg   Danny Hoch   Julie Kavner
Jason Kravits   Richard Libertini   Mark Linn-Baker   Max Gordon Moore
Patricia O'Connell   Allen Lewis Rickman   Grant Shaud   Marlo Thomas

Scenic Design	**Costume Design**	**Lighting Design**
Santo Loquasto	Donna Zakowska	Kenneth Posner
Sound Design	**Casting**	**Production Stage Manager**
Carl Casella	Cindy Tolan	Ira Mont
Production Management		**Press Representative**
Aurora Productions		Boneau/Bryan Brown
Associate Producer		**General Management**
The Weinstein Company		Richards/Climan, Inc.

directed by
John Turturro

The Producers wish to express their appreciation to the Theatre Development Fund for its support of this production.

11/21/11

(L-R): Danny Hoch and Jason Kravits in *Talking Cure*

Photo by Joan Marcus

Relatively Speaking

Cast Continued

Eddie .... GRANT SHAUD
Judy Spector .... CAROLINE AARON
Fay Roth .... JULIE KAVNER
Sam Roth .... MARK LINN-BAKER
Rabbi Baumel .... RICHARD LIBERTINI
Dr. Brill .... JASON KRAVITS
Sal Buonacotti .... DANNY HOCH
Paul Jessup .... BILL ARMY

UNDERSTUDIES

For Patient, Jerry Spector:
GRANT SHAUD
For Patient, Sal Buonacotti, Paul Jessup:
MAX GORDON MOORE
For Attendant, Assistant Funeral Director:
BILL ARMY
for Mother, Carla:
JULIA BROTHERS
For Doreen, Judy Spector, Fay Roth:
KATHERINE BOROWITZ
For Nanny:
ELIZABETH SHEPHERD
For Funeral Director:
JASON KRAVITS
For Nina Roth:
SARAH SOKOLOVIC
For Dr. Brill:
ALLEN LEWIS RICKMAN

(L-R): Grant Shaud, Marlo Thomas and Lisa Emery in *George Is Dead*

(L-R): Ari Graynor and Steve Guttenberg in *Honeymoon Motel*

Photos by Joan Marcus

Caroline Aaron
Judy Spector

Bill Army
Paul Jessup

Katherine Borowitz
Mother

Lisa Emery
Carla

Ari Graynor
Nina Roth

Steve Guttenberg
Jerry Spector

Danny Hoch
Patient, Sal Buonacotti

Julie Kavner
Fay Roth

Jason Kravits
Doctor, Dr. Brill

Richard Libertini
Rabbi Baumel

Mark Linn-Baker
Sam Roth

Max Gordon Moore
Attendant, Assistant Funeral Director

Patricia O'Connell
Nanny

Allen Lewis Rickman
Father, Funeral Director

Grant Shaud
Michael, Eddie

Marlo Thomas
Doreen

Julia Brothers
u/s Mother/Carla

Elizabeth Shepherd
u/s Nanny

Sarah Sokolovic
u/s Nina Roth

Ethan Coen
Playwright

Relatively Speaking

Elaine May
Playwright

Woody Allen
Playwright

John Turturro
Director

Santo Loquasto
Set Designer

Kenneth Posner
Lighting Design

Carl Casella
Sound Designer

Julian Schlossberg
Producer

David R. Richards, Tamar Haimes
Richards/Climan, Inc.
General Management

Roy Furman
Co-Producer

Bob Weinstein
The Weinstein
Company
Associate Producer

Harvey Weinstein
The Weinstein
Company
Associate Producer

STAFF FOR *RELATIVELY SPEAKING*

GENERAL MANAGEMENT
RICHARDS/CLIMAN, INC.
David R. Richards Tamar Haimes
Michael Sag   Kyle Bonder
Jessica Fried   Jaqueline Kolek

COMPANY MANAGER
Ron Gubin

GENERAL PRESS REPRESENTATIVE
BONEAU/BRYAN-BROWN
Chris Boneau   Joe Perrotta   Kelly Guiod

PRODUCTION MANAGEMENT
AURORA PRODUCTIONS, INC.
Gene O'Donovan   Ben Heller
Stephanie Sherline   Jarid Sumner
Liza Luxenberg   Anita Shah
Rebecca Zuber   Steven Dalton
Eugenio Saenz Flores   Isaac Katzanek
Melissa Mazdra

PRODUCTION STAGE MANAGER .... IRA MONT
Stage Manager .... Matthew Lacey
Associate Scenic Designer .... Jenny B. Sawyers
Graphic Artist .... Eric Helmin
Assistant Costume Designer .... Erika Ingrid Lilienthal
Associate Lighting Designer .... John Viesta
Assistant Sound Designer .... Josh Liebert
Production Assistant .... Kate Croasdale
Casting Associates .... Adam Caldwell, Ann Davidson
Casting Assistant .... Cynthia Degros
Assistant to the Director .... Nathan Brewer
Production Carpenter .... Jason Clark
Deck Automation Carpenter .... Ben Horrigan
Production Electrician .... Manuel Becker
Lighting Programmer .... Jay Penfield
Production Sound .... Wallace Flores
Props Coordinator .... Kathy Fabian/Propstar

Associate Props Coordinator .... Carrie Mossman/
Propstar
Head Props .... John Tutalo
Props Artisans .... Tim Ferro, Mary Wilson, Sarah Bird,
Cassie Dorland, John Estep,
Jessica Provencal
Wardrobe Supervisor .... Kay Grunder
Dresser .... Kim Prentice
Hair Supervisor .... Carmel Vargyas
Assistant to Mr. Schlossberg .... Ruth Better
Assistant to Ms. May .... Chantal Ribeiro
Assistant to Mr. Turturro .... Cameron Bossert
Advertising .... SERINO/COYNE/
Greg Corradetti, Marci Kaufman,
Tom Callahan, Joe Alesi,
Andrei Oleinik, Sarah Marcus
Digital Outreach & Website .... SERINO/COYNE/
Jim Glaub, Chip Meyrelles,
Laurie Connor, Kevin Keating, Ryan Greer,
Whitney Creighton, Mark Seeley
Marketing Service .... Type A Marketing/
Anne Rippey, John McCoy,
Robin Steinthal
Banking .... City National Bank/Michele Gibbons
Insurance .... DeWitt Stern Group Inc./
Peter Shoemaker, Anthony Pittari
Accountants .... Fried & Kowgios, CPA's LLP,
Robert Fried, CPA
Comptroller .... Elliott Aronstam
Legal Counsel .... Levine Plotkin & Menin LLP./
Loren H. Plotkin, Esq.;
Cris Criswell, Esq.
Payroll .... CSI/Lance Castellana
Production Photographer .... Joan Marcus
Opening Night Coordination .... Serino Coyne Events/
Suzanne Tobak, Chrissann Gasparro

Opening Night Party sponsored by MARINO WARE.

CREDITS
Scenery built, painted, electrified and automated by Show
Motion, Inc., Milford, CT. Scenery automation and show
control by Show Motion, Inc., Milford, CT, using the AC2
computerized motion control system. Lighting equipment
from PRG Lighting. Sound equipment from Sound
Associates. Flame treatment: Turning Star Inc. Specialty
props: Craig Grigg. Bridal wear supplied by Jane Wilson-
Marquis. Rehearsed at the Roundabout Rehearsal Studios.
Special thanks to Brooks Brothers and Solstiss Lace. "Till
There Was You," by Meredith Willson. Used by permission
of Frank Music Corp. and Meredith Willson Music, LLC
(ASCAP).

Earlier versions of *George Is Dead* were presented at the
George Street Playhouse and the Arizona Theatre
Company.

www.RelativelySpeakingBroadway.com

➤N◄
NEDERLANDER

Chairman	**James M. Nederlander**
President	**James L. Nederlander**

Executive Vice President
Nick Scandalios

Vice President	Senior Vice President
Corporate Development	Labor Relations
Charlene S. Nederlander	**Herschel Waxman**

Vice President	Chief Financial Officer
Jim Boese	**Freida Sawyer Belviso**

STAFF FOR THE BROOKS ATKINSON THEATRE
Theatre Manager .... Susan Martin
Treasurer .... Peter Attanasio
Associate Treasurer .... Elaine Amplo
House Carpenter .... Thomas Lavaia
Flyman .... Joe Maher
House Electrician .... Manuel Becker
House Propman .... Joseph P. DePaulo
House Engineer .... Reynold Barriteau

The Road to Mecca

First Preview: December 16, 2011. Opened: January 17, 2012.
Closed March 4, 2012 after 34 Previews and 56 Performances.

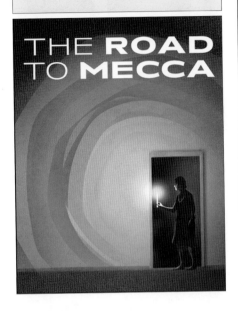

PLAYBILL

THE ROAD TO MECCA

An aging female sculptor attempts to remain vibrant and independent as age creeps up on her, and two friends advocate very different visions of her future.

CAST
(in order of appearance)

Miss Helen .... ROSEMARY HARRIS
Elsa Barlow .... CARLA GUGINO
Marius Byleveld .... JIM DALE

PLACE & TIME

The action takes place in the small Karoo village of
New Bethesda, South Africa,
autumn 1974.

UNDERSTUDIES

For Marius Byleveld:
MARTIN LaPLATNEY
For Miss Helen:
GORDANA RASHOVICH
For Elsa Barlow:
KAREN WALSH

Production Stage Manager:
ROY HARRIS
Stage Manager:
DENISE YANEY

AMERICAN AIRLINES THEATRE

ROUNDABOUTTHEATRECOMPANY

Todd Haimes, Artistic Director
Harold Wolpert, Managing Director
Julia C. Levy, Executive Director

Presents

Rosemary Harris   Carla Gugino

and

Jim Dale

in

THE ROAD TO MECCA

By

Athol Fugard

Set Design	*Costume Design*	*Lighting Design*	*Original Music and Sound Design*
Michael Yeargan	Susan Hilferty	Peter Kaczorowski	John Gromada
Hair & Wig Design	*Dialect Coach*	*Production Stage Manager*	*Production Management*
Paul Huntley	Barbara Rubin	Roy Harris	Aurora Productions
Casting		*General Manager*	*Press Representative*
Jim Carnahan, C.S.A. & Stephen Kopel		Denise Cooper	Boneau/Bryan-Brown

Associate Managing Director	*Director of Marketing & Sales Promotion*	*Director of Development*	*Founding Director*	*Adams Associate Artistic Director**
Greg Backstrom	David B. Steffen	Lynne Gugenheim Gregory	Gene Feist	Scott Ellis

Directed by

Gordon Edelstein

Produced by Special Arrangement with Signature Theatre Company.

Originally Produced by Yale Repertory Theatre, Lloyd Richards, Artistic Director
Major support for *The Road to Mecca* provided by Beth and Ravenel Curry.
*Generously underwritten by Margot Adams, in memory of Mason Adams.
Roundabout Theatre Company is a member of the League of Resident Theatres.
www.roundabouttheatre.org

1/16/12

(L-R): Jim Dale,
Carla Gugino,
Rosemary Harris

The Road to Mecca

Rosemary Harris
Miss Helen

Carla Gugino
Elsa Barlow

Jim Dale
Marius Byleveld

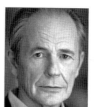

Martin LaPlatney
u/s Marius Byleveld

Gordana Rashovich
u/s Miss Helen

Karen Walsh
u/s Elsa Barlow

Athol Fugard
Playwright

Gordon Edelstein
Director

Michael Yeargan
Set Design

Susan Hilferty
Costume Design

Peter Kaczorowski
Lighting Design

John Gromada
*Original Music and
Sound Design*

Barbara Rubin
Dialect Coach

Paul Huntley
*Hair and Wig
Designer*

Jim Carnahan
Casting

Gene Feist
*Founding Director
Roundabout Theatre
Company*

Todd Haimes,
*Artistic Director
Roundabout Theatre
Company*

(L-R): Rosemary Harris,
Carla Gugino

Photo by Joan Marcus

Photo by Brian Mapp

BOX OFFICE
(L-R): Robert Morgan, Solangel Bido, Ted Osborne, Mead Margulies

The Road to Mecca

CREW
(L-R): Kat Martin, Dale Carman, Colyn Fiendel, Denise Yaney, Dann Wojnar, Glenn Merwede, Bobby Dowling, Brian Maiuri, Hannah Overton

ROUNDABOUT THEATRE COMPANY STAFF
ARTISTIC DIRECTOR ....TODD HAIMES
MANAGING DIRECTOR ....HAROLD WOLPERT
EXECUTIVE DIRECTOR ....JULIA C. LEVY
ADAMS ASSOCIATE
   ARTISTIC DIRECTOR ....SCOTT ELLIS

ARTISTIC STAFF
DIRECTOR OF ARTISTIC DEVELOPMENT/
   DIRECTOR OF CASTING ....Jim Carnahan
Artistic Consultant ....Robyn Goodman
Resident Director ....Doug Hughes
Associate Artists ....Mark Brokaw, Scott Elliott,
   Sam Gold, Bill Irwin, Joe Mantello,
   Kathleen Marshall, Theresa Rebeck
Literary Manager ....Jill Rafson
Senior Casting Director ....Carrie Gardner
Casting Director ....Stephen Kopel
Casting Associate ....Jillian Cimini
Casting Assistant ....Michael Morlani
Artistic Associate ....Amy Ashton
Literary Associate ....Josh Fiedler
The Blanche and Irving Laurie Foundation
   Theatre Visions Fund
      Commissions.......................David West Read,
       Nathan Louis Jackson
Educational Foundation of
   America Commissions ....Bekah Brunstetter,

      Lydia Diamond, Diana Fithian,
       Julie Marie Myatt
New York State Council
   on the Arts Commission ....Nathan Louis Jackson
Roundabout Commissions ....Helen Edmundson,
   Andrew Hinderaker, Stephen Karam,
   Steven Levenson, Matthew Lopez,
   Kim Rosenstock
Casting Interns ....Kyle Eberlein, Nick Gereffi,
   Rebecca Henning, Rachel Lee
Script Readers ....Jay Cohen, Shannon Deep,
   Ben Izzo, Alexis Roblan
Artistic Apprentice ....Joshua M. Feder

EDUCATION STAFF
EDUCATION DIRECTOR ....Greg McCaslin
Associate Education Director ....Jennifer DiBella
Education Program Manager ....Aliza Greenberg
Education Program Associate ....Sarah Malone
Education Assistant ....Holly Sansom
Education Dramaturg ....Ted Sod
Teaching Artists ....Josh Allen, Cynthia Babak,
   Victor Barbella, LaTonya Borsay,
   Mark Bruckner, Eric C. Dente, Joe Doran,
   Elizabeth Dunn-Ruiz, Carrie Ellman-Larsen,
   Deanna Frieman, Sheri Graubert, Melissa Gregus,
   Adam Gwon, Devin Haqq, Carrie Heitman,
   Karla Hendrick, Jason Jacobs, Alana Jacoby,

   Lisa Renee Jordan, Jamie Kalama, Alvin Keith,
   Erin McCready, James Miles, Nick Moore,
   Meghan O'Neil, Nicole Press, Leah Reddy,
   Amanda Rehbein, Nick Simone, Joe Skowronski,
   Heidi Stallings, Daniel Sullivan, Carl Tallent,
   Vickie Tanner, Laurine Towler, Jennifer Varbalow,
   Leese Walker, Gail Winar, Chad Yarborough
Teaching Artist Emeritus ....Reneé Flemings
Education Apprentice ....Kimberley Oria

EXECUTIVE ADMINISTRATIVE STAFF
ASSOCIATE MANAGING
   DIRECTOR..............................Greg Backstrom
Assistant Managing Director ....Katharine Croke
Assistant to the Managing Director ....Zachary Baer
Assistant to the Executive Director ....Nicole Tingir

MANAGEMENT/ADMINISTRATIVE STAFF
GENERAL MANAGER.......................Sydney Beers
General Manager,
   American Airlines Theatre................Denise Cooper
General Manager, Steinberg Center ....Rachel E. Ayers
Human Resources Director ....Stephen Deutsch
Operations Manager ....Valerie D. Simmons
Associate General Manager ....Maggie Cantrick
Office Manager ....Scott Kelly
Archivist ....Tiffany Nixon

The Road to Mecca

FINANCE STAFF
DIRECTOR OF FINANCE.................Susan Neiman
Payroll Director ....John LaBarbera
Accounts Payable Manager ....Frank Surdi
Payroll Benefits Administrator ....Yonit Kafka
Manager Financial Reporting ....Joshua Cohen
Business Office Assistant.....................Jackie Verbitski
Business Apprentice ....Kimberly Lucia

DEVELOPMENT STAFF
DIRECTOR OF
DEVELOPMENT ....Lynne Gugenheim Gregory
Assistant to the
Director of Development ....Liz Malta
Director, Institutional Giving ....Liz S. Alsina
Director, Individual Giving ....Christopher Nave
Associate Director, Individual Giving ....Tyler Ennis
Manager, Telefundraising ....Gavin Brown
Manager, Corporate Relations.................Sohyun Kim
Manager, Friends of Roundabout ....Marisa Perry
Manager, Donor Information Systems ....Lise Speidel
Special Events Associate ....Natalie Corr
Individual Giving Officer ....Joseph Foster
Individual Giving Officer ....Sophia Hinshelwood
Institutional Giving Assistant ....Brett Barbour
Development Assistant ....Martin Giannini
Special Events Assistant ....Amy Rosenfield
Development Apprentice ....Julie Erhart
Special Events Apprentice ....Genevieve Carroll

INFORMATION TECHNOLOGY STAFF
IT Associates ....Jim Roma, Cary Kim
DIRECTOR DATABASE
OPERATIONS ....Wendy Hutton

MARKETING STAFF
DIRECTOR OF MARKETING
AND SALES PROMOTION ....David B. Steffen
Associate Director of Marketing ....Tom O'Connor
Senior Marketing Manager ....Shannon Marcotte
Marketing Associate ....Eric Emch
Marketing Assistant ....Bradley Sanchez
Web Producer ....Mark Cajigao
Web Developer ....Daniel V. Gomez
Website Consultant ....Keith Powell Beyland
Director of Telesales
Special Promotions ....Marco Frezza
Telesales Manager ....Patrick Pastor
Marketing Apprentices...........................Julie Boor,
Bethany Nothstein

TICKET SERVICES STAFF
DIRECTOR OF
SALES OPERATIONS ....Charlie Garbowski, Jr.
Subscription Manager ....Bill Klemm
Box Office Managers ....Edward P. Osborne,
Jaime Perlman, Krystin MacRitchie,
Nicole Nicholson
Group Sales Manager ....Jeff Monteith
Assistant Box Office Managers ....Robert Morgan,
Joseph Clark, Andrew Clements,
Catherine Fitzpatrick

Assistant Ticket Services Managers ....Robert Kane,
Lindsay Ericson,
Jessica Pruett-Barnett
Customer Services Coordinator ....Thomas Walsh
Ticket Services ....Solangel Bido, Michael Bultman,
Lauren Cartelli, Adam Elsberry,
Joe Gallina, Kara Harrington,
Lindsay Hoffman, Nicki Ishmael,
Kiah Johnson, Kate Longosky,
Michelle Maccarone, Mead Margulies,
Laura Marshall, Chuck Migliaccio,
Carlos Morris, Kaia Rafoss, Josh Rozett,
Ben Schneider, Heather Siebert,
Nalane Singh, Ron Tobia,
Michael Valentine, Hannah Weitzman
Ticket Services Apprentice ....Jennifer Almgreen

SERVICES
Counsel ....Paul, Weiss,
Rifkind, Wharton and Garrison LLP,
Charles H. Googe Jr., Carol M. Kaplan
Counsel ....Rosenberg & Estis
Counsel ....Andrew Lance,
Gibson, Dunn, & Crutcher, LLP
Counsel ....Harry H. Weintraub,
Glick and Weintraub, P.C.
Counsel ....Stroock & Stroock & Lavan LLP
Counsel ....Daniel S. Dokos,
Weil, Gotshal & Manges LLP
Counsel ....Claudia Wagner/
Manatt, Phelps & Phillips, LLP
Immigration Counsel ....Mark D. Koestler and
Theodore Ruthizer
House Physicians ....Dr. Theodore Tyberg,
Dr. Lawrence Katz
House Dentist ....Neil Kanner, D.M.D.
Insurance ....DeWitt Stern Group, Inc.
Accountant ....Lutz & Carr CPAs, LLP
Advertising ....Spotco/
Drew Hodges, Jim Edwards,
Tom Greenwald, Kyle Hall, Josh Fraenkel
Interactive Marketing ....Situation Interactive/
Damian Bazadona, John Lanasa,
Eric Bornemann, Mollie Shapiro
Events Photography.................Anita and Steve Shevett
Production Photographer ....Joan Marcus
Theatre Displays.............King Displays, Wayne Sapper
Lobby Refreshments ....Sweet Concessions
Merchandising ....Spotco Merch/
James Decker

MANAGING DIRECTOR
EMERITUS ....Ellen Richard

Roundabout Theatre Company
231 West 39th Street, New York, NY 10018
(212) 719-9393.

GENERAL PRESS REPRESENTATIVE
BONEAU/BRYAN-BROWN
Adrian Bryan-Brown
Matt Polk   Jessica Johnson   Amy Kass

STAFF FOR THE ROAD TO MECCA
Company Manager ....Carly DiFulvio
Production Stage Manager ....Roy Harris
Stage Manager ....Denise Yaney

Production Management by ......Aurora Productions Inc./
Gene O'Donovan, Ben Heller,
Stephanie Sherline, Jarid Sumner,
Anthony Jusino, Anita Shah,
Liza Luxenberg, Steven Dalton,
Eugenio Saenz Flores, Isaac Katzanek,
Melissa Mazdra
Assistant Director ....Alexander Greenfield
Associate Scenic Designer ....Lauren Rockman
Assistant Scenic Designer ....Mikiko Suzuki MacAdams
Assistants to Mr. Yeargan ....Jinsun Kim,
Chien-Yu Peng, A. Ram Kim
Associate Costume Designer ....Marina Reti
Assistant Lighting Designers ....Peter Hoerburger,
Keri Thibodeau
Assistant Sound Designer ....Matthew Walsh
Production Properties Supervisor ....Peter Sarafin
Properties Shoppers ....Matt Hodges, Buist Bickley
Production Carpenter ....Glenn Merwede
Production Electrician ....Brian Maiuri
Running Properties ....Robert W. Dowling II
Sound Operator ....Dann Wojnar
Wardrobe Supervisor ....Susan J. Fallon
Dresser ....Kat Martin
Wardrobe Dayworker ....Dale Carman
Hair and Wig Supervisor ....Manuela LaPorte
Production Assistant ....Trisha Henson

CREDITS
Scenery built, painted and electrified by Showmotion, Inc.,
Milford, Connecticut. Additional painting by Scenic Artists
Studios. Additional prop and scenery fabrication by
Sightline Fabricators and Jeremy Lydic. Lighting equipment
by PRG Lighting. Sound equipment by Sound Associates.
Costumes constructed by Giliberto Designs and Euroco
Costumes. Custom knitting by Maria Ficalora. Distressing
by Hochi. Specialty makeup by Ashley Ryan. Special thanks
to Bra*Tenders for hosiery and undergarments.

Makeup provided by M•A•C Cosmetics.

AMERICAN AIRLINES THEATRE STAFF
Company Manager ....Carly DiFulvio
House Carpenter ....Glenn Merwede
House Electrician ....Brian Maiuri
House Properties ....Robert W. Dowling II
House Sound ....Dann Wojnar
IA Apprentice ....Hannah Overton
Wardrobe Supervisor ....Susan J. Fallon
Box Office Manager ....Ted Osborne
Assistant Box Office Manager ....Robert Morgan
House Manager ....Stephen Ryan
Associate House Manager ....Zipporah Aguasvivas
Head Usher ....Crystal Suarez
House Staff ....Lance Andrade, Christopher Busch,
Jeanne Coutant, Anne Ezell,
Denise Furbert, Maria Graves,
Lee Henry, Rebecca Knell,
Taylor Martin, Enrika Nicholas,
Jazmine Perez, Samantha Rivera,
Celia Torres, Alvin Vega, Felisha Whatts
Security ....Julious Russell
Additional Security provided by ....Gotham Security
Maintenance ....Jerry Hobbs, Daniel Pellew,
Sunil Jaggnanan, Neil Singh,
Magali Western
Lobby Refreshments ....Sweet Concessions

The Road to Mecca
SCRAPBOOK

Correspondent: Roy Harris, Production Stage Manager

When we began rehearsals on November 15, 2011, we knew we were in for a wonderful and unique experience. After all, we had three great actors—Rosemary Harris, Jim Dale, and Carla Gugino—two of whom are Tony Award winners, and a great script by the world-renowned South African playwright Athol Fugard. We also knew that we had a huge mountain to climb—many, many words, thankfully all beautiful, spoken by only two actors in the first act and all three in the second. Rehearsals were, frankly, a lot of good old hard work. Director Gordon Edelstein worked through each act beat by beat to discover the whys and wherefores of a South African artist, Miss Helen (Rosemary) who's come to a crossroads in her life. Elsa Barlow (Carla), her young English teacher friend, has driven 800 miles to the village of New Bethesda to help her make a life-changing decision. Helen's pastor Marius Byleveld (Jim) is invited for tea. The second act is a beautifully-paced confrontation between the conservative Afrikaner (the pastor) and the liberal young English teacher. We had a lively time in rehearsal trying to figure out these three remarkable characters.

We opened on Tuesday, January 17, to a rave review from *The New York Times'* Ben Brantley. "Rosemary Harris asks us to look close to find the creative soul within, and with the generosity of a great artist, she rewards us with the illusion that we have discovered the majesty of her character all by ourselves." Carla Gugino is "bracingly vital" and Jim Dale is "first-rate." The other reviews were mostly positive, a number of critics complained that the play is too long, but every critic saw the inherent power within.

Here are answers to some oft-asked questions about Broadway shows. Our favorite opening night gifts were various owls and candles, different sizes and shapes (there were 34 owls on the set and 24 real candles that got lit and extinguished at each performance). Favorite backstage ritual: Carla and Rosemary matching thumbs with stage manager Denise Yaney—they had to do it before every show. Favorite crew and stage managers' pastime at half-hour: "Wheel of Fortune" in the trap room Tuesdays-Fridays. Our favorite snack food: chocolate, adored by everybody in the company. Carla's opening night gift to each of us was a box of heavenly John Kelly Chocolates—dark chocolate with grey French sea salt. Yum! Behavior idiosyncratic to this company: Just as the curtain comes down at the end of the first act, all three actors remain onstage discussing how it went, the audience reaction, what lines were flubbed or forgotten, etc. Stage management had to practically herd them offstage so they could have a proper break. Our favorite therapy: Throat Coat and ginger tea. Throat

1. The cast (L-R): Carla Gugino, Jim Dale and Rosemary Harris, meet the press.
2. Costume designer Susan Hilferty and director Gordon Edelstein at the premiere party.
3. Curtain call on opening night (L-R) Gugino, Harris and Dale.

Coat was the tea that was consumed in both acts. The catchphrase that only the company would recognize: "Ready, steady, go." Rosemary taught us this—it's English in origin. In rehearsals, at the top of each act, the stage manager would say, "Ready, steady, go." The coolest thing about this experience: the chance to work with Rosemary, Jim, Carla, and Mr. Fugard himself, who was with us from the last days of rehearsal all through the preview period and opening night.

The highlight of doing a show at the Roundabout is the Sunday brunches hosted by Susan Fallon, head of wardrobe. Three or four days before each Sunday, Fallon chooses a theme—Waffles Sunday, Omelet Sunday, Breakfast Burritos, and Frittata Sunday, to name a few. Now, these brunches are known all over Broadway. If you work on a show at the Roundabout, you're fortunate to take part. They are phenomenal: three or four kinds of bacon usually fried by production carpenter Glenn Merwede, Fallon makes the main dish

that week right before your eyes, and also supplies hors d'oeuvres, crackers and cheese, and a salad. Actors, understudies, stage managers, et al, bring in anything they like: For instance, Denise Yaney is known all over the Rialto for her deviled eggs and her quiche. Roy Harris will gladly bring in his broccoli cheese cornbread, three ingredient salad (baby spinach, walnuts, and Granny Smith apples with a Dijon vinaigrette dressing), corn pudding—all three of which can be found in his most recent book, *Brunch over Broadway* (Broadway Cares/Equity Fights AIDS). House props Bobby Dowling would often offer various fresh breads from a neighborhood bakery—walnut, raisin, and pecan. And every once in a while, Gordana Rashovich (standby for Rosemary), brought her home-made baklava. Everyone connected to the show is invited—whether you bring something or no. The brunches are a great way to end the week.

A rewarding theatrical experience from beginning to end.

Rock of Ages

First Preview: March 17, 2009. Opened: April 7, 2009.
Still running as of May 31, 2012.

Drew and Sherrie are two starry-eyed kids who arrive in Los Angeles with dreams of becoming long-haired head-banging rock stars, but they have to learn a lot about life—and help save a rock club destined for the wrecker's ball—before their dreams can come true. This musical has an original story but a score of classic 1980s rock hits.

CAST
(in order of appearance)

Lonny	MITCHELL JARVIS
Justice	MICHELE MAIS
Dennis	ADAM DANNHEISSER
Drew	DAN DOMENECH
Sherrie	REBECCA FAULKENBERRY
Father	JEREMY WOODARD
Mother	MICHELE MAIS
Regina	JOSEPHINE ROSE ROBERTS
Mayor	ANDRE WARD
Hertz	BRET TUOMI
Franz	CODY SCOTT LANCASTER
Stacee Jaxx	JEREMY WOODARD
Waitress #1	ERICKA HUNTER
Reporter	EMILY WILLIAMS
Ja'Keith Gill	ANDRE WARD
Record Company Men	MITCHELL JARVIS/ ADAM DANNHEISSER
Sleazy Producer	JOEY CALVERI
Joey Primo	JOEY CALVERI
Candi	JOSEPHINE ROSE ROBERTS
Strip Club DJ	ANDRE WARD
Young Groupie	TESSA ALVES

Continued on next page

THE HELEN HAYES THEATRE

MARTIN MARKINSON   DONALD TICK

MATTHEW WEAVER   CARL LEVIN   JEFF DAVIS   BARRY HABIB   SCOTT PRISAND
MICHAEL COHL   REAGAN SILBER   S2BN ENTERTAINMENT   RELATIVITY MEDIA

in association with

JANET BILLIG RICH   HILLARY WEAVER
CORNER STORE FUND   RYAN KAVANAUGH   TONI HABIB
PAULA DAVIS   SIMON AND STEFANY BERGSON/JENNIFER MALONEY   CHARLES ROLECEK
SUSANNE BROOK   CRAIG COZZA   ISRAEL WOLFSON   SARA MERCER   JAYSON RAITT   MAX GOTTLIEB
MICHAEL MINARIK   DAVID KAUFMAN/JAY FRANKS   MICHAEL WITTLIN   PROSPECT PICTURES
LAURA SMITH/BILL BODNAR   WIN SHERIDAN   HAPPY WALTERS   MICHELE CARO   NEIL CANELL/JAY CANELL   MARIANO TOLENTINO
MARC BELL and THE ARACA GROUP

present

ROCK OF AGES

book by
CHRIS D'ARIENZO

starring
REBECCA FAULKENBERRY   DAN DOMENECH   ADAM DANNHEISSER   CODY SCOTT LANCASTER
MICHELE MAIS   JOSEPHINE ROSE ROBERTS   BRET TUOMI   *with* MITCHELL JARVIS *and* JEREMY WOODARD

TESSA ALVES   JOEY CALVERI   ERICKA HUNTER   TONY LePAGE
RALPH MEITZLER   JENNIFER RIAS   JUSTIN MATTHEW SARGENT   ANDRE WARD   EMILY WILLIAMS

scenery based on an original design by BEOWULF BORITT	*costume design* GREGORY GALE	*lighting design* JASON LYONS	*sound design* PETER HYLENSKI	*projection design* ZAK BOROVAY

hair/wig design TOM WATSON	*make-up design* ANGELINA AVALLONE	*casting* TELSEY + COMPANY	*production stage manager* MATTHEW DICARLO

assistant director ADAM JOHN HUNTER	*associate choreographer* ROBERT TATAD	*associate producer* DAVID GIBBS

general management ROY GABAY	*press representative* THE HARTMAN GROUP	*advertising & marketing* aka	*technical supervisor* TECH PRODUCTION SERVICES

music director HENRY ARONSON	*music coordinator* JOHN MILLER	*original arrangements* DAVID GIBBS

music supervision, arrangements & orchestrations by
ETHAN POPP

choreographed by
KELLY DEVINE

directed by
KRISTIN HANGGI

10/3/11

(L-R): Dan Domenech, Rebecca Faulkenberry

Photo by Paul Kolnik

Rock of Ages

Cast Continued

THE ENSEMBLE
TESSA ALVES, JOEY CALVERI,
ERICKA HUNTER,
ANDRE WARD, EMILY WILLIAMS

OFFSTAGE VOCALS
TONY LePAGE

UNDERSTUDIES
For Sherrie: TESSA ALVES, ERICKA HUNTER
For Drew: CODY SCOTT LANCASTER,
    TONY LePAGE
For Franz: TONY LePAGE,
    JUSTIN MATTHEW SARGENT
For Hertz: TONY LePAGE, RALPH MEITZLER
For Stacee Jaxx/Lonny/Dennis: JOEY CALVERI,
    TONY LePAGE
For Regina/Justice: TESSA ALVES,
    JENNIFER RIAS

SWINGS
TONY LePAGE, RALPH MEITZLER,
JENNIFER RIAS, JUSTIN MATTHEW
SARGENT

DANCE CAPTAIN
JENNIFER RIAS

BAND
Conductor/Keyboard: HENRY ARONSON
Guitar 1: JOEL HOEKSTRA
Guitar 2: TOMMY KESSLER
Drums: JON WEBER
Bass: WINSTON ROYE

Synthesizer Programming: RANDY COHEN
Music Coordinator: JOHN MILLER
Copyist: FIREFLY MUSIC SERVICE/
    BRIAN ALLAN HOBBS

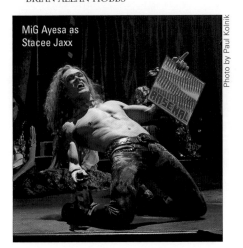

MiG Ayesa as
Stacee Jaxx

Photo by Paul Kolnik

Rebecca
Faulkenberry
Sherrie

Dan Domenech
Drew

Jeremy Woodard
Stacee Jaxx/Father

Mitchell Jarvis
Lonny

Adam Dannheisser
Dennis

Cody Scott Lancaster
Franz

Michele Mais
Justice/Mother

Josephine Rose
Roberts
Regina/Candi

Bret Tuomi
Hertz

Tessa Alves
Ensemble

Joey Calveri
Ensemble

Ericka Hunter
Ensemble

Tony LePage
Swing

Ralph Meitzler
Swing

Jennifer Rias
*Swing, Dance
Captain*

Justin Matthew
Sargent
Swing

Andre Ward
Ensemble

Emily Williams
Ensemble

Chris D'Arienzo
Book

Kristin Hanggi
Director

Rock of Ages

Kelly Devine
Choreographer

Beowulf Boritt
Original Scenery Design

Gregory Gale
Costume Design

Jason Lyons
Lighting Design

Peter Hylenski
Sound Design

Zachary Borovay
Projection Design

Tom Watson
Hair and Wig Design

Angelina Avallone
Make-up Design

Peter Fulbright
Tech Production Services
Technical Supervisor

Ethan Popp
Music Supervisor, Arranger, Orchestrator

John Miller
Music Coordinator

David Gibbs
Original Arrangements/ Guitar

Bernard Telsey
Telsey + Company Casting

Robert Tatad
Associate Choreographer

Adam John Hunter
Associate Director

Roy Gabay
General Manager

Matthew Weaver
Producer

Carl Levin
Producer

Jeff Davis
Producer

Barry Habib
Producer

Scott Prisand
Producer

Michael Cohl
Producer

Ryan Kavanaugh
Relativity Media, LLC (RML)
Producer

Toni Habib
Producer

Stefany Bergson
Producer

Jennifer Maloney
Producer

Jayson Raitt
Producer

Bill Bodnar
Producer

Mariano Tolentino
Producer

Marc Bell
Producer

Michael Rego, Hank Unger and Matthew Rego, The Araca Group
Producer

MiG Ayesa
Staccee Jaxx, Father

Jenifer Foote
Dance Captain, Swing

Rock of Ages

Michael Minarik
Swing

Paul Schoeffler
Hertz

Cassie Silva
Swing

Valerie Stanois
*Dance Captain,
Swing*

Becca Tobin
Swing

Genson Blimline
*Lonny, Record
Company Man*

Jenifer Foote
Swing

Lindsay Janisse
Swing

Michael Minarik
Swing

Emily Padgett
Sherrie

Josh Sassanella
Swing

Paul Schoeffler
Hertz

Ashley Spencer
Sherrie

Valerie Stanois
Swing

Katie Webber
*Waitress #1,
Ensemble*

Neka Zang
Reporter, Ensemble

STAGE MANAGEMENT
(L-R): Justin Scribner,
Matt DiCarlo,
Bryan Bradford

CREW
(L-R): Robert Lindsay,
Bob Etter
Matt Nieski,
Al Toth (House Props),
Joe Moritz,
Doug Purcell (House Carpenter),
Joe Beck (House Electrician)

Rock of Ages

Photo by Brian Mapp

FRONT OF HOUSE

(L-R): Karyn DeAndrade, Shani Murfin, Katherine Angulo, Robin Mates, Kimberley DeAndrade, Mia Fantaci, Anya Aliferis, Natasha Thomas, Berd Vaval, Jackie Munoz, Shykia Fields, Chiyo Sakai, Alan Markinson (House Mgr.), John Biancamano, Linda Maley, Margaret Flanagan, Helene Waldemarson

---

STAFF FOR *ROCK OF AGES*

GENERAL MANAGEMENT
ROY GABAY PRODUCTIONS
Roy Gabay   Mandy Tate
Bruce Kagel   Mark Gagliardi   Vic Kelman

COMPANY MANAGER
Daniel Kuney
Associate Company Manager ....Chris Aniello

GENERAL PRESS REPRESENTATIVE
THE HARTMAN GROUP
Michael Hartman
Leslie Papa   Whitney Holden Gore

CASTING
TELSEY + COMPANY
Bernie Telsey CSA, Will Cantler CSA,
David Vaccari CSA, Bethany Knox CSA,
Craig Burns CSA, Tiffany Little Canfield CSA,
Rachel Hoffman CSA, Justin Huff CSA,
Patrick Goodwin CSA, Abbie Brady-Dalton CSA,
David Morris, Cesar A. Rocha

TECHNICAL SUPERVISOR
TECH PRODUCTION SERVICES
Peter Fulbright
Colleen Houlehen   Mary Duffe
Kaitlyn Anderson

Production Stage Manager ....Matthew DiCarlo
Stage Manager ....Justin Scribner

Assistant Stage Manager ....Heather J. Weiss
Associate Director ....Adam John Hunter
Resident Director ....Adam Dannheisser
Production Manager ....Peter Fulbright
Production Management Associate ......Colleen Houlehen
Associate Scenic Designer ....Jo Winiarski
Assistant Scenic Designers ....Maiko Chii,
                                  Alexis Distler, Buist Bickley
Associate Costume Designer ....Karl Ruckdeschel
Assistant Costume Designers ....Julia Broer,
                                      Colleen Kesterson
Associate Lighting Designer ....Grant Wilcoxen
Assistant Lighting Designer ....Sean Beach
Assistant Lighting Designer ....Driscoll Otto
Assistant to Mr. Lyons ....Zach Pizza
Moving Light Programmer ....Marc Polimeni
Associate Sound Designer ....Keith Caggiano
Assistant Sound Designer ....Drew Levy
Associate Projection Designer ....Daniel Brodie
Assistant Projection Designer ....Austin Switser
Associate Choreographer ....Robert Tatad
Creative Advisor ....Wendy Goldberg
Production Carpenter ....Doug Purcell
Advance Production Carpenter ....Brian Munroe
Production Electrician ....Joseph Beck
Production Sound ....Phil Lojo
Head Mixer ....Robert Etter
Head Propman ....Roger Keller
Wardrobe Supervisor ....Wendall Goings
Dressers ....Michael Goodmark, Timothy Hanlon,
                                          Stacey Haynes
Stitcher/Laundry ....Pierre Parisi

Daywork/Band Dresser ....Thom Carlson
Hair & Wig Supervisor ....Renee Kelly
Production Assistant ....Shelley Miles
Production Intern ....Ashley Zednick
Script Supervisor ....Justin Mabardi
Executive for
   Corner Store Entertainment ....Tom Pelligrini
Production Associate ....Rebecca Breithaupt
Assistant to Mr. Levin ....Alexandra Bisker
Music Director/Conductor ....Henry Aronson
Music Coordinator ....John Miller
Assistant to John Miller ....Nichole Jennino
Production Vocal Coach ....Liz Caplan
Synthesizer Programmer ....Randy Cohen
Music Copying/
   Music Preparation ....Anixter Rice Music Service
Advertising & Marketing ....aka/
               Scott A. Moore, Clint Bond, Jr.,
               Liz Furze, Joshua Lee Poole,
               Janette Roush, Adam Jay,
         Jenna Bissonnette, Jacob Matsumiya
Internet Marketing and Strategy 87AM/
               Adam Cunningham, Lisa Egan,
                          Alexandra Bisker
Press Associates ....Katie Britton, Nicole Capatasto,
                   Tom D'Ambrosio, Juliana Hannett,
            Bethany Larsen, Emily McGill, Matt Ross,
                   Frances White, Wayne Wolfe
Production Photography ....Joan Marcus
Insurance ....Ventura Insurance Brokerage/
                                          Tick and Co.

Rock of Ages

Legal Counsel ....Sendroff and Baruch, LLP/
    Jason Baruch
Banking ....City National Bank
Payroll Service ....Checks and Balances
Accounting ....Fried & Kowgios Partners, CPAs, LLP
Bookkeeper ....Galbraith & Company
Additional New York
    Rehearsal ....Manhattan Theatre Club
Group Sales ....Broadway Inbound

CREDITS AND ACKNOWLEDGEMENTS

Avalon Salon & Day Spa, Gibson, Ernie Ball, Baldwin Piano, Vic Firth, Vans and The Spoon Group. Audio and video provided by PRG Secaucus. Scenery and automation by Showmotion, Inc., Milford, CT. Lighting equipment from Hudson/Christie Lighting, Mimi Bilinski. Costumes constructed by Jennifer Love Costumes. Custom leatherwear by www.rawhides.com. Shoes and boots constructed by T.O. Dey and Worldtone. Fabric painting and costume crafts by Jeffrey Fender. Hosiery and undergarments by Bra*Tenders. Keyboards by Yamaha. Additional scenery by Daddy-O. Dany Margolies

A special thanks to Trash and Vaudeville
for the rock 'n' roll gear.

MUSIC CREDITS

"Anyway You Want It" written by Steve Perry and Neal Schon. © Published by Lacey Boulevard Music and Weed High Nightmare Music.

"Beaver Hunt" written by David Gibbs and Chris Hardwick. Published by Feed the Pony Songs and Fish Ladder, Inc. (BMI).

"Can't Fight This Feeling" written by Kevin Cronin. © Published by Fate Music (ASCAP).

"Cum on Feel the Noize" written by Neville Holder and James Lea. © Barn Publishing (Slade) Ltd.

"Don't Stop Believin'" written by Jonathan Cain, Stephen Ray Perry, Neal J. Schon © Published by Weed High Nightmare Music and Lacey Boulevard Music.

"Every Rose Has Its Thorn" written by Bobby Dall, Bruce Anthony Johannesson, Bret Michael, Rikki Rocket. © All rights owned or administered by Universal Music-Z Songs on behalf of Cyanide Publ./BMI. Used by permission.

"The Final Countdown" written by Joey Tempest. © Screen Gems-EMI Music Inc.

"Harden My Heart" written by Marvin Webster Ross. © 1980 WB Music Corp. (ASCAP), Narrow Dude Music (ASCAP) and Bonnie Bee Good Music. All rights administered by WB Music Corp. All rights reserved. Used by permission.

"Heat of the Moment" written by Geoffrey Downes and John K. Wetton. © 1982 WB Music Corp. (ASCAP), Almond Legg Music Corp (ASCAP) and Pallan Music. All rights on behalf of itself and Almond Legg Music Corp. administered by WB Music Corp. All rights reserved. Used by permission.

"Heaven" written by Jani Lane, Erik Turner, Jerry Dixon, Steven Sweet and Joey Allen ©.

"Here I Go Again" written by David Coverdale and Bernard Marsden. © 1982 C.C. Songs Ltd. (PRS) and Seabreeze Music Ltd. Administered by WB Music Corp. (ASCAP). All rights reserved. Used by permission.

"High Enough" written by Jack Blades, Ted Nugent and Tommy R. Shaw. © Published by Bicycle Music Company, Broadhead Publishing and Wixen Music.

"Hit Me With Your Best Shot" written by E. Schwartz. © Sony/ATV Tunes LLC/ASCAP.

"I Hate Myself for Loving You" written by Desmond Child and Joan Jett. © All rights owned or administered by Universal-PolyGram Int. Publ., Inc./ASCAP. Used by permission.

"I Wanna Rock" written by Daniel Dee Snider. © All rights owned or administered by Universal Music-Z Melodies on behalf of Snidest Music/SESAC. Used by permission.

"I Want to Know What Love Is" written by Michael Leslie Jones. © Published by Somerset Songs Publishing, Inc.

"Just Like Paradise" written by David Lee Roth and Brett Tuggle. © Diamond Dave Music c/o RS Plane Music.

"Keep on Lovin' You" written by Kevin Cronin. © Published by Fate Music (ASCAP).

"Kiss Me Deadly" written by Mick Smiley. © Published by The Twin Towers Co. and Mike Chapman Publishing Enterprises.

"More Than Words" written by Nuno Bettencourt and Gary F. Cherone. © All rights owned or administered by Almo Music Corp. on behalf of Color Me Blind Music/ASCAP. Used by permission.

"Nothin' But a Good Time" written by Bobby Dall, Bruce Anthony Johannesson, Bret Michaels, Rikki Rocket. © All rights owned or administered by Universal Music-Z Songs on behalf of Cyanide Publ./BMI. Used by permission.

"Oh Sherrie" written by Steve Perry, Randy Goodrum, Bill Cuomo, Craig Krampf. © Published by Street Talk Tunes, April Music Inc & Random Notes, Pants Down Music and Phosphene Music.

"Renegade" written by Tommy Shaw. © All rights owned or administered by Almo Music Corp. on behalf of itself and Stygian Songs /ASCAP. Used by permission.

"The Search Is Over" written by Frank Sullivan and Jim Peterik. © Published by Ensign Music LLC (BMI). Used by permission. All rights reserved.

"Shadows of the Night" written by D.L. Byron. © Zen Archer/ASCAP.

"Sister Christian" written by Kelly Keagy. © Published by Bicycle Music Company.

"To Be With You" written by David Grahame and Eric Martin. ©EMI April Music, Inc. obo itself, Dog Turner Music and Eric Martin Songs (ASCAP).

"Too Much Time on My Hands" written by Tommy Shaw. © Stygian Songs/ASCAP.

"Waiting for a Girl Like You" written by Michael Leslie Jones and Louis Gramattico. © Published by Somerset Songs Publishing, Inc.

"Wanted Dead or Alive" written by Jon Bon Jovi and Richard S. Sambora. © All rights owned or administered by Universal-Polygram Int. Publ., Inc. on behalf of itself and Bon Jovi Publishing/ASCAP. Used by permission.

"We Built This City" written by Dennis Lambert, Martin George Page, Bernie Taupin and Peter Wolf. © All rights owned or administered by Universal-Polygram Int. Publ., Inc. on behalf of Little Mole Music Inc./ASCAP. Used by permission.

"We're Not Gonna Take It" written by Daniel Dee Snider. © All rights owned or administered by Universal Music-Z Melodies on behalf of Snidest Music/SESAC. Used by permission.

THE HELEN HAYES THEATRE STAFF

Owned and Operated by Little Theatre Group LLC
Martin Markinson and Jeffrey Tick

General Manager and Counsel ....Susan S. Myerberg
House Manager ....Alan R. Markinson
Engineer ....Hector Angulo
Treasurer ....David Heveran
Assoc. Gen. Manager ....Sharon Fallon
Assistant Treasurer ....Kenny Klein
Head Ushers ....Linda Maley, Berd Vaval,
    John Biancamano
Stage Door ....Ernest J. Paylor, Jonathan Angulo,
    Anthony Bethea
Accountant ....Chen-Win Hsu, CPA, PC
Intern ....Jacqueline Munoz

Helen Hayes Theatre is a proud member of the
Broadway Green Alliance

HEAD DOORMAN
Ernest Paylor

BOX OFFICE
Kenneth Klein

Photos by Brian Mapp

Rock of Ages
Scrapbook

Members of the cast rock out on the set.

Photo by Paul Kolnik

Correspondent: Tony LePage, Swing

Milestone: In November 2011, *Rock of Ages* celebrated becoming the 100th longest running show on Broadway! And we've been climbing the ladder fast ever since, and loving every second.

Understudy Anecdote: I think being a swing in this show is so much fun. The most I've done in a week is five different roles. It is particularly weird playing Hertz then Franz, father then son. There are voices in my head.

Most Exciting Celebrity Visitor: Jim Carrey was in with his family. We were so pumped! He said he loved the show and had a great time. It was so cool to see him laughing at what we did instead of the other way around.

Actor Who Performs the Most Roles in This Show: As a swing, I guess that would be me. I have now performed all eight male roles in the show: Drew, Lonny, Dennis, Franz, Hertz, Stacee Jaxx, The Mayor/JaKeith and Joey Primo. I love this job!

Actor Who Has Done the Most Performances in This Show: I think it would be Michele Mais, or "Maisey" as she is known. She has been in *Rock of Ages* since it began in Los Angeles, then Off-Broadway, and is still rockin' it every night.

Favorite Moment During Each Performance: There is something special about the intro to "Don't Stop Believin'." No matter how many times you perform it—when the piano starts, the audience roars, and the lighters go up, that's pretty magical.

Favorite In-Theatre Gathering Place: We love to get together in the greenroom and eat our lunch, watch football, and laugh…a lot. This cast is so close-knit and I would have it no other way!

Favorite Off-Site Hangout: We all go to The Glass House Tavern if we're in the mood for a post show "watering."

Favorite Snack Foods: I can't eat enough trail mix. The other thing is, somebody is always baking something. I don't know how it happens, but it's amazing! There is a constant flow of food in the greenroom: cookies, cupcakes…. Sensational stuff!

Mascot: No actual mascots, but if there was one it would have to be the baby llama. What's not to love about a baby llama?

Favorite Therapies: Ricolas, Bio Freeze and Jack Daniels.

Memorable Ad-Lib: Adam Dannheisser (hilarious individual): Someone was talking during a scene, and without missing a beat, he tells the audience member, "Looks like we need some more duct tape." The audience lost it… perfect!

Cell Phone Rings, Cell Phone Photos or Texting Incidents During a Performance: We have a pretty funny and "to the point" pre-show announcement, telling people that texting during the show makes them look like a "douchebag." So, that usually takes care of it.

Memorable Stage Door Fan Encounter: I was on for Lonny one night, covering Mitch Jarvis, and this guy came up to me and wanted a picture. He just kept yelling: Keith Stone!! I of course am not Mitch Jarvis (the spokesperson for Keystone beer—a.k.a. Keith Stone). So I told him I was the understudy, and the guy looked at me, paused and said, "Yeah… I'm still gonna tell my friends I saw Keith Stone."

Web Buzz: So exciting, especially with the movie coming out June 2012. Lots of great press everywhere! We got to perform on New Year's Eve in Times Square, and the Super Bowl Parade, so there are so many great YouTube videos to check out.

Fastest Costume Change: I would have to say that one goes to Franz. It happens onstage, and it is a tear away business suit into sparkly leotard situation and takes about 1 second. Off-stage, the girls have about a million, but Franz has the quickest one.

Busiest Day at the Box Office: We had our best week to date during Christmas when we broke the Helen Hayes Box Office record, I think we sold at 99 percent. The numbers were through the roof. It was so exciting to have such packed houses, and it continued all through the winter!

Heaviest/Hottest Costume: *Rock of Ages* has a few heavy ones. The "Wolfgang Von Colt" jacket that Drew wears is abnormally heavy. I think it's made of lead and sand and stitched with zinc, then soaked in lava.

Who Wore the Least: God love the girls of *Rock of Ages*! Not much is left to the imagination there, but they are all so beautiful and confident that it looks so amazing.

Sweethearts Within the Company: There are no relationships within the company, but there are a bunch of "crushes" for sure. I guess we all just get along so well, we love spending time together.

Memorable Directorial Note: Every once in a while you catch hysterical sound bites: "When you make out with the llama, could you cheat your face out?" "Could you try to shoot the panties further into the audience?" You know, stuff like that.

Tale From the Put-in: When Genson Blimline joined the cast, we were doing the opening number, and when he went into a slow, full split, the entire cast lost it! (And we still do during performances on occasion!)

Nicknames: E Wills, Marquez Revolanche, Adam "The Bear" Dannheisser (softball MVP reference), Mama Maisey.

Embarrassing Moments: When you have a cast full of mullets and fishnets and baby llamas… oh my…there is little that can happen to embarrass, but the audience can get pretty wild. As Stacee Jaxx stumbles his way through the audience in Act II, the ladies can get pretty aggressive! Good times!

Coolest Thing About Being in This Show: Doing this show is the most fun I have ever had! The cast members are all close friends and so incredible to be around. The show is hysterical and so easy to love, day in and day out and the music is the greatest! There is only one thing we can't do at *Rock of Ages*…lose.

Seminar

First Preview: October 27, 2011. Opened: November 20, 2011.
Closed: May 6, 2012 after 25 Previews and 191 Performances.

A group of young writers hires a former novelist as a private tutor. He turns out to be abrasive, insulting, crude and sexist—but he quickly sorts out the talented from the untalented and begins to encourage the seeming least of them toward greatness.

CAST
(in order of speaking)

Douglas .... JERRY O'CONNELL
Martin .... HAMISH LINKLATER
Kate .... LILY RABE
Izzy .... HETTIENNE PARK
Leonard .... ALAN RICKMAN

Alan Rickman is appearing with the permission of Actors' Equity Association.

STANDBYS
For Leonard: ROCCO SISTO
For Kate and Izzy: CHRISTINA PUMARIEGA
For Martin and Douglas: MATTHEW GREER

2011-2012 AWARD

THEATRE WORLD AWARD
For Outstanding Broadway
or Off-Broadway Debut
(Hettienne Park)

GOLDEN THEATRE
A Shubert Organization Theatre

Philip J. Smith, *Chairman*   Robert E. Wankel, *President*

Jeffrey Finn   Jill Furman

John N. Hart Jr. & Patrick Milling Smith

Roy Furman   David Ian   David Mirvish   Amy Nauiokas   James Spry

present

ALAN RICKMAN

in

SEMINAR

by

THERESA REBECK

Starring

LILY RABE   HAMISH LINKLATER
JERRY O'CONNELL   HETTIENNE PARK

Scenic & Costume Design	Lighting Design	Original Music & Sound Design
David Zinn	Ben Stanton	John Gromada

Casting	Press Representative	Advertising & Marketing	Production Manager
MelCap Casting	The Publicity Office	Serino/Coyne	Peter Fulbright

Production Stage Manager	Associate Producers	Executive Producer/General Manager
Charles Means	Matthew Schneider	101 Productions, Ltd.
	Wake Up Marconi	
	Jamie Kaye-Phillips	
	Charles Stone/Ben Limberg	

Directed by

SAM GOLD

The Producers wish to express their appreciation to the Theatre Development Fund for its support of this production. 11/20/11

(Center): Alan Rickman and the Company

Photo by Jeremy Daniel

Seminar

Alan Rickman
Leonard

Lily Rabe
Kate

Hamish Linklater
Martin

Jerry O'Connell
Douglas

Hettienne Park
Izzy

Rocco Sisto
Standby for Leonard

Christina Pumariega
Standby for Kate & Izzy

Matthew Greer
Standby for Martin & Douglas

Theresa Rebeck
Playwright

Sam Gold
Director

David Zinn
Scenic & Costume Designer

John Gromada
Original Music & Sound Designer

Wendy Orshan
101 Productions, Ltd
General Manager

Jeffrey Finn
Producer

Jill Furman
Producer

John N. Hart Jr.
Producer

Roy Furman
Producer

David Ian
Producer

David Mirvish
Producer

Charles Stone
Associate Producer

TRANSFER STUDENTS

Jeff Goldblum
Leonard

Zoe Lister-Jones
Kate

Justin Long
Martin

Hamish Linklater and Lily Rabe

Photo by Jeremy Daniel

Seminar

STAGE MANAGEMENT
Charles Means, Lisa Buxbaum

BOX OFFICE
Chip Jorgensen, Diane Lettieri

WARDROBE
Robert Guy, Tree Sarvay

Photos by Brian Mapp

CREW
Front Row (Seated L-R): Tree Sarvay, Lisa Buxbaum, Brad Gyorgak

Back Row (L-R): Rob Presley, Sylvia Yoshioka, Terry McGarty, Matt Maloney, Brian McGarty

Seminar

FRONT OF HOUSE STAFF
Back Row (L-R): Lars Jorgensen, Joyce Lumpkin, Brian Aviles, Patricia Byrne, Helen Bentley, Sheila Staffney, Susan Ann Treacy
Front Row (L-R): Yolanda Ayala, Jane Van Gelder, Thomas Jarus, Carolyne Jones-Barnes, Rita Russell, John Seid

STAFF FOR *SEMINAR*

GENERAL MANAGEMENT
101 PRODUCTIONS, LTD.
Wendy Orshan   Jeffrey M. Wilson
David Auster
Elie Landau

COMPANY MANAGER
Barbara Crompton

GENERAL PRESS REPRESENTATIVE
THE PUBLICITY OFFICE
Marc Thibodeau   Michael S. Borowski
Jeremy Shaffer

PRODUCTION MANAGER
TECH PRODUCTION SERVICES, INC.
Peter Fulbright   Mary Duffe
Colleen Houlehen   Sheena Crespo

CASTING
MELCAP CASTING
David Caparelliotis   Mele Nagler
Lauren Port   Christina Wright   Felicia Rudolph

Production Stage Manager	Charles Means
Stage Manager	Lisa Buxbaum
Assistant Director	Portia Krieger
Associate Set Designer	Josh Zangen
Associate Costume Designer	Jacob A. Climer
Associate Lighting Designer	Ken Elliott
Associate Sound Designer	Alex Neumann
Assistant Costume Designer	Matthew Simonelli
Assistant to the Set Designer	Michael Simmons
Assistant to the Costume Designer	Stefanie Genda
Production Props	Buist Bickley
Prop Shopper	Sarah Gosnell
Prop Painter	Emily Walsh
Prop Upholstery	Julia Sandy

Production Carpenter	Paul Wimmer
Production Electrician	Thomas Lawrey
Head Props	Rob Presley
Head Sound	Wayne Smith
House Carpenter	Terry McGarty
House Flyman	Thomas Anderson

House Electrician	Sylvia Yoshioka
House Properties	Leah Nelson
Wardrobe Supervisor	Robert Guy
Dressers	John Robelen, Tree Sarvay

Legal Counsel	Sendroff & Baruch, LLP/ Jason Baruch
Accountant	Fried & Kowgios/Robert Fried
Controller	Galbraith & Co Inc./Kenny Noth
Advertising	Serino/Coyne/ Sandy Block, Angelo Desimini, Matt Upshaw, Ryan Cunningham, Doug Ensign, Lauren Houlberg
Digital Outreach & Website	Serino/Coyne/ Jim Glaub, Chip Meyrelles, Laurie Connor, Kevin Keating, Whitney Creighton, Joe Reckley
Marketing & Opening Night Event	Serino/Coyne/ Leslie Barrett, Ian Weiss, Suzanne Tobak, Chrisann Gasparro
101 Productions, Ltd. Staff	Ashley Berman, Beth Blitzer, Thom Clay, Clinton Kennedy, Kathy Kim, Michael Rudd, Mary Six Rupert
101 Productions, Ltd. Intern	Annora Brennan
Press Intern	Lauren Wolman
Banking	City National Bank/ Anne McSweeney
Insurance	Tanenbaum Harber of Florida/ Carol Bressi-Cilona
Immigration	Visa Consultants/Lisa Carr Traffic Control Group/David King
Theatre Displays	King Displays, Inc.
Payroll Services	Castellana Services, Inc.
Production Photographer	Jeremy Daniel

CREDITS
Scenery built by ShowMotion, Inc. Lighting by PRG. Sound by Masque Sound. Custom furniture by SFDS. Music produced at OK Records, Nyack, NY; Greg Talenfeld, engineer. Special thanks to Bra*Tenders for hosiery and undergarments, Derek Lam Optics and Brett Anderson at Dockers.

Seminar rehearsed at Ballet Hispanico Studios.

SPECIAL THANKS
Nathan Gehan, Chris Morey, Ron Gubin,
Brett Anderson, Bobby Lucy,
Joseph Lembo, Laurence Waltman,
Story Fund LLC

AUTHOR'S THANKS
The author wishes to thank Jen Ikeda, Peter Scanavione, Rocco Sisto, Greg Keller and Zoe Lister-Jones.

www.SeminarOnBroadway.com

Energy-efficient washer/dryer courtesy of
LG Electronics.

THE SHUBERT ORGANIZATION, INC.
Board of Directors

Philip J. Smith	**Robert E. Wankel**
Chairman	President
Wyche Fowler, Jr.	**Dana Phillips**
Lee J. Seidler	**Michael I. Sovern**
Stuart Subotnick	

Elliot Greene	**David Andrews**
Chief Financial Officer	Senior Vice President Shubert Ticketing
Juan Calvo	**John Darby**
Vice President – Finance	Vice President – Facilities
Peter Entin	**Charles Flateman**
Vice President – Theatre Operations	Vice President – Marketing
Anthony LaMattina	**Brian Mahoney**
Vice President – Audit & Production Finance	Vice President – Ticket Sales

D.S. Moynihan
Vice President – Creative Projects

House Manager .... Carolyne A. Jones-Barnes

Shatner's World: We Just Live in It...

First Preview: February 14, 2012. Opened: February 16, 2012.
Closed March 4, 2012 after 2 Previews and 17 Performances.

Actor William Shatner, whose career included stints on Broadway, film and TV (notably the "Star Trek" series as Captain Kirk), recalls his life, passions, mistakes and triumphs in this solo show which retraces where his philosophy of "saying yes" has led him.

CAST
WILLIAM SHATNER

PROGRAM NOTE: ABOUT TONIGHT

A one-man show by definition is one man. I know we are all alone in life, and as much as we try to reach out to other people, fall in love, have children and keep social contacts alive, still we are alone and we die alone. Our life is pretty much a one-man show. And yet...we mask it with our flurries of activities and meetings, and texting and jokes and gossip and Pilates, all of it to hide our essential aloneness.

But there's no masking being the only one on stage. Oh God, how I wish I had dancing girls and acrobats, and a couple of timpani would help. But then that is a four-man show. This is me, telling stories. Oh sure, a few projections here and there but hey — it could work without them. Look as hard as you can, you can't find anyone else on stage.

The material needs to be interesting, observant, piquant and hopefully amusing. There needs to be contrast and color and rhythm and tempo. You need to hold the audience's attention. The actor has no aids like plot or conflict and all the essentials of dramatic plays. The lonely performer is responsible for all that.

And what about a little anxiety?

The actor going solo has a little more apprehension than is customary. No matter how many years one is in entertainment, the constant companion is fear of failure. That, my friend, is a cruel task master.

So here we are, the ultimate in theatre. A one-man show on Broadway. What a challenge.

The irony is that a one-man show doesn't come about through one man. There are many others without whom the endeavor would not exist. People like Larry Thompson, Trixstar and Mike Anderson, Spirit Works in Australia, and creative partners like Innovation Arts Entertainment. I am grateful to all of them.

William Shatner

THE MUSIC BOX
239 W. 45th Street
A Shubert Organization Theatre

Philip J. Smith, *Chairman*   **Robert E. Wankel,** *President*

INNOVATION ARTS & ENTERTAINMENT

Adam Troy Epstein   Seth Keyes

LARRY A. THOMPSON ORGANIZATION

Josh Sherman   Larry A. Thompson

Present

William Shatner
in

SHATNER'S WORLD
we just live in it...

Scenic Design	Lighting Design	Sound Design
EDWARD PIERCE	KEN BILLINGTON	PETER FITZGERALD

Press Representative	Advertising
BONEAU/BRYAN-BROWN	SPOTCO

Technical Supervisor	General Management	Production Stage Manager
AURORA PRODUCTIONS	BESPOKE THEATRICALS	PAUL J. SMITH

Directed by
SCOTT FARIS

2/16/12

William Shatner with a projected portrait of himself as Captain Kirk.

Photo by Joan Marcus

Shatner's World: We Just Live in It...

William Shatner

Photo by Joan Marcus

William Shatner

Scott Faris
Director

Edward Pierce
Scenic Design

Ken Billington
Lighting Design

Larry A. Thompson
Organization
Producer

Maggie Brohn
Bespoke Theatricals
General Manager

Amy Jacobs
Bespoke Theatricals
General Manager

Devin Keudell
Bespoke Theatricals
General Manager

Nina Lannan
Bespoke Theatricals
General Manager

BOX OFFICE
Robert D. Kelly, Bryan P. Cobb

Photos by Brian Mapp

CREW
(Clockwise from left:) Dennis Maher, Paul J. Smith, Gerald Stein Jr.,
William K. Rowland, John R. Carlotto, Kim Garnett, Heidi Neven

FRONT OF HOUSE STAFF
Front Row (L-R): Lottie Dennis,
Joseph Spezzano, Michael Concepcion,
Kenneth Kelley

Back Row (L-R): Jenna Scanlon,
Dennis Scanlon, Francis T. Sanabria,
John Seid, Jonathan Shulman

Missing: Joe Amato, Nick Fusco, John Himmel,
Thomas Murdoch, Edith Rosado,
Laura Scanlon

Shatner's World: We Just Live in It...

Scrapbook

Photo by Joseph Marzullo/WENN

1. William Shatner arrives with his wife Elizabeth Shatner for the opening night party at Sardi's restaurant.
2. Taking a bow at the premiere.
3. Shatner with director Scott Faris at Sardi's.

STAFF FOR *SHATNER'S WORLD*

GENERAL MANAGEMENT
BESPOKE THEATRICALS
Devin Keudell Amy Jacobs
Maggie Brohn Nina Lannan

COMPANY MANAGER
Heidi Neven

GENERAL PRESS REPRESENTATIVE
BONEAU/BRYAN-BROWN
Adrian Bryan-Brown Jackie Green
Michael Strassheim

PRODUCTION MANAGEMENT
AURORA PRODUCTIONS
Gene O'Donovan, Ben Heller,
Stephanie Sherline, Jarid Sumner,
Liza Luxenberg, Anita Shah, Anthony Jusino,
Steven Dalton, Eugenio Saenz Flores,
Isaac Katzanek, Aneta Feld, Melissa Mazdra

Production Stage Manager .... Paul J. Smith
Production Assistants .... Aaron Elgert, Alison Harma
Associate Lighting Designer .... Anthony Pearson

INNOVATION ARTS & ENTERTAINMENT STAFF

Chief Executive Officer .... Adam Epstein
Vice President/
Director of Programming .... Seth Keyes
Co-Vice President/
Event Marketing & Venue Logistics .... Todd Rossi
Co-Vice President/
Event Marketing & Venue Logistics .... Julie Chepy
Tour Director/
Marketing & Event Logistics .... Jaymes Kaiser
Tour Director/
Marketing & Event Logistics .... Nancy Rebek
Director of Production .... Jason Merder
Director of Accounting .... Lindsey Proper
Director of Design
& Creative Production .... Gina Knapik

Director of Patron Communication &
Ticketing Services .... Christy Warren
Project Manager .... Emily Dehm
Project Manager .... Melissa Buckley
Junior Designer .... Kate Terwilliger
Innovation Touring Group
President .... Josh Sherman

Production Electrician .... Neil McShane

Assistant to Mr. Shatner .... Kathleen Hays
Assistant to Mr. Thompson .... Robert J. Endara II
Advertising .... SPOTCO/Drew Hodges,
Jim Edwards, Tom Greenwald,
Stacey Maya
General Management
Associates .... Steve Dow, Libby Fox,
David Roth, Danielle Saks
General Management Interns .... Michelle Heller,
Jimmy Wilson
Press Associates .... Chris Boneau, Jim Byk,
Joe Perrotta, Matt Polk, Susanne Tighe,
Jessica Johnson, Aaron Meier,
Heath Schwartz, Kelly Guiod, Amy Kass,
Emily Meagher, Christine Olver, Holly Kinney,
Linnae Hodzic, Kevin Jones, Amanda Sales
Travel Agent .... Tzell Travel/The "A" Team,
Andi Henig
Theatre Displays .... King Displays, Inc.
Merchandise .... Max Merchandise, LLC
Video Segment Coordinator .... Ryan Tirrell
Production Photographer .... Joan Marcus

CREDITS

Scenery by Hudson Scenic Studio. Lighting and video equipment from PRG. Sound equipment by Sound Associates. TV commercial produced by Cinevative. Video clips: The American Film Institute, Comedy Central, International Olympic Committee and United States Olympic Committee, McGill University, Le Big Boss Productions, The National Film Board of Canada, NASA and George Takei.

MUSIC CREDITS

Thanks to ShoutFactory!, Brad Paisley, Ben Folds, Alan Wolmark, Adam Hamilton and Cleopatra Records.

Shatner's World originally rehearsed at Roundabout Rehearsal Studios.

www.ShatnersWorld.com

SPECIAL THANKS
Paul Camuso
Chris Cronin
Photos by Elizabeth Shatner
Mr. Shatner wears and thanks Carroll and Co., Beverly Hills

THE SHUBERT ORGANIZATION, INC.
Board of Directors

Philip J. Smith
Chairman

Robert E. Wankel
President

Wyche Fowler, Jr. **Diana Phillips**

Lee J. Seidler **Michael I. Sovern**

Stuart Subotnick

Chief Financial Officer .... Elliot Greene
Sr. Vice President, Ticketing .... David Andrews
Vice President, Finance .... Juan Calvo
Vice President, Human Resources .... Cathy Cozens
Vice President, Facilities .... John Darby
Vice President, Theatre Operations .... Peter Entin
Vice President, Marketing .... Charles Flateman
Vice President, Audit .... Anthony LaMattina
Vice President, Ticket Sales .... Brian Mahoney
Vice President, Creative Projects .... D.S. Moynihan
Vice President, Real Estate .... Julio Peterson

House Manager .... Jonathan Shulman

Sister Act

First Preview: March 24, 2011. Opened: April 20, 2011.
Still running as of May 31, 2012.

PLAYBILL®

A musical comedy adaptation of the 1992 film of the same title, about a nightclub singer on the run from the mob who transforms the lives of a convent full of nuns when she hides out among them.

CAST

(in order of appearance)

Deloris Van Cartier	PATINA MILLER
Michelle	RASHIDRA SCOTT
Tina	ALÉNA WATTERS
Curtis Jackson	KINGSLEY LEGGS
Joey	JOHN TREACY EGAN
Pablo	CAESAR SAMAYOA
TJ	DEMOND GREEN
Ernie	CHRIS BOHANNON
Joey Finnochio	DANNY STILES
Eddie Souther	CHESTER GREGORY
Cop	ALAN H. GREEN
Mother Superior	CAROLEE CARMELLO
Monsignor O'Hara	FRED APPLEGATE
Mary Robert	MARLA MINDELLE
Mary Patrick	SARAH BOLT
Mary Lazarus	AUDRIE NEENAN
Mary Martin-of-tours	TRISHA RAPIER
Mary Theresa	MADELEINE DOHERTY
Waitress	HOLLY DAVIS

ENSEMBLE

JENNIFER ALLEN, CHRIS BOHANNON, CHARL BROWN, HOLLY DAVIS, MADELEINE DOHERTY, ALAN H. GREEN, KIMBERLY MARABLE, MARISSA PERRY, TRISHA RAPIER, RASHIDRA SCOTT,

Continued on next page

⑤BROADWAY THEATRE

1681 Broadway
A Shubert Organization Theatre

Philip J. Smith, *Chairman*   Robert E. Wankel, *President*

WHOOPI GOLDBERG & STAGE ENTERTAINMENT
IN ASSOCIATION WITH
THE SHUBERT ORGANIZATION AND DISNEY THEATRICAL PRODUCTIONS

PRESENT

SISTER ACT

MUSIC	LYRICS	BOOK
ALAN MENKEN	GLENN SLATER	CHERI STEINKELLNER & BILL STEINKELLNER

ADDITIONAL BOOK MATERIAL
DOUGLAS CARTER BEANE

BASED ON THE TOUCHSTONE PICTURES MOTION PICTURE "SISTER ACT" WRITTEN BY JOSEPH HOWARD

STARRING
PATINA MILLER   CAROLEE CARMELLO

WITH

FRED APPLEGATE SARAH BOLT JOHN TREACY EGAN DEMOND GREEN CHESTER GREGORY
KINGSLEY LEGGS MARLA MINDELLE AUDRIE NEENAN CAESAR SAMAYOA

JENNIFER ALLEN CHRIS BOHANNON CHARL BROWN HOLLY DAVIS MADELEINE DOHERTY JACQUI GRAZIANO
ALAN H. GREEN CARRIE A. JOHNSON LOUISE MADISON KIMBERLY MARABLE MARISSA PERRY
ERNIE PRUNEDA TRISHA RAPIER T. OLIVER REID RASHIDRA SCOTT JENNIFER SIMARD
DANNY STILES CHELSEA MORGAN STOCK LAEL VAN KEUREN ROBERTA B. WALL ALÉNA WATTERS

SET DESIGN	COSTUME DESIGN	LIGHTING DESIGN	SOUND DESIGN
KLARA ZIEGLEROVA	LEZ BROTHERSTON	NATASHA KATZ	JOHN SHIVERS

CASTING	WIG AND HAIR DESIGN	PRODUCTION MANAGEMENT	PRODUCTION SUPERVISOR
TELSEY + COMPANY	DAVID BRIAN BROWN	AURORA PRODUCTIONS	STEVEN BECKLER

ORCHESTRATIONS	DANCE MUSIC ARRANGER	MUSIC DIRECTOR	MUSIC COORDINATOR
DOUG BESTERMAN	MARK HUMMEL	BRENT-ALAN HUFFMAN	JOHN MILLER

MUSIC SUPERVISOR, VOCAL AND INCIDENTAL MUSIC ARRANGEMENTS
MICHAEL KOSARIN

ORIGINAL PRODUCTION DEVELOPED IN ASSOCIATION WITH PETER SCHNEIDER & MICHAEL RENO

ASSOCIATE PRODUCER	PRESS	DIRECTOR OF CREATIVE DEVELOPMENT	GENERAL MANAGER	CO-EXECUTIVE PRODUCER
TOM LEONARDIS	THE HARTMAN GROUP	ULRIKE BURGER-BRUJIS	321 THEATRICAL MANAGEMENT	BEVERLEY D. MAC KEEN

PRODUCERS
WHOOPI GOLDBERG, JOOP VAN DEN ENDE, BILL TAYLOR & REBECCA QUIGLEY

CHOREOGRAPHER
ANTHONY VAN LAAST

DIRECTOR
JERRY ZAKS

ORIGINALLY PRODUCED BY PASADENA PLAYHOUSE, PASADENA, CA AND ALLIANCE THEATRE, ATLANTA, GA.

2/13/12

Patina Miller and The Company

Photo by Joan Marcus

Sister Act

MUSICAL NUMBERS

ACT ONE

"Take Me to Heaven" .... Deloris, Michelle, Tina
"Fabulous, Baby!" .... Deloris, Michelle, Tina
"Here Within These Walls" .... Mother Superior, Deloris
"It's Good to Be a Nun" .... Deloris, Mary Patrick, Mary Robert, Mary Lazarus, Nuns
"When I Find My Baby" .... Curtis, Joey, Pablo, TJ
"I Could Be That Guy" .... Eddie, Bums
"Raise Your Voice" .... Deloris, Mary Patrick, Mary Robert, Mary Lazarus, Nuns
"Take Me to Heaven" (Reprise) .... Deloris, Mary Patrick, Mary Robert, Mary Lazarus, Nuns

ACT TWO

"Sunday Morning Fever" .... Deloris, Mother Superior, Monsignor O'Hara, Eddie, Mary Patrick, Mary Robert, Mary Lazarus, Nuns, Workers
"Lady in the Long Black Dress" .... Joey, Pablo, TJ
"Haven't Got a Prayer" .... Mother Superior
"Bless Our Show" .... Deloris, Mary Patrick, Mary Robert, Mary Lazarus, Nuns
"The Life I Never Led" .... Mary Robert
"Fabulous, Baby!" (Reprise) .... Deloris, Eddie, Nuns, Fantasy Dancers
"Sister Act" .... Deloris
"When I Find My Baby" (Reprise) .... Curtis
"The Life I Never Led" (Reprise) .... Mary Robert
"Sister Act" (Reprise) .... Deloris, Mother Superior, Mary Patrick, Mary Robert, Mary Lazarus, Nuns
"Spread the Love Around" .... The Company

(L-R): Chester Gregory, Patina Miller

Photo by Joan Marcus

ORCHESTRA

Conductor:
MICHAEL KOSARIN
Associate Conductor:
BRENT-ALAN HUFFMAN
Assistant Conductor:
ARON ACCURSO
Concert Master:
SUZANNE ORNSTEIN
Violins:
MINEKO YAJIMA, ERIC DeGIOIA,
KRISTINA MUSSER
Cello:
ROGER SHELL
Woodwinds:
ANDREW STERMAN, MARC PHANEUF,
JACQUELINE HENDERSON

Trumpets:
CRAIG JOHNSON, SCOTT HARRELL
Trombones:
GARY GRIMALDI, JEFF NELSON
Guitar:
JOHN BENTHAL
Bass:
DICK SARPOLA
Drums:
RICH MERCURIO
Percussion:
MICHAEL ENGLANDER
Keyboards:
BRENT-ALAN HUFFMAN, ARON ACCURSO
Musical Coordinator:
JOHN MILLER

Cast Continued

JENNIFER SIMARD, DANNY STILES,
CHELSEA MORGAN STOCK,
LAEL VAN KEUREN, ROBERTA B. WALL,
ALÉNA WATTERS

SWINGS
JACQUI GRAZIANO, CARRIE A. JOHNSON,
LOUISE MADISON, ERNIE PRUNEDA,
T. OLIVER REID

DANCE CAPTAIN
LOUISE MADISON

ASSISTANT DANCE CAPTAIN
ERNIE PRUNEDA

UNDERSTUDIES
For Deloris:
KIMBERLY MARABLE, RASHIDRA SCOTT
For Mother Superior:
JENNIFER ALLEN, TRISHA RAPIER
For Curtis:
ALAN H. GREEN, T. OLIVER REID
For Mary Robert:
CHELSEA MORGAN STOCK,
LAEL VAN KEUREN
For Mary Patrick:
HOLLY DAVIS, MARISSA PERRY
For Mary Lazarus:
JENNIFER ALLEN, ROBERTA B. WALL
For Eddie, Pablo, TJ:
CHARL BROWN, ERNIE PRUNEDA
For Monsignor O'Hara, Joey:
CHRIS BOHANNON, DANNY STILES
For Ernie, Cop, Joey Finnochio:
ERNIE PRUNEDA, T. OLIVER REID
For Mary Martin-of-tours:
JENNIFER ALLEN, JENNIFER SIMARD
For Mary Theresa:
JENNIFER SIMARD, ROBERTA B. WALL
For Waitress:
JACQUI GRAZIANO, CARRIE A. JOHNSON,
LOUISE MADISON
For Michelle, Tina:
CARRIE A. JOHNSON, KIMBERLY MARABLE,
LAEL VAN KEUREN

Electronic Music Design:
ANDREW BARRETT/LIONELLA MUSIC LLC.

Sister Act

Patina Miller
Deloris Van Cartier

Carolee Carmello
Mother Superior

Fred Applegate
Monsignor O'Hara

Sarah Bolt
Mary Patrick

John Treacy Egan
Joey

Demond Green
TJ

Chester Gregory
Eddie Souther

Kingsley Leggs
Curtis Jackson

Marla Mindelle
Mary Robert

Audrie Neenan
Mary Lazarus

Caesar Samayoa
Pablo

Jennifer Allen
Ensemble

Chris Bohannon
Ernie, Ensemble

Natalie Bradshaw
Swing

Charl Brown
Ensemble

Holly Davis
Waitress, Ensemble

Madeleine Doherty
Mary Theresa

Jacqui Graziano
Swing

Alan H. Green
Cop, Ensemble

Carrie A. Johnson
Swing

Louise Madison
Swing, Dance Captain

Kimberly Marable
Ensemble

Marissa Perry
Ensemble

Ernie Pruneda
Swing

Trisha Rapier
Mary Martin-of-tours, Ensemble

T. Oliver Reid
Swing

Rashidra Scott
Michelle, Ensemble

Jennifer Simard
Ensemble

Danny Stiles
Joey Finnochio, Ensemble

Chelsea Morgan Stock
Ensemble

Lael Van Keuren
Ensemble

Roberta B. Wall
Ensemble

Aléna Watters
Tina, Ensemble

Alan Menken
Composer

Glenn Slater
Lyrics

Sister Act

Cheri Steinkellner
Book

Bill Steinkellner
Book

Douglas Carter Beane
Additional Book Material

Jerry Zaks
Director

Anthony Van Laast
Choreography

Klara Zieglerova
Set Design

Lez Brotherston
Costume Design

Natasha Katz
Lighting Design

John Shivers
Sound Design

Bernard Telsey
Telsey + Company
Casting

David Brian Brown
Wig & Hair Design

Gene O'Donovan
Aurora Productions
Production Management

Ben Heller
Aurora Productions
Production Management

Steven Beckler
Production Supervisor

Marcia Goldberg, Nancy Nagel Gibbs and Nina Essman
321 Theatrical Management
General Management

Michael Kosarin
Music Supervisor/ Vocal and Incidental Music Arranger/ Conductor

Doug Besterman
Orchestrations

Mark Hummel
Dance Music Arranger

Brent-Alan Huffman
Music Director

John Miller
Music Coordinator

Whoopi Goldberg
Producer

Joop van den Ende
Stage Entertainment
Producer

Philip J. Smith, Chairman,
The Shubert Organization
Producer

Robert E. Wankel
President,
The Shubert Organization
Producer

Bill Taylor
Producer

Rebecca Quigley
Producer

Tom Leonardis for Whoop Inc.
Associate Producer

Sheldon Epps
Artistic Director,
The Pasadena Playhouse
Original Production

Susan V. Booth
Artistic Director,
Alliance Theatre
Original Production

STAGE MANAGEMENT
(L-R:) Mary MacLeod, Steve Beckler, Jason Trubitt, Thomas Recktenwald

Photo by Brian Mapp

Sister Act

Victoria Clark
Mother Superior

Christina Decicco
Ensemble

Blake Hammond
*Ernie, Joey Finnochio
Ensemble*

Wendy James
Mary Martin-of-tours

Kevin Ligon
Ensemble

Corbin Reid
Ensemble

Lance Roberts
Swing

Melvin Abston
Cop, Ensemble

Aaron Kaburick
*Joey Finnochio,
Ensemble*

Jessica Sheridan
Ensemble

Raven-Symoné
Doloris Van Cartier

(L-R): Carolee Carmello, Raven-Symoné

STAGE DOOR
Fernando Sepulveda

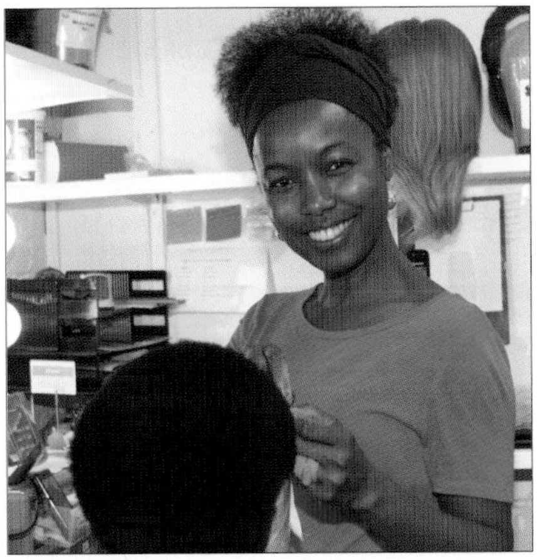

HAIR
Karen Dickenson

Photos by Brian Mapp

BOX OFFICE
Jimmy Toguville

FRONT OF HOUSE
Front Row (L-R): Lori Bokun, Barbara Arias

Middle Row (L-R): Mae Park, John Hall, Mattie Robinson, William Phelan, Lisa Maisonet

Top Row (L-R): Jorge Colon, Lou Santiago, William Denson, Ismeal Tirado

COMPANY MANAGEMENT
(L-R): Susan Brumley, Eric Cornell

CREW
(Clockwise from Back Left): Jim Ernest, Peter Becker, Scott Monroe, Steve Schroettnig, Pat Shea, Rick DalCortivo, David Gotwald, Gene Syzmanski, Bob Beimers, Dan Tramontozzi, Dominick Intagliato, Anmaree Rodibaugh, Declan McNeil, Paul Davila

Sister Act

Sister Act
SCRAPBOOK

Correspondent: Lance Roberts, Swing

Milestone Parties, Celebrations and/or Gifts: Birthdays are big at our theatre. Nothing better than seeing a cast member's birthday listed on the daily In/Out sheet. And it seems that Amy's Bread is the winner for cakes.

Most Exciting Celebrity Visitor and What They Did: Watching Miss Elaine Stritch leap out of her aisle seat and rush the stage and wave at the cast during the encore!

Actors Who Performed the Most Roles in This Show: The female swings.

Person Who Has Done the Most Shows: Kingsley Leggs has only missed three shows since we opened!

Special Backstage Ritual: We have an interfaith prayer circle outside of the male ensemble dressing room before most shows.

Favorite Moment During Each Performance (On Stage or Off): At the end of our show, audience members routinely wave their hands in the air like they are testifying at church!

Favorite In-Theatre Gathering Place: Half Hour Hot Topics in the male ensemble dressing room.

Favorite Off-Site Hangout: There aren't any seats, so we don't hang out inside, but several members of the cast and crew stop at Pie Face before AND after the show!!!!

Favorite Snack Foods: Baked goods from our stage manager Jason Trubitt's family.

Mascot: Patina Miller's dog, Bella.

Favorite Therapy: Chester Gregory likes to chew on licorice bark. Must work, because he sings those high notes flawlessly every performance!

Memorable Ad-Lib: You can't beat Victoria Clark talking to God about her problems as Mother Superior when Fred Applegate missed his cue as the Monsignor. He entered right before she was about to make a confession!

Memorable Stage Door Fan Encounter: About 50 teenagers sang "Fabulous, Baby!" as the cast came out of the stage door.

Web Buzz: We like that they call us "Stubbornly Successful"!

Latest Audience Arrival: We now have a few 7 PM performances. I was watching the show by the front of house monitors and a couple came halfway into the second act. When the usher told them that there were only 20 minutes left to the show, the couple said that they just needed to see some singing and dancing nuns and they would be satisfied. And that they got...in sequins!!!!!

Busiest Days at the Box Office: The week after President Obama stopped by the show.

Who Wore the Heaviest/Hottest Costume: That will always be Sister Mary Patrick.

Who Wore the Least: That will always be KiKi, KoKo or Kchi Kchi!

Catchphrase Only the Company Would Recognize: "Come on Bums!!!!"

Tales from the Put-in: T. Oliver Reid knew THREE roles one week BEFORE he officially started.

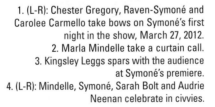

1. (L-R): Chester Gregory, Raven-Symoné and Carolee Carmello take bows on Symoné's first night in the show, March 27, 2012.
2. Marla Mindelle take a curtain call.
3. Kingsley Leggs spars with the audience at Symoné's premiere.
4. (L-R): Mindelle, Symoné, Sarah Bolt and Audrie Neenan celebrate in civvies.

Understudy Anecdote: I'm a swing (Lance Roberts) and play many roles. The first time that I went on for Charl as the Cabdriver, I didn't know that my pants were so huge. When Kingsley Leggs (as Curtis) told me to get out of his face, he scared the pants off of me...literally!!!

I ran and they fell right down!

Sweethearts Within the Company: Not many single company members, but one of President Obama's secret service men did date one of the nuns for a minute.

Best In-House Parody Lyrics: Sister Mary Robert sings "So, she stays here now," but we all sing "so, CHEESESTEAKS here now."

Company In-Joke: "Chamballa?, Yes, Chamballa!"

Nicknames: JTT, Bernie, Ambrose, Leggsly King, Stilays, CB, Sharl, Morrible.

Ghostly Encounters Backstage: At various times, different cast members will spot a shadowy figure at the back of the theatre during the show. It turns out, it is usually Jerry Zaks, our director, stopping in and dancing to the numbers.

Coolest Thing About Being in This Show: Makes me want to go to church...but haven't found one with a glitter Disco Mary yet!

Spider-Man Turn Off the Dark

First Preview: November 28, 2010. Opened: June 14, 2011.

Still running as of May 31, 2012.

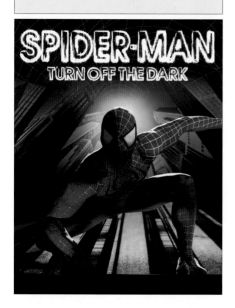

Given extraordinary powers by the bite of a genetically enhanced spider, Peter Parker resolves to do battle with the forces of evil and his nemesis, the Green Goblin, as Spider-Man in this musical based on the comic book character of the same name.

CAST

(in order of appearance)

Peter Parker/Spider-Man	REEVE CARNEY
Arachne	T.V. CARPIO
Mary Jane Watson	JENNIFER DAMIANO
Mrs. Gribrock	ISABEL KEATING

The Bullies

Flash	MATT CAPLAN
Kong	LUTHER CREEK
Meeks	CHRISTOPHER W. TIERNEY
Boyle	DWAYNE CLARK

Uncle Ben	KEN MARKS
Aunt May	ISABEL KEATING
MJ's Father	JEB BROWN
Norman Osborn/Green Goblin	PATRICK PAGE
Emily Osborn	LAURA BETH WELLS
J. Jonah Jameson	MICHAEL MULHEREN
Gangsters	MATT CAPLAN, DWAYNE CLARK, LUTHER CREEK
Hero Flyer	CHRISTOPHER W. TIERNEY
Purse Snatcher	SEAN SAMUELS

Reporters

Buttons	KEN MARKS
Bud	MATT CAPLAN
Stokes	JEB BROWN
Maxie	ISABEL KEATING

Continued on next page

FOXWOODS THEATRE

A LIVE NATION VENUE

Michael Cohl & Jeremiah J. Harris
Land Line Productions, Hello Entertainment/David Garfinkle/Tony Adams, Sony Pictures Entertainment
Norton Herrick and Herrick Entertainment, Billy Rovzar & Fernando Rovzar, Stephen Bronfman
Jeffrey B. Hecktman, Omneity Entertainment/Richard G. Weinberg
James L. Nederlander, Terry Allen Kramer, S2BN Entertainment, Jam Theatricals
The Mayerson/Gould/Hauser/Tysoe Group, Patricia Lambrecht, and Paul McGuinness

by arrangement with
Marvel Entertainment

present

SPIDER-MAN
TURN OFF THE DARK

Music and Lyrics by	Book by
Bono and The Edge	**Julie Taymor, Glen Berger & Roberto Aguirre-Sacasa**

Starring

Reeve Carney   Jennifer Damiano   T.V. Carpio   Patrick Page

Featuring

Michael Mulheren   Ken Marks   Isabel Keating   Jeb Brown
Matthew James Thomas   Laura Beth Wells   Matt Caplan   Dwayne Clark   Luther Creek

with

Kevin Aubin   Gerald Avery   Collin Baja   Marcus Bellamy   Emmanuel Brown   Jessica Leigh Brown   Daniel Curry   Erin Elliott   Craig Henningsen
Dana Marie Ingraham   Ayo Jackson   Joshua Kobak   Megan Lewis   Ari Loeb   Natalie Lomonte   Kevin C. Loomis   Kristen Martin   Jodi McFadden   Bethany Moore
Kristen Faith Oei   Jennifer Christine Perry   Kyle Post   Brandon Rubendall   Sean Samuels   Dollar Tan   Joey Taranto   Christopher W. Tierney

Scenic Design **George Tsypin**	Lighting Design **Donald Holder**	Costume Design **Eiko Ishioka**	Sound Design **Jonathan Deans**
Projection Design **Kyle Cooper**	Mask Design **Julie Taymor**	Hair Design **Campbell Young Associates** **Luc Verschueren**	Make-up Design **Judy Chin**
Aerial Design **Scott Rogers**	Aerial Rigging Design **Jaque Paquin**	Projection Coordinator / Additional Content Design **Howard Werner**	Prosthetics Design **Louie Zakarian**
Arrangements & Orchestrations **David Campbell**	Music Supervision **Teese Gohl**	Music Producer **Paul Bogaev**	Music Direction **Kimberly Grigsby**
Music Coordinator **Antoine Silverman**	Vocal Arrangements **David Campbell, Teese Gohl Kimberly Grigsby**		Additional Arrangements / Vocal Arrangements **Dawn Kenny & Rori Coleman**
Associate Scenic Design **Rob Bissinger**	Resident Director **Keith Batten**	Resident Choreographer **Jason Snow**	Production Stage Managers **C. Randall White** **Kathleen E. Purvis**
Casting Director **Telsey + Company**	Marketing Director **Len Gill**	Marketing **Keith Hurd**	Associate Producer **Anne Tanaka**
Press Representation **O & M Co.**	Production Management **Juniper Street Productions & MB Productions**	General Management **Alan Wasser - Allan Williams Aaron Lustbader**	Executive Producers **Glenn Orsher** **Stephen Howard** **Martin McCallum** **Adam Silberman**

Choreography and Aerial Choreography by
Daniel Ezralow

Additional Choreography by
Chase Brock

Creative Consultant
Philip Wm. McKinley

Original Direction by
Julie Taymor

6/14/11

(L-R): Patrick Page and Reeve Carney

Photo by Jacob Cohl

Spider-Man Turn Off the Dark

MUSICAL NUMBERS

ACT 1

"The Myth of Arachne" ....Peter
"Behold and Wonder" ....Arachne, Ensemble
"Bullying by Numbers" ....Peter, Bullies, High School Students
"No More" ....Peter, Mary Jane
"D.I.Y. World" ....Norman, Emily, Peter, Mary Jane,
High School Students, Lab Assistants
"Venom" ....Bullies
"Bouncing Off the Walls" ....Peter, High School Students
"Rise Above" ....Peter, Arachne, Ensemble
"Pull the Trigger" ....Norman, Emily, Viper Executives, Soldiers
"Picture This" ....Peter, Mary Jane, Norman, Emily

ACT 2

"A Freak Like Me Needs Company" ....Green Goblin, Ensemble
"If the World Should End" ....Mary Jane, Peter
"Sinistereo" ....Reporters
"Spider-Man!" ....Citizens of New York
"Turn Off the Dark" ....Arachne, Peter
"I Just Can't Walk Away" ....Mary Jane, Peter
"Boy Falls From the Sky" ....Peter
"I'll Take Manhattan" ....Green Goblin
"Finale – A New Dawn" ....Full Company

Cast Continued

Travis ....LUTHER CREEK
Robertson ....DWAYNE CLARK
Viper Executives.........................JEB BROWN,
DWAYNE CLARK,
LUTHER CREEK, KEN MARKS
The Sinister Six
Carnage ....COLLIN BAJA
Electro ....EMMANUEL BROWN
Kraven
the Hunter ...CHRISTOPHER W. TIERNEY
The Lizard ....BRANDON RUBENDALL
Swarm ....GERALD AVERY
Swiss Miss ....SEAN SAMUELS
Marbles ....LAURA BETH WELLS
Exterminator Flyer ....CRAIG HENNINGSEN
Green Goblin Flyer ....COLLIN BAJA
Citizens, Weavers, Students, Lab Assistants,
Reporters, Puppeteers, Spider-Men, Secretaries,
Soldiers ....GERALD AVERY, COLLIN BAJA,
MARCUS BELLAMY, EMMANUEL BROWN,
JEB BROWN, MATT CAPLAN,
DWAYNE CLARK, LUTHER CREEK,
CRAIG HENNINGSEN, DANA MARIE
INGRAHAM, AYO JACKSON,
ISABEL KEATING, NATALIE LOMONTE,
KEN MARKS, KRISTEN MARTIN,
JODI McFADDEN, BETHANY MOORE,
KRISTEN FAITH OEI,
JENNIFER CHRISTINE PERRY,

BRANDON RUBENDALL, SEAN SAMUELS,
DOLLAR TAN, CHRISTOPHER W. TIERNEY,
LAURA BETH WELLS
Ensemble Aerialists ....KEVIN AUBIN,
GERALD AVERY, COLLIN BAJA,
MARCUS BELLAMY, JESSICA LEIGH BROWN,
LUTHER CREEK, DANIEL CURRY,
ERIN ELLIOTT, CRAIG HENNINGSEN,
DANA MARIE INGRAHAM, AYO JACKSON,
ARI LOEB, NATALIE LOMONTE,
KRISTEN MARTIN, JODI McFADDEN,
BETHANY MOORE, KRISTEN FAITH OEI,
JENNIFER CHRISTINE PERRY,
BRANDON RUBENDALL, SEAN SAMUELS,
CHRISTOPHER W. TIERNEY

At certain performances, the role of
Peter Parker/Spider-Man will be played by
MATTHEW JAMES THOMAS.

UNDERSTUDIES

For Peter Parker/Spider-Man: MATT CAPLAN
For Mary Jane Watson: KRISTEN MARTIN
For Arachne: JODI McFADDEN, MEGAN LEWIS
For Norman Osborn/The Green Goblin:
JEB BROWN
For J. Jonah Jameson: KEVIN C. LOOMIS,
KEN MARKS
For Mrs. Gribrock: JESSICA LEIGH BROWN,
MEGAN LEWIS, LAURA BETH WELLS

For Flash, Kong: KYLE POST, JOEY TARANTO
For Boyle: COLLIN BAJA, KYLE POST,
SEAN SAMUELS, JOEY TARANTO
For Meeks: JOSHUA KOBAK, KYLE POST,
JOEY TARANTO
For Uncle Ben: KEVIN C. LOOMIS
For Aunt May: JESSICA LEIGH BROWN,
MEGAN LEWIS, LAURA BETH WELLS
For MJ's father: LUTHER CREEK,
KEVIN C. LOOMIS
For Gangsters: KEVIN AUBIN, DANIEL CURRY,
ARI LOEB, KYLE POST, JOEY TARANTO
For Buttons: KEVIN C. LOOMIS, KYLE POST
For Bud, Travis, Robertson: KEVIN C. LOOMIS,
KYLE POST, JOEY TARANTO
For Stokes: KEVIN C. LOOMIS, KYLE POST
For Maxie, Emily Osborn, Marbles:
JESSICA LEIGH BROWN, MEGAN LEWIS
For Viper Executives: MATT CAPLAN,
KEVIN C. LOOMIS, KYLE POST,
JOEY TARANTO
For Carnage: KEVIN AUBIN, DANIEL CURRY,
BRANDON RUBENDALL
For Electro: ARI LOEB, DOLLAR TAN
For Kraven the Hunter: KEVIN AUBIN,
DANIEL CURRY, JOSHUA KOBAK,
ARI LOEB
For The Lizard: KEVIN AUBIN, DANIEL
CURRY,
ARI LOEB
For Swarm: MARCUS BELLAMY, ARI LOEB
For Swiss Miss: KEVIN AUBIN, DANIEL CURRY,
BRANDON RUBENDALL

Dance Captains: ERIN ELLIOTT, ARI LOEB
Assistant Dance Captain: MARCUS BELLAMY

SWINGS

KEVIN AUBIN, JESSICA LEIGH BROWN,
DANIEL CURRY, ERIN ELLIOTT,
JOSHUA KOBAK, MEGAN LEWIS,
ARI LOEB, KEVIN C. LOOMIS,
KYLE POST, JOEY TARANTO

Matthew James Thomas is appearing with the
permission of Actors' Equity Association.

ORCHESTRA

Conductor: KIMBERLY GRIGSBY
Associate Conductor: CHARLES duCHATEAU
Guitars: ZANE CARNEY, MATT BECK,
BEN BUTLER
Basses: AIDEN MOORE,
RICHARD HAMMOND
Drums: JON EPCAR

Continued on next page

Spider-Man Turn Off the Dark

Orchestra Continued

Keyboards: BILLY JAY STEIN,
   CHARLES duCHATEAU
Percussion: JOHN CLANCY
Hammered Dulcimer/Percussion: BILL RUYLE
Concertmaster: ANTOINE SILVERMAN
Viola/Violin: CHRISTOPHER CARDONA
Cello: ANJA WOOD
Trumpets: DON DOWNS, TONY KADLECK
French Horn: THERESA MacDONNELL
Trombone/Tuba: MARCUS ROJAS
Reeds: AARON HEICK

Electronic Music Design: BILLY JAY STEIN
Music Coordination: ANTOINE SILVERMAN
Music Copying Supervisor: STEVEN M. ALPER
Music Copyists: BETTIE ROSS,
RUSSELL ANIXTER, STEVEN COHEN,
JODY JAROWEY, DON RICE, ROY WILLIAMS,
DAVID WOLFSON
Piano Vocal Score Coordination: MARK BAECHLE

Reeve Carney
*Peter Parker/
Spider-Man*

Jennifer Damiano
Mary Jane Watson

T.V. Carpio
Arachne

Patrick Page
*Norman Osborn/
Green Goblin*

Michael Mulheren
J. Jonah Jameson

Ken Marks
*Uncle Ben, Buttons,
Viper Executive,
Ensemble*

Isabel Keating
*Aunt May,
Mrs. Gribrock, Maxie*

Jeb Brown
*MJ's Father, Stokes,
Viper Executive,
Ensemble*

Matthew James
Thomas
*Peter Parker/
Spider-Man
Alternate*

Laura Beth Wells
*Emily Osborn,
Marbles, Ensemble*

Matt Caplan
*Flash, Gangster, Bud,
Ensemble*

Dwayne Clark
*Boyle, Gangster,
Robertson, Viper
Executive, Ensemble*

Luther Creek
*Kong, Gangster,
Travis, Viper
Executive, Ensemble*

Kevin Aubin
Swing

Gerald Avery
Swarm, Ensemble

Collin Baja
Carnage, Ensemble

Marcus Bellamy
*Assistant Dance
Captain, Ensemble*

Emmanuel Brown
Electro, Ensemble

Jessica Leigh Brown
Swing

Daniel Curry
Swing

Erin Elliott
*Dance Captain,
Swing*

Craig Henningsen
Ensemble

Dana Marie
Ingraham
Ensemble

Ayo Jackson
Ensemble

Joshua Kobak
Swing

Megan Lewis
Swing

Ari Loeb
*Dance Captain,
Swing*

Natalie Lomonte
Ensemble

Kevin C. Loomis
Swing

Spider-Man Turn Off the Dark

Kristen Martin
Ensemble

Jodi McFadden
Ensemble

Bethany Moore
Ensemble

Kristen Faith Oei
Ensemble

Jennifer Christine Perry
Ensemble

Kyle Post
Swing

Brandon Rubendall
The Lizard, Ensemble

Sean Samuels
Swiss Miss, Ensemble

Dollar Tan
Ensemble

Joey Taranto
Swing

Christopher W. Tierney
Meeks, Kraven the Hunter, Ensemble

Julie Taymor
Co-Book Writer, Original Direction, Mask Designer

Bono
Music & Lyrics

The Edge
Music & Lyrics

Philip Wm. McKinley
Creative Consultant

Glen Berger
Co-Book Writer

Roberto Aguirre-Sacasa
Co-Book Writer

Daniel Ezralow
Choreographer, Aerial Choreographer

Chase Brock
Additional Choreography

George Tsypin
Scenic Designer

Donald Holder
Lighting Designer

Eiko Ishioka
Costume Designer

Jonathan Deans
Sound Designer

Kyle Cooper
Projections Designer

Luc Verschueren, Campbell Young Associates
Hair Designers

Judy Chin
Make-up Designer

Scott Rogers
Aerial Designer

Jaque Paquin
Aerial Rigging Designer

Howard Werner
Projection Coordinator/ Additional Content Design

Rob Bissinger
Associate Scenic Designer

Keith Batten
Resident Director

Jason Snow
Associate/Resident Choreographer

David Campbell
Arrangements and Orchestrations, Vocal Arrangements

Teese Gohl
Music Supervisor

Paul Bogaev
Music Producer

Spider-Man Turn Off the Dark

Kimberly Grigsby
Music Director

Antoine Silverman
Music Coordinator

Rori Coleman
*Additional
Arrangements/
Vocal Arrangements*

Dawn Kenny
*Additional
Arrangements/
Vocal Arrangements*

Billy Jay Stein
*Electronic Music
Designer*

Bernard Telsey
Telsey + Company
Casting

Keith Hurd
Marketing

Ana Rose Greene, Guy Kwan, Joe DeLuise,
Hillary Blanken
Juniper Street Productions
Production Management

Mike Bauder
MB Productions
*Production
Management*

Alan Wasser
General Manager

Allan Williams
General Manager

Michael Cohl
Producer

Jeremiah J. Harris
Producer

David Garfinkle,
CEO,
Hello Entertainment
Producer

Norton Herrick
Producer

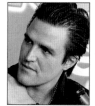
Billy Rovzar
Producer

Fernando Rovzar
Producer

Stephen Bronfman
Producer

Jeffrey B. Hecktman
Producer

Richard G. Weinberg,
Omneity
Entertainment
Producer

James L.
Nederlander
Producer

Terry Allen Kramer
Producer

Arny Granat
Jam Theatricals
Producer

Steve Traxler
Jam Theatricals
Producer

Frederic H.
Mayerson
The Mayerson/
Gould/Hauser/
Tysoe Group
Producer

James M. Gould
The Mayerson/
Gould/Hauser/
Tysoe Group
Producer

Ron Tysoe
The Mayerson/
Gould/Hauser/
Tysoe Group
Producer

Paul McGuinness
Producer

Glenn Orsher
Executive Producer

Stephen Howard
Executive Producer

Adam Silberman
Executive Producer

Julius C. Carter
*The Lizard, Purse
Snatcher, Ensemble
Aerialist*

Adam Ray Dyer
*Ensemble Aerialist,
Swing*

Spider-Man Turn Off the Dark

Rebecca
Faulkenberry
Mary Jane Watson

Drew Heflin
*Spider-Men, Swarm,
Ensemble Aerialist,
Swing*

Elizabeth Judd
*Spider-Men,
Ensemble Aerialist*

Reed Kelly
*Swiss Miss,
Ensemble Aerialist,
Soldier*

Heather Lang
*Soldier, Ensemble
Aerialist, Swing*

Leon Le
*Ensemble Aerialist,
Swing*

Katrina Lenk
Arachne

Kourtni Lind
*Spider-Men,
Ensemble Aerialist*

Paul McGill
*Electro, Spider-Men,
Soldier, Ensemble
Aerialst*

Maxx Reed
Electro, Spider-Men

Adam Roberts
*Carnage, Green
Goblin Flyer,
Ensemble Aerialist*

Christina Sajous
Archne

Emily Shoolin
*Emily Osborn, MJ's
Friend, Marbles,
Receptionist, Soldier*

Cassandra Taylor
Swing

Matthew Wilkas
*Flash, Bud,
Newsboy, Third
Gangster, Soldier*

2011-2012 AWARDS

OUTER CRITICS CIRCLE AWARDS
Outstanding Set Design
(George Tsypin)
Outstanding Costume Design
(Eiko Ishioka)

RICHARD SEFF AWARD
(Patrick Page)

Patrick Page

Photo by Jacob Cohl

(Reeve Carney (top) prepares to rescue Jennifer Damiano (suspended below bridge) in one of the scenic effects moments from the show.

Photo by Jacob Cohl

Spider-Man Turn Off the Dark

Photos by Brian Mapp

FRONT OF HOUSE
Row 1 (L-R): Gerald Spencer, Devon Howe, Ray Perez, Kyle Atterbury

Row 2 (L-R): Eric Paris, Adrian Zambrano, Mike Gregorek, Erich Jungwirth, David Chiu, Jessica Leal, Eric Grapatin, Denise Williams, Lalita Prashad, Rita Wozniak, Ashley Baker, Parveen Quresha, Jessica Bettini, Chris Casarino, Clarissa Abud, Jennifer Coolbaugh, Orlando Ortiz, Juan Thompson

Row 3 (L-R): Adam Sarsfield, Tony Lepore, Daniel Pivovar, Jessica Carollo, David Toombs, Chadd Wilson, Lisa Lamothe

Row 4 (L-R): Edward Griggs, John King, Alan Toribio, Eric Byrd, Martin Santiago, Jonathan Harris, Kate Gosnell, Andy Still

Row 5 (L-R): Tracy Moss, Will Norris, Greg Rose, Ryan Goodale, Jordon McDonough, Ana Fernandez, Elvin Rodriguez, Keldya Gordon, Cody Melton, Glenda Deabreu

CREW
Front Row (L-R): Jenny Slattery, Sandy Franck, Diana Calderazzo, Tiffany Hicks, Lacie Pulido, Jack Scott, Valerie Lai, Gonzalo Brea, Jack Anderson, John Santagata

Row 2 (Kneeling or Crouching) (L-R): Patrick O'Connor, Mark Davidson, Jeff Wener, Dave Fulton, Lisa Weiss, Angela Johnson, Stacy Scheiderman, Evelina Nervil, Michael Hannah, Michael Wilhoite, Philippe Vercruyssen, Karl Lawrence, Mike Bernstein, Tom Lowery, John Harris, Mike Norris

Back Row (L-R): Megan Henninger, Scott Sanders, Chris Morris, Valerie Spradling, John James, Jackie Freeman, Christel Murdock, Ron Tagert, Brian Hennings, Hugh Hardyman, Alan Grudzinski, Matty Lynch, Ron Rebentisch, John Warburton, Eric Dressler, Kris Keene, Tommy McDonough, Jimmy Harris

BOX OFFICE
(L-R): Michelle Smith,
Frances Destricher,
Danny Nitopi,
Spencer Taustine

Spider-Man Turn Off the Dark

STAFF FOR *SPIDER-MAN TURN OFF THE DARK*

GENERAL MANAGEMENT
ALAN WASSER ASSOCIATES

Alan Wasser	Allan Williams
Aaron Lustbader	Mark Shacket

PRODUCTION MANAGEMENT
JUNIPER STREET PRODUCTIONS
Hillary Blanken   Kevin Broomell
Guy Kwan   Ana Rose Greene   Alexandra Paull
Joseph DeLuise

MB PRODUCTIONS
Mike Bauder
Sonya Duveneck

TECHNICAL DIRECTOR
Fred Gallo

CASTING
TELSEY + COMPANY
Bernard Telsey CSA, Will Cantler CSA,
David Vaccari CSA
Bethany Knox CSA, Craig Burns CSA,
Tiffany Little Canfield CSA, Rachel Hoffman CSA,
Justin Huff CSA, Patrick Goodwin CSA,
Abbie Brady-Dalton CSA, David Morris, Cesar A. Rocha

COMPANY MANAGER
Marc Borsak

GENERAL PRESS REPRESENTATIVE
O&M CO.
Rick Miramontez
Andy Snyder   Jaron Caldwell
Elizabeth Wagner   Molly Barnett   Sam Corbett

Production Stage Manager	C. Randall White
Co-Production Stage Manager	Kathleen E. Purvis
Second Assistant	
Stage Managers	Sandra M. Franck, Andrew Neal, Jenny Slattery, Michael Wilhoite
Sub Stage Managers	Theresa A. Bailey, Valerie Lau-Kee Lai, Bonnie Panson
Associate Company Manager	Thom Mitchell
Assistant Company Manager	Lisa Guzman
Assistant Creative Consultant	Eileen F. Haggerty
Assistant Director	Dodd Loomis
Assistant Choreographer	Cherice Barton
Production Aerial Supervisor	Angela Phillips
UK Casting	Gillian Hawser

Set Design Creative Team:

Associate Scenic Designer	Rob Bissinger
Pop-up and Dimensional Design	Arturs Virtmanis
Illustration and Graphics	Baiba Baiba
Cityscape Graphics	Sergei Goloshapov

Assistant Set Design Team:

First Assistant Set Design	Anita La Scala
Graphic Art	Sia Balabanova, Rafael Kayanan
Pop-ups	Nathan Heverin
Model Makers	Eric Beauzay, Catherine Chung, Rachel Short Janocko, Damon Pelletier, Daniel Zimmerman

Draftsmen	Robert John Andrusko, Toni Barton, Larry W. Brown, Mark Fitzgibbons, Jonathan Spencer, Josh Zangen
Assistant Set Design	Tijana Bjelajac, Szu-Feng Chen, Heather Dunbar, Mimi Lien, Qin (Lucy) Lu, Robert Pyzocha, Chsato Uno, Frank McCullough
Previsualization	Lily Twining
Associate Costume Designer	Mary Nemecek Peterson
Assistant Costume Designers	Angela M. Kahler, Katie Irish
Costume Shoppers	Jennifer Adams, Dana Burkart, Cathy Parrott, Jen Raskopf
Associate Makeup Designer	Angela Johnson
Associate Lighting Designer	Vivien Leone
Assistant Lighting Designers	Caroline Chao, Carolyn Wong, Michael Jones
Assistant to the Lighting Designer	Porsche McGovern
Automated Lighting Programmer	Richard Tyndall
Assistant Video Designer	Sarah Jakubasz
Video Programmer	Phil Gilbert
Associate Sound Designers	Brian Hsieh, Keith Caggiano
Puppet and Mask Production Supervisor	Louis Troisi
Assistant Puppet and Mask Coordinator	Curran Banach
Automated Flying Programmer	Jason Shupe
Production Carpenter	Jack Anderson
Assistant Carpenters	Andrew Elman, Dave Fulton, Hugh Hardyman, Kris Keene, Matthew J. Lynch, Mike Norris, Geoffrey Vaughn
Production Electricians	Randall Zaibek, James Fedigan
Head Electrician	Ron Martin
Production Video Electricians	Jason Lindahl, Chris Herman
Production Sound Engineer	Simon Matthews
Head Sound Engineer	John Sibley
Assistant Sound Engineer	Dan Hochstine
Production Properties Supervisor	Joseph P. Harris, Jr.
Associate Properties Supervisor	Timothy M. Abel
E-Stop Personnel	Martin Garcia, Gonzalo Brea, Thomas Andrews
Production Wardrobe Supervisor	Michael D. Hannah
Assistant Wardrobe Supervisors	Christel Murdock, Sonya Wysocki
Dressers	Robert Belopede, Diana Calderazzo, Jackie Freeman, Rachel Garrett, Lyle Jones, Carrie Kamerer, Rosemary Keough, Shannon McDowell, Leslie Moulton, Daniel Mura, Kyle O'Connor, Michael Piscitelli, Jack Scott, Kyle Stewart, Ron Tagert, Arlene Watson, Cheryl Widner
Seamstress	Alejandra Rubinos
Laundry	William Hamilton
Hair Supervisor	John James
Assistant Hair Supervisor/ Assistant Hair Designer	Cory McCutcheon
Hairstylists	Therese Ducey, Brian Hennings
Production Makeup Supervisor	Angela Johnson
Assistant Makeup Supervisor	Tiffany Hicks
Production Photographer/Videographer	Jacob Cohl
Video Crew	Ben Nabors, Matt Kazman, Nora Tennessen

Cover Photo	Jacob Cohl
Lead Guitar Technician	Dallas Schoo
Additional Guitar Technician	Mike Vegas
Workshop Audio Engineers	Carl Glanville, Angie Teo
Vocal Coach	Don Lawrence
Dialect Coach	Deborah Hecht
Acting Coach	Sheila Grey
Technical Production Assistants	Sue Barsoum, Steve Chazaro, Kate DellaFera, Sonya Duveneck, Ania Parks, Alexandra Paull, Melissa Spengler, Kim Straatemeier
Production Assistants	Allison Cottrell, Hannah Dorfman, Amanda Johnson, Gregory Murray, Samantha Preiss, Danya Taymor, Raynelle Wright
Costume Interns	Yingshi June Lin, Tomke Von Gawinski
Physical Therapist	Heidi Green
Official Athletic Trainer	Prime Blueprint/ Dr. Edyth Heus
Consulting Producer	Jeffery Auerbach
Producing Consultant	Carl Pasbjerg
Executive Assistant to Michael Cohl	Jamie Forshaw
Executive Assistant to Jeremiah J. Harris	Stella Morelli
Executive Assistant to Glenn Orsher	Tricia Olson
Marketing Director	Len Gill
Marketing	Keith Hurd
Marketing Associate	Mary Caitlin Barrett
Advertising	Serino Coyne/ Nancy Coyne, Sandy Block, Angelo Desimini, Matt Upshaw
Website Design & Internet Marketing	Situation Interactive/ Damian Bazadona, John Lanasa, Jeremy Kraus, Victoria Gettler, Chris Powers
National Public Relations	Ken Sunshine/ Sunshine, Sachs & Associates
Sponsorship Consultant	Cary Chevat
Ticket Services Manager	Mike Rafael
Press Associates	Philip Carrubba, Jon Dimond, Richard Hillman, Yufen Kung
Press Interns	Michael Jorgensen, Chelsea Nachman, Alexandra H. Rubin
Legal Counsel	Ron Feiner, Esq., Beigelman, Feiner & Feldman Joseph T. Moldovan, Esq., Jack Levy, Esq., Joshua D. Saviano, Esq., Morrison Cohen LLP Dale Cendali, Esq.; Courtney Farkas, Esq. Kirkland & Ellis LLP
Accounting	Rosenberg, Neuwirth & Kuchner/ Chris Cacace, Marina Flom, Kirill Baytalskiy
General Management Associates	Mark Barna, Jake Hirzel
General Management Office	Hilary Ackerman, Nina Lutwick, Dawn Kusinski, Jennifer O'Connor
Insurance	DeWitt Stern Group/Pete Shoemaker
Banking	Signature Bank/Barbara von Borstel, Margaret Monigan, Mary Ann Fanelli, Janett Urena
Payroll	Castellana Services, Inc.

Spider-Man Turn Off the Dark

Transportation and Housing ......Road Rebel Touring and
Travel Services,
Alternative Business Accommodations,
The Mansfield Hotel

Group Sales
Broadway.com/1-800-Broadway

CREDITS AND ACKNOWLEDGMENTS

Scenery and scenic effects built and electrified by PRG Scenic Technologies, New Windsor, NY. Scenery painted by Scenic Art Studios, Cornwall, NY. Show control and scenic motion control featuring Stage Command Systems® by PRG Scenic Technologies, New Windsor, NY. Aerial effects equipment provided by Fisher Technical Services Inc. Video projection equipment, lighting equipment and sound equipment provided by PRG, Secaucus, NJ. Special effects executed by Excitement Technologies, Addison, TX. Softgoods built by I. Weiss and Sons Inc., Fairview, NJ. Props executed by the Spoon Group, Rahway, NJ; the Rollingstock Company, Sarasota, FL; the Paragon Innovation Group Inc., Toronto, ON; Illusion Projects, Las Vegas, NV; Beyond Imagination, Newburgh, NY; Cigar Box Studios Inc., Newburgh, NY; Czinkota Studios, Gardiner, NY; and Hamilton Scenic Specialty Inc., Dundas, ON. Media content created by Prologue Films. Puppets executed by Nathan Heverin, New Paltz, NY; Michael Curry Design Inc., Portland, OR; the Paragon Innovation Group Inc., Toronto, ON; Igloo Projects/Philip Cooper, Brooklyn, NY. Puppet assistance by Ilya Vett. Hauling by Clark Transfer Inc.; Michael O'Brien & Sons, Bronx, NY; and Prop Transport, New York, NY. Excerpt from "Manhattan" written by Richard Rodgers, Lorenz Hart, used by permission of Piedmont Music Company, publisher. "The Boy Falls From the Sky" lyrics by Bono and The Edge, music by U2, used by permission.

Costumes constructed by Parsons-Meares Ltd.

Additional costumes by Bill Hargate Costumes; Tom Talmon Studios; Artur & Tailors Ltd.; Danielle Gisiger; Valentina Kozhecksy; Arel Studio; Costume Armour, Cornwall, NY; Maria Ficalora Knitwear; and Jon Gellman Designs. Millinery by Monica Vianni, Arnold Levine. Costume crafts by Paragon Innovation Group Inc., Toronto, ON; James Chai, Philip Cooper, New York, NY; Signs and Shapes International. Custom shirts by L. Allmeier. Custom shoes by Jitterbug Boy, LaDuca Shoes, Montana Leather, Capri Shoes and World Tone. Digital printing and screen printing by Gene Mignola. Costume painting by Parmalee Welles-Tolkan, Mary Macy, Margaret Peot, Virginia Clow, Claudia Dzundza. Additional printing by Jeff Fender. Development painting by Hochi Asiatico.

IN MEMORY OF
Tony Adams

SPECIAL THANKS

Stan Lee, Anne Runolfsson, Thomas Schumacher, William Court Cohen, Trevor Bowen, Keryn Kaplan, Shan Lui, Liz Devlin, Catriona Garde, Susan Hunter, Missy Iredell, Michelle Lieu, Jennifer McManus, Principle Management Dublin and New York, Steve Lillywhite, David Toraya, Allen Grubman, Gil Karson, Larry Shire, Paul Wachter, Seth Gelblum, Michael West, Elliot Goldenthal, Jon Kilik, Michael Arndt, Bill Flanagan, Jennifer Lyne, Colin Farrell,

Susan Stroman, Eoin Colfer, Jake Bell, Don Lasker, Darryl Scherba, William Dailey, Michael O'Brien and Sons, Derek Mouton of MCD, Vox Amplification, Fender Guitars, Rickenbacker Guitars, to NS Design for the loan of the electric violin and cello, Roland, Tekserve, James Jones Hammered Dulcimers, David S. Weiss, M.D., Bruce Glikas.

Syfy
Official Media Partner

The Chrysler Building and its image are trademarks of Tishman Speyer Properties, LP and its affiliates and is used herein with permission.

Makeup provided by M·A·C Cosmetics

Rehearsed at the New 42nd Street Studios

Souvenir merchandise designed and created by
S2BN Entertainment
Norman Perry   Brahma Jade   Pete Milano
www.SpiderManOnBroadwaystore.com

Energy efficient washer/dryer courtesy of
LG Electronics

**To learn more about the production please visit
www.SpiderManOnBroadway.com**

HISTORY OF THE FOXWOODS THEATRE

The Foxwoods Theatre combines architectural preservation with state-of-the-art construction and technology. The spirit and character of New York's grandest historic theatres has been maintained and united with the technical amenities of a modern facility.

In 1997 the Ford Center for the Performing Arts was erected on the site of the legendary Lyric Theatre (1903; 1,261 seats) and Apollo Theatre (1920; 1,194 seats). The auditorium's interior design is based on historic elements from the Apollo Theatre. The Apollo's original ceiling dome, proscenium arch, and side boxes were removed, restored and re-installed (upon expansion for the larger scale of the new theatre) in the new auditorium. The side wall panels were created for acoustical considerations and designed to complement the historic features. New murals were commissioned to form a frieze over the new side boxes. Informally titled "Wings of Creativity," they were inspired by ancient Greek myths of Apollo, patron god of musicians and poets.

The lobby's design is based on historical elements of the Lyric Theatre. An elliptical dome from the Lyric was reproduced as the centerpiece of a new two-story atrium. The grand limestone staircase was designed to provide the flow and spirit of a grand theatre or opera house. The staircase railings feature lyre designs that were recreated from the original 43rd Street façade balcony rails. In the floor is a magnificent mosaic featuring comedy and tragedy masks inspired by sculptures on the historic 43rd St. façade. The 650-sq.-ft. mosaic includes 172,800 hand-cut pieces of marble from all over the world. At the top of the stairs is a medallion with the head of Zeus, taken from the Lyric's auditorium, and on the dress circle level, cold-painted windows (a stained glass technique) featuring a cupid design have been restored. The lighting in the lobby features the bare carbon filament light bulb, utilized in the early 20th century, to create a warm candlelight glow.

At 1,932 seats, the new theatre is one of Broadway's largest.

The Ford Center opened with the acclaimed musical *Ragtime*, followed by the Broadway revival of *Jesus Christ Superstar* and the award-winning revival of *42nd Street*. In 2005, the Ford Center was renamed the Hilton Theatre. Its premiere production was the musical *Chitty Chitty Bang Bang*, followed by the dance-inspired musical *Hot Feet*, the holiday spectacular *Dr. Seuss' How the Grinch Stole Christmas: The Musical*, *The Pirate Queen* and the new Mel Brooks' musical *Young Frankenstein*. In 2010, the Hilton Theatre was renamed the Foxwoods Theatre. We are pleased to welcome *Spider-Man Turn Off The Dark* to the Foxwoods stage.

FOXWOODS THEATRE

General Manager ....Erich Jungwirth
Assistant General Manager ....Sue Barsoum
House Manager ....Eric Paris
Facility Manager....................................Jeff Nuzzo
Assistant Facility Manager ....David Dietsch
Box Office Treasurer ....Spencer Taustine
Assistant Box Office Treasurer ....Michelle Smith
Head Carpenter ....James C. Harris
Head Electrician ....Art J. Friedlander
Head of Properties ....Joseph P. Harris Jr.
Head of Sound ....John R. Gibson
Staff Accountant ....Carmen Martinez
Staff Accountant ....Jill Johnson
Shipping/Receiving ....Dinara Kratsch
Administrative Assistant ....Brian Mahoney

FOXWOODS THEATRE

A Live Nation Venue

LIVE NATION ENTERTAINMENT

President and Chief Executive Officer ......Michael Rapino
President, North America Music, North ...Mark Campana
President, North America Music, South ....Bob Roux
Chairman, Northeast Region ....Jim Koplik
President, New York Music ....Kevin Morrow
Senior Vice President, Northeast Operations .....John Huff
Vice President Marketing, New York ....Jim Steen
Vice President Ticketing Operations ......Wayne Goldberg
President of Live Nation Network ....Russell Wallach
Chief Financial Officer ....Kathy Willard
President,
    North America Venues & Markets ....Ben Weeden
Senior Vice-President,
    North America Finance ....Kathy Porter
Vice President, Finance ....Dan Casale
Director of Accounting, Northeast ....Jennifer Douglas

About Live Nation Entertainment

Live Nation Entertainment (NYSE-LYV) is the largest live entertainment company in the world, connecting 200 million fans to 100,000 events in more than 40 countries, which has made Ticketmaster.com the number-three eCommerce website in the world. For additional information, visit www.livenation.com/investors.

Spider-Man Turn Off the Dark
SCRAPBOOK

Correspondent: Luther Creek, "Kong," "Gangster," "Travis," "Viper Executive," "Ensemble"

Company In-Jokes: When previews and rehearsals began to stretch into a territory formerly reserved for civil lawsuits, we found ourselves in the longest tech in Broadway history. As early as February, we began to exchange gag notions of when the seemingly most unbelievable and hilarious dates would be, in which we would still be rehearsing. The most absurd held that we would be rehearsing until June. Funny thing.

Mascot: The lovely and charming Sophie, a Maltese dog, companion of Patrick Page and his wife Paige Davis.

Memorable Ad-Lib: Green Goblin, in Act I: "Life is yours. So seize it! Forget following your DNA... I have no idea." We had been receiving entire speech changes during the day, yet performing the "old" show at night. It was more than a little disorienting.

Memorable Press Encounter: The much anticipated (and deserved) return of cast-member Christopher Tierney, who arrived to a stage door swarming with press.

What Did You Think of the Web Buzz on Your Show: We didn't realize. Has anyone been talking about the show?

Fastest Costume Change: From "Columbia University Professor" to "Newscaster" in 18 seconds, onstage, in full view of the audience.

Who Wore the Heaviest/Hottest Costume: "Kraven, the Hunter"!

Catchphrases Only the Company Would Recognize: "Tick... tick... Boom, boom, boom!" (etc., etc.)

Sweethearts Within the Company: Little Jodi McFadden and Gerald Avery!

"Gypsy of the Year" Skit: "Good as New" by Aiden Moore, Marcus Bellamy, Emmanuel Brown, Dana Marie Ingraham, Ayo Jackson, Ari Loeb and Natalie Lomonte.

Orchestra Member Who Played the Most Instruments: John Clancy (percussion) plays likely more than two dozen.

Orchestra Member Who Played the Most Consecutive Performances Without A Sub: It may have to be a tie between Jon Epcar (drums) and Zane Carney (lead guitar).

Memorable Directorial Notes: "Aunt May, could you go down on him?" "Mary Jane, I need you to put out more." This was in tech. It's a family show.

Understudy Anecdote: Actor I: "I saw a costume in the hallway racks with my name on it. I didn't even know I cover that part!" Actor II: "That would be funny if I hadn't just read my name in our PLAYBILL. Apparently, I am covering a part I had no idea I cover."

1. Bows at the long-delayed official opening night (L-R): T.V. Carpio, Reeve Carney, Jennifer Damiano, Patrick Page.
2. (L-R): Carpio, Page, Carney and Damiano out of makeup backstage.
3. Close-up of Page's makeup as the Green Goblin.
4. Page welcomes the show's 500,000th audience member, Jordan Muir (cap, center) along with parents Rob and Michelle onstage after the September 14, 2011 matinee.

Spider-Man Turn Off the Dark
SCRAPBOOK

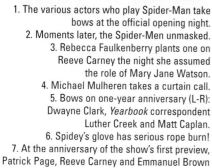

1. The various actors who play Spider-Man take bows at the official opening night.
2. Moments later, the Spider-Men unmasked.
3. Rebecca Faulkenberry plants one on Reeve Carney the night she assumed the role of Mary Jane Watson.
4. Michael Mulheren takes a curtain call.
5. Bows on one-year anniversary (L-R): Dwayne Clark, *Yearbook* correspondent Luther Creek and Matt Caplan.
6. Spidey's glove has serious rope burn!
7. At the anniversary of the show's first preview, Patrick Page, Reeve Carney and Emmanuel Brown with a model of the show's climactic battle.

Photo by Krissie Fullerton

Photos by Monica Simoes

Photo by Krissie Fullerton

Photo by Luther Creek

Photo by Krissie Fullerton

Photo by Krissie Fullerton

Photo by Krissie Fullerton

Stick Fly

First Preview: November 18, 2011. Opened: December 8, 2011.
Closed February 26, 2012 after 24 previews and 93 Performances.

PLAYBILL

The African-American LeVay family gathers at its home on Martha's Vineyard to meet the younger son's firebrand fiancee and the older son's white girlfriend. But stakes are raised even higher when a secret is revealed about two unexpected members of the household.

CAST
(in order of appearance)

Cheryl .... CONDOLA RASHAD
Taylor .... TRACIE THOMS
Spoon (Kent) LeVay .... DULÉ HILL
Flip (Harold) LeVay .... MEKHI PHIFER
Joe LeVay .... RUBEN SANTIAGO-HUDSON
Kimber .... ROSIE BENTON

The LeVay Home
Martha's Vineyard, 2005
Not Oak Bluffs

UNDERSTUDIES

For Joe LeVay:
JEROME PRESTON BATES
For Spoon (Kent) LeVay/Flip (Harold) LeVay:
DON GUILLORY
For Kimber:
GRETCHEN HALL
For Cheryl/Taylor:
ZAKIYA YOUNG

---

⑤ CORT THEATRE
138 West 48th Street
A Shubert Organization Theatre

Philip J. Smith, *Chairman*   **Robert E. Wankel,** *President*

NELLE NUGENT   ALICIA KEYS   SAMUEL NAPPI   REUBEN CANNON
JAY H. HARRIS/CATHERINE SCHREIBER   HUNTINGTON THEATRE COMPANY   DAN FRISHWASSER   CHARLES SALAMENO
SHARON A. CARR/PATRICIA KLAUSNER/RICK DANZANSKY   DAVEED D. FRAZIER/MARK THOMPSON

in association with
JOSEPH SIROLA   CATO AND NICOLE JUNE/MATTHEW AND SHAWNA WATLEY
ERIC FALKENSTEIN   KENNETH TEATON

present

DULÉ HILL   MEKHI PHIFER   TRACIE THOMS and RUBEN SANTIAGO-HUDSON

in

STICK FLY

by

LYDIA R. DIAMOND

also starring

ROSIE BENTON   CONDOLA RASHAD

Original Music
ALICIA KEYS

Scenic Design	Costume Design	Lighting Design	Sound Design
DAVID GALLO	**REGGIE RAY**	**BEVERLY EMMONS**	**PETER FITZGERALD**

Advertising & Marketing aka	Website & Social Media	Casting	Production Stage Manager
	BAY BRIDGE PRODUCTIONS	**MELCAP CASTING**	**ROBERT BENNETT**

Associate Producers	Production Management	Press Representative	General Manager
SARAHBETH GROSSMAN **MICHAEL MASO** **ERIKA ROSE**	**AURORA PRODUCTIONS**	**BONEAU/BRYAN-BROWN**	**PETER BOGYO**

Directed By
KENNY LEON

STICK FLY was developed in part at Chicago Dramatists and originally produced by Congo Square Theatre
and subsequently produced by McCarter Theatre Center. A further developmental production
directed by Kenny Leon was produced jointly by Arena Stage and the Huntington Theatre Company.

12/8/11

The Producers wish to express their appreciation to Theatre Development Fund for its support of this production.

(L-R): Ruben Santiago-Hudson, Condola Rashad, Mekhi Phifer, Dulé Hill, Tracie Thoms

Photo by Richard Termine

Stick Fly

Dulé Hill
Spoon (Kent) LeVay

Mekhi Phifer
Flip (Harold) LeVay

Tracie Thoms
Taylor

Ruben Santiago-
Hudson
Joe LeVay

Rosie Benton
Kimber

Condola Rashad
Cheryl

Jerome Preston
Bates
u/s Joe LeVay

Don Guillory
*u/s Flip (Harold)
LeVay/ Spoon (Kent)
LeVay*

Gretchen Hall
u/s Kimber

Zakiya Young
u/s Taylor/Cheryl

Lydia R. Diamond
Playwright

Kenny Leon
Director

Alicia Keys
*Producer, Original
Music*

David Gallo
Set Design

Peter Bogyo
General Manager

Kate Wilson
Voice Coach

Jay H. Harris
Producer

Catherine Schreiber
Producer

Dan Frishwasser
Producer

Sharon Carr
Producer

Patricia Klausner
Producer

Rick Danzansky
Producer

Mark Thompson
Producer

Joseph Sirola
Producer

Eric Falkenstein
Producer

Photo by Brian Mapp

CREW
Sitting (L-R): Scott DeVerna, Eileen Miller, Richard Gross, Lark Hackshaw, Lisa Alia, Anita Ali Davis
Standing (L-R): Tony Curtis, Jens McVoy, Jill Johnson, Vera Pizzarelli (photo), Peter Bogyo, Chris Morey,
Robert Bennett, Lonnie Gaddy

Stick Fly

BOX OFFICE STAFF
(L-R): Larry Staroff, Pete Damen

Photo by Brian Mapp

Stick Fly
SCRAPBOOK

Correspondent: Rosie Benton, "Kimber"

Opening Night Gifts: Stick Fly M&Ms from Alicia Keys. LeVay T-shirts from Ruben Santiago-Hudson

Most Exciting Celebrity Visitors: The cast of *The Mountaintop*.

Actor Who Has Done the Most Shows in His Career: Ruben Santiago-Hudson

Special Backstage Rituals: Prayer circle before show, ZIP ZAP ZOP.

Favorite Moments During Each Performance (On Stage or Off): Feeling the audience react to the secrets being revealed. Group scenes in the kitchen. Dancing backstage.

Favorite In-Theatre Gathering Place: Around Smitty and Tracie's dressing room for a Chipotle party.

Favorite Off-Site Hangout: 48 Lounge (across the street)

Favorite Snack Food: Leftover brunch from our amazing crew.

Mascot: Richard, the Saboteur.

Favorite Therapies: Singer's spray, humidifiers, Grether's Pastilles, whiskey.

Memorable Ad-Libs: "Dad, seriously, what's up with Dad?" and "Seems like homemade women are a family tradition...." and "Do we have Happy Time?"

Cell Phone Incidents During a Performance: We had a few actual phone calls happen. As in, people picked up the phone and answered it during the play.

Memorable Stage Door Fan Encounter: People traveling from all over the country to see us.

What the Cast Thought of the Internet Buzz on the Show: We are very proud of it, but we don't read too much about the show so we can stay focused.

Latest Audience Arrival: Act II

Fastest Costume Changes: Rosie into running gear, Condola out of bathrobe, Dulé running around the stage with his galleys.

Busiest Day at the Box Office: The week of the holidays they were all busy!

Who Wore the Heaviest/Hottest Costume: Condola and Tracie had two on at once some of the time.

Who Wore the Least: The whole cast was in their pajamas at some point during the play.

Catchphrases Only the Company Would Recognize: The Leon Lounge. "Playin' games." "Flip, please."

Memorable Directorial Notes: "I would have paid about $68 to see that." (This was early in rehearsal.) Or, "Don't kiss her ass."

Company In-Jokes: "M'am... Ma'am... CALM DOWN!" "The water ain't gonna be tasty." "Hey there, you there?" "Hey ya ya ya, nnghaaah."

Company Legend: Director Kenny Leon is a legend.

Understudy Anecdote: Don Guillory went on super early during tech and killed it.

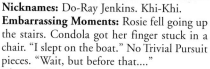

Nicknames: Do-Ray Jenkins. Khi-Khi.

Embarrassing Moments: Rosie fell going up the stairs. Condola got her finger stuck in a chair. "I slept on the boat." No Trivial Pursuit pieces. "Wait, but before that...."

The Coolest Thing About Being in This Show: The team effort from everyone. The whole theatre stayed positive and generous. Backstage, onstage, security, front of house...it takes a village!

1. (L-R): Condola Rashad, Rosie Benton, Ruben Santiago-Hudson, Alicia Keys, Lydia R. Diamond, Kenny Leon, Tracie Thoms, Dulé Hill and Mekhi Phifer at Hard Rock Cafe October 20, 2012 for a press event.
2. Phifer at Copacabana for the premiere party.
3. Rashad at Copacabana.
4. (L-R) Diamond, Keys and Leon at Hard Rock Cafe.
5. Opening night curtain call (L-R): Benton, Phifer, Thoms, Santiago-Hudson, Hill and Rashad.

A Streetcar Named Desire

First Preview: April 3, 2012. Opened: April 22, 2012.
Still running as of May 31, 2012.

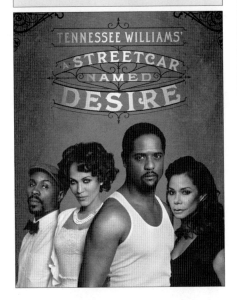

A revival of Tennessee Williams' Pulitzer-winning classic about faded Southern belle Blanche DuBois who loses the family plantation and is forced to come to live in squalor with her sister Stella and Stella's brutish husband Stanley, who represents all that is coarse and ugly in the world. The fragile Blanche doesn't last long in her harsh new surroundings and finds herself once again having to depend on "the kindness of strangers." This production is notable in part for its non-traditional casting.

CAST

(in order of appearance)

Stella	DAPHNE RUBIN-VEGA
Eunice	AMELIA CAMPBELL
Mexican Woman/ Neighbor	CARMEN de LAVALLADE
Stanley	BLAIR UNDERWOOD
Harold Mitchell (Mitch)	WOOD HARRIS
Blanche	NICOLE ARI PARKER
Steve	MATTHEW SALDÍVAR
Pablo	JACINTO TARAS RIDDICK
Young Collector	AARON CLIFTON MOTEN
Doctor	COUNT STOVALL
Matron	ROSA EVANGELINA ARREDONDO

PLACE:

French Quarter, New Orleans

TIME:

1952

Continued on next page

⊕ BROADHURST THEATRE

235 West 44th Street
A Shubert Organization Theatre

Philip J. Smith, *Chairman*   Robert E. Wankel, *President*

STEPHEN C. BYRD   ALIA M. JONES   ANTHONY LACAVERA
BET NETWORKS   HENRY G. JARECKI   SIMON SAYS ENTERTAINMENT   DANCAP PRODUCTIONS

in association with

LINDA DAVILA   PATRICIA & THOMAS BRANSFORD   THEATRE VENTURE INC.

present

BLAIR UNDERWOOD   NICOLE ARI PARKER
DAPHNE RUBIN-VEGA   WOOD HARRIS

in

with

AMELIA CAMPBELL   MATTHEW SALDÍVAR

ROSA EVANGELINA ARREDONDO   CARMEN de LAVALLADE   AARON CLIFTON MOTEN
JACINTO TARAS RIDDICK   COUNT STOVALL

SET DESIGN EUGENE LEE	COSTUME DESIGN PAUL TAZEWELL	LIGHTING DESIGN EDWARD PIERCE	SOUND DESIGN MARK BENNETT
CASTING TELSEY + COMPANY WILL CANTLER, CSA	FIGHT DIRECTION RICK SORDELET	VOCAL AND DIALECT COACH BETH McGUIRE	HAIR AND WIG DESIGN CHARLES G. LaPOINTE
PRESS REPRESENTATIVE SPRINGER ASSOCIATES PR	ADVERTISING AND MARKETING aka	GROUP SALES AND MARKETING WICG, INC. DONNA WALKER-KUHNE	TECHNICAL SUPERVISION JAKE BELL PRODUCTIONS SERVICES, LTD
PRODUCTION STAGE MANAGER LLOYD DAVIS, JR.	GENERAL MANAGER ROY GABAY	COMPANY MANAGER BRUCE KAGEL	

ASSOCIATE PRODUCERS

DARYL ROTH RANDOLPH STURRUP WALTER WHITE LINDEN RHOADS	PAULETTE MARTIN-CARTER ELLEN KRASS JACQUIE LEE ANTONY DETRE	KEISHA & TROY DIXON RENEE HUNTER STEPHEN JOHNSON CONSORTIUM VENTURES	SOCRATES MARQUEZ STEPHEN VALENTINE GEORGE WILLIAMS JESSICA ISAACS WILLIAM NETTLES

MUSIC COMPOSED BY
TERENCE BLANCHARD

DIRECTED BY
EMILY MANN

A STREETCAR NAMED DESIRE is presented by special arrangement with The University of the South, Sewanee, Tennessee. The Producers wish to express their appreciation to the Theatre Development Fund for its support of this production.

(L-R): Blair Underwood, Nicole Ari Parker and Daphne Rubin-Vega

Photo by Ken Howard

A Streetcar Named Desire

Cast Continued

UNDERSTUDIES

For Blanche, Stella:
ROSA EVANGELINA ARREDONDO
For Stanley, Mitch, Steve, Pablo, Doctor:
MOROCCO OMARI
For Eunice, Mexican Woman, Neighbor Woman,
Matron:
DANIELLE LEE GREAVES
For Young Collector:
J. MALLORY-McCREE

Blair Underwood
Stanley

Nicole Ari Parker
Blanche

Daphne Rubin-Vega
Stella

Wood Harris
Mitch

Amelia Campbell
Eunice

Matthew Saldívar
Steve

Rosa Evangelina
Arredondo
Matron

Carmen de Lavallade
*Mexican Woman/
Neighbor*

Aaron Clifton Moten
Young Collector

Jacinto Taras Riddick
Pablo Gonzales

Count Stovall
Doctor

Morocco Omari
*u/s Stanley, Mitch,
Steve, Pablo, Doctor*

Danielle Lee Greaves
*u/s Eunice/Mexican
Woman/Neighbor
Woman/Matron*

J. Mallory-McCree
u/s Young Collector

Tennessee Williams
Playwright

Emily Mann
Director

Terence Blanchard
Music

Jade King Carroll
Associate Director

Eugene Lee
Set Designer

Paul Tazewell
Costume Designer

Edward Pierce
Lighting Designer

Mark Bennett
Sound Designer

Charles Lapointe
Hair and Wig Design

Bernard Telsey
Telsey + Company
Casting

Rick Sordelet
Fight Director

Roy Gabay
General Manager

Camille A. Brown
Choreographer

Jake Bell
*Production
Supervisor*

Beth McGuire
*Vocal Director/
Dialect Coach*

A Streetcar Named Desire

Stephen Byrd
Producer

Alia M. Jones
Producer

Anthony LaCavera
Producer

Henry G. Jarecki
Producer

Ron Simons
SimonSays
Entertainment
Producer

Aubrey Dan
Dancap Productions
Producer

Linda Davila
Producer

Patricia & Thomas Bransford
Producers

Stewart F. Lane, Bonnie Comley
Producers

Photos by Brian Mapp

STAGE MANAGEMENT
(L-R): Hilary Austin, Lloyd Davis, Jr.

TICKET TAKERS, USHERS, PORTER and MERCHANDISE
Front Row (L-R): Henry Bethea, La'Shone Cleveland (Head Usher), Nancy Nunez (Porter), Merch Peter
Middle Row (L-R): Hugh Lynch, Nancy Reyes, Janice Beckwith
Back Row (L-R): Tony Lopez, Joshua Diaz, Aishah Kelly, Danielle Banyai

DOORMAN
Joe Trapasso, Jr.

CREW
Seated (L-R): Jamie Stewart, Moira Conrad,
Laura Koch, Cat Dee
Standing (L-R): Wallace Flores,
Charles J. DeVerna, Brian McGarty

A Streetcar Named Desire

HAIR AND WIG SUPERVISOR
Jamie Stewart

Photos by Brian Mapp

BOX OFFICE
(L-R): Noreen Morgan, Pete Jankunas, Jr.

STAFF FOR *A STREETCAR NAMED DESIRE*

GENERAL MANAGEMENT
ROY GABAY PRODUCTIONS
Roy Gabay   Mandy Tate
Daniel Kuney   Chris Aniello   Katrina Elliott
Mark Gagliardi   Lily Alia

COMPANY MANAGER
Bruce Kagel

GENERAL PRESS REPRESENTATIVE
SPRINGER ASSOCIATES PR
Gary Springer   Joe Trentacosta

PRODUCTION SUPERVISION
Jake Bell

CASTING
TELSEY + COMPANY
Bernie Telsey CSA, Will Cantler CSA,
David Vaccari CSA,
Bethany Knox CSA, Craig Burns CSA,
Tiffany Little Canfield CSA, Rachel Hoffman CSA,
Justin Huff CSA, Patrick Goodwin CSA,
Abbie Brady-Dalton CSA,
David Morris, Cesar A. Rocha, Andrew Femenella,
Karyn Casl, Kristina Bramhall, Jessie Malone

Production Stage Manager ....Lloyd Davis, Jr.
Assistant Stage Manager ....Hilary Austin
Associate Director ....Jade King Carroll
Assistant Director ....Shannon Cameron
Production Electrics ....Charles J. DeVerna
Production Carpenter ....Brian McGarty
Head Props ....J. Marvin Crosland
Production Sound Engineer ....Wallace Flores
House Props...................................Laura Koch
Wardrobe Supervisor ....Moira Conrad
Production Assistant ....Colleen M. Sherry
Production Assistant ....Trey Johnson
Associate Sound Designer ....Leon Rothenberg
Associate Sound Designer ....Danny Erdberg
Associate Lighting Designer ....Jonathan Spencer

Associate Costume Designer ....Sara Tosetti
Assistant Costume Designer ....Sarah Cubbage
Props Coordinator ....Kathy Fabian/Propstar
Props Associate ....Carrie Mossman
Props Associate ....Cassie Dorland
Production Electrician ....Brendan C. Quigley
Production Carpenter ....Richard Howard
Wardrobe Supervisor ....Moira Conrad
Dressers ....Catherine Dee, Anita Ali Davis
Hair and Wig Supervisor ....Jamie Stewart
Associate Scenic Designer ....Nick Francone
Assistant to Scenic Designer ....Patrick Lynch
Sound Design Intern ....Jake Zerrer
Vocal Director/Dialect Coach ....Beth McGuire
Assistant to the Director ....Pat Golden
Assistant Composer ....Mark Strand
Assistant Composer ....Joshua Johnson
Advertising and
   Marketing ....aka/Elizabeth Furze,
        Scott A. Moore, Melissa Marano,
        Bashan Aquart, Adam Jay, Erin Rech,
        Janette Roush, Sara Rosenzweig,
        Jen Taylor, Trevor Sponseller
Marketing and Group
   Sales ....Walker Communications Group/
        Donna Walker-Kuhne, Cherine Anderson
Production Photographer ....Ken Howard
Assistant to GM ....Mandy Tate
Press Associate ....Hafsa Mahfooz
Legal ....Donald C. Farber
Accounting ....Rosenberg, Neuwirth & Kuchner
Accountant ....Jana Jevnikar
Insurance ....Dewitt Stern Group
Banking....................................City National Bank
Payroll Service ....CSI/Lance Castellana

CREDITS

Scenery supplied by Stiegelbauer Associates Inc. Lighting
and sound equipment provided by Production Resource
Group. Vocal effects engineered at John Kilgor Studios. Ms.
Parker's clothing by Donna Langman Costumes, Ms.
Rubin-Vega's clothing by Jennifer Love Costumes, Mr.
Stovall's suit by Paul Chang Custom Tailors. Men's hats by
JJ Hatters. Additional menswear by DL Cerney. Vintage
clothing by New York Vintage and Autumn Olive. Painting
by Hochie Theatrical. Makeup provided by IMAN
Cosmetics.

SPECIAL THANKS

A Streetcar Named Desire would not have been possible
without the help and support of the following institutions
and individuals: New Orleans Tourism Marketing
Corporation (neworleansonline.com), Peter Dodenc of
HSBC USA Inc., Jeff Fasano, Lucian, Tom Fasano, Robin
Burgess, Lolis Elie, Dr. Kenneth Holditch, Faye Wattleton,
Connie Jackson, Peter Harvey, Willette Klushner, Rev. Dr.
Calvin O Butts, Marcus Samuelsson, Macy's, Bevolo Gas &
Electric Lights, B. Smith's, Lamar Williams, Laurence
George, Pamela Henry, Oz Scott, Amtrak, Pamela Monroe,
Lisa Pacino.

THE SHUBERT ORGANIZATION, INC.
Board of Directors

Philip J. Smith Chairman	**Robert E. Wankel** President
Wyche Fowler, Jr.	**Diana Phillips**
Lee J. Seidler	**Michael I. Sovern**

Stuart Subotnick

Chief Financial Officer ....Elliot Greene
Sr. Vice President, Ticketing ....David Andrews
Vice President, Finance ....Juan Calvo
Vice President, Human Resources ....Cathy Cozens
Vice President, Facilities ....John Darby
Vice President, Theatre Operations ....Peter Entin
Vice President, Marketing ....Charles Flateman
Vice President, Audit ....Anthony LaMattina
Vice President, Ticket Sales ....Brian Mahoney
Vice President, Creative Projects ............D.S. Moynihan
Vice President, Real Estate ....Julio Peterson

---

House Manager ....Hugh Barnett

Venus in Fur

First Preview: October 13, 2011. Opened: November 8, 2011 at the Samuel J. Friedman Theatre. On Hiatus December 19, 2011 to February 6, 2012. Reopened: Lyceum Theatre February 7, 2012. Still running as of May 31, 2012.

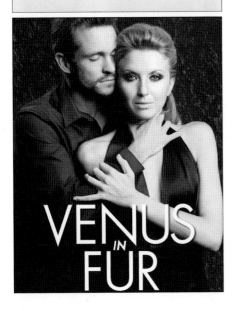

PLAYBILL®

VENUS IN FUR

A playwright gets more than he bargained for when an actress he is auditioning to portray a dominatrix in his new drama turns out to be far readier to play the role than he imagined.

CAST
(in alphabetical order)

Vanda ....NINA ARIANDA
Thomas ....HUGH DANCY

Stage Manager ....CARLOS MAISONET

UNDERSTUDIES

For Thomas: MARK ALHADEFF
For Vanda: VICTORIA MACK

Hugh Dancy is appearing with the permission of Actors' Equity Association pursuant to an exchange program between American Equity and UK Equity.

2011-2012 AWARD

TONY AWARD
Best Performance by an Actress
in a Leading Role in a Play
(Nina Arianda)

MANHATTAN THEATRE CLUB
SAMUEL J. FRIEDMAN THEATRE

ARTISTIC DIRECTOR
LYNNE MEADOW

EXECUTIVE PRODUCER
BARRY GROVE

JON B. PLATT

BY SPECIAL ARRANGEMENT WITH
SCOTT LANDIS

CLASSIC STAGE COMPANY

PRESENTS

VENUS IN FUR

BY
DAVID IVES

WITH
NINA ARIANDA   **HUGH DANCY**

SCENIC DESIGN
JOHN LEE BEATTY

COSTUME DESIGN
ANITA YAVICH

LIGHTING DESIGN
PETER KACZOROWSKI

SOUND DESIGN
ACME SOUND PARTNERS

FIGHT DIRECTION
THOMAS SCHALL

PRODUCTION STAGE MANAGER
WINNIE Y. LOK

CASTING
**NANCY PICCIONE &
JAMES CALLERI**

DIRECTED BY
WALTER BOBBIE

ARTISTIC PRODUCER
MANDY GREENFIELD

GENERAL MANAGER
FLORIE SEERY

DIRECTOR OF ARTISTIC DEVELOPMENT
JERRY PATCH

DIRECTOR OF MARKETING
DEBRA WAXMAN-PILLA

PRESS REPRESENTATIVE
BONEAU/BRYAN-BROWN

PRODUCTION MANAGER
JOSHUA HELMAN

ARTISTIC LINE PRODUCER
LISA McNULTY

DIRECTOR OF DEVELOPMENT
LYNNE RANDALL

Originally produced by Classic Stage Company, Artistic Director, Brian Kulick, Executive Director, Jessica R. Jenen.

Manhattan Theatre Club wishes to express its appreciation to Theatre Development Fund for its support of this production.

(L-R): Hugh Dancy, Nina Arianda

Photo by Joan Marcus

Venus in Fur

Nina Arianda
Vanda

Hugh Dancy
Thomas

Mark Alhadeff
u/s Thomas

Victoria Mack
u/s Vanda

David Ives
Playwright

Walter Bobbie
Director

John Lee Beatty
Scenic Design

Anita Yavich
Costume Design

Peter Kaczorowski
Lighting Design

Sten Severson, Tom Clark, Mark Menard, Nevin Steinberg
Acme Sound Partners
Sound Design

Thomas Schall
Fight Direction

Angelina Avallone
Makeup Design

Neil A. Mazzella/
Hudson Theatrical
Associates
*Technical
Supervision*

Lynne Meadow
*Artistic Director
Manhattan Theatre
Club, Inc.*

Barry Grove
*Executive Producer
Manhattan Theatre
Club, Inc.*

Scot M. Delman
Producer

Scott Landis
Producer

Jon B. Platt
Producer

Brian Kulick
*Artistic Director,
Classic Stage
Company
Producer*

Maggie Brohn
Bespoke Theatricals
*General
Management*

Amy Jacobs
Bespoke Theatricals
*General
Management*

Devin Keudell
Bespoke Theatricals
*General
Management*

Nina Lannan
Bespoke Theatricals
*General
Management*

Liv Rooth
u/s Vanda

(L-R): Hugh Dancy
and Nina Arianda

Photo by Joan Marcus

Venus in Fur

CREW
(L-R): Samuel Patt, Jeremy Von Deck, Louis Shapiro, Carlos Maisonet,
Natasha Steinhagen, Leah Redmond, Winnie Lok, Erin Moeller, Jeff Dodson (in photo)

BOX OFFICE
(L-R): Geoffrey Nixon, David Dillon

FRONT OF HOUSE STAFF
Front Row (L-R): Patricia Polhill, Jackson Ero, Richard Ponce, Cindy De La Cruz, Dinah Glorioso
Back Row (L-R): Cathy Burke, Jim Joseph, Christine Snyder, Wendy Wright, Ed Brashear, Enrique Cruz

Venus in Fur

MANHATTAN THEATRE CLUB STAFF

Artistic Director . . . . **Lynne Meadow**
Executive Producer . . . . **Barry Grove**
General Manager . . . . **Florie Seery**
Artistic Producer . . . . **Mandy Greenfield**
Director of Artistic Development . . . . **Jerry Patch**
Director of Artistic Operations . . . . **Amy Gilkes Loe**
Artistic Line Producer . . . . Lisa McNulty
Assistant to the Artistic Director . . . . Nicki Hunter
Assistant to the Artistic Producer . . . . Megan Dieterle
Assistant to the Executive Producer . . . . . . Emily Hammond
Director of Casting . . . . **Nancy Piccione**
Casting Associate . . . . Kelly Gillespie
Casting Assistant . . . . Darragh Garvey
Literary Manager/
   Sloan Project Manager . . . . Annie MacRae
Literary Associate . . . . Alex Barron
Artistic Administrative Assistant . . . . Elizabeth Rothman
Director of Development . . . . **Lynne Randall**
Director, Individual Giving . . . . Emily Fleisher
Director, Special Events . . . . Kristina Hoge
Manager, Individual Giving . . . . Josh Martinez-Nelson
Manager, Institutional Giving . . . . Andrea Gorzell
Manager, Corporate &
   Government Relations . . . . Laurel Bear
Development Associate/
   Individual Giving . . . . Laura Petrucci
Development Associate/
   Institutional Giving . . . . Ryan Fogarty
Development Associate/
   Special Events . . . . Allison Taylor
Patrons' Liaison . . . . Kaity Neagle
Director of Marketing . . . . **Debra Waxman-Pilla**
Assistant Marketing Director . . . . Becca Goland-Van Ryn
Marketing Manager . . . . Caitlin Baird
Director of Finance . . . . **Jessica Adler**
Director of Human Resources . . . . **Darren Robertson**
Business Manager . . . . Ryan Guhde
Business & HR Associate . . . . Andrew Kao
Business Assistant . . . . Lauren Amira
IT Manager . . . . Mendy Sudranski
Systems Analyst . . . . Andrew Dumawal
Studio Manager/Receptionist . . . . Thatcher Stevens
Associate
   General Manager . . . . **Lindsey Sag**
Company Manager/NY City Center . . . . Julia Baldwin
General Management Assistant . . . . Gillian Campbell
Director of
   Subscriber Services . . . . **Robert Allenberg**
Subscriber Services Manager . . . . Kevin Sullivan
Subscriber Services
   Representatives . . . . Mark Bowers,
                                             Tim Salamandyk,
                                    Rosanna Consalvo Sarto,
                                              Amber Wilkerson
Director of Telesales and
   Telefunding . . . . **George Tetlow**
Telesales and Telefunding Manager . . . . Terrence Burnett
Telemarketing Staff . . . . Stephen Brown,
                                    Kel Haney, Molly Thomas,
                                              Allison Zajac-Batell
Director of Education . . . . **David Shookhoff**
Assistant Education Director/
   Coordinator, Paul A. Kaplan Theatre
      Management Program . . . . Amy Harris
                                              Education Assistant/
TheatreLink Coordinator . . . . Nora DeVeau-Rosen

MTC Teaching Artists . . . . Stephanie Alston,
                                    Chris Ceraso, Charlotte Colavin,
                                    Dominic Colon, Allison Daugherty,
                                    Andy Goldberg, Kel Haney, Elise Hernandez,
                                    Jeffrey Joseph, Julie Leedes, Kate Long,
                                    Andres Munar, Melissa Murray,
                                    Angela Pietropinto, Alexa Polmer,
                                    Carmen Rivera, Judy Tate,
                                    Candido Tirado, Liam Torres, Joe White
Theatre Management Interns . . . . Holli Campbell,
                                    Cindy De La Cruz, Olivia Haas,
                                    Leora Kanner, Scott Kaplan,
                                    Samantha Kindler, Jane Madden,
                                    Amber McCleerey, Aleeza Sklover,
                                    Nick Trotta, Alyssa Weldon

---

Production Manager . . . . **Joshua Helman**
Associate Production Manager . . . . Bethany Weinstein
Assistant Production Manager . . . . Kevin Service
Properties Supervisor . . . . **Scott Laule**
Assistant Properties Supervisor . . . . Julia Sandy
Props Carpenter . . . . Peter Grimes
Costume Supervisor . . . . **Erin Hennessy Dean**

GENERAL PRESS REPRESENTATION
BONEAU/BRYAN-BROWN
Chris Boneau   Aaron Meier
Christine Olver   Emily Meagher

Script Readers . . . . Aaron Grunfeld,
                              Clifford Lee Johnson III, Liz Jones,
                              Rachel Lerner-Ley, Rachel Slaven

SERVICES
Accountants . . . . ERE, LLP
Advertising . . . . SpotCo/Drew Hodges,
                              Tom Greenwald, Jim Edwards,
                              Tom McCann, Beth Watson, Tim Falotico
Web Design . . . . SpotCo Interactive/
                              Sara Fitzpatrick, Michael Crowley,
                              Marc Mettler, Meghan Ownbey
Legal Counsel . . . . Charles H. Googe, Jr.;
                              Carol M. Kaplan/
                              Paul, Weiss, Rifkind,
                              Wharton and Garrison LLP
Real Estate Counsel . . . . Marcus Attorneys
Labor Counsel . . . . Harry H. Weintraub/
                              Glick and Weintraub, P.C.
Immigration Counsel . . . . Theodore Ruthizer/
                              Kramer, Levin, Naftalis & Frankel, LLP
Sponsorship
   Consultant . . . . Above the Title Entertainment/
                              Jed Bernstein
Insurance . . . . DeWitt Stern Group, Inc./
                              Anthony Pittari
Maintenance . . . . Reliable Cleaning
Production Photographer . . . . Joan Marcus
Event Photography . . . . Bruce Glikas
Cover Photograph . . . . Jason Bell
Cover Design . . . . SpotCo
Theatre Displays . . . . King Displays

PRODUCTION STAFF FOR *VENUS IN FUR*
Company Manager . . . . **Erin Moeller**
Production Stage Manager . . . . **Winnie Y. Lok**
Stage Manager . . . . Carlos Maisonet
Mary Mill Directing Fellow . . . . Ross Evans

Make-Up Designer . . . . Angelina Avallone
Vocal Coach . . . . Deborah Hecht
Associate Scenic Designer . . . . Kacie Hultgren
Assistant Costume Designer . . . . Nicole Jescinth Smith
Assistant Lighting Designer . . . . Gina Scherr
Associate Sound Designer . . . . Jason Crystal
Hair/Make-Up Supervisor . . . . Natasha Steinhagen
Lighting Programmer . . . . Jay Penfield
Production Assistant . . . . Samantha Flint

---

FOR THE THEATRICAL DEVELOPMENT CORPORATION
Executive Producer . . . . Jessica Jenen
Assistant to Jon B. Platt . . . . Terrie Lootens Hyde
Legal Counsel . . . . Davis Wright Tremaine LLP/
                              M. Graham Coleman, Esq.

CREDITS
Scenery fabrication by Hudson Scenic Studio. Lighting
equipment provided by PRG Lighting. Sound equipment
provided by Masque Sound. Costumes executed by John
Kristiansen New York Inc.

SPECIAL THANKS
Flora Stamatiades

MUSIC CREDITS
"Gallery Piece" by Kevin Barnes ©Apollinaire Rave (BMI).
Administered by Bug Music, Inc.

For more information visit
www.ManhattanTheatreClub.org

MANHATTAN THEATRE CLUB
SAMUEL J. FRIEDMAN THEATRE STAFF
Theatre Manager . . . . **Jim Joseph**
Assistant House Manager . . . . Richard Ponce
Box Office Treasurer . . . . **David Dillon**
Assistant Box Office Treasurers . . . . Jeffrey Davis,
                                              Geoffrey Nixon
Head Carpenter . . . . Chris Wiggins
Head Propertyman . . . . Timothy Walters
Sound Engineer . . . . Louis Shapiro
Master Electrician . . . . Jeff Dodson
Wardrobe Supervisor . . . . Leah Redmond
Apprentices . . . . Sam Patt, Jeremy Von Deck
Chief Engineer . . . . Deosarran
Maintenance Engineers . . . . Ricky Deosarran,
                                              Maximo Perez
Security . . . . Allied Barton
Lobby Refreshments . . . . Sweet Concessions

Photo by Joan Marcus

(L-R): Nina Arianda,
Hugh Dancy

Venus in Fur
SCRAPBOOK

Correspondent: Winnie Y. Lok, Production Stage Manager

Memorable Opening Night Notes: We got so many notes from the Broadway community! They were all special in their own way and we felt really welcomed.

Opening Night Gifts: From David Ives: a riding crop.

From Hugh and Nina: a dog collar.

Most Exciting Celebrity Visitors: A slew of them including Michael Kors, Anna Wintour, Henry Winkler, Cherry Jones, Mike Nichols, Frances McDormand, Joel Coen.

Henry Winkler called Nina "an angel" and said he wanted to marry her.

Anna Wintour was worried about Hugh getting slapped in the face twice during the show.

Special Backstage Rituals: Everyone has their own ritual, but cast and crew like to fist-bump or elbow-bump the calling SM as they file past to backstage at the top of show.

Favorite Moment (On Stage or Off): Alejandro, our honey bear, greets Nina with open arms after each performance.

Favorite In-Theatre Gathering Places: Hugh's dressing room after the show has the comfy chair and whiskey bar.

Nina's dressing room for meals and to sign *Playbill*s and posters. (She has a candle that smells really nice!)

SM Office for chocolates and self-adhesive laminating sheets.

Favorite Off-Site Hangout: Balkanika in Hell's Kitchen.

Favorite Snack Food: Pepperidge Farm Milanos!!!

Mascot: Our lovely doggie Miyokko.

Favorite Therapy: Throat-Coat Tea with honey (lovingly named "hottie toddies" by Carlos, our ASM).

Record Number of Cell Phone Rings, Cell Phone Photos or Texting Incidents During a Performance: We seemed to have more cell phones ring during previews for some reason. I think the record was five to seven for one performance. Our house staff is really vigilant so if they see any cell phones on, they catch the patron right away.

Other Disruptions During a Performance: On our third preview, the only moving set piece on stage—the door—wouldn't open for Nina's entrance. Hugh and Nina continued their lines for the scene while our ASM and crew and Nina kicked and jangled the door to no avail. We finally had to stop the show for about five minutes while we got the door open. The weird thing was that it opened and closed fine during pre-show and for Hugh's entrance three minutes before.

Internet Buzz on the Show: Our press department did a great job with that. There didn't seem to be a website we would go to that didn't have an ad or banner for our show!

Latest Audience Arrival: Due to the content of the show, our last late seating break is about 20 minutes in. We limited it to that because anyone arriving after that point may not understand what was going on.

Fastest Costume Change: Because this show takes place in real time (no transitions), Nina and Hugh handle all the costume changes on stage and by themselves.

Busiest Day at the Box Office: We broke MTC box office sales the day after we opened!

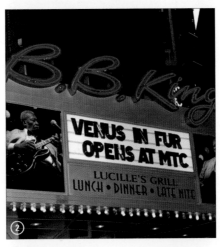

1. (L-R): Director Walter Bobbie, co-stars Nina Arianda and Hugh Dancy, and playwright David Ives on opening night.
2. Marquee of B.B. King's nightclub on 42nd Street where the cast party was held.
3. Dancy and Arianda take curtain call at the premiere.
4. Arianda and Dancy at B.B. King's.

Who Wore the Least: Nina, at one point, is wearing just a bustier, garters, stockings and boots. She wins!

Catchphrase Only the Company Would Recognize: "Unless it's double-sided!"

Coolest Thing About Being in This Show: It's a pretty small company so we all get along really well. It's really a family here.

Photos by Joseph Marzullo/WENN

War Horse

First Preview: March 15, 2011. Opened: April 14, 2011.
Still running as of May 31, 2012.

PLAYBILL

A young man braves the battlefields of World War I in order to retrieve his pet horse who has been sold to the cavalry, in Lincoln Center Theater's transfer of the hit National Theatre production. This production is notable for its arresting physical design, especially the horses—huge puppets manipulated by multiple puppeteers simultaneously.

CAST

THE HORSES

Joey as a foal ....STEPHEN JAMES ANTHONY,
     DAVID PEGRAM, LEENYA RIDEOUT
Joey ....JOBY EARLE, ARIEL HELLER,
     ALEX HOEFFLER, JESLYN KELLY,
     JONATHAN DAVID MARTIN,
     PRENTICE ONAYEMI, JUDE SANDY,
     ZACH VILLA or ENRICO D. WEY
Topthorn .. JOBY EARLE, JOEL REUBEN GANZ,
     ARIEL HELLER, ALEX HOEFFLER,
     TOM LEE,
     JONATHAN CHRISTOPHER MacMILLAN,
     JUDE SANDY, ZACH VILLA,
     or ENRICO D. WEY
Coco ....JOBY EARLE, JOEL REUBEN GANZ,
     ALEX HOEFFLER,
     JESLYN KELLY, TOM LEE,
     JONATHAN DAVID MARTIN,
     ZACH VILLA, or ENRICO D. WEY
Heine ....SANJIT DE SILVA, BHAVESH PATEL

THE PEOPLE (in order of speaking)
Song Woman ....KATE PFAFFL
Song Man ....LIAM ROBINSON
Continued on next page

Continued on next page

LINCOLN CENTER THEATER AT THE VIVIAN BEAUMONT

under the direction of
André Bishop and **Bernard Gersten**

NATIONAL THEATRE OF GREAT BRITAIN
under the direction of
Nicholas Hytner and **Nick Starr**
in association with
Bob Boyett   War Horse LP
presents
National Theatre of Great Britain production

WarHorse

based on the novel by **Michael Morpurgo**
adapted by **Nick Stafford**
in association with **Handspring Puppet Company**
with (in alphabetical order)

Stephen James Anthony   Zach Appelman   Alyssa Bresnahan   Richard Crawford
Sanjit De Silva   Matt Doyle   Austin Durant   Joby Earle   Joel Reuben Ganz   Ariel Heller
Peter Hermann   Alex Hoeffler   Brian Lee Huynh   Jeslyn Kelly   Ian Lassiter   Tom Lee
Jonathan Christopher MacMillan   Jonathan David Martin   Boris McGiver   Seth Numrich
Prentice Onayemi   Bhavesh Patel   David Pegram   Kate Pfaffl   Stephen Plunkett
Leenya Rideout   Liam Robinson   Jude Sandy   Hannah Sloat   T. Ryder Smith   Zach Villa
Elliot Villar   Cat Walleck   Enrico D. Wey   Madeleine Rose Yen

sets, costumes & drawings	puppet design, fabrication and direction	lighting
Rae Smith	**Adrian Kohler with Basil Jones** for Handspring Puppet Company	**Paule Constable**

director of movement and horse movement	animation & projection design
Toby Sedgwick	**59 Productions**

music	songmaker	sound	music director
Adrian Sutton	**John Tams**	**Christopher Shutt**	**Greg Pliska**

associate puppetry director	artistic associate	production stage manager	casting
Mervyn Millar	**Samuel Adamson**	**Rick Steiger**	**Daniel Swee**

NT technical producer	NT producer	NT associate producer	NT marketing	Boyett Theatricals producer
Katrina Gilroy	**Chris Harper**	**Robin Hawkes**	**Alex Bayley**	**Tim Levy**

managing director	production manager	executive director of development & planning	director of marketing	general press agent
Adam Siegel	**Jeff Hamlin**	**Hattie K. Jutagir**	**Linda Mason Ross**	**Philip Rinaldi**

directed by
Marianne Elliott and **Tom Morris**

Sponsor

Leadership Support from The Jerome L. Greene Foundation.
Major Support from Ellen and Howard Katz in honor of Marianne Elliott,
Florence and Robert Kaufman, The Blanche and Irving Laurie Foundation,
and The National Endowment for the Arts.
Generous Support from Laura Pels International Foundation for Theater and
The Henry Nias Foundation courtesy of Dr. Stanley Edelman.
National Theatre is supported by Arts Council England

American Airlines®
250 Cities. 40 Countries.
Official Airline

Supported by
ARTS COUNCIL ENGLAND

11/14/11

(L-R): David Pegram,
Seth Numrich,
Ariel Heller,
Madeleine Rose Yen,
Peter Hermann

Photo by Paul Kolnik

War Horse

UNDERSTUDIES

For Joey as a foal: BRIAN LEE HUYNH, HANNAH SLOAT, CAT WALLECK

For Song Woman, Song Man: LEENYA RIDEOUT

For Lt. Nicholls, Cpt. Stewart: ZACH APPELMAN, SANJIT DE SILVA

For Arthur: RICHARD CRAWFORD, AUSTIN DURANT

For Billy: STEPHEN JAMES ANTHONY, DAVID PEGRAM

For Albert: STEPHEN JAMES ANTHONY, MATT DOYLE

For Ted: AUSTIN DURANT, BHAVESH PATEL

For Chapman Carter: PETER HERMANN, ELLIOT VILLAR

For Allan: PETER HERMANN, IAN LASSITER

For Thomas Bone: IAN LASSITER, DAVID PEGRAM

For Rose: LEENYA RIDEOUT, CAT WALLECK

For Priest: SANJIT DE SILVA, ELLIOT VILLAR

For Sgt. Thunder: AUSTIN DURANT, BORIS McGIVER

For Pvt. Taylor: STEPHEN JAMES ANTHONY, ZACH APPELMAN

For Paulette: LEENYA RIDEOUT, HANNAH SLOAT

For Soldat Schnabel: BHAVESH PATEL, LIAM ROBINSON

For Hauptmann Müller: T. RYDER SMITH, ELLIOT VILLAR

For Soldat Klausen: IAN LASSITER, STEPHEN PLUNKETT

For Dr. Schweyk, Taff: IAN LASSITER, BHAVESH PATEL

For Oberst Strauss: IAN LASSITER, BORIS McGIVER

For Sgt. Fine: BRIAN LEE HUYNH, BHAVESH PATEL

For Unteroffizier Klebb: RICHARD CRAWFORD, SANJIT DE SILVA

For Emilie: KATE PFAFFL, HANNAH SLOAT

For Manfred: BORIS McGIVER, T. RYDER SMITH

For Matron Callaghan: ALYSSA BRESNAHAN, CAT WALLECK

For Annie: KATE PFAFFL, CAT WALLECK

For Vet. Ofc. Martin: STEPHEN PLUNKETT, ELLIOT VILLAR

For Heine: IAN LASSITER

Ensemble: BEN GRANEY, ISAAC WOOFTER

Cast Continued

Lieutenant James Nicholls ....STEPHEN PLUNKETT
Arthur Narracott ....T. RYDER SMITH
Billy Narracott ....MATT DOYLE
Albert Narracott..................SETH NUMRICH
Ted Narracott......................BORIS McGIVER
Chapman Carter ....AUSTIN DURANT
Allan ....ELLIOT VILLAR
Thomas Bone ....BHAVESH PATEL
John Greig ....JOBY EARLE, JOEL REUBEN GANZ, ALEX HOEFFLER, or JONATHAN DAVID MARTIN
Rose Narracott ....ALYSSA BRESNAHAN
Priest...............................PETER HERMANN
Captain Charles Stewart ......BRIAN LEE HUYNH
Sergeant Thunder..........RICHARD CRAWFORD
Private David Taylor ....DAVID PEGRAM
Paulette ....CAT WALLECK
Soldat Schnabel ....ZACH APPELMAN
Hauptmann Friedrich Müller ..PETER HERMANN
Soldat Klausen.......................ELLIOT VILLAR
Doctor Schweyk ....SANJIT DE SILVA
Oberst Strauss ....BHAVESH PATEL
Sergeant Fine ....ZACH APPELMAN
Unteroffizier Klebb ....STEPHEN PLUNKETT
Emilie ....MADELEINE ROSE YEN
Taff ....SANJIT DE SILVA
Manfred..........................AUSTIN DURANT
Matron Callaghan ....LEENYA RIDEOUT
Annie Gilbert ....HANNAH SLOAT
Veterinary Officer Martin ....IAN LASSITER

Goose ....JOBY EARLE, JONATHAN CHRISTOPHER MacMILLAN or JUDE SANDY

Villagers of Devon and Soldiers are played by members of the company.

Assistant Stage Managers ....BRIAN BOGIN, AMY MARSICO

Seth Numrich

Photo by Paul Kolnik

War Horse

Stephen James
Anthony
Joey as a foal

Zach Appelman
*Soldat Schnabel,
Sergeant Fine*

Alyssa Bresnahan
Rose Narracott

Richard Crawford
Sergeant Thunder

Sanjit De Silva
*Heine, Doctor
Schweyk, Taff*

Matt Doyle
Billy Narracott

Austin Durant
*Chapman Carter,
Manfred*

Joby Earle
*Joey, Topthorn,
Coco, John Greig,
Goose*

Joel Reuben Ganz
*Topthorn, Coco, John
Greig*

Ariel Heller
Joey, Topthorn

Peter Hermann
*Priest, Hauptmann
Friedrich Müller*

Alex Hoeffler
*Joey, Topthorn,
Coco, John Greig*

Brian Lee Huynh
*Captain Charles
Stewart*

Jeslyn Kelly
Joey, Coco

Ian Lassiter
*Veterinary Officer
Martin*

Tom Lee
Topthorn, Coco

Jonathan
Christopher
MacMillan
Topthorn, Goose

Jonathan David
Martin
*Joey, Coco, John
Greig*

Boris McGiver
Ted Narracott

Seth Numrich
Albert

Prentice Onayemi
Joey

Bhavesh Patel
*Heine, Thomas Bone,
Oberst Strauss*

David Pegram
*Joey as a foal,
Private David Taylor*

Kate Pfaffl
Song Woman

Stephen Plunkett
*Lieutenant James
Nicholls,
Unteroffizier Klebb*

Leenya Rideout
*Joey as a foal,
Matron Callaghan*

Liam Robinson
Song Man

Jude Sandy
*Joey, Topthorn,
Goose*

Hannah Sloat
Annie Gilbert

T. Ryder Smith
Arthur Narracott

Zach Villa
Joey, Topthorn, Coco

Elliot Villar
Allan, Soldat Klausen

Cat Walleck
Paulette

Enrico D. Wey
Joey, Topthorn, Coco

Madeleine Rose Yen
Emilie

War Horse

Ben Graney
Understudy

Isaac Woofter
Understudy

Michael Morpurgo
Author

Nick Stafford
Adaptor

Adrian Kohler
Handspring Puppet
Company
*Puppet Direction,
Design and
Fabrication*

Basil Jones
Handspring Puppet
Company
*Puppet Direction,
Design and
Fabrication*

Marianne Elliott
Director

Tom Morris
Director

Rae Smith
*Set, Costumes,
Drawings*

Paule Constable
Lighting

Leo Warner
59 Productions
*Animation and
Projection Design*

Mark Grimmer
59 Productions
*Animation and
Projection Design*

Lysander Ashton
59 Productions
*Animation and
Projection Design*

Peter Stenhouse
59 Productions
*Animation and
Projection Design*

Adrian Sutton
Music

John Tams
Songmaker

Christopher Shutt
Sound

Greg Pliska
Music Director

Mervyn Millar
*Associate Puppetry
Director*

Samuel Adamson
Artistic Associate

Drew Barr
Resident Director

Paul Huntley
*Hair and Wig
Designer*

Thomas Schall
Fight Director

Gillian Lane-Plescia
Dialect Coach

Kate Wilson
Vocal Coach

Bob Boyett

Nicholas Hytner
*Director, National
Theatre of Great
Britain*

André Bishop
*Artistic Director
Lincoln Center
Theater*

Bernard Gersten
*Executive Producer,
Lincoln Center
Theater*

Michael Braun
*Veterinary Officer
Martin*

Harlan Bengel
Understudy

Toby Billowitz
Joey, Topthorn, Coco

Lute Breuer
Joey, Topthorn, Coco

War Horse

Hunter Canning
Joey as a foal

Anthony Cochrane
Chapman Carter, Manfred

Andrew Durand
Albert Narracott

Leah Hofman
Joey, Topthorm

Ben Horner
Veterinary Officer Martin

Tessa Klein
Paulette

David Lansbury
Hauptmann Müller

David Manis
Arthur Narracott

Nat McIntyre
Heine, Thomas Bone, Oberts Strauss

Geoffrey Allen Murphy
Understudy

Andy Murray
Ted Narracott

Tommy Schrider
Heine, Doctor Schweyk, Taff

Jessica Tyler Wright
Song Woman

Katrina Yaukey
Matron Callaghanv

STAGE MANAGEMENT
From Top (L-R):
Karen Evanouskas
(Production Assistant),
Rick Steiger
(Production Stage Manager),
Brian Bogin
(Assistant Stage Manager),
Christopher R. Munnell
(Assistant Stage Manager)

Photos by Brian Mapp

FRONT OF HOUSE
Front Row (L-R): Susan Lehman,
Diane Nottle, Mim Pollock,
Margareta Shakeridge, Paula Gallo

Back Row (L-R): Jerry Sodano,
Officer Douglas Charles, Nick Andors,
Jeff Goldstein, Cayte Thorpe

MAKE-UP DESIGNER AND HAIR SUPERVISOR
Cynthia Demand

WARDROBE
Front Row (L-R:) Adam Adelman, Terry LaVada, Sarah Rochford

Back Row (L-R): Donna Holland, Peggy Danz Kazdan, Patti Luther,
Joe Godwin, Holly Nissen, Greg Holtz, Abby Bailey

Not pictured: Lynn Bowling (Wardrobe Supervisor),
James Nadeaux, Ros Wells (dressers)

War Horse

Photo by Brian Mapp

CREW

Front Row (L-R): Bruce Rubin (Electrician/Board Operator), Luis Lojo (Deck Sound), Adam Smolenski (Deck Sound), Brant Underwood (Deck Automation), Greg Cushna (Flyman), Kyle Barrineau (Props), Nick Irons (Follow Spot), Rudy Wood (Props), Andrew Belits (Carpenter)

Back Row (L-R): Marc Salzberg (Production Soundman), Bill Burke (Projection Technician), John Weingart (Production Flyman), Mark Dignam (Props), Frank Linn (Automation Tech), Joe Pizzuto (Pyro Technician), Pat Merryman (Production Electrician), Jeff Ward (Follow Spot Operator), Kevin McNeill (Carpenter), Bill Nagle (Production Carpenter), Karl Rausenberger (Production Propman)

Not Pictured: Dan Rich (Follow Spot Operator), John Ross (Props), John Howie (Carpenter), Ray Skillin (Deck Carpenter)

LINCOLN CENTER THEATER

ANDRÉ BISHOP   BERNARD GERSTEN
ARTISTIC DIRECTOR   EXECUTIVE PRODUCER

ADMINISTRATIVE STAFF

MANAGING DIRECTOR ....ADAM SIEGEL
  General Manager ....Jessica Niebanck
  Associate General Manager ....Meghan Lantzy
  General Management Assistant ....Laura Stuart
  Facilities Manager ....Alex Mustelier
  Associate Facilities Manager ....Michael Assalone
GENERAL PRESS AGENT ....PHILIP RINALDI
  Press Associates ....Barbara Carroll,
                                      Amanda Dekker
PRODUCTION MANAGER ....JEFF HAMLIN
  Associate Production Manager ....Paul Smithyman
EXECUTIVE DIRECTOR OF DEVELOPMENT
  & PLANNING ....HATTIE K. JUTAGIR
  Associate Director of Development ......Rachel Norton
  Manager of Special Events and
    LCT Young Angels ....Karin Schall
  Grants Writer ....Neal Brilliant
  Manager, Patron Program ....Sheilaja Rao
  Assistant to the Executive Director of
    Development & Planning ......Raelyn R. Lagerstrom
  Development Associate/Special Events & LCT
    Young Angels ....Jennifer H. Rosenbluth-Stoll
  Development Assistant/
    Individual Giving ....Sydney Rais-Sherman
DIRECTOR OF FINANCE ....DAVID S. BROWN
  Controller ....Susan Knox
  Systems Manager ....Stacy Valentine
  Finance Assistant ....Kristen Parker
DIRECTOR OF MARKETING LINDA MASON ROSS
  Associate Director of Marketing ......Ashley M. Dunn
  Digital Marketing Associate ....Rebecca Leshin
  Marketing Assistant ....John Casavant

DIRECTOR OF EDUCATION ....KATI KOERNER
  Associate Director of Education ....Alexandra Lopez
  LEAD Project Manager ....Andrea Dishy
Assistant to the Executive Producer ......Barbara Hourigan
Office Manager ....Brian Hashimoto
Messenger ....Esau Burgess
Reception ....Anna Strasser, Michelle Metcalf

ARTISTIC STAFF

ASSOCIATE DIRECTORS ......GRACIELA DANIELE,
                            NICHOLAS HYTNER,
                            JACK O'BRIEN,
                            SUSAN STROMAN,
                            DANIEL SULLIVAN
RESIDENT DIRECTOR .... BARTLETT SHER
DRAMATURG and DIRECTOR,
  LCT DIRECTORS LAB ....ANNE CATTANEO
CASTING DIRECTOR ....DANIEL SWEE, CSA
MUSICAL THEATER
  ASSOCIATE PRODUCER ....IRA WEITZMAN
ARTISTIC DIRECTOR/LCT3 ....PAIGE EVANS
  Artistic Administrator ....Julia Judge
  Casting Associate ....Camille Hickman
  Lab Assistant ....Kate Marvin

HOUSE STAFF

HOUSE MANAGER ....RHEBA FLEGELMAN
  Production Carpenter ....William Nagle

Production Electrician ....Patrick Merryman
Production Soundman ....Marc Salzberg
Production Propertyman ....Karl Rausenberger
Production Flyman ....John Weingart
House Technician ....Linda Heard
Chief Usher ...................................M.L. Pollock
Box Office Treasurer ....Fred Bonis
Assistant Treasurer ....Robert A. Belkin

SPECIAL SERVICES

Advertising ....Serino-Coyne
                      Jim Russek, Roger Micone,
                    Nick Nolte, Alexandra Rubin
Principal Poster Artist ....James McMullan
Counsel ....Peter L. Felcher, Esq.;
                    Charles H. Googe, Esq.;
                  and Carol Kaplan, Esq. of
    Paul, Weiss, Rifkind, Wharton & Garrison
Counsel ....Lazarus & Harris LLP
Immigration Counsel ....Theodore Ruthizer, Esq.;
                    Mark D. Koestler, Esq.
    of Kramer, Levin, Naftalis & Frankel LLP
Labor Counsel ....Michael F. McGahan, Esq.
    of Epstein, Becker & Green, P.C.
Auditor............................Frederick Martens, C.P.A.
                    Lutz & Carr, L.L.P.
Insurance ....Jennifer Brown of
                    DeWitt Stern Group
Photographer ....Paul Kolnik
Video Services ....Fresh Produce Productions/
                    Frank Basile
Travel ....Tygon Tours
Consulting Architect...........................Hugh Hardy,
    H3 Hardy Collaboration Architecture
Construction Manager ....Yorke Construction
Payroll Service ....Castellana Services, Inc.
Merchandising ....Marquee Merchandise, LLC/
                    Matt Murphy
Lobby Refreshments ....Sweet Concessions

STAFF FOR *WAR HORSE*

COMPANY
  MANAGER ..JESSICA PERLMETER COCHRANE
Assistant Company Manager ....Rachel Scheer
Associate Puppetry Director ....Mervyn Millar
Resident Director ....Drew Barr

War Horse

Resident Puppetry Director ....Matt Acheson
Movement Associate ....Adrienne Kapstein
US Associate Set Designer ....Frank McCullough
UK Associate Costume Designer ....Johanna Coe
US Associate Costume Designer ....Sarah Laux
UK Associate Lighting Designer ....Nick Simmons
US Associate Lighting Designer ....Karen Spahn
UK Associate Sound Designer ....John Owens
US Assistant Sound Designer ....Bridget O'Connor
UK Puppetry Technician ....Ed Dimbleby
Automated Light Programmer ....Victor Seastone
Projection Programmer ....Benjamin Pearcy
Props ....Faye Armon
Fight Captain ....Ian Lassiter
Make-Up Designer ....Cynthia Demand
Wardrobe Supervisor ....Lynn Bowling
Dressers ....Adam Adelman, Peggy Danz,
Richard Gross, Donna Holland,
Shannon Koger, Erick Medinilla,
James Nadeaux, Sarah Rochford,
Rosie Wells, Kristi Wood
Hair Supervisor ....Cynthia Demand
Physical Therapy ....PhysioArts/Jennifer Green
Orthopedist ....David S. Weiss, MD
Production Assistants ....Christopher R. Munnell,
Deanna Weiner
Child Guardian ....John Mara

Fight Director ....Thomas Schall

Dialect Coach ....Gillian Lane-Plescia

Vocal Coach ....Kate Wilson

Hair and Wig Design ....Paul Huntley

Official Accordion Sponsorship by Saltarelle

Incidental Music
Recorded at Sear Sound, NY
Recording Engineer: Gary Maurer
Copyist: Steve Cohen
Jim Lake ....Trumpet, Cornet
Angela Gosse ....Trumpet, Cornet
Judy Yin-Chi Lee ....Horn, Alto Horn
Hitomi Yakata ....Trombone, Euphonium
Richard Heckman ....Clarinet, Flute

NATIONAL THEATRE
Nicholas Hytner ....Director
Nick Starr ....Executive Director
Lisa Burger ....Finance Director
John Campbell ....Director of Production,
Technical and Engineering
Chris Harper ....Producer
Katrina Gilroy ....Technical Producer
Robin Hawkes ....Associate Producer
Racheli Sternberg ....Producing Assistant
Alex Bayley ....Marketing

Supported by the National Theatre's
War Horse Production Office.

Additional thanks to the National Theatre's Marketing,
Digital, Graphics and Finance departments.

CREDITS
Scenery by Hudson Scenic Studio. Tank by Scott Fleary.
Costumes by National Theatre Costume department.
Officer uniform tailoring by Mark Costello. Tailoring by
Roxy Cressy. Additional tailoring by Kirstie Robinson.
Footwear supervision by National Theatre Footware
department. English and German uniforms supplied by
Khaki Devil. U.S. alterations by James Nadeaux. Additional
U.S. alterations by John Kristiansen, NY. Additional
costume supplies by Costume Store, Vintage Shirt
Company and Silvermans. Costume aging and distressing
by Jeff Fender Studio. Sound and video equipment by
Sound Associates. Lighting equipment from PRG Lighting.
Props by National Theatre Props department. Technical
drawings by Tim Crowdy. Violin provided by David Gage
String Instruments.

Visit WarHorseOnBroadway.com

For groups of 20 or more:
Caryl Goldsmith Group Sales
(212) 889-4300

Peter Hermann (standing) and Elliot Villar

Photo by Paul Kolnik

War Horse
SCRAPBOOK

Correspondent: Katrina Yaukey, "Matron Callaghan"

Most Exciting Celebrity Visitors: Angela Lansbury, Ryan Gosling, Eva Mendes, Angela Bassett and Courtney B. Vance stayed and hung out. Matthew Broderick offered the number for his back surgeon once the show closes.

Special Backstage Rituals: Singing "Rolling Home" every night at half hour to get the ensemble in sync with one another. Some of the horse teams do breathing exercises/horse noises to get into the life of the horse.

Favorite Moments: Transformation or the death of Topthorn. Barbed Wire. Any time Joel hurts himself. Napping on the pontoon during intermission.

Favorite In-Theatre Gathering Place: Between shows on two show days or after rehearsals people convene in the lobby of the Beaumont. After the shows there may or may not be gatherings in the Stables (the horse teams' dressing room) or dressing rooms number 5, 6, and 10.

Favorite Off-Site Hangouts: Henry's up on 105th. Occasionally people go to Lincoln Park or the Emerald Inn.

Favorite Snack Foods: Banana Pudding from Magnolia, Burrito Box, Chia Seeds, Coconut Water, and Seal milk.

Mascots: We have several. Flossy with the long face, Charger the kinkiest guy in Minnesota, and War Turkeys.

Favorite Therapies: The company offers PT, massage, and acupuncture regularly. Ball-ee. Risk. The Rumble Rollers.

Most Memorable Ad-Lib: Nin Nin Nin Nin. Das Fuhrer. Ja. Ja. Ja. My orderly is queasy Major. Oh you like it you big baby. What's up Miss Bangs. My orderly is sick Colonel.

Memorable Press Encounter: Neil Patrick Harris rode Joey at the Tony awards.

Latest Audience Arrival: Kanye came late and left after the first act. Leonardo DiCaprio also came late and also left after intermission.

Catchphrases Only the Company Would Recognize: Boning Grieg. The Bloody Whizbangs. Shirkin Cowards. 1st Paulette. Welcome to SoreHorse.

Memorable Stage Door Fan Encounters: An Italian self-produced playwright came and handed out his own self-published play. Also, after his first appearance as the head of Joey, Jonathan Christopher MacMillan met a fan outside the stage door who was hoping for a tour. He and the lovely Carina Waye would eventually date.

Nicknames: LIT, JJL, JJT, RAJ, Bangs and Serena. Buddy Booker. Woofy. G-Spot. BeBop. Lizbeth.

Understudy Anecdote: Elliot Villar broke his leg onstage as Friedrich and finished the show.

Embarrassing Moments: Several horses have had pants split right down the back and have to finish an entire act with their pants split open.

Company In-Jokes: Joel gets hurt a lot. Anything from *Top Gun*.

1. Backstage at the Beaumont (L-R): Zach Villa, Isaac Woofter, Geoffrey Allen Murphy and Jonathan Christopher MacMillan.
2. (L-R): *Yearbook* correspondent Katrina Yaukey, Tessa Klein and Leah Hofmann.
3. (L-R): David Lansbury, Madeleine Rose Yen, and Tessa Klein.

Memorable Directorial Notes: John Tams saying that we sounded too Broadway and then a year later saying we sounded like pirates.
"In this scene, the important thing to remember, and this goes for the whole play, which isn't to say that this is a rule, we don't do rules, but truly, and with the constant reminder to follow your own compass, we need to go through this scene later."

Coolest Thing About Being in This Show: The people.

Other Memorable Moments: There was a Seeing Eye dog in the audience that began barking at Joey. Also, Tom Lee had to sprint out of the theatre when his wife went into labor.

Wicked

First Preview: October 8, 2003. Opened: October 30, 2003.
Still running as of May 31, 2012.

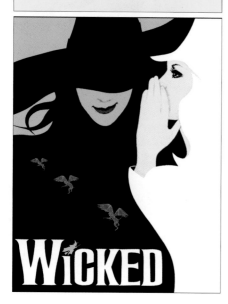

This imaginative "prequel" to The Wizard of Oz traces the friendship of two young women of Oz, Elphaba and Glinda, and how events beyond their control transform them into the familiar Wicked Witch of the West and Good Witch of the North. Dorothy, the Scarecrow and other beloved Oz characters don't arrive until nearly the end, but reveal fascinating backstories of their own. The show also offers a surprise from the early life of the Wizard himself, and explores what it really means to be "wicked."

THE CAST
(in order of appearance)

Glinda .... CHANDRA LEE SCHWARTZ
Witch's Father .... SEAN McCOURT
Witch's Mother .... LINDSAY JANISSE
Midwife .... KATHY SANTEN
Elphaba .... JACKIE BURNS
Nessarose .... JENNY FELLNER
Boq .... TAYLOR TRENSCH
Madame Morrible .... RANDY DANSON
Doctor Dillamond .... TOM FLYNN
Fiyero .... RICHARD H. BLAKE
Ozian Official .... SEAN McCOURT
The Wonderful Wizard of Oz .... P.J. BENJAMIN
Chistery .... MARK SHUNKEY
Monkeys, Students, Denizens of the Emerald City,
  Palace Guards and
  Other Citizens of Oz .... NOVA BERGERON,
    JERAD BORTZ, CAROLINE BOWMAN,

Continued on next page

Continued on next page

⇥N⇤ GERSHWIN THEATRE

UNDER THE DIRECTION OF
JAMES M. NEDERLANDER AND JAMES L. NEDERLANDER

Marc Platt
Universal Pictures
The Araca Group   and   Jon B. Platt

David Stone

present

WICKED

Music and Lyrics   Book
Stephen Schwartz   **Winnie Holzman**

Based on the novel by Gregory Maguire

starring

Jackie Burns   Chandra Lee Schwartz

also starring

Richard H. Blake

Jenny Fellner   Tom Flynn   Taylor Trensch

Alicia L. Albright Nova Bergeron Jerad Bortz Caroline Bowman
Kristina Fernandez Zach Hanna Lindsay Janisse Jesse JP Johnson
Colby Q. Lindeman Sean McCourt Jonathan McGill Brian Munn Lindsay K. Northen
Desi Oakley Rhea Patterson Nathan Peck Alexander Quiroga Adam Sanford
Kathy Santen Mark Shunkey Heather Spore Brian Wanee Jonathan Warren
Bud Weber Betsy Werbel Robin Wilner Briana Yacavone

and

Randy Danson   **P.J. Benjamin**

Settings	Costumes	Lighting	Sound
Eugene Lee	**Susan Hilferty**	**Kenneth Posner**	**Tony Meola**
Projections	Wigs & Hair	Production Supervisor	Technical Supervisor
Elaine J. McCarthy	**Tom Watson**	**Thom Widmann**	**Jake Bell**
Music Arrangements	Music Director	Dance Arrangements	Music Coordinator
Alex Lacamoire &	**Bryan Perri**	**James Lynn Abbott**	**Michael Keller**
Stephen Oremus			
Associate Set Designer	Special Effects	Associate Choreographer	Associate Director
Edward Pierce	**Chic Silber**	**Corinne McFadden Herrera**	**Lisa Leguillou**
Casting	Production Stage Manager	General Management	Press
Telsey + Company	**Marybeth Abel**	**321 Theatrical Management**	**The Hartman Group**

Executive Producers
Marcia Goldberg & Nina Essman

Orchestrations
William David Brohn

Music Supervisor
Stephen Oremus

Musical Staging by
Wayne Cilento

Directed by
Joe Mantello

Grammy Award-winning Original Cast Recording on DECCA BROADWAY

3/5/12

Chandra Lee Schwartz
as Glinda

Wicked

MUSICAL NUMBERS

ACT I

"No One Mourns the Wicked" ....Glinda and Citizens of Oz
"Dear Old Shiz" ....Students
"The Wizard and I" ....Morrible, Elphaba
"What Is This Feeling?" ....Galinda, Elphaba and Students
"Something Bad" ....Dr. Dillamond and Elphaba
"Dancing Through Life" ....Fiyero, Galinda, Boq, Nessarose, Elphaba and Students
"Popular" ....Galinda
"I'm Not That Girl" ....Elphaba
"One Short Day" ....Elphaba, Glinda and Denizens of the Emerald City
"A Sentimental Man" ....The Wizard
"Defying Gravity" ....Elphaba, Glinda, Guards and Citizens of Oz

ACT II

"No One Mourns the Wicked" (reprise) ....Citizens of Oz
"Thank Goodness" ....Glinda, Morrible and Citizens of Oz
"The Wicked Witch of the East" ....Elphaba, Nessarose and Boq
"Wonderful" ....The Wizard and Elphaba
"I'm Not That Girl" (reprise) ....Glinda
"As Long As You're Mine" ....Elphaba and Fiyero
"No Good Deed" ....Elphaba
"March of the Witch Hunters" ....Boq and Citizens of Oz
"For Good" ....Glinda and Elphaba
"Finale" ....All

ORCHESTRA

Conductor: BRYAN PERRI
Associate Conductor: DAVID EVANS
Assistant Conductor: BEN COHN

Concertmaster: CHRISTIAN HEBEL
Violin: VICTOR SCHULTZ
Viola: KEVIN ROY
Cello: DANNY MILLER
Harp: LAURA SHERMAN
Lead Trumpet: JON OWENS
Trumpet: TOM HOYT
Trombones: DALE KIRKLAND,
     DOUGLAS PURVIANCE
Flute: HELEN CAMPO
Oboe: TUCK LEE
Clarinet/Soprano Sax: JOHN MOSES
Bassoon/Baritone Sax/Clarinets: CHAD SMITH
French Horns: THEO PRIMIS,
     CHAD YARBOROUGH
Drums: MATT VANDERENDE
Bass: KONRAD ADDERLEY
Piano/Synthesizer: BEN COHN
Keyboards: PAUL LOESEL, DAVID EVANS
Guitars: RIC MOLINA, GREG SKAFF
Percussion: ANDY JONES

Music Coordinator: MICHAEL KELLER

Photo by Joan Marcus

Jackie Burns as Elphaba,
sings "Defying Gravity."

KRISTINA FERNANDEZ, ZACH HANNA,
LINDSAY JANISSE, JESSE JP JOHNSON,
COLBY Q. LINDEMAN, SEAN McCOURT,
JONATHAN McGILL, LINDSAY K. NORTHEN,
RHEA PATTERSON, NATHAN PECK,
ALEXANDER QUIROGA, ADAM SANFORD,
MARK SHUNKEY, HEATHER SPORE,
BRIAN WANEE, BUD WEBER,
BETSY WERBEL, ROBIN WILNER

UNDERSTUDIES and STANDBYS

Standby for Glinda:
KATE FAHRNER
Understudy for Elphaba:
CAROLINE BOWMAN
Understudy for Glinda:
LINDSAY K. NORTHEN, HEATHER SPORE
For Fiyero:
JERAD BORTZ, BUD WEBER
For the Wizard and Dr. Dillamond:
SEAN McCOURT, BRIAN MUNN
For Madame Morrible:
KATHY SANTEN, BETSY WERBEL
For Boq:
ZACH HANNA, JESSE JP JOHNSON
For Nessarose and Midwife:
ROBIN WILNER, BRIANA YACAVONE
For Chistery:
BRIAN WANEE, JONATHAN WARREN
For Witch's Father and Ozian Official:
BRIAN MUNN, ALEXANDER QUIROGA
For Witch's Mother/Midwife:
ALICIA L. ALBRIGHT, ROBIN WILNER
For Midwife:
DESI OAKLEY

SWINGS:

BRIAN MUNN, DESI OAKLEY,
BRIANA YACAVONE

Dance Captains/Swings:
JONATHAN WARREN, ALICIA L. ALBRIGHT

Wicked

Jackie Burns
Elphaba

Chandra Lee
Schwartz
Glinda

Randy Danson
Madame Morrible

P.J. Benjamin
The Wizard

Richard H. Blake
Fiyero

Jenny Fellner
Nessarose

Tom Flynn
Dr. Dillamond

Taylor Trensch
Boq

Kate Fahrner
Standby for Glinda

Alicia L. Albright
Dance Captain,
Swing

Nova Bergeron
Ensemble

Jerad Bortz
Ensemble

Caroline Bowman
Ensemble

Kristina Fernandez
Ensemble

Zach Hanna
Ensemble

Lindsay Janisse
Witch's Mother;
Ensemble

Jesse JP Johnson
Ensemble

Colby Q. Lindeman
Ensemble

Sean McCourt
Witch's Father/
Ozian Official

Jonathan McGill
Ensemble

Brian Munn
Swing

Lindsay K. Northen
Ensemble

Desi Oakley
Swing

Rhea Patterson
Ensemble

Nathan Peck
Ensemble

Alexander Quiroga
Ensemble

Adam Sanford
Ensemble

Kathy Santen
Midwife

Mark Shunkey
Chistery

Heather Spore
Ensemble

Brian Wanee
Ensemble

Jonathan Warren
Dance Captain

Bud Weber
Ensemble

Betsy Werbel
Ensemble

Robin Wilner
Ensemble

Wicked

Briana Yacavone
Swing

Stephen Schwartz
Music and Lyrics

Winnie Holzman
Book

Joe Mantello
Director

Wayne Cilento
Musical Staging

Eugene Lee
Scenic Designer

Susan Hilferty
Costume Designer

Kenneth Posner
Lighting Designer

Tony Meola
Sound Designer

Elaine J. McCarthy
Projection Designer

Tom Watson
Wig and Hair Designer

Joe Dulude II
Makeup Designer

Thom Widmann
Production Supervisor

Jake Bell
Technical Supervisor

Stephen Oremus
Music Supervisor; Music Arrangements

William David Brohn
Orchestrations

Alex Lacamoire
Music Arrangements

James Lynn Abbott
Dance Arrangements

Michael Keller
Music Coordinator

Edward Pierce
Associate Scenic Designer

Chic Silber
Special Effects

Corinne McFadden Herrera
Associate Choreographer

Bernard Telsey
Telsey + Company
Casting

Gregory Maguire
Author of Original Novel

Marcia Goldberg, Nancy Nagel Gibbs and Nina Essman,
321 Theatrical Management
General Management

Michael Rego, Hank Unger and Matthew Rego,
The Araca Group
Producer

Marc Platt
Producer

Jon B. Platt
Producer

David Stone
Producer

ALUMNI
2011-2012

Aaron J. Albano
Ensemble

Todd Anderson
Swing

Etai BenShlomo
Boq

Wicked

Al Blackstone
Ensemble

Cristy Candler
Nessarose

Catherine Charlebois
Swing

Katie Rose Clarke
Glinda

Michael DeVries
Ensemble

Jennifer DiNoia
Standby Elphaba

Maia Evwaraye
Griffin
Ensemble

Kathy Fitzgerald
Madame Morrible

Anthony Galde
Swing

Kristen Gorski-
Wergeles
*Witch's Mother,
Ensemble*

Kevin Jordan
Swing

Ryan Patrick Kelly
Swing

Kelly Lafarga
Swing

Kyle Dean Massey
Fiyero

Tom McGowan
*Th Wonderful Wizard
of Oz*

Mark Myars
Swing

Eddie Pendergraft
Ensemble

Amanda Rose
Ensemble

Josh Rouah
Ensemble

Constantine Rousouli
Ensemble

Libby Servais
Swing

Stephanie Torns
Ensemble

Teal Wicks
Elphaba

Laura Woyasz
Standby Glinda

TRANSFER
STUDENTS
2011-2012

Todd Anderson
Swing

Etai BenShlomo
Boq

Michael DeVries
*Witch's Father, Ozian
Official, Ensemble,
Swing*

Adam Grupper
*The Wonderful
Wizard of Oz*

David Hull
Ensemble

Eddie Pendergraft
Ensemble

Amanda Rose
Swing

John Schiappa
*Witch's Father, Ozian
Official, Ensemble*

392

Wicked

Photos by Brian Mapp

FRONT OF HOUSE STAFF
Front Row (L-R): Mariana Casanova, Michele Belmond, Carmen Rodriguez, Lorraine Lowrey, Jean Logan, Susan Sunday, Rick Kaye, Jacob Korder, Marilyn Luby, Albert Cruz, Brenda Denaris

Back Row (L-R): Joyce Pena, Peggy Boyles, Heather Farrell, Leonila Guity, Greg Woolard, Eileen Roig, Eric Brown, Alex Kehr, Joe Ortenzio, David Pena, Siobhan Dunne, Philippa Koopman

STAGE AND COMPANY MANAGEMENT
Top Row (L-R): Shawn Pennington, Jennifer Marik
Bottom Row (L-R): Adam Jackson, Christy Ney, Susan Sampliner

WARDROBE
Front Row (L-R): Kevin Hucke, Kathe Mull, Randy Witherspoon, James Byrne

Back Row (L-R): Karen Lloyd, Bobbye Sue Albrecht, Laurel Parrish, Teri Pruitt, Michael Michalski, Alyce Gilbert

HAIR AND MAKEUP
(L-R): Barbara Rosenthal, Nora Martin, Brittnye Batchelor, Craig Jessup, Rob Harmon, Cheri Tiberio

Wicked

CREW
(L-R): Jeff Sigler, Henry Brisen, Neil McShane, Kevin Anderson, Augie Mericola (with magic potion), Steve Caputo, Larry Doby, John Riggins, Mark Illo

STAFF FOR WICKED

GENERAL MANAGEMENT
321 THEATRICAL MANAGEMENT
Nina Essman   Nancy Nagel Gibbs
Marcia Goldberg

GENERAL PRESS REPRESENTATIVE
THE HARTMAN GROUP
Michael Hartman
Tom D'Ambrosio   Frances White

CASTING
TELSEY + COMPANY
Bernie Telsey CSA, Will Cantler CSA,
David Vaccari CSA, Bethany Knox CSA,
Craig Burns CSA, Tiffany Little Canfield CSA,
Rachel Hoffman CSA, Justin Huff CSA,
Patrick Goodwin CSA, Abbie Brady-Dalton CSA,
David Morris, Cesar A. Rocha, Andrew Femenella,
Karyn Casl, Kristina Bramhall, Jessie Malone

TECHNICAL SUPERVISION
JAKE BELL PRODUCTION SERVICES LTD.

COMPANY MANAGER .... SUSAN SAMPLINER

PRODUCTION
  STAGE MANAGER .... MARYBETH ABEL

Stage Manager .... Jennifer Marik
Assistant Stage Managers .... Christy Ney,
                                                Shawn Pennington
Associate Company Manager .... Adam Jackson
Assistant Director .... Paul Dobie
Dance Supervisor .... Patrick McCollum
Assistant to Mr. Schwartz .... Michael Cole
Assistant Scenic Designer .... Nick Francone
Dressing/Properties .... Kristie Thompson

Scenic Assistant .... Christopher Domanski
Oz Map Design .... Francis Keeping
Draftsman .... Ted LeFevre
Set Model Construction .... Miranda Hardy
Associate Costume Designers .... Michael Sharpe,
                                              Ken Mooney
Assistant Costume Designers .... Maiko Matsushima,
                                              Amy Clark
Costume Coordinator .... Amanda Whidden
Wig Coordinator .... J. Jared Janas
Associate Lighting Designer .... Karen Spahn
Associate Lighting Designer/
  Automated Lights .... Warren Flynn
Assistant Lighting Designer .... Ben Stanton
Lighting Assistant .... Jonathan Spencer
Associate Sound Designer .... Kai Harada
Sound Assistant .... Shannon Slaton
Projection Programmer .... Mark Gilmore
Assistant Projection Designer .... Anne McMills
Projection Animators .... Gareth Smith,
                                              Ari Sachter Zeltzer
Special Effects Associate .... Aaron Waitz
Associate Hair Designer .... Charles LaPointe
Fight Director .... Tom Schall
Flying Effects .... ZFX Flying Illusions
Production Carpenter .... Rick Howard
Head Carpenter .... C. Mark Overton
Deck Automation Carpenter .... William Breidenbach
Production Electrician .... Robert Fehribach
Head Electrician .... Brendan Quigley
Deck Electrician/Moving Light Operator .... Craig Aves
Follow Spot Operator .... Valerie Menz
Production Properties .... George Wagner
Property Master .... Joe Schwarz
Assistant Property Master .... Augie Mericola
Production Sound Engineer .... Douglas Graves
Sound Engineer .... Jordan Pankin
Assistant Sound Engineer .... Jack Babin
Production Wardrobe Supervisor .... Alyce Gilbert

Assistant Wardrobe Supervisor .... Kevin Hucke
Dressers .... Bobbye Sue Albrecht, Dennis Birchall,
                      James Byrne, Dianne Hylton, Nancy Lawson,
                      Michael Michalski, Kathe Mull, Laurel Parrish,
                      Teresa Pruitt, Barbara Rosenthal, Jason Viarengo,
                      Randy Witherspoon
Hair Supervisor .... Nora Martin
Assistant Hair Supervisor .... Ryan P. McWilliams
Hairdressers .... Jenny Pendergraft, Cheri Tiberio
Makeup Design .... Joe Dulude II
Makeup Supervisor .... Craig Jessup
Music Preparation Supervisor .... Peter R. Miller,
                                            Miller Music Service
Synthesizer Programming .... Andrew Barrett for
                                            Lionella Productions, Ltd.
Rehearsal Drummer .... Gary Seligson
Music Intern .... Joshua Salzman
Production Assistants .... Timothy R. Semon,
                                            David Zack
Advertising .... Serino Coyne/Greg Corradetti,
                                            Joaquin Esteva
Marketing .... Betsy Bernstein
Online Marketing .... Situation Interactive
Website .... Istros Media Corporation
Merchandise .... The Araca Group
Theatre Display .... King Displays
Group Sales .... Nathan Vernon (646-289-6885)
Banking .... JP Morgan Chase Bank/
                                            Salvatore A. Romano
Payroll .... ADP/Automatic Data Processing, Inc.
Director of Finance .... John DiMeglio
Production Administrator .... Robert Brinkerhoff
Accountant .... Robert Fried, C.P.A.
Insurance .... AON/Albert G. Ruben Insurance
Legal Counsel .... Loeb & Loeb/Seth Gelblum
Legal Counsel for Universal Pictures .... Keith Blau
Physical Therapy .... Encore Physical Therapy, P.C.
Orthopaedist .... David S. Weiss, MD
Onstage Merchandising .... George Fenmore, Inc.

Wicked
SCRAPBOOK

Correspondent: Jonathan Warren, Dance Captain

Major Backstage Projects: 2011-2012 has brought the completion of a project by Eddie Pendergraft. Eddie designed and painted an amazing mural spanning three floors in one of the Gershwin stairwells. The mural includes paintings of many of the characters of *Wicked*, including Elphaba, Glinda, The Wizard, Madame Morrible, Chistery, and the Citizens of the Emerald City. These characters are woven in with paintings of the landscape of *Wicked*, such as the cornfields, the Fallen House, the Quoxwood trees, and the poppy fields—all with Elphaba flying high above. The mural will hopefully be a part of the Gershwin for years and years to come.

Marybeth Abel, our PSM, also started The *Wicked* Hall of Fame this year. As each cast member leaves the show, their name goes up on the wall as part of the Shiz University alumni. To date, the names have made their way from the ground floor to the second floor. It is one of the highlights of a backstage tour.

Wicked has also brought a run of engagements, weddings and pregnancies in the past. It seems the women's ensemble are all in step with one another, and the excitement has found its way throughout the building. The list of engagements/weddings includes: Lindsay Northen, Heather Spore, Briana Yacavone, Kristen Gorski-Wergeles, Lindsay Janisse and Dominick Amendum, Eddie Pendergraft, Susan Sampliner and Tom Flynn. The

A detail from Eddie Pendergraft's mural of scenes from *Wicked* that adorn the three-story backstage staircase at the Gershwin Theatre.

pregnancies have begun with Kristen Gorski-Wergeles and Maia Evwaraye-Griffin. Everyone's got the bug....

Mascot/Most Exciting Celebrity Visitor: Some of the women's ensemble deemed a stuffed frog our show mascot—her name is "Fifi the Frog." Christian Bale came to the show this year, and brought his family with him. After the

show, while one of the ensemble members was giving them a tour, Christian's daughter tried to steal "Fifi the Frog" from the dressing room table.

Memorable Fan Gift: Donna Vivino, our Elphaba Standby, tells how she received a green witch Christmas ornament. When she turned it around, she found that the back of the dress had

---

Makeup provided by MAC Cosmetics

MARC PLATT PRODUCTIONS
Adam Siegel, Greg Lessans, Joey Levy, Jared LeBoff, Nik Mavinkurve, Conor Welch, Claire Wihnyk, Keri DeVos

STONE PRODUCTIONS
David Stone   Patrick Catullo   Aaron Glick

321 THEATRICAL MANAGEMENT
Susan Brumley, Mattea Cogliano-Benedict, Eric Cornell, Tara Geesaman, Jason Haft, Andrew Hartman, Brent McCreary, Alex Owen, Rebecca Peterson, Greg Schaffert, Ken Silverman, Haley Ward

UNIVERSAL PICTURES
President & COO, Universal Studios ....Ron Meyer
Chairman ....Adam Fogelson
Co-Chairman ....Donna Langley
Vice-Chairman ....Rick Finkelstein
President, Universal Pictures ....Jimmy Horowitz

Wicked is a proud member of the Broadway Green Alliance

To find out more about the world of *Wicked* and to take our Broadway survey, visit www.wickedthemusical.com.

CREDITS
Scenery built by F&D Scene Changes, Calgary, Canada. Show control and scenic motion control featuring Stage Command Systems© and scenery fabrication by Scenic Technologies, a division of Production Resource Group, New Windsor, NY. Lighting and certain special effects equipment from Fourth Phase and sound equipment from ProMix, both divisions of Production Resource Group LLC. Other special effects equipment by Sunshine Scenic Studios and Aztec Stage Lighting. Video projection system provided by Scharff Weisberg Inc. Projections by Vermilion Border Productions. Costumes by Barbara Matera Ltd., Parsons-Meares Ltd., Scafati, TRICORNE New York City and Eric Winterling. Millinery by Rodney Gordon and Lynne Mackey. Shoes by T.O. Dey, Frederick Longtin, Pluma, LaDuca Shoes NYC, and J.C. Theatrical. Flatheads and monkey wings built by Michael Curry Design Inc. Masks and prosthetics by W.M. Creations, Inc., Matthew W. Mungle and Lloyd Matthews; lifecasts by Todd Kleitsch. Fur by Fur & Furgery. Undergarments and hosiery by Bra*Tenders, Inc. Antique jewelry by Ilene Chazanof. Specialty jewelry and tiaras by Larry Vrba. Custom Oz accessories by LouLou Button. Custom screening by Gene Mignola. Certain props by John Creech Designs and Den Design Studio. Energy-efficient washers courtesy of LG Electronics. Additional hand props courtesy of George Fenmore. Confetti supplied by Artistry in Motion. Puppets by Bob Flanagan. Musical instruments from Manny's and Carroll Musical Instrument Rentals. Drums and other percussion equipment from Bosphorus, Black Swamp,

PTECH, D'Amico and Vater. Emer'gen'C provided by Alacer Corp. Rehearsed at the Lawrence A. Wien Center, 890 Broadway, and the Ford Center for the Performing Arts.

NEDERLANDER

Chairman ....James M. Nederlander
President ....James L. Nederlander

Executive Vice President
Nick Scandalios

Vice President   Senior Vice President
Corporate Development   Labor Relations
Charlene S. Nederlander   **Herschel Waxman**

Vice President   Chief Financial Officer
Jim Boese   **Freida Sawyer Belviso**

STAFF FOR THE GERSHWIN THEATRE
MANAGER ....RICHARD D. KAYE
Assistant Manager ....Susan Sunday
Treasurer ....John Campise
Assistant Treasurer ....Anthony Rossano
Carpenter ....John Riggins
Electrician ....Henry L. Brisen
Property Master ....Mark Illo
Flyman ....Dennis Fox
Fly Automation Carpenter ....Michael J. Szymanski
Head Usher ....Martha McGuire Boniface

Wicked
Scrapbook

been purposefully ripped open and the doll had a hairy butt.

Actor Who Performed the Most Roles in This Show: Brian Wanee, our onstage cross-over swing (in and out of the show), has performed the most roles—somewhere around 12.

Who Has Done the Most Shows: Kristen Gorski-Wergeles is our only remaining original cast member. To date (in late February 2012) she has marked 2974 performances.

Special Backstage Rituals: Spirit leader, Kathy Fitzgerald, liked to have the cast "circle-up" at the top of the show. The circle usually consisted of her...and her alone.

Favorite Moment During Each Performance (On Stage or Off): Watching Joe Schwarz, our head prop man, joggling Nessa's joystick. She goes round and round and round.

Favorite Off-Site Hangout: On any given night, you can probably still find one of the company members having a glass of wine after the show at Sosa Borella.

Favorite Snack Food: There is always a tub of peanut butter-filled pretzels in the stage management office. Sometimes you just need a salty peanut butter fix.

Favorite Therapy: The favorite therapy around *Wicked* is an oxidative bath. It has been referred to as "The Crazy Bath" and "The Explosive Bath." When someone is starting to get sick, a 20-minute hot bath filled with 64 oz. of hydrogen peroxide and a cup of Epsom salt is the suggested remedy. Don't try this at home.

Incident During a Performance: A lady was handily pleasing her Valentine in Row 3 and we were all attending the performance.

Memorable Ad-Lib: "Hold your center, Elphaba!" —Brian Wanee during Elphaba's dance in the OzDust Ballroom.

Memorable Stage Door Fan Encounter: Tom McGowan had a fan say to him, "I saw you in

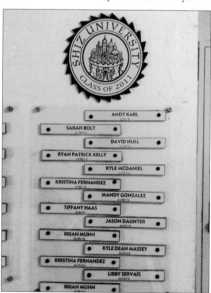

Backstage plaque remembering cast members who have "graduated."

More of Eddie Pendergraft's three-story backstage mural of scenes from *Wicked* so fellow cast members never have to leave Oz, even when offstage. Above, the burning of Shiz University. Below, the field of enchanted poppies.

Portland, and you are getting better."

Latest Audience Arrival: 10:15! Our show comes down 25 minutes later. Better late than never!

Fastest Costume Change: Crew getting out of blacks.

Heaviest/Hottest Costume: Most of our costumes are made out of upholstery fabric...who's hot in that??

Who Wore the Least: Maia Evwaraye-Griffin to, from, outside, inside the dressing room. Just about anywhere.

Catchphrases Only the Company Would Recognize: "¡Trabajo!" "Krow!" "Ecreif!"

Favorite Hangout in the Theatre: With Professor Plum in the greenroom with the remote control.

Orchestra Member Who Played the Most Instruments: Andy Jones, our percussionist, plays 59 instruments during the course of the show. He has an extra instrument for decoration.

Orchestra Member Who Played the Most Consecutive Performances Without a Sub: Greg Skaff played 112 consecutive performances between July 19 and October 23.

Memorable Directorial Notes: "No one's watching the dancers anyway." "This week you're on 8, not 6. And next week it will be back to 6."

Company In-Jokes: We don't laugh here. We're always about the work.

Understudy Anecdote: Bud Weber hit his head on the wall and almost gave himself a concussion during his first performance on as Fiyero.

Nicknames: Marybeth Abel loves to nickname the cast and crew. Here are some of the favorites:

Constantine Rousouli—Stan Risotto
Jennifer DiNoia—Jenny Any-Dots
Jon Warren—Jonny Ony-Dots
Brendan Quigley—Quigs
Nova Bergeron—Nova Scotia
Jordan Pankin—Jordissimo
Jesse JP Johnson—John Jacob Jingleheimer Schmidt
Jerad Bortz—Show Crush

Ghostly Encounters Backstage: Nathan Peck got tapped on the shoulder before his front of house monkey flight one evening. When he turned around, no one was standing near him. Later, when he told people about it, Kevin Hucke mentioned that he had the same experience throughout the years in the same location. It is rumored and believed to be the ghost at the Gershwin.

Coolest Thing About Being in This Show: It's a government job.

Two Stephen Schwartz musicals played at theatres in the same building during 2011-2012.

Wit

First Preview: January 5, 2012. Opened: January 26, 2012.
Closed March 17, 2012 after 24 Previews and 60 Performances.

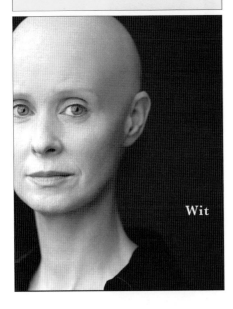

PLAYBILL

Wit

A scholar of John Donne's poetry discovers new and deeper meaning in the verses when she undergoes treatment for terminal cancer.

CAST

(in order of appearance)

Vivian Bearing, Ph.D. ....CYNTHIA NIXON
Harvey Kelekian, M.D./
   Mr. Bearing ....MICHAEL COUNTRYMAN
E.M. Ashford, D. Phil. ....SUZANNE BERTISH
Susie Monahan,
   R.N., B.S.N. ....CARRA PATTERSON
Lab Technicians/Students/
   Fellows .....PUN BANDHU, JESSICA DICKEY,
      CHIKÉ JOHNSON, ZACHARY SPICER
Jason Posner, M.D. ....GREG KELLER

Stage Manager ....KELLY BEAULIEU

TIME:
1995
PLACE:
A university hospital

UNDERSTUDIES

For Susie Monahan, R.N., B.S.N.:
JESSICA DICKEY
For Vivian Bearing, Ph.D./E.M. Ashford, D. Phil.:
ELIZABETH NORMENT
For Lab Technicians/Students/Fellows:
IRENE SOFIA LUCIO
For Harvey Kelekian, M.D./Mr. Bearing:
STEPHEN SCHNETZER
For Jason Posner, M.D.:
ZACHARY SPICER

Manhattan Theatre Club
Samuel J. Friedman Theatre

Artistic Director
Lynne Meadow

Executive Producer
Barry Grove

Presents

Wit

by
Margaret Edson

with

Pun Bandhu   Suzanne Bertish   Michael Countryman
Jessica Dickey   Chiké Johnson   Greg Keller
Cynthia Nixon   Carra Patterson   Zachary Spicer

Scenic Design	Costume Design	Lighting Design
Santo Loquasto	Jennifer von Mayrhauser	Peter Kaczorowski

Sound Design	Specialty Staging Consultant	Production Stage Manager
Jill BC Du Boff	J. David Brimmer	Barclay Stiff

Directed by
Lynne Meadow

Artistic Producer
Mandy Greenfield

General Manager
Florie Seery

Director of Artistic Development	Director of Marketing	Press Representative	Production Manager
Jerry Patch	Debra Waxman-Pilla	Boneau/Bryan-Brown	Joshua Helman

Director of Casting	Artistic Line Producer	Director of Development
Nancy Piccione	Lisa McNulty	Lynne Randall

Produced in New York City by MCC Theater (Bernard Telsey and Robert Lupone, *Executive Directors*; William Cantler, *Associate Director*), Long Wharf Theatre, and Daryl Roth, with Stanley Shopkorn, Robert G. Bartner and Stanley Kaufelt. Lorie Cowen Levy, *Associate Producer*; Roy Gabay, *General Manager*.

New York production originally premiered at Long Wharf Theatre, New Haven, Connecticut. Doug Hughes, *Artistic Director*; Michael Ross, *Managing Director*.

Originally produced by South Coast Repertory, David Emmes, *Producing Artistic Director*; Martin Benson, *Artistic Director*.

Manhattan Theatre Club wishes to express its appreciation to Theatre Development Fund for its support of this production.

1/26/12

(L-R): Pun Bandhu, Chiké Johnson, Jessica Dickey, Zachary Spicer, Greg Keller, Cynthia Nixon, Michael Countryman

Photo by Joan Marcus

Wit

Cynthia Nixon
Vivian Bearing, Ph.D.

Michael Countryman
*Harvey Kelekian,
M.D./Mr. Bearing*

Suzanne Bertish
*E. M. Ashford,
D. Phil.*

Carra Patterson
*Susie Monahan,
R.N., B.S.N.*

Pun Bandhu
*Lab Technician/
Student/Fellow*

Jessica Dickey
*Lab Technician/
Student/Fellow*

Chiké Johnson
*Lab Technician/
Student/Fellow*

Zachary Spicer
*Lab Technician/
Student/Fellow*

Greg Keller
Jason Posner, M.D.

Irene Sofia Lucio
*u/s Lab Technicians/
Students/Fellows*

Elizabeth Norment
*u/s Vivian Bearing,
Ph. D./E.M. Ashford,
D. Phil.*

Stephen Schnetzer
*u/s Harvey Kelekian,
M.D./Mr. Bearing*

Margaret Edson
Playwright

Lynne Meadow
*Director/
Artistic Director,
Manhattan Theatre
Club*

Santo Loquasto
Scenic Design

Jennifer Von
Mayrhauser
Costume Design

Peter Kaczorowski
Lighting Design

Jill BC Du Boff
Sound Design

J. David Brimmer
Fight Director

Barry Grove
*Executive Producer,
Manhattan Theatre
Club*

Photo by Brian Mapp

FRONT OF HOUSE STAFF
Front Row (L-R): Patricia Polhill, Lyanna Alvarado, Camille Vazquez, Tiffany Santucci, Dinah Glorioso

Back Row (L-R): Wendy Wright, Christine Snyder, Ed Brashear, Richard Ponce, Bridget Leak, Jim Joseph

Wit

SECURITY GUARD
Kemjika Iwuagwu

BOX OFFICE STAFF
(L-R): David Dillon, Geoffrey Nixon

CREW
Clockwise from upper left: Michael Countryman (Actor), Lou Shapiro (Sound), Kelly Beaulieu (Stage Manager), Erin Moeller (Company Manager), Shonté Walker, Jodi Jackson, Tim Walters (Head Props), Jeremy Von Deck (Apprentice), Sam Patt (Apprentice), Vaughn Preston (Automation), Suzanne Bertish (Actor), Thomas Bertsch (Wardrobe).

Wit

MANHATTAN THEATRE CLUB STAFF

Artistic Director	**Lynne Meadow**
Executive Producer	**Barry Grove**
General Manager	**Florie Seery**
Artistic Producer	**Mandy Greenfield**
Director of Artistic Development	**Jerry Patch**
Director of Artistic Operations	**Amy Gilkes Loe**
Artistic Line Producer	Lisa McNulty
Assistant to the Artistic Director	Nicki Hunter
Assistant to the Executive Producer	Emily Hammond
Assistant to the Artistic Producer	Megan Dieterle
Director of Casting	**Nancy Piccione**
Casting Associate	Kelly Gillespie
Casting Assistant	Darragh Garvey
Literary Manager/	
Sloan Project Manager	Annie MacRae
Literary Associate	Alex Barron
Artistic Administrative Assistant	Elizabeth Rothman
Director of Development	**Lynne Randall**
Director, Individual Giving	Emily Fleisher
Director, Special Events	Kristina Hoge
Manager, Individual Giving	Josh Martinez-Nelson
Manager, Institutional Giving	Andrea Gorzell
Development Associate/	
Individual Giving	Laura Petrucci
Development Associate/	
Institutional Giving	Ryan Fogarty
Development Associate/	
Special Events	Allison Taylor
Patrons' Liaison	Kaity Neagle
Director of Marketing	**Debra Waxman-Pilla**
Assistant Marketing Director	Becca Goland-Van Ryn
Marketing Manager	Caitlin Baird
Director of Finance	**Jessica Adler**
Director of Human Resources	**Darren Robertson**
Business Manager	Ryan Guhde
Business & HR Associate	Andrew Kao
Business Assistant	Lauren Amira
IT Manager	Mendy Sudranski
Systems Analyst	Andrew Dumawal
Studio Manager/Receptionist	Thatcher Stevens
Associate	
General Manager	**Lindsey Sag**
Company Manager/	
NY City Center	Samantha Kindler
General Management Assistant	Gillian Campbell
Director of	
Subscriber Services	**Robert Allenberg**
Subscriber Services Manager	Kevin Sullivan
Subscriber Services	
Representatives	Mark Bowers,
	Tim Salamandyk,
	Rosanna Consalvo Sarto,
	Amber Wilkerson
Director of Telesales and	
Telefunding	**George Tetlow**
Telesales and Telefunding Manager	Terrence Burnett
Telesales and Telefunding Staff	Stephen Brown,
	Kel Haney, Molly Thomas,
	Allison Zajac-Batell
Director of Education	**David Shookhoff**
Assistant Education Director/	
Coordinator, Paul A. Kaplan Theatre	
Management Program	Amy Harris
Education Assistant/	
TheatreLink Coordinator	Nora DeVeau-Rosen
MTC Teaching Artists	Stephanie Alston,

David Auburn, Chris Ceraso,
Charlotte Colavin, Dominic Colon,
Allison Daugherty, Andy Goldberg,
Kel Haney, Elise Hernandez,
Jeffrey Joseph, Julie Leedes, Kate Long,
Andres Munar, Melissa Murray,
Angela Pietropinto, Alexa Polmer,
Carmen Rivera, Judy Tate,
Candido Tirado, Liam Torres, Joe White

Theatre Management Interns	Cindy De La Cruz,
	Scott Kaplan, Ben Kawaller,
	Elizabeth Marvin, Schuyler Rooth,
	Aleeza Sklover, Nick Trotta,
	Alyssa Weldon, Amanda Williams,
	Caroline Young, Emily Yowell

Production Manager	**Joshua Helman**
Associate Production Manager	Bethany Weinstein
Assistant Production Manager	Kevin Service
Properties Supervisor	**Scott Laule**
Assistant Properties Supervisor	Julia Sandy
Props Carpenter	Peter Grimes
Costume Supervisor	**Erin Hennessy Dean**

GENERAL PRESS REPRESENTATION
BONEAU/BRYAN-BROWN

Chris Boneau	Aaron Meier
Christine Olver	Emily Meagher

Script Readers	Aaron Grunfeld,
	Clifford Lee Johnson III, Liz Jones,
	Rachel Lerner-Ley, Thomas Park,
	Rachel Slaven

SERVICES

Accountants	ERE, LLP
Advertising	SpotCo/Drew Hodges,
	Tom Greenwald, Jim Edwards,
	Tom McCann, Beth Watson, Tim Falotico
Web Design	SpotCo Interactive/
	Sara Fitzpatrick, Michael Crowley,
	Marc Mettler, Meghan Ownbey
Legal Counsel	Charles H. Googe, Jr.;
	Carol M. Kaplan/
	Paul, Weiss, Rifkind,
	Wharton and Garrison LLP
Real Estate Counsel	Marcus Attorneys
Labor Counsel	Harry H. Weintraub/
	Glick and Weintraub, P.C.
Immigration Counsel	Theodore Ruthizer/
	Kramer, Levin, Naftalis & Frankel, LLP
Sponsorship	
Consultant	Above the Title Entertainment/
	Jed Bernstein
Insurance	DeWitt Stern Group, Inc./
	Anthony Pittari
Maintenance	Reliable Cleaning
Production Photographer	Joan Marcus
Event Photography	Bruce Glikas
Cover Photograph	Jason Bell
Cover Design	SpotCo
Theatre Displays	King Displays

PRODUCTION STAFF FOR WIT

Company Manager	**Erin Moeller**
Production Stage Manager	**Barclay Stiff**
Stage Manager	Kelly Beaulieu

Mary Mill Directing Fellow	Kel Haney
Projection Designer	**Rocco DiSanti**
Wig Design	Paul Huntley
Make-Up Designer	Angelina Avallone
Assistant Scenic Designer	Antje Ellermann
Assistant Costume Designer	Leslie Bernstein
Costume Intern	Heather Carey
Assistant Lighting Designer	Gina Scherr
Assistant Sound Designer	Janie Bullard
Lighting Programmer	Marc Polimeni
Spot Light Operator	Sean Kane
Automation Operator	Vaughn Preston
Specialty Staging Assistants	Dan O'Driscoll,
	Turner Smith, Rin Allen,
	Mitchell McCoy
Hair/Make-Up Supervisor	Natasha Steinhagen
Production Assistants	Aaron Elgart,
	McKenzie Murphy

CREDITS

Scenery fabrication by Global Scenic Studios. Lighting equipment provided by PRG Lighting. Sound equipment provided by Masque Sound. Projection equipment by Scharff Weisberg. Makeup provided by M•A•C.

The Divine Poems by Donne, edited by Gardner (2001), one line, by permission of Oxford University Press. *The Runaway Bunny* by Margaret Wise Brown, copyright 1942 by Harper and Row Publishers. Text copyright renewed 1970 by Roberta Brown Rauch.

MTC thanks the following people for sharing their experience with the company of *Wit*: Cathy Handy, Ph.D., R.N., AOCN; Theresa Brown, R.N.; and Jeanette Kent and the Oncology Nursing Society.

For more information visit
www.ManhattanTheatreClub.org

**MANHATTAN THEATRE CLUB
SAMUEL J. FRIEDMAN THEATRE STAFF**

Theatre Manager	**Jim Joseph**
Assistant House Manager	Richard Ponce
Box Office Treasurer	**David Dillon**
Assistant Box Office Treasurers	Dustin Eastwood,
	Geoffrey Nixon
Head Carpenter	Chris Wiggins
Head Propertyman	Timothy Walters
Sound Engineer	Louis Shapiro
Master Electrician	Jeff Dodson
Wardrobe Supervisor	Leah Redmond
Apprentices	Sam Pratt, Jeremy Von Deck
Chief Engineer	Deosarran
Maintenance Engineers	Ricky Deosarran,
	Maximo Perez
Security	Allied Barton
Lobby Refreshments	Sweet Concessions

Wit
SCRAPBOOK

Correspondents: Jessica Dickey, Pun Bandhu, Zachary Spicer and Chiké Johnson, "Lab Technicians/Students/Fellows," a.k.a. "The Code Team."

Memorable Opening Night Faxes and Notes: It was so fun to see all the notices from the other Broadway shows! All of us on the Code Team made our Broadway debuts with *Wit*, and it was cool to realize what a community Broadway really is, how the different shows cheer each other on and bowl together and such!

Opening Night Gifts: Lynne gave us all *Wit* hats, which Jessie wore every time she ran in Central Park between shows (good advertising).

Most Exciting Celebrity Visitor and What He Said: Ian McKellen. We're all major fans and we rushed down to meet him at Cynthia's dressing room, and Cynthia shook his hand and said, "Thank you for coming." To which he replied in his amazing Ian McKellen way, "Oh I didn't come to see you, but I couldn't help noticing you.... Well done."

Special Backstage Ritual: We didn't do this much during the run, but during the rehearsals Lynne would have the company stand in a circle and hold hands and pass the pulse. At first it was delightful in a BFA program kind of way, but it came to be a special ritual for the company, and one which defined our energy and intention as a cast.

Favorite Moment During Each Performance (On Stage or Off): The company bow. The amount of catharsis and gratitude that the audience expresses to Cynthia and the company through their teary standing ovations every performance was a true privilege to witness and be a part of.

Favorite In-Theatre Gathering Place: Definitely the ladies' dressing room up top—Cynthia would often come and chat before the show, cast meetings were often held there, this is where we passed the pulse during tech—a lotta good vibes in that room.

Favorite Off-Site Hangout: GLASS HOUSE TAVERN!! A huge shout-out and thanks to Kevin and Chris and the entire staff at Glass House. They took amazing care of us!!! The food is incredible and the staff is fantastic. Great atmosphere.

Favorite Snack Food: Any kind of cookie.

Fastest Costume Change: Pun had a specific hairdo for each of his ensemble characters. It was subtle, but required a great deal of attention each costume change. :)

Catchphrase Only the Company Would Recognize: The Code Team wanted to start an advertising campaign: "*Wit*—you'll need a Code Team too!"

Coolest Thing About Being in This Show: We had the coolest stage management team EVER. Barclay and Kelly kept it real.

1. (L-R): Author Margaret Edson, star Cynthia Nixon and director Lynne Meadow at the opening night party at B.B. King Blues Club and Grill.
2. The "Code Team" (and *Yearbook* correspondents) on opening night (L-R): Zachary Spicer, Pun Bandhu, Jessica Dickey and Chiké Johnson.
3. Nixon onstage for curtain call at the premiere.
4. Cast member Carra Patterson at B.B. King's.

The following shows closed shortly after the start of the 2011-2012 season with no changes to their casts from the previous year's Playbill Broadway Yearbook. *For complete details and photographs from these shows, please consult the 2010-2011 edition.*

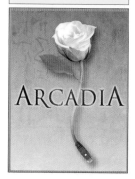

First Preview: February 26, 2011.
Opened: March 17, 2011.
Closed June 19, 2011 after 20 Previews and 108 Performances.

First Preview: March 11, 2011.
Opened: March 31, 2011.
Closed July 3, 2011 after 23 Previews and 108 Performances.

First Preview: February 21, 2011
Opened: March 22, 2011.
Closed July 10, 2011 after 25 Previews and 95 Performances.

First Preview: April 4, 2011.
Opened: April 25, 2011.
Closed June 25, 2011 after 21 Previews and 72 Performances.

First Preview: December 17, 2010.
Opened: January 13, 2011.
Closed June 26, 2011 after 30 Previews and 189 Performances.

First Preview: March 13, 2010.
Opened: April 11, 2010.
Closed June 12, 2011 after 34 Previews and 489 Performances.
Transferred to Off-Broadway.

First Preview: March 15, 2011.
Opened: April 11, 2011.
Closed July 17, 2011 after 28 Previews and 112 Performances.

First Preview: April 19, 2011.
Opened: April 27, 2011.
Closed July 10, 2011 after 10 Previews and 86 Performances.

First Preview: April 1, 2011.
Opened: April 28, 2011.
Closed June 19, 2011 after 30 Previews and 60 Performances.

Events

Broadway Bares XXI: "Masterpiece"

June 19, 2011 at Roseland Ballroom

Broadway Bares XXI: Masterpiece, the annual Burlesque-style celebration of Broadway's buffest bodies, broke last year's record by raising $1,103,072 for Broadway Cares/Equity Fights AIDS over two performances at the Roseland Ballroom.

Josh Rhodes, assistant choreographer for *The Drowsy Chaperone*, directed the fundraiser. 192 Broadway dancers brought art to life as they recreated classic works such as Michelangelo's *David*, Da Vinci's *The Last Supper*, Monet's *Water Lillies*, Munch's *The Scream* and Wood's *American Gothic*, to name a few.

This year's show featured performances by guest stars from many current and Broadway recent shows, including Robin De Jesús, David Hyde Pierce, Beth Leavel, Judith Light, Patina Miller, Rory O'Malley, Jim Parsons, Roger Rees and Christopher Sieber, plus journalist Michael Riedel.

1. Mistress of Ceremonies Beth Leavel (*Baby It's You!*) and David Hyde Pierce (*La Bête*).
2. Patina Miller (*Sister Act*) singing "The Final Masterpiece" as the cast recreates Seurat's *A Sunday Afternoon on the Island of La Grande Jatte*.
3. Nikka Graff Lanzarone kicks up her heels as a very naughty *Whistler's Mother* in the opening number "Going, Going, Gone."
4. Joshua Buscher (*Priscilla Queen of the Desert*) as *Washington Crossing the Delaware*.
5. The Broadway Bares Dancers with their auction paddles at the ready.

Broadway Barks 13

July 9, 2011 in Shubert Alley

Broadway Barks 13, the annual pet adopt-a-thon to benefit New York City animal shelters was held in Shubert Alley and hosted by founders Mary Tyler Moore and Bernadette Peters.

With an assist from Broadway stars, pets from 27 New York City animal shelters and adoption agencies looking for good homes were on parade. Some "celebrity dog walkers" lending a leash included Nick Adams, Bill Berloni, Kerry Butler, Bobby Cannavale, Reeve Carney, Sutton Foster, Joel Grey, John Benjamin Hickey, Jackie Hoffman, Nikki M. James, Patina Miller, Michael Mulheren, John Larroquette, Andrew Rannells and Will Swenson.

1. Mary Tyler Moore, Nell Newman, Bernadette Peters and friends.
2. Brad Oscar.
3. Aaron Tveit.

Broadway Meows 3

July 18, 2011 at Don't Tell Mama

The third annual Broadway Meows concert to benefit the Humane Society of New York was produced by Dennis Fowler and directed by Laura Pestronk, featuring songs by composer/lyricist Seth Bisen-Hersh. Bisen-Hersh began the concert in 2009 as way of saying thanks to the Humane Society for saving his cat, Smee.

Front Row (L-R): Lanene Charters, Sean Patrick Doyle, Seth Bisen-Hersh, Rori Nogee, Crystal Davidson, Lara Janine, Russell Fischer
Middle Row (L-R): Joi Danielle Price, Mackenzie Thomas, Olivia Oguma, Ryan Link, Stephanie Klemons, Brian Childers, Brian Shaw, Kristen Beth Williams, Garrett Long, Kimberly Faye Greenberg, Elisa Winter
Back Row (L-R): Brian Charles Rooney, Nathan Freeman

Roundabout Theatre Company *She Loves Me*

December 5, 2011 at Stephen Sondheim Theatre

As he did in 1993, Scott Ellis directed *She Loves Me* for Roundabout Theatre Company, this time to celebrate Roundabout's 20th anniversary of producing on Broadway and to benefit its programs, including its musical theatre initiative.

Kelli O'Hara and Josh Radnor (TV's "How I Met Your Mother") led an all-star cast which also included Peter Bartlett, Gavin Creel, Victor Garber, Jane Krakowski, Michael McGrath and Rory O'Malley all under the baton of conductor Paul Gemignani.

On hand to take a bow were Joe Masteroff (libretto) and Sheldon Harnick (lyrics). Composer Jerry Bock passed away in 2010.

(L-R): Victor Garber, Josh Radnor, Joe Masteroff, Sheldon Harnick, Kelli O'Hara and cast

Broadway in Bryant Park

Summer Thursdays 2011 in Bryant Park

Cast members from *Sister Act, Catch Me If You Can, Mary Poppins, Million Dollar Quartet, Rock of Ages, Anything Goes, Jersey Boys, Hair, Billy Elliot, Mamma Mia!, Newsical, The Fantasticks, Stomp* and other Broadway and Off-Broadway shows rocked Bryant Park at lunchtime Thursdays throughout the summer.

The free outdoor concert series gives the public samples from current shows.

(L-R): Caesar Samayoa, John Treacy Egan and Demond Green of *Sister Act*

Broadway Softball League Championship

August 25, 2011 at Hecksher Fields in Central Park

After two championships games, the team from *Rock of Ages* beat the *Catch Me If You Can* team 5-2 to win the 2011 Broadway Softball League championship, in a game that was forced to end early due to the rainy weather.

The win came after 16 weeks of Thursday afternoon softball games in Central Park, played by teams consisting of employees from more than two dozen Broadway shows and organizations at Hecksher Fields.

High-fives are exchanged between the teams from *Catch Me If You Can* and *Rock of Ages*.

Broadway Flea Market and Grand Auction

September 25, 2011 at West 44th Street and Times Square

The 25th Annual Broadway Flea Market and Grand Auction raised a total of $547,658 for Broadway Cares/Equity Fights AIDS. Held in its traditional West 44th Street location, for the first time it also included the Times Square pedestrian plaza on Broadway between West 43rd and 44th Streets.

Sixty-three tables selling a variety of theatre memorabilia raised $273,886. The tables that raised the most money this year were those hosted by *Wicked* ($15,367) and *Follies* ($14,819).

Earlier in the day, a series of half-hour silent auctions included 140 items and raised $59,365. Musical phrases handwritten and signed by Broadway composers proved most popular. The top item sold was *Godspell*'s "Day by Day" musical phrase, written and signed by Stephen Schwartz, selling for $3,500.

The Grand Auction included both live and silent auctions, as well as instant-experience "flash auctions," which were new this year. The live auction included 63 "lots" and raised $201,500. The top draw was a walk-on in *The Phantom of the Opera*, which went for $10,500 to two bidders, raising $21,000. The popular Autograph Table and Photo Booth raised $16,500, with more than 60 actors donating their time to meet with fans and help support BC/EFA.

Two top live auction items raised $10,000 each: A one-of-kind autographed photograph of the late Elizabeth Taylor, taken by Rivka Katvan during the 1981 production of *The Little Foxes*. It was autographed by the acting legend exclusively for Broadway Cares shortly before her death earlier this year; and a set visit to "Modern Family" in Los Angeles, coordinated by Broadway favorite Jesse Tyler Ferguson.

1. Tony Sheldon (*Priscilla*) is in the pink.
2. Melissa Errico, Ron Raines (*Follies*) and Gina Tognoni (*The Guiding Light*).
3. Judith Light and Thomas Sadoski of *Other Desert Cities*.
4. Joshing around with Josh Gad and Nikki M. James (*The Book of Mormon*).
5. Lindsay Mendez and Hunter Parrish (*Godspell*).
6. Charles Busch and Carole Shelley (*Billy Elliot*).

The 85th Macy's Thanksgiving Day Parade

November 24, 2011 on Broadway and West 34th Street.

In addition to floats, balloons and those high-kicking Rockettes, Macy's annual Thanksgiving Day Parade also included performances by the casts of Broadway shows, providing some high kicks of their own. This year's performances were by *Anything Goes*, "The Brotherhood of Man" with Daniel Radcliffe and the cast of *How to Succeed...*, *Memphis* ("Radio") featuring Adam Pascal, *Newsies* ("King of New York"), *Priscilla Queen of the Desert* ("I Love the Nightlife"), Patina Miller, Carolee Carmello and the *Sister Act* cast ("Spread the Love") and Reeve Carney, Patrick Page and the cast of *Spider-Man: Turn Off the Dark*.

Spider-Man takes a break from his gig at the Foxwoods Theatre to fly through the streets of New York.

Hulaween

October 28, 2011 at the Waldorf-Astoria Hotel

Bette Midler hosted her annual costume gala at the Waldorf-Astoria Hotel to benefit the New York Restoration Project. NYRP is dedicated to transforming open spaces throughout the city into green oases.

On hand to help with the festivities were Judy Gold, Master of Ceremonies, Michael Kors, who judged the costumes, and a collection of celebrities from the stage and concert hall. The evening honored Douglas Durst and Benjamin F. Needell, Esq. and featured a special performance by Stevie Wonder.

1. (L-R): Margo McNabb Nederlander and Jimmy Nederlander as Eva and Juan Perón.
2. Stevie Wonder and Bette Midler.

Broadway Recycled

April 22, 2012 at Joe's Pub

The third annual Earth Day concert, *Broadway Recycled*, presented by At Hand Theatre and highlighting songs cut from Broadway musicals, was held at Joe's Pub as a benefit for At Hand and the Broadway Green Alliance.

The concert, directed by Jennifer Ashley Tepper with musical direction by Julie McBride, featured performances by Alexis Field, J. Michael Friedman, Annie Golden, Randy Graff, Curt Hansen, Jessica Kent, Kait Kerrigan, Nikka Lanzarone, Jeremy Morse, Jacey Powers, Krysta Rodriguez, Jason Tam, Marty Thomas, Kate Wetherhead, Jason SweetTooth Williams, Robert Hancock, Megan McGinnis and Alex Wyse.

The cast of Broadway Recycled

Broadway Bears XV

March 18, 2012 at BB King Blues Club & Grill

The 15th edition of Broadway Bears, the annual auction of handmade, one-of-a-kind, theatrically costumed teddy bears, raised a record-setting $198,300 benefiting Broadway Cares/Equity Fights AIDS. The cumulative fundraising total for the 15 annual editions of this event stands at $2,048,427. This year's edition was billed as the event's grand finale.

The top bid for the 2012 auction went to a recreation of the horse Joey from the Tony Award-winning *War Horse*. Designed by Barak Stribling and Jamie Filippelli and based on the working drawings the Handspring Puppet Company used for the Broadway production, the Joey bear came complete with his own bear handlers. Seth Numrich, who starred as Albert in the Broadway production, signed the bear and helped lead the live auction bidding to an unprecedented $20,000 final price tag.

Two bidders fought for *The Lion King*'s Simba bear, designed by Katie Falk, Ilya Vett and Islah Abdul-Rahiim and signed by director/costume designer Julie Taymor. Winning bid: $18,000.

The bikini-clad bear representing Bette Midler's 1975 Broadway *Clams on the Half Shell Revue* arrived in her very own clam shell. Designed by Kevin Phillips, this Broadway bear snatched a high bid of $7,000.

Hugh Jackman signed the bear designed by Matthew Hemesath, which was dressed in the Peter Allen costume that opened Jackman's second act. It sold for $5,000.

1. Designer Kevin Phillips with the bear representing Bette Midler's Divine Miss M.
2. The Hugh Jackman/Peter Allen bear.
3. Joey from *War Horse* with his bear handlers.
4. *Spider-Man*'s Patrick Page with the Simba bear from *The Lion King*.

Photos by Monica Simoes

Broadway Beauty Pageant

March 19, 2012 at Symphony Space

Andrew Chappelle, Mr. *Mamma Mia!*, was crowned as winner of the sold out, sixth annual Broadway Beauty Pageant held March 19, 2012 at Symphony Space. The event raised a record $75,000 to benefit the Ali Forney Center, which provides shelter to homeless LGBT youth in New York City.

The evening featured Andrew Chappelle (*Mamma Mia!*), Wilkie Ferguson III (*Porgy and Bess*), Corey Mach (*Godspell*), Jesse Swimm (*Mary Poppins*) and Anthony Wayne (*Priscilla Queen of the Desert*). Brent Barrett (*Chicago*) and past Pageant winners Frankie James Grande (*Mamma Mia!*), Michael Cusumano (*Chicago*) and Anthony Hollock (*Hair*) also performed.

The contestants went head-to-head in front of a panel of celebrity judges, but ultimately, the final vote was the hands of the audience. The judges were Jackie Hoffman (*The Addams Family*), pop culture columnist Michael Musto and Tonya Pinkins (*Caroline, or Change*). The evening was hosted by four-time Tony nominated and Drama Desk Award-winning actress Tovah Feldshuh.

The Broadway Beauty Pageant was written and conceived by Jeffery Self and directed by Ryan J. Davis, with musical direction by Christopher Denny.

Photo by Gustavo Monroy

Broadway Beauty Andrew Chappelle

Roundabout Theatre Company Gala: From Stage to Screen

March 12, 2012 at the Hammerstein Ballroom

Rob Marshall, a Tony, Academy Award, Golden Globe nominee and four-time Emmy Award winner, received the Roundabout Theatre's Jason Robards Award for Excellence in the Theatre at RTC's gala called, appropriately, *From Stage to Screen*. The evening, hosted by Martin Short and directed and choreographed by Rob's sister, director Kathleen Marshall, with musical direction by David Krane, included performances by Bernadette Peters, Richard Gere, Christine Baranski, Boyd Gaines, Victor Garber, Donna Murphy and Kelli O'Hara.

1. (L-R): John DeLuca and Rob Marshall.
2. (L-R): Vanessa Williams and Kristin Chenoweth.

Broadway Originals!

October 16, 2011 at The Town Hall

The Seventh Annual *Broadway Cabaret Festival*, created, written and hosted for The Town Hall by Scott Siegel, kicked off with an afternoon titled *Broadway Originals!* The concert, directed by Scott Coulter, featured performers reprising songs they introduced either in the original Broadway production or revival.

Some of those who reprised their roles include Tony Award winners Tammy Grimes (*The Unsinkable Molly Brown*), Yvonne Constant (*La Plume de Ma Tante*) and Daisy Eagan (*The Secret Garden*).

(L-R): Marva Hicks, Vanessa A. Jones and Ramona Keller "The Radio Ladies" from *Caroline, or Change*.

Seventh Annual Fred Ebb Award

November 28, 2011 in the Penthouse Lobby of the American Airlines Theatre

Composer-lyricist Jeff Blumenkrantz was named recipient of the seventh annual Fred Ebb Award, an honor for rising musical theatre songwriters. The award includes $50,000, one of the largest prizes for American dramatic writing. The award was presented to Jeff by Bebe Neuwirth, a veteran of Ebb's *Chicago*.

The Fred Ebb Foundation (Mitchell Bernard, trustee) in association with the Roundabout Theatre Company (Todd Haimes, artistic director) gives the awards, established by the late Tony Award-winning lyricist of *Chicago, Cabaret, Zorba, Kiss of the Spider Woman* and other shows.

1. (L-R): Jeff Blumenkrantz and Bebe Neuwirth.
2. (L-R): John Kander, Margery Gray Harnick and Sheldon Harnick.

23rd Annual "Gypsy of the Year"

December 5 and 6, 2011 at the New Amsterdam Theatre

Literally auctioning the shirt off his back at performances of *Hugh Jackman Back on Broadway* helped Tony-winning Australian native Hugh Jackman to raise a one-show record of $857,740 as part of the 23rd Annual Gypsy of the Year competition, pushing the total for the 2011 Broadway Cares/Equity Fights AIDS fundraising event to a new overall record of $4,895,253.

Jackman's share of the total was so large—more than twice the next largest total ($325,935 raised by *How to Succeed in Business Without Really Trying*)—that the judges took him out of the competition and gave him a Special Award for the effort.

A farewell performance from the cast of *Billy Elliot* earned the soon-to-close musical the title of 2011 Gypsy of the Year/Best Stage Presentation.

Jackman was on hand with Daniel Radcliffe (*How to Succeed*), Bernadette Peters (*Follies*) and host Seth Rudetsky to hand out the awards. A total of 52 other Broadway, Off-Broadway and touring shows raised the rest of the money in six weeks of curtain-call appeals at theatres across New York and around the country.

A highlight of this year's event was the opening number, featuring a reunion of the original 1972 Broadway cast of the musical *Grease*. Thirteen original performers including Barry Bostwick, Carole Demas and Adrienne Barbeau (original Danny, Sandy and Rizzo, respectively) led a chorus of younger dancers in a medley of hits from the score.

Among other Broadway shows that performed dances or skits: *The Addams Family, Anything Goes, Chicago, Mamma Mia, Memphis, The Lion King, The Phantom of the Opera, Sister Act, Spider-Man: Turn Off the Dark.*

1. (L-R): Hugh Jackman, Daniel Radcliffe and Bernadette Peters present the awards.
2. Members of the original cast of *Grease* reunite and sing a medley from the show's score.
3. Leslie Uggams appears in "June," the skit from *Anything Goes*.
4. (L-R): Rob Bartlett, Rose Hemingway and Christopher J. Hanke of *How to Succeed* perform a skit about injuries, "Do the F**ing Show."
5. Young members of the *Mary Poppins* cast perform the "Junior" version of *Who's Afraid of Virginia Woolf?*
6. Gypsies from *Chicago* perform "*Chicago* Now and Forever."
7. Seth Rudetsky compares singing styles.

Broadway Backwards

March 5, 2012 at the Al Hirschfeld Theatre

Photos by Joseph Marzullo/WENN

Broadway Backwards, now in its seventh year, raised a record-breaking $329,000 to benefit Broadway Cares/Equity Fights AIDS and The Lesbian, Gay, Bisexual & Transgender Community Center (the Center).

The format, men singing songs traditionally sung by women and women singing those written for men, added another twist this year with a storyline featuring "leading ladies" Robin De Jesús and Jason Michael Snow. Created and directed by Rob Bartley with musical direction by Mary-Mitchell Campbell, the story follows the meeting and budding romance of the characters played by De Jesús and Snow, who duetted on "Old Fashioned Wedding." Throughout the night, Broadway luminaries contributed their musical talents. Included were Charles Busch ("If He Walked Into My Life"), Andrew Rannells ("The Music That Makes Me Dance"), Sierra Boggess and Elizabeth Stanley ("Tonight"), Jim Brochu and Harvey Evans ("It's Never Too Late to Fall in Love"), Jessie Mueller ("She Wasn't You"), Mario Cantone ("What Did I Have That I Don't Have"), Barrett Foa and Telly Leung ("I Still Believe") and Betty Buckley ("Not While I'm Around"/ "Johanna"/ "My Friends")

1. Cicily Daniels.
2. (L-R): Robin De Jesús and Jason Michael Snow.
3. (L-R): Anthony Fedorov and Brian Charles Rooney.
4. Betty Buckley.

Manhattan Theatre Club's Spring Gala

April 30, 2012 at Cipriani 42nd Street

Nina Arianda and Hugh Dancy hosted MTC's Spring Gala, which honored Glenn Britt and Time Warner Cable for their continued support of the organization. Jeremy Jordan, Corbin Bleu and the cast of *Godspell*, Tony Award winner Adriane Lenox, The Craze from *One Man, Two Guvnors*, Josh Young and the cast of *Jesus Christ Superstar*, the cast of *Leap of Faith*, Judy Kaye and Michael McGrath from *Nice Work If You Can Get It* and Dee Roscioli and Andrew Samonsky of *Murder Ballad*, a new musical in development at MTC, provided the entertainment for the evening.

Dignitaries included Lynne Meadow (MTC Artistic Director), and Barry Grove (MTC Executive Producer), as well as Margaret Colin, currently in the MTC production of *The Columnist,* and Marlo Thomas.

Photos by Monica Simoes

1. (L-R): Hosts Hugh Dancy and Nina Arianda.
2. The Craze from *One Man, Two Guvnors*.
3. (L-R): Lynne Meadow, Glenn Britt, Marlo Thomas and Barry Grove.

Miscast 2012

March 26, 2012 at the Hammerstein Ballroom

Comic Lewis Black hosted the MCC Theatre's Miscast 2012 gala, held at the Hammerstein Ballroom. The evening honored the authors of the musical *Carrie*: Michael Gore (composer); Dean Pitchford (lyricist) and Lawrence D. Cohen (book). A host of Broadway stars performed songs from shows and roles in which they would never ordinarily be cast.

Performers featured were Jonathan Groff ("The Music That Makes Me Dance"/*Funny Girl* and with the dancing ensemble, "Anything Goes"), Nicole Parker ("Soliloquy"/*Carousel*), Nikki M. James ("What More Can I Say"/*Falsettos*), Walter Bobbie ("If He Walked Into My Life"/*Mame*), Megan Hilty ("Mean to Me"/*Ain't Misbehavin'*), Josh Gad & Rory O'Malley ("For Good"/*Wicked*), Constantine Maroulis ("Home"/*The Wiz*; "And I Am Telling You I'm Not Going"/*Dreamgirls*), Jan Maxwell ("The Confrontation"/*Jekyll & Hyde*), Adriane Lenox ("When She Loved Me"/*Toy Story 2*) and Nicole Parker ("On My Own"/*Les Misérables*).

1. Megan Hilty.
2. Nikki M. James.
3. The cast of *Carrie*.
4. (L-R): Jonathan Groff and Walter Bobbie.

The Actors Fund Gala

May 21, 2012 at the New York Marriott Marquis Hotel

The 2012 Actors Fund Gala honored Tony and Emmy Award-winning artist/activist Harry Belafonte, acting duo Anne Meara and Jerry Stiller, and real-estate developer David Steiner.

Belafonte (*John Murray Anderson's Almanac*) was honored for his "lifelong career as artist and activist" with the Lee Strasberg Artistic Achievement Award, while Stiller and Meara received The Actors Fund Medal of Honor for their "long-time commitment to The Fund." David Steiner, a trustee since 2006, also received The Fund's Medal of Honor for his "service to the national human services organization."

1. Harry Belafonte.
2. Anne Meara and Jerry Stiller.

Photos by Monica Simoes

The 26th Annual Easter Bonnet Competition

April 23 and 24, 2012 at the Minskoff Theatre

The 26th annual Broadway Cares/Equity Fights AIDS Easter Bonnet Competition raised $3,677,855 in six weeks of nightly curtain-call appeals, the third-highest total in the history of the event. The sum was revealed at the second of two performances, held at the Minskoff Theatre, of skits, songs and dances that make up the unique fundraiser-show.

The total was just shy of last year's $3.70 million and was raised by 52 participating Broadway, Off-Broadway and touring shows. The top Broadway fundraising award went to *The Book of Mormon* which rang up $286,725. The Broadway play that raised the most was *Other Desert Cities* at $71,965.

Ricky Martin (*Evita*), Audra McDonald (*The Gershwins' Porgy and Bess*) and Eric McCormack (*Gore Vidal's The Best Man*) presented the performance/bonnet awards. Outstanding bonnet design went to the Broadway company of *Mamma Mia!*

As they did in 2011, the two touring companies of the musical *Wicked* took the top fundraising awards among national tours. The "Emerald City" company earned $280,504 and the "Munchkinland" company (the last two years' top fundraiser) was a runner-up, collecting $166,434 in the fight against AIDS.

The company of Broadway's *The Lion King* took the top prize for bonnet presentation, with "Hallelujah Harlem," tapping and singing gospel in 1920s period clothes. Church women in big hats combined them to make a bonnet resembling the marquee of the iconic Apollo Theatre.

1. The Broadway company of *Mamma Mia!* picked up the prize for outstanding bonnet design.
2. Dancers Responding to AIDS perform "Boys, Boys, Boys."
3. Awards presenters Eric McCormack (*Gore Vidal's The Best Man*), Audra McDonald (*The Gershwins' Porgy and Bess*) and Ricky Martin (*Evita*).
4. The cast of *Spider-Man: Turn Off the Dark* poke fun at their show's history of technical problems.
5. All the bonnets are displayed in the finale.
6. Christie Brinkley and Tony Yazbeck (*Chicago*).

The Antoinette Perry (Tony) Awards

June 10, 2012 at the Beacon Theatre

Photos by Joseph Marzullo/WENN

*O*nce, *Clybourne Park, The Gershwins' Porgy and Bess* and *Arthur Miller's Death of a Salesman* won the major production categories at the 2012 Antoinette Perry "Tony" Awards.

The 66th annual awards, representing excellence in Broadway theatre for the 2011-2012 season, were presented at the Beacon Theatre in a ceremony hosted by Neil Patrick Harris and broadcast on CBS-TV. The nominees and recipients of the 66th Annual Tony Awards follow. Winners are listed in **boldface**, with an asterisk (*).

Best Musical
Leap of Faith
Newsies
Nice Work If You Can Get It
***Once**

Best Play
***Clybourne Park* by Bruce Norris**
Other Desert Cities by Jon Robin Baitz
Peter and the Starcatcher by Rick Elice
Venus in Fur by David Ives

Best Revival of a Musical
Evita
Follies
***The Gershwins' Porgy and Bess**
Jesus Christ Superstar

1. (L-R): Brendan Griffin, Frank Wood, Crystal A. Dickinson, author Bruce Norris, Annie Parisse, Christina Kirk, Damon Gupton, Jordan Roth (Producer) of Best Play winner *Clybourne Park.*
2. (L-R): James Corden (Best Actor-Play), Audra McDonald (Best Actress-Musical), Nina Arianda (Best Actress-Play) and Steve Kazee (Best Actor-Musical)
3. Enda Walsh (Best Book of a Musical) and Martin Lowe (Best Orchestrations) of *Once.*
4. John Tiffany (Best Direction of a Musical) of *Once.*

The Tony Awards

Best Revival of a Play
*Arthur Miller's Death of a Salesman
Gore Vidal's The Best Man
Master Class
Wit

Best Performance by an Actor in a Leading Role in a Musical
Danny Burstein, *Follies*
Jeremy Jordan, *Newsies*
*Steve Kazee, *Once*
Norm Lewis, *The Gershwins' Porgy and Bess*
Ron Raines, *Follies*

Best Performance by an Actress in a Leading Role in a Musical
Jan Maxwell, *Follies*
*Audra McDonald, *The Gershwins' Porgy and Bess*
Cristin Milioti, *Once*
Kelli O'Hara, *Nice Work If You Can Get It*
Laura Osnes, *Bonnie & Clyde*

Best Best Performance by an Actor in a Leading Role in a Play
*James Corden, *One Man, Two Guvnors*
Philip Seymour Hoffman, *Arthur Miller's Death of a Salesman*
James Earl Jones, *Gore Vidal's The Best Man*
Frank Langella, *Man and Boy*
John Lithgow, *The Columnist*

Best Performance by an Actress in a Leading Role in a Play
*Nina Arianda, *Venus in Fur*
Tracie Bennett, *End of the Rainbow*
Stockard Channing, *Other Desert Cities*
Linda Lavin, *The Lyons*
Cynthia Nixon, *Wit*

Best Performance by an Actor in a Featured Role in a Musical
Phillip Boykin, *The Gershwins' Porgy and Bess*
Michael Cerveris, *Evita*
David Alan Grier, *The Gershwins' Porgy and Bess*
*Michael McGrath, *Nice Work If You Can Get It*
Josh Young, *Jesus Christ Superstar*

Best Performance by an Actress in a Featured Role in a Musical
Elizabeth A. Davis, *Once*
Jayne Houdyshell, *Follies*
*Judy Kaye, *Nice Work If You Can Get It*
Jessie Mueller, *On a Clear Day You Can See Forever*
Da'Vine Joy Randolph, *Ghost the Musical*

Best Performance by an Actor in a Featured Role in a Play
*Christian Borle, *Peter and the Starcatcher*
Michael Cumpsty, *End of the Rainbow*
Tom Edden, *One Man, Two Guvnors*
Andrew Garfield, *Arthur Miller's Death of a Salesman*
Jeremy Shamos, *Clybourne Park*

1. Deborra-Lee Furness presented husband Hugh Jackman with a Special Tony Award.
2. Michael McGrath, winner Best Featured Actor-Musical (*Nice Work If You Can Get It*).
3. On the red carpet: Tony host Neil Patrick Harris (R) with his husband, David Burtka.
4. Judy Kaye, winner Best Featured Actress-Musical (*Nice Work If You Can Get It*).

Best Performance by an Actress in a Featured Role in a Play
Linda Emond, *Arthur Miller's Death of a Salesman*
Spencer Kayden, *Don't Dress for Dinner*
Celia Keenan-Bolger, *Peter and the Starcatcher*
*Judith Light, *Other Desert Cities*
Condola Rashad, *Stick Fly*

Best Direction of a Musical
Jeff Calhoun, *Newsies*
Kathleen Marshall, *Nice Work If You Can Get It*
Diane Paulus, *The Gershwins' Porgy and Bess*
*John Tiffany, *Once*

Best Direction of a Play
Nicholas Hytner, *One Man, Two Guvnors*
Pam MacKinnon, *Clybourne Park*
*Mike Nichols, *Arthur Miller's Death of a Salesman*
Roger Rees and Alex Timbers, *Peter and the Starcatcher*

Best Choreography
Rob Ashford, *Evita*
*Christopher Gattelli, *Newsies*
Steven Hoggett, *Once*
Kathleen Marshall, *Nice Work If You Can Get It*

Best Scenic Design of a Musical
*Bob Crowley, *Once*
Rob Howell and Jon Driscoll, *Ghost the Musical*
Tobin Ost and Sven Ortel, *Newsies*
George Tsypin, *Spider-Man Turn Off The Dark*

Best Scenic Design of a Play

John Lee Beatty, *Other Desert Cities*
Daniel Ostling, *Clybourne Park*
Mark Thompson, *One Man, Two Guvnors*
*Donyale Werle, *Peter and the Starcatcher*

Best Costume Design of a Musical
*Gregg Barnes, *Follies*
ESosa, *The Gershwins' Porgy and Bess*
Eiko Ishioka, *Spider-Man: Turn Off the Dark*
Martin Pakledinaz, *Nice Work If You Can Get It*

Best Costume Design of a Play

The Tony Awards

Best Costume Design of a Play
William Ivey Long, *Don't Dress for Dinner*
Paul Tazewell, *A Streetcar Named Desire*
Mark Thompson, *One Man, Two Guvnors*
Paloma Young, Peter and the Starcatcher

Best Lighting Design of a Musical
Christopher Akerlind, *The Gershwins' Porgy and Bess*
Natasha Katz, *Follies*
Natasha Katz, Once
Hugh Vanstone, *Ghost the Musical*

Best Lighting Design of a Play
Jeff Croiter, Peter and the Starcatcher
Peter Kaczorowski, *The Road to Mecca*
Brian MacDevitt, *Arthur Miller's Death of a Salesman*
Kenneth Posner, *Other Desert Cities*

Best Sound Design of a Musical
Acme Sound Partners, *The Gershwins' Porgy and Bess*
Clive Goodwin, Once
Kai Harada, *Follies*
Brian Ronan, *Nice Work If You Can Get It*

Best Sound Design of a Play
Paul Arditti, *One Man, Two Guvnors*
Scott Lehrer, *Arthur Miller's Death of a Salesman*
Gareth Owen, *End of the Rainbow*
Darron L. West, Peter and the Starcatcher

Best Book of a Musical
Lysistrata Jones, Douglas Carter Beane
Newsies, Harvey Fierstein
Nice Work If You Can Get It, Joe DiPietro
***Once*, Enda Walsh**

Best Original Score (Music and/or Lyrics) Written for the Theatre
Bonnie & Clyde, Music: Frank Wildhorn, Lyrics: Don Black
***Newsies*, Music: Alan Menken, Lyrics: Jack Feldman**
One Man, Two Guvnors, Music & Lyrics: Grant Olding
Peter and the Starcatcher
Music: Wayne Barker, Lyrics: Rick Elice

Best Orchestrations
William David Brohn and Christopher Jahnke, *The Gershwins' Porgy and Bess*
Bill Elliott, *Nice Work If You Can Get It*
Martin Lowe, Once
Danny Troob, *Newsies*

Special Tony Award for Lifetime Achievement in the Theatre
Emanuel Azenberg

Tony Honors for Excellence in the Theatre
Freddie Gershon
Artie Siccardi
TDF Open Doors

Isabelle Stevenson Award
Bernadette Peters

Regional Theatre Tony Award
The Shakespeare Theatre Company, Washington, D.C.

Special Tony Awards
Actors' Equity Association
Hugh Jackman

Here's a tally of the 2012 Tony Award winners:
Once 8
Peter and the Starcatcher 5
Newsies 2
Nice Work If You Can Get It 2
Arthur Miller's Death of a Salesman 2
The Gershwins' Porgy and Bess 2
Follies 1
One Man, Two Guvnors 1
Other Desert Cities 1
Clybourne Park 1
Venus in Fur 1

1. Winners of Best Original Score Alan Menken (L) and Jack Feldman (*Newsies*).
2. Judith Light, winner Best Featured Actress-Play (*Other Desert Cities*).
3. Laura Bell Bundy with Christopher Gattelli, and his Tony for Best Choreography (*Newsies*).
4. Christian Borle, winner Best Featured Actor-Play (*Peter and the Starcatcher*).

Other Theatre Awards

Covering the 2011-2012 Broadway Season

PULITZER PRIZE FOR DRAMA

Water by the Spoonful by Quiara Alegría Hudes (Off-Broadway)

NY DRAMA CRITICS' CIRCLE AWARDS

Best Play: *Sons of the Prophet* (OB)
Best Musical: *Once*
Best Foreign Play: *Tribes* (OB)
Special Citations: Signature Theatre Company; Mike Nichols for his contribution to the theatre.

DRAMA DESK AWARDS

Outstanding Play: *Tribes* (OB)
Outstanding Musical: *Once*
Outstanding Revival of a Play: *Death of a Salesman*
Outstanding Revival of a Musical: *Follies*
Outstanding Actor in a Play: James Corden, *One Man, Two Guvnors*
Outstanding Actress in a Play: Tracie Bennett, *End of the Rainbow*
Outstanding Actor in a Musical: Danny Burstein, *Follies*
Outstanding Actress in a Musical: Audra McDonald, *The Gershwins' Porgy and Bess*
Outstanding Featured Actor in a Play: Tom Edden, *One Man, Two Guvnors*
Outstanding Featured Actress in a Play: Judith Light, *Other Desert Cities*
Outstanding Featured Actor in a Musical: Michael McGrath, *Nice Work If You Can Get It*
Outstanding Featured Actress in a Musical: Judy Kaye, *Nice Work If You Can Get It*
Outstanding Director of a Play: Mike Nichols, *Death of a Salesman*
Outstanding Director of a Musical: John Tiffany, *Once*
Outstanding Choreography: Christopher Gattelli, *Newsies The Musical*
Outstanding Music: Alan Menken, *Newsies The Musical*
Outstanding Lyrics: Glen Hansard and Markéta Irglová, *Once*
Outstanding Book of a Musical: Joe

Guests at the Theatre World Awards (L-R): Harvey Evans, Lee Roy Reams and Jim Brochu.

DiPietro, *Nice Work If You Can Get It*
Outstanding Music in a Play: Grant Olding, *One Man, Two Guvnors*
Outstanding Revue: *The Best Is Yet to Come: The Music of Cy Coleman*
Outstanding Set Design: Jon Driscoll, Rob Howell and Paul Kieve, *Ghost The Musical*
Outstanding Costume Design: Gregg Barnes, *Follies*
Outstanding Lighting Design: Brian MacDevitt, *Death of a Salesman*
Outstanding Sound Design in a Musical: Acme Sound Partners, *The Gershwins' Porgy and Bess*
Outstanding Sound Design in a Play: John Gromada, *Gore Vidal's The Best Man*
Outstanding Solo Performance: Cillian Murphy, *Misterman* (OB)
Outstanding Orchestrations: Martin Lowe, *Once*
Unique Theatrical Experience: *Gob Squad's Kitchen (You've Never Had It So Good)* (OB)
Outstanding Ensemble Performances: The cast of *Sweet and Sad* (OB)
Special Award to Mary Testa
Special Award to Nick Westrate (OB)
Special Award to New Victory Theatre (OB)
Sam Norkin Off-Broadway Award to Stephen Karam (OB)

OUTER CRITICS CIRCLE AWARDS

Outstanding New Broadway Play: *One Man, Two Guvnors*
Outstanding New Broadway Musical: *Once*
Outstanding New Off-Broadway Play: *Sons of the Prophet* (OB)
Outstanding New Off-Broadway Musical: *Queen of the Mist* (OB)
Outstanding Book of a Musical (Broadway or OB): *Once*
Outstanding New Score (Broadway or OB): *Newsies*

Outstanding Revival of a Play: *Death of a Salesman*
Outstanding Revival of a Musical: *Follies*
Outstanding Director of a Play (Lucille Lortel Award): Nicholas Hytner, *One Man, Two Guvnors*
Outstanding Director of a Musical: John Tiffany, *Once*
Outstanding Choreographer: Christopher Gattelli, *Newsies*
Outstanding Set Design: George Tsypin, *Spider-Man: Turn Off the Dark*
Outstanding Costume Design: Eiko Ishioka, *Spider-Man: Turn Off the Dark*
Outstanding Lighting Design: Hugh Vanstone, *Ghost: The Musical*
Outstanding Actor in a Play: James Corden, *One Man, Two Guvnors*
Outstanding Actress in a Play: Tracie Bennett, *End of the Rainbow*
Outstanding Actor in a Musical: Danny Burstein, *Follies*
Outstanding Actress in a Musical: Audra McDonald, *The Gershwins' Porgy and Bess*
Outstanding Featured Actor in a Play: James Earl Jones, *Gore Vidal's The Best Man*
Outstanding Featured Actress in a Play: Spencer Kayden, *Don't Dress for Dinner*
Outstanding Featured Actor in a Musical: Michael McGrath, *Nice Work If You Can Get It*
Outstanding Featured Actress in a Musical: Judy Kaye, *Nice Work If You Can Get It*
Outstanding Solo Performance: Denis O'Hare, *An Iliad* (OB)
John Gassner Award (New American Play): Jeff Talbott, *The Submission* (OB)

THE DRAMA LEAGUE AWARDS

Distinguished Production of a Play: *Other Desert Cities*
Distinguished Production of a Musical: *Once*

Stockard Channing co-hosted the 78th Annual Drama League awards luncheon where her show, *Other Desert Cities*, was named Distinguished Production of a Play.

Other Theatre Awards

Covering the 2011-2012 Broadway Season

Liza Minnelli beams at the crowd upon accepting her Douglas Watt Lifetime Achievement Award at the Fred and Adele Astaire Awards ceremony.

Distinguished Revival of a Play: *Death of a Salesman*
Distinguished Revival of a Musical: *Follies*
Distinguished Performance Award: Audra McDonald, *The Gershwins' Porgy and Bess*

THEATRE WORLD AWARDS

For Outstanding Broadway or Off-Broadway debuts:
Tracie Bennett, *End of the Rainbow*
Phillip Boykin, *The Gershwins' Porgy and Best*
Crystal A. Dickinson, *Clybourne Park*
Russell Harvard, *Tribes* (OB)
Jeremy Jordan, *Bonnie & Clyde*
Joaquina Kalukango, *Hurt Village* (OB)
Jennifer Lim, *Chinglish*
Jessie Mueller, *On a Clear Day You Can See Forever*
Hettienne Park, *Seminar* and *The Intelligent Homosexual's Guide to Capitalism & Socialism with a Key to the Scriptures* (OB)
Chris Perfetti, *Sons of the Prophet* (OB)
Finn Wittrock, *Death of a Salesman*
Josh Young, *Jesus Christ Superstar*
Dorothy Loudon Award for Excellence: Susan Pourfar, *Tribes* (OB)

CLARENCE DERWENT AWARDS

From Actors' Equity for "most promising female and male performers on the New York metropolitan scene."
Susan Pourfar, *Tribes* (OB)
Finn Wittrock, *Death of a Salesman*

RICHARD SEFF AWARDS

From Actors' Equity, to "female and male character actors 50 years of age or older."
Laila Robins, *The Lady from Dubuque* (OB)
Patrick Page, *Spider-Man: Turn Off the Dark*

OTHER ACTORS' EQUITY AWARDS

Joe A. Callaway Award for best performances in a classic play in the New York metropolitan area: Danai Gurira of *Measure for Measure* (OB) and Derek Smith of *The Witch of Edmonton* (OB)
St. Clair Bayfield Award for the best supporting performance by an actor in a Shakespearean play in the New York metropolitan area: Nick Westrate, *Love's Labor's Lost*
ACCA Award for Outstanding Broadway Chorus: the cast of *The Scottsboro Boys*
Paul Robeson Award for "a person who best exemplifies the principles by which Mr. Robeson lived": James Earl Jones of *Gore Vidal's The Best Man*

THE IRENE SHARAFF AWARDS

From the Theatre Development Fund, for outstanding costume design.
Robert L.B. Tobin Award for Sustained Excellence in Theatrical Design: Lloyd Burlingame
Artisan Award: Lynn Pecktal
Lifetime Achievement Award for Costume Design: Carrie Robbins
Young Master Award: Mathew LeFebvre
Special Memorial Tribute: William Eckart and Jean Eckart

FRED AND ADELE ASTAIRE AWARDS

Excellence in Choreography on Broadway: Ronald K. Brown, *Porgy & Bess*
Best Female Dancer on Broadway: Lisa Nicole Wilkerson, *Porgy & Bess*
Best Male Dancer on Broadway: Leslie Odom, Jr., *Leap of Faith*
Douglas Watt Lifetime Achievement Award: Liza Minnelli

HENRY HEWES DESIGN AWARDS

Announced in January 2012 for work in the 2010-2011 Season
Scenic Design: John Lee Beatty for *The Whipping Boy* (OB)
Costume Design: William Ivey Long for *The School for Lies* (OB)
Lighting Design: Jeff Croiter for *Peter and the Starcatcher* (OB)
Notable Effects: David Rockwell and Batwin+Robin for scenery and projections for *The Normal Heart*

GRAMMY AWARD

Best Musical Theatre Album: *Book of Mormon*

A gathering of Pulitzer Prize winners at the opening of 2011 winner *Clybourne Park* (L-R): Quiara Alegría Hudes (*Water by the Spoonful*, 2012), Marsha Norman (*'night, Mother*, 1983), Bruce Norris (*Clybourne Park*) and Tom Kitt (*Next to Normal*, 2010).

Faculty

Faculty

The Shubert Organization

Philip J. Smith
Chairman and co-CEO

Robert E. Wankel
President and co-CEO

Photos by Ben Strothmann

Coalition of Broadway Unions and Guilds (COBUG)

Photo by Brian Mapp

Seated (L-R): Frank Connolly, Jr. (Local 817), Gene McElwain (Local 751), Carol Bokun (Local 306), Tony DePaulo (IATSE International), Nick Kaledin (ATPAM). Standing (L-R): Steve Gelfand (AFM), Kirk Kelly (Local 30), Andy Friedman (Local 32BJ), Laura Penn (SDC), Rick Berb (Actors' Equity), Lawrence Paone (Local 751), Dan Dashman (Local 798), K.C. Boyle (Local 802), John Seid (Local 306), Bart Daudelin (Local 764), Carl Mulert (USA Local 829), David Faux (Dramatists Guild), Mauro Melleno (SDC), Elizabeth Miller, Patrick Langevin (USA 829), Evan Shoemake (SDC).

Faculty

The Nederlander Organization

James M. Nederlander
Chairman

James L. Nederlander
President

Nick Scandalios
*Executive
Vice President*

Photo courtesy Nederlander Organization

All photos by Anita & Steve Shevett except where otherwise noted.

Freida Belviso
*Chief Financial
Officer*

Jim Boese
Vice President

Susan Lee
*Chief Marketing
Officer*

Jack Meyer
*Vice President
Programming*

Charlene S.
Nederlander
*Vice President
Corporate
Development*

Kathleen Raitt
*Vice President
Corporate Relations*

Herschel Waxman
*Senior Vice
President
Labor Relations*

Tony Award Productions

Alan Wasser
General Manager

Allan Williams
General Manager

Photos by Brian Mapp

Faculty

JUJAMCYN THEATERS

Faculty

The Broadway League

Paul Libin
Chair

Charlotte St. Martin
Executive Director

Seated in Front Row (L-R): Julia Davis, Leslie Dock, Roxanne Rodriguez, Laura Fayans, Jennifier Stewart, Keith Halpern

Second Row: Chelsi Conklin, Lindsay Florestal, Mel Lauer, Ben Pesner, Kayla Kreidell, Christina Boursiquot, Charlotte St. Martin, Kendra Srebro

Back Row (L-R): Josh Cacchione, Colin Gibson, Erica Ryan, Jean Kroeper, Chris Brockmeyer, Neal Freeman, Chris Brucato, Mark Smith, Karen Hauser, Rachel Reiner, Robert Davis, Ed Sandler, Zenovia Varelis, Jason Laks

Manhattan Theatre Club

Front Row (L-R): Nancy Piccione, Jerry Patch, Florie Seery, Barry Grove, Lynne Meadow, Mandy Greenfield, Amy Loe, Elizabeth Rothman, Lindsey Sag
Second Row (L-R): David Shookhoff, Caitlin Baird, Becca Goland-Van Ryn, Annie MacRae, Jessica Adler, Gillian Campbell, Ryan Fogarty, Debra Waxman, Josh Martinez-Nelson, Nicki Hunter, Andy Kao
Third Row (L-R): Lynne Randall, Megan Dieterle, Thatcher Stevens, Rosanna Consalvo Sarto, Tim Salamandyk, Amber Wilkerson, Patricia Leonard, Andrea Gorzell Hickey, Amy Harris, Laura Petrucci, Kaity Neagle, Alex Barron, Emily Hammond, Samantha Kindler
Back Row (L-R): Michael Bateman, Kevin Sullivan, Mark Bowers, Darragh Garvey, Ryan Guhde, Lisa McNulty, Kelly Gillespie

Faculty

The Roundabout Theatre Company

Seated (L-R): Harold Wolpert (Managing Director), Todd Haimes (Artistic Director), Julia Levy (Executive Director)
Standing (L-R): Steve Deutsch, Susan Neiman, Daniel Gomez, Wendy Hutton, Greg McCaslin, Lynne Gugenheim Gregory, Sydney Beers, Greg Backstrom, Denise Cooper, Jill Rafson, Nicholas Caccavo, Valerie Simmons, Thomas Mygatt

The Dodgers

Floor (L-R): Jessica Ludwig, Pamela Lloyd, Andrew Serna
Chairs (L-R): Linda Wright, Annie Van Nostrand, Laurinda Wilson, Mariann Fresiello, Flora Johnstone, Lauren Freed, Sally Campbell Morse, Michael David, Paula Maldonado, Jessica Morris
Standing (L-R): Tony Lance, West Hyler, Jeff Parvin, Scott Dennis, Abigail Kornet, Edward Strong, Lauren Mitchell, Hunter Chancellor, Ashley Tracey, John Haber
Not pictured: Jennifer F. Vaughan, Anne Ezell, Jennie Mamary

Faculty

IATSE Local One, Stagehands

Seated (L-R): Chairman, Board of Trustees Paul F. Dean, Jr., Recording-Corresponding Secretary Robert C. Score, President James J. Claffey, Jr., Vice President William Walters, Treasurer Robert McDonough

Standing (L-R): Television Business Manager Edward J. McMahon, III, Theatre Business Manager Mickey Fox, Theatre Business Manager Kevin McGarty, Television Business Manager Robert C. Nimmo, Trustee Daniel D. Dashman, Trustee William Ngai

Stage Directors and Choreographers Society

Standing (L-R): Ronald H. Shechtman (Counsel), Mauro Melleno, John Rando, Adam Levi, Randy Anderson, Kim Rogers, Doug Hughes, Cole Jordan, Walter Bobbie

Middle Row (L-R): Laura Penn (Executive Director), Barbara Wolkoff, Elizabeth Miller, Karen Azenberg (Board President), Michele Holmes, Lisa Peterson, Kristy Cummings

Seated (L-R): Susan H. Schulman, Wendy Goldberg, Robert Moss, Seret Scott, Sue Lawless

Faculty

Actors' Equity Association

Nick Wyman
President

Mary McColl
Executive Director

Photos by Stephanie Masucci

NATIONAL COUNCIL
Front Row (L-R):
Secretary-Treasurer Sandra
Karas, First VP Paige Price,
Second VP Rebecca Kim Jordan

Back Row (L-R):
President Nick Wyman,
Third VP Ira Mont

Photo by Brian Mapp

**AEA STAFF
SIXTEENTH FLOOR**
Front Row (L-R) Jack Goldstein,
Anne Fortuno, Marie Gottschall,
Frank Horak, Stuart Levy

Middle Row (L-R): Joe De Michele,
Flora Stamatiades, Karen
Nothmann, Chris Williams, Jenifer
Hills, Stephanie Masucci.

Back Row (L-R): David Lotz,
Robert Fowler, Karen Master,
Doug Beebe, Jen Michaud

STAFF
Front Row (L-R) Kathy Mercado,
Cathy Jayne, Michelle Lehrman,
Maria Cameron, Mary-Kate Gilrein,
Valerie LaVarco

Middle Row (L-R): Pearl Brady,
Louise Foisy, Adeola Adegbola,
Joanna Spencer, Laura Schuman,
Alessandra Williams-Bellotti,
Tripp Chamberlain

Back Row (L-R): Kenneth Naanep,
Barry Rosenberg, Jessica Palermo,
Walt Kiskaddon, Joe Erdey,
David Shaerf, Megan Rogers,
Russell Lehrer

Photo by Brian Mapp

Photo by Brian Mapp

STAFF
Front Row (L-R): Elisabeth Stern,
Sierra Pasqaule, Courtney Godan,
Kristine Arwe, Chris Bennett,
Jillian Moss

Middle Row (L-R): Courtney Scott,
John Fasulo, Sylvina Persaud,
Jeff Morris, Jeffrey Bateman,
Melissa Colgan,
Lawrence Lorczak

Back Row (L-R): Gary Dimon,
Dragica Dabo, Beverly Sloan,
Dave Thorn, Dwane Upp

Faculty

Dramatists Guild

DRAMATISTS GUILD COUNCIL-STEERING COMMITTEE
Seated (L-R): Peter Parnell (Vice President), Stephen Schwartz (President), Marsha Norman, John Weidman

Standing (L-R): David Ives, David Lindsay-Abaire, Craig Carnelia

Not pictured: Theresa Rebeck (Treasurer), Julia Jordan, Doug Wright (Secretary), David Auburn

STAFF
(L-R): Joey Stocks, Rebecca Stump, Tari Stratton, Roland Tec, Gary Garrison, Patrick Shearer, Caterina Bartha, David Faux, Amy Von Vett, Ralph Sevush, Rachel Roouth, Seth Cotterman (seated on floor)

Association of Theatrical Press Agents and Managers

Front Row (L-R): Adam Miller, Gregg Arst, Barbara Carroll, Susan Elrod (Manager Chapter Chair)

Back Row (L-R): Nick Kaledin (Secretary-Treasurer), David Gersten (Press Agent Chapter Chair), Kevin McAnarney, Penny Daulton (Vice-President), Rina Saltzman, Shirley Herz, Jeremy Shaffer, Robert Nolan

Not pictured: David Calhoun (President), Jonathan Shulman, Steve Schnepp

Faculty

Theatrical Teamsters, Local 817

OFFICE STAFF
Seated (L-R): Allison Hammond, Marg Marklin, Tina Gusmano, Kathy Kreinbihl

Standing (L-R): Christine Harkerss, Margie Vaeth

EXECUTIVE BOARD
Seated: Thomas J. O'Donnell (President)

Standing (L-R): James Leavey (Recording Secretary), Michael Hyde (Trustee), Charles Spillane Jr. (Trustee), Francis J. Connolly Jr. (Secretary Treasurer), Edward Iacobelli (Sr.-Vice President), Kevin Keefe (Trustee)

IATSE Local 306 Motion Picture Projectionists, Video Technicians and Allied Crafts (Ushers)

Seated (L-R): Lorraine Lowrey, Carol Bokun, Rita Russell, Donna Vanderlinden, Lori Prager-Kupferberg

Standing (L-R): Stephen Coco, Kenneth Costigan, Maria Rivierzo, Joseph Rivierzo, Helen Bentley, Barry Garfman, John Seid, RoseAnn Cipriano, Michael Satran.

Faculty

Treasurers & Ticket Sellers Union, IATSE Local 751

Photos by Brian Mapp

EXECUTIVE COUNCIL
Seated (L-R): Noreen Morgan, Gene McElwain (President), Lawrence Paone (Secretary-Treasurer, Business Agent)

Standing (L-R): A. Greer Bond, John Nesbitt, Patricia DeMato, John Toguville, Harry Jaffie, Fred Santore, Jr., Robert Begin, Stanley Shaffer, Frank M. Loiacono, Matthew Fearon (Vice President)

OFFICE STAFF
Seated: Stephanie Swisher and Patricia Quiles

Standing (L-R): James Sita, Lawrence Paone, Gene McElwain

Theatrical Wardrobe Union, IATSE Local 764

First Row (L-R): Joanne Viverto, Christopher Lavin, Barbara Hladsky, Paula Cohen, Anita Ellis, Liz Deutsch, Bart Daudelin, Patricia Sullivan, Vangeli Kaseluris
Second Row (L-R): Maura Clifford, Jesse Galvin, Yleana Nuñez, Sonya Wysocki, Danajean Cicerchi, Pinky Pusillo, Karen Whittaker, Mark Klein, Paul Drost, Susan Garcia
Back Row (L-R): Scott Harrington, Shannon Koger, Jenna Krempel, Rodd Sovar, Dennis Birchall, Mary Ferry, Patricia White, James Swift, Anita Ali Davis, Frank Gallagher, Terry LaVada, Adam Adelman, Warren Wernick, Binh Hoong, Ashley Green, Julie Fernandez, Michael Gemignani, Rochelle Friedman

Faculty

Broadway Cares/Equity Fights AIDS

Front Row (L-R): Denise Roberts Hurlin, Yvonne Ghareeb, R. Keith Bullock, Dennis Henriquez, Josh Blye
Second Row (L-R): Madeline Reed, Carol Ingram, Lucky Lai, Andy Halliday, Cat Domiano, Tim Sullivan, Ngoc Bui, Ed Garrison, Larry Cook
Back Row (L-R): Tom Viola, Dex Ostling, Danny Whitman, Nathan Hurlin, Joe Norton, Michael Graziano, Peter Borzotta, Dan Perry, Lane Beauchamp, Rose James, Aaron Waytkus, Roy Palijaro, Chris Kenney, Chris Davis, Ryan Walls, Skip Lawing, Chris DeLuise, Chris Gizzi

American Theatre Wing

BOARD OF DIRECTORS AND STAFF
Seated (L-R): Jack O'Brien, Sondra Gilman, Enid Nemy, Dasha Epstein, Pia Lindstrom
Standing (L-R): Peter Schneider, William Craver, David Brown, David Henry Hwang, Heather A. Hitchens, Theodore S. Chapin, Alan Siegel, William Ivey Long, Joanna Sheehan, Raisa Ushomirskiy, Randy Ellen Lutterman, Gail Yancosek, Rachel Schwartz, Kenny Gallo

Faculty

Theatre Development Fund and TKTS

TDF STAFF

First Row (L-R): Craig Stekeur, Joey Haws, Vickie Alvarez, Patrick Berger, Christopher Reichheld, Michael Buffer, Howard Marren

Second Row (L-R): Christophe Mentor, Stephen Cabral, Lisa Carling, Michael Naumann, Victoria Bailey, Joy Cooper, David LeShay

Third Row (L-R): Thomas Westerman, George Connolly, Tina Kirsimae, Paula Torres, Denyse Owens, Catherine St. Jean, Julie Williams, Sal Polizzi, JoAnn Gall, Sheela Kangal

Fourth Row (L-R): Pierre LaFontant, Deborah Stein, Michael Yaccarino, Rob Neely, Doug Smith, Joseph Cali, Fran Polino, Tymand Staggs, Costas Michalopoulos, Thomas Adkins, Sarah Aziz, Robert Gore

Fifth Row: (L-R): Ginger Meagher, Mark Blankenship

TKTS TREASURERS
Front: Ann Ramirez
Middle (L-R): Raj Sharma, Gale Sprydon
Back (L-R): Bill Castellano (Head Treasurer), Shirley Martignetti, Tom Waxman

TKTS COSTUME COLLECTION
(L-R): Mark Runion, Stephen Cabral, Joanne Haas, Jennifer Hurlbert, Joey Haws, Craig Stekeur

Faculty

The Actors Fund

Photo by Brian Mapp

BOARD OF TRUSTEES
Seated (L-R): Abby Schroeder, Jomarie Ward, Phyllis Newman, Honey Waldman, Steve Kalafer, Anita Jaffe

Standing (L-R): Marc Grodman, M.D., Paul Libin, Lee H. Perlman, Lin-Manuel Miranda, Martha Nelson, Philip S. Birsh, Dale C. Olson, Janice Reals Ellig, Bebe Neuwirth, Ken Howard, Joyce Gordon, Nick Wyman, Chairman Brian Stokes Mitchell, Stewart F. Lane

Not Pictured: John A. Duncan, Jr., Philip J. Smith, Alec Baldwin, Annette Bening, Jed W. Bernstein, Jeffrey Bolton, Ebs Burnough, John Breglio, James J. Claffey, Jr., Nancy Coyne, Merle Debuskey, Rick Elice, Marc Hostetter, Kate Edelman Johnson, Michael Kerker, Matthew Loeb, Kristen Madsen, Kevin McCollum, James L. Nederlander, Harold Prince, Roberta Reardon, Charlotte St. Martin, Thomas Schumacher, David Steiner, Edward D. Turen, Tom Viola, Joseph H. Wender, B.D. Wong, George Zuber

NEW YORK STAFF
Seated (L-R): Amy Wilder, Wallace Munro, Caroline Parrone, Jay Haddad, Louie Anchondo, Ryan Dietz, Alice Vienneau, John Torres, Holly Wheeler, Ell Miocene, Richard Renner

Standing (L-R): Robyn Cucurullo, Courtney Toumey, Samuel A. Smith, David Engelman, Barbara Toy, Carol Wilson, Cassandra Kohilakis, Amy Picar, Stephen Joseph, Gloria Jones, Ashley Kumer, Elizabeth Avedon, Jennifer Anglade, Kent Curtis, Timothy Pinckney, Billie Levinson, Charlene Nurse, Susan Varon, Kathy Schrier, Ricardo Montero, Dalin Rivera, Susan Fila, Julia Peters, Robert Farrior

Photo by Brian Mapp

Photo courtesy The Actors Fund

WESTERN COUNCIL
Seated (L-R): Charlotte Rae, Jomarie Ward, Dale C. Olson, Kate Edelman Johnson, Joni Berry, Marguerite Ray, Jane A. Johnston

Standing (L-R): Daniel Henning, Joseph Ruskin, Bryan Unger, Danny Goldman, Theo Bikel, John Holly, William Thomas, Ilyanne Morden Kichaven, Richard Herd, Pam Dixon, Bridget Hanley, David Rambo, James Karen, Scott Roth

Not pictured: John Acosta, Barbara Allyne Bennet, B. Harlan Boll, Ilene Graff, Henry Polic II, Ken Werther, Mary Lou Westerfield, David Young

LOS ANGELES STAFF
Seated (L-R): Meg Thomas, Ze'ev Korn, Keith McNutt, Tracey Downs, Joanne Webb

Standing (L-R): TaNisha Harris, Angelique Prahalis, Daniel Kitowski, Frank Salamone, Ted Abenheim, Heather Vanian, John Mattson, Laura Campbell, Gregory Polcyn, Emmanuel Freeman, Joey Shanley, Karen Hanen, Caitlin Sorenson, Robin LaBorwit, Jan Kees Van Der Gaag, Mallory Morehead

Photo courtesy The Actors Fund

Faculty

Boneau/Bryan-Brown

Chris Boneau

Adrian Bryan-Brown

Jim Byk

Brandi Cornwell

Jackie Green

Kelly Guiod

Linnae Hodzic

Jessica Johnson

Kevin Jones

Amy Kass

Holly Kinney

Emily Meagher

Aaron Meier

Christine Olver

Joe Perrotta

Matt Polk

Amanda Sales

Heath Schwartz

Michael Strassheim

Susanne Tighe

Faculty

O & M Co.

Photo by Bruce Glikas

Front Row (L-R): Jaron Caldwell, Rick Miramontez, Chelsea Nachman, Molly Barnett
Middle Row (L-R): Michael Jorgensen, Jon Dimond, Richard Hillman
Back Row (L-R): Elizabeth Wagner, Philip Carrubba, Andy Snyder

The Hartman Group

Photo by Brian Mapp

(L-R): Michael Hartman, Emily McGill, Matt Ross, Whitney Holden Gore, Juliana Hannett, Nicole Capatasto, Bethany Larsen, Frances White, Colgan McNeil, Wayne Wolfe, Leslie Papa, Tom D'Ambrosio

Faculty

Richard Kornberg & Associates

Richard Kornberg

Don Summa

Billy Zavelson

Danielle McGarry

Jeffrey Richards Associates

Front Row (L-R): Steven Strauss,
Michael Crea, Irene Gandy,
Alana Karpoff, Will Trice,
Jeremy Scott Blaustein

Back Row (L-R): Thomas Raynor,
Andy Drachenberg, Jeffrey Richards,
Christopher Pineda, Ryan Hallett

The Publicity Office

Standing: Jeremy Shaffer

Seated: (L-R) Marc Thibodeau
and Michael Borowski

Springer Associates

(L-R): Joe Trentacosta, Gary Springer

Faculty

J. AQUINO
TRACK & FIELD

K. BARDWIL
KEY CLUB

M. BARRY
BADMINTON

W. BEISHIR
DETENTION

A. BIZJAK
JAZZ TEAM

J. BODLEY
ROCK BAND

K. CAROTHERS
HEAD OF THE PLASTICS

A. CATALA
ABSTINENCE CLUB

R. COHEN
MUSIC CONSERVATORY

J. COOPER
MANGA CLUB

D. COX
HISTORICAL SOCIETY

G. CRADDOCK
EAGLE SCOUTS

T. CREWS
VALEDICTORIAN

M. CROWLEY
THESPIANS

A. CRUZ
GLEE CLUB

A. DAVIS
BLACK HISTORY CLUB

M. DELMORE
BABYSITTERS CLUB

A. EISENHOWER
SWIM TEAM

L. ELLIS
SHAMPOO CLUB

T. FALOTICO
WATER POLO

C. FENTON
THATCHERITE

S. FITZPATRICK
CHEERLEADING

D. FORKIN
SCIENTOLOGY

J. FOX
A.M. ANNOUNCEMENTS

J. FRAENKEL
HILLEL

T. FRANCIS
STUDY CLUB

R. GASKINS
DRILL TEAM

C. GOFF
MOST TALKATIVE

G. GREEN
PEP SQUAD

M. HAINES
JUNIOR STATESMEN

K. HALL
WEIGHTLIFTING

L. HU
SCIENCE OLYMPIAD

P. JEFFREY
SCI-FI BOOK CLUB

SpotCo Class of 2012

L. JOHNSON
DANCE TEAM

R. KOLB
TAXIDERMY

S. LADD
TEACHER'S PET

N. LINDEMAN
PING PONG

D. HODGES
PRINCIPAL

J. EDWARDS
VICE PRINCIPAL

B. BERK
DEAN OF STUDENTS

T. GREENWALD
AV SQUAD

T. McCANN
EQUINE CLUB

M. McCRACKEN
NERD

J. McNICHOLAS
BROADCAST CLUB

M. METTLER
CLOGGING

W. MITCHELL
DRAMA SOCIETY

T. MOSER
BRAVO CLUB

C. NEWHOUSE
SOUTHERN BELLES

M. OWNBEY
CHEESE CLUB

N. PRAMIK
LINGUISTICS

D. PRESTON
MATHLETES

K. RATHBUN
QUIZ BOWL CAPTAIN

M. RHEAULT
WRESTLING

I. ROSEN
GUIDANCE COUNSELOR

A. ROTHENBERG
COLOR GUARD

S. ROTHSTEIN
PLAYWRITING CLUB

V. SAINATO
DEBATE

S. SANTORE
CROSS COUNTRY

C. SCHWITZ
FIRST TEAM ALL-STATE

C. SEES
CLASS CLOWN

C. SHALOIKO
SKI CLUB

R. SIMNOWITZ
HOME ECONOMICS

C. SKENE
COMPUTER CLUB

D. SNYPE
BALLET FOLKLORICS

J. SOCHACZEWSKI
EXCHANGE STUDENT

C. SOGLIUZZO
TEAM SPIRIT

S. SOSNOWSKI
FENCING

C. SPINNEY
QUEEN BEE

B. STANSELL
ETIQUETTE CLUB

D. SUYAMA
SOCCER

L. TAYLOR
APIARIST CLUB

N. TILLMANNS
CAT CLUB

N. VENNERA
BOXING CLUB

E. VICIOSO
BAND

B. WATSON
YOUNG DEMOCRATS

J. WECHSLER
SPEED-WALKING CLUB

E. WU
CLUB

Faculty

JOE ALESI **ANDY** APOSTOLIDES **HAILEY** APTER **LESLIE** BARRETT **DAVID** BARRINEAU **WILLIAM** BELL **SUMEET** BHARATI

SANDY BLOCK **CHRISTY** BORG **DANIELLE** BOYLE **MATT** BRITT **DENISE** BROWN **TOM** CALLAHAN **JAMIE** CAPLAN

JEFF CARROLL **CRYSTAL** CHASE **JONATHAN** CHIN **MICHAEL** CLAEYS **LAURIE** CONNOR **MONICA** CORONEL **GREG** CORRADETTI

BRUCE COUNCIL **NANCY** COYNE **WHITNEY** CREIGHTON **ANDREA** CUEVAS **RANDY** CUMBERBATCH **SIMONE** BOYD DeCASTRO **ANGELO** DESIMINI **DOUG** ENSIGN **JON** ERWIN **ELYSE** FAMILETTI

MAUREEN FAY **JOE** FIGLIOLA **CHERI** FONTANEZ **NICOLE** FRANCOIS **JENNA LAUREN** FREED **CHRISSANN** GASPARRO **EMILY** GENDUSO **JIM** GLAUB **IFAT** GOLAN **RYAN** GREER

PETER GUNTHER **CHRISTINA** HERNANDEZ **MIKHAIL** HERRERA **KIM** HEWSKI **KEVIN** HIRST **LAUREN** HOULBERG **ARTURO** IRIZARRY **VANESSA** JAVIER **KARA** JENKINS **SCOTT** JOHNSON

ROBERT JONES **JACQUI** KAISER **LEORA** KANNER **MARCI** KAUFMAN **KEVIN** KEATING **MARY** KEKLLAS **ZACK** KINNEY **ZHANNA** KIRTSMAN **JON** LAPRADE **JIM** LAZOS

JEAN LEONARD **ADINA** LEVIN **AGATHA** MACIEJEWSKI **SERGE** MAKAROV **JACK** MARCIANO **SARAH** MARCUS **KAT** MAROTTA **CHRIS** MARTIN **KEVIN** MEERE **CHIP** MEYRELLES

ROGER MICONE **CATHERINE** MIGUEIS **BRANDON** MIKOLASKI **DAVID** MOLINA **ROSA** MONSERRAT **SHAWNA** MONSON **JARED** NARBER **DREW** NEBRIG **SOFIA** NISNEVICH **RAY** NOELLE

NICK NOLTE **ANDREI** OLEINIK **TEE** PANTON **BRAD** PATTINIAN **CHUCK** PLATT **MIKE** RAFAEL **JOE** RECKLEY **CATHERINE** REID **ALEXANDRA** RUBIN **JIM** RUSSEK

DIANA SALAMEH **BETH** SCHEFFLAN **MARK** SEELEY **JUSTIN** STANFORD **CAROLINE** THOMPSON **SUZANNE** TOBAK **ALHAGIE** TOURAY **MATT** UPSHAW **IAN** WEISS **GINGER** WITT

ABBY WOLBE **SCOTT** YAMBOR **JASON** ZAMMIT **DANA** ZELL

SERINO/COYNE 2011-2012
It's **SHOW** TIME.

Faculty

ADAM KENWRIGHT

ELIZABETH FURZE

SCOTT MOORE

ADAM NEUMANN

ADAM JAY

ANDREW DAMER

BASHAN AQUART

BRADLEY HAMILTON

CRISTINA MARIE

ELIE BERKOWITZ

ELIZABETH FINDLAY

ELIZABETH RUBLEIN

ERIK ALDEN

ERIN RECH

FLORA PEI

GREG COLEMAN

JACOB MATSUMIYA

JANETTE ROUSH

JANICE SAVAGE

JENNA BISSONNETTE

JEN TAYLOR

JENNIFER SIMS

JOEY BOYLES

JONATHAN LANG

MARIA MYLONA

MARY LITTELL

MATEO MORENO

MEGHAN BARTLEY

MELISSA MARANO

NISHI CHAWLA

PIPPA BEXON

RICHARD ARNOLD

ROBERT POSTOTNIK

SEAN POMPOSELLO

TREVOR SPONSELLER

VICTORIA VOLOVIK

aka
2012

Faculty

THE BROADWAY CHANNEL™
One on the aisle and a backstage pass to the best of Broadway

Kate Shindle with Julie Andrews at the 2008 Tony Awards

Ken Hege

Matthew Hege

Jackie Bales

Kate Shindle

Betty Alvarez

Diovon Pelicot

Brian Piccirillo

John Sawina

Paul Dokuchitz

Keith Hurd

Isa Goldberg

Andy McGibbon

Faculty

Playbill

Philip S. Birsh
Publisher

Arthur T. Birsh
Chairman

Clifford S. Tinder
*Senior Vice President/
Publisher, Classic Arts
Division*

Joan Alleman Birsh
*Corporate Vice
President*

Blake Ross
*Editor-in-Chief
Playbill*

Photo by Brian Mapp

MANHATTAN OFFICE
Front Row (L-R): Jose Ortiz, Blake Ross, Michael Gioia, Clifford S. Tinder, Tiffany Feo

Second Row (L-R): Esvard D'Haiti, Jill Boriss, Jennifer Brown, Talaura Harms, Adam Hetrick, Stephanie Bradbury, Jon Goldman

Third Row (L-R): Oldyna Dynowska, Wanda Young, Theresa Holder, Brynn Cox, Maude Popkin, Diane Niedzialek, Travis Ferguson, Yadira Mitchell, Mark Ezovski

Fourth Row (L-R): Harry Haun, Andrew Ku, Kelechi Ezie, Anderson Peguero, Clara Barragán, Glenn Shaevitz, Arturo Gonzalez

Back Row: (L-R): Robert Viagas, David Gewirtzman, Matt Blank, Andrew Gans, Damian Fowler, Alex Near, Glenn Asciutto

Not Pictured: Louis Botto, Diana Leidel, Ari Ackerman, Silvija Ojols, Jolie Schaffzin, James Cairl, Joseph Marzullo, Kesler Thibert, Kenneth Jones, Julie Cohen

Faculty

Playbill

PLAYBILL.COM
Seated (L-R): Blake Ross, Andrew Gans, Kenneth Jones
Standing (L-R): Adam Hetrick, Mark Ezovski, Michael Gioia, Matt Blank, Andrew Ku, David Gewirtzman

PLAYBILLEDU.COM
(L-R): Jill Boriss, Theresa Holder, Robert Viagas, Stella Fawn Ragsdale

Not Shown: Sarah Jane Arnegger, Patricia Catenne, Heather Dudenbostel, Kelechi Ezie, Karen Master, Steven McCasland, Andrew Rusli

PLAYBILL VAULT
Seated (L-R): Megan Dekic, Brynn Cox

Standing (L-R): Andrew Ku, David Gewirtzman, Travis Ferguson, Jennifer Brown

Not Shown: Nicholas Betito, Jared Eberlein

Louis Botto
Columnist

Harry Haun
Columnist

Jennifer Lanter
Columnist

Mervyn
Rothstein
Columnist

Seth Rudetsky
Columnist

Mark Shenton
*London
Correspondent*

Robert Simonson
*Senior
Correspondent*

Steven Suskin
Columnist

Faculty

Playbill

ACCOUNTING
(Clockwise from front left): Lewis Cole, Theresa Bernstein, James Eastman, JoAnn D'Amato, John LoCascio
Not pictured: Beatriz Chitnis

Carolina Diaz
*Florida Production
Manager*

Photo by Brian Mapp

Regional Advertising Salespersons

Kenneth R. Back
*Sales Manager
Cincinnati*

Elaine Bodker
*Sales
St. Louis*

Bob Caulfield
*Sales
San Francisco*

Margo Cooper
*Sales Manager
St. Louis*

Betsy Gugick
*Sales Manager
Dallas*

Ron Friedman
*Sales Manager
Columbus*

Tom Green
*Sales
Florida/Texas, etc.*

Ed Gurien
*Sales
Florida/Dallas*

Karen Kanter
*Sales Manager
California*

Michel Manzo
*Sales Manager
Philadelphia*

Marilyn A. Miller
*Sales Manager
Minneapolis*

Judy Pletcher
*Sales Manager
Washington, DC*

Kenneth Singer
*Sales Manager
Houston*

Jill Wettersten
*Sales Manager
Chicago*

Not Pictured: Nancy Hardin, Donald Roberts and Jeff Ross.

Faculty

Playbill / Woodside Offices

CLASSIC ARTS DIVISION and PROGRAM EDITORS
Seated (L-R): Kristy Bredin, Pam Karr, Claire Mangan
Standing (L-R): Brian Libfeld, William Reese, Joseph Conroy, Scott Hale

Photos by Brian Mapp

PRODUCTION
(L-R): Benjamin Hyacinthe, Patrick Cusanelli, Amy Asch, Sean Kenny
Not Pictured: Maria Chinda, David Porrello, Andrew Rubin, Judy Samelson

DAY CREW

Front Row (L-R):
Nancy Galarraga,
David Rodriguez,
Janet Moti,
Arnold Jaklitsch,
Rodrigo Garcia,
Ray Sierra

Back Row (L-R):
Steve Ramlall,
Lidia Yagual,
Larry Przetakiewicz,
James Anticona,
Scott Cipriano,
Robert Cusanelli,
Steve Ryder,
Frank Divirgilio

Photo courtesy Jill Napierala

PLAYBILLSTORE.COM
(L-R): Jill Napierala, Craig Fogel, Bruce Stapleton, Yajaira Marrero, and
Rebecca Miller

NIGHT CREW
Kneeling (L-R): Frank Dunn, Pablo Yagual
Standing (L-R) Anna Rincon, Bernard Morgan, Francisco Montero,
James Ayala, Joseph Gurrieri, Ken Gomez, Elias Garcia

In Memoriam

June 2011 to May 2012

Ray Aghayan
Tom Aldredge
Cris Alexander
Ray Aranha
John Arden
Jeffrey Ash
Doe Avedon
Robert Baines
Fred Baker
Jean Banks
Emery Battis
Doris Belack
Price Berkley
Zina Bethune
Helen Beverley
Roberts S. Blossom
Paul Bogart
Florence Bray
Tommy Brent
Thomas Martell Brimm
Lynn Brinker
Graham Brown
Anne Diamond
    Brownstone
Phil Bruns
George Byrne
Michael Cacoyannis
Chris Calloway
Gilbert Cates
Shirley Chambers
Diane Cilento
Leonardo Cimino
Liviu Ciulei
Dick Clark
Jeff Conaway
Sam Coppola
Norman Corwin
Ted D'Arms
Shelagh Delaney
Henry Denker
Stephen Douglass
Margaret Ruth Draper
William Duell
Irving Elman
Peter Falk
James Farentino
Aniko Farrell
Mary Fickett

Broadway Dims Its Lights

Broadway theatres dimmed their marquee lights this season upon the passing of the following theatre personalities, listed here along with the date the honor was accorded: Circle in the Square co-founder Theodore Mann, February 24, 2012. Critic Howard Kissel, February 28, 2012. *Mary Poppins* composer Robert B. Sherman (Disney theatres), March 6, 2012.

Leo Friedman
Martha Flynn
Clebert Ford
Roger Franklin
Dan Frazer
Edgar "Buddy" Freitag
Jonathan Frid
Alan Fudge
Marcia Gardner
Margaret Gathright
Ben Gazzara
Earle Gister
Bruce Gordon
Donald Grody
Ulu Grosbard
Michael Hall
John Hallow
Roger Hamilton
Edward W. Hastings
Michael Hastings
Vaclav Havel
Gardner Hayes
Mary C. Henderson
Tresa Hughes
Katherine Hull
Maureen Hurley
Eiko Ishioka
William C. Jackson
Charles Jaffe
Davy Jones
Robert Karl
Tom Kelly
Marketa Kimbrell
Howard Kissel
Fran Landesman
Jerry Leiber
Judy Lewis

Christina Lind
George Lindsey
Mort Lindsey
Michael Lipton
Peggy Craven Lloyd
Anne Lommel
Phyllis Love
Ralph Lowe
Donald Lyons
Jet MacDonald
Laurie Main
Theodore Mann
George Martin
Ray Mason
Anna Massey
George McGrath
Sid Melton
Paul Michael
John Milligan
David I. Mitchell
Harry Morgan
Felix Munso
Tom Murrin
Gene Myers
John Neville
Patricia Neway
Melva Niles
Sam Norkin
Virginia Payne
Rose Pickering
Alice Playten
Lee Pockriss
David Pressman
Joe Pullara
Joyce Redman
Paul E. Richards
Linda Robbins

Cliff Robertson
Steve Roland
Philip Rose
Herbert Rubens
Beatrice Salten
Terry Saunders
Tom Sawyer
Bill Schelble
Maurice Sendak
Jack Sevier
Robert B. Sherman
Patricia Sigris
Bradshaw Smith
Harold Smith
Betty Spitz
Milton Stanzler
Morgan Sterne
Tony Stevens
Warren Stevens
Leonard Stone
Alan Sues
Grant Sullivan
Henry Sutton
John Swearingen
Yasuko Tamaki
Florence Tarlow
Clarice Taylor
Beatrice Terry
Giorgio Tozzi
Paul Trueblood
Margaret Tyzack
Renata Vaselle
Michael Wager
Mike Wallace
Daniel Watkins
Berenice Weiler
Bernard West
David Wheeler
Jane White
Kenneth White
Dick Anthony Williams
Nicol Williamson
Ethel Winter
Googie Withers
Edwin Judd Woldin
John Wood
Evelyn Wyckoff

Index

Index

Index

Index

Index

Index

Index

Index

Index

Index

Index

Index

Index

Index

Index

Index

Index

Index

Index

Index

Index

Index

Index

Index